THE ROUTLEDGE HANDBOOK ON
THE AMERICAN DREAM

The Routledge Handbook on the American Dream: Volume 2 explores the social, economic, and cultural aspects of the American Dream in both theory and reality in the twenty-first century. This collection of essays brings together leading scholars from a range of fields to further develop the themes and issues explored in the first volume.

The concept of the American Dream, first expounded by James Truslow Adams in *The Epic of America* in 1931, is at once both ubiquitous and difficult to define. The term perfectly captures the hopes of freedom, opportunity, and upward social mobility invested in the nation. However, the American Dream appears increasingly illusory in the face of widening inequality and apparent lack of opportunity, particularly for the poor and ethnic, or otherwise marginalized, minorities in the United States. As such, an appreciation of the importance of the American Dream through both theoretical analyses and empirical studies, whether qualitative or quantitative, is crucial to understanding contemporary America.

Like the first volume of *The Routledge Handbook on the American Dream*, this collection will be of great interest to students and researchers in a range of fields in the humanities and social sciences.

Robert C. Hauhart is a Professor in the Department of Society and Social Justice, Saint Martin's University, USA.

Mitja Sardoč is a Senior Research Associate at the Educational Research Institute, Ljubljana, Slovenia, where he is a member of the Educational Research program.

THE ROUTLEDGE HANDBOOK ON THE AMERICAN DREAM

Volume II

Edited by

Robert C. Hauhart
and Mitja Sardoč

NEW YORK AND LONDON

Cover image: Ericka Birkenstein, Theorie Photography and Rob Edmondson

First published 2023
by Routledge
605 Third Avenue, New York, NY 10158

and by Routledge
4 Park Square, Milton Park, Abingdon, Oxon, OX14 4RN

Routledge is an imprint of the Taylor & Francis Group, an informa business

Library of Congress Cataloging-in-Publication Data
Names: Hauhart, Robert C., 1950- editor. | Sardoéc, Mitja, editor.
Title: The Routledge handbook on the American Dream / edited by Robert C.
Hauhart and Mitja Sardoéc.
Description: New York, NY : Routledge, 2021.
Identifiers: LCCN 2020052765| ISBN 9780367895990 (hardback : vol. 1) | ISBN
9781032352961 (hardback : vol. 2) | ISBN 9780367896003 (paperback : vol.
1) | ISBN 9781032352978 (paperback : vol. 2) | ISBN 9781003020028 (ebook :
vol. 1) | ISBN 9781003326243 (ebook : vol. 2)
Subjects: LCSH: American Dream. | Social mobility--United States. | Social
values--United States. | Quality of life--United States. | United
States--Social conditions--21st century. | United States--Economic
conditions--21st century. | United States--Civilization--21st century.
Classification: LCC HN59.2 .R685 2021 | DDC 306.0973--dc23
LC record available at https://lccn.loc.gov/2020052765

ISBN: 978-1-032-35296-1 (hbk)
ISBN: 978-1-032-35297-8 (pbk)
ISBN: 978-1-003-32624-3 (ebk)

DOI: 10.4324/9781003326243

Typeset in Bembo
by KnowledgeWorks Global Ltd.

CONTENTS

Contents

FIGURES

viii

TABLES

ACKNOWLEDGMENTS

This project began during my period of affiliation with the Research Centre of the Slovenian Academy of Sciences and Arts, Ljubljana, in 2019 under the auspices of the Council for the International Exchange of Scholars' Fulbright Scholars Program. I would like to express my appreciation to those administrators, country and region managers, members of the grants committee, and peer reviewers at the Fulbright Program who made my experience there possible. This work would not have been created without the international exchange the Program fostered.

In Slovenia, I am indebted to Professor Oto Luthar, Director of the Research Centre, for his willingness to have the Centre act as my Fulbright host. Dr. Luthar, a highly regarded historian of Slovenia's past, must also manage the large and programmatically diverse Research Centre, a premier social science and humanities research institute in Slovenia. Still, Dr. Luthar found time to be a genial host and personally facilitated many details related to my stay. For this, and many other gestures of support, I am very grateful. Dr. Luthar's support created the opportunity for this jointly edited Slovene-American project to come together and facilitated the inclusion of important scholarly work by both Slovene and American contributors, among others.

In the United States, I would like to thank Kate Boyle, Provost, and Jeff Crane, former Dean of the College of Arts and Sciences at Saint Martin's (now at Humboldt State University), for actively supporting a regular program of sabbatical leaves, as well as unexpected leaves for recipients of grants like the Fulbright Scholar Award. Saint Martin's has established itself as a small but vibrant center of learning in the Pacific Northwest, and it is largely due to good administrative leadership that Saint Martin's has prospered. In this regard, I should acknowledge the prudent financial stewardship of our outgoing president of the University, Dr. Roy Heyndericks. I would also like to thank our editors at Routledge, Dean Birkenkamp, and, more recently, Michael Gibson.

Finally, I would like to give special thanks to my friend and co-editor, Mitja, our contributors to both volumes of the *Handbook*, who have collegially shared with us their own learning, and my personal supporters – Diane Wiegand, Jeff Birkenstein, Rossitsa Terzieva-Artemis (Rossie), Julia McCord Chavez, and many, many others too numerous to name.

Robert C. Hauhart

Acknowledgments

★ ★ ★

As a multivolume publishing project, *The Routledge Handbook on the American Dream* has accumulated considerable debt from the hard work and generosity of institutions and individuals around the world. I would first like to express my indebtedness to the Educational Research Institute in Ljubljana (Slovenia), my home for the last 25 years. As a member of its Educational Studies research program and member of the Center for the Philosophy of Education, I have benefited from the platform they provide to exchange ideas and research results. I would also like to thank colleagues who have found Volume I of this publishing project an invaluable research and study tool. In particular, I would like to express my gratitude to Prof. Michael Sandel, whose international academic bestseller, *The Tyranny of Merit*, I adopted as the centerpiece for a book symposium to address many of the issues the *Handbook* has raised anew. This scholarly detour has had an important galvanizing effect on my research on the American Dream.

Prof. Robert C. Hauhart has been an ideal co-editor and colleague whose high standards of academic publishing and superb editorial skills have made all the difference in bringing this publishing project to a successful conclusion. Both the contributors to this volume and those using it for research purposes have much to be thankful for due to his efforts. I would also like to thank our former editor at Routledge, Dean Birkenkamp, for his unflagging support of this project which grew beyond our initial expectation. Without his commitment, neither of the two volumes of the *Handbook* would have been possible. I would finally like to thank my wife, Mojca, and our two sons, Žiga and Jakob, for their enduring patience with my various publishing ventures. I truly appreciate their support and encouragement.

Any sequel, this one included, faces the obvious challenge of being compared to the original that preceded it. It is my firm belief that Volume II of *The Routledge Handbook on the American Dream* is a felicitous and successful follow-up to Volume I. The papers we have included offer vigorous analyses of issues, both old and new, with respect to the American Dream. Most importantly perhaps, this publishing project pays justice to the disciplinary and global richness that scholarly work on the American Dream has generated. Our fervent hope is that both volumes of the *Handbook* contribute to continuing new research and active discussions.

Mitja Sardoč

PREFACE

Volume II of *The Routledge Handbook on the American Dream* brings together 19 chapters by some of the leading scholars working on issues related to the American Dream today. This volume, like its *prequel*, aims to fill a lacuna in academic research on various issues associated with the American Dream and gather together authoritative chapters so that they are easily accessible. The diversity of approaches to the study of the American Dream and the variegated research methods the contributors have employed add a distinctively interdisciplinary character to this reference work. The chapters are listed under six main headings: *Economic Success and Upward Economic Mobility and the American Dream*; *Contemporary Issues in American Dream Studies*; *Migration and the Immigrant American Dream*; *Marginalized Americans and the American Dream*; *The American Dream Goes Global?*; and *Sustainability and the American Dream*.

The introductory chapter by Robert Hauhart and Mitja Sardoč ("Theorizing the American Dream") reassesses the role of theory in making sense of the American Dream. It provides an overview of the most important developments in this area of scholarly research and traces its intellectual history to some of the most prominent scholars who wrote on this phenomenon. As we accentuate, "[t]he persistence of the American dream, whether in popular culture or in rarefied academic research, is a testament to its vitality, its global diffusion, and its sustainability."

The section on *Economic Success and Upward Economic Mobility and the American Dream* includes seven chapters. The first by Tsedale M. Melaku is entitled "In Pursuit of the Elusive American Dream: Black Woman Professionals." Melaku argues that it is a misperception that "race is no longer central to the experiences of racially subordinated groups." She, like many others, believes that the idea that the United States is "post-racial" since the election of President Obama is ill-founded and misguided. Likewise, Melaku challenges the idealized notion of the American Dream. Time and again, she points out that events from the past decade are a testament to the fact that a post-racial society, like the American Dream itself, is a myth. "[B]y looking at the challenges and narratives of Black professionals who are perceived as having broken through barriers to achieve educational and socioeconomic advancements, and yet still face significant challenges reaching the pinnacle of their profession," Melaku refutes the easy complacency that has infused some conversations about race in the contemporary United States. Indeed, Prof. Melaku's concludes that "Black women professionals face incredible obstacles gaining entry to elite law firms, as well as accessing professional development and advancement opportunities, further thwarting this notion of the American dream." Her argument is a powerful one and offers a necessary corrective to the uncritical assessments offered too easily by other writers.

Karen Ho's chapter "Markets, Finance, Whiteness, and the American Dream" takes a closer look at the phenomenon of financialization, one of the main factors that has accelerated inequality as well as eroded the very idea of the American Dream. In particular, she focuses her attention on some of the "key causes of the American Dream's breakdown" and points to the divergent [or even conflicting] experiences of the American Dream by different communities in the United States. As she emphasizes, "[t]o better understand contemporary socioeconomic decline, as well as the politics of resentment, and scapegoating, it is crucial to examine the cultural workings of markets and finance and their interconnections with the formation of the American Dream. Specifically, we must ask, and answer, how hierarchies and exclusions, framed simply as 'the free market,' have made the American Dream possible for some while eliding its unequal conditions for many."

In his chapter "Earning Rent with Your Talent: American Inequality Rests on the Power to Define, Transfer and Institutionalize Talent" Jonathan J.B. Mijs puts the notion of talent at the center of contemporary discussions of the American Dream. His examination offers both an in-depth presentation of the merit-based dimension of the American Dream as well as an insight into the non-meritocratic aspects of talent, although there are many such elements that form what we might call talents' structural anatomy. As Mijs argues, "talent is a major means through which people seek rent in modern-day America. Talent today is what inherited land was to feudal societies; an unchallenged source of symbolic and economic rewards. Whereas God sanctified the aristocracy's wealth, contemporary privilege is legitimated by meritocracy." Yet, serious questions remain as to whether merit can ever be satisfactorily measured and evaluated, thereby raising the possibility that what is called merit or talent is only more or less a euphemism for class-based performative features that reproduce inequality and nothing more.

The chapter "From American Dream to Nordic Realities?" by Ingrid Christensen, John Erik Fossum, and Bent-Sofus Tranøy presents in detail a case study of the Nordic Model in comparison to the United States' neoliberal capitalism with regard to their respective effectiveness in developing an economic and social foundation for achieving the American Dream. As the authors describe their chapter, they wish to "examine[s] whether and to what extent the Nordic region has surpassed today's America on two of the most central tenets of the American Dream, defined as individualism and equal opportunity." Their findings are intriguing. This approach offers fertile ground for future research on issues related to intergenerational mobility, fairness, and the merit-based conception of distributive justice, whether in a comparative perspective or at the conceptual level.

The chapter by Mitja Sardoč and Vladimir Prebilič entitled "Equality, Opportunity and the American Dream" provides an insight into the centrality of the merit-based concept of distributive justice for the national dream narrative. Based on extensive research on issues associated with this phenomenon, the essay examines the intricate relationship between the American Dream and the issue of equality of opportunity. The authors first outline the "standard" interpretation of the American Dream as the most tangible materialization of the idea of equality of opportunity and then discuss the promise of the American Dream emanating from its commitment to a merit-based conception of distributive justice. Their essay also examines some criticisms that address the alleged failure of the American Dream and its decreasing vitality. The concluding section sets the stage for possible future research on the intricate relationship between these two ideas and the vitality of the American Dream itself.

In her chapter, "What 'American' Dream? Contemporary Reflections," Melanie E. L. Bush provides a much-needed contemplation regarding the source of the American Dream ethos in the genealogy of the inherent connections "between coloniality and the founding and rise of the United States as a hegemonic power." Thus, she examines the emergence of world capitalism, the establishment and rise of nation-states, and white supremacy/Euro-dominance as necessary precursors to the materialist conception of the American Dream that many in the first world are able to live. As Bush poignantly emphasizes, the American Dream is one of its most visible manifestations of the American century and arguably could only have been envisioned once these sources of support were in place. This chapter then explores some of the challenges contemporary crises have posed with regard to whether or not the idea of the American Dream can, or even should be, put forward as a societal ideal.

The concluding chapter of this section by Karyn Lacy starts from the "standard" interpretation of the American Dream and its narrative of economic success leading to upward social mobility. Yet, as she emphasizes, "[w]hile scholars tend to argue that today's middle class is struggling to stay afloat, by many accounts, the black middle class is at greater risk than other groups of sliding back down the class ladder. Put simply, some scholars worry that the black middle class will be unable to reproduce itself over time, that is, to pass their class position on to their children." In this chapter, she questions the very foundations of this conclusion by pointing out that the weakness of this approach is a monolithic conception of the black middle class as its key distinguishing characteristic. In particular, she focuses her attention "on intraclass distinctions within the group to show that not all middle class blacks face the prospect of downward mobility." By making this important intellectual maneuver, she reveals "the (often hidden) mechanisms by which two distinct groups of middle-class blacks attempt to put their children in position to achieve the dream."

The next section, entitled *Contemporary Issues in American Dream Studies*, includes two chapters. In her contribution "What (American) Dreams are made of: Disney's Fairy Tale Narratives," Tracey Mollet points to the intrinsic connection between the American Dream and the Disney organization's fairy tale narratives. As she emphasizes, "[i]n all of its fairy tales of the twentieth and twenty-first centuries, the Walt Disney Studios works to sell its audiences the national myth of the United States at any one given historical moment, constructing a vision of America as the site of happily ever after." Mollet's analysis deftly re-invigorates an oft-neglected feature of the iconic narrative: the fact that it is, after all, conceded to be and labeled a "dream" suggests that examining other fairy tales may well be one of the most fruitful forms of review and assessment. It is, after all, the myth-like enticement of the American Dream that has provided much of its rhetorical resonance. Like a good fairy tale, the dream's wish-fulfillment nature may be the source of its greatest strength.

Maxine Eichner's chapter, "The Free-Market Family," challenges the progressive and emancipatory promise of the American Dream by focusing on a policy shift beginning in the 1970s, i.e. "that families should obtain the resources they need privately through the market, without the help of government." As she emphasizes, "[f]ive decades of this 'free market family policy' show that this approach has undercut and corroded the well-being of families from the bottom of the economic ladder to the top, and decimated the Dream's promise." Through a comprehensive summary of US policy initiatives and economic data, Eichner effectively illustrates just how this devaluation of American family life took place.

Our third section, *Migration and the Immigrant American Dream*, brings together two chapters. In their contribution, "A Twenty-First Century African Immigrant View of the American Dream: Challenges and Opportunities," Enock Ariga Marindi and Robert C. Hauhart pick up a neglected phenomenon associated with migration, that of African immigrants to the United States in the late twentieth and twenty-first centuries. They draw similarities between this contemporary phenomenon and earlier waves of immigration to the United States, revealing that immigrants as historically distant as the nineteenth-century Irish, early twentieth-century eastern Europeans, and those from sub-Saharan African nations from the 1960s to today, often face similar vicissitudes that are rooted in their foreign-ness, their cultural distinctiveness, and, in the latter case, their obvious racial heritage. Marindi's field interviews of African respondents in both the United States and Uganda offer compelling contemporary support for their argument.

Steve Wilson's chapter, "The Boys from Little Mexico Redux: Dreaming the Immigrant Dream," builds on his previously published book, *The Boys from Little Mexico: A Season Chasing the American Dream* (Beacon 2010), where he chronicled the "stories of many boys who were first generation immigrants from Mexico, several of them illegal, and documented the challenges they faced in succeeding, academically, socially, and financially, in the United States." In 2021, Wilson re-interviewed "a number of the players, coaches, school administrators, and parents he first met and spoke with in 2005, offering an invaluable insight into American Dreams in the making. While many of the boys – now men – he was able to interview could claim some success in the United States, the personal cost they experienced in doing so was often notable. Like sub-Saharan African immigrants addressed in the previous chapter, assimilation and pursuit of the dream often induce cultural dislocation and a remaking of identity, a process that cannot be accomplished without ambivalence and pain.

The next section addresses *Marginalized Americans and the American Dream.* The section brings together four chapters discussing diverse communities that share oft-neglected narratives in relation to the American Dream. In her chapter, "Incorporation and Disruption: What Fictional Narratives Reveal About the Realities of the American Dream, " Elda María Román argues that "ethno-racial cultural producers often employ the upward mobility narrative as a way in which to critique values barring collectivist gains, [such as those embodied] in individualism, capitalism, and white supremacy." Part of her contribution expands on her book *Race and Upward Mobility* where she accentuates that "the four character types often recurring in upward mobility narratives – *status seekers, gatekeepers, mediators,* and *conflicted artists* – serve as allegorical pathways of incorporation and disruption, demonstrating how the boundaries of the American dream are upheld and contested."

In her chapter "The American Dream and Muslim Americans: (Im)Possibilities and Realities of Pursuing the Dream," Arshia Anwer focuses on the Muslim American population within the United States and their engagement with the American Dream from economic, political, and sociocultural viewpoints. The main part of this chapter "explores American Muslims (who, as a population category, are not homogenous, a frequent mis-understanding) and their access to and attainment of the American Dream." Anwer's most distinctive contribution, though, is her carefully informed description of issues "that lead to Muslim Americans' exclusion to access and/or attainment of the American dream," a story that each of the groups addressed in this section has had to experience at one time or another.

Theodore Greene's rich and interesting chapter "Gay Neighborhoods: Reimagining the Traditional Conception of the American Dream" explores "how LGBTQ+ Americans have accessed the American dream by producing and maintaining iconic gay neighborhoods." Greene's summary history illustrates, without stepping away from his principal thesis, just how similar the journeys of formerly maligned and marginalized groups – from LGBTQ Americans to Black Americans to those of various ethnic heritages – are alike. While a number of these groups were forcibly segregated, LGBTQ+ Americans learned that their communal strength could change their exclusion and turn it into a form and provide a space for the creation of supportive, gay-friendly districts. In the course of doing so, sections of urban environments were often reborn, becoming magnets not only for LGBQT+ Americans but for revived, diverse, multi-cultural neighborhoods that now represent forms of cosmopolitan urbanism that model what livable communities can be like in our cities of the twenty-first century.

The chapter by Joan Maya Mazelis entitled "The American Dream: Rhetoric of Opportunity and Reality of Exclusion" picks up a paradox inherent in the very idea of the American Dream. As she expresses eloquently, "[t]hough the American Dream is ostensibly about opportunity and openness, it is based on exclusion. The American Dream is exclusionary not only because of practices that further inequality and perpetuate disadvantage. The American Dream has been built on a premise of exclusion, particularly an exclusion founded on a racial hierarchy, and this exclusion is an intended feature of our society." This assertion, as the author emphasizes, is key to a correct and comprehensive understanding of what the American Dream actually propagates.

The section *The American Dream Goes Global?* includes a chapter by Iva Kosmos entitled "'Good Living' and Immigrants in the Literature of Aleksandar Hemon: Toward the Humble Dream." She examines in detail the writings of a Bosnian-American writer Aleksandar Hemon and his public figure as portrayed in mass media. Nevertheless, she argues that these types of portrayals offer a reductionist picture of those who arrive in the United States and make it. She considers in this chapter the "narrative tools Hemon uses to deconstruct the myth: the juxtaposition of distinct social realities and historical periods." Ironically enough, as Iva Kosmos accentuates, "Hemon's literary conclusions are confirmed in reality shaped by the contemporary press: his public presentation is still based on the story of the American dream, in spite of his literary debunking of the myth."

The final section of Volume II of *The Routledge Handbook on the American Dream* (*Sustainability and the American Dream*) brings together two chapters. LaTonya J. Trotter's contribution ("A Dream Deferred: Professional Projects as Racial Projects in US Medicine") examines a controversial practice of erecting barriers to exclude Black people and white women from professional medicine for most of the twentieth century. As she argues, "these exclusionary practices were not simply historical artifacts, but that investments in gendered forms of whiteness were at the heart of medicine's strategy for achieving the American Dream." She takes a closer look at the figure of the American physician as "an icon of white, elite masculinity" and its transformation. As she writes, "[c]onceptualizing professional projects as racial projects is important not just for understanding the past, but for understanding new forms of stratification in the medical workplace specifically, and in the labor market as a whole."

Robert C. Hauhart's chapter "Status Maintenance, Mobility, and the Persistence of Class Barriers to Achieving the American Dream" delves into the question of "whether there is more, or less, upward economic mobility in U.S. society now as compared to previous decades." In his chapter, Hauhart suggests that the focus on economics obscures the fact that the operative measure for upward or downward mobility should be membership in a class. He then proceeds to answer the question posed by relying on indicia of class membership in the course of examining a selection of extant studies of the working, lower, middle, and upper middle classes in the United States. It is apparent from the studies that movement among classes is very limited, whether within a generation or intergenerationally. In making this argument, Hauhart relies on well-known field studies by McLeod (2009), Bettie (2014), Ray (2017), Shankar (2019), and Dhingra (2020). He concludes that the barriers and boundaries these authors describe as marking the lines between classes are relatively impermeable based on the careful observations made in the field.

The American Dream has proven itself to be a durable cultural touchstone for American citizens and for those who wish to journey to the United States seeking a better way of life. We hope the collection of papers offered here illuminates both the strengths and the cultural perils of a belief in the American Dream.

Robert C. Hauhart and Mitja Sardoč

CONTRIBUTORS

Arshia Anwer, PhD, is an Assistant Professor of communication at Manhattan College with research interests in the areas of religious communication, intercultural communication, philosophy of communication, and integrated marketing communication. She has worked in the marketing communication and higher education fields in a variety of marketing, editing, and teaching roles. Her work has been published in *Gender, Race and Social Identity in American Politics* (Lexington Books, 2019), and *An Encyclopedia of Communication Ethics: Goods in Contention*, as well as the *Explorations in Media Ecology* journal.

Melanie E. L. Bush, PhD, MPH is a Professor at Adelphi University and a Research Associate, Department of Sociology Centre for Sociological Research and Practice, University of Johannesburg. She is the author of *Tensions in the American Dream: Rhetoric, Reverie or Reality* (Temple University Press, 2015, with Roderick D. Bush), *Everyday Forms of Whiteness: Understanding Race in a "Post-Racial" World* (Rowman and Littlefield, 2004, 2011), and lead editor of and contributor to *Rod Bush: Lessons from a Radical Black Scholar on Liberation Love and Justice* (2019). She has published and presented widely on racism, nation, education, political economy, and social movements. Dr. Bush is co-chair of the May First Movement Technology Board and serves on the Peoples Strike National Organizing Committee.

Ingrid Christensen is a Research Assistant at the ARENA Centre for European Studies, University of Oslo. She holds a bachelor's degree in Politics and International Relations from the University of Kent and is currently a master's student in the Theory and Practice of Human Rights at the University of Oslo. As part of her master's degree, she was an intern at the Norwegian Centre for Human Rights. During her bachelor's degree, she spent one academic year at Towson University in the United States. Her academic interests include human rights issues related to gender, democracy and the rule of law, refugee protection, and minority rights. Her master's thesis focuses on gender and transitional justice processes in Kosovo.

Maxine Eichner is the Graham Kenan Distinguished Professor of Law at the University of North Carolina School of Law. Professor Eichner is the author of *The Free-Market Family: How the Market Crushed the American Dream (and How It Can Be Restored)* (Oxford, 2020), winner of the 2021 PROSE award for best scholarly work on economics, which considers the harsh effects that market forces are having on American families today, as well as *The Supportive State: Families, Government, and America's Political Ideals* (Oxford, 2010). She earned a BA and J.D. from Yale University and a PhD in Political Science from the University of North Carolina.

John Erik Fossum (MA, UCSB; PhD, UBC) is a Professor at the ARENA Centre for European Studies, University of Oslo, Norway. He has published widely on issues of federalism, identity, democracy, and constitutionalism in the EU and Canada. He is the project coordinator for the H2020-project EU3D – Differentiation, Dominance, Democracy in EU (2019–2023). Most recent books: *Squaring the Circle on Brexit – Could the Norway Model Work?* (Bristol University Press, 2018), with Hans Petter Graver; *Diversity and Contestations over Nationalism in Europe and Canada*, (Palgrave MacMillan, 2018), co-edited with Riva Kastoryano and Birte Siim, and *Towards a Segmented European Political Order*, co-edited with Jozef Batora (Routledge, 2020). He published the article Fossum, J.E. "Europe's American Dream," *European Journal of Social Theory* 12(4): 483–504 (2009), and the chapter "Is the Nordic Model more compatible with the American Dream than present-day United States?" in Volume I of the *Routledge Handbook on the American Dream*.

Theo Greene is an Assistant Professor of Sociology at Bowdoin College. His research and teaching interests lie at the intersection of sexuality, urbanism, and culture. Greene's research broadly uses sexual communities to understand how urban redevelopment shapes and reconfigures how individuals conceptualize, identify to, and participate in local communities. His current book project, entitled *Not in MY Gayborhood: Gay Neighborhoods and the Rise of the Vicarious Citizen* (under contract with Columbia University Press), explores the persistence of iconic gay neighborhoods in Washington, DC, through ephemeral acts of placemaking by nonresidential community actors (vicarious citizens).

Robert C. Hauhart is a Professor in the Department of Society and Social Justice, Saint Martin's University, USA, where he teaches courses in sociology, criminology, social justice, law, and literature. His research focuses on the concept of the American Dream in twentieth and twenty-first-century sociology, as well as research and writing on multiple themes, including the American Dream, in American literature. In 2019, he was a recipient of a Fulbright Scholar Award to teach and research the American Dream at the Slovenian Academy of Sciences and Arts (ZRC SAZU) in Ljubljana, where he maintains an association as a visiting research fellow. He is the author of several books, including *The Lonely Quest: Constructing the Self in the Twenty-First Century United States* (Routledge, 2018) and *Seeking the American Dream: A Sociological Inquiry* (Palgrave Macmillan, 2016), which was nominated for the Pacific Sociological Association's Distinguished Scholarship Award in 2017. He is also co-editor of *American Writers in Exile* (Salem Press 2015); *Social Justice in American Literature* (Salem Press, 2017); *European Writers in Exile* (Lexington Books, 2018); *Connections and Influences Between the Russian and American Short Story* (Lexington Books, 2021); *The Routledge Handbook of the American Dream: Volume 1* (Routledge, 2021), and *Significant Food in American Literature* (University of Georgia Press, forthcoming 2023). He is the co-author (with Jon Grahe, Pacific Lutheran University, of *Designing and Teaching Undergraduate Capstone Courses* (Jossey-Bass/Wiley, 2015).

Karen Ho is an Associate Professor of Anthropology at the University of Minnesota, Twin Cities, and ethnographically studies Wall Street and the culture of finance. Her research centers on the problematic of understanding and representing financial markets, sites that are resistant to cultural analysis. Her domain of interest is the anthropology of economy, with specific foci on finance capital, capitalism, globalization, corporations, socioeconomic inequalities, and comparative ethnic and feminist studies. Her book, *Liquidated: An Ethnography of Wall Street* (Duke University Press, 2009), was based on three years of fieldwork among investment bankers and major financial institutions. Recent publications include "Gens: A Feminist Manifesto for the Study of Capitalism" (Theorizing the Contemporary Series, Cultural Anthropology Online, co-authored, 2015); "Markets, Myths, and Misrecognitions: Economic Populism in the Age of Financialization and Hyperinequality (Economic Anthropology, 2018); "What Happened to Social Facts?" (American Anthropologist, co-edited, 2019); "In the Name of Shareholder Value: Origin Myths of Corporations and Their Ongoing Implications" (Seattle Law Review, 2020); "Why the Stock Market Is Rising Amidst a Pandemic and Record, Racialized Inequality" (American Ethnologist online, 2020). Her latest work is especially concerned with the ongoing ramifications of financialization-gone-wild: increased socio-economic inequality, racialized extraction and scapegoating, and planetary unsustainability.

Iva Kosmos is a Researcher at ZRC SAZU, Institute of Culture and Memory Studies (Ljubljana, Slovenia). Kosmos graduated from the University of Zagreb (2015), was a Fulbright fellow at UW-Madison (2014), and a guest researcher at the Center for South East European Studies at the University of Graz (2016–2017). She graduated with a thesis on contemporary post-Yugoslav writers in the international literary market. The core of her interest lies at the intersection of cultural production, art, and society; recently, she is focused on memory politics of remembering the former Yugoslavia in art and everyday practices. She has published in Slovenian, Croatian and international journals and editions, including *East European Politics and Societies, The Slavonic and East European Review,* and the monograph *The Media of Memory* (Brill, 2020). She co-edited the monograph *Stories from Tin Cans: History of Canning Fish Industry in Northeast Adriatic* (in Slovenian, translated to Croatian, 2020).

Karyn Lacy is an Associate Professor of Sociology at the University of Michigan. She is a Ford Fellow and was a Visiting Scholar at the Russell Sage Foundation. Her work focuses on the black middle class, race relations, residential segregation, identity, parental socialization, and suburban inequality. She is the author of the award-winning book *Blue-Chip Black: Race, Class, and Status in the New Black Middle Class*, selected for the Zora Canon, a compilation of the top 100 books written by black women from 1850 to the present. Lacy's public writing has appeared in the *New York Times, Vox, Public Seminar,* and the *Chronicle of Higher Education.*

Enock Ariga Marindi holds a Bachelor of Theology degree from Bugema University (Uganda 2003), a Master of Science degree in counseling psychology from Bugema University (Uganda 2011), a post-graduate degree in teacher education from Kyambogo University (Uganda 2014), and a Masters' Degree in Theology from Luther Seminary (USA) 2018). The author emigrated from his homeland to the United States in 2016 and lived in the United States for three years. He presently resides in Uganda and is a lecturer at Uganda Martyrs University Nkozi, teaching psychology and counseling in the School of Social Sciences. He also conducts a private practice. He has openly published his academic thesis on Research Gate.

Joan Maya Mazelis is the author of *Surviving Poverty: Creating Sustainable Ties Among the Poor*, an associate professor of sociology in the Department of Sociology, Anthropology and Criminal Justice at Rutgers University – Camden, an affiliated scholar at Rutgers – Camden's

Center for Urban Research and Education, a member of the Scholars Strategy Network, and a Faculty Affiliate at the University of Wisconsin's Institute for Research on Poverty. Her work focuses on poverty, inequality, and social ties. Her current project, funded by the National Science Foundation, is a collaborative, mixed methods, longitudinal research on student debt, the transition to adulthood, and inequality.

Tsedale M. Melaku is a sociologist, Assistant Professor of Management at Zicklin School of Business, Baruch College (CUNY), and author of *You Don't Look Like a Lawyer: Black Women and Systemic Gendered Racism*, which reflects the emphasis of her scholarly interests on race, gender, class, workplace inequities, intersectionality, and organizations. Dr. Melaku's work has been featured in the *Harvard Business Review, New York Times, The Washington Post, Bloomberg Law, Inside Higher Ed, Fortune, Teen Vogue*, and other outlets. Her interdisciplinary research on women in the workplace unites three strands of significant sociological inquiry: diversity in the workplace, women in positions of leadership, and the impact of systemic racism on advancement opportunities. Dr. Melaku is working on her second book, *The Handbook on Workplace Diversity and Stratification*, while further developing her inclusion tax and invisible labor clause theories. To learn more, follow her on Twitter, @TsedaleMelaku, or visit her website, www.tsedalemelaku.com.

Jonathan J. B. Mijs (PhD) is an Assistant Professor of Sociology at Boston University and a Veni fellow at the Erasmus University Rotterdam. His work uses ethnography, experiments, and quantitative analysis of survey data to investigate how, in a post-industrial society increasingly driven by inequalities, beliefs in meritocracy are developed and sustained. His broader interest is in the interplay between structural and agentic forces that shape the course of people's lives. His research has been published in *Social Problems, Sociology of Education*, and the *Socio-Economic Review*, and has been featured in the *Washington Post, The Guardian*, and the *Financial Times*.

Tracey Mollet is a Lecturer in Media and Communication, University of Leeds, UK. Her research interests include Disney animation, American cultural history, and nostalgia in contemporary American television. She has published widely on Disney animation and American popular culture and is the author of *Cartoons in Hard Times: The Animated Shorts of Disney and Warner Brothers in Depression and War 1933–1945* (Bloomsbury Academic, 2017), *A Cultural History of the Disney Fairy Tale: Once Upon an American Dream* (Palgrave Macmillan, 2020) and co-editor of *Investigating Stranger Things: Upside Down in the World of Mainstream Cult Entertainment* (Palgrave Macmillan, 2021).

Vladimir Prebilič (PhD) is an Associate Professor at the Faculty of Social Sciences, University of Ljubljana (Slovenia). He lectures on Defense Geography, Military History, and Basics of European Union courses for undergraduate students and Geopolitics for postgraduate students. As the research project leader, he works in the field of patriotism, active citizenship, military history, local self-government, non-military threats to security, and crisis management. He published numerous articles in international journals and is a regular lecturer at the Council of Europe on transparency, political ethics, and anti-corruption behavior of political elites.

Elda María Román is an Associate Professor in the English Department, University of Southern California. She studies race, class, literature, and media. Her book *Race and Upward Mobility: Seeking, Gatekeeping, and Other Class Strategies in Postwar America* (Stanford UP, 2017) examines class dynamics in Black and Mexican American literature, TV, and film from 1940s to 2000s.

Mitja Sardoč is a Senior Research Associate at the Educational Research Institute, Ljubljana, Slovenia, where he is a member of the Educational Research program. His research interests include citizenship education, patriotism, multiculturalism, toleration, radicalization and violent extremism, talents and distributive justice, and equality of opportunity. He is the editor of numerous books, including, most recently, *Handbook of Patriotism* (Springer, 2020), *The Impacts of Neoliberal Discourse and Language in Education: Critical Perspectives on a Rhetoric of Equality, Well-Being, and Justice* (Routledge, 2021), *The Palgrave Handbook of Toleration* (Palgrave Macmillan, 2021), *Making Sense of Radicalization and Violent Extremism: Interviews and Conversations* (Routledge, 2022), and *Talents and Distributive Justice* (Routledge, 2022). He is also co-editor of *The Routledge Handbook of the American Dream: Volume 1* (2021) and Managing Editor of the *Theory and Research in Education* journal.

Bent Sofus Tranøy is a Professor of Political Science at Inland Norway University of Applied Sciences and at Kristiania University College. He has published in the fields of Comparative Political Economy, Public Policy, Organization Theory, and History of Science. He is currently editing a book on Great Policy Success in the Nordics for OUP together with Paul t'Hart and a pan-Nordic team of editors. Among recent publications are: "Failing forward in financial stability regulation" (with Eirik T. Stendstad) and "The ECB – Unchecked transgressions and formal extensions" (with Ingrid Hjertaker), both in *Handbook on EU Crisis* (Palgrave Macmillan, 2021). "Equality as a driver of inequality? Universalistic welfare, generalised creditworthiness and financialised housing markets." *West European Politics* (2019) (with Ingrid Hjertaker and Mary Ann Stamsø); "The Norwegian Petroleum Fund as institutionalised self-restraint," in *Great Policy Successes: How Governments Get It Right in a Big Way at Least Some of the Time* (OUP, 2019) (with Camilla B. Øvald and Ketil Raknes); "Illusions of convergence: The persistent simplification of a wicked crisis" in *Towards a Segmented European Political Order* (Routledge, 2020) and "Thinking about Thinking about Comparative Political Economy: From Macro to Micro and Back." *Politics & Society* (2018) (both with Herman Schwartz).

LaTonya J. Trotter is an Associate Professor with the University of Washington's Department of Bioethics and Humanities. She is a sociologist of medicine whose work explores the relationship between changes in the organization of medical work and the reproduction of racial, economic, and gender inequality. Her first book, *More Than Medicine: Nurse Practitioners and the Problems They Solve for Patients, Health Care Organizations, and the State*, questions the common view of the NP as a physician stand-in, illustrating how NPs are creating new possibilities for what the medical encounter could be while showing the depth of the crisis of care we face.

Steve Wilson is an independent scholar and author, most notably of *The Boys from Little Mexico: A Season Chasing the American Dream* (Beacon Press, 2010).

1

INTRODUCTION

Theorizing the American Dream

Robert C. Hauhart and Mitja Sardoč

"A pearl necklace! She wanna a pearl necklace!"
"Pearl Necklace"
Written by Frank Lee Beard, Joe Michael Hill, Billy F Gibbons (ZZ Top)[1981] 2014
From the Album ZZ Top: The Very Baddest

★ ★ ★

Something of great importance became clear. We are deeply unsure about our proper place in the world, are largely unaware of our doubts and logic, and thus continue fervently to pursue victory and shun loss.
Winning: Reflections on an American Obsession
Franceso Duina 2013, 98

The American Dream has been called the most iconic statement of a people's aspirations ever devised and, not infrequently, a myth. What drives these radically different assessments of the American Dream? Can theory help us understand the American Dream and the role it plays in American society? We will argue in this brief introduction that the sociological perspective is ideally constituted to successfully analyze the American Dream and situate it fruitfully within the parameters of what we already know about how American society is organized.

What Is the American Dream?

The American dream has eluded precise and exact definition for nearly 100 years. Hochschild (1995, 15), in her seminal *Facing Up to the American Dream*, notes, " ... the American dream has been attached to everything from religious freedom to a home in the suburbs, ... " Quoting John Locke ("In the beginning, all the world was America."), Hochschild observes that Locke's paean to the new continent "[evoked] the unsullied newness, infinite possibilities, limitless resources that are commonly understood to be the essence of the 'American dream'" (15). She goes on, " ... the phrase elicits for most Americans some variant of Locke's fantasy – a new world where anything can happen and good things might" (15). Indeed, the idea is so resonant that F. Scott Fitzgerald nearly quotes it verbatim in *The Great Gatsby*

DOI: 10.4324/9781003326243-1

([1925] 2004), but without citing Locke. Nick Carraway, the narrator, and Gatsby are driving to New York City from Long Island in Gatsby's limousine, "a rich cream color, bright with nickel, swollen here and there in its monstrous length with its triumphant hat-boxes and supper-boxes and tool-boxes, and terraced with a labyrinth of wind-shields that mirrored a dozen suns" (64). Nick observes, "The city seen from the Queensboro Bridge is always the city seen for the first time, in its first wild promise of all the mystery and the beauty of the world" (64). In the book, in the manner in which symbols are created and dispensed in literary works, New York City stands for all of America. Returning to the text, Nick meditates on the grandeur and awe the scene has evoked, "'Anything can happen now that we've slid over this bridge,' I thought; "anything at all … " (65).

Faced with imposing her own definition on these mythic conceptions, Hochschild retreats to more functional ground, electing to identify the concept as consisting merely of a series of "tenets about achieving success" (15). In certain respects, we have been poorer for it ever since.

Hochschild's emphasis on achieving success as the core of the American Dream did not break new ground. As many commentators on the American Dream have observed, certainly a dominant theme within American life from the age of discovery through colonization up to and including today has been a concern with earthly success and its antithetical corollary, failure (Alger [1868] 1962; Duina 2013; Hauhart 2016). Commonly, identifying success as the central component of the American Dream has led commentators to envision it, and then calculate it, principally in financial terms. For example, no less a figure than Robert Merton defined success in achieving the American Dream in solely pecuniary terms in what some have claimed is the most read, most cited, and most celebrated American sociological essay ever written, "Social Structure and Anomie" (1938). Moreover, Merton himself was not standing alone, outside of the American experience or on the far edge of mainstream thinking on the issue. The historian Cal Jillson (2004, 16) succinctly sums up his overview of early colonial settlement in North America by remarking, "The first settlers into North America came either for quick wealth or to live in ways not permitted them at home." It is not material, as he immediately informs the reader that those who came for easy wealth were "almost invariably disappointed" (16). Merton (1938), in his famous essay, went on to contend that it was the American Dream, and perhaps most especially the pecuniary form in which it was most commonly pursued, that led the United States' most potent myth to become the source of both energetic, often commercial, development within the United States and unlawful ambition.[1] Others interested in analyzing crime and criminogenesis adopted Merton's core insight, although they elaborated upon it in ways he did not forecast (see, for example, Messner and Rosenfeld 2012).

These two features of Merton's original pecuniary definition – its tendency to disappoint (often rather quickly) and its easy conversion into a "grab the wealth by any means" formula – have led many sociologists, political scientists, and others to define, and then operationalize, the economic orientation of the American Dream differently. Thus, later commentators, including Hochschild (1995), have redefined the American Dream as an aspiration for upward mobility rather than merely a fervid pursuit of ready cash (Putnam 2015; Rank, Hirschl, and Foster 2014). Still, even in this approach, upward mobility is most often analyzed purely in economic terms, disregarding the complexity that a discussion of social mobility would introduce. The distinctiveness this variation introduced was simply to view the achievement as financially successful only if it was intergenerational (Hochschild 1995, 44–45).

One variation on the predominant economic success model, as we suggest above, is those writers who emphasize social mobility and social status rather than solely measuring upward mobility only according to upward economic mobility (Sorokin 1959). There is, of course, typically a close connection between the two. Weber (Gerth and Mills 1946, 183), for example, was adamant that "the factor that creates 'class' is unambiguously economic interests." At the same time, one can hardly dispute the fact that Weber was conscious of the importance that factors other than the purely economic held for one's life chances. Thus, Weber recognized that the level of infrastructure and technological development of society generally underpinned what he termed "entrepreneurial" (182, 185) opportunity, representing "the kind of services that can be offered in the market" (182). These distinctions helped Weber differentiate "status groups" from classes so that members of a similar status share a "specific *style of life*" with others "who wish to belong to the circle" (187; emphasis in original). Indeed, status honor distributed along the dimensions inherent in a *style of life* can, and often does, establish ritualized conventions to the effect that "every rational economic pursuit" is an active *disqualifier* for *social mobility* rather than a basis for upward mobility (191). Milner (1994) was a particularly astute observer of this phenomenon with respect to Indian society. There, too much obvious absorption in the quest for earthly material benefits would signal that one was unfit for inclusion in a more exalted status group. In Indian culture, grasping for money and economic gain, no less than achieving it, was a social disqualifier, and one would be excluded from attaining the rise in society one sought.

The import for discussions of the American Dream, therefore, is simply that achieving economic upward mobility is not synonymous with achieving upward social mobility. The latter depends, in greater part, on what we have come to regard as acquisition of a very specific form and extent, of "cultural capital" (sometimes called "human capital") rather than simply "capital" (Bourdieu and Passeron [1977] 1990). One reason that this approach has not received more interest, perhaps, is the fact that status competition is immeasurable and infinite. Relying on quantitative measures of the very tangible, economic form of capital greatly simplifies the comparative task of deciding whether, or not, a person or group have moved upward. Status groups simply establish their own esoteric standards and measure exclusion and inclusion according to their own idiosyncratic rating scales. As Slater (1990, 13) comments, the "competitive quest for progressively more rare and expensive symbols" is "a quest that is ultimately futile ..., " whether the signifying symbols are social or cultural in nature. One can simply never have enough of the right ones, and the "right ones" are always subject to being redefined at any time.

There have also been authors who have diverged from this general approach in which success in "moving upward" in society, whether economically, socially, or both, is no longer the key element. Indeed, at least one author reframed his definition of the American Dream to minimize the role of achievement without entirely abandoning that element. These authors have refocused the concept principally by broadening the definition of the American Dream rather than narrowing it. One such author is the earliest print commentator on the American Dream, James Truslow Adams. In doing so, Adams left us a definition that rivals any of those offered by more contemporary authors.

Adams, in the epilogue to his book *The Epic of America* ([1931] 1933), having summarized in broad strokes the discovery of the western hemisphere through settlement of the English colonies, the American war of rebellion, and the 150-year history of the United States (at the time he was writing) in a brisk 300 pages, reflected on the American Dream's meaning. Surveying what Americans had achieved, Adams spoke positively of advances in the sciences, in medicine, in humanitarian reforms, and with respect to contributions toward a more just world order. Noting that "many of these things are not new" (1933: 317), he went on to say:

> ... and if they were all the contributions which America had to make, she would have meant only a place for more people, a spawning ground for more millions of the human species. ...

If, as I have said, the things already listed were all we had had to contribute, America would have made no distinctive and unique gift to mankind. But there has been the American *dream*, that dream of a land in which life should be better and fuller and richer for every man, with opportunity for each according to his ability or achievement. It is a difficult dream for the European upper classes to interpret adequately, and too many of us ourselves have grown weary and mistrustful of it. It is not a dream of motor cars and high wages merely, but a dream of a social order in which each man and each woman shall be able to attain to the fullest stature of which they are innately capable, and be recognized by others for what they are, regardless of the fortuitous circumstances of birth or position.

Adams went on, page after page, to say a great deal more. His statement of the dream, eschewing materialism as its central component, focused instead on a just social order in which each man or woman might fulfill his or her inherent potential as a human being. Although Adams' definition struck a different note than earlier, and many later conceptions, and became popular among some of those who study American life, does it really matter? Has our obsession with the American Dream, however defined, done much of anything to make it more realizable? Have we made housing more affordable in the last 70 years? Are college completion rates higher? Are real wages higher than in the late 1960s? Moreover, has our quality of life improved, however one might measure it? Are we more loving? Is political discourse more cordial and more often directed at the common good? These, and many other, questions suggest that perhaps we still do not understand the cultural context in which the American Dream exists and the nature of its influence on American society, let alone its global reach.

Understanding the Nature of the American Dream in Cultural Context

The American Dream, as Fitzgerald (2004) understood (and as most advertisers understand today), is about limitless, optimistic yearning for a nearly paradisiacal life, place, position, experience, or moment. Some, consistent with the pecuniary vision of the dream, seek income and wealth as the means by which they will find themselves in a favored position, one where they can enjoy the fruits of American beneficence and avoid the niggardly means the United States affords the poor. Others seek income and wealth as only instrumental values, ones that will affirm and secure their social status, enabling them to sample, display, and benefit from cultural capital in all its forms. Some, like Gatsby, seek income and wealth as instrumental in obtaining an even less realizable goal than mere social status; in his case, Gatsby sought upward economic mobility so he could win the utter and complete love of a woman that would return him, if only for a moment, to some lost idea of himself from his past (2004, 110). Regardless of the specific content of one or another version of the American Dream, there seem to be investigations of each that suggest none of them may ultimately be achievable, even for the briefest moment, no matter the number and amount of resources or skill or energy applied to the pursuit.[2]

How then can we account for the American Dream's sustained grip on the American imagination? In Marxian terms, the function of the American Dream is perhaps understood best as a twist on the concept of false consciousness. For Lukács (1971), whose work on reification contributed most to illuminating the frame of false consciousness, the working class can only develop a true class consciousness when it sheds its illusions by grasping the true nature of its situation. One can argue by analogy that one can only appreciate the meaning of the American Dream by grasping its mythical role in sustaining cultural and economic competition within the context of a highly stratified, capitalist society. The fact that the meaning of the American Dream is left to the eye of the observer yields a cloudy ethereality that obscures the fact of its indefiniteness. As a consequence, the concept projects a gauzy film over the actual workings of American society, akin to the false consciousness that clouds the vision of the working class in Marxian analysis.

Returning to Hochschild's (1995, 15–16) detailed examination of the meaning of the American Dream, she contends it is best defined as an interwoven series of tenets about achieving success without specifying what success actually means. Its nebulous elasticity is encompassed in four succinct propositions according to Hochschild: anyone can pursue the dream with a "reasonable anticipation" of achieving it, so long as the aspirant engages in the hard work necessary, and doing so is virtuous and a worthy goal in and of itself (18–24). Hochschild notes that at the time of her writing, belief in the viability of the American Dream was widespread, noting that polling at the time showed that "… two thirds of the poor [believe] that Americans like themselves 'have a good chance of improving our standard of living'" (19, citing Ladd 1993). Hochschild, however, is not easily lured into a ready appreciation of the dream; rather, she is attuned to its potential weaknesses, which she elucidates succinctly in as few as a dozen pages.

Briefly, Hochschild notes that it has hardly ever been true that everyone can pursue their dream equally in the United States, as many have been excluded from doing so (26). Similarly, the likelihood one can "reasonably" anticipate achieving success is highly dependent on the nature of the success identified and the availability of opportunities and resources that can lead to the successful outcome envisioned (27–30). The premise that success will result from the effort invested by chasers of the dream fails to apprehend the contingent nature of most human undertakings. While effort may well be a necessary ingredient in any successful venture, it is clearly not a sufficient element in and of itself (30). The fact is that outside forces, human folly, and innumerable other intervening factors will have a bearing on the outcome of any enterprise. Finally, the Dream makes a virtue of winning and, by implication, a sin of losing (30–34). This emphasis on success without any appreciation of the barriers that impede it inspires even the poor to blame the poor for their condition (as well as people blaming themselves) (31). As Hochschild observes, "Devaluing losers allows people to maintain their belief that the world is fundamentally just, even when it patently is not" (31). Surely, former President Trump's appeal to a wide range of Americans is attributable in large part to this sociological phenomenon.

Hochschild is especially attuned to the problem of specifying the point at which a person can stop striving because they have achieved the success they have sought. She relies on Tocqueville in this regard, who observed:

> In America I have seen the freest and best educated of men in circumstances the happiest to be found in the world; yet it seemed to me that a cloud habitually hung on their brow, and they seemed serious and almost sad even in their pleasures.
>
> The chief reason for this is that … [they] never stop thinking of the good things they have not got.
>
> *255; citing and quoting Tocqueville, Democracy in America 1969, 536*

As Hochschild (255) correctly notes, "The dream is ambiguous not only on how much achievement counts as success but also on what kind of achievement ought to be pursued." Ultimately, this inherent ambiguity makes the American Dream a "choose-your-own" ideology. It has the seductive effect of permitting anyone and everyone to feel a strong sense of positive community and belonging and to believe in the American Dream. In short, it permits Americans to share a dream in an economic order that is otherwise very isolating and, in many obvious respects, unequal and patently unfair.

These reflections and sources are the inspiration for many, if not most, of the scholarly efforts that follow. The persistence of the American Dream, whether in popular culture or in rarefied academic research, is a testament to its vitality, its global diffusion, and its sustainability. The chapters that follow offer tentative answers to many of the questions the American Dream has posed. Where persuasive answers seem less readily available, our contributors offer intriguing analyses based on the best research available.

Notes

1 Fitzgerald used this same insight in *The Great Gatsby* as well, although he did so 13 years in advance of Merton, by telling the shorthand story of Meyer Wolfsheim as "the man who fixed the World's Series back in 1919" (Fitzgerald 2004, 73).
2 This is suggested merely by the titles commonly chosen by serious scholars analyzing the Dream: *Pursuing the American Dream* (Jillson 2004); *Chasing the American Dream* (Rank, Hirschl, and Foster 2014); *Seeking the American Dream* (Hauhart 2016); and many others.

References

Adams, James Truslow. [1931] 1933. *The Epic of America*. Garden City: Garden City Books.

Alger, Horatio Jr. [1868] 1962. *Ragged Dick, or Street Life in New York with Boot-Blacks, and Mark, the Match Boy*. New York: Collier Books.

Beard, Frank Lee, Joe Michael Hill, and Billy F Gibbons (ZZ Top). [1981] 2014. "Pearl Necklace" in *The Very Baddest (of ZZ Top)*. Los Angeles: Rhino/Warner.

Bourdieu, Pierre, and Jean-Claude Passeron. [1977] 1990. *Reproduction in Education, Society and Culture*. London: Sage.

Duina, Francesco. 2013. *Winning: Reflections on an American Obsession*. Princeton: Princeton University Press.

Fitzgerald, F. Scott. [1925] 2004. *The Great Gatsby*. New York: Scribner.

Gerth, H. H. and C. Wright Mills. 1946. *From Max Weber: Essays in Sociology*. New York: Oxford University Press.

Hauhart, Rober C. 2016. *Seeking the American Dream: A Sociological Inquiry*. New York: Palgrave Macmillan.

Hochschild, Jennifer L. 1995. *Facing Up to the American Dream: Race, Class and the Soul of the Nation*. Princeton: Princeton University Press.

Jillson, Cal. 2004. *Pursuing the American Dream: Opportunity and Exclusion over Four Centuries*. Lawrence: University Press of Kansas.

Ladd, Everett. 1993. "Thinking about America," *Public Perspective*, 4(5):19–34.

Lukács, Georg. 1971. *History and Class Consciousness: Studies in Marxist Dialectics*. Cambridge: MIT Press.

Merton, Robert K. 1938. "Social Structure and Anomie," *American Sociological Review*, 3(5):672–82.

Messner, Steven and Richard Rosenfeld. 2012. *Crime and the American Dream*. Belmont: Thomson/Wadsworth.

Milner, Murray, Jr. 1994. *Status and Sacredness: A General Theory of Status Relations and an Analysis of Indian Culture*. New York: Oxford University Press.

Putnam, Robert D. 2015. *Our Kids: The American Dream in Crisis*. New York: Simon and Schuster.

Rank, Mark, Thomas A. Hirschl, and Kirk A. Foster. 2014. *Chasing the American Dream: Understanding What Shapes Our Fortunes*. New York: Oxford University Press.

Slater, Philip. 1990. *The Pursuit of Loneliness*. Boston: Beacon Press.

Sorokin, Pitirim A. 1959. *Social and Cultural Mobility*. New York: Free Press.

Tocqueville, Alexis de. [1848] 1969. *Democracy in America* (One Volume; J.P. Mayer, ed.). New York: Doubleday.

PART I

Economic Success and Upward Economic Mobility and the American Dream

2

IN PURSUIT OF THE ELUSIVE AMERICAN DREAM

Black Woman Professionals

Tsedale M. Melaku

A Call to Action

2020 has called a lot into question and re-focused our attention on the long-standing inequities faced by Black people across America. The COVID-19 global pandemic, the murders of George Floyd, Breonna Taylor, and Ahmad Arbery by police and emboldened whites,[1] and the ensuing protests have systemically highlighted the impenetrable mechanisms that prevent Black people from not only accessing the *American Dream* but dying disproportionately from the nightmare of being Black in America. This year has called into question the declarations made not only by organizations professing to support racial justice[2] but also those made by the Founding Fathers and inscribed in the framework of the US Constitution, particularly the Declaration of Independence asserting: "We hold these truths to be self-evident, that all men are created equal, that they are endowed by their Creator with certain unalienable Rights, that among these are Life, Liberty and the pursuit of Happiness (US 1776)." Granted these words were written in consideration of white, male landowners, understanding that class, status, race, and gender played a significant role in conceptualizing whom these words were meant for. However, 2020 yearns for a reimagining of these words, to become fully realized, we must recognize how this *American Dream* remains but a dream, always elusive for many Black people in the United States.

It has been proclaimed that the *American Dream* is very much alive, this proclamation is often called upon to manifest through Barack Obama's presidency.[3] The idea that race is no longer central to the experiences of racially subordinated groups has been ill-founded and misguided. The myth of the *American Dream* has been challenged and continues to ring hollow for many Black people in America. Within the past ten years, the notion of a post-racial society[4] is, in fact, the myth that has been broken by the reality of the persistent discriminatory practices that lead to racial inequality, including the killing of Black people leading to the Black Lives Matter Movement; Executive Order 13769 Protecting the Nation from Foreign Terrorist Entry ("Muslim Ban"); Immigration and Customs Enforcement ("ICE") detention camps and family separations; and criminal justice inequities that disproportionately impact Black, Indigenous, and People of Color (BIPOC) to name a few.[5]

The structural foundation of what it means to pursue the *American Dream* is imperfect and not realized for all racial groups at the same level. Over racist practices have been subsumed

DOI: 10.4324/9781003326243-3

by subtle mechanisms that perpetuate racial inequality in American institutions, often maintained by white moderates and liberals who purport to be progressive in support of racial equity.[6] In this chapter, I illustrate this by looking at the challenges and narratives of Black professionals who are perceived as having broken through barriers to achieve educational and socioeconomic advancements and still face significant obstacles reaching the pinnacle of their profession. Through the lens of Black women lawyers, who are significantly marginalized in white institutional spaces and encounter the most difficulty rising to the rank of partner in elite law firms,[7] I challenge the idealized notion of the *American Dream*. My research highlights how Black women professionals face incredible challenges gaining entry to elite law firms, as well as accessing professional development and advancement opportunities, further thwarting this notion of the *American Dream*.

What is the *American Dream*?

Systemic racism is deeply rooted in American institutions controlling the resources that prevent access to the *American Dream* and negatively impact the life chances of Black people in America.[8] Running and navigating is very much a reality that many Black people continue to face today. Running toward the *American Dream* while navigating racist practices embedding across political, economic, social, and educational institutions preventing them from accessing the *dream* is endemic to the Black experience. What is this *dream*? I am profoundly impacted by the *American Dream* dreamt by my parents. As Ethiopian refugees in the 1980s, they dreamt of a land of opportunity where our abilities would lead to a better life than the one they were forced to leave. Like many immigrants who come to America, they dreamt that with hard work, determination, and access to education,[9] their children would fulfill the *dream*. For all intents and purposes, their *American Dream* was fulfilled by the *promise* of opportunity for their children.

Many people come to understand the *American Dream* as access to opportunity to become successful and live a better life. In *Facing Up to the American Dream: Race, Class, and the Soul of the Nation*, Jennifer L. Hochschild (1995)[10] thoroughly examines the differences in how Black and white Americans perceive access to opportunity and success for themselves as well as others. In Hochschild's attempt to explicate the common beliefs among Black and white Americans about the *American Dream*, the varied ways in which race complicates the *dream*, and the differences in how access to the *dream* is perceived by both groups, she articulates four tenets of the *American Dream*: (1) anyone can pursue their dream; (2) there is a reasonable anticipation of success; (3) this success depends on your will to work hard and your abilities; and finally, that (4) success is associated with virtue.[11] Hochschild's findings indicate that white Americans believe the *American Dream* is attainable for everyone, with discrimination not as prevalent as in the past. On the other hand, Black Americans perceive the *American Dream* to be mainly attainable to those who are not Black, with discrimination remaining persistent.

What is fascinating is that although the *dream* is elusive for Black people, the class variation among Black people also creates a varied response in terms of who buys into the *dream*. Poor Blacks were more likely to buy into the *American Dream*, while middle-class Blacks were less optimistic.[12] Race and class complicate the *dream*. The bootstrap mentality focusing on an individual agency that is part of the ideological push of the *American Dream* neglects the real strictures driven by systemic racism within American institutions. This feeds into the myth of the *American Dream*.[13] The notion that if you work hard enough, you will be successful and that those who are successful are virtuous plays into the narrative that those who succeed deserve their success. Interestingly, poor Blacks were also more likely to buy into this notion that hard work leads to success, and individual agency, to the detriment of social structures that impede on individual abilities to access opportunity. Therefore, we cannot deny the impact of racist social structures detailed in American history that prevent Black people from accessing the *American Dream*.

History Has Its Eye on the *American Dream*

The history of the United States is marred with the story of African Americans being forced to run and navigate. Forced into slavery on stolen land, Black bodies were used to build the *American Dream* for whites in America.[14] The wealth and privilege Black people amassed for whites in a system deliberately designed to keep the *dream* out of reach for those who were perceived as non-white is immeasurable. The American institution of slavery created an incredible divide between whites and Blacks through property ownership. Upon emancipation, the yolk of promised lands and opportunities quickly dried up or was never fulfilled. Running from abject poverty and destitution, Black people were forced into sharecropping and subsistence farming[15] which barely staved off hunger, let alone allowed them to save and build. Attempts to navigate this type of fraught living, combined with the continuous threat of racial violence, forced many Black people to migrate to northern and mid-western states, leading to the Great Migration.[16] However, the hope of opportunity was met with segregation, racial violence, limited access to jobs, and the reality that the *dream* to build was yet again out of reach for most Black people. This theme of running and navigating is strewn across American history and continues to be prevalent today.

Perhaps the best investigation into the plight of Black people in America fighting for access to the *American Dream* is through the work of William Edward Burghardt Du Bois. Sociologists aptly acknowledge the tremendous impact of Du Bois' book, *The Philadelphia Negro: A Social Study* (1899),[17] as one of the first works to historically record and sociologically examine the experiences of Black people in America[18] and the problems realizing the *American Dream*. Existing research thoroughly analyzes how American sociological perspectives can illuminate the influence of the *American Dream*.[19] Du Bois was one of the most influential Black scholars of the 20th century, notably known as the most prominent in sociology. In his 1940 "unofficial" autobiography, *Dusk of Dawn: An Essay Toward an Autobiography of a Race Concept*,[20] Du Bois provides detailed information on his personal life, focusing on his childhood upbringing and educational ambitions. During his early academic career, Du Bois primarily focused on the social sciences and used this science to frame his argument for the betterment of the Black race.[21] He believed that by doing a scientific analysis of the Black population, it would influence whites to intervene on behalf of Black people, which in turn, would bring about social change that would improve their condition in America.

Subsequently, Du Bois' first book, *The Philadelphia Negro: A Social Study* (1899),[22] is an intense social scientific study of the Black population residing in the Seventh Ward of Philadelphia. This was the first study ever done on a Black community in America, using comprehensive qualitative and quantitative analysis as a method of collecting data on the social, economic, political, and religious life of Black people in this section of Philadelphia.[23] Du Bois attempted to awaken the white consciousness of America as a means of effecting positive social change for the Black community. *The Philadelphia Negro* is Du Bois' social conservative reform appeal to white advocates for the social improvement of Blacks through changing institutions that upheld racist ideology by excluding Blacks and upholding Jim Crow laws. At the time, he believed that these conditions would only change with the help of whites.[24] However, Du Bois would later modify his views on how he would be able to effect change.

The Problem with Accessing the *American Dream*

As the times would have it, the late 1890s into the 20th century was the height of brutality visited upon the Black population and Du Bois began to realize that using a social
science approach in order to appeal to whites for help may not be enough. With the persistence of Jim Crow laws, lynchings, disenfranchisement, and riots; Du Bois recognized
that Black people could only change their condition through activism, such as protesting.
In *The Souls of Black Folk: Essays and Sketches* (1903),[25] Du Bois proclaims a uniqueness of
African American salvation, recognizing that "the problem of the Twentieth Century is the
problem of the color-line."[26] This color-line, presented in physical racial appearance, is the
foundation of the denial of access to resources, benefits, and privileges afforded to whites –
to Black people. This is what keeps Black people from accessing the *American Dream*. In
showing the historical struggles of Black people through slavery, reconstruction, and the fall
of reconstruction, Du Bois outlines the hardships Black people endured as a result of failed
US policies. Policies that did not successfully provide freed enslaved people with economic
opportunity of growth and educational development,[27] all of which is necessary to access the
American Dream.

Recognizing the fact that the playing field must be leveled, while racial discrimination[28]
and practices used to keep Black people from the *dream* has to be interrogated, we cannot
ignore the actions of the government. The United States' public investments and historical programs, such as the Homestead Act of 1862, which gave farmland, the Servicemen's
Readjustment Bill of 1944 ("GI Bill"), which provided education, and the Veteran's
Administration Mortgage, which gave loans for homeownership were only accessible to
whites.[29] All of these strategic government interventions created a gap in generational wealth
favoring whites while stymying the wealth building potential of racially subordinated groups
in the US, as well as the opportunity to access the *American Dream*. The structured social
programs put in place to help white Americans reach the *dream* speaks directly to the benefits
and privileges of being white in America. Race has always been a critical factor of the
American Dream.

The creation of housing segregation in the United States is another key factor that perpetuates
the barriers Black people face trying to access the *dream*. The separation of different groups
of people into distinct neighborhoods was birthed in the early 1900s. Racial segregation
developed precisely out of racial violence carried out by whites to prevent Blacks from living
in white neighborhoods. Racially restrictive neighborhood covenants that legally protected
whites who aimed to ensure that property leases or sales would be restricted to whites[30] also
played a significant role in keeping white neighborhoods exclusively white. Homeownership
is a cornerstone of the *American Dream*, and by preventing Black people from buying homes,
this specifically stifled their access to accumulating home equity, tax savings, economic stability, and other varying benefits that build wealth. Discriminatory practices in lending,
including redlining, housing covenants, limited access to Federal Housing Administration
loans, predatory lending, and subprime loans, all contribute to making the *American Dream*
both elusive and illusive for Black people in America.[31] This funnels into housing, education,
income, labor market, health, and criminal justice inequities that disproportionately impact
Black communities.

The COVID-19 global pandemic and racial upheaval in America have shown a glaring
light on racial inequities that continue to impact the life chances of Black people in America.
As Dr. Martin Luther King, Jr. preaches in his July 4, 1965 sermon,[32] segregation, and

discrimination, endemic racist practices must be rooted out in order to make the *American Dream* a reality for all Americans:

> Now there's another thing that we must never forget. If we are going to make the *American dream* a reality, (*Yes*) we are challenged to work in an action program to get rid of the last vestiges of segregation and discrimination. This problem isn't going to solve itself, however much [*word inaudible*] people tell us this…History is the long story of the fact (*Yes*) that privileged groups seldom give up their privileges without strong resistance, and they seldom do it voluntarily. And so if the *American dream* is to be a reality, we must work to make it a reality and realize the urgency of the moment. And we must say now is the time to make real the promises of democracy. Now is the time to get rid of segregation and discrimination…Now is the time to make the United States a better nation. (*Yes*) We must live with that, and we must believe that.[33]

Dr. Martin Luther King Jr's words ring true today as it did 55 years ago. COVID-19 and the continued abject brutalization of Black people in America at the hands of emboldened whites[34] and police officers has awakened what has always been a problem too difficult to address substantively: *the seamless proliferation of racism within American institutions*. From the streets to the halls, racism has thrived, stalling access to medical care, education, housing, wealth building, jobs, justice, and equity for Black people.

As is demonstrated in my study examining the experiences of Black women lawyers in elite law firms, many perceive the *dream* to be elusive based on the daily, subtle racial and gender aggressions they continue to experience. Black professionals in white institutional spaces have a front-row seat in seeing how racism and discrimination work to paralyze Black people's social, political, and economic advancement. In analyzing Black women's experiences, we must engage how systemic gendered racism works to create nuanced oppressive experiences that are unique to their social location.[35] The ways that race and gender overlap, combine and intersect are critical to understanding Black women's access to the *American Dream*.

Gender at Play – Impact on Women Professionals

Arlie Hochschild and Anne Machung (1989)[36] describe the unpaid labor women perform at home in addition to the paid labor they engage in at work as the *second shift*. As though the *second shift* was not hard enough on women in America, the COVID-19 global pandemic compounds the level of visible and invisible labor women face in varying workplaces in America. Women across the country must contend with the fact that they not only have to maintain their "day" jobs but must now multi-task in a way that requires them to become full-time teachers, full-time mothers, full-time cooks, and full-time cleaners all at once.[37] Schools closing and distance learning becoming our new normal has changed the everyday labor associated with working full-time and managing a household. Similar to Hochschild's findings, women continue to be primarily responsible for childcare and household work, in addition to their everyday jobs.[38] While some progress[39] has been made since Hochschild's study to help women advance in corporate America, the present situation – absent of any external and often costly scaffolds such as nannies, after-school programs, or housekeepers – renders women into their historical default mode as the primary caretaker of children and home.[40]

Historically and culturally in society, women and men are socially programmed to fit within gender roles that posit women as caregivers and men as providers.[41] Numerous studies suggest that this exists precisely because of the gender stereotypes that "derive from the discrepant distribution of men and women in social roles both in the home and at work."[42] Research on homeschooling indicates that mothers are the "she-fault" parent during this pandemic, arguing that the expectation that child-rearing and homeschooling is "women's work" is proving to be a reality for many during this global health crisis.[43] Today this translates into the majority of the housework and caretaking responsibilities disproportionately falling on the shoulders of women while they also maintain their "day" jobs.[44] The added labor required to do this level of work will undoubtedly lead to various outcomes, but one that really concerns many is the demise of the potential opportunity and access for women in the workplace. This lack of access is also compounded by the fact that unemployment has soared to unprecedented levels,[45] which is expected to disproportionately affect women and racially subordinated communities, as was seen during the 2008 Great Recession.[46] This will continue to make the *American Dream* elusive for Black women to access.

Intersections of Race and Gender at Play – Impact on Black Women Lawyers

The COVID-19 global pandemic has magnified the ways in which systemic racism is embedded within American institutions, including political, economic, social, educational, legal, and medical systems.[47] The incredible loss of life suffered among Black and Latinx communities highlights the racial disparities that exist in accessing medical services, working essential jobs, limited financial resources, poverty, food insecurity, and housing inequities. All of these factors produce social conditions that perpetuate racial inequalities.[48] Women of color, and Black women particularly, fare worse than any other group during COVID-19 with compounded challenges associated with racial and gender inequities.[49] There is no doubt that the global pandemic has had a significant impact on women of color accessing advancement opportunity as they work from home. What does this mean in terms of remote work and the recognition of invisible work done? Although working from home may have appealed to many, it was appealing in so far as school was in session and employees had the space and time to focus on the work. The added physical, emotional and cognitive labor women are required to take on will have deleterious effects on their advancement prospects, undoubtedly making it even harder to reach the *American Dream*, and especially for women of color.[50]

Scholarship focusing on the salience of race, gender, class, and varying other axes of identity, points to the uniqueness of the experiences of women of color.[51] Intersectional approaches that take into account how racial and gender oppression create nuanced and often disadvantageous outcomes for women of color are critical to understanding the experiences that marginalize and silence this group.[52] Focusing on the experiences of Black women provides insight on the major barriers women of color face accessing professional development, mentor and sponsorship relationships, and networking opportunities that would facilitate their advancement in organizations.[53]

The theme of running and navigating becomes even more prevalent in the experiences of Black professionals in white spaces. Black women navigating white institutional spaces, and working to reach the *American Dream* has always been a site of contention.[54] The "double burden" Black women face based on the deeply entrenched racial and gender discrimination that permeates law firms creates concrete barriers to their ability to navigate successfully.[55] It was already hard enough to gain access while physically being present in the workplace, where Black women are rendered invisible by existing practices.[56] The global pandemic has intensified the barriers Black women are forced to contend with today.

In my study examining the experiences of Black women in elite law firms, I argue that there are specific challenges to their advancement that result from race and gender overlapping, intersecting, and/or combining. I conceptualize that an *invisible labor clause* exists in the employment contract of Black women that requires them to perform, added, invisible, uncompensated labor to maintain their positions and to navigate daily racialized and gendered aggressions in the firm.[57] This invisible labor manifests in the form of an organizational *inclusion tax*, highlighting the economic value of the invisible labor performed without compensation or recognition. The *inclusion tax* represents the additional resources Black women are forced to "spend," such as money, time, mental, and emotional energy to not only be included in white spaces but also to resist and/or adhere to white norms.[58] The *inclusion tax* is further theorized to specifically manifests in emotional, cognitive, financial, and relational labor.[59]

Women's Work Pre and Post-COVID-19

Prior to COVID-19, the Black women interviewed in my study stressed that unlike many of their male counterparts, they did not have the convenience of having another person (i.e. a partner) take on the essential daily "home" work required to maintain their households, while still maintaining their rigorous work responsibilities.[60] Daily home "work" includes cleaning, cooking, laundry, dry cleaning, paying bills, grocery shopping, managing childcare, school responsibilities, and much more. And where available, many women have to procure these services from outside networks of support in order to maintain their demanding work schedules.[61] As a result of COVID-19, these very networks and systems of support are removed with the burden falling on women to take up the task of managing two shifts simultaneously at once, often performing a *third shift* in order to mitigate the potentially negative effects on work and home. If these same issues have already created significant attrition rates for women in firms prior to this pandemic, it is only fair to deduce that this current climate, which prevents systems of support from existing, will lead to even higher rates of attrition among all women, but particularly for women of color.[62]

Jocaste, a fifth year-associate, describes this disparity as the "double shift:"

> I don't have a wife at home who takes care of all my business. That was one thing that I think was very annoying to a lot of us women. Because most of the men worked late, and male partners assigned work. And it was great that they [men] got stuff done at home because they had a wife at home who could take care of all their stuff. Not us; we don't have wives. We're the wives, or we're single or what have you, so laundry doesn't get done, cooking doesn't get done, bills don't get paid. All of those things that they rely on their women, I hate saying that, but their wives to do. We just didn't have the liberty, and it was very frustrating because there was no recognition of the fact that women, for better or for worse, have this sort of double shift. We need to work, but we also, to the extent we have someone at home, we're still in that role of wife, girlfriend, mother, whatever it is where we have things to do at home. There was no acknowledgment of that and not at the other firms I was at either.
>
> *Melaku 2019a, 55*

As depicted in Jocaste's narrative, the *inclusion tax* manifests in the cognitive and emotional labor she is forced to engage in attempting to navigate the firm and the politics surrounding gender expectations at home and in the workplace. The care work that is disproportionately on women to maintain home and hearth while rigorously sustaining their work responsibilities is unacknowledged and detrimental to their professional development and advancement opportunities. The *American Dream* cannot be realized for Black women if the additional labor they are saddled with to be in white spaces is not acknowledged and mitigated to prevent them from getting derailed while pursuing an upward career trajectory.

While the present COVID-19 pandemic poses very real problems for everyone working remotely with their children, partners, families, pets, and home life converging in one[63] – the fact remains that before the pandemic working remotely has always posed different perceptions for women as compared to men and will continue to do so. When women work from home, there is a gendered and racial framing[64] that operates to create bias, assumptions, and narratives that they are hanging out with their children or doing non-work-related tasks or personal errands such as getting their nails done. On the other hand, when men are working from home, they are presumed to be working hard. Kallisto, a sixth-year associate in the study, poignantly calls out presumptions about women working outside of the office and the double standard that exists with men, saying:

> I was on a deal one time with a partner who I absolutely loved. This partner, he was great, and we're on the phone, we're trying to reach counsel on the other side, and he's like, "Oh, she's probably out just getting her nails done. Why is she not answering her phone?" And I thought to myself, "If this was a male, he would never assume that the reason why this male is not answering this call is because of anything other than something being work-related." But for a woman, and this happened often, and this is just a small example because this used to always happen with women on the other side of deals in positions of power, the partners would always assume that they were not responsive for superficial reasons. But the male, it was because they were busy with other clients, and they were just busy. They must be busy. And that bothered me so much. And it happened often, but when it happened with this partner, it made me particularly upset because...even a good/bad situation, it's still bad. It still stinks, and even the best of the partners here think of women subtly in a way, that women in positions of power are dillydallying and off taking care of kids, when I know clients have called you [the partner], and you've asked me to redirect the call because you're on a roller coaster right now. So why are you assuming?
>
> *Melaku 2019a, 87*

The amount of invisible labor required to maneuver gender stereotypes, as depicted by Kallisto, is exhausting, discouraging, and unstainable. Like proactive policies that should already support Black women in physical workspaces, in remote workspaces, there needs to be the acknowledgment that invisible, unpaid labor exists and is exacerbated. Although these professionals are not in the firm's physical offices, they are maintaining their jobs while doing "home" work, which again will inevitably affect how Black women access networking and professional development opportunities. Work/Life balance efforts have always been challenging, but the dilemma is now exacerbated by both converging in time and space. Unless organizations are willing to regress and force women to choose between personal responsibilities, professional development, and career advancement, they must recognize the impact of gendered stereotypes on work and home expectations.

For Black women professionals, gendered stereotypes are compounded by existing racial narratives about their competence, work habits, drive, and desire to be successful, all of which derive from the white racial framing entrenched within structures that are systemically racist.[65] Therefore, although Black women professionals are in large part perceived to have "made it" or are living the *American Dream* because of their educational attainments and entry into white spaces, they are still prevented from reaching the pinnacle of their profession. The path to the coveted position of partner in law firms is marred with the subtle yet pernicious inequalities that produce a steep *inclusion tax* in the form of uncompensated, invisible labor. This uncompensated and unrecognized invisible labor works to keep Black women professionals entrenched in mitigating daily racialized and gendered aggressions.

Black at Work in the Time of BLM and Racial Upheaval

As Jennifer L. Hochschild (1995)[66] finds in her study on the *American Dream*, Black middle-class respondents recognized that although they may be perceived as having gained access to white spaces, they are often recipients of pervasive discriminatory practices that hinder their ability to advance. The subtle nature of racism in law firms is incredibly pervasive with cultural and structural barriers it imposes when it comes to advancing lawyers of color.[67] There are various factors that negatively impact the trajectory of Black associates in corporate law firms that stem from subconscious stereotypes and biases that manifest in white institutional spaces.[68] However, the racialized social structure law firms are built upon is the crux of why white privilege and power continue to proliferate, maintaining a racial hierarchy that benefits whites over all other racial groups.[69]

The experiences of Black lawyers can be explained by considering how a "new racism" permeates within social and institutional structures in American society that rely on a color-blind racist ideology.[70] Color-blind racist ideology works to explain contemporary racial inequality as the outcome of nonracial dynamics, emphasized in four critical frames, including *abstract liberalism, cultural racism, minimization of racism,* and *naturalization*.[71] The importance of each frame is that it justifies and reproduces racial inequality without outwardly appearing racist. Essentially, color-blind racist ideology provides whites with an opportunity to engage in subtle forms of discriminatory practices that maintain and reinforce white privilege and power without being labeled as racists.[72] This is a critical point when considering how many white progressives actually perpetuate racial inequality within organizations.[73]

One of the core themes throughout my interviews with Black women lawyers centers on the subtle ways they experience racism, which makes it very difficult for them to navigate their firms. These daily racial and gender aggressions have a cumulative effect that negatively impacts their lived experiences and career trajectories. Black associates often feel isolated and are required to make others comfortable with their difference and presence.[74] The recent verified complaint filed by a Black associate formerly employed at a major law firm[75] outlines the dismissive nature of firm practices that ingeniously engage in racial bias creating significant barriers for Black lawyers' professional development and advancement. It is one of many examples of how Black lawyers are marginalized in white spaces.[76] Specific practices by law firms minimize the effects of racism by blaming those victimized for their victimization,[77] as well as systemically removing them from gaining access to training, substantive work, mentor/sponsor relationships, networking, and various other opportunities to advance.[78]

The countless killings of Black people during the global pandemic amplifies the ways that they are forced to continue to fight two viruses simultaneously in America, COVID-19, and racism. The story today penetrating the lives of Black people is one where they are running and navigating, running from the COVID-19 disease while continuously navigating the plague of racism. In the wake of racial upheaval in America, organizations across the nation have publicly stepped out with press releases in support of racial justice, reaffirming commitments to diversity, equity and inclusion.[79] The efficacy of these statements is called into question when considering the experiences of Black people in organizational spaces.

Being a Black person in a predominately white institution impacts how people perceive them and how that effects inclusion. In this moment of racial upheaval, Black people have been called upon to relive their racial traumas for public learning and consumption. Practices that do not address systemic racism embedded within the structure of the organization are the problem. Law firms and other varying organizations need to recognize that public statements of support ring hollow when the experiences of Black professionals are not addressed within their organizations. Pipeline narratives that continue to argue that there is "a very limited pool of Black talent to recruit from"[80] or that Black professionals are not interested in working in law firms perpetuate racial inequality.[81]

Being one of the very few Black people in white spaces lead to white narratives of affirmative action that label Black people as diversity hires, perpetuating arguments that they are not qualified to be in white spaces.[82] Presumptions of incompetence[83] that are embedded in appearance limit the advancement opportunities of Black professionals because it often works to impede access to professional development and relationship building with mentors and sponsors.[84] It also works to make Black professionals hypervisible when marginal mistakes are made, and invisible when recognition of good work is warranted.[85] This hypervisibility and invisibility, as a result of being one of very few Black people, work to simultaneously marginalize and silence Black women in white spaces. Therefore being an outsider comes with very real emotional, mental, and physical labor required to manage other people's perceptions of you to be included, which is an invisible labor.

The experiences of the Black women interviewed continuously reflect how they were forced to adjust to the expectation of making others comfortable with their difference and presence, paying an *inclusion tax* to be included in white spaces. The recognition that racism exists, whether intended or not and the hidden mechanisms that perpetuate it is just as important as understanding the impact of these mechanisms on Black professionals. Discriminatory practices are built into the ways that organizations operate primarily to maintain the status quo.[86] This inevitably limits the potential for Black lawyers to reach the pinnacle of their profession and hinders their ability to fully access the *American Dream*.

Conclusion

The first step that needs to be taken is the recognition that the *American Dream* can never be realized unless accountability there is for the marred history that is continuously amplified by the racial inequities pervasive in the everyday lives of Black people in America. Recommendations that managers, employers, and organizations as a whole can take on include understanding that women, women of color, and Black women particularly are disproportionately burdened by the "home" work necessary to maintain their households; and recognizing that support networks that were in place, such as nannies, caretakers, families, or schools are presently unavailable for many families – women – to utilize. Organizations have an opportunity to make substantive changes by targeting racial and gender inequities, biased performance metrics, instituting flexible work schedules, and supporting development and advancement prospects for Black women, especially working mothers – creating space for a more equitable workplace.

If organizations do not make intentional and targeted changes that will shift the wave of inequity magnified during this dual pandemic, the *American Dream* will continue to remain elusive for Black professionals and Black women specifically. Running from racial discrimination, gender stereotypes, limited access, and unequal resources, all while navigating white institutional spaces imbedded with racist mechanisms that perpetuate inequities, will continue to remain the dominant narrative centering Black professionals in America – unless we face the reality of our past, present, and future.

Notes

1 Aaron Ross Coleman, "Black Bodies Are Still Treated as Expendable," *Vox*, June 5, 2020, https://www.vox.com/2020/6/5/21277938/ahmaud-arbery-george-floyd-breonna-taylor-covid.
2 Tsedale M. Melaku and Angie Beeman, "Academia Isn't a Safe Haven for Conversations about Race and Racism," *Harvard Business Review*, June 25, 2020, https://hbr.org/2020/06/academia-isnt-a-safe-haven-for-conversations-about-race.
3 Jonathan Charteris-Black, *Politicians and Rhetoric: The Persuasive Power of Metaphor* (Basingstoke: Palgrave Macmillan, 2005); Jeffrey Nesoff, "The Myth of a Post-Racial Society after the Obama Presidency," *Facing History and Ourselves*, February 8, 2017, https://facingtoday.facinghistory.org/the-myth-of-a-post-racial-society-after-the-obama-presidency; Michael Tesler, *Post-Racial or Most-Racial?: Race and Politics in the Obama Era* (Chicago, IL: University of Chicago Press, 2016); and Randall Kennedy, *The Persistence of the Color-Line: Racial Politics and the Obama Presidency* (New York: Pantheon, 2011).
4 Charteris-Black, *Politicians and Rhetoric: The Persuasive Power of Metaphor*; Nesoff, "The Myth of a Post-Racial Society after the Obama Presidency"; Tesler, *Post-Racial or Most-Racial?: Race and Politics in the Obama Era*; and Kennedy, *The Persistence of the Color-Line: Racial Politics and the Obama Presidency*.
5 Black Lives Matter, "Herstory," BLM, Accessed September 28, 2020, https://blacklivesmatter.com/herstory/; American Civil Liberties Union, "Timeline of the Muslim Ban," *ACLU*, Accessed September 28, 2020, https://www.aclu-wa.org/pages/timeline-muslim-ban; Southern Poverty Law Center, "Family Separation under the Trump Administration – A Timeline," *SPLC*, Accessed September 28, 2020, https://www.splcenter.org/news/2020/06/17/family-separation-under-trump-administration-timeline; and Michelle Alexander, *The New Jim Crow: Mass Incarceration in the Age of Colorblindness* (New York: The New Press, 2012).
6 Tsedale M. Melaku "Amy Cooper, White Privilege and the Murder of Black People," *Fair Observer*, June 2, 2020, https://www.fairobserver.com/region/north_america/tsedale-melaku-amy-cooper-white-privilege-abstract-liberalism-george-floyd-death-protests-us-news-15161/; Angie Beeman, "Walk the Walk but Don't Talk the Talk: The Strategic Use of Color-Blind Ideology in an Interracial Social Movement Organization," *Sociological Forum* 30, no. 1 (2015): 127–47, https://doi.org/10.1111/socf.12148.
7 Tsedale M. Melaku, *You Don't Look Like a Lawyer: Black Women and Systemic Gendered Racism* (Lanham, MD: Rowman & Littlefield, 2019).
8 Joe R. Feagin, *Systemic Racism: A Theory of Oppression* (New York: Routledge, 2006).
9 Jennifer L. Hochschild, *Facing Up to the American Dream: Race, Class and the Soul of the Nation* (Princeton, NJ: Princeton University Press, 1995), 16.
10 Hochschild, *Facing Up to the American Dream*.
11 Hochschild, *Facing Up to the American Dream*, 15–25.
12 Hochschild, *Facing Up to the American Dream*, 80.
13 John Archer, "The Resilience of Myth: The Politics of the *American Dream*," *Traditional Dwellings and Settlements Review* 25, no. 2 (2014): 7–21, Accessed September 2, 2020, http://www.jstor.org/stable/24347714.
14 Feagin, *Systemic Racism*; and Joe R. Feagin, *Racist America: Roots, Current Realities, and Future Reparations*, 2nd ed. (New York: Routledge, 2010).
15 Feagin, *Systemic Racism*, 128–9.
16 Feagin, *Systemic Racism*, 131.
17 W.E.B. Du Bois and Isabel Eaton, *The Philadelphia Negro: A Social Study* (Philadelphia, PA: University of Pennsylvania Press, 1899).

18 Aldon D. Morris, *The Scholar Denied: W.E.B. Du Bois and the Birth of Modern Sociology* (Oakland, CA: University of California Press, 2015).

19 Sandra L. Hanson and John Kenneth White, *The American Dream in the 21st Century* (Philadelphia, PA: Temple University Press, 2011); Robert C. Hauhart, "American Sociology's Investigations of the *American Dream*: Retrospect and Prospect," *The American Sociologist* 46, no. 1 (2015): 65–98, https://doi.org/10.1007/s12108-015-9253-1.

20 W.E.B. Du Bois and Irene Diggs, *Dusk of Dawn: An Essay Toward an Autobiography of Race Concept* (New Brunswick: Transaction Publishers, 2011).

21 Du Bois and Diggs, *Dusk of Dawn: An Essay Toward an Autobiography of Race Concept*.

22 Du Bois and Eaton, *The Philadelphia Negro*.

23 Du Bois and Eaton, *The Philadelphia Negro*.

24 Du Bois and Eaton, *The Philadelphia Negro*.

25 W.E.B. Du Bois, *The Souls of Black Folk: Essays and Sketches* (Chicago: A.C. McClurg & Co., 1903).

26 Du Bois, *The Souls of Black Folk*, VII, 13, 40.

27 Du Bois, *The Souls of Black Folk*.

28 Adia Harvey Wingfield and Koji Chavez, "Getting in, Getting Hired, Getting Sideways Looks: Organizational Hierarchy and Perceptions of Racial Discrimination," *American Sociological Review* 85, no.1 (2020): 31–57, https://journals.sagepub.com/doi/pdf/10.1177/0003122419894335.

29 Feagin, *Systemic Racism*, 3.

30 Feagin, *Systemic Racism*, 126.

31 Jacob S. Rugh, Len Albright, and Douglas S. Massey, "Race, Space, and Cumulative Disadvantage: A Case Study of the Subprime Lending Collapse," *Social Problems* 62, no. 2 (2015): 186–218, https://doi.org/10.1093/socpro/spv002.

32 Martin Luther King, Jr., "The *American Dream*," The Martin Luther King, Jr., Research and Education Institute, July 9, 2014, https://kinginstitute.stanford.edu/king-papers/publications/knock-midnight-inspiration-great-sermons-reverend-martin-luther-king-jr-4.

33 King, "The *American Dream*."

34 Melaku, "Amy Cooper, White Privilege and the Murder of Black People."

35 Adia Harvey Wingfield, *Doing Business with Beauty: Black Women, Hair Salons, and the Racial Enclave Economy* (Lanham, MD: Rowman & Littlefield, 2008).

36 Arlie Russell Hochschild and Anne Machung, *The Second Shift: Working Parents and the Revolution at Home* (New York: Viking, 1989).

37 Brittni Frederiksen, Ivette Gomez, Alina Salganicoff, and Usha Ranji, "Coronavirus: A Look at Gender Differences in Awareness and Actions," *Kaiser Family Foundation*, March 20, 2020, https://www.kff.org/coronavirus-covid-19/issue-brief/coronavirus-a-look-at-gender-differences-in-awareness-and-actions/.

38 Hochschild and Machung, *The Second Shift*; and Robin J. Ely and Irene Padavic, "What's Really Holding Women Back?," *Harvard Business Review*, February 19, 2020, https://hbr.org/2020/03/whats-really-holding-women-back.

39 Ely and Padavic, "What's Really Holding Women Back."

40 Tital Alon, Matthias Doepke, Jane Olmstead-Rumsey, and Michèle Tertilt, "The Impact of COVID-19 on Gender Equality," *Covid Economics*, CEPR Press 4, April 2020: 62–85, https://doi.org/10.3386/w26947.

41 Jonathan Gershuny, Michael Bittman, and John Brice, "Exit, Voice, and Suffering: Do Couples Adapt to Changing Employment Patterns?," *Journal of Marriage and Family* 67, no. 3 (2005): 656–65, https://doi.org/10.1111/j.1741-3737.2005.00160.x.

42 Tanja Hentschel, Madeline E. Heilman, and Claudia V. Peus, "The Multiple Dimensions of Gender Stereotypes: A Current Look at Men's and Women's Characterizations of Others and Themselves," *Frontiers in Psychology* 10 (2019): 2, https://doi.org/10.3389/fpsyg.2019.00011.

43 Kate Henley Averett, "Moms Are the 'She-Fault' Parent during This Pandemic," *Scary Mommy*, March 27, 2020, https://www.scarymommy.com/coronavirus-homeschooling-disproportionate-burden-women/.

44 Jessica Bennett, "'I Feel Like I Have Five Jobs': Moms Navigate the Pandemic," *New York Times*, March 20, 2020, https://www.nytimes.com/2020/03/20/parenting/childcare-coronavirus-moms.html.

45 Scott Horsley, "One for the History Books: 14.7% Unemployment, 20.5 Million Jobs Wiped Away," *National Public Radio*, May 8, 2020, https://www.npr.org/sections/coronavirus-live-updates/2020/05/08/852430930/one-for-the-history-books-14-7-unemployment-20-5-million-

jobs-wiped-away; Anu Madgavkar, Olivia White, Mekala Krishnan, Deepa Mahajan, and Xavier Azcue, "COVID-19 and Gender Equality: Countering the Regressive Effects," *McKinsey & Company*, July 15, 2020, https://www.mckinsey.com/featured-insights/future-of-work/covid-19-and-gender-equality-countering-the-regressive-effects.

46 Cynthia Fuchs Epstein and Abigail Kolker, "The Impact of the Economic Downturn on Women Lawyers in the United States," *Indiana Journal of Global Legal Studies* 20, no. 2 (2013): 1169, https://doi.org/10.2979/indjglolegstu.20.2.1169; and Kori Hale, "The Economic Impact of COVID-19 Will Hit Minorities the Hardest," *Forbes*, March 17, 2020, https://www.forbes.com/sites/korihale/2020/03/17/the-economic-impact-of-covid-19-will-hit-minorities-the-hardest/#1218a08310c0.

47 Feagin, *Systemic Racism*.

48 Whitney N. Laster Pirtle, "Racial Capitalism: A Fundamental Cause of Novel Coronavirus (COVID-19) Pandemic Inequities in the United States," *Health Education and Behavior*, April 26, 2020, https://doi.org/10.1177/1090198120922942; Angel Gurría, "Commentary: COVID-19 Is Compounding Housing Inequities Worldwide. How to Fix That," *Fortune*, July 31, 2020, https://fortune.com/2020/07/31/covid-housing-impact-affordability-sustainability/.

49 Lucy Erickson, "The Disproportionate Impact of COVID-19 on Women of Color," *Society for Women's Health Research*, April 30, 2020, https://swhr.org/the-disproportionate-impact-of-covid-19-on-women-of-color/; Casey McDermott, "Black Women Are Affected Disproportionately by COVID-19 in N.H., New Data Show," *New Hampshire Public Radio*, August 13, 2020, https://www.nhpr.org/post/black-women-are-affected-disproportionately-covid-19-nh-new-data-shows#stream/0.

50 Jocelyn Frye, "On the Frontlines at Work and at Home: The Disproportionate Economic Effects of the Coronavirus Pandemic on Women of Color," *Center for American Progress*, April 23, 2020, Accessed September 2, 2020, https://www.americanprogress.org/issues/women/reports/2020/04/23/483846/frontlines-work-home/.

51 Destiny Perry, Paulette Brown, and Eileen Letts, *Left Out and Left Behind: The Hurtles, Hassles, and Heartaches of Achieving Long-Term Legal Careers for Women of Color*, American Bar Association (ABA) Commission on Women in the Profession (Chicago: IL American Bar Association, 2020); The NALP Foundation for Law Career Research and Education and The Center for Women in Law, *Women of Color: A Study of Law School Experiences*, 2020; Melaku, *You Don't Look Like a Lawyer*; Adia Harvey Wingfield, *Flatline: Race, Work and Healthcare* (Oakland, CA: University of California Press, 2019); Beeman, "Walk the Walk but Don't Talk the Talk;" Janet E. Gans Epner, *Visible Invisibility: Women of Color in Law Firms*, American Bar Association (ABA) Commission on Women in the Profession (Chicago, IL: American Bar Association, 2006); Kimberlé Crenshaw, "Mapping the Margins: Intersectionality, Identity Politics, and Violence against Women of Color," *Stanford Law Review* 43, no. 6 (1991): 285–320, https://doi.org/10.2307/1229039.

52 Patricia Hill Collins, *Black Feminist Thought: Knowledge, Consciousness, and the Politics of Empowerment*, (New York: Routledge, 2000); Patricia Hill Collins, "It's All in the Family: Intersections of Gender, Race and Nation," *Hypatia* 13, no. 3 (1998): 62–82, http://www.jstor.org/stable/3810699; Crenshaw, "Mapping the Margins;" Philomena Essed, *Understanding Everyday Racism: An Interdisciplinary Approach* (London, England: Sage, 1991); Denise Segura, "Chicanas and the Triple Oppressions in the Labor Force," in *Chicana Voices: Intersection of Class, Race, and Gender*, ed. Teresa Cordova and the National Association of Chicana Studies Editorial Committee (Austin, TX: Center for Mexican American Studies, 1984), 47–65; Patricia Hill Collins, "Learning from the Outsider within: The Sociological Significance of Black Feminist Thought," *Social Problems* 33, no. 6 (1986): 14–32, https://doi.org/10.2307/800672.

53 Melaku, *You Don't Look Like a Lawyer*.

54 Enobong Hannah Branch, *Opportunity Denied: Limiting Black Women to Devalued Work* (New Brunswick, NJ: Rutgers University Press, 2011); Sharon Harley, *Sister Circle: Black Women and Work* (New Brunswick, NJ: Rutgers University Press, 2002).

55 Feagin, *Racist America*; Yanick St. Jean and Joe R. Feagin, *Double Burden: Black Women and Everyday Racism* (Armonk, NY: M. E. Sharpe, 1998).

56 Melaku, *You Don't Look Like a Lawyer*.

57 Melaku, *You Don't Look Like a Lawyer*, 16–18; Tsedale M. Melaku, "Why Women and People of Color in Law Still Hear 'You Don't Look Like a Lawyer,'" *Harvard Business Review*, August 7, 2019, https://hbr.org/2019/08/why-women-and-people-of-color-in-law-still-hear-you-dont-look-like-a-lawyer.

58 Melaku, *You Don't Look Like a Lawyer*, 16–18; Tsedale M. Melaku, "Why Women and People of Color Still Hear."

59 Melaku, "Black women in white institutional spaces: The invisible labor clause and the inclusion tax," *American Behavioral Scientist* 66, 11(2022): 1512–1525. https://doi.org/10.1177/00027642211066037.

60 Melaku, *You Don't Look Like a Lawyer*, 55–56, 58.

61 Melaku, *You Don't Look Like a Lawyer*, 49–76.

62 Vault and Minority Corporate Counsel Association, 2019 *Vault/MCCA Law Firm Diversity Survey*, 2019, https://www.mcca.com/wp-content/uploads/2020/03/2019-Vault_MCCA-Law-Firm-Diversity-Survey-Report.pdf; National Association for Law Placement (NALP), *2019 Report on Diversity in U.S. Law Firms* (Washington, DC: National Association of Law Placement), https://www.nalp.org/uploads/2019_DiversityReport.pdf; Melaku, *You Don't Look Like a Lawyer*; Deepali Bagati, *Women of Color in U.S. Law Firms: Women of Color in Professional Services Series* (New York: Catalyst, 2009).

63 Adam Gorlick, "The Productivity Pitfalls of Working from Home in the Age of COVID-19," *Stanford News*, March 30, 2020, https://news.stanford.edu/2020/03/30/productivity-pitfalls-working-home-age-covid-19/; Anna Fazackerley, "Women's Research Plummets during Lockdown – but Articles from Men Increase," *The Guardian*, Guardian News and Media, May 12, 2020. https://www.theguardian.com/education/2020/may/12/womens-research-plummets-during-lockdown-but-articles-from-men-increase; Nicholas Bloom, James Liang, John Roberts, and Zhichun Jenny Ying, "Does Working from Home Work? Evidence from a Chinese Experiment," *The Quarterly Journal of Economics* 30 (2015): 165–218, https://doi.org/10.1093/qje/qju032.

64 Joe R. Feagin, *The White Racial Frame: Centuries of Racial Framing and Counter-Framing*, 2nd ed. (New York: Routledge, 2013); Wingfield, *Doing Business with Beauty*; Feagin, *Systemic Racism*.

65 Feagin, *The White Racial Frame*; Feagin, *Racist America*; Feagin, *Systemic Racism*.

66 Hochschild, *Facing Up to the American Dream*.

67 David B. Wilkins and Mitu G. Gulati, "Why Are There So Few Black Lawyers in Corporate Law Firms? An Institutional Analysis," *California Law Review* 84 (May 1996): 493–625. http://nrs.harvard.edu/urn-3:HUL.InstRepos:13548823.

68 Wendy Leo Moore, *Reproducing Racism: White Spaces, Elite Law Schools, and Racial Inequality* (Lanham, MD: Rowman & Littlefield, 2008).

69 Victor Ray, "A Theory of Racialized Organizations," *American Sociological Review* 84, no. 1 (2019): 26–53, https://doi.org/10.1177/0003122418822335; Moore, *Reproducing Racism*; Feagin, *Systemic Racism*; Eduardo Bonilla-Silva, "Rethinking Racism: Toward a Structural Interpretation," *American Sociological Review* 62, no. 3 (1997): 465–80, https://doi.org/10.2307/2657316.

70 Eduardo Bonilla-Silva, *Racism without Racists: Color-Blind Racism and the Persistence of Racial Inequality in America*, 4th ed. (Lanham, MD: Rowman & Littlefield, 2014).

71 Bonilla-Silva, *Racism without Racists*, 74–99.

72 Bonilla-Silva, *Racism without Racists*, 76.

73 Beeman, "Walk the Walk but Don't Talk the Talk."

74 Melaku, *You Don't Look Like a Lawyer*.

75 Bloomberg Law, Kaloma Cardwell v. Davis Polk & Wardwell LLP; United States District Court for the Southern District of New York. Case 1:19-cv-10256. Filed 11/04/2019: 1–87.

76 Melaku, *You Don't Look Like a Lawyer*; Wilkins and Gulati, "Why Are There So Few Black Lawyers in Corporate Law Firms?."

77 Bonilla-Silva, *Racism without Racists*.

78 Melaku, *You Don't Look Like a Lawyer*.

79 Melaku and Beeman, "Academia Isn't a Safe Haven for Conversations about Race and Racism."

80 Chris Isidore and Matt Egan, "Wells Fargo CEO Apologizes for Saying the Black Talent Tool Is Limited," *CNN Business*, September 23, 2020, https://hbr.org/2019/11/why-so-many-organizations-stay-white.

81 Monique R. Payne-Pikus, John Hagan and Robert L. Nelson, "Experiencing Discrimination: Race and Retention in America's Largest Law Firms," *Law & Society Review* 44, no. 3–4 (2010): 553–84, https://doi.org/10.1111/j.1540-5893.2010.00416.x.

82 Melaku, *You Don't Look Like a Lawyer*; Moore, *Reproducing Racism*.

83 G. Gutiérrez y Muhs, Y.F. Niemann, C.G. González, and A.P. Harris, *Presumed Incompetent: The Intersections of Race and Class for Women in Academia* (Logan, UT: Utah State University Press, 2012).

84 Melaku, *You Don't Look Like a Lawyer*.

85 Ashleigh Shelby Rosette and Robert W. Livingston, "Failure Is Not an Option for Black Women: Effects of Organizational Performance on Leaders with Single versus Dual-Subordinate Identities," *Journal of Experimental Social Psychology* 48, no. 5 (2012): 1162–7, https://doi.org/10.1016/j.

jesp.2012.05.002; Wilkins and Gulati, "Why Are There So Few Black Lawyers in Corporate Law Firms?"

86 Ray, "A Theory of Racialized Organizations"; Victor Ray, "Why So Many Organizations Stay White," *Harvard Business Review*, November 19, 2019, https://hbr.org/2019/11/why-so-many-organizations-stay-white.

References

Alexander, Michelle. *The New Jim Crow: Mass Incarceration in the Age of Colorblindness*. New York: The New Press, 2012.

Alon, Titan, Matthias Doepke, Jane Olmstead-Rumsey, and Michèle Tertilt. "The Impact of COVID-19 on Gender Equality." Covid Economics, CEPR Press 4, April 2020: 62–85. https://doi.org/10.3386/w26947.

American Civil Liberties Union. "Timeline of the Muslim Ban." ACLU. Accessed September 28, 2020. https://www.aclu-wa.org/pages/timeline-muslim-ban.

Archer, John. "The Resilience of Myth: The Politics of the *American Dream*." *Traditional Dwellings and Settlements Review* 25, no. 2 (2014): 7–21. Accessed September 2, 2020. http://www.jstor.org/stable/24347714.

Averett, Kate Henley. "Moms Are the 'She-Fault' Parent during This Pandemic." Scary Mommy. March 27, 2020. https://www.scarymommy.com/coronavirus-homeschooling-disproportionate-burden-women/.

Bagati, Deepali. *Women of Color in U.S. Law Firms: Women of Color in Professional Services Series*. New York: Catalyst, 2009.

Beeman, Angie. "Walk the Walk but Don't Talk the Talk: The Strategic Use of Color-Blind Ideology in an Interracial Social Movement Organization." *Sociological Forum* 30, no. 1 (2015): 127–47. https://doi.org/10.1111/socf.12148.

Bennett, Jessica. "'I Feel Like I Have Five Jobs': Moms Navigate the Pandemic." *New York Times*. March 20, 2020. https://www.nytimes.com/2020/03/20/parenting/childcare-coronavirus-moms.html.

Black Lives Matter. "Herstory." *BLM*. Accessed September 28, 2020. https://blacklivesmatter.com/herstory/.

Bloom, Nicholas, James Liang, John Roberts, and Zhichun Jenny Ying. "Does Working from Home Work? Evidence from a Chinese Experiment." *The Quarterly Journal of Economics* 30 (2015): 165–218. https://doi.org/10.1093/qje/qju032.

Bloomberg Law, Kaloma Cardwell v. Davis Polk & Wardwell LLP; United States District Court for the Southern District of New York. Case 1:19-cv-10256. Filed 11/04/2019: 1–87.

Bonilla-Silva, Eduardo. "Rethinking Racism: Toward a Structural Interpretation." *American Sociological Review* 62, no. 3 (1997): 465–80. https://doi.org/10.2307/2657316.

Bonilla-Silva, Eduardo. *Racism without Racists: Color-Blind Racism and the Persistence of Racial Inequality in America*. 4th ed. Lanham, MD: Rowman & Littlefield, 2014.

Branch, Enobong Hannah. *Opportunity Denied: Limiting Black Women to Devalued Work*. New Brunswick, NJ: Rutgers University Press, 2011.

Charteris-Black, Jonathan. *Politicians and Rhetoric: The Persuasive Power of Metaphor*. Basingstoke: Palgrave Macmillan, 2005.

Coleman, Aaron Ross. "Black Bodies Are Still Treated As Expendable." *Vox*, June 5, 2020. https://www.vox.com/2020/6/5/21277938/ahmaud-arbery-george-floyd-breonna-taylor-covid.

Collins, Patricia H. "Learning from the Outsider within: The Sociological Significance of Black Feminist Thought." *Social Problems* 33, no. 6 (1986): 14–32. https://doi.org/10.2307/800672.

———. "It's All in the Family: Intersections of Gender, Race and Nation." *Hypatia* 13, no. 3 (1998): 62–82. http://www.jstor.org/stable/3810699.

———. *Black Feminist Thought: Knowledge, Consciousness, and the Politics of Empowerment*. New York: Routledge, 2000.

Crenshaw, Kimberlé. "Mapping the Margins: Intersectionality, Identity Politics, and Violence against Women of Color." *Stanford Law Review* 43, no. 6 (1991): 285–320. https://doi.org/10.2307/1229039.

Du Bois, W.E.B. *The Souls of Black Folk: Essays and Sketches*. Chicago: A.C. McClurg & Co., 1903.

Du Bois, W.E.B, and Isabel Eaton. *The Philadelphia Negro: A Social Study*. Philadelphia, PA: University of Pennsylvania Press, 1899.

Du Bois, W.E.B., and Irene Diggs. *Dusk of Dawn: An Essay Toward an Autobiography of a Race Concept.* New Brunswick, NJ: Transaction Publishers, 2011.

Ely, Robin J., and Irene Padavic. "What's Really Holding Women Back?" *Harvard Business Review.* February 19, 2020. https://hbr.org/2020/03/whats-really-holding-women-back.

Essed, Philomena. *Understanding Everyday Racism: An Interdisciplinary Approach.* London, England: Sage, 1991.

Epstein, Cynthia Fuchs, and Abigail Kolker. "The Impact of the Economic Downturn on Women Lawyers in the United States." *Indiana Journal of Global Legal Studies* 20, no. 2 (2013): 1169. https://doi.org/10.2979/indjglolegstu.20.2.1169.

Erickson, Lucy. "The Disproportionate Impact of COVID-19 on Women of Color." *Society for Women's Health Research.* April 30, 2020. https://swhr.org/the-disproportionate-impact-of-covid-19-on-women-of-color/.

Fazackerley, Anna. "Women's Research Plummets during Lockdown – but Articles from Men Increase." *The Guardian.* May 12, 2020. https://www.theguardian.com/education/2020/may/12/womens-research-plummets-during-lockdown-but-articles-from-men-increase.

Feagin, Joe R. *Systemic Racism: A Theory of Oppression.* New York: Routledge, 2006.

———. *Racist America: Roots, Current Realities, and Future Reparations.* 2nd ed. New York: Routledge, 2010.

———. *The White Racial Frame: Centuries of Racial Framing and Counter-Framing.* 2nd ed. New York: Routledge, 2013.

Frederiksen, Brittni, Ivette Gomez, Alina Salganicoff, and Usha Ranji. "Coronavirus: A Look at Gender Differences in Awareness and Actions." *Kaiser Family Foundation.* March 20, 2020. https://www.kff.org/coronavirus-covid-19/issue-brief/coronavirus-a-look-at-gender-differences-in-awareness-and-actions/.

Frye, Jocelyn. "On the Frontlines at Work and at Home: The Disproportionate Economic Effects of the Coronavirus Pandemic on Women of Color." *Center for American Progress.* April 23, 2020. Accessed September 2, 2020. https://www.americanprogress.org/issues/women/reports/2020/04/23/483846/frontlines-work-home/.

Gans Epner, Janet E. *Visible Invisibility: Women of Color in Law Firms.* American Bar Association (ABA) Commission on Women in the Profession. Chicago, IL: American Bar Association, 2006.

Gershuny, Jonathan, Michael Bittman, and John Brice. "Exit, Voice, and Suffering: Do Couples Adapt to Changing Employment Patterns?" *Journal of Marriage and Family* 67, no. 3 (2005): 656–65. https://doi.org/10.1111/j.1741-3737.2005.00160.x.

Gorlick, Adam. "The Productivity Pitfalls of Working from Home in the Age of COVID-19." *Stanford News.* March 30, 2020. https://news.stanford.edu/2020/03/30/productivity-pitfalls-working-home-age-covid-19/.

Gurría, Angel. "Commentary: COVID-19 Is Compounding Housing Inequities Worldwide. How to Fix That." *Fortune.* July 31, 2020. https://fortune.com/2020/07/31/covid-housing-impact-affordability-sustainability/.

Gutiérrez y Muhs, G., Y.F. Niemann, C.G. González, and A.P. Harris. *Presumed Incompetent: The Intersections of Race and Class for Women in Academia.* Logan, UT: Utah State University Press, 2012.

Hale, Kori. "The Economic Impact of COVID-19 Will Hit Minorities the Hardest." *Forbes.* March 17, 2020. https://www.forbes.com/sites/korihale/2020/03/17/the-economic-impact-of-covid-19-will-hit-minorities-the-hardest/#1218a08310c0.

Harley, Sharon. *Sister Circle: Black Women and Work.* New Brunswick, NJ: Rutgers University Press, 2002.

Hanson, Sandra L., and John Kenneth White. *The American Dream in the 21st Century.* Philadelphia, PA: Temple University Press, 2011.

Hauhart, Robert C. "American Sociology's Investigations of the *American Dream*: Retrospect and Prospect." *The American Sociologist* 46, no. 1 (2015): 65–98. https://doi.org/10.1007/s12108-015-9253-1.

Hentschel, Tanja, Madeline E. Heilman, and Claudia V. Peus. "The Multiple Dimensions of Gender Stereotypes: A Current Look at Men's and Women's Characterizations of Others and Themselves." *Frontiers in Psychology* 10 (2019). https://doi.org/10.3389/fpsyg.2019.00011.

Hochschild, Jennifer L. *Facing Up to the American Dream: Race, Class and the Soul of the Nation.* Princeton, NJ: Princeton University Press, 1995.

Hochschild, Arlie Russell, and Anne Machung. *The Second Shift: Working Parents and the Revolution at Home.* New York: Viking, 1989.

Horsley, Scott. "One for the History Books: 14.7% Unemployment, 20.5 Million Jobs Wiped Away." *National Public Radio.* May 8, 2020. https://www.npr.org/sections/coronavirus-live-updates/2020/05/08/852430930/one-for-the-history-books-14-7-unemployment-20-5-million-jobs-wiped-away.

Isidore, Chris, and Matt Egan. "Wells Fargo CEO Apologizes for Saying the Black Talent Tool is Limited." *CNN Business.* September 23, 2020. https://hbr.org/2019/11/why-so-many-organizations-stay-white.

Kennedy, Randall. *The Persistence of the Color Line: Racial Politics and the Obama Presidency.* New York: Pantheon, 2011.

King, Jr., Martin Luther. "The *American Dream.*" The Martin Luther King, Jr., Research and Education Institute. July 9, 2014. https://kinginstitute.stanford.edu/king-papers/publications/knock-midnight-inspiration-great-sermons-reverend-martin-luther-king-jr-4.

Madgavkar, Anu, Olivia White, Mekala Krishnan, Deepa Mahajan, and Xavier Azcue. "COVID-19 and Gender Equality: Countering the Regressive Effects." *McKinsey & Company.* July 15, 2020. https://www.mckinsey.com/featured-insights/future-of-work/covid-19-and-gender-equality-countering-the-regressive-effects.

Melaku, T. M. (2022). Black Women in White Institutional Spaces: The Invisible Labor Clause and The Inclusion Tax. *American Behavioral Scientist,* 66(11), 1512–1525. https://doi.org/10.1177/00027642211066037.

Melaku, Tsedale M. "Why Women and People of Color in Law Still Hear 'You Don't Look Like a Lawyer.'" *Harvard Business Review.* August 7, 2019b. https://hbr.org/2019/08/why-women-and-people-of-color-in-law-still-hear-you-dont-look-like-a-lawyer.

Melaku, Tsedale M. "Amy Cooper, White Privilege and the Murder of Black People." *Fair Observer.* June 2, 2020. https://www.fairobserver.com/region/north_america/tsedale-melaku-amy-cooper-white-privilege-abstract-liberalism-george-floyd-death-protests-us-news-15161/.

Melaku, Tsedale M., and Angie Beeman. "Academia Isn't a Safe Haven for Conversations about Race and Racism." *Harvard Business Review.* June 25, 2020. https://hbr.org/2020/06/academia-isnt-a-safe-haven-for-conversations-about-race.

McDermott, Casey. "Black Women Are Affected Disproportionately by COVID-19 in N.H., New Data Show." *New Hampshire Public Radio.* August 13, 2020. https://www.nhpr.org/post/black-women-are-affected-disproportionately-covid-19-nh-new-data-shows#stream/0.

Moore, Wendy Leo. *Reproducing Racism: White Spaces, Elite Law Schools, and Racial Inequality.* Lanham, MD: Rowman & Littlefield, 2008.

Morris, Aldon D. *The Scholar Denied: W.E.B. Du Bois and the Birth of Modern Sociology.* Oakland, CA: University of California Press, 2015.

National Association for Law Placement (NALP). *2019 Report on Diversity in U.S. Law Firms.* Washington, DC: National Association of Law Placement. https://www.nalp.org/uploads/2019_DiversityReport.pdf.

Nesoff, Jeffrey. 2017. "The Myth of a Post-Racial Society after the Obama Presidency." Facing History and Ourselves: Facing Today: A Facing History Blog. February 8, 2017. https://facingtoday.facinghistory.org/the-myth-of-a-post-racial-society-after-the-obama-presidency.

Payne-Pikus, Monique R., John Hagan, and Robert L. Nelson. "Experiencing Discrimination: Race and Retention in America's Largest Law Firms." *Law & Society Review* 44, no. 3–4 (2010): 553–84. https://doi.org/10.1111/j.1540-5893.2010.00416.x.

Perry, Destiny, Paulette Brown, and Eileen Letts. *Left Out and Left Behind: The Hurtles, Hassles, and Heartaches of Achieving Long-Term Legal Careers for Women of Color.* American Bar Association (ABA) Commission on Women in the Profession. Chicago, IL: American Bar Association, 2020.

Pirtle, Whitney N. Laster. "Racial Capitalism: A Fundamental Cause of Novel Coronavirus (COVID-19) Pandemic Inequities in the United States." *Health Education and Behavior.* April 26, 2020. https://doi.org/10.1177/1090198120922942.

Ray, Victor. "A Theory of Racialized Organizations." *American Sociological Review* 84, no. 1 (2019): 26–53. https://doi.org/10.1177/0003122418822335.

Ray, Victor. "Why So Many Organizations Stay White." *Harvard Business Review.* November 19, 2019. https://hbr.org/2019/11/why-so-many-organizations-stay-white.

Rosette, Ashleigh Shelby, and Robert W. Livingston. "Failure is Not an Option for Black Women: Effects of Organizational Performance on Leaders with Single Versus Dual-Subordinate Identities." *Journal of Experimental Social Psychology* 48, no. 5 (2012): 1162–7. https://doi.org/10.1016/j.jesp.2012.05.002.

Rugh, Jacob S., Len Albright, and Douglas S. Massey. "Race, Space, and Cumulative Disadvantage: A Case Study of the Subprime Lending Collapse." *Social Problems* 62, no. 2 (2015): 186–218. https://doi.org/10.1093/socpro/spv002.

Segura, Denise. "Chicanas and the Triple Oppressions in the Labor Force." pp. 47–65 in *Chicana Voices: Intersection of Class, Race, and Gender*, edited by Teresa Cordova and the National Association of Chicana Studies Editorial Committee. Austin, TX: Center for Mexican American Studies, 1986.

Southern Poverty Law Center, "Family Separation under the Trump Administration – A Timeline." SPLC. Accessed September 28, 2020. https://www.splcenter.org/news/2020/06/17/family-separation-under-trump-administration-timeline.

St. Jean, Yanick, and Joe R. Feagin. *Double Burden: Black Women and Everyday Racism.* Armonk, NY: M. E. Sharpe, 1998.

Tesler, Michael. *Post-Racial or Most-Racial?: Race and Politics in the Obama Era.* Chicago, IL: University of Chicago Press, 2016.

The NALP Foundation for Law Career Research and Education and the Center for Women in Law. *Women of Color: A Study of Law School Experiences*, 2020.

Vault and Minority Corporate Counsel Association. *2019 Vault/MCCA Law Firm Diversity Survey.* 2019. https://www.mcca.com/wp-content/uploads/2020/03/2019-Vault_MCCA-Law-Firm-Diversity-Survey-Report.pdf.

Wingfield, Adia Harvey. *Doing Business with Beauty: Black Women, Hair Salons, and the Racial Enclave Economy.* Lanham, MD: Rowman & Littlefield, 2008.

Wingfield, Adia Harvey. *Flatline: Race, Work and Healthcare.* Oakland, CA: University of California Press, 2019.

Wingfield, Adia Harvey, and Koji Chavez. "Getting in, Getting Hired, Getting Sideways Looks: Organizational Hierarchy and Perceptions of Racial Discrimination." *American Sociological Review* 85, no.1 (2020): 31–57. https://journals.sagepub.com/doi/pdf/10.1177/0003122419894335.

Wilkins, David B., and Mitu G. Gulati. "Why Are There So Few Black Lawyers in Corporate Law Firms? An Institutional Analysis." *California Law Review* 84 (May 1996): 493–625. http://nrs.harvard.edu/urn-3:HUL.InstRepos:13548823.

3

MARKETS, FINANCE, WHITENESS, AND THE AMERICAN DREAM

Karen Ho

Introduction

Over the past four decades, financialization has accelerated inequality and undermined the American Dream's conditions of possibility – yet the role played by financialization has been elided in the American imagination, largely due to the power of market discourse and racialized resentment. Compounding the analytical difficulties in making sense of contemporary financial-market-generated downward mobility, the American Dream has long been naturalized as the result of "market" workings and meritocracy. Moreover, the promises of the American Dream have always been contested, uneven, and contradictory. To better understand contemporary socioeconomic decline, as well as the politics of resentment and scapegoating, it is crucial to examine the cultural workings of markets and finance and their interconnections with the racialized formations of the American Dream. Specifically, we must ask and answer how hierarchies and exclusions, framed simply as "the free market," have made the American Dream possible for some while obfuscating its unavailability to many. To the extent that markets and finance (and oftentimes, economy and globalization) have been brought into the conversation as central to either the making or the demise of the American Dream, they are framed in the abstract, without a corresponding socioeconomic explanation of the ways in which the American Dream, markets, and finance have harmonized to construct and maintain unequal dreams.

Over the past 40 years, the growing dominance of finance, which has both restructured corporations in favor of investors and executives at the expense of labor and aligned the socioeconomic safety net to the financial markets, has wreaked havoc on the American Dream (Ho 2014; Lazonick 2013; Lin and Tomaskovic-Dewey 2013). Inequality in the US has surpassed the levels of the Great Depression, with the top 20 percent of households owning almost 90 percent of all privately held wealth, while the net worth of the bottom 40 percent was negative in 2010 (Cooper 2014). The past few decades have witnessed a massive transfer of income *to* the wealthiest 1 percent, and finance, in particular, has catalyzed the very mechanisms that have allowed the top centile to capture "60 percent of the total increase of US national income" from 1977 to 2007 (Piketty 2014, 297). Since the Great Recession of 2008, Wall Street (the recipient of the largest bailout in US history) and the wealthy have not only recovered but have surged to new heights (Mirowski 2013; Piketty 2020). Wall Street's

DOI: 10.4324/9781003326243-4

approach since then is exemplified by the adage of never letting a good crisis go to waste: the financial services industry in New York – having been bailed out – witnessed ongoing growth and profitability. By 2017, Wall Street had returned to pre-financial crisis heights, and average salaries, including bonuses, had reached a "staggering $403,100, "the highest since 2008" and the highest of any state in the nation[1] (Office of the New York State Comptroller 2018).

I have long argued that the exponential increase of wealth inequality in the US has been fueled by the growing ability of elite finance to access and unlock the accumulated productive assets embedded in such sites as corporations and houses (Ho 2020a). Corporations, for example, have been restructured and downsized, converted into financial assets, and redistributed as capital toward the top, thereby reducing the number of people who can lay claim to them for their livelihoods (Lin and Tomaskovic-Dewey 2013). In the past 40 years, as corporations were increasingly financialized and correspondingly downsized and restructured according to the dictates of shareholder value, the previously normative socioeconomic concept of longstanding, stable employment was jettisoned (Ho 2020b; Stout 2012). Jobs and careers were often replaced by short-term, flexible, "gig" positions that showcased the new cultural value that employment (and employees) existed *outside* of the corporation, which was now seen as beholden only to its stock price, institutional shareholders, investors and financial advisors, and financial markets. Corporations, now governed by the concerns of finance, are interested not in the welfare of workers, employment, or even long-term productivity but in mergers and acquisitions and financial deal-making to boost stock prices and financial fees (Ho 2009). Correspondingly, those whose wealth accumulation occurs through financial channels and markets (such as dominant financial interests and the top portion of the 1 percent) have benefited since the 1980s, and even more since 2008, from the ongoing restructuring of corporations and the appropriation of formerly distressed assets, such as foreclosed homes (Derickson et al. 2021). On the flipside, most workers have experienced wage stagnation since 1979. They have been shut out from job security and upward mobility, and home ownership rates are lower than they were 25 years ago (Choi et al. 2018).

In the face of rising inequality generated by the past four decades of financialization, it is crucial to direct our analysis back to the American Dream, its overall dismantling as well as its stark unevenness. Though difficult to grasp, there has been *no progress* made toward reducing the wealth gap between Black and White in the past 60 years: "[T]he gap between the finances of blacks and whites is still as wide in 2020 as it was in 1968, when a run of landmark civil rights legislation culminated in the Fair Housing Act in response to centuries of unequal treatment of African Americans in nearly every part of society and business" (Kuhn et al. 2018; Long and Van Dam 2020).[23] What does it mean when the American Dream is increasingly precarious for most, and yet BIPOC communities, especially African Americans and immigrants of color, are increasingly scapegoated and blamed for "special treatment" even as they experience significant downward mobility and the economic gap between them and Euro-Americans has not narrowed in over a half-century? How do those who have enjoyed the dream's largesse interpret its deterioration versus those who have been equally compelled by the dream yet have been systematically excluded? Because this dream has historically been both broad-based for normative categories of Americans *and* hierarchically exclusive for many minority and marginalized communities, its recent erosion and newfound unreliability are simultaneously jarring and expected. Figuring out that the boat is leaking and that, in fact, some parts of the boat have long been underwater and never repaired is central to the task of understanding the state of the American Dream today. To do so requires briefly revisiting the post-WWII era when the American Dream looked to many like a rising tide lifting everyone's boats.

The post-war years brought the most robust period in US history of shared relative prosperity and declining inequality between rich and poor (Piketty 2020). It was a result not of corporate largesse but rather of protracted social struggles, including various social liberation protests and movements, progressive taxation and other government policies, multiple crises produced by two world wars, anti-imperial resistance to ongoing empire-building, and unprecedented federal investments from the New Deal to the GI Bill. All these developments were necessary to achieve such socioeconomic conditions, as critical, historical, and social-science scholarship has amply demonstrated (Ortner 2011; Piketty 2014, 2020; Yanagisako 2018). A period of consensus politics around the welfare state enabled the US to create stable institutions and safety nets and to expand access to home ownership on a mass scale, albeit for limited social categories (such as normative White men who fit the nuclear family imagination); when socioeconomic policy centered around "family values" were challenged, these critiques galvanized alliances between neoliberal and social conservative social movements to double-down on the normative family in the late 20th century and beyond (Brodkin 1998; Canaday 2011; Cooper 2017; Katznelson 2005). Nevertheless, it is worth noting that these post-WWII infrastructures provided the basis for what Gerald Davis calls a "society of organizations" in which civil rights, Black power, feminist, and queer social movements struggled for socioeconomic inclusion and the right to participate and succeed in the job market (Davis 2009; Laird 2006; MacLean 2006). And, through such demands, these institutions "just as they were about to be dismantled [through financialization] – had become important sites in the struggle for middle-class employment equality by women and people of color who had previously been excluded from such privileged workplaces" (Ho 2014). It was, unfortunately, precisely at this moment of traction, when various markets and corporate ladders were opened to minority communities, that neoliberal financialization intervened to dismantle the very institutions that were becoming more "inclusive" (Ho 2014; Laird 2006; Sennett 2006).

It is important to establish, then, that differently positioned communities will have divergent nostalgias for the American Dream: those who bemoan what has been lost and those who ongoingly question (and yearn for) that which was never implemented. Specifically, the conditions that made (White) middle-class wealth creation possible included access to quality jobs and corporate ladders as well as federal underwriting and guaranteeing of mortgages, which helped to construct a mass market in housing and became the central avenue for wealth accumulation in favored households. Neither avenue of accumulation, through upwardly-mobile employment or through homeownership, was made widely available to BIPOC communities. Moreover, when Wall Street and other banking institutions finally made mortgages available to the formerly redlined, the methodology had radically changed. Instead of low-rate, stable, and guaranteed mortgages as provided through the post-WWII GI Bill (combined with living-wage jobs and GI business loans that allowed mortgages to be paid), the recipe became one of "predatory inclusion" (see Taylor 2019), and the offerings were not subsidized but rather, "subprime" loans. It is thus not surprising that the wealth gap between Black people and White people never really closed after the civil rights movements. Promises of upward mobility were structured around reliable and secure corporations, yet these stable, paternalistic corporations have largely been dismantled and no longer form an avenue to middle-class possibilities even for many of those previously included, with the situation even worse for the marginalized (Davis 2016; Ho 2014).

At the same time, the state and high finance have collaborated, not always advertently, to outsource roles that the government used to provide (such as helping to underwrite, secure, and regulate "safety net" payments to retirements and homes) to the financial markets and short-term investors in ways that eventually eroded their stability by overly profiteering and commodifying these payments. These structural transformations, however, have escaped scrutiny (Krippner 2011; Stout 2019). For example, reactionary conservatism and right-wing populism's targeting and scapegoating of marginalized communities further obscure the roles of finance and government in this neoliberal outsourcing, which dismantled socioeconomic institutions in ways that favor the elite (Bessire and Bond 2017; Fraser 2017). Elsewhere, I have made the argument that this "reactionary populism ... that has led to Trumpism arose out of real grievances against neoliberal financialization and globalization yet has conflated the policies and practices that benefit the financial elite with the demands of marginalized and minoritized group." These "misrecognitions" have led to an "economic populism mistakenly organize[d] around the fake culprit of reverse discrimination and special rights"; thus one of the tasks of a critical economic anthropology is to analyze the "confounding layers of obfuscation imposed by dominant narratives" and to "unpack these resentments and illuminate their relation to the financialization of the US and global social economy" (Ho 2018, 148–50).

In this chapter, I want to focus on the mythologies of financial markets and the ways in which these ideologies and narratives, when entangled and co-constituted by the corresponding myths of the American Dream, double down on the erasure of uneven power relations, further eliding the conditions of possibility of markets as well as the American Dream. In other words, the *longue durée* assumption that markets are acultural and "free," bolstered by the extent to which naturalized discourses of American meritocracy and market conceptualizations are mutually constitutive of each other, obscures the workings of finance by enshrouding it within other dominant myths. As such, because one of the central origin myths of financialization is that (supposedly free) markets solidified the American Dream throughout the 20th century, it is even more difficult to both challenge the problematic presumption that (financial) markets are an unequivocal force for socioeconomic prosperity, and interrogate the role of financialization in intensifying socioeconomic inequality.

Markets, Meritocracy, Whiteness, and the American Dream

One of the key origin myths of the American Dream, then, is the naturalization of markets and the corresponding erasure of the central role of the state, institutions, and elite networks in the workings and expansion of markets and in empowering some communities and social categories for success. The effect of this myth has been that only a particular construct of presumably meritocratic, hard-working individuals interacting "one on one" with supposedly neutral markets is *seen* and understood as instantiating the American Dream (Chen 2022; Lane 2011; Markovits 2019; McNamee 2018; Newman 1999). If the explicit roles of society and the state in generating an "inclusive" market of upward mobility *for some* have largely been rendered invisible, then those historically included in the American Dream only recognize the bootstrapping story of the self-made man. The flipside of the American Dream's exclusion of many marginalized categories and communities was its seductive storytelling to a broad spectrum of White men, who have been led to believe that their success was due primarily to their hard work as individuals freely navigating autonomous markets.

This origin myth is important to critique *in light of downward mobility*, especially for the previously and relatively enfranchised in the current context of growing insecurity and inequality writ large. In fact, I would argue that it is crucial to interrogate what those who are socialized into the cultural expectations and worldviews of the American Dream will do *when the dream is dismantled*. To better understand everything from intensifying (White) resentment to the scapegoating of the marginalized, from grievance politics to the rise of populism and alternative facts, critical scholars must continue to question the visceral ramifications of dreams based on relative privilege, monopoly, and hierarchy. What unfolds when these dreams are themselves eroded, not in favor of equity, but instead in the form of intensified inequality?

The fiction of the American Dream was part and parcel of a larger socialization process that framed a particular understanding of upward mobility. Over 30 years ago, anthropologist Katherine Newman, in *Falling from Grace: The Experience of Downward Mobility in the American Middle Class*, conceptualized the narrow purview of the "true believers" in the American Dream: those whose worldviews were forged by their successes, and whose understanding of their current struggles is still shaped by the same discourses. Specifically, Newman, who carried out extensive ethnographic research on white-collar (and predominantly White male) managers who were experiencing downsizing for the first time in the late 1980s, argued that displaced managers are "trapped in a cultural maze" in that they are "not in rebellion against the business culture in which they have been nurtured ... [rather], they are its true believers" (Newman 1999, 75). Framing these cultural assumptions as "meritocratic individualism," she argues that this worldview had previously worked for (and comforted) management, as it "justifies the view that they rose to higher positions because of sheer ability and hard work. It encourages the notion that social inequality is an expression of the natural order of things ... " (Newman 1999, 77). However, "[w]hen the successful fall from grace, this ideology boomerangs" in the sense that it is used against the individual victim, not in the pursuit of greater reflexivity or understanding of the larger social order, but toward self (and other)-blame.

Newman goes on to explain the larger ramifications of this worldview for managers:

> Because they have been steeped in the tenets of the managerial worldview, they cannot avoid its condemnation of their character or conduct. They prosecute themselves on its behalf, turning criticisms against themselves and against one another: victims blaming victims ...
>
> *Newman 1999, 75*

Newman's framing is crucial for understanding how "markets" have strategically substituted for meritocratic individualism and vice versa. In this dominant American social imaginary, markets, meritocracy, individualism, and hard work are deployed and utilized so interchangeably that they have *proxied* for one another and have served as mutually reinforcing justifications and rationales. Conceptually substituting (and rendering interchangeable) "markets" and "meritocratic individualism" allows seemingly autonomous processes and social ideals to be cloaked and protected by each other: the biases of markets are translated as meritorious and virtuous, and the cultural inequalities embedded in meritocratic individualism are anonymized as just the market. It is instructive to explicitly recognize that the "main motif" of meritocratic individualism infusing American managerial culture is that of "the market," and since the main cultural belief undergirding "the market" is that it is an acultural, autonomous process, it is not surprising that anything conflated with "the market" can elide its own cultural presence. Newman's explanation of the consequences of this cultural framework demonstrates the central problematic for both critical social analysts and recently displaced White male managers:

> [I]f individuals are responsible for their own destinies, there is no one else to blame in case of failure. If the market rewards the competent and casts out the inefficient, unemployment is perforce a judgment of one's abilities. It is a testament to the strength of this business culture that unemployed managers assert and reassert these

values, even though this brings criticism down upon themselves and others in the same predicament.

Newman 1999, 77

Remarkably, over two decades later, anthropologist Carrie Lane studied a similar demographic and set of circumstances – White-male, white-collar employees laid off in the high-tech industry – and found that while meritocratic individualism had transformed into a neoliberal, "career management" ideology, these workers continued to be true believers in the free markets and in the power of individual self-management and responsibility despite intensifying insecurity. They "espouse[d] a doggedly resilient faith … in individual agency" and "the efficiency and justness of the free market" and believed that in the face of ubiquitous insecurity, engagement in the market was the "means by which one can best position oneself to succeed in an increasingly globalized and competitive world" (Lane 2011, 4–5, 13). Specifically, Lane argues that because employees no longer have any expectation of job security, they do not blame themselves for unemployment (unlike Newman's interlocuters, where meritocratic individualism and the relative newness of insecurity demanded self-blame). But, similar to Newman's study, they *also* do not seriously question pro-market ideology or blame the market, which continues to serve as the arbiter of meritocracy. In fact, Lane argues that pro-market, neoliberal socialization has ironically propelled these high-tech white-collar workers to conceptualize rampant insecurity not as a major socioeconomic problem but as a catalyst for empowerment, as an "empowering alternative to dependence," and antidote to complacency (Lane 2011, 13). This problematic cultural reasoning serves to double-down on and legitimize the market as the solution to (not one of the culprits of) contemporary insecurity and inequality.

In this important contemporary twist, while Lane's high-tech employees almost never "criticized their employers for disloyalty," they often cast aspersions on co-workers who complained too much, who acted like dependent children (Lane 2011, 39). Such a framing allows the neoliberal employee to play the meritocratic hero, to embody the entrepreneurial "company of one" who can claim individual self-reliance and masculine agency that allow the weathering and navigating of insecure employment in stark contradistinction to "dependent" people. The consequences of this conceptual model are far-reaching. First, relatively privileged, high-tech workers who are recently laid off reproduce and occupy the ideological position of the corporation: the institution and dominant market actors escape blame, individual responsibility is heralded, and those who grumble are derided as fostering dependency. "Job seekers have internalized the logic of the corporation," Lane points out, in ways that shield corporations and markets from critique and rehearse the aura of inevitability and the invisible hand of markets (Lane 2011, 51). Second, this neoliberal ideology produces an ideal type and a scapegoat, disciplining against particular desires and critiques. As Lane argues, by stigmatizing the "very act of seeking secure employment" as weak, victim-seeking behavior and itself productive of dependency, these employees ventriloquize the problematic, neoliberal narrative (Lane 2011, 46). They accept the argument that it is precisely those naively and misguidedly "looking for security in an insecure world," those who critique insecurity and demand protections, who deserve the blame (Lane 2011, 55). Moreover, this construction of an "other" to the well-managed neoliberal self not only absolves corporations but also blames "government" and those who protest for governmental reform and regulation as "too socialist," as undermining "security and prosperity" and "re-creat[ing] the situation of dependence and vulnerability" (Lane 2011, 57–60). In these scenarios, insecurity itself is cast as both a naturalized occurrence of blameless markets and problematically mobilized to serve a social Darwinist ideology. When markets, seen as neutral, are let off the hook, we are left with individual-shaming and other-blaming, with government elites, as conservative and neoliberal rhetoric would have it, picking "winners and losers." Importantly, the precarities and institutional deconstruction wrought by financialization and financial market actors – key catalysts in downward mobility – go largely unseen.

Not surprisingly, this "neoliberal" mindset is not merely imbued with racialized undertones – it is entirely shaped and empowered by racist hierarchies. Interestingly enough, Carrie Lane's interlocuters foreshadowed the conceptual frame that instigates polarization, scapegoating, and racialized resentment in the contemporary moment through the construction of a problematic binary of capitalist individualists and socialist dependents, self-reliant entrepreneurs versus protesters supported by government largesse. An instructive way to apprehend the connection between neoliberal self-reliance and racialized scapegoating is through a mechanism of what sociologist Allison Pugh calls "displacing."

Allow me to explain. First, Allison Pugh, in her trenchant ethnographic exploration *The Tumbleweed Society: Working and Caring in an Age of Insecurity*, explores rampant socio-economic insecurity by demonstrating the extent to which intimate lives are also shaped and upended by insecure employment. Studying variously positioned workers who must nevertheless navigate a "one-way honor system" (where their own commitments to the workplace are not reciprocated by their employers), Pugh documents how these "betrayals" shape the burdens of care and the meanings of commitment at home (Pugh 2015, 5–9). She insightfully demonstrates that precarious workers (including those relatively privileged, but especially those facing downward mobility who had been afforded the American Dream) are caught up in a neoliberal market ideology of "personal responsibility, self-sufficiency, and independence" such that they must look "anywhere but at the employer" for support (Pugh 2015, 32). Their shame, grief, and frustration are often expressed "not at work but at home," which makes them prime candidates for "displacing" (Pugh 2015, 33, 88). In other words, the "doomed nobility" of the lonely and suffering worker is not contained within the self; rather, self-blame ebbs and flows and can shift toward anger and resentment elsewhere. As Pugh describes, "displacing is a way for workers to feel their feelings, but without aiming them at the forces at work that they view as more implacable, impervious, and inevitable" (Pugh 2015, 31, 88).

In these contexts, a multi-scalar kind of displacement occurs. On the one hand, these predominantly White male workers, parents, and family members that Pugh interviews often aim these hurt "feelings at their intimate partners, animated by a powerful sense of other people's duty at home" (Pugh 2015, 88). Simultaneously, it structurally follows that many similarly positioned workers also engage in a "collective displacing" where "feminists and people of color" are blamed for the "economic changes undertaken by political and economic elites" (Pugh 2015, 91). In both contexts, "others" are framed for not fulfilling their "duty" – not at home, not in reproductive labors, not in the world, and this structure of feeling is expressed and affectively embodied in the figure of the "angry white man" (Pugh 2015, 89–93). Rather than recognize the gendered and racialized privileges they still enjoy, they often displace their unfulfilled expectations onto their intimate lives and deploy an erroneous narrative about racialized others whose supposed dependence and penchant for protest threaten to disrupt their ahistorical understandings of how their successes were structured in the first place. As Pugh concludes,

> Job security has rent the fabric of men's duty narrative, with its onslaught on the dependability of their provisioning, raising questions about what men can and should

be counted on to contribute …. [S]ome 'angry white men,' betrayed at work and at home, displace their feelings about work onto their intimate partners, in reflection of their gendered expectations of duty. Pugh 2015, 107

"Given the primacy of work as a moral measure," they further displace their anger about work onto various others (Pugh 2015, 108). Without the tools to mobilize a critique against financialization and the historical linkages between racialized and gendered protections and corporate and market successes, insecurity culture instead breeds narratives of an impossible self-reliance that explodes and devolves blame elsewhere.

In this context, the critical and specific analysis of the construction of Whiteness in the post-civil-rights era, as well as in the Trump era, is also necessary. Almost twenty years ago, critical race theorist Howard Winant observed that in the late 20th century, American Whiteness – for the first time – experienced a period of crisis and confusion, what he calls "white racial dualism" (Winant 1997, 40). Specifically, he explains that the partial successes of the civil rights movements called out White supremacy and Whiteness to such an extent that Whiteness could no longer be considered superior, invisible, and normal. Through the counterclaims of the excluded and the other, White racial identity emerged as "contradictory" and fissured (Winant 1997, 40–1). Those who clung to it sought to maintain privilege while simultaneously recognizing that contemporary law and culture were *supposed* to be "color-blind." Winant explains that when Whites and Whiteness – previously constructed as unproblematically superior *and* as the unracialized default – are explicitly racialized by the other and called out as dominant and privileged, a crisis of Whiteness ensues. Whiteness, when explicitly framed as "difference," as a visible color, is destabilized and anxious, no longer self-evident as singularly hegemonic and coherent, with the uncontested right to self-definition.[4] The result can be reactionary, and the "anxieties" are "articulate[d] … in racial terms" and felt as "disadvantage" (Winant 1997, 42, 49). For instance, the contemporary resurgence of White supremacy is often problematically understood as resistance to White "victimization" in the sense that after the civil rights movement, many Whites presumed that racism (not to mention engrained hierarchical institutional structures) had magically disappeared. The official emergence of the discourse of colorblindness thereby constituted evidence of the existence of a newly equal playing field (Bonilla-Silva 2014). Of course, if one imagines that equality of opportunity already exists, then any attempt at amelioration (or even calling out racism) becomes, ipso facto, evidence of "reverse discrimination" (Wellman 1997).

This foreboding sense that Whiteness was poised to become even more reactionary has been vindicated in the 20 years since Winant's conclusion that the racial dualism of Whiteness was rendering it unstable. In 2019, political scientist Ashley Jardina found that 30–40 percent of the White population in the US is gravitating toward White identity politics, toward interest and focus on White "racial solidarity" and a belief that the benefits of Whites as a group are "endangered" (Jardina 2019, 4, 8). In other words, some Whites are responding to a fractured racial identity *and* socioeconomic precarity by engaging in social activism *as Whites.* Now, precisely because Whites continue to be institutionally and structurally privileged and White identity has historically been about power and hierarchy, racial solidarity for Whites is not equivalent to solidarity for BIPOC communities. In fact, as Jardina observes, White racial solidarity is not an "inconsequential" developing of stronger racial identities; rather, this phenomenon cannot be separated from racial prejudice and resentment and is centrally about the protection of "power and status" (Jardina 2019, 5–6). At the same time, Jardina is quick to point out that these White racial attitudes are not self-understood as "prejudice," although the central motivation is often to protect "their group's collective interests and to maintain its status" (5, 7). In other words, when it comes to Whiteness, given its origins in a hierarchical social order designed to protect White claims and monopoly position in society, group solidarity and "collective interest" are not innocent and cannot be disentangled from uneven power relations. As Jardina, who takes care to contextualize White voices and worldviews, explains, the activation of White identity is inseparable from its hierarchical contexts, where downward mobility is presumed to be a White loss because of *others'* gain. (Again, just because White gains were historically made possible through the exclusions of others does not mean that marginalized communities have fared well in the wake of generalized socioeconomic precarity.) Jardina writes,

> White racial solidarity is also associated with perceptions of group competition and alienation. Whites who adopt greater levels of racial identity or consciousness are more likely to see the world in zero-sum terms. They view their own group as in competition with non-whites, and they believe that economic and political gains for these out-groups come at the expense of their own group. These whites also feel a sense of grievance. They believe their group has not gotten its fair share, and that they, as whites, are owed more than they have been given. At the same time, many white identifiers recognize that their group has captured certain advantages. White identity is defined both by an anxiety about encroachment from other groups, and a recognition that being white has its privileges...*But* white identity is *activated* in a very different manner – it is a product of the belief that resources are zero-sum, and that the success of non-whites will come at the expense of whites.
>
> (Jardina 2019, 262–3, 268 emphasis mine)

It is the zero-sum ideology and the preservation of inequality central to White identity that needs to be dismantled: if Whites continue to believe that they "will be the losers in this game," then the seductiveness of White identity and White power grows (Jardina 2019, 268).

Moreover, one of the conundrums of understanding White identity, especially of White grievance politics and scapegoating of others, is the failure to recognize the incommensurability of Whiteness as a category with other racialized categories. For example, Jardina argues that one point of irritation among Whites (especially "white identifiers") is their perceived inability to "celebrate whiteness" when "others" are allowed to celebrate their identities. "White identified" people did not understand why "other groups have their own celebrations" (i.e. people of color) but "celebrating whiteness" is historically problematic (Jardina 2019, 136). Specifically, Whites who embraced "white identity politics" "appeared resentful of that idea that expressing their identity would be seen, unfairly, as problematic or even racist":

> ... [M]any whites ... have observed other racial groups organize around their race, establish race-based student organizations on college campuses, and honor their racial heritage. Some whites wonder why they cannot openly celebrate their race in the way they believe blacks and other racial minorities are able to do. A common refrain during February is, "Why is there an African-American History month, but not a White History month?" Many whites seem to ask this question with sincerity, and not because they align themselves with ... white supremacists ... Instead, they think that racial equality means that they, too, ought to be able to recognize their racial group. These whites complain that the very rejection of whites' ability to do so is yet another example of the way in which whites are unfairly maligned in the United States.
>
> *Jardina 2019, 137–8*

Further context is necessary to better understand this important source of discontent. As discussed, first, the identity and category of Whiteness have been based on supremacy, not on *longue durée* ethnic, cultural ties to ancestral communities. It was not until *after* the civil rights movement, as historian Matthew Frye Jacobson importantly points out, that White Americans began to deploy and identify with various European ethnicities to distance themselves from Whiteness given the larger societal challenges to White privilege (Jacobson 2008; see also, hooks 1992). European-American ethnicities, which had largely been assimilated and traded away for the privileges of Whiteness and Americanness in suburbia, were now being claimed as a reaction and resistance to the civil rights movements. Advertently or inadvertently, these deployments allow Euro-ethnic immigrant narratives to be equated with the experiences of racialized minorities, erasing the fact of White privilege (Gallagher 2003). Importantly, this newfound, "post-civil-rights-reactive" focus on ethnicity by people who can also belong to the category "White" allows them to unmark themselves as bearers of White privilege. Given Whiteness' historical role as a requirement for Americanness and the historical deployment of White ethnicity to distance from or deny contemporary racism, neither celebrating Whiteness nor celebrating Euro-ethnicities can be a solution to "post-civil rights" alienation, as Whiteness is neither a marginalized racialized identity in need of empowerment nor an ethnicity; rather, it is a claim to hierarchical power.

In sum, understanding the mutual constitution of Whiteness, markets, and the American Dream allows us to better untangle White-identity grievance politics, especially how the myths and misrecognitions surrounding how neoliberal markets got (get) made, who/what they privilege, and how they change over time have fueled reactionary populism. When governmental policies and investments helped to shape housing markets, higher educational opportunities, and stable jobs for upwardly mobile working- and middle-class White men in paternalistic, Fordist companies, this was framed as simply the American Dream and the free market. Thus, when downward mobility hits, the constructed nature of the "free market," Whiteness, and racial hierarchies are not, in turn, noticed or implicated. Rather, the cultural hegemony of the narrative of independence so well-documented by Newman, Lane, and Pugh fuels resentment toward those framed as "dependent," although (and ironically) those dubbed "dependent" have historically *not* been recipients of corporate or governmental largesse. As previously privileged groups experience a crisis of expectations and a reordering of their social world, they turn toward scapegoating and resentment, misdirected toward multiple others. In this context, it is crucial to better excavate the extent to which the historical accrual of wealth through seemingly free, open, and fair markets that exemplified the American Dream, such as the housing and job markets in the US, were explicitly subsidized through racism.

The Accrual of Wealth through the Housing Market

The "free market" in housing in the US did not organically and a-culturally emerge out of a human need for housing in the suburbs: it was actively constructed and made possible through the federal underwriting of mortgage loans that came in the forms of subsidies, insurance, and loan guarantees to a variety of state-sponsored and private lenders, and only made available to a particular prototype of "citizen" – the White male breadwinner.[5] Much critical scholarship, especially in history, ethnic studies, and sociology, has unpacked the multiple ways in which property and housing have played an outsized role in producing the entrenched wealth gap between Whites and people of color, especially African Americans, in the process constructing and consolidating Whiteness, conflating Whiteness and suburbia, and engendering segregation and urban unrest (Brodkin 1998; Freund 2006; Kruse 2007; Massey and Denton 1993; Oliver and Shapiro 2006; Taylor 2019). As historian David Freund has demonstrated, the Federal Home Loan Bank System (FHLB), Home Owners' Loan Corporation (HOLC), and Federal Housing Authority (FHA) provided unprecedented socioeconomic subsidies as part of the New Deal and the WWII-era GI Bill. Through these agencies, the federal government created a mass market in housing where none existed previously and established parameters that shaped how value could accrue, who could accrue it, and who and what were worthy of investment in the first place.[6] In other words, the market in housing was predicated on the notion of the "invest-ability" of normative White males and the crucial importance of creating valuable infrastructure to transform this category of persons into stable breadwinners, as they were understood as the cornerstones of the social economy (Canaday 2011). Not only was the housing market created through and subsidized because of the socioeconomic imaginaries that cohered to these categories and trajectories, but also, as a result, only certain categories of people, imbued as repositories of value, were able to accumulate wealth (Harris 2013; Oliver and Shapiro 2006). Over time, particular cultural values, aesthetics, identities, imaginaries, and categories came to be seen as indistinguishable from the functioning of the market itself.

My analysis here relies on the recognition of two underlying conditions of the housing market. First, it is important to acknowledge that who was allowed to enter the housing market in the first place not only shaped the color of wealth for generations but also the very politics and categories of belonging and upward mobility in the US. Second, the terms and rules of the market in property dictated that the accumulation of value would be directly linked to and singularly dependent upon both Whiteness and segregation. Although multiple social movements coalesced to challenge this state of affairs by supporting the 1968 Fair Housing Act, which prevented the federal government from using explicitly racist language in loan underwriting manuals, the legislation had limited effect (Taylor 2019; Wiggins 2020). By this time, the housing market and the rules of value had been so deeply structured around race and gender that these factors continue to shape the market into the contemporary era. Thus, in this section, I seek to go beyond the notion that the central problematic mechanism of the housing market was simply its exclusion of certain categories of people. Focusing only on their exclusions would reproduce a problematic approach to markets where the market mechanisms appear as though they are not themselves racialized and gendered, and the only issue is who is, or is not, allowed to enter. In this scenario, the simple *inclusion* of people of color would fix housing markets, for the normative assumption is that markets are expressions of neutral, free commerce, and the only problem is gatekeeper bias. A careful analysis suggests otherwise.

The investment in normative White men as a category deserving of the full benefits of citizenship went hand in hand with the construction of the housing market. I use citizenship here in the sense of "cultural citizenship," a pivotal concept honed by anthropologists such as Renato Rosaldo and Aihwa Ong that offers a more capacious approach to citizenship beyond the legal definition of sociopolitical membership with attendant rights and responsibilities. Rosaldo and Ong use "cultural citizenship" to highlight the importance of cultural hierarchies and "differences" in shaping hegemonic criteria for belonging, and they approach citizenship not as a single status granted by the state but a set of contested social processes of "self-making and being made" where both the state and multiple subjects are being shaped and produced (Ong 1996; Rosaldo 1993, 1999). In the case of the GI Bill – a collection of the "most far-reaching pieces of social policy legislation in the twentieth century [that] open[ed] up education and home-ownership" – only normative White men were considered proper candidates for the property ownership that was considered integral to cultural citizenship, even White men with no wealth, collateral, or so-called credit histories (Canaday 2011, 140). As historian Margot Canaday writes, "the disciplinary story not often told is the denial of these benefits to almost all African Americans, most women, and white men who 'were dishonorably discharged for homosexuality'" while serving in WWII (Canaday 2011, 140–1). Drawing from the particular and significant exclusion of suspected White gay men, Canaday points out that the primary societal (and socioeconomic) goal at the time was to settle White men in nuclear families after wartime, such was the fear of "deviant" wanderers with few socioeconomic prospects (Canaday 2011, 137–40). The key mechanism devised for rooting men in this way was to construct a coveted and hegemonic category of cultural citizenship for men considered worthy of investment (i.e. normative White, heterosexual men writ large, White veterans in particular), a category whose members would be amply rewarded under a dominant heterosexual family model in which the married man with a "dependent" wife would become the upwardly mobile breadwinner.

The GI Bill, then, by actively ushering particular identity categories into the market and welfare state, helped to produce certain kinds of valued categories and practices. Because the "magnitude" of benefits was so unprecedented – the GI Bill "represented a staggering 15 percent of the federal budget, and veterans constituted nearly one-half of the student body in colleges and universities across the country" in the immediate post-war era – it became a large-scale opportunity for social engineering, to construct and steer the desired citizenry (Canaday 2011, 140–2). The market in housing, along with education grants, loans to start businesses, and training/access to living wage jobs, was central to post-war planning, and these efforts led to a once-in-a-century "expansion" yet also "contraction" of the full benefits of the American Dream and who deserved them. These advantages were open to working and middle-class White men as never before but were exclusive to the social positionality of White male heads of households. Importantly, Canaday notes that the process of connecting heterosexuality and Whiteness to "first-class citizenship" and using "sexual identity" as a criterion for benefits also helped to construct the "closet," precisely because homosexual men could still become beneficiaries through their Whiteness, but only if closeted. In sum, the federal government, through unprecedented social provisioning for normative White men, helped to create and regulate socioeconomic categories, identities, and markets.

In this first stage of the creation of the mid-20th-century housing market, the extent of racialized exclusion in the housing market is telling. As the extraordinary video documentary *Race: The Power of an Illusion poignantly details,* "Between 1934 and 1962, the federal government underwrote 120 billion dollars in new housing. Less than 2% went to non-whites" (Adelman 2003). This totalizing exclusion meant that African Americans, for example, were completely locked out of this "market," with access mainly to public rentals or predatory contract-for-deed loans, which were never intended to build equity in homes but rather to extract income (Satter 2009). As such, the very beginning of the post-war housing market was defined through associating *value* with Whiteness and, in stark contrast, framing Blackness as *anti-value.* Despite the fact that it was a single housing market (in the sense that only Whites could engage as buyers and sellers), Whiteness and Blackness were both deeply shaped through the construction of an exclusionary market in housing. Race, in other words, became one of the central factors in constituting and influencing the housing market, not to mention housing prices and long-term real estate value.

Once single-family homes were mainly populated by nuclear families with White male heads of household, it was precisely the Whiteness of neighborhoods that became their most salient feature on the housing market. The gains of the various social movements of the 1960s, especially the Fair Housing Act, did widen access to the housing market although what continued unabated was the central importance of race (in particular Whiteness and Blackness) and racism (in particular the hierarchical cultural concepts of purity and contamination) in the making and functioning of housing markets. Specifically, segregation from Blackness was, for decades, perhaps up to and including the present, a socioeconomic necessity for success in the market. In other words, producing value and ensuring a healthy market necessitated the active protection of the "integrity" of property values, which was understood to depend on exclusive, homogenous Whiteness.

Just as segregation provides a key window into the structure of the US housing market, its attempted integration further reveals the fabric and workings of this market. Importantly, because housing value was still premised on segregated Whiteness even after the Fair Housing Act, "the Black population needed to be contained or segregated to preserve property values for white homeowners" (Taylor 2019, 6). Even as the social movements of the 1960s ushered in an apparent drawback of the redlining policies of the FHA and other loan-granting institutions, the cultural assumptions embedded within and constituting housing markets did not markedly change. Instead of a single housing market pre-1970s (with the segregation of African Americans into only rental possibilities and predatory rent-to-own schemes), the launch of "low-income home ownership programs" that utilized federal subsidies and loan guarantees, akin to what had been made available to Whites two generations earlier, created a "dual housing market" (Adelman 2003; Taylor 2019, 3). African Americans were mainly steered away from suburbs and toward overpriced, often dilapidated, urban homes that did *not* appreciate in value. In this context, the "shift from federal redlining to inclusion" did not end systemic housing racism; rather, the housing market substituted exclusion for what African-American Studies scholar Keeanga-Yamahtta Taylor brilliantly dubs "predatory inclusion," which became a "continuation of older predatory practices in combination with the invention of wholly new means of economic exploitation of African Americans in the US housing market" (Taylor 2019, 7).

It is crucial to understand that once the housing market technically became open to all, it continued to be structured through the cultural-economic rules of race and racial hierarchies, yet these unequal conditions were elided through normative and neutralizing market discourse that obscured the actual circumstances. For example, let us take the common "economic" concept of supply and demand, which is predominantly understood to be the primary shaper of housing prices (and housing value) in the US. Given that segregation and exclusion are not simply historical contexts but engines generating value, it is not surprising that these dynamics also, in turn, shape our understanding and interpretation of supply and demand and therefore limit our comprehension of the very structure of "markets."

Specifically, in the US housing market, segregation was (and continues to be) structured as a positive cultural value: the association of Whiteness with desirability and invest-ability, in stark contradistinction to Blackness defined as risk and contaminant. In essence, real estate imperatives demanded not only the separation of Whiteness from Blackness but also the tyrannical exclusion of African Americans to maintain and reproduce the relationship between Whiteness and exclusivity. Moreover, these structural relationships are deeply sedimented and reproduced: the large majority of potential homebuyers continue to be White because it is White households that have acquired savings, material connections to family inheritances and networks, a historical monopoly on stable careers, and access to federally guaranteed and affordable bank mortgages and federal grants. In fact, according to the National Association of Realtors in 2019, approximately 85 percent of homebuyers are White.[7] Given the extent to which White homebuyers have been both socialized into Whiteness, that is, into segregation as a key cultural value *and* into the "possessive investment in whiteness" where socioeconomic value coheres to exclusive Whiteness, it comes as no surprise that in making home purchasing decisions, they are mainly buying homes in neighborhoods where "whiteness as property" can be realized (Harris 1993; Lipsitz 2006).[8] In other words, given these larger social contexts, over 80 percent of the homebuying population is demanding houses in all-White neighborhoods (Adelman 2003). As such, the demand in these "desirable neighborhoods" skyrockets, and the supply dwindles. In tandem, when a neighborhood integrates, over 80 percent of the homebuying population is *no longer looking* for houses in that neighborhood. Demand plummets. As normative economics predicts, housing prices in integrated (as well as all-minority) neighborhoods fall while those in all-White neighborhoods rise until an equilibrium is reached (Adelman 2003).[9] And yet, in a direct challenge to economic orthodoxy, it is not autonomous rational individuals navigating the market according to an a priori logic of supply and demand, but rather racism embedded in culture, specifically notions of White exclusivity and Blackness as contamination that *centrally and singularly* shape supply and demand and buyers' desires and choices. In other words, race (and the role White supremacy and anti-Blackness play in shaping housing values and the importance of "location, location, location," even for individuals who attempt to resist this paradigm) are key to understanding what centrally moves and constructs the housing market.

For African Americans, then, the consequences of ownership and the value of their housing were starkly divergent from those of their White counterparts. As Keeanga-Yamahtta Taylor insightfully observed,

> Midcentury narrative of normative whiteness embodied in conceptions of the suburban-based nuclear family shaped the perceptions of *home* as an expression of *use value* within white communities. Conversely, developing narratives concerning perceived domestic dysfunction within Black living spaces – whether nonnormative family structures or poverty or dilapidated living structures – cast Black dwellings as incapable of achieving the status of home, thus reducing them to their base exchange value. Where white housing was seen as an asset developed through inclusion and the accruable possibilities of its surrounding property, Black housing was marked by its distress and isolation, where value was extracted, not imbued.
>
> (Taylor 2019, 11, original emphasis)

In this grounded analysis, whereas White-owned houses can achieve the "status of home," which Taylor understands as "use value," Black dwellings are "reduced" to their "base exchange value." She sets up a tension between use value and exchange value to showcase the stark difference between White-owned houses, which could be "developed" by exploiting their White-dominated contexts and thus "achiev[e] the status of home" versus Black-owned houses, where skewed and isolated contexts destroyed their potential as repositories of value.

While these insights are crucial, this argument can be constructively extended to provide further analytical power. For much of the post-WWII period (and continuing on into the contemporary moment, although deindustrialization, disinvestment, and financialization increasingly affect the value stability of previously "reliable" neighborhoods), White homeowners *also* reaped the benefits of exchange value because as their homes stored and accrued value, they helped to catalyze a *liquid* marketplace, in which property could be (relatively) easily bought and sold should the owners seek to realize its value. The houses of Black homeowners stagnated or declined in value precisely because they were framed as less desirable in terms of the condition (integration) and location (close to Blackness) of the neighborhood. As such, their homes were less likely to be sold, i.e. rendered illiquid, were not incorporated into a robust market, and thus could not realize their potential exchange value.

This social fact – that Black-owned houses were often kept from both achieving the status of home and reaping, for their owners, the rewards of exchange – leads me to the following point: only houses owned by Whites (mostly men) in exclusively or predominantly White neighborhoods could faithfully *realize* their value in the housing market. Houses owned by White people in all-White neighborhoods were homes with "use value," places that could be lived and invested in without imminent and continual fear of extraction, predation, and collapse of value. They were also *assets* with present and future "exchange value." The flipside was also true: Blackness was understood as anti-value, as contamination, and integration was understood as the destruction of value; Black-owned houses were not quite home and were also not quite stable assets. As such, for African Americans, the housing market simply did not quite *work*, even at the seemingly basic level of "real estate" exchange value.

The housing market has been dependent on Whiteness for value retention and growth, and as middle-class and upper middle-class White households saw their wealth appreciate through rising home prices due to White homogeneity and exclusivity, Black-owned homes in predominantly African American neighborhoods did not correspondingly rise in value, despite the homeowners' hard work and perseverance. And yet all this was somehow lost on most White homeowners. Historian David Freund's prescient article "Marketing the Free Market: State Intervention and the Politics of Prosperity in Metropolitan America" compellingly explains why the principles of White homogeneity, segregation, and exclusivity as the triadic components of the "free market in housing" are not understood or represented as such, especially by White homeowners (Freund 2006). The normative response of "it's just the market" or "that is how real estate economics work" is telling evidence that from the very outset of co-constituting the housing market, the state, which subsidized and underwrote the market in housing and constructed Whiteness as investible, erased its own cultural tracks. As Freund argues, "Paradoxically, the state helped popularize the myth that its policies did not construct and facilitate the housing market and suburban growth" but rather simply "'unleashed' existing but latent, market forces," and "[n]ot surprisingly this free-market story was embraced by the beneficiaries of federal largesse, most enthusiastically by an expanding, and increasingly suburban, white middle class" (Freund 2006, 12–3). Even in critical scholarship, the assumption is that the state facilitates and stabilizes "existing" markets, that states react, that states prevent monopoly control or attempt to (re)distribute scarce resources – but not that states *create* markets. It thus comes to no surprise that "[c]ountless whites came to believe that the state had no right to intervene in the economy or in their local communities," especially to "rectify" contemporary inequality, "because the state helped convince them that it had not intervened in the past" (Freund 2006, 14). Through the state's active self-erasure and its relentless promotion of free-market narratives, markets – framed as neutral, autonomous, and free of intervention – came to proxy for racism in the mid to late 20th century.

Segregation became, then, a political problem, not one that was produced and constituted by markets. The state "validated and disseminated a new economic theory about the relationship between race and property: the claim that the laws of free markets required the racial segregation of residence" (Freund 2006, 21). This particular logic then became "conventional wisdom among white businesspeople and consumers, encouraging them to portray racial exclusion not as a byproduct of their racial preferences, but rather as an inexorable market imperative ... " (Freund 2006, 21). In other words, Whiteness was the main qualification for participation and success in the housing market, yet markets justified exclusion without invoking the principle of racial difference. The state simultaneously spread the story that it did not "interfere" with free markets while every aspect of the housing market points to race. If mainly White properties accrue value, and if White properties can only accrue value if they abide by and enforce segregation, then segregation becomes the rule of the market.

Parallels to the "Job Market"

Eliding the race-inflected cultural processes that construct markets leads to misrecognition of the main causes of socioeconomic inequality. When exclusion, hierarchy, and privileged networks are understood as simply "the market," and individuals are seen as climbing the socioeconomic ladder through pluck, luck, talent, and hard work (meritocracy), then there is no unequal structure or systemic racism in the American Dream. While, earlier in this chapter, the housing market served as a key example of both the "marketing of markets" as free and fair *and* the epistemological and structural consequences of such a misrepresentation of foundational inequalities, there is a remarkable consistency in format and strategy across multiple markets in the US. Take "the job market," for example. Historian Nancy MacLean explains that central to the architecture of the American social economy has been an "entrenched culture of exclusion that long restricted to white men nearly every one of the nation's most desirable jobs at all class levels, whether skilled operative and craft jobs, the professions, or managerial positions" (MacLean 2006, 7). In fact, "workplace segregation by race, sex, and sometimes national origin" was so ingrained and naturalized that it became a "way of life for most Americans," taken so thoroughly for granted that "[m]embers of a single demographic seemed assigned almost by nature to job categories such as maid, salesman, carpenter, secretary, migrant farm worker, flight attendant, or executive" (MacLean 2006, 7–8). As such, the very term "job market," like the housing market, is a misnomer.

It can be quite mind-blowing to confront the socioeconomic fact that historically, and until the 1960s and beyond, there was really no such thing as a "job market," much less one that was open, free, and fair – at least if one considers that competition is inherent to the notion of a job market. Job categories were largely about separation and even confinement, as well as status, hierarchy, and typecasting. It is thus not surprising that when African American-led civil rights[10] and other social movements challenged the conflation of particular categories of people with particular jobs, these transformations "upset every location in the hierarchy" (MacLean 2006, 9). Given that "employers and policymakers constructed a labor market biased toward men, especially white men, and devised social welfare policy that shored up male-dominated households while weakening others," then, for all intents and purposes, the main group that could officially participate in the labor market was White men (MacLean 2006, 16). It would thus not be an exaggeration to underscore that this internal job sorting and placement did not resemble what we imagine as a job market since "direct interracial competition for jobs" was virtually nonexistent (MacLean 2006, 18).

Further, as MacLean reminds us, "[w]hat kept the whole system intact was employers' conviction that they could do as they wished with their own resources, a conviction backed by a legal system that defined the rules of the industrial order" (MacLean 2006, 21). The private "right" of businesses to discriminate worked hand in hand with the discursive strategy of framing an exclusionary network as a free market. Moreover, this expression of the freedom of contract, linked to the "nation's founding commitment to the rights of property," was further bolstered and naturalized by the discourses and practices of meritocratic individualism, which enshrined "the popular success myth" that led the majority of White men to "imagine themselves" and their relatives and friends as "someday sitting in the boss's chair"

(MacLean 2006, 21–2). The equating of White male monopoly with "freedom of hiring" and meritocracy helped to reproduce the ongoing fictions of the American Dream, allowing for both seemingly neutral market justifications and the realization of upward mobility for some (MacLean 2006, 21).

The ongoing reverberations of hierarchical, segregated, and exclusive job segmentations into the contemporary moment are extensive and worth unpacking. It is important to emphasize what critical scholars have long demonstrated and what many mainstream observers continue to fail to understand: White male employees and "others" did not usually *compete* in the same "job markets": the former's job placements were largely exclusive and protected. As such, the very notion of marginalized categories of workers "taking away their jobs" is largely a structural fiction. In fact, as American Studies scholar David Roediger has long demonstrated, Black and White workers did not occupy the same job space, so to speak. In Roediger's brilliant study, *Wages of Whiteness: Race and the Making of the American Working Class*, he cautions against assuming that it was job competition that intensified Irish American, working-class resentment against newly emancipated African American workers. He argues, rather, that most of the job competition came from other White ethnic immigrants, that is, immigrants who had even more of a claim to Whiteness than the Irish, because "free Blacks were *not* effective competitors for jobs" (Roediger 1991, 147, original emphasis). Roediger notes that African Americans were not only slotted into specific niches but also that "Blacks were so much less able to strike back," as they were "'despised with impunity.'" Given this context, "Irish Catholic immigrants quickly learned that Blacks in America ... could be victimized with efficacy ... and [w]hat was most noteworthy to free Blacks at the time, and probably should be noteworthy to historians, was the relative ease with which Irish-Americans 'elbowed-out' African-Americans from unskilled jobs" (Roediger 1991, 148).

Importantly, one of the key lessons that Irish Americans (and many not-quite-White European American ethnics) learned in navigating the racial hierarchies of the US is that socio-economic security and upward mobility for immigrants *necessitated* the claiming of Whiteness (and the affordances that come with the privileges of Whiteness). As Roediger demonstrates, when Irish immigrants and Irish Americans advocated for belonging *as Irish* (which was itself a denigrated category), they were much less successful than when they advocated *as Whites*. He states that it was "easier ... for the Irish to defend jobs and rights as 'white' entitlements instead of as Irish ones" (Roediger 1991, 148). Crucially, yet tragically, the structural pressure that allowed for the Irish to move up the ladder to Whiteness was *distance from* Blackness. As Roediger details, while Irish Americans faced intense discrimination as Irish, the more they adopted "American" mores, which centrally included cultural-economic disassociation from and racism toward Black folks, the more they grew into Whiteness. Given that the social category of Whiteness in American culture was largely defined and understood as "not Black" (and thus not constructed to be subject to enslavement), one of the key strategies for upward mobility was to separate from and castigate Blackness. Thus dual "job markets" developed to prevent competition from non-Whites (tracking "others" into entirely segregated jobs and professions), rather than a free and fair space for all to compete.

Writing about job conflicts throughout much of the mid-20th century, sociologist Edna Bonacich argues that the two-fold strategies of nationalist exclusion on the one hand and ethnicized and racialized segregations and monopolies on the other prevented privileged workers from having to occupy the same spaces as "cheaper" workers. Researching the historical moment when capital and labor policies were being reconstituted in the wake of shifting immigration restrictions and emergent civil rights movements, Bonacich shows that even in the context of growing US wealth and global market dominance in the post-WWII era, when mainstream assumptions often picture a rising tide lifting all boats, employment and job placement in the US continued to practice a "labor market split" in which "the differentially priced workers ideally never occupy the same position" (Bonacich 1972, 555). Such out-of-sight and out-of-mind segregations and segmentations thus sidelined confrontations about our unequal arrangements, monopolies, and lack of competition. When entire groups and social categories, organized primarily by race and gender, are tracked into specific kinds and classes of job positions, rather than having a job market where multiple categories and classes intersect, compete, and intermingle, the US (along with other states with apartheid-like systems and histories) constructed a hierarchical "caste" system that was problematically marketed and cloaked as a "free" market.

As sociologist Deirdre Royster, following Bonacich, explains and sums up: "[I]n this violent and multifaceted racial stratification system, which privileged whites of all classes …. [w]hite workers developed two strategies to preserve race-based privileges in the labor market: exclusion and caste system" (Royster 2003, 32). In practice, "nonwhite workers were prevented from participating in the labor pool, and employers were … unable to undercut the position and wage rates of dominant white workers by hiring cheaper nonwhite workers," because the two categories were framed as and constructed into separate spheres, one relatively protected, the other incommensurately precarious. Royster concluded that the resulting aims in the social economy characterized by exclusion and hierarchy were to "monopolize" *both* good jobs *and* the "the acquisition of skills" and apprenticeships to procure such jobs, to "prevent the immediate use of cheaper labor as undercutters or strikebreakers in times of crisis," and to "weaken the cheaper labor group politically" (Royster 2003, 33).

Alongside exclusionary and caste strategies, critical legal scholar Daria Roithmayr makes the case that privileged organizing and the implementation of reactionary cartels were also central to maintaining socioeconomic job hierarchies and monopolies. Roithmayr argues that despite the taken-for-granted assumptions of neoclassical economic theory that "free" market competition eventually eliminates discrimination (because discrimination is too costly and prevents businesses from taking full capitalist/profitable advantage), such theories have failed because they have not taken seriously enough the importance of collective, cartel-like action on the part of the privileged, the durability of a caste system, and the structural reproductive effects of stratification over time. In particular, Roithmayr states that "the concept of a racial cartel turns this neoclassical story on its head" because the explicit usage of the term "cartel" shines a spotlight on anti-competitive, White collective action (Roithmayr 2014, 29). As a cartel, a "group of actors who work together to extract monopoly profits by manipulating price and limiting competition," the collectivity of White actors who make up "the market" are not simply interested in competition, finding "the best person" for the job, or searching for the best price. This is why market economies do not "naturally" abolish racism (Roithmayr 2014, 30). Roithmayr explains that contrary to the assumption that employers, in their continual pursuit of cheap labor, would refuse anti-competitive antics that drove up the costs of labor, Whites have instead engaged in "collusion by social groups to obtain monopoly control over the market by excluding competitors" (Roithmayr 2014, 32). While White workers also relied on the fact that most employers were themselves socialized into the entitled and protectionist space of Whiteness, they were also able to make this bargain work for the employer because Whites "shift[ed] the cost of segregation from its perpetrators to its victims." This means that the corresponding under-compensation of African Americans, through their expropriated labor, made up the difference for uncompetitively paying Whites more (Roithmayr 2014, 30). Moreover, Roithmayr makes the point that this arrangement was not fleeting: these racial cartels remained stable because White cartels induced "their members to deploy the same anti-competitive strategy, to monitor each other's compliance, and to continue to cooperate even when they are tempted to defect or free-ride" (Roithmayr 2014, 32). Because economists were too ensconced in the neoclassical mindset, they did not "focus on whites' collective action in engaging in such conduct" and thus did not realize that "whites engaged in cartel conduct for their own economic gain" (Roithmayr 2014, 30).[11]

Finally, it is important to recognize the extent to which these sedimented structures (job exclusions, castes, cartels, and hierarchies) have set the stage for the ongoing reproduction of job market inequalities. One key manifestation is how job networks, trainings, and apprenticeships work. There exists a direct connection between the size, density, and efficiency of networks and persistent inequality: "Social networks distribute a great deal of value because they enable a network member to draw direct support from their closest contacts, and also indirect support from a more loosely connected group of contacts" (Roithmayr 2014, 84). Given that the "probability that a job seeker gets referred for the job will depend on many links each jobseeker has to the next layer up in the hierarchy, and on how well linked the succeeding layers are as one moves up the hierarchy" (Roithmayr 2014, 85), it is not surprising that the racially segregated employment and housing structures that produced similar networks would be key in maintaining racial hierarchies and exclusion. Race shapes "size and density of a social network" as well as "how insular network ties" are (Roithmayr 2014, 89-90). For example, "compared to whites, black and Latino job seekers have networks that are smaller in size and have fewer links per person to potential employment" and are "far more likely to reside in the layers of the hierarchy at the bottom, far from direct access to employment" (Roithmayr 2014, 89). Not only are marginalized networks less connected to the upper reaches of the job hierarchy, but also these networks tend to be "very tightly knit," meaning that the job seeker's contacts are not likely to be widely dispersed and diffuse enough to catalyze a connection not already known to the job seeker. Such networks, while supportive, are unlikely to be highly connective or provide "market" traction farther up the hierarchy, and as such, historically marginalized communities may be "less successful on the job market because these groups cannot bridge the structural holes in their networks" (Roithmayr 2014, 90). Not surprisingly, "[i]t turns out that a relatively narrow range of connectivity makes all the difference between a network that has enough pathways for a jobseeker to connect to a job and a network that disintegrates before the jobseeker can connect to employment" (Roithmayr 2014, 86).

Similarly, Deirdre Royster makes the crucial point that not only are White male networks denser, relatively secure, and composed of both bosses and workers, with enough men at the high end of the hierarchy, but also that these networks *actually operate differently* and divergently when encountering Blackness than they do with respect to Whiteness. Through Royster's ethnographic research on how White working-class networks exclude Black men, she found that the networks of younger White men worked in ways that spurred connectivity, gave context, and showed faith. Mistakes were overlooked, chances were taken on young men, side jobs turned into trade jobs, interviews were granted, and hiring could happen "on the spot" (Royster 2003, 145). When these White networks encountered Black men, the opposite happened – hiring was never on the spot, mistakes were remembered, interviews were required for even the most menial tasks, connections were not taken up, recommendations and contexts were not given. In other words, White male fraternity was the necessary ingredient for the network to actually work *as a network*; with that ingredient missing, there was no connectivity, no efficiency to the network.

Importantly, Royster demonstrated that White contacts and members of the network could make recommendations without considering the racial patterns in the job setting and could recommend young White men for jobs for which they had little training. They could take risks with referrals and recommendations without backlash or repercussions, as baseline flexibility and overlooking of mistakes were sutured into the very framing of (White) capabilities. Not surprisingly, White networks did not spring into action for young Black men, and correspondingly, the sparse Black networks were unable to make recommendations because Black contacts paid the price (exacted by White networks) for recommending young Black workers who did not "fit" well.

Therefore, part of the success of White male networks is that they simply proxied for the workings of the markets; they were expansive, connective, elastic, and forgiving of failure, and yet understood and represented as neutral. Black networks had to be effectively disguised, and to the extent that African American men received any institutional or educational support, it was through the state, through "visible" intervening hands. In fact, according to Royster, when White networks were explicitly mentioned or called out (in terms of connections, introductions, who said "hi" to whom), it did not weaken the myth of the invisible hand. To the contrary, meager Black networks became marked as unfair and distasteful and could be used to undermine and put at risk the very Black workers who had to rely on them. As Royster explains, White raced networks do not appear "exclusive to white beneficiaries" who wrongly assume that many opportunities go to minorities, and it is precisely this assumption that serves as a strong disincentive to include Black men in predominantly White networks (Royster 2003, 178). The minstrelsy of reverse discrimination accusations prevents the potential sharing of White male networks for Black men*, and* they also discourage White support of important ameliorative policies like affirmative action.

As examined earlier in this chapter, when financialization and corporate restructuring engendered massive job outsourcing and the dismantling of job benefits and stability, almost all job categories were affected, even those of the formerly protected; of course, the "cheaper" and "non-White" positions were often either dismantled (creating structural unemployment) or further downgraded into low-wage service sector jobs with few ladders for upper mobility. Importantly, the valued skills training attached to middle-class jobs (which were themselves associated with the formerly protected and upwardly mobile workers) were deeply racialized and gendered and were not transferred to low-wage labor categories. Given this larger context in the contemporary moment where corporations and institutions shoulder less responsibility for apprenticeship and training opportunities, it is not surprising that informal contacts, background and interpersonal networks, and cultural capital have become even more important (Sennett 2006). Individualized inetworks – formed over time and strengthened through spatial proximity to cultural homology – are more crucial for job referrals, placement, and upward mobility than ever. With the gutting of institutions, those who had newly won "inclusion" were jettisoned. The downsizing of bureaucracy had the unintended consequence of undermining countervailing efforts from institutions to create less biased ladders and systems of hiring and promotion, and demanded that job seekers rely on already-existing background networks, which, as this chapter demonstrates, further heightens inequality.

Toward a Conclusion: Financialization, the Unreliability of "Markets," and the Rise of Expropriation

In the contemporary moment, financialization plays a central role in the undermining of the American Dream for most. In the late 20th and early 21st centuries, financiers worked with corporate executives and large investment funds to constantly buy and sell companies with little to no regard for the welfare of the millions of workers whose jobs were eliminated in the

process. Financiers who "closed the deal" reaped enormous fees, and socioeconomic dislocation was shifted downstream. This ongoing process of restructuring some of the key socioeconomic institutions of upward mobility has dismantled the ladder to the middle class. As I
have queried elsewhere, how can there be institutional mobility and security when the very
institutions that have been charged with this task in capitalist society have been liquidated
(see Ho 2014)?

The financialization of corporate America also sundered the fraternal expectations and
cross-class bonds of upward mobility between working-class, middle-class, and elite White
men. Until the late 20th century, normatively racialized and gendered markets did, in
fact, create space for upward mobility, allowing less privileged White men access to wider
networks. It is precisely because of this prior expectation that the reactionary populism and
corresponding scapegoating of the Trump era (and the decades leading up to it) frame itself
as a response to the betrayal of fraternal Whiteness by elite men. The cross-class kinship
between privileged and less privileged White men can no longer be robustly counted on
for job security and mobility, leading to the kinds of White-supremacist social violence –
shrouded in frames of victimization – that can occur when expected networks and kinship
ties are no longer guaranteed.

With financialization, for many working and middle-class Whites, their prior understanding
of "the market" – as a free and neutral marketplace, as the American Dream, as an arena for
hard work, opportunity, and upward mobility – was upended. Globalization and minorities
were often called forth as scapegoats (Ho 2018).[12] Philosopher Nancy Fraser insightfully dubs
these developments as indicative of an era of "financialized capitalism," when the distinctions
between "exploitation" and "expropriation" have collided (Fraser 2016). If that sounds overly
abstract, allow me to explain. As many critical scholars have outlined, especially in work on
racial capitalism and critical Black studies,[13] the expropriation of labor, peoples, resources, and
lands through enslavement, colonialism, and settler colonialism is what fueled the making
of empires, wealthy elites, and industrial capitalism itself. This scholarship has importantly
shown that such theft, dependent on the construction of racism, sexism, differential value, and
multiple forms of hierarchy, was not a "one-time" world-historical event but an ongoing set
of processes and structures that ripple into the present day.

In parallel, it was precisely through the accumulations made possible by the "unfree origins
of capitalism" that the possibility of waged exploitation, based on the prototype of "citizen-
workers" who could sell their labor in the industrial marketplace, materialized (Fraser 2016;
Rockman 2005). The "racializing dynamic of capitalist society" was "crystallized in the
'mark' that distinguishes *free subjects of exploitation* from *dependent subjects of expropriation*," which
in turn "correlate[ed] with the color line" as well as relationships between core and peripheries (not to mention multiple peripheries within the core) (Fraser 2016, 169–72, original
emphasis). It was through the ongoing expropriation of resources – the land, materials, and
labor that elite capitalists could procure for "free" – that "exploitation of metropolitan industrial workers" became profitable, and the result was that for the long colonial period into the
20th century, not only was expropriation the condition of possibility for the relative privileges
of exploitation, but also the two forms of capture and labor were intimately interrelated yet
widely divergent in terms of the bodies and categories that inhabited them (Fraser 2016, 174).
From the early 20th century into the post-WWII era, with the strengthening of benefits and
stability, not to mention welfare-state-managed inclusion, many White men rose in status
and were cushioned from the precarities of wage exploitation. Although resistance and social
movements allowed some workers in marginalized communities to move away from expropriation, the mark of expropriation was still precedent for people of color, especially Black

workers, as "expropriation combined with exploitation" and "segmenting labor markets ... exact[ed] a confiscatory premium from racialized labor"[14] (Fraser 2016, 175).

Using the concepts of expropriation and exploitation, Fraser argues that in the US, at the supposed height of the American Dream, the middle classes were "shielded by their status as citizen-workers," and BIPOC communities and women differentially navigated the lines between expropriation and exploitation, occasionally making headway without being able to fully shed their marked and lower-value status (Fraser 2016, 176). On top of these inequalities, in the contemporary moment, financialization has (re)unleashed the processes of expropriation writ large, as capital generated by corporations and other institutions are "captured" to such an unequal extent by wealthy financial actors. Since Wall Street helped to reduce corporations into mere appendages of their stock prices, the larger socioeconomic ramifications have been devastating: the accumulated repositories of wealth stored in corporations have been redistributed to powerful investors. The goods and services, the buildings and factories, the employees and communities – all prior "stakeholders" of the corporation, whose value accrued due to input from labor – were all downsized in favor of the shareholders and the financial institutions who act in their name. Employees have been written out of the corporate social contract, with a truncation of both their upward mobility (and security) and their claims to share in corporate profits, because under financialization, the corporation is reframed as "belonging" solely to the shareholders. In today's financial worldview, corporations are financial assets belonging to elite investors, and ordinary workers are relegated to the gig economy. And when those who helped to build, sustain, and grow the corporation are excised from it, losing job security while receiving none of the proceeds, it is not far-fetched to argue that their work is now increasingly "expropriated."

It is precisely the encroachment of the techniques of expropriation into areas that have previously been protected and the intensification of expropriation in marginalized communities that have rendered the present so jarring and upending. As Fraser explains, in the "present regime of racialized accumulation, which I call 'financialized capitalism'," "expropriation is on the rise, threatening to dwarf exploitation again as a source and driver of capital expansion ... afflicting not only its traditional subjects but also those who were previously shielded by their status as citizen-workers" (Fraser 2016, 176). Fraser continues,

> In financialized capitalism .... [i]n place of the earlier, sharp divide between expropriable subjects and exploitable citizen-workers, there appears a continuum. At one end lies the growing mass of defenseless, expropriable subjects; at the other, the dwindling ranks of protected exploited citizen-workers. At the center sits a figure, already glimpsed in the previous era, but now generalized: the *expropriable-and-exploitable citizen-worker*, formally free but acutely vulnerable. No longer restricted to peripheral populations and racial minorities, this hybrid figure is becoming the norm in much of the historic core. Nevertheless, the expropriation/exploitation continuum remains racialized, as people of color are still disproportionately represented at the expropriative end of the spectrum.
>
> (Fraser 2016, 176, original emphasis)

In other words, the distinction between exploitation and expropriation, while blurred among the relatively marginalized and the hyper-marginalized, is perhaps increasingly relevant in explaining the separation between the hyper-wealthy and "the rest." Financialization has continually remade the gaps between rich and poor, between White privilege and non-White insecurity, and between valued economic resources and useless forms of nature and humanity. In creating safety and wealth for a few, financialization seals the fate of those who live outside their (often flimsy) enclosures. And yet, those who had presumed that their safety and prosperity were guaranteed by "neutral" markets as well as the expropriation of others and outsourcing elsewhere have aired grievances against the collapse of the American Dream and called for the restoration of their own safety and prosperity. These aggrieved reactionaries would rather "shatter our nation than share it," to quote inaugural poet Amanda Gorman, even as their protests misrecognize how we came to be in this mess in the first place. In the face of financialization and hyperinequality, perhaps this excavation into the problematic conditions of possibility of markets, Whiteness, and the American Dream can generate thicker, rather than zero-sum, solidarities across multiple communities.

Notes

1 It is worth noting that in 2021, in the heights of the pandemic, *Wall Street* reported near-all-time record earnings, with average salaries, including bonuses, at $438,000, the highest of any industry by far (New York State Comptroller 2021).

2 According to figures adjusted for inflation from the historical Survey of Consumer Finances, "In 1968, a typical middle-class black household had $6,674 in wealth compared with $70,786 for the typical middle-class white household," and in "2016, the typical middle-class black household had $13,024 in wealth versus $149,703 for the median white household, an even larger gap in percentage terms" (Long and Van Dam 2020). https://www.washingtonpost.com/business/2020/06/04/economic-divide-black-households/

3 In this chapter, I have consciously decided to capitalize both "Black" and "White" to denote the particularity, artificiality, and constructedness of racialized categories. While many newspapers, professional academic organizations, and critical scholars have regularized the capitalization of "Black" since the 2020 murder of George Floyd to convey precisely its historical specificity, its power as a collective identity, and its social constructedness, *not its naturalness*, there has been little consensus on the capitalization of "White." As Philosopher and African Americanist cultural theorist Kwame Anthony Appiah presciently discusses, the sticking point is the taken-for-granted normativity of Whiteness: it is not usually capitalized both because White people usually take their race for granted and because of the social danger of elevating the hierarchical and dominant aspect of Whiteness with a capital letter (Appiah 2020). And yet, given that one of the central interventions of this chapter is to thwart the reproduction of White privilege by preventing its socioeconomic and psychological status as invisible norm and as neutral, non-raced standard, then capitalizing White is one small stylistic step in not exempting White people from their "troubling history" through treating it as a particular, accountable, and situated category, not a taken-for-granted, objective fact or description (Appiah 2020). https://www.theatlantic.com/ideas/archive/2020/06/time-to-capitalize-blackand-white/613159/. It is important to note, however, that, throughout the chapter, when I quote other authors, I keep their capitalizations and conventions used at the time of publication intact.

4 It is also interesting to note that in this discussion of race, Whiteness, and markets, the formerly unquestioned position of Whiteness is precisely what we continue to reproduce in our analyses of markets. In that sense, it is crucial to unpack the discourse of "free markets" in the US using the critical approach to Whiteness that has importantly highlighted its ability to self-define as both normative and superior. Keeping in mind "white racial dualism," we might similarly call out "free market dualism," where free market promotors continue to double-down on claims of market rationality, superiority, and normativity, despite the fact that we see an increasing challenge to market self-presentations as "neutral" through the highlighting of privileged networks and categories. Of course, such privileged market networks continue to be rendered invisible through normative market discourse.

5 In this section, I use citizen in a cultural, not a legal, sense, and later in the chapter, I explain how the term "cultural citizenship" is a more apt term. Specifically, while people of color and women are US "citizens" in a legal sense, they have not been included in the full benefits of cultural citizenship, as the hierarchical standard for inclusion and belonging have long been that of normative White men. I thus use "citizen" to denote not so much legal citizenship but full treatment

as citizens. It is also important to note that indigenous communities have long critiqued the very notion of citizenship and inclusion as contradictory and problematic, given that the US nation-state is situated on stolen land and depends on the colonial repression of native sovereignties. Seeking "inclusion" has offered limited multicultural recognition, not real decoloniality; rather, the effects have been to assuage and accommodate settler colonial guilt and hierarchical relations (Hayes 2018).

6　There is perhaps no better example of a market fundamentally shaped and operationalized by racism and racial inequality than the growth of the housing market in the US from the post-depression era into the contemporary moment. It is important to remember that before the 1930s, there was *no mass market* in housing, as the financial concept and instrument of mortgages – and the federal subsidies, guarantees, and insurance which made this financing possible – did not yet exist. For the most part, only the wealthy who could buy housing outright – without the benefit of a 30-year mortgage – were homeowners. However, in the wake of the Great Depression and especially after WWII with the GI Bill, the federal government (through the creation of the Federal Housing Authority's subsidies and insurance for banking institutions, which in turn financed low-interest, 30-year mortgages) seeded a new market in housing for a particular category of people, White men of varying class positions.

7　https://www.nar.realtor/sites/default/files/documents/2019-home-buyers-and-sellers-generational-trends-report-08-16-2019.pdf

8　Interestingly enough, in a recent presentation, sociologist Zaire Dinzey-Flores argues that Whiteness and a particular White aesthetic imbue the home staging and design preparation for sale in the housing market, noting that culturally marked homes are framed as less desirable than homes that are represented as neutral, new, and modern, which are terms associated with the erasures and unmarked normativities of Whiteness (Dinzey-Flores, Zaire. 2022. "Visionaries Wanted: Listing Race in *New* Brooklyn Real Estate." Presentation at the Department of Chicano and Latino Studies, University of Minnesota).

9　This insight into racism as a key mover of supply and demand comes from the critically acclaimed documentary, *Race: The Power of an Illusion.* (See Adelman, Larry. 2003. *Race: The Power of an Illusion.* California Newsreel.)

10　MacLean writes: "[F]rom their history African Americans developed an unusually radical and universalistic vision of justice and grounded it in mainstream American values. In these years, blacks focused on living-wage jobs for all as critical to advancement, and they worked more than any other population with organized labor. Building broad coalitions, they argued for measures to assist other victims of discrimination and pressed for active efforts by the national government to promote economic equality for all Americans to a degree that was not true of other peoples of color, of white women, or of working-class white men" (MacLean 2006, 4). "[L]egal freedom, formal equality, was not enough. Rather, genuine inclusion – full belonging as Americans – required participation in the economic mainstream – namely, access to good jobs at all levels once reserved for white men alone" (MacLean 2006, 5).

11　In a similar manner, the earlier example of housing markets – where White homeowners helped to institute and police segregation, and were bolstered by laws, government policies, and the disciplining of realtors and White sellers who might have attempted to defy the cartel – demonstrates that overall, Whites benefited from housing market cartels, as their segregated properties accrued value over time. Even if this accrual was modest, mortgage interest could be deducted from taxes, and monthly payments cohered to the owner. As Roithmayr states, "[W]hite association members enjoyed a monopoly on the higher property values," and "keep[ing] neighborhoods all white was in their best interests as well" (Roithmayr 2014, 36).

12　For those scapegoated – many marginalized communities in the US who never laid claim to post-WWII prosperity, their incipient inroads into liberal inclusion were stunted by post-civil-rights backlash, not to mention "neoliberal" socioeconomic policies and practices that favored the already well-resourced and highly pedigreed. As such, they face continued exclusion and downward mobility, an erosion of the meager programs designed for amelioration, and further blame for the new insecurities facing the (majority White) middle classes.

13　See, for example, Leroy and Jenkins (2021), Melamed (2015), and Robinson (2000).

14　Similarly, "[w]ith political independence, some postcolonials managed to raise their status from expropriable subject to exploitable citizen-worker, but precariously and on inferior terms" (Fraser 2016, 175).

References

Adelman, Larry. 2003. *Race: The Power of an Illusion*. California Newsreel.

Appiah, Kwame Anthony. 2020. "The Case for Capitalizing the B in Black. *The Atlantic*. June 2020. https://www.theatlantic.com/ideas/archive/2020/06/time-to-capitalize-blackand-white/613159/ (accessed August 2022).

Bessire, Lucas, and David Bond. 2017. "Introduction: The Rise of Trumpism." *Cultural Anthropology* (blog). January 18. https://culanth.org/fieldsights/1031-introduction-the-rise-of-trumpism (accessed January 2022).

Bonacich, Edna. 1972. "A Theory of Ethnic Antagonism: The Split Labor Market." *American Sociological Review* 37(5): 547–59.

Bonilla-Silva, Eduardo. 2014. *Racism without Racists: Color-Blind Racism and the Persistence of Racial Equality in America*, 4th edition. Lanham, MD: Rowman & Littlefield Publishers, Inc.

Brodkin, Karen. 1998. *How the Jews Became White Folks and What That Says About Race in America*. New Brunswick, NJ: Rutgers University Press.

Canaday, Margot. 2011. *The Straight State: Sexuality and Citizenship in Twentieth-Century America*. Princeton, NJ: Princeton University Press.

Chen, Victor Tan. 2022. "The Mirage of Meritocracy and the Morality of Grace." In *Routledge Handbook on the American Dream: Volume 1*, edited by Robert C. Hauhart and Mitja Sardoc. New York: Routledge.

Choi, Jung Hyun et al. 2018. "Millenial Homeownership: Why Is It So Low, and How Can We Increase It?" *Urban Institute Research Report*. July 2018. https://www.urban.org/sites/default/files/publication/98729/millennial_homeownership_0.pdf (accessed August 2021).

Cooper, Marianne. 2014. *Cut Adrift: Families in Insecure Times*. Berkeley, CA: University of California Press.

Cooper, Melinda. 2017. *Family Values: Between Neoliberalism and the New Social Conservatism*. New York: Zone Books.

Davis, Gerald. 2009. "The Rise and Fall of Finance and the End of the Society of Organizations." *Academy of Management Perspectives* 23(3): 27–44.

Davis, Gerald. 2016. *The Vanishing American Corporation: Navigating the Hazards of the new Economy*. San Francisco: Berrett-Koehler Publishers.

Derickson, Kate et al. 2021. "Private Equity Firms: The New Landlord." https://marketfailure.substack.com/p/private-equity-firms-the-new-landlord

Fraser, Nancy. 2016. "Expropriation and Exploitation in Racialized Capitalism." *Critical Historical Studies* 3(1): 163–78.

Fraser, Nancy. 2017. "The End of Progressive Neoliberalism." *Dissent*. January 2. https://www.dissentmagazine.org/online_articles/progressive-neoliberalism-reactionary-populism-nancy-fraser (accessed January 2022).

Freund, David. 2006. "Marketing the Free Market: State Intervention and the Politics of Prosperity in Metropolitan America." In *The New Suburban History*, edited by Kevin Kruse and Thomas Sugrue, 11–32. Chicago, IL: University of Chicago Press.

Gallagher, Charles. 2003. "Playing the White Ethnic Card: Using Ethnic Identity to Deny Contemporary Racism." In *White Out: The Continuing Significance of Racism*, edited by Ashley W. Doane and Eduardo Bonilla-Silva, 145–58. New York: Routledge.

Harris, Cheryl. 1993. "Whiteness as Property." *Harvard Law Review* 106(8): 1710–91.

Harris, Dianne. 2013. *Little White Houses: How the Postwar Home Constructed Race in America*. Minneapolis, MN: University of Minnesota Press.

Hayes, Katherine. 2018. "The Carceral Side of Freedom." *International Journal of Heritage Studies* 25(7): 641–55.

Ho, Karen. 2009. *Liquidated: An Ethnography of Wall Street*. Durham, NC: Duke University Press.

Ho, Karen. 2014. "Corporate Nostalgia? Managerial Capitalism from a Contemporary Perspective." In *Corporations and Citizenship*, edited by Greg Urban, 267–88. Philadelphia, PA: University of Pennsylvania Press.

Ho, Karen. 2018. "Markets, Myths, and Misrecognitions: Economic Populism in the Age of Financialization and Hyperinequality." *Economic Anthropology* 5: 148–50.

Ho, Karen. 2020a. "Why the Stock Market Is Rising Amidst a Pandemic and Record, Racialized Inequality." In *Intersecting Crises*, edited by Calynn Dowler, American Ethnologist website, 12 October, https://americanethnologist.org/panel/pages/features/pandemic-diaries/

introduction-intersecting-crises/why-the-stock-market-is-rising-amidst-a-pandemic-and-record-racialized-inequality/edit.

Ho, Karen. 2020b. "In the Name of Shareholder Value: Origin Myths of Corporations and Their Ongoing Implications." *Seattle University Law Review* 43: 609–30.

hooks, bell, ed. 1992. "Representations of Whiteness." *Black Looks: Race and Representation*. Boston, MA: South End Press.

Jacobson, Matthew Frye. 2008. *Roots Too: White Ethnic Revival in Post-Civil Rights America*. Cambridge, MA: Harvard University Press.

Jardina, Ashley. 2019. *White Identity Politics*. Cambridge, UK: Cambridge University Press.

Katznelson, Ira. 2005. *When Affirmative Action Was White: An Untold History of Racial Inequality in Twentieth Century America*. New York: W.W. Norton & Company.

Krippner, Greta. 2011. *Capitalizing on Crisis: The Political Origins of the Rise of Finance*. Cambridge, MA: Harvard University Press.

Kruse, Kevin. 2007. *White Flight: Atlanta and the Making of Modern Conservatism*. Princeton, NJ: Princeton University Press.

Kuhn, Moritz et al. 2018. "Income and Wealth Inequality in America, 1949–2016." *Institute Working Paper* 9. June 14. https://www.minneapolisfed.org/research/institute-working-papers/income-and-wealth-inequality-in-america-1949-2016 (accessed January 2020).

Laird, Pamela. 2006. *Pull: Networking and Success Since Benjamin Franklin*. Cambridge, MA: Harvard University Press.

Lane, Carrie. 2011. *A Company of One: Insecurity, Independence, and the New World of White-Collar Unemployment*. Ithaca, NY: Cornell University Press.

Lazonick, William. 2013. "The Financialization of the U.S. Corporation: What Has Been Lost, and How It Can Be Regained." *Seattle University Law Review* 36: 857–908.

Leroy, Justin, and Dustin Jenkins, eds. 2021. *Histories of Racial Capitalism*. New York: Columbia University Press.

Lin, Ken-Hou, and Donald Tomaskovic-Dewey. 2013. "Financialization and U.S. Income Inequality." *American Journal of Sociology* 118(5): 1284–329.

Lipsitz, George. 2006. *The Possessive Investment in Whiteness: How White People Profit from Identity Politics*. Temple University Press: PA, Philadelphia.

Long, Heather, and Andrew Van Dam. 2020. "The Black-White Economic Divide Is as Wide as It Was in 1968." *The Washington Post*. June 4. https://www.washingtonpost.com/business/2020/06/04/economic-divide-black-households/ (accessed January 2022).

MacLean, Nancy. 2006. *Freedom Is Not Enough: The Opening of the American Workplace*. Cambridge, MA: Harvard University Press.

Markovits, Daniel. 2019. *The Meritocracy Trip: How America's Founding Myth Feeds Inequality, Dismantles the Middle Class, and Devours the Elite*. New York: Penguin Press.

Massey, Douglas, and Nancy Denton. 1993. *American Apartheid: Segregation and the Making of the Underclass*. Cambridge, MA: Harvard University Press.

McNamee, Stephen. 2018. *The Meritocracy Myth*. Lanham, MD: Rowman & Littlefield.

Melamed, Jodi. 2015. "Racial Capitalism." *Critical Ethnic Studies* 1(1): 76–85.

Mirowski, Phillip. 2013. *Never Let a Serious Crisis Go to Waste: How Neoliberalism Survived the Financial Meltdown*. London: Verso.

New York State Comptroller. 2018. "The Securities Industry in New York City." September 2018. osc.state.ny.us/files/reports/osdc/pdf/report-6-2019.pdf (accessed November 2021).

New York State Comptroller. 2021. "The Securities Industry in New York City." October 2021. osc.state.ny.us/files/reports/osdc/pdf/report-12-2022.pdf (accessed November 2021).

Newman, Katherine. 1999. *Falling from Grace: Downward Mobility in the Age of Affluence*. Berkeley, CA: University of California Press.

Oliver, Melvin, and Thomas Shapiro. 2006. *Black Wealth/White Wealth: A New Perspective on Racial Inequality*, 2nd edition. New York: Routledge.

Ong, Aihwa. 1996. "Cultural Citizenship as Subject-Making: Immigrants Negotiate Racial and Cultural Boundaries in the United States." *Current Anthropology* 37(5): 737–62.

Ortner, Sherry. 2011. "On Neoliberalism." *Anthropology of This Century*. Available at: http://aotcpress.com/articles/neoliberlism (accessed January 2022).

Piketty, Thomas. 2014. *Capital in the Twenty-First Century*. Cambridge, MA: The Belknap Press of Harvard University Press.

Piketty, Thomas. 2020. *Capital and Ideology.* Cambridge, MA: The Belknap Press of Harvard University Press.

Pugh, Allison. 2015. *The Tumbleweed Society: Working and Caring in an Age of Insecurity.* Oxford: Oxford University Press.

Robinson, Cedric. 2000 [1983]. *Black Marxism: The Making of the Black Radical Tradition,* Chapel Hill, NC: University of North Carolina Press.

Rockman, Seth. 2005. "The Unfree Origins of American Capitalism." In *The Economy of Early America: Historical Perspectives and New Directions,* edited by Cathy Matson, 335–61. University Park, PA: Penn State University Press.

Roediger, David. 1991. *The Wages of Whiteness: Race and the Making of the American Working Class.* London: Verso.

Roithmayr, Daria. 2014. *Reproducing Racism: How Everyday Choices Lock in White Advantage.* New York: New York University Press.

Rosaldo, Renato. 1993. *Culture and Truth: The Remaking of Social Analysis.* Boston, MA: Beacon Press.

Rosaldo, Renato. 1999. "Cultural Citizenship, Inequality, and Multiculturalism." In *Race, Identity, and Citizenship: A Reader,* edited by Rodolfo Torres, Louis Mirón, and Jonathan Inda, 253–61. Malden, MA: Blackwell.

Royster, Deirdre. 2003. *Race and the Invisible Hand: How White Networks Exclude Black Men from Blue Color Jobs.* Berkeley, CA: University of California Press.

Satter, Beryl. 2009. *Family Properties: Race, Real Estate, and the Exploitation of Black Urban America.* New York: Metropolitan Books.

Sennett, Richard. 2006. *The Culture of the New Capitalism.* New Haven, CT: Yale University Press.

Stout, Lynn. 2012. *The Shareholder Value Myth: How Putting Shareholders First Harms Investors, Corporations, and the Public.* San Francisco: Berrett-Koehler Publishers.

Stout, Noelle. 2019. *Dispossessed: How Predatory Bureaucracy Foreclosed on the American Middle Class.* Berkeley, CA: University of California Press.

Taylor, Keeanga-Yamahtta. 2019. *The Race for Profit: How Banks and the Real Estate Industry Undermined Black Ownership.* Chapel Hill, NC: University of North Carolina Press.

Wellman, David. 1997. "Minstrel Shows, Affirmative Action Talk, and Angry White Men: Marking Racial Otherness in the 1990s." In *Displacing Whiteness: Essays in Social and Cultural Criticism,* edited by Ruth Frankenburg. Durham, NC: Duke University Press.

Wiggin, Benjamin. 2020. *Calculating Race: Racial Discrimination in Risk Assessment.* New York: Oxford University Press.

Winant, Howard. 1997. "Behind Blue Eyes: Whiteness and Contemporary U.S. Racial Politics." *Off White: Readings on Power, Privilege, and Resistance,* edited by Michelle Fine et al. New York: Routledge.

Yanagisako, Sylvia. 2018, "Accumulating Family Values," Goody Lecture 2018. Available at: https://www.eth.mpg.de/5317376/Goody_Lecture_2018.pdf (accessed August 2020).

4

EARNING RENT WITH YOUR TALENT

American inequality rests on the power to define, transfer, and institutionalize talent

Jonathan J.B. Mijs

Introduction

Capital makes the world go round. Those who own it reap the rewards. Many of the largest companies in the world are in car manufacturing (Toyota, Volkswagen), petroleum refining (Exxon Mobil, Royal Dutch Shell), and other industries that rely on copious amounts of capital. Social science research describes how ownership of capital is a major source of wealth inequality (Keister and Moller 2000; Killewald, Pfeffer, and Schachner 2017; Piketty 2014). Scholarship points to the unfair advantages capital ownership provides, such as the ability to extract rent beyond its productive value (Atkinson 2015; Sørensen 1996, 2000; Weeden and Grusky 2014). Moreover, capital is passed down intergenerationally to sons and daughters whose only accomplishment is being born to the right set of parents. Some of the wealthiest people in the world today owe their fortune to their family business. From the Waltons (Walmart) and Bettencourts (L'Oréal) to the Mars family and the Koch brothers, today's rich belong to the same social groups, networks, and families as those who held the reins generations ago (Chetty et al. 2014; Pfeffer and Killewald 2018).

While scholars, journalists, and politicians are scrutinizing the ownership, transmission, and use of capital, much of modern-day inequality has a different guise. Whereas we disapprove of the plutocracy of capital, we celebrate the meritocracy of talent (Littler 2018; Mijs 2020, 2021; Mulligan 2018b). The last decades have seen the rise of companies based on little more than great ideas and a top 1 percent of athletes, pop stars, managers, and executive officers, whose fortunes derive from their unique set of skills and abilities. Today, six out of the ten largest equities in the Standard & Poor 500 are IT companies built on the creativity, entrepreneurship, and hard work of extraordinary individuals. We speak of talent when an athlete outperforms the competition, when a young politician rises through the ranks of their party, or when two guys in a garage[1] set up what turns out to be one of the largest companies in the world. We laud talent, we love those who have it, and we loathe our own limits; if only we had come up with that idea first, we'd be the Bill, Larry, Sheryl, or Oprah with a billion dollars to our name.

There is a shadow side to the meritocracy of talent. In the world of talent, success is driven by good ideas, ambition, and hard work. Inequality simply reflects their uneven

DOI: 10.4324/9781003326243-5

distribution: some of us are brighter, aim higher, and work harder. It is a compelling story, but one with cruel consequences. When talent is the basis for success and differences in talent are the source of economic fortune, what right do we have to complain about inequality and its excesses? Looking at society through the lens of talent equates success with merit and failure with incompetence. Talent consecrates people's privileged place in society (Accominotti 2018; Khan 2010). Talent today is what inherited land was to feudal societies; an unchallenged source of symbolic and economic rewards. Whereas God sanctified the aristocracy's wealth, contemporary privilege is legitimated by talent. Consequently, today's inequalities are as striking as ever, yet harder to challenge than ever before.

In this chapter, I argue that talent and capital have much more in common than meets the eye. I will show that the economic gains of talent rely on a process of rent-seeking previously reserved for the owners of capital. In what follows, I give a brief history of rent to show how the return on talent relies on three processes, none of which are meritocratic: (1) just like capital, talents are intergenerationally transmitted from parents to children; (2) further, what constitutes talent relies on the definitional power of powerful gatekeepers who decide which traits to reward and which to discard; (3) moreover, talents are structural, not individual traits; their economic returns are institutionalized in privileged positions. In sum, I will show that inequality is produced by the ways in which talent is defined, transmitted, and sustained by the moral deservingness we attribute to the accomplishments of talents.

A Short History of Rent

The word rent, to most people, is a reminder of their monthly commitment to a landlord or landlady; the price that comes with the roof over their head. For others, it is a source of income: property owners extract rent by letting real estate to people or businesses willing to pay more than their upkeep requires. We tend to associate the term real estate with houses and the agents selling them, but it actually refers to buildings as well as land. Whereas it is ownership of the former that is especially important in today's urban societies, for most of human history, land has been the primary source of income and wealth.

Economic theory describes how, starting with David Ricardo's law of rent. Ricardo (1817) defines rent as the individual benefits accrued by owning land over and above its productive quality. Land, if used for agricultural purposes, for instance, has a productive quality. Ownership of the land, however, has its own benefit: the ability to extract additional returns in the form of rent. Such benefits derive from artificial limits to the supply of an asset, like in a monopoly (see Marshall 1895). Given a fixed supply of land, the owners can extract returns that greatly exceed its value in a competitive market.

Whereas Ricardo's law of rent continues to inform economic thought, the industrial revolution and the coming of post-industrial society (Bell 1973) meant the concept of rent required an update. Jacob Mincer (1958), Theodore Schultz (1960), and, most notably, Gary Becker (1962) provide the foundation for that by taking the concept of capital to the labor market and to the realm of education. Human capital theory states that our minds and bodies are potential sources of rent as well. To Becker, human capital is how most modern citizens make a living; the market rewards people's investments in productive skills, knowledge, habits, and traits:

> Schooling, a computer training course, expenditures of medical care, and lectures on the virtues of punctuality and honesty [are] capital. That is because they raise earnings, improve health, or add to a person's good habits over much of his lifetime. Therefore, economists regard expenditures on education, training, medical care, and

so on as investments in human capital. They are called human capital because people cannot be separated from their knowledge, skills, health, or values in the way they can be separated from their financial and physical assets.

Becker 2002

Whereas the focus of human capital theory is on the productive quality of education and health, minds and bodies can also be a source of rent. For one, the supply of human capital is artificially limited. As Becker and others have acknowledged, people are not equally positioned to reap the rewards of investments in human capital. Potential investments in human capital are limited by financial constraints, which are a function of the cost of schooling (and the cost of health, among other productive qualities) and opportunities to invest, i.e. the availability of and access to pre-schools, private tutoring and extracurricular activities, elite colleges, etc. Simply put, you can't accumulate human capital if you cannot afford school or get in.

The human capital equation, however, is missing a crucial variable, to which I now turn. Rent-seeking in the age of human capital rests on talent.

Returns = Investment * Talent

No amount of schooling will turn a half-wit into a genius. Equally, Einstein may have written his theory of relativity even if he hadn't graduated from high school (which, some sources suggest, he barely did).[2] In other words, some talent is required for schooling to make an impact. In fact, there are good reasons to suspect that a higher level of available talent is likely to produce greater returns on the invested education.

To start, schools are set up to cater specifically to students' talents, either by adjusting the level and pace of learning to students' abilities or by differentiating instruction altogether by sorting students into general and honor's classes, vocational and academic tracks, and other forms of grouping based on ability (Domina, Penner, and Penner 2017; Mijs 2011; Van de Werfhorst and Mijs 2010). Moreover, a student's talents determine whether particular educational opportunities are or aren't available. For instance, remedial classes are offered only to students with learning difficulties, while a great deal of talent is required for a person to be given the opportunity of receiving an Ivy League education as elite institutions purposefully keep enrollment low (more on this point below).

In short, *real* returns on education equal investment *times* talent. Minds and bodies become a source of rent when ideas and skills are deemed unique talents which merit a reward beyond their productive qualities. In what follows, I show that there is nothing necessary or natural about talent's economic returns. Just like other forms of capital, talents (1) are intergenerationally transferred; (2) rely on being so defined by powerful gatekeepers; and (3) are institutionalized in positions of privilege and protected professions.

We Receive Our Talents from Our Parents

Reflective of the classical Greek meaning of the word τάλαντον (money), we receive our talents from our parents. Academic ability, IQ, health, height, and physical attractiveness are just a few of the many traits unequally distributed by the rigged lottery of birth (Fischer et al. 1996; Rimfeld et al. 2018). On top of the genetic gains of birth are a set of social skills – or "cultural capital" to use Bourdieu's (1984) term. Children acquire from their parents and from their *social milieu* more generally, traits and manners, a sense of entitlement or constraint, and a level of (dis)comfort with adults and authorities, which makes school a much more productive space for some than for others. Upper (middle) class parents tend to instill in their children the cultural capital to set them up well for tests and exams (Bourdieu 1984; Yamamoto and Brinton 2010), dream big and aim high (Jackson 2013; Lareau 2011), and assure that teachers give them the attention they demand (Calarco 2011, 2018).

In Bourdieu's words, by failing to take into account the investments already made within the family,

> [Human capital theorists] let slip the best hidden and socially most determinant educational investment, namely, the domestic transmission of cultural capital. Their studies of the relationship between academic ability and academic investment show that they are unaware that ability or talent is itself the product of an investment of time and cultural capital.
>
> *Bourdieu 1986, 244–5*

In other words, talent is inherited, in the strict sense, to the extent that our intellectual ability, health, and other productive traits are based on the genetic makeup we receive from our parents. In a broader sense as well, children's talents depend on their parents (Smeeding, Erikson, and Jäntti 2011). Children rarely make investment decisions themselves; the amount of time, attention, and resources parents commit to education ("shadow education") greatly impacts their children's human capital accumulation (Buchmann, Condron, and Roscigno 2010). Taken together, there are vast and consequential differences in people's opportunity to benefit from human capital and extract rent because of the unequal distribution of talent and early investments therein. Talents, in short, are far from the individual quality we make them to be; talent, like capital, is transferred, sustained, and cultivated across generations.

Talent Is Whatever Is So Defined

When Ivy League colleges invented American Football around 1880, a new set of talents was created with it. Some such talents travel better than others; being a good football (soccer) player may earn you respect and, if you're good enough, a living in as many as 200 countries with professional football leagues. Being good in *American Football*, by contrast, means much more in one country than anywhere else.

The portability of talent points to a crucial quality: talent's meaning and payoff are context-specific, varying across place and over time.[3] What is true for American Football is true for musical craft and artistic talent; and even for the traits that people value in others. As I have argued elsewhere (Mijs 2016:20), what constitutes merit is historically contingent and institutionally specific:

> Manliness, aggression, asceticism and (bi)sexuality, for instance, were considered important traits for men to have in Sparta, 400 B.C., and display of such traits was rewarded with social status (De Botton 2005). In Western Europe anno 479, in contrast, pacifism, vegetarianism and asexuality were considered meritocratic traits (ibid.). Similarly changes in meritocratic traits over time are described with regard to the rise of court society (Elias 1939), in the evaluation of American social science and humanities scholarship (Tsay et al. 2003), as well as between men and women today (Prentice and Carranza 2002).

What is termed, considered, and concomitantly rewarded as productive traits, skills, and knowledge depends on how such are defined by society's gatekeepers. So does the opportunity to earn rent with your talent.

A powerful empirical illustration of this insight comes from Karabel's (2005) archival research at Harvard, Princeton, and Yale. Digging through their archives, he uncovered detailed minutes and reports describing how in the post-World War II era, these elite institutions discussed and devised strategies for keeping out unwanted groups of students while keeping their gates open to the students they wanted to have. How? By defining merit in ways that their preferred students could meet but others couldn't. First, they included "character" in the admission criteria as a way to exclude Catholics, then they introduced additional requirements in the form of recommendation letters and personal interviews as a means to weed out the uninitiated. As a means of last resort, they incorporated athleticism into their definition of merit to raise the barrier for purportedly physically unfit Jewish students.

The take-away from Karabel's study is that definitions of talent are never neutral; how we define qualities like talent, character and merit always benefits some groups of people while putting others at a disadvantage. Consequently, an important basis of rent-seeking lies with those who are in a position to define talent. The definition of talent does not stop at the front gate; schools continuously draw boundaries between groups of students (e.g. "vocational," "academic," "gifted," "at-risk") (Golann 2015). For those fortunate to fit the mold, these boundaries can produce powerful credentials (degrees) and distinctions (e.g. "magna cum laude"). In the worst-case scenario, they lead to a student's expulsion, the long-term consequences of which have been described as a "school-to-prison pipeline" (Kim, Losen, and Hewitt 2010; Mittleman 2018; Welch and Payne 2018).

This definitional power extends far beyond the realm of education into the world of literature (Franssen and Kuipers 2013), fashion (Mears 2010), business (Khurana 2002), and, as we will see below, sports.

Talents Are Institutionalized in Positions of Privilege

Some definitions of talent fluctuate; others are more stable. The main process by which definitions are made to stick is through institutionalization: the rent-producing quality of talent is incorporated in positions that generate rent. Simply put, in order to turn your labor power into money, you need a job or a market for your services. Without either, your hard work and talent will go unrewarded.

Sports offer a good illustration of this process. The ability to jump high, dribble, and throw a bouncing ball was institutionalized in the sport of basketball in 1891. Before that time, playing basketball was just that: play. With the institutionalization of the sport, that ability became a skill, and with the establishment of the National Basketball Association in 1946, that skill became a productive quality. As the sport's popularity grew, its valuation rose. Today, a professional basketball player in America can make as much as $45 million in a season, not taking into account the lucrative sponsorship deals that supplement athletes' salaries.

That dollar figure is the result of a very long process of rent creation. In fact, that process is still ongoing. Every number of years, players and teams come together to negotiate just how much their talents are worth. Players today make a lot more than what they made a few decades ago, and players in the US make a multitude of what players in other countries make. The difference is the level of institutionalization of the sport and the rent creation that came with it. Rent, in sports, is the difference between an athlete with and one without a job. Whereas the difference in skills, effort, and talent may be minimal, the difference in reward is likely to be enormous. Owing to "superstar" markets (Rosen 1981), a very small group of athletes (Lewis and Yoon 2018), college graduates (Clotfelter 2017), fashion models (Mears 2011), and rock stars (Krueger 2005) takes home a disproportional part of the pie. As Mulligan (2018a:178) puts it, superstar earnings "drive a wedge between contribution and desert."

In more mundane spheres of life as well, people benefit from institutionalized positions of privilege. Certain professions, for instance, are protected by what Freidson (1970, 2001) calls "labor market sheltering": strategies for limiting entry into certain professional groups, such as bar exams for lawyers and board exams for doctors. Such practices allow for professional groups to extract advantages beyond the market value of their human capital. Besides deciding who gains entry into these professions, through such entry requirements, occupational societies set limits to the number of people allowed into their profession, thereby putting a cap on the supply-side of the equation that sets their wages.

Another way occupational groups establish rent-seeking is by institutionalizing demand for their services through government licensing and other forms of occupational closure (Sørensen 1996). When you go to court, you would do well to get an attorney. In fact, in most countries, you will be provided with one, if needed, on the government's dime. Less obvious is the need, institutionalized in many countries around the world, for a (notary) lawyer when purchasing a house, accepting an inheritance, merging two businesses, translating a government document, or transferring an Internet domain. All these monopolistic services derive from government regulation successfully fought for by occupational groups and societies (see Abbott 1988).

Yet another source of rent-seeking is in hiring and pay-setting institutions that do not operate on market principles. CEO wages are set by a board of directors who have an interest in appeasing the person whose salary they control (Bebchuk and Fried 2009; Weeden and Grusky 2014). When a board of directors hires a CEO, they may in earnest be picking the most meritorious candidate. They are unlikely, however, to have a lot to choose from. The pool of candidates is limited by a long list of structural forces that keep people from rising through the corporate ranks (Khurana 2002). The CEO market, in other words, is a closed market:

> Closure generates an artificial scarcity of candidates who are considered for the CEO job. The function of closure is not only to limit the competitive field in this way but also to set the terms of competition and to assign the rewards for work done in accordance with these limits. It creates the rules of the game, constituting the boundaries by which people will be judged and criticized. At its core, then, the external CEO labor "market" operates as a circulation of elites within a single, sealed-off system relying on socially legitimated criteria that—contrary to conventional economic wisdom—are not to be confused with relevant skills for the CEO position.
>
> *Khurana 2002, 205*

In sum, many of the accomplishments celebrated as individual feats, in fact, reflect the privileged positions people occupy. Such positions depend on a long process of institutionalization through which occupational groups such as lawyers, doctors, and basketball players, have established rent-seeking privileges. In short, it's not people and their talents, but talents and their people.

Conclusion

A growing elite in modern societies has made its wealth not based on their birthright, inherited fortune, or by manifest market manipulations. Today's elite is a meritocracy of great ideas and entrepreneurship and the special talents of artists, athletes, and managerial miracle workers. Or so the story goes.

In this chapter, I have argued that talent, in fact, relies on structural advantages that have nothing to do with the market nor with merit. The accomplishments of talent rely first on the intergenerational transmission of genetic and cultural endowments from parents to their children. Parents, moreover, provide the cultural competence and economic resources to cultivate their children's productive traits – or lack the means to. In short, both the distribution of and investment in talent depend on the lottery of birth.

The returns on talents further depend on which talents are recognized and rewarded. As illustrated by the history of sports, an American Football player before 1880 was just a guy running around with an egg-shaped ball and a harness on. Today, he can make millions of dollars, given that he's privileged to be playing for an NFL team. Talents, in other words, are institutionally specific and historically contingent. Much power resides with the persons and institutions that guard the gates of talent.

The opportunity to earn rent from your talent rests on institutional forces. For a person to make an income based on their work, they need a job or market to work. Certain types of work have a payoff that far exceeds their market value. The talents of lawyers, managers, athletes, and artists have been institutionalized in their respective vocations by processes of social closure. Closure artificially limits entry into professions and occupations, increases demand for services, and manipulates their pay to maximize the return on talent. In short, it may be more accurate to speak of talents and their people than of people and their talents.

Whereas a further exploration of the topic falls beyond the scope of this chapter, it merits mentioning that the undeserved advantages of inheritance, rent-definition, and rent-creation, discussed in this chapter, seamlessly coexist with capitalism – best illustrated perhaps by the countless examples of such instances in contemporary America. The neoliberal emphasis on market, competition, and responsibility has helped elevate talent to what is arguably society's most celebrated trait (Hall and Lamont 2013; Littler 2018). "Investing" in talent and preventing its "waste" has become a major policy focus in advanced capitalist societies (OECD 2008; see Mijs 2016:16–7) and deemed the best hope for international development (World Bank 2010). Paradoxically, then, pro-market ideology has come to support and celebrate an enemy of the market, economic rent, under the thin veil of talent.

In conclusion, when we buy and sell the myth that today's billionaires started with nothing but a garage and a great idea, we miss the moral means for scrutinizing inequality. Looking at wealth and status as the accomplishments of individual talent removes the ground for public debate and political action. Talent cannot be faulted, nor can it be taxed. Recognizing the socially constructed nature of talent and its institutionalized power is the first and necessary step for an interrogation of the economic and symbolic returns on talents in contemporary society.

Notes

1 "We started our company out of our garage" serves to convey the notion that all a successful enterprise needs is a good idea and a lot of hard work. It has become such a common phrase that it is now referred to as the garage trope. It features as the origin myth of Amazon, Google, Apple, Microsoft, and Hewlett-Packard, among other companies (https://www.inc.com/drew-hendricks/6-25-billion-companies-that-started-in-a-garage.html).

2 Einstein did not master French, which was a required topic in his Swiss high school. This is also the most probable reason he failed to gain admission to the prestigious Federal Technical Institute in Zurich. Biographers, however, note that Einstein showed early signs of his brilliance in high school and also point to the role of his home environment where "manipulations of electricity and magnetism were a daily preoccupation helped set him on a road that led to his first relativity theory" (https://www.nytimes.com/1984/02/14/science/einstein-revealed-as-brilliant-in-youth.html).

3 Another way to express this quality of talent is to think of it, in Bourdieusian terms, as field-specific capital; i.e. the qualities and traits that pay off in a particular (structural) setting (Lamont and Lareau 1988).

References

Abbott, Andrew. 1988. *The System of Professions: An Essay on the Division of Expert Labor.* Chicago, IL: University of Chicago Press.

Accominotti, Fabien. 2018. "Consecration as a Population-Level Phenomenon." *American Behavioral Scientist* 65(1): 9–24. doi: 10.1177/0002764218800144.

Atkinson, Anthony B. 2015. *Inequality. What Can Be Done?* Cambridge, MA: Harvard University Press.

Bebchuk, Lucian A., and Jesse M. Fried. 2009. *Pay without Performance: The Unfulfilled Promise of Executive Compensation.* Cambridge, MA: Harvard University Press.

Becker, Gary S. 1962. "Investment in Human Capital: A Theoretical Analysis." *Journal of Political Economy* 70: 9–49.

Becker, Gary S. 2002. "Human Capital." In *The Concise Encyclopedia of Economics*, edited by D.R. Henderson. Indianapolis, IN: Liberty Fund.

Bell, Daniel. 1973. *The Coming of Post-Industrial Society: A Venture in Social Forecasting.* New York: Basic Books.

Bourdieu, Pierre. 1984. *Distinction: A Social Critique of the Judgement of Taste.* Cambridge, MA: Harvard University Press.

Bourdieu, Pierre. 1986. "The Forms of Capital." In *Handbook of Theory and Research for the Sociology of Education*, edited by J.F. Richardson, 241–58. New York: Greenwood Press.

Buchmann, Claudia, Dennis J. Condron, and Vincent J. Roscigno. 2010. "Shadow Education, American Style: Test Preparation, the SAT and College Enrollment." *Social Forces* 89(2): 435–61. doi: 10.1353/sof.2010.0105.

Calarco, Jessica McCrory. 2011. "'I Need Help!' Social Class and Children's Help-Seeking in Elementary School." *American Sociological Review* 76(6): 862–82. doi: 10.1177/0003122411427177.

Calarco, Jessica McCrory. 2018. *Negotiating Opportunities: How the Middle Class Secures Advantages in School.* New York: Oxford University Press.

Chetty, Raj, Nathaniel Hendren, Patrick Kline, Emmanuel Saez, and Nicholas Turner. 2014. "Is the United States Still a Land of Opportunity? Recent Trends in Intergenerational Mobility." *American Economic Review* 104(5): 141–7. doi: 10.1257/aer.104.5.141.

Clotfelter, Charles T. 2017. *Unequal Colleges in the Age of Disparity.* Cambridge, MA: Harvard University Press.

De Botton, Alain. 2005. *Status Anxiety.* New York: Vintage.

Domina, Thurston, Andrew Penner, and Emily Penner. 2017. "Categorical Inequality: Schools as Sorting Machines." *Annual Review of Sociology* 43(1): 311–30. doi: 10.1146/annurev-soc-060116-053354.

Elias, Norbert. 1939. *The Civilizing Process: The History of Manners.* Oxford: Blackwell Publishing.

Fischer, Claude S., Michael Hout, Martin Sanchez Jankowski, Samuel R. Lucas, Ann Swidler, and Kim Voss. 1996. *Inequality by Design: Cracking the Bell Curve Myth.* Princeton, NJ: Princeton University Press.

Franssen, Thomas, and Giselinde Kuipers. 2013. "Coping with Uncertainty, Abundance and Strife: Decision-Making Processes of Dutch Acquisition Editors in the Global Market for Translations." *Poetics* 41(1): 48–74.

Freidson, Eliot. 1970. *Profession of Medicine: A Study of the Sociology of Applied Knowledge.* Chicago, IL: University of Chicago Press.

Freidson, Eliot. 2001. *Professionalism, the Third Logic: On the Practice of Knowledge.* Chicago, IL: University of Chicago Press.

Golann, Joanne W. 2015. "The Paradox of Success at a No-Excuses School." *Sociology of Education* 0038040714567866. doi: 10.1177/0038040714567866.

Hall, Peter, and Michèle Lamont. 2013. *Social Resilience in the Neoliberal Era.* Cambridge: Cambridge University Press.

Jackson, Michelle. 2013. *Determined to Succeed?: Performance versus Choice in Educational Attainment.* Palo Alto, CA: Stanford University Press.

Karabel, Jerome. 2005. *The Chosen: The Hidden History of Admission and Exclusion at Harvard, Yale, and Princeton.* Boston, MA: Houghton Mifflin Harcourt.

Keister, Lisa A., and Stephanie Moller. 2000. "Wealth Inequality in the United States." *Annual Review of Sociology* 26(1): 63–81. doi: 10.1146/annurev.soc.26.1.63.

Khan, Shamus Rahman. 2010. *Privilege: The Making of an Adolescent Elite at St. Paul's School.* Princeton, NJ: Princeton University Press.

Khurana, Rakesh. 2002. *Searching for a Corporate Savior: The Irrational Quest for Charismatic CEOs.* Princeton, NJ: Princeton University Press.

Killewald, Alexandra, Fabian T. Pfeffer, and Jared N. Schachner. 2017. "Wealth Inequality and Accumulation." *Annual Review of Sociology* 43: 379–404.

Kim, Catherine Y., Daniel J. Losen, and Damon T. Hewitt. 2010. *The School-to-Prison Pipeline: Structuring Legal Reform.* New York: New York University Press.

Krueger, Alan B. 2005. "The Economics of Real Superstars: The Market for Rock Concerts in the Material World." *Journal of Labor Economics* 23(1): 1–30. doi: 10.1086/425431.

Lamont, Michele, and Annette Lareau. 1988. "Cultural Capital: Allusions, Gaps and Glissandos in Recent Theoretical Developments." *Sociological Theory* 6(2): 153–68. doi: 10.2307/202113.

Lareau, Annette. 2011. *Unequal Childhoods: Class, Race, and Family Life, Second Edition with an Update a Decade Later.* Berkeley, CA: University of California Press.

Lewis, Michael, and Yeujun Yoon. 2018. "An Empirical Examination of the Development and Impact of Star Power in Major League Baseball." *Journal of Sports Economics* 19(2): 155–87. doi: 10.1177/1527002515626220.

Littler, Jo. 2018. *Against Meritocracy: Culture, Power and Myths of Mobility.* London: Routledge.

Marshall, Alfred. 1895. *Principles of Economics.* London: Macmillan.

Mears, Ashley. 2010. "Size Zero High-End Ethnic: Cultural Production and the Reproduction of Culture in Fashion Modeling." *Poetics* 38(1): 21–46.

Mears, Ashley. 2011. *Pricing Beauty: The Making of a Fashion Model.* Berkeley, CA: University of California Press.

Mijs, Jonathan J.B. 2011. "Van Terecht Onrecht Naar Pluriform Talent." *Beleid En Maatschappij* 38(3): 327–33.

Mijs, Jonathan J.B. 2016. "The Unfulfillable Promise of Meritocracy: Three Lessons and Their Implications for Justice in Education." *Social Justice Research* 29(1): 14–34. doi: 10.1007/s11211-014-0228-0.

Mijs, Jonathan J.B. 2021. "The Paradox of Inequality: Income Inequality and Belief in Meritocracy Go Hand in Hand." *Socio-Economic Review* 19(1): 7–35. doi: 10.1093/ser/mwy051.

Mijs, Jonathan J.B. 2021. "Earning Rent with Your Talent: Modern-Day Inequality Rests on the Power to Define, Transfer and Institutionalize Talent." *Educational Philosophy and Theory* 53(8): 810–18. doi: 10.1080/00131857.2020.1745629.

Mincer, Jacob. 1958. "Investment in Human Capital and Personal Income Distribution." *Journal of Political Economy* 66: 281–302.

Mittleman, Joel. 2018. "A Downward Spiral? Childhood Suspension and the Path to Juvenile Arrest." *Sociology of Education* 91(3): 183–204. doi: 10.1177/0038040718784603.

Mulligan, Thomas. 2018a. "Do People Deserve Their Economic Rents?." *Erasmus Journal for Philosophy and Economics* 11(2): 163–90. doi: 10.23941/ejpe.v11i2.338.

Mulligan, Thomas. 2018b. *Justice and the Meritocratic State.* New York: Routledge.

OECD. 2008. *The Global Competition for Talent. Mobility of the Highly Skilled.* Paris: Organisation for Economic Co-operation and Development.

Pfeffer, Fabian T., and Alexandra Killewald. 2018. "Generations of Advantage. Multigenerational Correlations in Family Wealth." *Social Forces* 96(4): 1411–42. doi: 10.1093/sf/sox086.

Piketty, Thomas. 2014. *Capital in the Twenty-First Century.* Cambridge, MA: Harvard University Press.

Prentice, Deborah A., and Erica Carranza. 2002. "What Women and Men Should Be, Shouldn't Be, Are Allowed to Be, and Don't Have to Be: The Contents of Prescriptive Gender Stereotypes." *Psychology of Women Quarterly* 26(4): 269–81. doi: 10.1111/1471-6402.t01-1-00066.

Ricardo, David. 1817. *On the Principles of Political Economy, and Taxation.* London: J. Murray.

Rimfeld, Kaili, Eva Krapohl, Maciej Trzaskowski, Jonathan R.I. Coleman, Saskia Selzam, Philip S. Dale, Tonu Esko, Andres Metspalu, and Robert Plomin. 2018. "Genetic Influence on Social Outcomes during and after the Soviet Era in Estonia." *Nature Human Behaviour* 2(4): 269. doi: 10.1038/s41562-018-0332-5.

Rosen, Sherwin. 1981. "The Economics of Superstars." *The American Economic Review* 71(5): 845–58.

Schultz, Theodore W. 1960. "Capital Formation by Education." *Journal of Political Economy* 68(6): 571–83.

Smeeding, Timothy, Robert Erikson, and Markus Jäntti, eds. 2011. *Persistence, Privilege, and Parenting. The Comparative Study of Intergenerational Mobility.* New York: Russell Sage Foundation.

Sørensen, Aage B. 1996. "The Structural Basis of Social Inequality." *American Journal of Sociology* 101(5): 1333–65.

Sørensen, Aage B. 2000. "Toward a Sounder Basis for Class Analysis." *American Journal of Sociology* 105(6): 1523–58.

Tsay, Angela, Michèle Lamont, Andrew Abbott, and Joshua Guetzkow. 2003. "From Character to Intellect: Changing Conceptions of Merit in the Social Sciences and Humanities, 1951–1971." *Poetics* 31(1): 23–49. doi: 10.1016/S0304-422X(03)00002-0.

Van de Werfhorst, Herman G., and Jonathan J.B. Mijs. 2010. "Achievement Inequality and the Institutional Structure of Educational Systems: A Comparative Perspective." *Annual Review of Sociology* 36: 407–28.

Weeden, Kim A., and David B. Grusky. 2014. "Inequality and Market Failure." *American Behavioral Scientist* 58(3): 473–91. doi: 10.1177/0002764213503336.

Welch, Kelly, and Allison Ann Payne. 2018. "Latino/a Student Threat and School Disciplinary Policies and Practices." *Sociology of Education* 91(2): 91–110. doi: 10.1177/0038040718757720.

World Bank. 2010. *Talent Abroad Promoting Growth and Institutional Development at Home: Skilled Diaspora as Part of the Country.* Washington, DC: World Bank.

Yamamoto, Yoko, and Mary C. Brinton. 2010. "Cultural Capital in East Asian Educational Systems The Case of Japan." *Sociology of Education* 83(1): 67–83. doi: 10.1177/0038040709356567.

5

FROM AMERICAN DREAM TO NORDIC REALITIES?

Ingrid Christensen, John Erik Fossum, and Bent Sofus Tranøy

Introduction

James Truslow Adams, in his Epic of America, spells out his vision of the American Dream:

> that dream of a land in which life should be better and richer and fuller for everyone, with opportunity for each according to ability or achievement. It is a difficult dream for the European upper classes to interpret adequately, and too many of us ourselves have grown weary and mistrustful of it. It is not a dream of motor cars and high wages merely, but a dream of social order in which each man and each woman shall be able to attain to the fullest stature of which they are innately capable, and be recognized by others for what they are, regardless of the fortuitous circumstances of birth or position.
>
> *Adams 1959 [1931], 374*

We see from this that Adams' notion of the American Dream is not confined to material wealth but to human flourishing broadly speaking. Individualism in the sense of basic equal rights and equality of opportunity are vital preconditions for such flourishing. Further, the European settlers sought to leave behind a stratified social order and conceived of America as exceptionally well-suited for such human flourishing; hence, the notion of American exceptionalism.

The American Declaration of Independence and the Constitution codified an essential tenet of the American Dream, namely that persons cannot develop to their potential unless they possess a set of basic individual rights and freedoms that protect them from undue incursions from governments and from other individuals, groups, and collectives. Those basic rights should also enable citizens to understand themselves as the ultimate authors of the laws that they are subject to, hence popular sovereignty. Every individual should be free to pursue life, liberty, and happiness. Such a pursuit should not be reserved for the few or the privileged but should be universally available. Two preconditions for this are (a) basic rights and popular sovereignty and (b) equality of opportunity. The American Dream thus arguably resides in two aspects of equality: equal basic rights and equal opportunities. Equal basic individual rights give legal protection to individualism and ensure a measure of freedom. Equality of opportunity ensures that all will be able to pursue their life chances. The notion of equal

DOI: 10.4324/9781003326243-6

opportunity posits that some compensatory measures (forms of government intervention) are necessary to ensure that all have the same opportunities since people do not have the same starting points. There is no space in the American Dream for the third notion of equality (the first being equal basic rights and the second equal opportunity), equality of results, which posits that people who are different nevertheless end up with the same and implies significant state or public interventions such as redistribution of resources and various forms of compensation.

American Exceptionalism holds that there is something distinctive or unique to America. Manifest Destiny posits that America is destined for something great. Taken together these two notions hold that there are particularly germane conditions for a freedom-seeking individualism in America.

The question that we pose here is whether (parts of) Europe may not only have caught up with America on the core counts of the American Dream but may, in fact, have surpassed America. More precisely, we argue that the Nordic region is a particularly relevant site for discussing this. An important reason is that there are certain identifiable Nordic values that are institutionalized within and across the five states that make up the Nordic region. These are referred to as the Nordic Model, a distinct Nordic approach to democracy, and a social market economy. Our claim is that the two core components that mark the American Dream, individualism and equal opportunity resonate strongly with the values that underpin the Nordic Model, even if the Nordic Model is based on a different calibration of these. As was shown (Fossum 2021), the Nordic Model does not, as is often thought or claimed, especially by the American Right, downplay individualism by imposing a repressive system for ensuring equality of results over and above equal opportunity. The Nordic Model is not anti-capitalist; it seeks to direct capitalism toward humane ends, to develop a socioeconomic and political context that is conducive for human flourishing, individual and societal.

In this chapter, we will complement the analysis of the ideational congruence between the American Dream and the Nordic Model that was presented in Fossum (2021). The purpose is to establish whether or the extent to which the facts on the ground in the Nordic region suggest that this region is closer to the core tenets of the American Dream than is contemporary America.

In the following, we develop more specific indicators and operationalize these; and check them against the cases. Our approach is *not* to compare the situation in the US against the situation in the Nordic region; we are interested in identifying *convergence with or deviation from* the core dimensions of the American Dream in the US and in the Nordic region. There are, as we will show, significant differences between the US and the Nordic region, which will likely affect the transferability of lessons from one setting to the other. Nevertheless, since the American Dream combines universalizable (individualism and equal opportunity) and context-specific features (American exceptionalism), our approach clarifies the role of context in today's world. If the Nordic region is closer to the core tenets of the American Dream than is the contemporary US, the issue for the US is to clarify how it should reform itself to approach a similar result. The Nordic experience provides relevant information on the direction of that travel.

American Exceptionalism and Nordic–US Differences

We are interested in probing Nordic–US convergence and divergence on the key tenets of the American Dream. For that, we need to know more about the role of American exceptionalism in the contemporary era. Our argument is that many of the elements of US exceptionalism that are particularly relevant for individualism and equality of opportunity have been whittled down, given that much of Europe has caught up with the US, although how this has occurred is quite instructive. In addition, there are differences between the US and the Nordics that give new meaning to American exceptionalism in today's world.

The most obvious differences between the US and the Nordic region are geographical location, size, and global influence. The US occupies much of the North American continent and has only two close neighbors, Canada and Mexico. The Nordic region is not in the same way sheltered by geography. It occupies a corner of North Western Europe and has land-based borders with Russia and Germany. The critical difference in size[1] and power (as, for instance, measured in military spending[2]) means that the US's ability to influence global developments but also to isolate itself from the rest of the world has been radically different from what has been the case in the Nordic countries. This central global role is arguably the most important element of American exceptionalism in today's world.

In what sense do differences in size and influence matter for the US's and the Nordics' relations to the American Dream? They do, in the sense that the US has been the single most important *architect* (rule-maker and upholder) of the post-war political, legal, and economic framework for global governance, along military, economic, social, and legal lines, including the establishment of the post-war system of international law and governance (UN, GATT then WTO, etc.), whereas the Nordic countries have to a large extent been global and regional *rule-takers*. In other words, a key element ensuring rights-based individualism convergence between the US and the Nordic region stems from the fact that the US has contributed to establish and uphold an international and regional-European system of rights that the Nordic states have incorporated in their constitutional-legal arrangements.

This development matters to how we understand convergence. One form of convergence is for the Nordics to approximate to the US; the other is for both the US and the Nordics to *converge on rights-based individualism*. In this latter case, the issue is not how similar or different the US and the Nordics are, as such, but whether both are oriented toward rights-based individualism. It is this latter form of convergence that we focus on here.

Given their limited size and lack of military prowess, the Nordic states have a strong interest in a legally regulated and predictable global context that curtails great powers and the scope for power politics. The US, as a key setter of global terms, is in a qualitatively different position. For the US, especially when it was the sole super-power, it was a matter of balancing constraints imposed by others (which were quite weak); subject itself to various forms of self-bind; and shirk or modify rules and norms to suit its own interests. This balancing act has varied over time.[3] America's near-global presence and its many interventions abroad entail a high exposure to volatile situations and conflicts, with a significant likelihood for international conflicts and problems "spilling over" to the domestic arena. The latter was readily apparent in the 9/11 terrorist attacks, which prompted a significant US military engagement in the Middle East, notably the NATO-led invasions of Afghanistan and the invasion of Iraq.

This US global role and exposure – amplified by the fact that it to a large extent relies on force and military acumen – has a significant impact on the American ability to uphold a rights-based world and respect for human rights, be it the types of weapons employed or the use of torture or unlawful imprisonment (Guantanamo), or rendition flights. A global super-power, even if wholly committed to human rights, would experience severe challenges to uphold them as long as the world does not uphold human rights.

The American global role also weighs in on the American economy and the balance between the civilian and the military components of the economy. It is useful to remind ourselves that despite the supply-side rhetoric, Reaganomics was a version of "military

Keynesianism"(Peterson and Estenson 1985, 448) and testifies to the central importance of the military in the US economy but also in US domestic society. One might wonder if the significant American global presence and interventions over the last several decades have "militarized" American society. One assumption is that this affects citizens' understanding of the social contract, what type of role they attribute to government, and how they perceive of government (including the issue of trust). We have not examined this systematically here.

One assumption that we will try to shed some light on is that the American global role and exposure have implications for the type of social problems and challenges that American society and the public sector grapple with. For instance, the large number of war veterans, some of whom are traumatized and suffer from physical and mental problems,[4] weighs in on the welfare arrangements and probably also impacts levels of violence in American society.

The American global role and exposure stand in stark contrast to the Nordic states that have seen military retrenchment (significant reductions in their standing armies and the number of conscripts) and have very few persons in active military engagements (even if there are some led by NATO, the UN, and the EU). In any case, the Nordic states' propensity to "import" problems from other parts of the world due to military interventions is dramatically different from that of the US.

Intrinsic to American exceptionalism has been America's great attraction to the rest of the world as a haven of freedom and opportunity, whereas the Nordic states have a long history of exporting population surpluses, not the least to the US (there are more people of Norwegian ancestry in the US than in present-day Norway). In the last few decades, however, Europe's attractiveness has increased greatly. The Nordic states have become more multicultural due to immigration,[5] with Sweden having the highest rate and the most liberal policy.[6]

Today's form of American exceptionalism is closely associated with the US's central global role. We have already suggested that this role comes with some forms of vulnerability (including importing conflicts and generating social problems). With regard to economic factors, the sheer size of the American economy suggests that the US does not need to be globally adaptive in any way remotely resembling the Nordic countries. The ability to adapt to a dynamic and changing global context is a trait that Peter Katzenstein (1985) attributes to small states such as the Nordic states. For the US, there is no similar externally imposed imperative due to the sheer size of the US internal market and the US' own resource wealth and ease of access to resources from its immediate neighborhood (especially the resource-rich Canada). US military adventures, however, have greatly indebted the US state; hence the US debt burden may be a source of external vulnerability.

The US has, throughout the post-war period, been Europe's security guarantor through NATO and through the US's support for European post-war reconstruction and the European integration project (the latter with the notable exception of the Trump presidency). The Nordic states have all become closely affiliated with the EU even if they have chosen different paths (Denmark, Sweden, and Finland are EU members, whereas Iceland and Norway are affiliated through the European Economic Area Agreement and a host of other agreements (for an overview of these see Fossum and Graver 2018). All five Nordic states are, however, wholly integrated in the EU's internal market, and all Nordic citizens are EU *economic citizens* (Olsen 2014).

This section has shown that American exceptionalism in today's world gravitates around the US's exceptionally influential global role and presence. That, on the one hand, has fostered a rules-based convergence with Europe and, on the other hand, a range of possible forms of divergence given that the US' global role also exposes it to a whole range of problems and challenges that sets it apart from the Nordic states. It follows from this that the Trump presidency represented a deviation both domestically (through its authoritarian and nepotistic onslaught) and internationally (through its systematic attempts at undermining the world order that the US had played such a fundamental role in creating).

Before proceedings to assess whether there is Nordic – US convergence on the American Dream, we need to underline the presence of several historically based and deeply entrenched forms of injustice which in many ways are litmus tests for the American Dream.

Historically Entrenched forms of Injustice and Discrimination

In the US, it is difficult to discuss the American Dream without paying explicit attention to "the two Americas," which refers to the fact that America remains deeply divided by color and race. It has taken very long indeed for the Declaration of Independence's insistence on equal inalienable rights to have any bite on the plight of the descendants of slaves and on the plight of Native Americans. As will become apparent below, this historical form of structural domination still figures strongly across all the indicators of individualism and equality of opportunity that we present and assess. This fact, more than the US's great ethnic, linguistic, and cultural diversity,[7] stands out as an exception because it flies in the face of both of the two core tenets of the American Dream that we identify, individual rights and equality of opportunity.

Historian George Fredrickson, in his presidential address (1998), pointed to how ingrained this problem is in America's mindset: "By midcentury, it had become customary to celebrate the nation's tolerance for the diverse religions and cultural preferences of white ethnic groups. At the same time, relations between whites and people of color, especially African Americans, continued to be framed by a racial-caste hierarchy based (at least in the minds of the upper caste) on biological rather than cultural differences. Latinos were in an ambiguous, intermediary position -not quite white but not clearly nonwhite. Privately and in their basic attitudes, a substantial fraction of white Americans (possibly a silent majority) still adheres to this pre-1960s conception of racial hierarchy, and a militant fringe speaks and acts aggressively on its behalf, but the doctrines associated with it are no longer acceptable in public discourse" (Fredrickson 1998, 860). The Trump presidency appears to have given at least some credence to those that wanted to reintroduce such doctrines into the public discourse.

In Scandinavia, there is no similar history of slavery, even if Scandinavians participated in the slave trade. Domestically speaking, the historical absence of feudalism stands out from the rest of Western Europe as a historical resource for individualism (Sørensen and Stråth 1997). Discrimination based on ethnicity has historically been directed against the Sámi people, the indigenous people in Norway and Sweden (and Finland),[8] and ethnic minorities but they were not deprived of rights in ways remotely reminiscent of slavery. Since the 1960s, when immigration increased to Scandinavia, discrimination against ethnic minorities has remained an important challenge. In today's Scandinavia, the most serious transgressions are in violations of international law bent on protecting asylum seekers and refugees.

Patterns of historically entrenched structural domination and discrimination have not merely been directed at minorities; across both the US and Scandinavia, they have been directed at the majority: women who also today continue to experience discrimination due to their gender.[9] In all four countries, gender-based discrimination against women manifests itself in employment, political participation, and family relations. Men experience gender-based discrimination in other areas, as we will show, for instance, in the criminal justice system, and especially in the US.

Discrimination based on race or ethnicity often intersects with other relations, such as gender. Therefore, the need to adopt an intersectional perspective is apparent, both with reference to the US and Scandinavia. For instance, policies that improve the opportunities of some women may decrease equality for other women (Borchorst and Siim 2002, 91). While we would have liked to include an intersectional approach to all of our discussions, some areas lack data on how race, ethnicity, and gender intersect, especially on an aggregate level.

The contemporary US also shows that yesterday's successful gender equality battles may be tomorrow's defeats. Even though the US has a general prohibition on discrimination against women, legislation aiming to restrict women's sexual and reproductive rights have been implemented over the past decades (Amnesty International 2021a). A particularly concerning trend in the US is the implementation of policies that aim to restrict women's right to have an abortion. Since 1973, abortion had been generally protected under the *Roe v. Wade* judgement (Ziegler 2022). However, the Supreme Court overturned the judgment on 24 June 2022, meaning that millions of women in the US will lose the right to an abortion (Amnesty International 2022). The example of the recent law passed in Texas demonstrates this problem. A law that generally prohibits abortion after six weeks went into effect on September 1, 2021 (Liptak, Goodman and Tavernise 2021). The Texas abortion law will prohibit the abortion of around 87 percent of procedures and will likely reduce women in Texas' access to safe abortions, including for pregnancies resulting from rape (Liptak, Goodman and Tavernise 2021). This law follows a trend in restricting women's right to sexual and reproductive health, which has severe negative consequences (Human Rights Watch 2021a). The World Health Organization (2022, chap 1) views "comprehensive abortion care" as an essential health service that ensures women's rights to "…the highest possible level of health" and bodily autonomy. Moreover, restricting access to abortion does not reduce women's willingness to have an abortion, but leads to higher health risks (World Health Organization 2022, chap 1). For instance, unsafe abortions are connected to higher maternal death and other negative health consequences (World Health Organization 2022, chap 1). The attack on women's rights raises questions about the US's commitment to rights-based equality, which is a key tenet of the American Dream.

The rationale for presenting these historically entrenched instances of structural racism, domination, and discrimination – in many cases upheld through basic rights deprivations or through attributing an inferior legal status to persons or groups (the legal category of slave[10]) – is to underline that convergence along the lines of the American Dream must include explicit efforts to reduce or abrogate such instances of historical injustice.

Is There Convergence on the American Dream?

Our approach in the following is: (a) to disaggregate the two core dimensions of individualism and equal opportunity, (b) to identify points of convergence between the US and the Nordic countries on the key tenets of the American Dream, and (c) to identify important deviations from the two key dimensions of the American Dream in the US and the Nordic region.

The Nordic region consists of five states: Denmark, Finland, Iceland, Norway, and Sweden. Our collection of detailed data has focused on the three Scandinavian states (Denmark, Norway, and Sweden) and the US. Especially Sweden has been most closely associated with the Nordic Model in the US. Danish, Norwegian, and Swedish are very closely related languages; all Scandinavians understand each other and can talk to each other in their own native language. That is not the case with Finnish and Icelandic. Iceland is also a much smaller state and has special issues due to its limited population size. We have therefore focused on those three countries that we have the best access to and that we understand the best within the Nordic region.

The American Dream Unpacked: Individualism

The American Dream is steeped in a culture of individualism that reflects the sense of liberation that immigrants felt when arriving to America from Europe. That sense was amplified by the presence of the wide-open American frontier. Today there is no such open frontier, and Europe has caught up with the US in terms of decline of hierarchies of order and meaning previously organized by church, state, monarchy, and aristocracy. Europe, especially its Western part, is a site of democracy, basic rights, and a standard of living that does not deviate much from America's in terms of GDP as measured in purchasing power parities.[11] In addition, the Nordic region has, historically speaking, a more pronounced individualist legacy than the rest of Europe, not the least due to the absence of feudalism in the Nordic region (Sørensen and Stråth 1997).

An Important development and pattern of American-European convergence is that basic individual rights have become critical elements in how modern societies understand personhood and the role of the individual – as a rights-holder. A person's rights and legal status matter greatly to how that person is understood and recognized in society. We, therefore, cannot study individualism with reference to culture alone but need to understand how this legal rights-based development gives shape to the modern culture of individualism.

An important source of European-American convergence with a direct bearing on individualism is the post-war development of international law and human rights, associated with the UN and regional systems of governance such as the European Union, not the least because the US played an important role in erecting this system. American individualism, as noted above, is not only about rights; but it is also about self-determination. That has implications for American-European convergence, in the sense that the development of international law and rights has altered our understanding of states and state sovereignty: "[i]nternational law recognizes powers and constraints, and rights and duties, which have qualified the principle of state sovereignty in a number of important respects; sovereignty per se is no longer a straightforward guarantee of international legitimacy. Entrenched in certain legal instruments is the view that a legitimate state must be a democratic state that upholds certain common values" (Held *et al.* 1999, 65). As will be further documented in the section below, an important convergence implication is that European states have opened their legal and political systems to this international (and European) legal rights-based development (Fossum and Menéndez 2011).

US–Nordic Individualism Convergence?

With regard to individualism, our focus is on basic rights, including civil rights and rights to equal political participation, organization, and voice, as well as social and economic rights. Further, we look briefly at how (strictly) freedom of expression is regulated. More specifically, we are interested in the extent to which rights are tailored to individuals rather than to groups and communities; the scope of rights in terms of how binding they are on states; and the range and composition of rights, especially the relationship between civil and political versus social, economic, and cultural. Our assumption is that the American Dream's individualism is clearly orientated toward civil and political rights; beyond that are only those rights that ensure equality of opportunity. An important question is whether that rules out social and economic rights or whether such rights might, in fact, be such calibrated as to contribute to equality of opportunity.

Further, we are interested in individualism translated into rights to ensure that every person is acknowledged as a stakeholder in the system of governing with formal rights to participate and organize. With this is meant clear and transparent rules for who is able to vote in elections; that such rights are universal and available to all citizens (subject to certain age requirements); that citizens have the right to organize and take part in political life; and that the electoral system is fair in that it is tailored to ensure that votes are counted equally as far as possible.

All four countries' constitutions offer protection for civil and political rights. The principle of non-discrimination is fundamental to human rights law and recognized in the US and Scandinavia.[12] That all persons are equal before the law entails that discrimination based on race, color, sex, language, religion, political opinion, and nationality should be prohibited.[13] Constitutional rights-protection in the US and Denmark is primarily limited to civil and political rights, while Norway and Sweden today protect a range of civil, political, economic, and social rights in constitutional and other parts of domestic law. However, in practice, Denmark generally protects economic and social rights in a manner comparable to Norway and Sweden (Ojanen 2018, 137). With the exception of Norway, the Nordic countries generally speaking differ from the US when it comes to judicial restraint, which has historically been lacking in Denmark and Sweden. Instead, the Nordic countries have favored "constitutional legislative supremacy" and an idea of democracy as majority rule, according to Tuomas Ojanen (2018, 139). However, improvements in judicial safeguards have been installed in the Scandinavian countries, especially in the 1990s, due to a profound influence of the European Convention on Human Rights (ECHR) and the UN human rights treaties, which have shaped Denmark's, Norway's, and Sweden's legal systems. The US domestic system has not been similarly shaped by international human rights norms, however, the US had judicial safeguards in place from the "beginning."

The Scandinavian states allow for a more active state role in ensuring individual rights than the US. This aspect has led to a difference in the prioritization and scope of individual rights. The Nordic states are far more explicitly attentive to the notion that economic, social, and cultural rights are important for realizing an individual's self-fulfillment and other basic rights than is the US, even though economic and social rights are not "visible" in Danish legislation (but protected in practice).

Some key rights include the right to work; the right to a fair wage; the right to form and join trade unions; the right to social security; the right to an adequate standard of living; the right to the highest attainable standard of physical and mental health; and the right to education (UN General Assembly 1966b). While these rights seem to place considerable obligations on states, they do not require the state to guarantee that individuals are, for example, employed or healthy. Instead, states that grant their citizens economic and social rights have an obligation to provide favorable conditions that provide individuals with equal opportunities and access to basic services (Bantekas and Oette 2020, Chap. 9).

As noted above, an intrinsic part of trans-Atlantic individual rights-based convergence is the fact that international and regional human rights treaties have significantly influenced rights-protection in Scandinavia after 1950, and the three countries are strong supporters of these documents. For instance, Denmark, Norway, and Sweden are founding members of the Council of Europe and contributed to the development of the ECHR (Ojanen 2018, 136–140). The three states have further accepted the jurisdiction of the European Court of Human Rights (ECtHR). This is significant as the judgments by the ECtHR are legally binding on the member states, as opposed to the monitoring treaty bodies of the UN (Council of Europe 1950, sec. II; OHCHR no date). In addition to the ECHR, Denmark, Norway, and Sweden have ratified several of the regional conventions under the Council of Europe. For example, they have ratified the Convention on Preventing and Combating Violence Against Women and Domestic Violence (Istanbul Convention), and Norway and Sweden have ratified the European Social Charter (Council of Europe 2021b, 2021a).

The strong support for international human rights is also visible in the ratification status of the nine core UN human rights treaties, which highlights these states' tendency to commit to international legal standards. Norway and Denmark have ratified eight of the core treaties, with the notable exception of the International Convention on the Protection of the Rights of All Migrant Workers and Members of Their Families (CMW) (UN Human Rights Treaty Bodies no date). Sweden has ratified seven of the UN treaties, with the exception of the Convention for the Protection of All Persons from Enforced Disappearance (CED) and CMW (UN Human Rights Treaty Bodies no date). The three countries have also ratified the International Covenant on Economic, Social, and Cultural Rights (ICESCR) (UN Human Rights Treaty Bodies no date).

Even though the Scandinavian countries have not incorporated all treaties into domestic law, the engagement with international human rights has influenced judicial practices. When it comes to understanding their obligations to protect and respect individual rights, they tend to follow similar practices to that of international and regional courts (Ojanen 2018, 142–146).

The lack of incorporation of the ICESCR into domestic law in, especially Denmark and, to some extent, Sweden is somewhat surprising, as the Scandinavian countries are known for their social democracy and welfare provisions, granting extensive support to their populations (Esping-Andersen 2015, 125). Despite the limited protection of these rights in the constitutional structures, Denmark and Sweden generally meet their positive obligations under the ICESCR (Ojanen 2018, 139). Therefore, in order to understand the protection of individual rights in a society, the general public discourse and governmental practices must be taken into account (Lomell and Smith 2017, 197). For example, Lomell and Smith (2017, 197–198) argue that the public, in general, has started to invoke a human rights language with the purpose of ensuring that the government upholds its positive obligations, such as protection from non-state actors, rather than seeking protection from government involvement. Therefore, active engagement from the public and politicians is vital for rights-protection, in addition to judicial review. Even though there are some serious human rights problems in the Scandinavian countries, such as when it comes to the use of detention in prisons, gender-based violence, and asylum protection, the three countries are generally seen as complying with human rights. For instance, Denmark, Norway, and Sweden have received comparatively few judgments by the ECtHR on violations of the Convention (European Court of Human Rights 2021).

A similar engagement with international human rights and, in particular, economic, social, and cultural rights is not found in the US. Moreover, the constitutional protection of rights in the US has generally not been modernized since the Bill of Rights was adopted, even though they have been expanded to apply to the entire US population.

While the US played a key role in the drafting of the Universal Declaration of Human Rights (UDHR) and other UN human rights treaties, it has ratified significantly fewer treaties than Denmark, Norway, and Sweden (UN Human Rights Treaty Bodies no date). Of the nine core human rights treaties, the US has only ratified three: the International Covenant on Civil and Political Rights (ICCPR), the International Convention on the Elimination of All Forms of Racial Discrimination (CERD), and the Convention against Torture (CAT) and Other Cruel Inhuman and Degrading Treatment or Punishment (UN Human Rights Treaty Bodies no date). In addition, it has ratified the two optional protocols to the Convention on the Rights of the Child (CRC) (UN Human Rights Treaty Bodies no date). The US has further signed, but not ratified, the Convention on the Elimination of All Forms of

Discrimination against Women (CEDAW), the ICESCR, and the CRC (UN Human Rights Treaty Bodies no date).

While Denmark, Norway, and Sweden engaged more broadly and deeply with international human rights after the 1990s, the US continued to place considerable emphasis on civil and political rights found in its own legal structure (Beetham 1995, 43). Economic and social rights have not received significant attention or protection in the American system, especially in comparison to the Scandinavian countries.

The US has been particularly ambivalent when it comes to economic and social rights after 1948. For instance, the US supported and contributed to the drafting of the ICESCR, and it was signed in 1977, along with the ICCPR (Whelan and Donnelly 2007, 924–932). While the Senate approved the ICCPR in 1992 with extensive reservations and declarations, the ICESCR has never been approved (MacNaughton and McGill 2012, 366–367). Approval from the Senate is necessary for the ratification of treaties in the US. American opposition to economic and social rights is visible in its responses at the international level. The US has expressed the view that these guarantees should not be defined as *rights* but rather that states should aspire to grant their citizens such securities (Bantekas and Oette 2020, 415; Whelan and Donnelly 2007, 924–932).

Despite its unwillingness to ratify the ICESCR, the US engages to some extent with UN procedures that monitor compliance with the UN Charter and the UDHR, which contain provisions on economic and social rights (MacNaughton and McGill 2012, 370–372). Moreover, because the US has signed the ICESCR, it cannot act in contradiction with the purpose of this treaty. During the US's Universal Periodic Review (UPR) under the UN Human Rights Council in 2010, the report by the US government covered the implementation of economic and social rights in the US, referring to President Roosevelt's so-called "Four Freedoms" (MacNaughton and McGill 2012, 378–381). However, the US was criticized for failing to account for the gap between law and reality on the ground (MacNaughton and McGill 2012, 379–380). During the UPR, the US accepted recommendations from other UN member states to ensure equal socioeconomic, work, and education opportunities, along with a range of recommendations tied to civil and political rights (MacNaughton and McGill 2012, 380). While the US highlighted that it will fulfill these rights progressively, it is an important development that the US recognized these rights as applying within its borders (MacNaughton and McGill 2012, 381).

Further, whereas the federal government does not provide economic and social rights, state constitutions are generally more accepting of such rights (MacNaughton and McGill 2012, 378). All of the US states guarantee the right to public education (at least primary education) and a majority take responsibility for providing welfare provisions (MacNaughton and McGill 2012, 378). For example, the Supreme Court of Appeals of West Virginia referred to the UDHR when it recognized the fundamental right to education (MacNaughton and McGill 2012, 388). Vermont has also relied on a human rights framework when developing its heath care (MacNaughton and McGill 2012, 388–390).

As seen, there is some commitment to economic and social rights in the US. However, they are not seen as individual rights that everyone is entitled to on the same basis as civil and political rights, neither in the legal system nor in practice. The US does not respect and support economic and social rights on the same level as the Scandinavian countries. In this connection, it is important to underline that there are no grounds for asserting that the manner in which the Scandinavian states uphold social and economic rights has negative implications for equal opportunity. If anything, social and economic rights are meant to give support to policies bent on fostering equal opportunity.

Freedom of Expression in the US and Scandinavia

The US and the Scandinavian states differ in their interpretation and hierarchical understanding of basic rights with reference to freedom of expression. This example shows that while the US and the Scandinavian countries value individual rights, these rights receive different prioritization and protection. The US grants a higher protection of freedom of expression, leading to a higher acceptance of hate speech and inflammatory speech. The Scandinavian states place greater importance on meeting their obligations under international human rights treaties, which has led to prohibitions on discriminatory and hate speech to protect ethnic, national, and sexual minorities.

The US Constitution lays out freedom of expression in the First Amendment, along with freedoms of religion and association. The amendment does not specify the scope of freedom of expression. Therefore, the courts, and particularly the US Supreme Court, have an important role in interpreting this right (Barendt 2007, 49). The amendment is framed as a direct obligation for the state, theoretically only applying to Congress, to not interfere with individuals' freedom of expression rather than giving the right to individuals. However, the Supreme Court interprets the Amendment to entail individual rights as well (Barendt 2007, 49). In the case *Gillow* v. *New York* in 1925, the Supreme Court held that freedom of expression must be protected from interference by the states and the federal government (Barendt 2007, 50). Moreover, the Supreme Court accepts that the freedom is not absolute and can be subject to limitations when it conflicts with other fundamental rights. The US Supreme Court balances this right against other important basic rights and interests, including public order, national security, and the right to a fair trial (Barendt 2007, 51).

Nonetheless, the US places considerable value on the freedom of expression, placing it high in comparison to other fundamental individual rights (Barendt 2007, 51). For example, the Supreme Court holds that freedom of expression shall include expressions that insult or disturb (as does the ECHR), as long as it does not cause considerable harm (Boyle 2001, 489). The understanding of the protection of freedom of expression is influenced by the suspicion of the government found in the US (Barendt 2007). Consequently, the federal and state governments must firmly explain why restrictions on freedom of expression are necessary and justified. When it comes to so-called content-based restrictions on a specific topic, it is particularly challenging for the state or federal government to pass laws or regulations. However, the Supreme Court has been more willing to accept regulations that are considered content-neutral (Barendt 2007).

The US does not accept direct incitement to violence as falling under freedom of expression. Another striking aspect is that freedom of expression is generally seen as a right against the state and not against private companies, such as media corporations, which can determine who has access to their platforms (Bangstad 2012).

The US's interpretation of freedom of expression conflicts, to some extent, with its obligations under international human rights treaties, which hold that state parties have an obligation to restrict this right in certain aspects. For instance, article 20 of ICCPR contains an obligation to prohibit certain expressions, such as war propaganda and "advocacy of national, racial or religious hatred that constitutes incitement to discrimination ..." (UN General Assembly 1966a, art. 20(1,2)). In order to protect freedom of expression, the US has submitted reservations to any provision that would require it to limit the right (UN Treaty Collection 2021a, 2021b).

While the right to freedom of expression is considered fundamental in the Scandinavian states, they permit restrictions to this right in line with international human rights treaties (Ojanen 2018).

Even though ECHR is open to the limitation to freedom of expression, under article 10, the ECtHR places great emphasis on its importance. For instance, in the case of *Erdoğdu and Ince v. Turkey*, the ECtHR held that "[f]reedom of expression constitutes one of the essential foundations of a democratic society and one of the basic conditions for its progress and for each individual's self-fulfilment" (European Court of Human Rights 1999, para. 47(i)). Any restriction must be prescribed by law and considered "necessary in a democratic society" consequently, the restriction must serve a legitimate purpose and be proportionate (Council of Europe 1950, para. art. 10; Ojanen 2018). Norwegian law reflects the understanding of the ECtHR and other international human rights treaties. For instance, article 100 of the Norwegian Constitution states that "[l]imitations to this right may be prescribed by law to protect the privacy of the individual or for other weighty reasons" (Norwegian Ministry of Justice and Public Security 1814, art. 100). In order to meet Norway's obligations under the ICCPR and CERD, the Norwegian Penal Code sections 185 and 186 prohibit discriminatory and hate speech on the basis of skin color, nationality, ethnicity, religion, sexual orientation, gender identity, or disability (Norwegian Ministry of Justice and Public Security 2021, art. 185–186). The Danish Constitution similarly highlights that freedom of expression carries duties and responsibilities that can be restricted under law (Denmark 1849, art. 77). The Swedish Constitution allows for restrictions in order to meet Sweden's obligation under human rights law (Sveriges Riksdag 2016).

The presentation thus far has pointed to two central concerns: one is the extent to which a given state imposes constraints on freedom of speech and the criteria and justifications involved. The other is who persons and groups should be protected against: the state only or societal actors as well. The latter brings up an important issue pertaining to individualism-relevant rights-based convergence, namely whether the individual person remains at the center of attention as the main legal subject. In that context, there are certain alarming US developments that find some resonance in Europe. We will illustrate that with the US Supreme Court ruling *United Citizens versus Federal Election Commission* (2010). The verdict starts by saying that "[t]he Federal Election Campaign Act ('the Act') prohibits corporations and labor unions from using their general treasury funds to make electioneering communications or for speech that expressly advocates the election or defeat of a federal candidate. 2 U.S.C. §441b. An electioneering communication is generally defined as 'any broadcast, cable or satellite communication' that is 'publicly distributed' and refers to a clearly identified federal candidate and is made within 30 days of a primary or 60 days of a general election. 2 U.S.C. §434(f)(3) (A) and 11 CFR 100.29(a)(2)" (US Federal Election Committee no date b). In his assessment of this ruling, Woody Clermont (2010, 481–482) situates this ruling within what he refers to as: "the growing movement that has allowed corporations to exercise the cherished rights of American citizens – reflecting the migration of the constitutional system away from an individual prerogative, and toward placing greater and greater emphasis on the rights of amorphous, faceless organizations through a favorable, judicially activist interpretation of the law." The ruling greatly increases the scope for corporations to shape communication and, by implication, freedom of speech and influence election campaigning. As such, it appears to represent a two-pronged attack on core individualist foundations. There is a development of "market citizenship" in Europe as well, through, for instance, the central role business corporations occupy in EU law, but this does not as easily as in the US translate into political influence in election campaigns.

Finally, explicit attempts at free speech subversion were seen when former President Donald Trump actively tried to discredit, undermine, and assault the free press in the US, including its independence from the government. These were efforts we associate with authoritarians not democrats and suggest that a return of Mr. Trump to power in DC will have serious repercussions not only for freedom of speech and the press but for US constitutional democracy *tout court*.

The analysis thus far suggests that the post-war period has seen a clear rule-based trans-Atlantic convergence, especially since the Scandinavian countries have incorporated international law into their constitutional systems. Even if this has also meant that their legal systems have incorporated social and economic rights, this does not, in a fundamental sense, detract from the individualist core of their legal systems. The critical issue for individualism then is, as the last paragraph above has suggested, the developments that reduce the centrality of the individual person as the main legal subject by, for instance, including corporations. In a similar vein as the next section will show are developments that undermine rights or use law to generate legally sanctioned status differences between individuals.

Constraints on or Limits to Individualism

With regard to constraints on basic rights, we have identified a range of relevant factors. For all of these, it matters whether they are particularly targeted at or have especially strong effects on vulnerable groups or groups that have historical legacies of exclusion, marginalization, or discrimination. In this context, the US stands out with its historical legacy of slavery. In addition, all four countries have historical legacies of discrimination and domination directed at women. These forms of historical oppression serve to color and gender-code constraints on individualism and equality of opportunity; thus compelling us to consider whether or the extent to which countries have been able to remove such historical patterns of oppression and injustice.

One set of factors pertains to whether the state is equipped with undue powers to interfere in persons' lives, including incarceration without due cause or without proper procedure. Police violence and police brutality figure here, especially if directed at certain groups or visible minorities. As part of our assessment, we include the death sentence to check if it is color-coded and because the effects of a miscarriage of justice are irreversible.

Further is the issue of whether there are provisions for obtaining and losing voting rights that are restrictive, color-coded, or otherwise discriminatory. This may include voting registration procedures that increase the bar for participating in elections (Jim Crow laws), gerrymandering, and manipulating constituency bounds.

Since we are interested in individualism as a core value of the American Dream, the assessment of constraints should not be confined to a technical presentation of existing legal provisions but must "place the law in social context" so-to-speak. The provisions governing election financing may serve as an illustration: to what extent do the rules open up space for wealthy persons and corporations to translate their economic power into political influence? The more money permeates the political process, the more acute this problem is. In the previous section, we showed how the rights to freedom of expression are gradually shifted away from individuals to, for instance, corporations.

External Forms of Rights Deprivations

One of the most explicit instances of rights deprivations has taken place within the international realm - through how states have dealt with foreigners (asylum seekers). During the US's war on terror, launched in the aftermath of the terrorist attacks against the US on September 11, 2001, the US has routinely acted outside international law and actively undermined human rights. The extent of the human rights violations committed against terrorist suspects has had a global scope. The use of extra-ordinary rendition (the extrajudicial transfer between states), indefinite secret detention centers, and systematic use of torture (termed enhanced interrogation methods) are well documented (The Rendition Project 2019, 17). Rendition aircraft carried prisoners, interrogators, and other US officials, creating a network between so-called "black sites." For instance, Abu Zubaydah was rendered at least seven times including to Thailand, Poland, Morocco, Lithuania, Afghanistan, and Guantanamo (The Rendition Project 2019, 19)· Some prisoners were shackled, hooded, beaten, and placed in coffins during transfer. Prisoners were also denied legal representation and could be held for years. At least 780 terrorist suspects have been detained at the US military base at Guantanamo (Weill and Robinson 2020, 257). Only a few persons have had their cases reviewed by a court (Whitmer 2006, 172).

The extensive use of drone strikes (especially under Presidents Obama and Trump) has caused civilian deaths. Counter-terrorism laws of surveillance and monitoring have disproportionately affected Muslims due to their religion and ethnicity (Amnesty International no date). Scholars such as Aradau (2007) and Johns argue that the US's behavior in the war on terror has been particularly problematic in that it has attempted to redefine and reinterpret international law, in effect undermining it (Johns 2013, 32–40). The US is a party to the UN CAT, which clearly prohibits any action that may amount to torture or other cruel, inhuman, or degrading treatment under any circumstance. The US's behavior of engaging in torture and extraordinary rendition is a clear violation of international human rights law.

In relation to what was said above about US exceptionalism, it is interesting to note that some scholars argue that the US used "exceptionalism" as a rhetoric to justify the war on terror, arguing that the US is an exceptionally "good" state, allowing it to use exceptional measures. This has developed into a discourse that has been used to justify and rationalize the war on terror and the need to use military means to combat terrorism based on ideas of American exceptionalism (De Schutter 2019, 244). Even if the Scandinavian states did not engage in most of the US's practices, Denmark and Norway, as members of NATO, and Sweden have supported the US's War on Terror. For instance, the three states supported the NATO-led invasion of Afghanistan in 2001, and Denmark and Norway were involved in the Libyan intervention in 2011.

Another instance that is at least a grey zone in terms of rights deprivation is found in aspects of how notably but not exclusively Denmark relates to asylum-seekers. One aspect pertains to denial of asylum-seekers' claims so as to reduce the number of asylum seekers. Another is that the Danish government has launched a controversial proposal aiming to create reception centers in non-EU states, leaving other states with the responsibility of processing asylum claims (Preisler 2021). The UNHCR "… strongly urges Denmark to refrain from establishing law and practices that would minimize and shift its asylum and protection obligations to third countries" (UNHCR 2021b, p. 2 (para. 7)). In 2020, the number of displaced persons was at a record high, meaning that Denmark (and other European countries) are currently unwilling to act to protect refugees and asylum seekers (UNHCR 2021a). In 2020, the Council of Europe's Committee for the Prevention of Torture (CPT) published a report that was highly critical of Denmark's administrative migration detention centers, which hold rejected asylum seekers or persons who have likely committed a crime that will lead to expulsion (Council of Europe 2019, 53). Migrants were reportedly held in prison-like conditions and the CPT holds that "a carceral environment" should be avoided, as those that are detained have not been convicted of a crime (Council of Europe 2019, 54).

In the following, we turn to internal forms of rights deprivation.

Internal Forms of Rights Deprivations: Losing Individual Rights

In the US, a significant portion of inmates and individuals with a criminal record is denied the right to vote. Totally, 48 of the states and the District of Colombia (the exceptions are Maine and Vermont) do not allow inmates to vote in elections (Alexander 2012, 158). The following section draws heavily on the work of Michelle Alexander (2012). Many states further deny released prisoners the right to take part in elections ranging from a few years to the rest of their life (Alexander 2012, 158). Former inmates automatically lose their right to vote when they are released from prison, and in those states that do allow individuals with a criminal record to vote, there are many barriers to restoring this right. In several states, there is a fee that must be paid to restore the right to vote, however, in practice, this can be particularly challenging for those with a criminal record. For instance, persons that are released from prison often have a low income and are required to pay multiple state agencies, such as probation departments and legal institutions. This means that in practice, many are never able to restore the right to vote and are denied the opportunity to participate in elections. Of particular concern is that it is not uncommon to go to prison for smaller offenses that can lead to political disenfranchisement for life (Alexander 2012, 159).

In addition to losing the right to vote, former felons often struggle to find employment and housing, as they often lose the right to public benefits and federal welfare provisions. For instance, many forms require an applicant to inform if they have a criminal record, such as when applying for jobs, rental agreements, universities, and mortgages. Moreover, due to the failure of the state government to support former felons, it is easy to return to prison, including for minor offenses (Alexander 2012, 141). The police can legally monitor, stop and search a former inmate, which increases the likelihood of being subjected to police violence (Alexander 2012, 140–143).

While the consequences of having a criminal record affect all ethnic groups in the US, black Americans are excessively hit due to the high incarceration rate. Alexander compares the discrimination taking place in the criminal justice system with the Jim Crow laws (Alexander 2012). She argues that the massive increase in incarceration means that a significant part of the black population is affected today. For example, African Americans constitute around 90 percent of those sentenced to prison for a drug offense in Illinois, while white Americans are rarely arrested. Additionally, in Chicago, an estimated 55 percent of the black adult male population has a criminal record and "young black men are more likely to go prison than to college" (Alexander 2012, 190).

The likelihood of losing fundamental rights is far higher in the US than in the Scandinavian countries (or other democratic states). While it is possible to lose the right to vote in Norway, this is rare (Stortinget 2020). A person can lose the right to vote if they have committed a serious criminal offense, such as treason, attempted to overthrow the government, or committed election fraud. However, the maximum time a person can lose this right is up to ten years (Stortinget 2020). For instance, Norwegians who volunteered to fight for the German Wehrmacht during World War II lost their right to vote for a set time period after the war, being sentenced with treason.

Violations of Children's Rights

The US is the only country that has not ratified the CRC (Mehta 2015). While the US generally complies with most provisions of the CRC, serious violations of children's human rights occur in the criminal justice system. Many children face the criminal justice system at a very young age. Around 14 states do not have an age of criminal responsibility, meaning that young children can be subject to strict punishments and long sentences. The American Civil Liberties Union (ACLU) reports that children as young as six have been arrested in schools with handcuffs for minor disturbances, such as drawing on school property (Mehta 2015). Children are also confined in adult prisons, placing them at risk of physical and sexual violence (Mehta 2015). Even children placed in juvenile prisons face major challenges, as they are not focusing on rehabilitation. According to the ACLU, the US is the only country in the world where children can be sentenced to life in prison without the possibility of parole (Mehta 2015). Similar to general incarceration, children with minority backgrounds are disproportionately targeted. While the US Supreme Court has taken steps to improve children's rights, such as by no longer applying the death penalty to those under the age of 18, the US's protection of children remains insufficient and runs contrary to the CRC.

Prison Incarceration and Recidivisms

The American prison system does not only deprive persons of rights; incarceration rates and patterns testify to structural racism and discrimination. The US has the world's highest number of incarcerated persons per capita (Benecchi 2021). While around 300,000 persons were in prison in 1972, the number increased to around two million in 2010 (Alexander 2012, 6). In 2021, the US continues to imprison an estimated two million individuals, which means that the US has both the highest rate of prisoners per capita and the largest number in the world (Statista Research Department 2021). Figure 5.1 shows the rate of prisoners in the Scandinavian countries and the US, demonstrating how much of an outlier the US is:

According to data from the UN Office on Drugs and Crime, the rate of women in prisons was significantly lower than men within each country. In the Scandinavian countries, the rate of incarcerated men was more than 15 times that of women in 2010. For the US, the rate of men was 11 times that of women in the same year.

In the US, the incarceration rates point to forms of racial discrimination. In 2018, data from the Department of Justice shows that black Americans have the highest state and federal imprisonment rate with 1,134 per 100,000 black citizens. The rate of black men was estimated

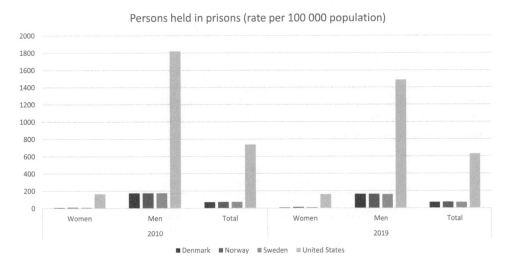

Figure 5.1 Persons held in prisons (rate per 100,000 population in 2010 and 2019).[14]

Source: UN Office on Drugs and Crime (2019).

to be 5.8 times that of white men, while the rate of black women was 1.8 times that of white women (Carson 2020, 1).

Even though the rate of imprisoned black Americans has decreased since 2008, this group continues to face discrimination due to their ethnicity. For instance, in some states in the US, the rate of black men charged with drug-related crimes is 20 to 50 times that of white men (Alexander 2012,7–9). Alexander argues that the police targeted black Americans as part of the War on Drugs by focusing on poorer neighborhoods that are predominately black (Alexander 2012, 182–185). This is one factor that has led to the massive increase in incarceration rates. Moreover, black and Latino Americans are more likely to be sentenced to prison than white Americans convicted of similar crimes (American Civil Liberties Union 2014, 1). Additionally, black men, on average, receive a 20 percent longer sentence than white men convicted of a comparable crime (American Civil Liberties Union 2014, 1). The situation is particularly worrying for those serving longer sentences, where black Americans are heavily overrepresented. For instance, the ACLU estimated that in 13 states and the federal system, black Americans totaled over 60 percent of those serving life sentences, despite only constituting around 13 percent of the US population (American Civil Liberties Union 2014, 2). In the federal system, the number is as high as 71.3 percent of those on life sentences without the possibility of parole (American Civil Liberties Union 2014, 2).

According to ACLU, the devastating situation of mass incarceration in the US is a result of racial discrimination taking place "at every stage of the criminal justice system" (American Civil Liberties Union 2014). Black Americans are more often stopped, interrogated, and searched than white Americans (American Civil Liberties Union 2014, 2). They are further denied meaningful legal representation and can be pressured to plead guilty, leading to higher incarceration rates and longer sentences (Alexander 2012, 185–186).

Another major challenge is recidivism in the US (Benecchi 2021). Due to a lack of job opportunities and financial support for housing and food, many people end up being incarcerated again (Benecchi 2021). For example, after five years, 77 percent of former prisoners are, on average, arrested for a new crime (Sipes no date). Liz Benecchi (2021) argues that the main reason explaining the high number of persons that reenter prisons is a limited focus on rehabilitation, which leads to a neglect of mental health problems. American prisons do not prepare individuals for reentering society. For instance, there are few opportunities for work training or education (Benecchi 2021).

Benecchi (2021) compares the US recidivism rate to Norway, which has the lowest recidivism rate in the world at 20 percent. For instance, Norway's maximum-security prison, Halden Fengsel, aims to reintegrate persons into society by focusing on securing housing, employment, and a social network prior to leaving the prison (Benko 2015). The Scandinavian countries further treat and protect their prisoners better than the US. For example, according to the UN Office on Drugs and Crime, the US struggles with occurrences of intentional homicide in prisons, as seen in Table 5.1.

Table 5.1 Rate of victims of intentional homicide per 100,000 prisoners

	2010	*2014*
Denmark	0	0
Norway	0	0
Sweden	0	0
United States	4.6	5.5

Source: UN Office on Drugs and Crime (2016).

The figures show that the US had a rate of 5.5 intentional homicides per 100,000 prisoners in 2014, which had increased from 4.6 in 2014. In the same time period, almost no persons were killed in Scandinavian prisons.

Election Manipulation: Gerrymandering, Barriers to Political Participation, and Excessive Spending

While the US system is generally seen as democratic (fair), the electoral system can be subject to manipulation by what has been termed partisan gerrymandering. This concerns the process of redrawing the borders of electoral districts for Representatives of the House and state legislators, supervised by elected officials. The process often takes place after each decennial census of the US population. As the US states are free to determine voting rules, some states have implemented strict identification laws and fewer polling places, making it more difficult for Americans to participate in elections.[15] Many states also prohibit Americans with a criminal record to vote, as we discussed above. These processes, laws, and policies, including gerrymandering, have been criticized for leading to the further marginalization of ethnic and racial minorities.

Attempts to alter restrictions on voting rights are currently ongoing in the US and pose important challenges for American democracy. Republicans, in particular, are currently leading a process to implement additional restrictions on voting prior to the 2022 mid-term election (Schouten 2021). In 2021, the Republican Party has proposed more than 250 laws aiming to limit available options for voting (Gardner, Rabinowitz and Stevens 2021). According to CNN, the Brennan Center's Democracy Program had documented 34 bills restricting voting accessibility and rights in 19 states (Schouten 2021). The Republican Party appears bent on continuing the process of passing the proposed bills in 2022. The proposed restrictions include stricter ID requirements, reduced hours to vote, reducing the opportunity to vote by mail or to vote early (Gardner, Rabinowitz and Stevens 2021). For instance, Georgia, that is seen as a "red state" and was flipped by President Joe Biden in 2020, has reduced the number of available ballot drop boxes (Schouten 2021). The Republican party justifies the proposed changes in voting legislation as necessary to ensure confidence in elections following the 2020 presidential election. While the Trump administration and other Republicans questioned the outcome of the 2020 election, these claims are entirely unsubstantiated (Schouten 2021). That this is a serious political onslaught is further reflected in the fact that the Republican party has targeted states that were not contested by Trump during the 2020 election (Gardner, Rabinowitz and Stevens 2021).

In contrast, if we look at Norway, it does not leave scope for a similar process of gerrymandering, as public officials do not determine the electoral districts. There is also a requirement to ensure that polling stations are easily accessible to all citizens, including persons with disabilities (Norwegian Ministry of Local Government and Modernisation 2002).

With regard to election campaign spending, Table 5.2 below shows that ability to raise funds is a major de facto requirement for political participation. Here "money talks" so loudly that it skews the entire electoral process in favor of the money collectors and the large-scale donors.

The table shows that Joe Biden raised more than 1 billion USD for his presidential campaign, while Donald Trump raised around 750 million USD.

Police Brutality

The level of police brutality in the US further highlights the issue of racial discrimination, which has gained international attention after the police killed George Floyd on May 24,

Table 5.2 2020 Presidential election in USD (for the time period 2019–2020)

	Joe Biden (D)	*Donald Trump (R)*
Total individual contributions	823,098,083.37	458,351,485.61
Party committee contributions	8,200	0
Other committee contributions	563,064.21	846,953.30
Transfer from other authorized committees	243,411,324.12	275,176,528.12
Total offsets to expenditures	7,021,943.40	6,374,755.93
Other receipts	77,360.93	3,600,506.30
Total receipts	**1,074,179,976.03**	**744,350,229.26**

Source: US Federal Election Commission (no date a).

2020, leading to widespread protests across the country (and outside) (Amnesty International 2021b). While the US government does not report or collect data on police brutality, private organizations, such as Mapping Police Violence, record the number of people killed by police officers in the US (Human Rights Watch 2021b; Mapping Police Violence 2021).

Data by Mapping Police Violence shows a disproportionate targeting of ethnic minorities. A total of 1,126 people were killed in 2020, with the vast majority (96 percent) being killed in police shootings (Mapping Police Violence no date). However, officers were only charged in 16 of the cases (Mapping Police Violence no date). While black Americans only constitute 13 percent of the US population, black persons accounted for 27 percent of those killed in 2020, as seen in Table 5.3 (Mapping Police Violence no date):

We may conjecture that there is a relationship between police killings and the nature and length of police training. The US police stands out as having considerably less basic training than the police in Denmark, Sweden, and Norway, visualized in Table 5.4:

In contrast to the US, the Scandinavian countries require recruits to go through extensive basic training that can last from around 2.5 years to 3 years, normally with an option to continue their education. For instance, in Norway, police officers qualify for a master's program.

An accompanying feature we conjecture is the contents and orientation of the training. In the US, the length of police training varies by state level. The US Department of Justice provides an overview of the training of 135,000 recruits that entered basic training programs for state and local enforcement between 2011 and 2013. Around 48 percent received training from academics based on a model that was more oriented on a stress than a non-stress approach. Stress-based training is inspired by a military-oriented model and is centered on intensive "physical demands and psychological pressure" (Reaves 2016). Only 18 percent received training by academics that was more centered on a non-stress approach, focusing on academic achievement, physical training, and supportive environment. Around 34 percent received a balanced approach. Finally, given that basic law enforcement training lasted on average 21 weeks (840 hours), excluding field training (Reaves 2016, 3), and a significant amount of

Table 5.3 2020 Police violence report (percentage)

	Police killings 2020	*US population*
Black	27	13
Hispanic	21	17
White	48	63
Other	4	7

Source: Mapping Police Violence (2021, no date).

Table 5.4 Basic training requirements for police

	Time
Denmark (Politi no date)	Around 2.5 years (university level)
Norway (Politihøgskolen no date b)	3 years (university level, bachelor's degree)
Sweden (Polisen 2020)	Around 2.5 years (university level)
United States (Reaves 2016)	Around 21 weeks (depends on state)

that time is spent on training with firearms and the use of physical force, there appears little scope for socializing police officers in the social skills that conflict-reduction requires. If we look at the training in Norway in comparison, a central aspect is based on crime prevention and how to address persons in vulnerable situations, aiming to ensure safety, including community safety (Politihøgskolen no date a).

Death Penalty

The death penalty was abolished in Denmark, Norway, and Sweden after World War II, whereas the US continues to practice the death penalty. However, over the past years, there has been a reduction in the number of executions in the US (Pew Research Center 2021). Nevertheless, it is interesting that a majority of citizens in a society with such a strong libertarian tradition as the US is willing to grant the state the power to decide over life and death.

A recent report by the Death Penalty Information Center, a non-profit organization that provides information and analysis on issues related to the death penalty in the US, argues that the death penalty has been applied discriminatory against ethnic minorities (Ndulue 2020). Historically, black persons have been disproportionately executed and were often subject to more painful executions than white persons were (Ndulue 2020, 28). A study released in 2000 showed that 89 percent of defendants in death penalty cases were persons of color (American Civil Liberties Union 2014, 7). A key issue is related to racial discrimination in jury selection in death penalty cases (American Civil Liberties Union 2014, 10). For instance, several black defendants have been tried before all-white juries, which often results in capital punishment (American Civil Liberties Union 2014, 10). The Death Penalty Information Center holds that the counties that continue to apply the death penalty excessively target racial and ethnic minorities (Ndulue 2020, 28).

While the US Supreme Court held in *Atkins v. Virginia* that executions of "mentally retarded criminals" are unconstitutional (US Supreme Court 2002), persons with serious mental illnesses and disabilities can receive capital punishment, according to the ACLU (2021). For instance, Lisa Montgomery was executed in 2020 despite having PTSD and brain damage because of sexual violence and torture that she experienced as a child, according to ACLU (Stubbs 2021). Such punishment is considered "cruel and unusual punishment," prohibited under the Eight Amendment (US Supreme Court 2002). ACLU argues that several of the executions in 2020 were unconstitutional (Stubbs 2021).

All methods of execution in the US have a high risk of amounting to torture and extreme pain (American Civil Liberties Union 2021). The ACLU further holds that 173 innocent prisoners on death row have been released between 1973 and 2016 (American Civil Liberties Union 2021). Almost four persons are, on average, exonerated per year (since 1973) (Death Penalty Information Center 2021).

Roger Hood (according to Hodgkinson) makes several arguments for why states have increasingly abolished the death penalty after World War II: it violates the right to life; it is not an efficient deterrent against crime; administration of the death penalty is highly problematic (also in "developed states"), and it gives out "confused moral messages" (Hodgkinson 2009, 11–12). One central argument against the death penalty is the execution of innocent persons (Hodgkinson 2009, 12).

It is interesting to note that the ECtHR had held that death row in the US can amount to torture and inhuman treatment, violating article 3 of the ECHR. The ECtHR states that parties cannot return a person to the US if they risk the death penalty, however, it is not the death penalty itself that is the main issue, but rather the inhumane conditions of being on death row (European Court of Human Rights 1989, paras. 92–99). In the following we will discuss the other key aspect of the American Dream, equal opportunity.

The American Dream Unpacked: Equality of Opportunity

What do we mean by "Equality of Opportunity"? How should we operationalize this concept in order to compare to what degree societies approximate or deviate strongly from this normative ideal embedded in the American Dream?

One obvious and quite tangible proxy for equality of opportunity is social mobility. This measure tells us something about the *probability* that you will enter a different economic group than that which you were born into. In order to get a better handle on equality of opportunity, we can ask what variables impact social mobility? Evenly distributed access to affordable education of a reasonable quality seems like an obvious candidate. Therefore, we will discuss educational systems below. But what other factors should be considered? One possible point of entry is to engage further with the notion of social mobility at a conceptual level.

Social mobility entails upside possibilities and downside risks: The empirically unattainable but theoretically valuable notion of perfect social mobility requires that as many people experience a drop through the socioeconomic strata as those that experience "promotion." The underlying idea is that if no biases or privileges impact how you "end up" in terms of economic circumstances – i.e. when we have a perfectly level playing field – each individual has the same chance to realize the potential given by their innate talent and willingness to work. From this, we can establish that equality of opportunity is intimately linked to risk and thus probabilities. Therefore, we can expand our argument and ask, to what degree do Scandinavian and US welfare institutions, and societies in general, protect their citizens from life risks?

We will look at data on social mobility and distribution of income and wealth. Then we turn to the institutions that do or do not provide social protection and education. Loosely speaking, we can think of these four factors as the independent variables in our argument. The logic being that our prime measure of equality of opportunity is social mobility, while this outcome is fundamentally shaped by various risk mitigating or exacerbating institutions and patterns related to inequality, social protection, and education. In principle assigning values to these variables does not, however, exhaust the topic of how well a given regime opens or closes opportunities and possibilities for the individual. This is so because a country can produce a strong performance along these dimensions and still be relatively poor. But as we have already made clear above, the Scandinavian countries and the US are among the richest countries in the world. And with a partial exception for Sweden, there is not much daylight between the per capita GDP performance (measured by Purchasing Power Parities) of the four of them.

Social Mobility Indicator

First, a caveat: While social mobility is a useful proxy for equality of opportunity, research in this field does not adequately include information on women. Studies on social mobility included here tend to consider connections between the income of father and son (most common) and of father and daughter,[16] while the connections between mother and daughter, and mother and son remain unexplored. Additionally, studies that do include women are often based on comparatively less data than for men.[17] Therefore, the findings in these studies are not sufficient to determine social mobility, as it remains limited to primarily male perspectives.

The problem with the male bias in research on social mobility and welfare systems is that the male perspective is presented as the "norm" or presumed starting point of analysis, while research on women becomes something separate, seen as "the other." Therefore, we underline that the data on social mobility is male centered.

Following from this shortcoming, the focus on income and education leaves out other variables that have a larger impact on women's lives in comparison to men. For example, women continue to carry out the majority of unpaid work, including taking care of children and cleaning, which negatively impacts their opportunities to take on paid work and political participation (UN Women 2017). Therefore, in order to examine how the US and Scandinavia compare to the ideal of equality of opportunity, it is necessary to look at other variables. As institutions in both the US and Scandinavia are male oriented,[18] we examine how state policies influence gender (in)equality, such as promotion of female employment, gender gap, parental leave, childcare, and maternal health.

The literature reviewed here reveals five tendencies of particular interest to us: Firstly, all available studies agree that the Scandinavian states have a higher social mobility than the US, especially in terms of upward mobility from the bottom quintile. In other words, Scandinavia has succeeded in reducing the link between the income of fathers and the sons and daughters of those born into the lowest quintile. The US has low social mobility in absolute terms, and compared to the Scandinavian states, it is particularly low for those at the bottom (Jäntti *et al.* 2006; Landersø and Heckman 2017).

Secondly, it is sticky at the top: In the US and the Scandinavian countries, being born into the top quintile significantly increases your chances of living your adult life in affluence. An interesting difference between US males and individuals of both genders in Scandinavia and women from the US is that while those in the latter two groups have a probability slightly below 20 percent of "relegation" to the lowest quintile, the corresponding risk for US males born at the top is significantly lower (is less than 10 percent). This implies, and this is our third observation, that US women born at the top are more exposed to "relegation" than their male counterparts. One likely interpretation of this is that women are more dependent on their husbands' wages in order to preserve their income status.

Our fourth observation is that in the US, the middle class, and in particular the upper middle class, is the most socially mobile group measured by *intergenerational income elasticity* (IGE), a coefficient that captures the statistical connection between parents' income and their children's income in later life. Lastly, social mobility in the US is tied to racial and ethnic background. There is a higher mobility among white Americans than black Americans.

We will return to these points when we discuss the impact of the various structures and institutions that impact life risk and, therefore, mobility. Furthermore, we group these factors under four headings: Economic inequality (including housing); social protection (including health), education and employment, and family policies. Recognizing the role of gender and other identities, including intersectionality, we emphasize that persons' opportunities are influenced by this aspect. A shortcoming of the aggregated data presented on the gender pay gap and employment is that women are presented as one group, not separating between ethnicities or race. However, we highlight the ways in which such discrimination can take shape by looking at inequality, housing, health, education, and employment in the US.

Studies show that the Scandinavian countries have higher social mobility than the US. This is illustrated in the study by Jäntti et al. from 2006, which considers income mobility among father and son, and father and daughter. Measured in terms of IGE, where a higher value indicates lower social mobility, men in the US (0.517) had considerably lower mobility in comparison to Denmark (0.071), Norway (0.155), and Sweden (0.258) (Jäntti *et al.* 2006, 13). While mobility is higher for women in the US (0.283), women are more mobile in Denmark (0.034), Norway (0.114), and Sweden (0.191).

While overall mobility is higher in the Scandinavian states, the conditional probability of ending up in the lowest and highest quintile provides further insight into the mobility in the four countries (Jäntti *et al.* 2006, 18):

Tables 5.5 and 5.6 indicate two notable findings. First, the US has exceptionally low mobility for men at the bottom, an estimated 42 percent remain in the lowest quintile. In comparison, around 25 percent remain at the bottom in Denmark and Sweden and 28 percent in Norway. Second, fewer men and women of the lowest group make it to the top in the US, around 10 percent, while more than 14 percent reach the top quintile in Denmark, Norway, and Sweden.

If we look at the distribution of men and women fathered by men in the highest income group, visualized in Tables 5.7 and 5.8, we observe similarities between the four countries

Table 5.5 Distribution of men with father in the quintile lowest group (percentages) (conditional probability of being in the extreme diagonal and antidiagonal cells)

	Denmark	Norway	Sweden	US
Bottom	24.7	28.2	25.8	42.2
Top	14.4	11.9	10.9	7.9

Source: Jäntti *et al.* (2006, 18).

Table 5.6 Distribution women with father in lowest quintile group (percentages)

Quintile	Denmark	Norway	Sweden	US
Bottom	23.5	23.8	23.9	25.6
Top	16	14.3	14.5	9.7

Table 5.7 Distribution of women with father in the highest quintile group (percentages)

	Denmark	Norway	Sweden	US
Bottom	17.2	17.1	16.5	18
Top	32.0	31.3	32.3	33.8

Table 5.8 Distribution of men with father in the highest quintile group (percentages)

	Denmark	Norway	Sweden	US
Bottom	15.3	14.6	16.3	9.5
Top	36.3	35.4	37.1	36

as more than 30 percent of women and more than 35 percent of men remain at the top. Therefore, being born into the top quintile increases the likelihood of securing a high income to a significant degree. However, there are noteworthy differences between men and women in the US. While only around 9 percent of men from the top "relegate" to the bottom, the rate of women is almost twice that of men (18 percent). One factor that might explain this trend is that women's income is more influenced by their marriage status than vice versa.[19] However, as noted above, the findings on women are based on comparatively less data than for men, meaning that these numbers do not show the complete picture.

In the previous paragraphs, we have demonstrated that the Scandinavians have higher mobility, especially for the bottom than the US, even though there is low mobility at the top in all countries. These findings have also been supported in later studies.[20] Another interesting finding relates to the middle class in the US. A 2018 study by Palomino, Marrero, and Rodríguez shows that sons born into the bottom quantiles have especially low mobility (IGE of 0.645 and 0.567 for the 0.1 and 0.2 quantiles), meaning their opportunities to "move up" are strongly conditioned by their parents' income (Palomino, Marrero and Rodríguez 2018, 148–149). Similarly, mobility is low at the top quantiles (IGE of 0.424 and 0.476 for the 0.8 and 0.9 quantiles). However, the mobility of the middle quantiles is significantly higher, which is illustrated in Figure 5.2.

Therefore, sons with parents in the upper-middle part have higher mobility, being less conditioned by their parents' income than sons at the bottom and the top.

As we have seen, the US stands out as having low social mobility in comparison to the Scandinavian countries, even though its middle class is relatively mobile. In addition, social mobility is linked to race and ethnicity in the US. Academics have identified that black

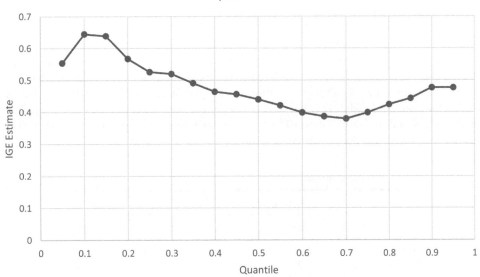

Figure 5.2 IGE by quantiles: Pooled regression analysis for the 1980–2010 period (baseline) in the US.[21]

Source: Data collected from Palomino, Marrero and Rodríguez (2018, 356–357).

Americans, in particular, have a lower mobility compared to white Americans.[22] Bhattacharya and Mazumder (2011, 335) argue, based on the relationship between the income of father and son, that the comparatively low upward mobility of black Americans is a key factor explaining the "interracial gap in economic status." Moreover, Chetty et al. (2014, 1607–1608) found that mobility was lower for all ethnicities in areas where large proportions of African Americans live, which is likely linked to the legacy of racial segregation.

These findings indicate that the US faces key challenges regarding direct and indirect forms of racial discrimination. For instance, African Americans have historically faced serious barriers in terms of employment, education, and wealth accumulation (Fox 2016, 708). In the following sections, we emphasize how past injustices committed against minorities in the US continue to negatively impact their opportunities.

Inequality

Inequality impacts social mobility through several mechanisms. The crudest mechanism is the transfer of capital through inheritance. This concerns various types of assets from stocks and bonds to housing. While it is widely accepted that education is important for channeling income inequality, it is less powerful when seeking to explain wealth gaps. Nordli Hansen and Toft (2021) hold that different social segments use different types of opportunity hoarding when class privilege is transmitted. While cultural capital is associated with education, families rich in money capital teach their children skills related to the use of leverage and tax planning. At the other end of the scale, poverty obviously impacts life chances since poor children can be hurt by social exclusion, the need to work, and downright hunger.

General differences in income inequality between the US and Scandinavian countries can be seen in Table 5.9, which is based on aggregated data from the OECD. The table contains an overview of the Gini coefficient and the so-called S80/S20 ratio, which is based on the ratio of the average income of the top quintile (top 20 percent) and those that have an average income of the bottom quintile (bottom 20 percent).

The table highlights that in 2017, the US had a higher Gini coefficient, which was 0.390 in 2017 and a higher S80/S20 ratio with 8.4. In 2017, the S80/S20 ratio for the US was twice that of Denmark (3.8), Norway (4.0), and Sweden (4.2). The Gini coefficient of the Scandinavian countries is relatively similar in Denmark (0.264), Norway (0.262), and Sweden (0.282). Data from the OECD shows that income inequality has remained relatively stable in the US between 2013 and 2017, whereas there has been a small increase in income inequality in all three Scandinavian countries. The US is, nevertheless, characterized by much higher income inequality than the Scandinavian countries.

Table 5.9 Income inequality

	Gini coefficient		S80/S20	
	2013	*2017*	*2013*	*2017*
Denmark	0.254	0.264	3.6	3.8
Norway	0.252	0.262	3.8	4.0
Sweden	0.268	0.282	4.0	4.2
United States	0.396	0.390	8.6	8.4

Source: OECD (2021c).

Ratio of children whose income falls below the poverty line

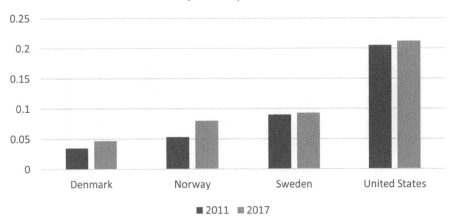

Figure 5.3   Ratio of children whose income falls below the poverty line, taken as half the median household income of the total population.[24]

Source: OECD (2021g).

Large income inequalities are intuitively associated with poverty, even if, in principle, it does not have to be that way. Since we are interested in equality of opportunity, child poverty is of particular interest to us. In fact, Esping-Andersen (2015, 137) argues that the eradication of child poverty is the main factor explaining a more equal opportunity structure in the Scandinavian countries.[23]

If we consider aggregated data from the OECD, the Scandinavian countries have been more successful in ensuring that children do not grow up in poverty than the US. As of 2017, the US's child poverty ratio remains higher than that of Denmark, Norway, and Sweden. Figure 5.3 shows that the US's child poverty ratio is more than twice that of Denmark, Norway, and Sweden.

Another worrying aspect of child poverty in the US is that black and Hispanic children are overrepresented in comparison to white and Asian children. As seen in Figure 5.4, the rate of black children living in poverty was close to 40 percent in 2013, while the rate was around 10 percent for Asian and white (not Hispanic) children. The rate of Hispanic children was also high at around 30 percent in 2013 (US Census Bureau 2021c). Even though the ratio of children living in poverty decreased between 2013 and 2020, the rate of Hispanic and black children far exceeds that of white and Asian children.

In addition to child poverty, the countries' general poverty rate is also of interest, as it impacts exposure to risk and, as we shall see, protection against it through mechanisms related to eligibility and ability to buy insurance. The poverty rate can be seen in Figure 5.5.

While all four countries had an increase in the poverty rate between 2013 and 2017, the US stands out with a particularly high rate. Similar to child poverty, general poverty in the US also shows differences depending on ethnic background, which is visible in Figure 5.6 (US Census Bureau 2021c). For example was the rate of Hispanic and black Americans living in poverty was more than twice that of white (not Hispanic) and Asian Americans.

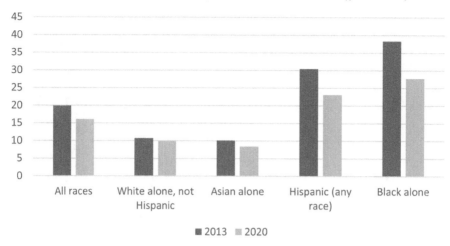

Figure 5.4 Poverty status of people under the age of 18 based on race and ethnicity in the US.[25]

Source: US Census Bureau (2021c).

As seen in the previous sections, the US has relatively high income inequality and poverty rate. The high ratio of children below the poverty line is particularly worrying, which likely negatively impacts their possibilities for gaining access to education and other mechanisms that improve their life conditions. Moreover, poverty disproportionality affects minority groups in the US. If we consider these indicators in connection with social mobility, those born at the bottom in the US are more likely to remain at the bottom and to live in poverty than what is the case in the Scandinavian countries.

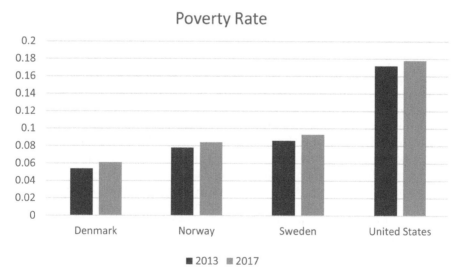

Figure 5.5 Poverty rate measured as the ratio of the number of people whose income falls below the poverty line, taken as half the median household income of the total population.

Source: OECD (2021g).

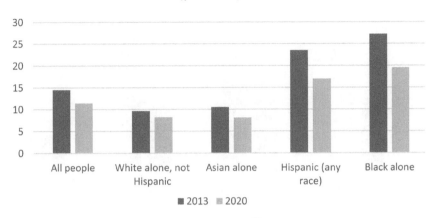

Figure 5.6 Poverty status by race and ethnicity in the US.[26]

Source: US Census Bureau (2021c).

Income vs. Wealth Inequality[27]

Wealth is extremely unevenly distributed in the US, even more so than income. Top 10 percent hold 70.7 of net personal wealth (while their income share is 45.5). The top one percent holds 34.9 (the corresponding income share is 18.8 percent), while the bottom 50 combined hold 1.5 percent of net wealth (and take home 13.3 percent of income) (WID 2020). After the publication in English of Piketty's (2014) Capital in the 20th century, inequality has risen on the academic and political agenda, but inter-racial inequality has, while acknowledged, not received the same amount of attention, at least not in Europe.[28]

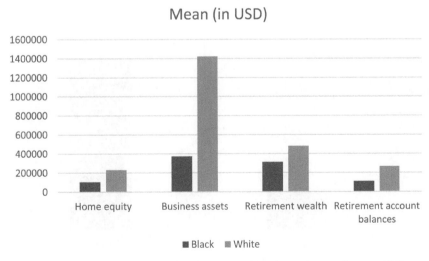

Figure 5.7 Share of US households with specific assets and conditional mean, by race, 2019.

Source: Weller and Figueroa (2021, 10).

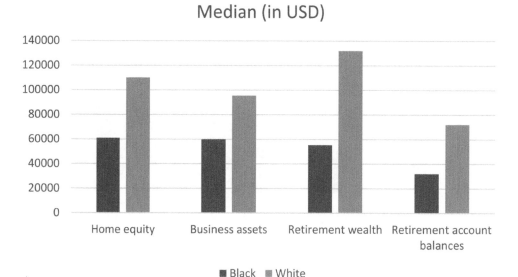

Figure 5.8 Share of US households with specific assets and median values of major assets, by race, 2019.

Source: Weller and Figueroa (2021, 10).

The single most striking fact is that white Americans hold more wealth than black Americans across all categories, as seen in Figures 5.7 and 5.8. A second observation is that this difference, while still substantial, is somewhat reduced as we move from mean to the median as our chosen indicator. This reflects the gross intra-white inequalities, which are also contained in the "colorblind" wealth inequality statistics given above. The third fact we want to highlight is the relative difference observed in the wealth category that is smallest in terms of the sums

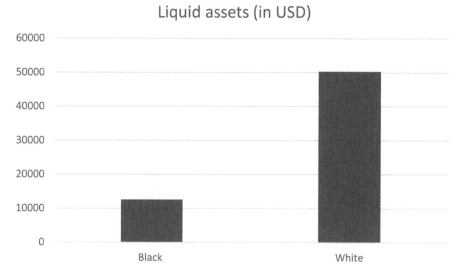

Figure 5.9 US households and distribution of liquid assets, by race, 2019.

Source: Weller and Figueroa (2021, 10).

involved, namely liquid assets, as visualized in Figure 5.9. Cash holdings and the like are the first buffer and what matters most for those living on the margin. While the median black household had only 1,300 USD in liquid savings, white households' median score on this measure was 7,850 USD as of 2019. This difference in financial vulnerability was important when the Pandemic struck. As Weller and Figueroa (2021) observe: "Black households were typically much less prepared for the pandemic and the myriad financial emergencies it created, including layoffs, caregiving needs, and worsening health outcomes"

Comparisons with the dramatically unequal US can pale Scandinavian income inequality into insignificance. Nonetheless, they deserve attention: As in many other countries, there are tendencies toward a trifurcation where the top runs away (particularly evident in Norway) and the bottom is left behind (particularly evident in Sweden) (Barth *et al.* 2020). While initial debates on inequality often talked in general terms, more recent contributions have shown that income and wealth inequality are not strongly associated and that countries with low income inequality may have very high levels of wealth inequality (e.g. Balestra and Tonkin 2018; Pfeffer and Waitkus 2021). In the OECD's database, the bottom 40 percent of households receive approximately 20 percent of generated income on average among OECD countries but hold only 3 percent of net wealth. Wealth is more concentrated at the top than income is. Among OECD countries, the top 10 percent doubles its share when you move from income to wealth. The top 10 percent of households in OECD countries hold, on average, 52 percent of net wealth, but "only" 24 percent of total income is held by the top 10 percent of the income distribution (Balestra and Tonkin 2018, 7).

Scandinavian wealth data paint the same picture; they indicate that these are less egalitarian societies than what the income data shows. Compared to income data, wealth data is hard to come by and often contested. Researchers, therefore, have to estimate the distribution of wealth, and there are different opinions about what should count toward wealth and how best to measure it. One topic is the value of using household wealth surveys in countries where no good administrative and tax data exist, as these surveys tend to overcount the rich. Another is whether or not to include the value of occupational and social security pensions.

Different wealth estimates used in Credit Suisse's reports, the OECD Wealth Distribution Database, and Piketty's World Income Database yield somewhat different rankings of the three Scandinavian countries (see Balestra and Tonkin 2018; Credit Suisse 2017; Zucman 2016). Yet even the lowest estimates of wealth inequality in Scandinavia show that these countries do not stand out in wealth inequality data as they still do in income inequality – even Sweden, with its rapidly rising income inequality, remains in the OECD's top ten most equal countries where income is concerned (OECD 2015).

This could be due to the fact that wealth data is more accurate in Scandinavia, given better administrative and tax register data, whereas other countries rely on household surveys. This could mean that current wealth inequality data more correctly represents wealth inequality in Scandinavia yet significantly undercounts wealth inequalities in countries such as the US. Norway still has a wealth tax and thus has comparatively good data on wealth, and Norwegian wealth inequality data are considered to be of high quality compared to most other countries (Zucman 2016, 39). While Denmark removed its wealth tax in 1996, it still collects comparatively good wealth data. A partial exception is Sweden, which does not have equally good wealth data, and is, in fact, not included in the OECD Wealth Distribution Database.

Yet, while it may be the case that other countries' wealth inequality may be systematically higher than reported, Scandinavian wealth inequality is still high in absolute terms and perhaps especially problematic given the ideals of the Nordic model. While Scandinavian wealth data may be comparatively better, these data still suffer from not counting "hidden" wealth.

Using data from the Swiss leaks, the Panama Papers, and data from tax amnesty programs in all three Scandinavian countries, Alstadsæther, Johannesen and Zucman (2019) show that while tax evasion on average is low in Scandinavia compared with other countries, the richest 0.01 percent of Scandinavian households evade 25 percent of their taxes. If this is the case, the top wealth share in Scandinavia is even higher than the comparatively good wealth data suggests.

Housing Wealth[29]

In Scandinavia, most people are still middle class in terms of income, and middle class people hold most of their wealth in houses. This is important both for individuals and households and for the economy as such. In Norway, for instance, the total housing stock (at market prices in 2019) has been estimated to be worth about 2.7 times that of Norway's GDP (Eggum and Røed Larsen 2021, 4). Pfeffer and Waitkus (2021) find the distribution of housing equity is most closely related to wealth inequality, further underscoring the importance of looking at housing market developments as a potential threat to social democratic models in Scandinavia. Interestingly, in the OECD dataset, countries with low homeownership rates on average have higher wealth inequality, even when the level of income inequality is low (Causa *et al.* 2019, 8–9).

This is because owning property leads to wealth accumulation and serves as financial security (Goodman and Mayer 2018; Mathä, Porpiglia and Ziegelmeyer 2017). Mathä, Porpiglia and Ziegelmeyer (2017) argue that homeownership is especially important for the middle quantiles measured by wealth. The homeownership rate in the US and the Scandinavian countries is comparable, with the exception of Norway.

Figure 5.10 shows that in 2019, Denmark had the lowest homeownership rate with 60.8 percent owning their home, while the US had a slightly higher rate of 65.4 percent in 2021. Norway stands out with a particularly high rate of 80.3 percent as of 2019. A report by OECD on Housing Tenure showed that Norway has an exceptionally high number of owners with

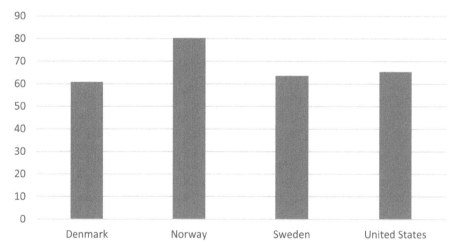

Figure 5.10 Homeownership rate in 2019.[30]

Source: Based on data from Eurostat (2021) (Denmark, Norway, and Sweden) and US Census Bureau (2021a) (the US).

mortgage, estimated around 50 percent (OECD no date, 1). The report also showed that there is a large difference based on wealth and income in all countries, meaning that those at the top measured by income are more likely to own property (OECD no date, 3). For example, around 95 percent of the top quantile own their dwelling in Norway (OECD no date, 3). These findings hold that a majority of individuals in the Scandinavian countries and the US do own their homes.

This illustrates that average ownership rates do not tell the full story. In the US, for example, there are large differences in the homeownership rate of minorities. In 2021, only 44 percent of black households owned their own home, while the rate was 74.2 percent of non-Hispanic white households, as seen in the Figure 5.11. The rate of black Americans was the lowest of all measured ethnicities in the US, however, the rate of Hispanic and Asian, Native, Hawaiian, and Pacific Americans was also lower than for white Americans.

This data supports findings of racial discrimination in the housing market in the US. Besbris and Faber (2017) found that real estate agents in New York perpetuate racial or ethnic segregation, meaning they often make decisions based on the potential buyer's ethnicity. For instance, real estate agents were more present in wealthier neighborhoods than in poorer neighborhoods, which tend to be non-Hispanic white and Asian neighborhoods (Besbris and Faber 2017, 870). As real estate agents in the US serve a key role in determining which neighborhoods viewers will see, their work is central to the "distribution of people in the housing market," meaning they have incentives to "steer" (Besbris and Faber 2017, 850). Discrimination in the housing market has severely negative impacts on minorities in the US, which reduces their opportunities and possibilities to accumulate wealth and financial security at the same level as non-Hispanic whites.

A similar, if not ethnicity-based mechanism can be found in Scandinavian housing markets. While wages have been rising across the income distribution, housing prices have been rising even more. Sweden ranked third globally on price-to-income ratio in 2018. Norway ranked

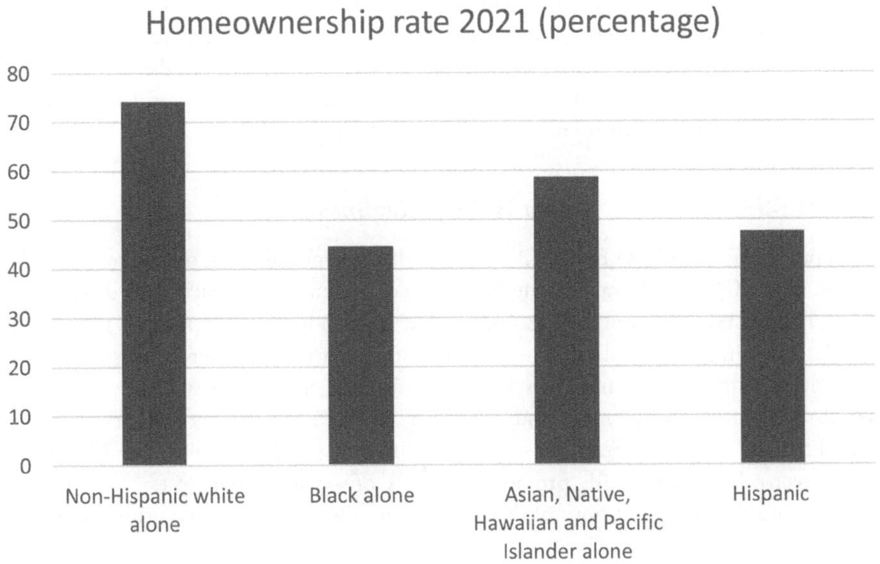

Figure 5.11 Homeownership rates by ethnicity in the US.

Source: Based on data from US Census Bureau (2021d).

9th, and Denmark 19th (having come down following their housing bust in 2009). Increased unaffordability has not yet caused a decline in homeownership, but we have seen an increase in debt levels and in the reliance on parental help.

As house prices continue to rise faster than wages, inequality dynamics are set in motion. Two fault lines are deepened in this process. The first is generational, between older haves and younger have-nots. This, in turn, increases the demand for help from "The Bank of Mum and Dad" (BoMad). The second fault line is geographical. Financialization and urbanization may not be causally linked, but they are running in tandem, widening the price gap between urban and non-urban property. In the Norwegian case, this trend was documented and highly specified based on a sample of 77,000 properties over the 2007–2019 period found large generational and geographic differences in capital gains (Eggum and Røed Larsen, 2021). They found firstly that the earlier you bought, the stronger the capital gains, and secondly, that there were large differences between those who held properties in Oslo versus those outside the capital. The most pronounced difference in terms of equality of opportunity thus appears between those seeking entry into urban markets with and without parents possessing urban housing capital that will be passed on to the next generation.

The Norwegian case suggests that homebuyers with parental help enter the market with less debt and far more valuable housing than those without. For those renting, rents are high and without the tax subsidies offered to house owners. In 2018, Norway ranked first on rental unaffordability (median rents as percentage of disposable income) in the OECD. Sweden was fourth, and Denmark ninth (Balestra and Tonkin 2018). Denmark and Sweden still have some rent controls, but in all three countries, we see an increased risk of getting stuck in a renter's trap, that is inability to get on the property ladder at all (Tranøy *et al.* 2020).

Scandinavian countries have traditionally had sets of policies that make it easier for the young to leave the parental home early (Flynn 2020). However, the first-time buyer may now find it more and more difficult to get on the property ladder. Even on a median income, a single person household can today find it difficult to buy even a small apartment in one of the three Nordic capitals without parental help. Those at the top of the income distribution, who already own their primary dwelling, will increasingly see property as an attractive investment and an important part of their asset portfolio (along with stocks and bonds). When this is an investment in residential property, we can expect a growth in the buy-to-let market and a higher proportion of landlords owning more than one property.

Two Welfare-Regimes

Since the publication of Gøsta Esping-Andersen's (1990) seminal work on welfare capitalisms, the notion of the US as a liberal and the Nordic one as social democratic, this distinction has been the obvious starting point for exercises such as ours. The key difference is that while the Nordics have several – often flat rate – universalistic institutions where inclusion is granted through citizenship, the US model is residual, meaning that those who are not provided welfare through their employment and purchases made in the market are served by means tested and modest programs. Another important difference is that while in the Nordic states, the public sector has traditionally provided the bulk of services itself, in the US, the private sector dominates service provision, with what this entails in terms of variation of both price and quality.

Some scholars have questioned the received view of the US regime (Alber 2010; Howard 2021). Not so much arguing against the notion that the welfare state for the poor is residual as a warning against underestimating how the middle class is served by a "hidden welfare state." It is hidden because it is a no-show in statistical measures that do not include tax expenditures. This spending subsidizes and bolsters the value of the health and pension programs provided by employers. In addition to tax expenditures, Alber argues that when comparing social spending, analysts should also factor in how much welfare states claw back of what they spend by taxing benefits. Furthermore, regulation in the form of governments mandating private employers to provide benefits and charitable giving is not irrelevant for this discussion.

In a later contribution, Esping-Andersen argues that the main purpose of the Nordic model has not been to achieve equality of outcome or necessarily high social mobility, but rather that welfare provisions have been implemented to achieve other goals, such as general social protection and income maintenance (Esping-Andersen 2015, 125). However, there has been a shift at the end of the 20th century, when the Nordic states implemented education reforms, efforts to eradicate child poverty, and promote female employment and parental leave with the goal of promoting equality of opportunity (Esping-Andersen 2015, 125). Comparatively, the Scandinavian countries place greater emphasis on such policy goals than other states (Esping-Andersen 2015, 125).

If one disregards the net effect of how the tax system is used, the Scandinavian welfare states look much larger and more generous than the US welfare regime. This is interesting if one wants to compare how much of a society's resources is spent on welfare. For us, however, the more pertinent question is, generous to whom? That is, what groups are shielded from life risk, and to what degree?

The US economy is considerably more unequal and volatile than the Scandinavian countries' economies (Alesina and Glaeser, 2006). Not being sufficiently protected against risks, such as against the cost of unemployment and illness, can be especially damaging for those at the bottom quantiles in a volatile economy. When looking at the states' social expenditure, we can see clear differences in how much the US, on the one hand, and the Scandinavian countries, on the other, spend on pensions, health care, unemployment, labor market programs, housing, family provisions, and other social policy areas.

Table 5.10 shows that the four countries spend more on social protection today than in 1980. In 2019, Denmark spent the most on social programs with 28.3 percent of its GDP, whereas the US spent the least with 18.7 percent. Norway and Sweden spent around 25 percent in 2019. While the Scandinavian countries have a range of social programs, the US's spending goes primarily to social security and Medicare (Alber, 2010, 107).

Social Security

Social security protects individuals against financial insecurity and poverty. The US does not have comparatively lower expenditure in all areas. When it comes to public expenditure on

Table 5.10 Social Expenditure (percentage of GDP)

	1980	1990	2000	2005	2010	2015	2016	2017	2018	2019
Denmark	20.3	21.9	23.8	25.2	29.6	29.9	29.3	29.2	28.7	28.3
Norway	16.1	21.6	20.4	20.7	22.1	24.8	26.0	25.2	24.4	25.3
Sweden	24.5	26.9	26.5	27.1	25.9	26.2	26.6	26.0	25.8	25.5
United States	12.9	13.2	14.1	15.5	19.1	18.5	18.6	18.4	18.2	18.7

Source: OECD (2021e).

Table 5.11 Public expenditure on old-age and survivors' cash benefits (percentage of GDP)

	1980	1990	2000	2005	2010	2015	2017
Denmark	5.7	6.1	6.3	6.5	7.1	8.1	8.0
Norway	4.5	5.5	4.7	4.8	5.2	6.6	6.9
Sweden	6.6	7.2	6.8	7.2	7.2	7.1	7.2
United States	6.0	5.8	5.7	5.7	6.6	7.0	7.1

Source: OECD (2021e).

old-age and survivors cash benefits, the US spends around the same as the Scandinavian countries measured in percentage of GDP, which can be seen in Table 5.11.

Through the social security program in the US, in 2022, "workers with maximum-taxable earnings" can receive a monthly benefit of up to 2,364 USD if retiring at age 62 and up to 3,568 if retiring at age 67 (US Social Security Administration, no date b). The highest benefit is for those retiring at age 72, granting a benefit of 4,194 USD. The key difference here centers on how you qualify. In the Scandinavian countries, all citizens are guaranteed a minimum pension independently of your status in the labor market, while in the US you have to pay in, in order to qualify for social security. The other key difference is the way tax breaks for supplementary pensions are structured. US tax expenditures for supplementary pensions are de facto more excluding (if your employer does not provide pension benefits, you have no access) and thus have a stronger middle class and upwards bias than corresponding schemes in Scandinavia.

In addition to the previously mentioned schemes in the US, persons with disabilities or over the age of 65 with limited income may qualify for Supplemental Security Income (SSI) (US Social Security Administration no date a). While coverage differs between the states, in 2021, individuals and children that qualify for SSI could receive up to 794 USD, and couples could receive up to 1,191 USD per month. In contrast to social security benefits, the Supplement Security Income is not based on previous earnings.

If we also consider unemployment benefits, the generosity of the four countries differs to some extent. Data from 2020 shows that Denmark had the most generous benefits, with a replacement rate of 82 in unemployment benefits after two months, six months, and one year (OECD 2021a). Norway had a replacement rate of 68 after two months, six months, and one year, while the rate drops significantly to 23 after five years. Sweden has a consistent replacement rate regardless of how long a person has been unemployed with 59 percent. While the US is relatively generous after two months with a rate of 54, it stands out as it barely grants unemployment benefits after six months. However, the replacement rate differs depending on the state. For instance, Alabama has a replacement rate that is 1/26th of previous income, the minimum income is 45 USD per month, and the maximum is 275 USD (Yin, Wheatley and Tuytel 2020). In comparison, persons living in Massachusetts can receive a weekly benefit of up to 50 percent of previous earnings. The minimum benefit amounts to 98 USD, and the maximum benefit could be up to 1,234 USD.

Even though the US has unemployment benefits, the aggregated data from OECD does not capture the fact that few unemployed Americans actually receive these benefits. According to Pew Research Center, only around 29 percent of unemployed Americans received benefits in March 2020 (Desilver 2020). Massachusetts had the highest share of unemployed receiving benefits with around 66 percent, while this was the case for around 8 percent of unemployed living in Florida (Desilver 2020).

Health Care

Spending on social programs does not alone determine how effectively life risks are mitigated. This is strikingly clear if one compares health care costs relative to performance in the US. Health care in Denmark, Norway, and Sweden is based on universal access and bar a small co-pay element, free and provided by the public sector. The US system is based on a mixture of private insurance and public programs, such as Medicaid. According to data from the OECD (2021e), the US spends a higher percentage of its GDP on health care than any other OECD country. In 2019, Germany was second in terms of expenditure on health with 11.7 percent of its GDP, which was still considerably lower than the US, which spent 16.8 percent of its GDP (OECD 2021e). In a recent comparison of health care system performance in 11 high income countries (Schneider *et al.* 2021), the US came last by a huge margin. It ranked last on access to care, administrative efficiency, equity, and health care outcomes but second on measures of care process. Norway topped the table, Sweden achieved an average score, while the US was an outlier. Much more expensive, much worse results.

As seen in Figure 5.12, the US spends around 6 percentage points more of its GDP on health care than Denmark, Norway, and Sweden. Or put differently: The US spends about 50 percent more of its GDP on health. In 2018, data from the US government shows that 91.5 percent of Americans are part of some form of health plan, 67.3 percent have private insurance, and 34.4 percent are part of a public plan, such as Medicare or Medicaid (US Census Bureau 2019). However, around 8.5 percent or 27 million people do not have any form of health insurance, meaning they are particularly vulnerable in case they are injured or sick. There is a higher share of uninsured in the bottom quintile, increasing their vulnerability if they fall sick (Alber 2010, 109).

The US has several health care plans, the three main pillars of which are Medicaid for the poorest, Medicare for the elderly, and employer-based plans (Alber 2010, 108). While Medicare and Medicaid are public programs, beneficiaries still pay "premiums" to have access to health care. On top of this, the sums involved for deductibles or co-pay are at a completely different

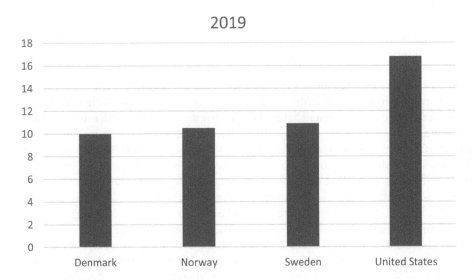

Figure 5.12 Expenditure on health (share of GDP).

Source: OECD (2021e).

level in the US compared to the Scandinavian countries. Thus, a relatively poor person with insurance will still most likely go broke if he or she is afflicted by a serious illness in the US.

Medicare is a federal health insurance program for Americans over the age of 65, some young persons with disabilities, and people with end-stage renal disease. The "premium" varies depending on whether a person or a spouse has paid so-called Medicare taxes (US Government no date b). In 2021, if a person has not paid Medicare taxes for a certain amount of time, he or she will have to pay up to 471 USD per month for "hospital insurance," which includes hospital stays, stay in nursing facility, and hospice care. In order to get additional coverage, so-called "medical insurance" that covers doctors' service, medical supplies, and outpatient care, all beneficiaries must pay at least 148 USD per month (US Government no date b). Despite the costs of paying for Medicare, 99 percent of those over the age of 64 have insurance (Keisler-Starkey and Bunch 2021, 5).

Medicaid is an option for Americans with limited income and resources, funded by the federal and state governments and administered by the state governments (US Government no date a). While there are some general federal requirements, states can determine if they want to offer certain optional benefits, meaning that coverage varies greatly between states (US Government no date a). The coverage of Medicaid was expanded with the Patient Protection and Affordable Care Act (Obamacare), giving the option for states to include adults who fall under 138 percent of the poverty line (Keisler-Starkey and Bunch 2021, 9).

However, 15 states did not expand the eligibility of Medicaid, consequently, individuals in these states are more likely to be uninsured (Keisler-Starkey and Bunch 2021, 9). In 2020, around 17 percent were uninsured in the bottom quintile in "expansion states," while almost 38 percent were uninsured in the bottom quintile in "non-expansion states" (Keisler-Starkey and Bunch 2021, 10). Those that fall below "100 percent of poverty," meaning the bottom quintile in the US, are in general more likely to lack health insurance. While only 3.4 percent were uninsured at the top quintile, 17.2 percent have no form of insurance at the bottom quintile (Keisler-Starkey and Bunch 2021, 9). This means that Medicaid does not cover those that fall below the poverty line, despite being developed to assist Americans with limited income and resources.

There are also large differences based on ethnicity and "nativity." In 2020, only 7.7 percent of non-Hispanic whites lacked insurance, while 14.3 percent of black Americans and 24.9 percent of Hispanics were uninsured (Keisler-Starkey and Bunch 2021, 13).

When it comes to having equal opportunities, having employer-based health insurance limits individuals' opportunities to change jobs, meaning that the employer holds significant power over its employees. Moreover, they are particularly vulnerable if they become unemployed. For example, around 5.4 million Americans lost their health insurance between February and May of 2020 due to the COVID-19 pandemic, putting them at additional financial risks if, for example, hospitalized from COVID-19 (Stolberg 2021). While a majority most likely qualify for Medicare, affording the premium costs to get access to coverage is not realistic for many (Stolberg 2021). (As health care is not tied to employment in Denmark, Norway, and Sweden, individuals have the opportunity of changing jobs without worrying about losing affordable access to health care). This section on health care in the US demonstrates that high expenditure on health does not necessarily translate into high coverage.

That the US health care system falls behind the systems in Denmark, Norway, and Sweden is particularly visible when looking at maternal health. Data from the World Health Organization (WHO) shows that the US has an exceptionally high rate of maternal mortality in comparison to the Scandinavian states and other Western European states (World Health Organization 2021b). The aggregated numbers are presented in Figure 5.13.

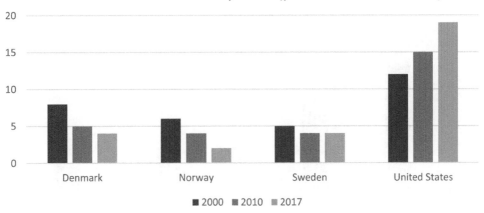

Figure 5.13 Maternal mortality ratio (per 100,000 live births).

Source: World Health Organization (2021b).

Figure 5.13 shows that the US stands out in comparison to Denmark, Norway, and Sweden. In 2017, the maternal mortality ratio was around five times higher in the US than it was in Denmark and Sweden. In 2017, Norway had the lowest maternal mortality ratio with 2 deaths per 100,000 live births, compared to 19 in the US. Another striking aspect is that the mortality ratio in the US has progressively increased between 2000 and 2017, while it decreased in Denmark, Norway, and Sweden. While the Centers for Disease Control and Prevention are unsure of the reasons behind the increase in the mortality rate, which can be due to improved data collection rather than a worsening of maternal health, it is beyond doubt that American women are more likely to die giving birth than women in Denmark, Norway, and Sweden (Centers for Disease Control and Prevention 2020).

Data from the Centers for Disease Control and Prevention further reveals the extent of racial discrimination in the US and how it affects individuals' health. While this chapter does not examine all differences between health outcomes of minorities in the US, the example of maternal mortality highlights the worrying consequences of underlying racial inequalities. Figure 5.14 presents data from Centers for Disease Control and Prevention on pregnancy-related mortality ratio for the years 2014–2017.

The figure shows that the US has a particularly high mortality ratio for black women, measured in deaths per 100,000 live births, with 41.7 compared to 13.4 for white women and 11.6 for Hispanic or Latino women. Black women in the US are, on average, three times more likely to die giving birth than white women in the US. In comparison to the Scandinavian countries, this ratio is ten times higher than in Denmark and Sweden and more than twenty times higher than in Norway (as the Norwegian ratio is very low).

Studies on maternal health tend to highlight the connection to the infant mortality ratio,[31] which demonstrates another area of differences between the US and the Scandinavian states worth considering here. Data from the WHO details the infant mortality ratio, referring to the likelihood of a child dying between birth and age one (World Health Organization 2021a).

These data show that the infant mortality ratio decreased in all four countries between 1990 and 2019, while the US's mortality rate has been significantly higher than the rate in Denmark, Norway, and Sweden. In 2019, the US had a rate of 5.56 of infants dying per 1,000

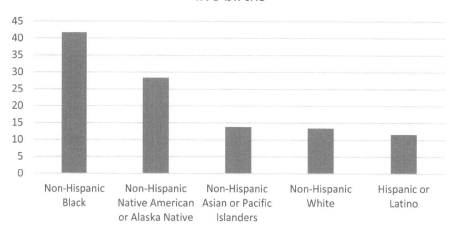

Pregnancy-related mortality ratio per 100 000 live births

Figure 5.14   Pregnancy-related mortality ratio by ethnicity United States 2014–2017.

Source: Centers for Disease Control and Prevention (2020).

living birth, while Norway had the lowest rate with 1.98, followed by Sweden with a rate of 2.08 and Denmark with a rate of 3.24.

The poorer health of American women in comparison to women in Scandinavian countries is related to the general state of the American health care system and, for minority women, racial discrimination, which affects their civil, political, economic, and social rights, as discussed above. Human rights organizations, such as Human Rights Watch, continue to underline that women in the US die from preventable maternal deaths, as well as gynecological cancer-related deaths (Human Rights Watch 2020). Therefore, minority women in the US face additional challenges and health consequences primarily due to their ethnicity. The findings in this section also demonstrate that the US lags behind the Scandinavian countries when it comes to ensuring women's basic right to health overall.

In the previous section, we have discussed issues relating to female health in the US. If we briefly consider general trends in health and quality of life, we notice further challenges and differences between the four countries. For instance, aggregated data from the OECD shows that life expectancy is lower in the US than in Denmark, Norway, and Sweden (OECD 2022). All four countries have a higher life expectancy for women than men, as seen in Figure 5.15. In 2019, men in the US had the lowest life expectancy at birth at 76, compared to 80 for men in Denmark, 81 for men in Norway, and 82 for men in Sweden.

According to data from the CDC, black Americans had a lower life expectancy than white and Hispanic Americans (Arias, Tejada-Vera and Ahmad 2021). For example, in 2020, the life expectancy of black men was 68 compared to 77 for Hispanic men and 76 for white men (Arias, Tejada-Vera and Ahmad 2021). This gap indicates that racial discrimination has serious consequences for the overall health of black Americans.

When it comes to quality of life, the suicide rates in all four countries show that they currently face serious challenges regarding mental health. In 2021, data from the World Population Review (2021), based on the WHO, held that the US had the highest suicide rate with 16.1 per 100,000 people. The rate was comparatively high in Sweden, which had a rate

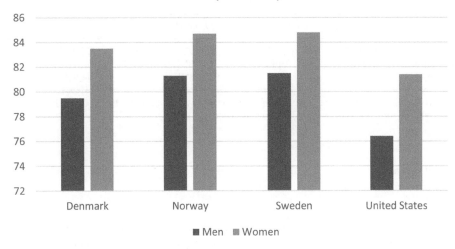

Figure 5.15 Life expectancy at birth.

Source: OECD (2022).

of 14.7 per 100,000 people. Denmark, with a rate of 10.7, and Norway, 11.8, had the lowest suicide rate. However, all four countries have a higher rate than the world's average (9.48).

Despite the high suicide rate, the Scandinavian countries are ranked among the "happiest countries in the world," according to the World Population Review (2021), based on the World Happiness Report. The index relies on six variables: GDP per capita, "social support," "healthy life expectancy," "freedom to make your own life choices," "generosity of the general population," and perception of corruption in the country (World Population Review 2021). While the index generalizes the conditions in the four countries, it highlights differences in how well they ensure a good quality of life for their citizens. In 2021, Denmark was ranked second, Norway ranked sixth, and Sweden seventh.[32] The US received a comparable lower ranking at 19 out of 146 countries (World Population Review 2021).

Education and Employment

Education is often the first factor referred to by analysts seeking to explain social mobility. Certain forms of education, such as a high rate of civic literacy, are an important source of social capital that matters to politics and political participation as well as to the sustenance of complex and comprehensive welfare states. The Nordic states score high on civic literacy, which matter for the public support for comprehensive, complex publicly funded welfare arrangements.[33]

In the following, we focus on education's role in social mobility. Recent research indicates that education tends to hold for income mobility, while education impacts wealth mobility much less, if at all. The relevance of education for a discussion of life risk is not, however, restricted to income and wealth effects. It can also impact health outcomes (via learned habits and knowledge about how lifestyle impacts health, working hours, and risk of falling in harm's way at work).

Some studies show that the influence of family background on educational attainment is similar in some Scandinavian countries; Denmark and the US (Landersø and Heckman 2017).

Table 5.12 The odds of attaining upper-secondary education among children of low educated fathers. Comparing three cohorts (logistic odds ratios)

	United States	United Kingdom	Denmark	Norway	Sweden	Germany
1970s cohort	0.115***	0.185***	0.449**	0.661*	0.320**	0.094***
1950s cohort	0.097***	0.153***	0.248***	0.447**	0.164***	0.067***
1940s cohort	0.133***	0.162***	0.213***	0.205***	0.091***	0.098***

Source: IALS. Cohort 1 is born after 1970; cohort 2, 1955–1964; cohort 3, in the 1940s. Controls for cognitive abilities, sex, and immigrant status (cited in Esping-Andersen (2015)).

Notes:

★=0.05,

★★=0.01,

★★★=0.001 or better.

IALS: International Adult Literacy Survey (from Esping-Andersen (2015))

Esping-Andersen, however, holds that the Scandinavian countries had improved social mobility in education (Esping-Andersen 2015). He argues that Scandinavian countries have improved the opportunities for those at the bottom to have access to higher education, which does not necessarily reduce the wealth gap. Nordli Hansen and Toft (2021) found that education is not a factor explaining wealth gaps, while it does impact income equality.

The following presents evidence from Esping-Andersen's study, highlighting the role of education and intergenerational income mobility (Table 5.12). Through an examination of the three birth cohorts (father-son) from 1940s, 1950s, and 1970s in Denmark, Germany, Norway, Sweden, the United Kingdom, and the US, Esping-Andersen found that the likelihood of a son attaining education based on the father's social origin was comparatively low in Denmark and Norway in the 1940s, while Sweden had a stronger social origin effect than the US.

Implementation of education reforms appears to have had an effect in Sweden for those born in the 1970s, where the odds of attaining upper-secondary education of children of low educated fathers had by then greatly surpassed that of the US. The odds of attaining higher education have also greatly improved in Denmark and Norway for those born in the 1970s; it had tripled in Norway and doubled in Denmark in comparison to those born in the 1940s. For the US, the odds for those born in the 1970s had slightly decreased. Therefore, the difference between the Scandinavian countries and the US is significant: those born in the 1970s were four times more likely to obtain upper-secondary education in Denmark, six times more likely in Norway, and three times more likely in Sweden than in the US when looking at children of low educated fathers (Esping-Andersen 2015, 128). The higher odds in the Scandinavian countries coincide with the implementation of public investment in education, directly by expanding the institutions that provide higher education, but also indirectly through student financing and student welfare (Esping-Andersen 2015, 128). However, it is difficult to attribute the precise effect of education reform as income equalization and reduction of poverty took place at the same time (Esping-Andersen 2015, 128).

Esping-Andersen has also collected newer data on Denmark, Norway, France, Italy, and Spain from the EU-SILC database of 2006 (Esping-Andersen 2015, 130). He highlights that it is challenging to determine the social origin effects of younger generations in terms of income, as it might be too early to measure their "generational" income (Esping-Andersen 2015, 130). The higher education level can be seen as a measure of the indirect origin effect (Esping-Andersen 2015, 130).

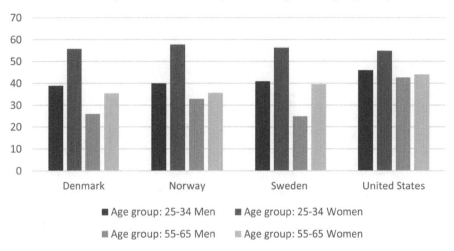

Tertiary education in percentage of age group

Legend:
- ■ Age group: 25-34 Men
- ■ Age group: 25-34 Women
- ■ Age group: 55-65 Men
- ■ Age group: 55-65 Women

Figure 5.16   Tertiary education in percentage of age group (2019 or latest available).

Source: OECD (2021f).

When examining the current education rate in the US and the Scandinavian countries, we identify that all four countries have a comparable education rate for the age group of 25–34 for both genders measured, see Figure 5.16. Moreover, the US had a comparatively higher percentage of individuals with higher education among those aged between 55 and 65.

However, educational attainment in the US differs between ethnicities. In 2015, based on data from the US Census Bureau, educational attainment was highest among Asian Americans, while black and Hispanic Americans had significantly lower attainment (Ryan and Bauman 2016, 2). In 2015, over 50 percent of Asian Americans over the age of 24 had a bachelor's degree or more, while this was the case for around 35 percent of white (non-Hispanic). In comparison, only an estimated 20 percent of black Americans and 15 percent of Hispanic Americans had obtained a bachelor's degree or more.

Figure 5.17 indicates that Asian and white (non-Hispanic) are more likely to have access to higher education than black and Hispanic Americans.[34] This aspect has negative implications on the opportunities of black and Hispanic Americans.

If we return to looking at gender and employment, an interesting point is that more women than men take tertiary education in all four countries, which should, in theory, increase their possibilities of earning a higher income. While women are relatively well educated, fewer women than men are employed in the four countries, as seen in Table 5.13.

The employment rate of men was similar across all four countries in 2019. However, Denmark, Norway, and the US have a gender gap with a lower rate of women being employed. The largest gap between men and women is found in the US. In 2000, the US had a gap of 12.84 percentage points. In Denmark, the gap was 9.2 in favor of men. Similarly, Norway had a gender gap of 7.7 percentage points in 2000. Sweden had the smallest gap, which decreased from 4.1 percentage points in 2000 to 3.4 in 2019. In 2019, the reduction of the gender gap appears to be a result of a decrease in the employment rate of men rather than an increase in women's employment rate in Denmark, Norway, and the US, while Sweden increased its employment rate of both women and men between 2000 and 2019.

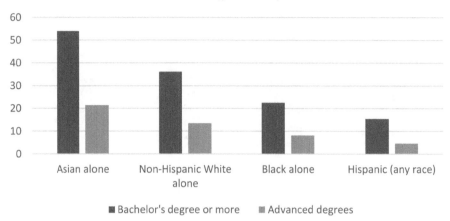

Educational Attainment of the Population Aged 25 and Older (percent) in 2015

■ Bachelor's degree or more   ■ Advanced degrees

Figure 5.17   Educational attainment of the population aged 25 and older (percent) in 2015 in the US.

Source: US Census Bureau (2021b).

Nonetheless, while the employment rate in the US and Scandinavian countries is comparable, there are significant differences in terms of hours in paid work, as seen in Figure 5.18. For instance, few Scandinavians work long hours, i.e. exceeding 50 hours per week, while this is not the case in the US, particularly for American men. In 2019, whereas less than one percent of women worked long hours in all Scandinavian countries, the US had a rate of 6.71. In 2019, the rate for Scandinavian men was less than 3, while the US's rate was 15.04. This shows that the Scandinavian countries have a "better" work-life balance.

Another aspect when it comes to time spent in employment is connected to the full-time employment rate. Americans are more likely to work full-time than Scandinavians. In 2019, data from OECD (Figure 5.19) on full-time equivalent employment rates shows that the US had the highest rate of full-time employment for men and the second highest rate for women, after Sweden (OECD 2021e), illustrated below.

With the exception of Sweden, fewer women in Denmark and Norway are employed in full-time positions than in the US. Teigen and Skjeie also note that the Scandinavian

Table 5.13   Employment rate in percentage of working age population (age 15–64)

	Employment rate			
	2000		2019	
	Men	*Women*	*Men*	*Women*
Denmark	80.9	71.7	78.1	72.2
Norway	81.3	73.6	77.4	73.1
Sweden	76.3	72.2	78.8	75.4
United States	80.6	67.8	76.5	66.3

Source: OECD (2021b).

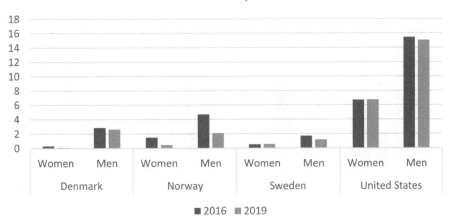

Figure 5.18   Employment rate.

Source: OECD (2021b).

countries have a fairly large proportion of women employed in part-time work (Teigen and Skjeie 2017, 135). While part-time positions may be a reason explaining the comparatively higher female employment rate in the Scandinavian countries, this is not necessarily a positive trend when it comes to achieving gender equality in this area (Teigen and Skjeie 2017, 135). For instance, it can reduce the demand for full-time positions in the labor market, leading to fewer opportunities for securing full-time work (Teigen and Skjeie 2017, 135).

As we have seen, more women have higher education than men in the respective countries. However, women continue to make less money. In 2019, based on data from the OECD

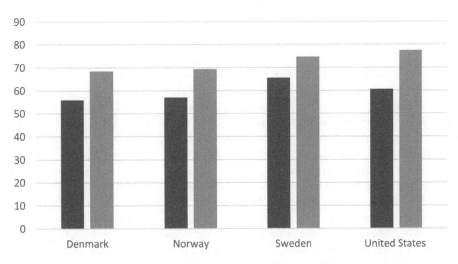

Figure 5.19   Full-time equivalent employment rate (40 hours per week), those 15–64.

Source: OECD (2021e).

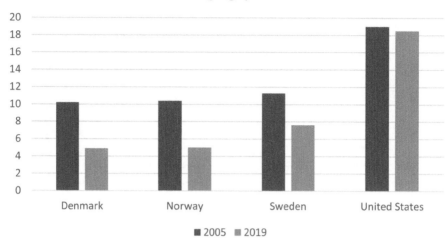

Figure 5.20   Gender wage gap at median: Based on gross earnings of full-time employees by earnings deciles (upper limits).

Source: OECD (2021e).

(2021e), the gender wage gap was drastically higher for all the examined quintiles in the US than the gap in Denmark, Norway, and Sweden. For the wage gap at the median, all four countries decreased their gap between 2005 and 2019. Sweden had the largest gap of the Scandinavian countries with 7.6 in 2019, which was still lower than the US's gap at 18.5. This constitutes a gap that is more than twice that of Sweden and three times the gap of Denmark and Norway, as visualized in Figure 5.20.

As Figure 5.20 shows, the US stands out with a comparatively high gender wage gap at the median. Another worrying aspect is the difference in pay gap attributable to ethnicity and gender in the US. According to a report by Pew Research Center, which looks at median hourly earnings, black Americans earned 75 percent as much as white Americans, while women only earned 83 percent as much as men in 2015 (Patten 2016) Asian men had the highest hourly earnings at the median (24 USD), followed by white men (21 USD). These two groups out-earned women and black and Hispanic men. Hispanic women had the lowest hourly earnings (12 USD), which was marginally lower than the earnings of black women (13 USD). In comparison, black men earned 15 USD, and Hispanic men earned 14 USD on average in 2015 (Patten 2016). As we saw above, black and Hispanic Americans have lower rates of tertiary education than white and Asian Americans, which could potentially explain the significant pay gap. Having said that, gender and ethnicity have an impact on a person's earnings also among those who have a bachelor's degree or more (Patten 2016). For instance, black and Hispanic women earn around 70 percent per hour of that of white men with similar education, while white women, black men, and Hispanic men earn around 80 percent of that of white men (Patten 2016). This example shows that women and minority groups, with the exception of Asian men, face additional barriers when it comes to employment in the US in comparison to white men. This was especially the case of minority women, who experienced discrimination due to both their ethnicity or race and gender.

Based on the data presented here, it is clear that the Scandinavian countries have achieved more equality between the genders in terms of employment and wage, in addition to having a better work-life balance than the US. However, none of the countries has achieved a gender balance, still placing women at a disadvantage in comparison to men.

Family Policies

While the US has implemented some measures to enhance women's opportunities, the Scandinavian countries outperform the US when it comes to family policies to enhance gender equality, economic equity, and maternal health, as seen above. Despite shortcomings in all four states, it is beyond doubt that the US falls behind the Scandinavian countries when it comes to meeting its obligations to ensure the rights of women.

The welfare provisions in the Scandinavian countries, including parental leave and subsidized childcare, are often emphasized as a factor explaining the high inclusion of women in paid work in these countries (Teigen and Skjeie 2017, 125–126).

Family policies that aim to reduce or alter women's share of unpaid work and childcare, in which women carry a disproportionate burden, can increase their opportunities in employment and political participation. Moreover, they are beneficial to men, increasing their opportunity to, for example, take part in their children's lives. While Denmark, Norway, and Sweden have generous universal childcare systems and provisions for parental leave (Esping-Andersen 2015, 126; Teigen and Skjeie 2017, 140), similar provisions are absent in the US. The family policies differ significantly between the US and Scandinavia. In Scandinavia, these policies have generally improved women's opportunities to take part in employment on a similar basis as men (even though there is still a gap), while the lack of such policies negatively influences women's opportunities in the US. We identified a particularly striking difference between the US and the Scandinavian countries when it comes to parental leave arrangements.

The US stands out – not only in comparison to the Scandinavian countries but also to the rest of the OECD countries – in that it is the only state that does not offer women paid maternity leave at a national level (OECD 2019, 2). Instead, the US offers an option for unpaid maternity leave. The Family and Medical Leave Act of 1993 grants employees the right to 12 weeks of unpaid leave if they work for a private company with more than 49 employees; for a public agency; or for an elementary or secondary school (US Department of Labor 2012). However, academic studies show that only 59 percent of American workers are eligible for coverage under the Act due to many restrictions (Van Niel *et al.* 2020, 113). Besides the limited option for unpaid maternity leave, some women have access to private maternity leave, but only an estimated 16 percent of employees employed in the private sector have access to paid leave (Van Niel *et al.* 2020, 113).

In addition to the federal provisions for unpaid leave, some US states have taken steps to implement arrangements for paid leave (National Partnership for Women & Families 2021). These provisions are meager by Scandinavian standards, ranging between 4 and 12 weeks (National Partnership for Women & Families 2019, 2021). Therefore, women in the US face obstacles when it comes to income security, making it overall more challenging to stay employed or work on a similar basis to men (since women, as a rule, continue to carry the main responsibility for children).

In contrast to the US, the Scandinavian countries offer generous paid parental leave arrangements, which in 2016 ranged from around 49 to 69 weeks (Teigen and Skjeie 2017, 140). In order to ensure that parental leave is divided between each parent, Norway and Sweden have specific quotas for each parent. For example, in 2021, 15 weeks are reserved for each parent, while 16 weeks can be shared between the parents at a benefit rate of 100 percent parental benefit in Norway (Arbeids- og Velferdsetaten (NAV) 2021). The provisions of parental leave in Denmark, Norway, and Sweden provide the family with more flexibility and a secure income. As we mentioned above, the Scandinavian countries provide a better balance between work and leisure time than the US.

Academic studies have particularly highlighted that parental leave in particular grants significant individual and societal benefits. For instance, it provides wage stability to parents, encourages employment, reduces maternal and child mortality, improves the physical health of children, and reduces the likelihood of hospitalization of mother and child post-birth (England, Levine and Mishel 2020; Esping-Andersen 2015; Van Niel *et al.* 2020). As we discussed in the previous sections, the maternal and child mortality ratio was higher in the US than in the Scandinavian countries.

Conclusion

In this chapter, we have critically examined the question as to whether the Nordic region has moved closer to the core tenets of the American Dream than contemporary America. We conceptualized the American Dream as individualism, equality of opportunity, and American exceptionalism. Two important post-war developments are particularly relevant for this examination, as we have shown. One is that American exceptionalism today is dramatically different from that when the American Dream was initially conceived. Today's exceptionalism stems mainly from the US's role as the dominant global superpower and international rule-setter. This exceptionalism has had an ambiguous effect on America's ability to pursue the American Dream. On the one hand, the American role in global rule-making has fostered rights-based individualism convergence across the Atlantic, a pattern that, also for other reasons, has resonated particularly well with Western Europe and the Nordic region. At the same time, there is a dark side to this form of US exceptionalism, in that the US shirks international and domestic rules and norms and violates individual rights. As we have shown, the US is not alone in rights deprivations; the Scandinavian countries also violate rights, especially in relation to asylum-seekers and migrants. Nevertheless, there is a clear difference in magnitude. The question this raises is: what type of global role for America is compatible with the American Dream?

Our conclusion is that with regard to rights-based individualism, the Nordic region fares overall better than the US. To what extent does that also apply to the equality of opportunity? Tying the different threads of our discussion of factors that condition equality of opportunity together, we can distinguish between how the US and Scandinavian systems distribute life risks and protection against them and how they structure the opportunities that individual citizens face.

On all three scores, the Scandinavian countries approximate the ideals inherent to the American Dream better than the US does. Having said that, from the upper echelons of the middle class and upwards the US system works fine. Those least exposed to risk, with the richest opportunity structure, are also well protected. They also have access to some of the best health services in the world, with high but for them affordable premiums and deductibles. The unfavorable comparison with the ideals of the American Dream is revealed when we consider that larger parts of the US population face more grave life risks with less protection and poorer opportunities than what is the case for people placed similarly in the Scandinavian social structure.

To consider the extreme cases can be instructive. If you are a black child growing up in a deprived neighborhood, chances are that the quality of schooling you get is very poor, that gangsters are more likely role models than engineers and doctors (never mind hedge fund managers) and if you, through talent, hard work and good guidance and teaching manage to get enough scholarships to enter a good tertiary educational institution, you may still need to work double digit hours a week in order to supplement your student loans and scholarships. And more dramatically, you are still just a few academic or behavioral missteps away from falling back to where you came from. Or you may face the choice between going back and caring for a (poorly insured) sick parent or staying on in school. Either way, there is no safety net to allow you to bounce back onto the trajectory you have been striving for. Then consider a white middle class youth who has taken the broader set of more ample chances offered with the intention of following in the footsteps of the role models he or she has grown up among but who then fails academically. In this case, there is every chance that your family will take you in, pay for therapy and/or tutoring, send you to Europe or ask you to go work for a year until you have matured sufficiently to go back to school.

In the Scandinavian countries, reflecting less dramatic disparities of income and resources, the situation can be bad enough, but on average poor kids are less poor and the deprived neighborhoods less deprived. The middle-class role models may still be absent, but the worst schools are less bad than in the US, illness in the family is not financially ruinous and student loans are universally available and closer to being sufficient, in particular when we take into consideration that tertiary education in the main is free of charge.

The paragraphs above can come across as waxing lyrical about the merits of the Scandinavian model. If so, this is an unintended consequence of simultaneously holding both systems up against the standards set by our operationalization of the American Dream. In order to counter this effect somewhat, it is useful to remind ourselves of the evolution of Scandinavian housing markets over the last 30 to 35 years. If the trends we have outlined continue, we can expect Scandinavian wealth inequality to increase and the importance of inheritance along with it. As prices in the three capitals and other major cities continue to grow faster than national averages, there will also be an increasing urban-rural divide in the value of inheriting family property. The compound effect of these two phenomena is being felt by many of the often well-educated young people from rural areas who are trying to settle in major cities, thus negatively affecting exactly the open opportunity structure and social mobility we have highlighted as the core feature of the Scandinavian model when held up against the American Dream.

In a similar vein, we can qualify somewhat our celebratory description of gender equality in the Scandinavian countries by reminding ourselves of how women from ethnic minorities have fared. The Scandinavian states' policies and push for gender equality have been termed "state feminism" (Siim and Skjeie 2008, 323). State feminism in Scandinavia is founded on achieving education and labor market participation, public childcare, parental leave, and equal political participation, seen as "women friendly" (Siim and Skjeie 2008, 323). Keskinen, Dís Skaptadóttir and Toivanen (2019) argue that the dominant narrative of the Nordic region is one of cultural homogeneity, which is seen as a condition for social cohesion. However, state feminism is increasingly criticized for viewing women as a homogenous group with the same priorities and needs, leaving out significant groups (Knobblock and Kuokkanen 2015; Siim and Skjeie 2008, 324). For example, Sámi feminism has addressed how oppressive national policies and racism have shaped gender relations in the Sámi communities in Norway, Sweden, and Finland (Knobblock and Kuokkanen 2015, 275). For instance, domestic violence and the goal of ensuring that children learn the Sámi language are key concerns for Sámi women (Knobblock and Kuokkanen 2015, 277). The idea of ethnic and cultural homogeneity has been imposed on minorities through repressive policies in all three Scandinavian countries and is particularly visible in the treatment of the Sámi people in Norway and Sweden (and Finland) (Keskinen, Dís Skaptadóttir and Toivanen 2019, 3–4). Consequently, the aggregated data presented here does not adequately reflect the opportunities of individuals belonging to minority groups.

Notes

1 The total population of the five countries that make up the Nordic region is around 27 million, whereas the total US population is around 331 million. (Source: Population, total (data.worldbank. org)). The landmass that makes up the Nordic region is 1,217,168 km^2, whereas the US size is 9,147,420 km^2 (Source: land area (km^2) (data.worldbank.org)).

2 The total GNI (Atlas method) of the Nordic region is 1,644,402,780,000 USD, whereas the total US GNI is 21,640,511,020,000 USD (https://data.worldbank.org/indicator/NY.GNP.ATLS.CD). US military spending is 778 billion USD; Nordic is 18.6 billion USD (https://sipri.org/sites/default/files/2021-04/fs_2104_milex_0.pdf).

3 The Trump administration apparently sought to combine global retrenchment with global rule and norm shirking/undermining.

4 For instance, the US has in total around 20 million living veterans (2018). Source: Veteran Population – National Center for Veterans Analysis and Statistics (va.gov). The number of veterans with PTSD varies depending on when and where they served, according to the US Department of Veterans Affairs. Source: How Common is PTSD in Veterans? – PTSD: National Center for PTSD (va.gov). Around 11–20 percent of those that served in Operations Iraqi Freedom and Enduring Freedom have been diagnosed with PTSD. From the Gulf War Desert Storm, the number is around 12 out of every 100 veterans, while around 15 percent of Vietnam War veterans have been diagnosed. A cause of PTSD for those serving in the US military (in addition to combat and stress situations) is military sexual trauma. An estimated 23 percent of women serving in the US military have reported a sexual assault. Around 55 percent of women and 38 percent of men have experienced sexual harassment. Around 19.6 percent of veterans have a disability connected to their service in the US military. Source: The Disability of Veterans (census.gov) p. 4.

5 According to Pew Research Centre, the following contains the percentage of the state's foreign-born population in 2017 https://www.pewresearch.org/global/interactives/international-migrants-by-country/: (US has taken more historically). Denmark: 11 percent (doubled since 1990); Finland: 6 percent (doubled since 2000); Norway: 15 percent (more than doubled since 2000); Sweden: 18 percent (doubled since 1990); and US: 14 percent (increase with 6 percent since 1990). The US has a population of 44.8 million foreign-born, which is the highest number globally https://www.pewresearch.org/fact-tank/2020/08/20/key-findings-about-u-s-immigrants/.

6 Sweden host by far the most refugees as a proportion of the total population in Europe with 2.6 percent. (In comparison, Lebanon 19.5 percent and Jordan 10.5 percent.) https://www.nrc.no/perspectives/2020/the-10-countries-that-receive-the-most-refugees/. US hosts around 773,000 refugees, which is around 0.23 percent of its population.

7 For an overview of racial and ethnic diversity in the US, including at state level, see: Racial and Ethnic Diversity in the US: 2010 Census and 2020 Census.

8 The Sámi people live in Norway, Sweden, Finland, and Russia.

9 See, for instance: World Economic Forum (2021) and Amnesty International (2021a).

10 United States Slave Law – Oxford Handbooks.

11 GDP per capita, PPP (current international $) | Data (worldbank.org).

12 Except for voting rights, the US Constitution does not explicitly prohibit discrimination on the basis of sex (Murphy, 2018, pp. 937–938). However, other forms of legislation prohibit sex-based discrimination in different sectors, such as employment.

13 See ICCPR, art. 26.

14 Norway: no data for 2019, collected for 2018.

15 An overview of these different provisions is found here: Welcome (votingrightslab.org). The following overview shows how states have moved in different directions: Map Of Voting Bills By State, Restrictions And Expansions: NPR.

16 One study also included both parents and son (not daughter) (Palomino, Marrero and Rodríguez, 2018).

17 This was the case for the study by Jäntti *et al.* (2006, p. 19).

18 See (Skjeie and Teigen, 2005) for Scandinavia.

19 Preliminary results by Palomino, Marrero and Rodríguez (2018, p. 353) suggest that the income mobility of women in the US, measured by IGE, depends on whether they are married.

20 See, for example Esping-Andersen (2015) (Norway and Denmark) and Landersø and Heckman (2017) (Denmark and the US).

21 The study relies on data from the Panel Study of Income Dynamics (PSID) and uses conditional Quantile Regression.

22 See, for example Bhattacharya and Mazumder (2011), Chetty *et al.* (2014), and Fox (2016).

23 See also Scruggs and Allan (2008).

24 No data for 2011 for Sweden and the US, collected for 2013.

25 Data from 2013 is classified as 2013(3) (US Census Bureau, 2021b).

26 Data from 2013 is classified as 2013(3) (US Census Bureau, 2021b).

27 This section draws heavily on joint but unpublished work with Ingrid Hjertaker (Hjertaker and Tranøy, 2021).

28 Oliver and Shapiro (2006, p. 69) argue that there are major differences between the wealth of black and white Americans, who hold that financial wealth is the so-called "buried fault line of the American social system."

29 Several paragraphs in this section draw heavily on joint but unpublished work with Ingrid Hjertaker (Hjertaker and Tranøy, 2021).

30 Data for the US is from 2021.

31 See, for instance: Maternal and Child Health Journal (https://www.springer.com/journal/10995).

32 Finland was ranked at the top, while Afghanistan received the lowest score.

33 For an excellent and very comprehensive assessment of civic literary, see Milner (2002).

34 For differences between sex, race, and ethnicity, see (US Census Bureau, 2021a).

References

Adams, James Truslow. 1959. *The Epic of America*. Boston: Little, Brown and Company, (1931[1959]).

Alber, Jens. 2010. "What the European and American welfare states have in common and where they differ: Facts and fiction in comparisons of the European social model and the United States." *Journal of European Social Policy*, *20*(2), 102–25. https://doi.org/10.1177/0958928709358791.

Alesina, Alberto, and Edward L. Glaeser. 2006. "Why are welfare states in the US and Europe so different?" *Horizons Stratégiques*, *2*(2), 51–61. https://doi.org/10.3917/hori.002.0051.

Alexander, Michelle. 2012. *The New Jim Crow*. New York: The New Press.

Alstadsæter, Annette, Niels Johannesen and Gabriel Zucman. 2019. "Tax evasion and inequality." *American Economic Review*, *109*(6), 2073–2103.

American Civil Liberties Union. 2014. "Written Submission of the American Civil Liberties Union on Racial Disparities in Sentencing Hearing on Reports of Racism in the Justice System of the United States Submitted to the Inter-American Commission on Human Rights." https://www.aclu.org/sites/default/files/assets/141027_iachr_racial_disparities_aclu_submission_0.pdf.

———. 2021. "Capital Punishment." https://www.aclu.org/issues/capital-punishment#latest.

Amnesty International. 2021a. "Gender, Sex and Identity." https://www.amnestyusa.org/issues/gender-sexuality-identity/.

———. 2021b. "Police Violence." https://www.amnesty.org/en/what-we-do/police-brutality/.

———. (no date) "National Security & Human Rights." https://www.amnestyusa.org/issues/national-security/.

Amnesty International. 2022. "USA: Supreme Court Decision to Overturn Roe v. Wade Marks Grim Milestone in History of the United States." June 24, 2022. https://www.amnesty.org/en/latest/news/2022/06/supreme-court-decision-overturn-roe-wade/.

Aradau, Claudia. 2007. "Law transformed: Guantánamo and the 'other' exception." *Third World Quarterly*, *28*(3), 489–501. https://doi.org/10.1080/01436590701192298.

Arbeids- og Velferdsetaten (NAV). 2021. "About Parental Benefit." https://familie.nav.no/om-foreldrepenger.

Arias, Elizabeth, Betzaida Tejada-Vera and Farida Ahmad. 2021. "Provisional Life Expectancy Estimates for January through June, 2020." Centers for Disease Control and Prevention. https://www.cdc.gov/nchs/data/vsrr/VSRR10-508.pdf.

Balestra, Carlotta and Richard Tonkin. 2018. "Inequalities in Household Wealth across OECD Countries: Evidence from the OECD Wealth Distribution Database." OECD Statistics and Data Directorate Working Paper Series, 88.

Bangstad, Sindre. 2012. "Failing to protect minorities against racist and/or discriminatory speech." *Nordic Journal of Human Rights*, *30*(4), 483–514.

Bantekas, Ilias and Lutz Oette. 2020. *International Human Rights Law and Practice*. 3rd ed. Cambridge: Cambridge University Press.

Barendt, Eric. 2007. *Freedom of Speech*. 2nd ed. Oxford: Oxford University Press. https://doi.org/10.1093/acprof:oso/9780199225811.001.0001.

Barth, Erling, Kalle Moene and Axel West Pedersen. 2020. "Rising inequality in the egalitarian Nordics." In George Fischer and Robert Strauss (eds.), *Europe's Income, Wealth, Consumption, and Inequality*, 218–45. Oxford: Oxford University Press.

Beetham, David. 1995. "What future for economic and social rights?" *Political Studies*, XLIII, 41–60. https://doi.org/10.4324/9781315199955-5.

Benecchi, Liz. 2021. "Recidivism Imprisons American Progress." *Harvard Political Review*, August 8, 2021. https://harvardpolitics.com/recidivism-american-progress/.

Benko, Jessica. 2015. "The Radical Humaneness of Norway's Halden Prison." *The New York Times*, March 26, 2015. https://www.nytimes.com/2015/03/29/magazine/the-radical-humaneness-of-norways-halden-prison.html.

Besbris, Max and Jacob William Faber. 2017. "Investigating the relationship between real estate agents, segregation, and house prices: Steering and upselling in New York state." *Sociological Forum*, *32*(4), 850–73. https://doi.org/10.1111/socf.12378.

Bhattacharya, Debopam and Bhashkar Mazumder. 2011. "A nonparametric analysis of black–white differences in intergenerational income mobility in the United States: Intergenerational income mobility." *Quantitative Economics*, *2*(3), 335–79. https://doi.org/10.3982/QE69.

Borchorst, Anette and Birte Siim. 2002. "The women-friendly welfare states revisited." *Nordic Journal of Feminist and Gender Research*, *10*(2), 90–8. https://doi.org/10.1080/080387402760262186.

Boyle, Kevin. 2001. "Hate speech – the United States versus the rest of the world?" *Maine Law Review*, *53*(2), 487.

Carson, E. Ann. 2020. "Prisoners in 2018." US Department of Justice. https://bjs.ojp.gov/content/pub/pdf/p18.pdf.

Causa, Orsetta, Nicholas Woloszko and David Leite. 2019. "Housing, Wealth Accumulation and Wealth Distribution: Evidence and Stylized Facts." OECD Economics Department Working Papers, 1588. https://doi.org/10.1787/86954c10-en.

Centers for Disease Control and Prevention. 2020. "Pregnancy Mortality Surveillance System." https://www.cdc.gov/reproductivehealth/maternal-mortality/pregnancy-mortality-surveillance-system.htm?CDC_AA_refVal=https%3A%2F%2Fwww.cdc.gov%2Freproductivehealth%2Fmaternalinfanthealth%2Fpregnancy-mortality-surveillance-system.htm.

Chetty, Raj, Nathaniel Hendren, Patrick Kline and Emmanuel Saez. 2014. "Where is the land of opportunity? The geography of intergenerational mobility in the United States." *The Quarterly Journal of Economics*, *129*(4), 1553–1623. https://doi.org/10.1093/qje/qju022.

Clermont, Woody R. 2010. "Business Associations Reign Supreme: The Corporatist Underpinnings of Citizens United v. Federal Election Commission." *Thomas M. Cooley Law Review*, *27*(3): 477–508.

Council of Europe. 1950. "European Convention for the Protection of Human Rights and Fundamental Freedoms (European Convention on Human Rights)." https://www.echr.coe.int/documents/convention_eng.pdf.

———. 2019. "Report to the Danish Government on the Visit to Denmark Carried out by the European Committee for the Prevention of Torture and Inhuman or Degrading Treatment or Punishment." https://rm.coe.int/1680996859.

———. 2021a. "Chart of Signatures and Ratifications of Treaty 163." https://www.coe.int/en/web/conventions/full-list?module=signatures-by-treaty&treatynum=163.

———. 2021b. "Chart of Signatures and Ratifications of Treaty 210." https://www.coe.int/en/web/conventions/full-list?module=signatures-by-treaty&treatynum=210.

Credit Suisse. 2017. "Global Wealth Report 2017", ZurichCredit Suisse AG, Research Institute.

Death Penalty Information Center. 2021. "Facts about the Death Penalty." https://documents.deathpenaltyinfo.org/pdf/FactSheet.pdf.

Denmark. 1849. Danmarks Rigets Grundlov (as Amended in 1953).

De Schutter, Olivier. 2019. *International Human Rights Law: Cases, Materials, Commentary.* 3rd ed. Cambridge: Cambridge University Press.

Desilver, Drew. 2020. "Not All Unemployed People Get Unemployment Benefits; in Some States, Very Few Do." *Pew Research Center*, April 24, 2020. https://www.pewresearch.org/fact-tank/2020/04/24/not-all-unemployed-people-get-unemployment-benefits-in-some-states-very-few-do/.

Eggum, Terje and Erling Røed Larsen. 2021. "Is the Housing Market an Inequality Generator?" Housing Lab Working Paper Series 2021 | 2.

England, Paula, Andrew Levine and Emma Mishel. 2020. "Progress toward gender equality in the United States has slowed or stalled." *Proceedings of the National Academy of Sciences of the United States of America*, 117(13), 6990–7. https://doi.org/10.1073/pnas.1918891117.

Esping-Andersen, Gøsta. 1990. *The Three Worlds of Welfare Capitalism.* Princeton: Princeton University Press.

Esping-Andersen, Gøsta. 2015. "Welfare regimes and social stratification." *Journal of European Social Policy*, 25(1), 124–34. https://doi.org/10.1177/0958928714556976.

European Court of Human Rights. 2021. "Overview 1959-2020 ECHR." https://www.echr.coe.int/Documents/Overview_19592020_ENG.pdf.

European Court of Human Rights (GC). 1999. Case of Erdoğdu and Ince v. Turkey. (App. Nos. 25067/94 and 25068/94).

European Court of Human Rights (Plenary). 1989. Case of Soering v. the United Kingdom (Appl. No. 14038/88).

Eurostat. 2021. "Distribution of Population by Tenure Status, Type of Household and Income Group – EU-SILC Survey." https://ec.europa.eu/eurostat/databrowser/view/ILC_LVHO02__custom_1794566/default/table?lang=en.

Flynn, Lindsay B. 2020. "The young and the restless: housing access in the critical years." *West European Politics*, 43(2), 321–43.

Fossum, John Erik. 2021. "Is the Nordic model more compatible with the American dream than present-day United States?" In Robert C. Hauhart and Mitja Sardoč (eds.), *The Routledge Handbook on the American Dream Volume 1*, 105–20. New York: Routledge.

Fossum, John Erik and Hans Petter Graver. 2018. *Squaring the Circle on Brexit – Could the Norway Model Work?* Bristol: Bristol University Press.

Fossum, John Erik and Agustín José Menéndez. 2011. *The Constitution's Gift – A Constitutional Theory for a Democratic European Union.* Boulder: Rowman and Littlefield.

Fox, Liana E. 2016. "Parental wealth and the black-white mobility gap in the U.S." *Review of Income and Wealth*, 62(4), 706–23. https://doi.org/10.1111/roiw.12200.

Fredrickson, George M. 1998. "Presidential address: America's diversity in comparative perspective." *The Journal of American History*, 85(3), 859–75.

Gardner, Amy, Kate Rabinowitz and Harry Stevens. 2021. "How GOP-Backed Voting Measures Could Create Hurdles for Tens of Millions of Voters." *Washington Post*, March 11, 2021. https://www.washingtonpost.com/politics/interactive/2021/voting-restrictions-republicans-states/.

Goodman, Laurie S. and Christopher Mayer. 2018. "Homeownership and the American Dream." *Journal of Economic Perspectives*, 32(1), 31–58. https://doi.org/10.1257/jep.32.1.31.

Held, David, Anthony McGrew, David Goldblatt and Jonathan Perraton. 1999. *Global Transformations: Politics, Economics and Culture.* Cambridge: Polity Press.

Hjertaker, Ingrid and Bent Sofus Tranøy. 2021: "A model but not a home: Wealth inequality and housing in Scandinavia," Paper presented at The Fourth Nordic Challenges Conference, Reconsidering the Nordic Models in an Age of Polarization, Boston University | November 5–6, 2021.

Hodgkinson, Peter. 2009. "Capital punishment: Improve it or remove it?" In Peter Hodgkinson and William A. Schabas (eds.), *Capital Punishment: Strategies for Abolition*. Cambridge: Cambridge University Press. https://doi.org/10.1017/CBO9780511489273.001.

Howard, Christopher. 2021. *The Welfare State Nobody Knows.* Princeton: Princeton University Press.

Human Rights Watch. 2020. "United States: Event of 2019." https://www.hrw.org/world-report/2020/country-chapters/united-states.

———. 2021a. "The Right of Everyone to Sexual and Reproductive Health: Challenges and Opportunities during Covid-19." https://www.hrw.org/news/2021/06/10/right-everyone-sexual-and-reproductive-health-challenges-and-opportunities-during.

———. 2021b. "United States: Events of 2020." https://www.hrw.org/world-report/2021/country-chapters/united-states.

Jäntti, Markus, Bernt Bratsberg, Knut Røed, Oddbjørn Raaum, Eva Österbacka, Anders Björklund and Tor Eriksson. 2006. "American Exceptionalism in a New Light: A Comparison of Intergenerational Earnings Mobility in the Nordic Countries, the United Kingdom and the United States." IZA Discussion Paper, 1938: 1–40. https://docs.iza.org/dp1938.pdf.

Johns, Fleur. 2013. *Non-Legality in International Law: Unruly Law*. Cambridge: Cambridge University Press. https://doi.org/10.1017.

Katzenstein, Peter J. 1985. *Small States in World Markets – Industrial Policy in Europe*. Ithaca: Cornell University Press.

Keisler-Starkey, Katherine and Lisa N Bunch. 2021. "Health Insurance Coverage in the United States: 2020." US Census Bureau. https://www.census.gov/content/dam/Census/library/publications/2021/demo/p60-274.pdf.

Keskinen, Suvi, Unnur Dís Skaptadóttir and Mari Toivanen. 2019. "Narrations of Homogeneity, Waning Welfare States, and the Politics of Solidarity." In Suvi Keskinen, Unnur Dís Skaptadóttir, and Mari Toivanen (eds.), *Undoing Homogeneity in the Nordic Region: Migration, Difference, and the Politics of Solidarity*. London: Routledge. https://doi.org/10.4324/9781315122328.

Knobblock, Ina and Rauna Kuokkanen. 2015. "Decolonizing feminism in the North: A conversation with Rauna Kuokkanen." *Nordic Journal of Feminist and Gender Research*, *23*(4), 275–81. https://doi.org/10.1080/08038740.2015.1090480.

Landersø, Rasmus and James J. Heckman. 2017. "The Scandinavian fantasy: The sources of intergenerational mobility in Denmark and the US." *Scandinavian Journal of Economics*, *119*(1), 178–230. https://doi.org/10.1111/sjoe.12219.

Liptak, Adam, J. David Goodman and Sabrina Tavernise. 2021. "Supreme Court, Breaking Silence, Won't Block Texas Abortion Law." *New York Times*, September 1, 2021.

Lomell, Heidi Mork and Peter Scharff Smith. 2017. "Rettssosiologi." In Andreas Føllesdal, Morten Ruud, and Geir Ulfstein (eds.), *Menneskerettigheter Og Norge: Rettsutvikling, Rettsliggjøring Og Demokrati*. Oslo: Universitetsforlaget.

MacNaughton, Gillian and Mariah McGill. 2012. "Economic and social rights in the United States: Implementation without ratification Universal Declaration of Human Rights, which has since become." *Northeastern University Law Journal*, *4*(2), 365–406.

Mapping Police Violence. 2021. "Police Violence Map." 2021. https://mappingpoliceviolence.org.
———. no date. "2020 Police Violence Report." https://mappingpoliceviolence.org.

Mathä, Thomas Y., Alessandro Porpiglia and Michael Ziegelmeyer. 2017. "Household wealth in the euro area: The importance of intergenerational transfers, homeownership and house price dynamics." *Journal of Housing Economics*, *35*, 1–12. https://doi.org/10.1016/j.jhe.2016.12.001.

Mehta, Sarah. 2015. "There's Only One Country That Hasn't Ratified the Convention on Children's Rights: US." *American Civil Liberties Union*, November 20, 2015. https://www.aclu.org/blog/human-rights/treaty-ratification/theres-only-one-country-hasnt-ratified-convention-childrens.

Milner, Henry. 2002. *Civic Literacy – How Informed Citizens Make Democracy Work*. Hanover and London: University Press of New England.

Murphy, Bridget L. 2018. "The equal rights amendment revisited." *Notre Dame Law Review*, *94*(2), 937–958.

National Partnership for Women & Families. 2019. "Paid Leave Works: Evidence from State Programs." https://www.nationalpartnership.org/our-work/resources/economic-justice/paid-leave/paid-leave-works-evidence-from-state-programs.pdf.

National Partnership for Women & Families. 2021. "State Paid Family and Medical Leave Insurance Laws." https://www.nationalpartnership.org/our-work/resources/economic-justice/paid-leave/state-paid-family-leave-laws.pdf.

Ndulue, Ngozi. 2020. "Enduring Justice: The Persistence of Racial Discrimination in the U.S. Death Penalty." *Death Penalty Information Center*. https://documents.deathpenaltyinfo.org/pdf/Enduring-Injustice-Race-and-the-Death-Penalty-2020.pdf.

Nordli Hansen, Marianne and Maren Toft. 2021. "Wealth accumulation and opportunity hoarding: Class-origin wealth gaps over a quarter of a century in a Scandinavian country." *American Sociological Review*. https://doi.org/10.1177/00031224211020012.

Norwegian Ministry of Justice and Public Security. 1814. The Constitution of the Kingdom Norway (English Translation) (as Amended in 2020). LOV-1814-05-17. https://lovdata.no/dokument/NLE/lov/1814-05-17.

Norwegian Ministry of Justice and Public Security. 2021. Lov 1 juli 2021 om straff (straffeloven) (Penal Code). https://lovdata.no/dokument/NLE/lov/2005-05-20-28/KAPITTEL_2#KAPITTEL_2.

Norwegian Ministry of Local Government and Modernisation. 2002. Act Relating to Parliamentary and Local Government Elections (Election Act) (English Translation). Norway: LOV-2002-06-28-57.

OECD. 2015. "Sweden Policy Brief [OECD Better Policies Series]." https://www.oecd.org/sweden/sweden-achieving-greater-equality-of-opportunities-and-outcomes.pdf.

OECD. 2019. "PF2.1. Parental Leave Systems." https://www.oecd.org/els/soc/PF2_1_Parental_leave_systems.pdf.

OECD. 2021a. "Benefits in Unemployment, Share of Previous Income (Indicator)." https://doi.org/10.1787/0cc0d0e5-en.

———. 2021b. "Employment Rate (Indicator)." https://doi.org/10.1787/1de68a9b-en.

———. 2021c. "Income Inequality (Indicator)." https://doi.org/10.1787/459aa7f1-en.

———. 2021d. "Net Childcare Costs." https://doi.org/10.1787/e328a9ee-en.

———. 2021e. "OECD Statistics." https://stats.oecd.org.

———. 2021f. "Population with Tertiary Education (Indicator)." https://doi.org/10.1787/0b8f90e9-en.

———. 2021g. "Poverty Rate (Indicator)." https://doi.org/10.1787/0fe1315d-en.

———. 2022. "Life Expectancy at Birth." https://doi.org/10.1787/27e0fc9d-en.

———. no date. "HM1.3 Housing Tenures." https://www.oecd.org/els/family/HM1-3-Housing-tenures.pdf.

OHCHR. no date. "Human Rights Bodies." https://www.ohchr.org/EN/HRBODIES/Pages/HumanRightsBodies.aspx.

Ojanen, Tuomas. 2018. "Human Rights in Nordic Constitutions and the Impact of International Obligations." In Helle Krunke and Björg Thorarensen (eds.), *The Nordic Constitutions: A Comparative and Contextual Study*, 133–66. Oxford: Hart Publishing.

Oliver, Melvin L. and Thomas M. Shapiro. 2006. *Black Wealth/White Wealth: A New Perspective on Racial Inequality*. New York: Routledge.

Olsen, Espen D.H. (2014). "Utenforskapets" paradoks: mot et depolitisert statsborgerskap? In Erik O. Eriksen and John E. Fossum (eds.), *Det norske paradoks – Om Norges forhold til Den europeiske union*, 134–52. Oslo: Universitetsforlaget.

Palomino, Juan C., Gustavo A. Marrero and Juan G. Rodríguez. 2018. "One size doesn't fit all: A quantile analysis of intergenerational income mobility in the U.S. (1980–2010)." *Journal of Economic Inequality*, 16(3), 347–67.

Patten, Eileen. 2016. "Racial, Gender Wage Gaps Persist in U.S. despite Some Progress." *Pew Research Center*. https://www.pewresearch.org/fact-tank/2016/07/01/racial-gender-wage-gaps-persist-in-u-s-despite-some-progress/.

Peterson, Wallace C. and Paul S. Estenson. 1985. "The Recovery: Supply-Side or Keynesian?" *Journal of Post Keynesian Economics*, 7(4): 447–62.

Pew Research Center. 2021. "Most Americans Favor the Death Penalty Despite Concerns About Its Administration."

Pfeffer, Fabian T. and Nora Waitkus. 2021. "The wealth inequality of nations." *American Sociological Review*, 86(4), 567–602. https://doi.org/10.1177/00031224211027800.

Piketty, Thomas. 2014. *Capital in the 21st Century*. Cambridge: Harvard University Press.

Polisen. 2020. "Utbildningsplan för Polisprogrammet." https://www.sh.se/download/18.35738f6f170c016f8e724615/1584614664900/Utbildningsplan%20för%20Polisprogrammet%20kull%20VT20%20-%20(giltig%20fr.om.%201%20januari%202020).pdf.

Politihøgskolen. no date a. "Bachelor – Police Studies." https://www.politihogskolen.no/en/bachelor/.

Politihøgskolen. no date b. "Finn Ditt Studium." https://www.politihogskolen.no.

Politi. no date. "Politiets Basisuddannelse." https://politi.dk/politiskolen/politiets-basisuddannelse.

Preisler, Marie. 2021. "Is Denmark's proposed refugee legislation unrealistic?" *Nordic Labour Journal*. http://www.nordiclabourjournal.org/nyheter/news-2021/article.2021-02-23.5268588151.

Reaves, Brian A. 2016. "State and Local Law Enforcement Training Academies, 2013." US Department of Justice. https://bjs.ojp.gov/content/pub/pdf/slleta13.pdf.

Ryan, Camille L. and Kurt Bauman. 2016. "Educational Attainment in the United States: 2015." US Census Bureau. https://www.census.gov/content/dam/Census/library/publications/2016/demo/p20-578.pdf.

Schneider, Eric C., Arnav Shah, Michelle M. Doty, Roosa Tikkanen, Katharine Fields and Reginald D. Williams II, A. (2021) *Reflecting Poorly – Health Care in the U.S. Compared to Other High-Income Countries*, Mirror, Mirror 2021, New York: The Commonwealth Fund.

Schouten, Fredreka. 2021. "State Legislators Gear up to Pass a 'Tidal Wave' of Voting Restrictions Ahead of Crucial 2022 Midterms." *CNN*, December 22, 2021. https://edition.cnn.com/2021/12/21/politics/gop-state-officials-prepare-new-wave-of-voting-restrictions/index.html.

Scruggs, Lyle A. and James P. Allan. 2008. "Social stratification and welfare regimes for the twenty-first century: Revisiting the three worlds of welfare capitalism." *World Politics*, *60*(4), 642–64. https://doi.org/10.1353/wp.0.0020.

Siim, Birte and Hege Skjeie. 2008. "Tracks, intersections and dead ends: Multicultural challenges to state feminism in Denmark and Norway." *Ethnicities*, *8*(3), 322–44. https://doi.org/10.1177/1468796808092446.

Sipes, Leonard A. Jr. no date. "Offender Recidivism and Reentry in the United States." *Crime in America*, December 19, 2021. https://www.crimeinamerica.net/offender-recidivism-and-reentry-in-the-united-states/.

Skjeie, Hege and Mari Teigen. 2005. "Political Constructions of Gender Equality: Travelling Towards … a Gender Balanced Society?" *Nordic Journal of Feminist and Gender Research*, *13*(3), 187–97. https://doi.org/10.1080/08038740600590004.

Statista Research Department. 2021. "Countries with the Largest Number of Prisoners per 100,000 of the National Population, as of May 2021." https://www.statista.com/statistics/262962/countries-with-the-most-prisoners-per-100-000-inhabitants/.

Stolberg, Sheryl Gay. 2021. "Millions Have Lost Health Insurance in Pandemic-Driven Recession." *The New York Times*, July 13, 2021. https://www.nytimes.com/2020/07/13/us/politics/coronavirus-health-insurance-trump.html.

Stortinget. 2020. "Folkestyret." https://www.stortinget.no/no/Stortinget-og-demokratiet/Storting-og-regjering/Folkestyret/.

Stubbs, Cassandra. 2021. "Atrocities of the Federal Death Penalty." *American Civil Liberties Union*, 2 February 2021. https://www.aclu.org/news/capital-punishment/atrocities-of-the-federal-death-penalty/.

Sveriges Riksdag. 2016. "The Constitution of Sweden: The Fundamental Laws and the Riksdag Act (English Translation)." https://www.riksdagen.se/globalassets/07.-dokument–lagar/the-constitution-of-sweden-160628.pdf.

Sørensen, Øystein and Bo Stråth (eds.). 1997. *The Cultural Construction of Norden*. Oslo: Scandinavian University Press.

Teigen, Mari and Hege Skjeie. 2017. "The Nordic Gender Equality Model." In Oddbjørn Knutsen (ed.), *The Nordic Models in Political Science: Challenged, but Still Viable?*. Bergen: Vigmostad & Bjørke, Fagbokforlaget.

The Rendition Project. 2019. "CIA Torture Unredacted: Chapter One." https://www.therenditionproject.org.uk/documents/RDI/190710-TRP-TBIJ-CIA-Torture-Unredacted-Ch1.pdf.

Tranøy, Bent Sofus, Mary Ann Stamsø and Ingrid Hjertaker. 2020. "Equality as a driver of inequality? Universalistic welfare, generalised creditworthiness and financialised housing markets." *West European Politics*, *43*(2), 390–411.

UN General Assembly. 1966a. "International Covenant on Civil and Political Rights." United Nations: Treaty Series, vol. 999, p. 171. https://www.ohchr.org/en/professionalinterest/pages/ccpr.aspx.

UN General Assembly. 1966b. "International Covenant on Economic, Social and Cultural Rights." United Nations: Treaty Series, vol. 993, p. 3. https://www.ohchr.org/en/professionalinterest/pages/cescr.aspx.

UN Human Rights Treaty Bodies. no date. "View the Ratification Status by Country or by Treaty." https://tbinternet.ohchr.org/_layouts/15/TreatyBodyExternal/Treaty.aspx.

UN Office on Drugs and Crime. 2016. "Victims of Intentional Homicide in Prison: 2016." https://dataunodc.un.org/data/homicide/Homicide in prison.

UN Office on Drugs and Crime. 2019. "Persons Held in Prisons: 2019." https://dataunodc.un.org/data/Prison/Persons%20held%20in%20prison.

UN Treaty Collection. 2021a. "International Convention on the Elimination of All Forms of Racial Discrimination." https://treaties.un.org/Pages/ViewDetails.aspx?src=IND&mtdsg_no=IV-2&chapter=4&clang=_en.

———. 2021b. "International Covenant on Civil and Political Rights." https://treaties.un.org/Pages/ViewDetails.aspx?chapter=4&clang=_en&mtdsg_no=IV-4&src=IND.

UNHCR. 2021a. "Refugee Data Finder." https://www.unhcr.org/refugee-statistics/.

———. 2021b. "UNHCR Observations on the Proposal for Amendments to the Danish Alien Act (Introduction of the Possibility to Transfer Asylum-Seekers for Adjudication of Asylum Claims and Accommodation in Third Countries)." https://www.refworld.org/docid/6045dde94.html.

UN Women. 2017. "Women in the Changing World of Work." https://interactive.unwomen.org/multimedia/infographic/changingworldofwork/en/index.html

United States Government. no date a. "Eligibility." https://www.medicaid.gov/medicaid/eligibility/index.html.

———. no date b. "What's Medicare?" https://www.medicare.gov/what-medicare-covers/your-medicare-coverage-choices/whats-medicare.

US Census Bureau. 2019. "Number and Percentage of People by Type of Health Insurance: 2017 and 2018." https://www2.census.gov/programs-surveys/demo/tables/p60/267/table1.pdf.

———. 2021a. "Current Population Survey/Housing Vacancy Survey." 2021. https://www.census.gov/housing/hvs/files/qtr221/hown221.jpg.

———. 2021b. "Educational Attainment in the United States: 2020." https://www.census.gov/data/tables/2020/demo/educational-attainment/cps-detailed-tables.html.

———. 2021c. "Historical Poverty Tables: People and Families – 1959 to 2020." https://www.census.gov/data/tables/time-series/demo/income-poverty/historical-poverty-people.html.

———. 2021d. "Quarterly Residential Vacancies and Homeownership." https://www.census.gov/housing/hvs/files/currenthvspress.pdf.

US Department of Labor. 2012. "Fact Sheet #28: The Family and Medical Leave Act."

US Federal Election Commission. no date a. "Campaign Finance Data." https://www.fec.gov/data/.

———. no date b. "Citizens United v. FEC." https://www.fec.gov/legal-resources/court-cases/citizens-united-v-fec/.

US Social Security Administration. no date a. "Supplemental Security Income (SSI) Overview." https://www.ssa.gov/ssi/text-over-ussi.htm.

———. no date b. "Workers with Maximum-Taxable Earnings." https://www.ssa.gov/oact/cola/examplemax.html.

US Supreme Court. 2002. "Atkins v. Virginia 536 U.S. 304." https://supreme.justia.com/cases/federal/us/536/304/.

Van Niel, Maureen Sayres, Richa Bhatia, Nicholas S. Riano, Ludmila De Faria, Lisa Catapano-Friedman, Simha Ravven, Barbara Weissman, et al. 2020. "The impact of paid maternity leave on the mental and physical health of mothers and children: A review of the literature and policy implications." *Harvard Review of Psychiatry*, 28(2), 113–26. https://doi.org/10.1097/HRP.0000000000000246.

Weill, Sharon and Mitchell Robinson. 2020. "Military Courts and Terrorism: The 9/11 Trial before the Guantanamo Bay Military Jurisdiction." In Ben Saul (ed.), *Research Handbook on International Law and Terrorism*. Cheltenham: Edward Elgar Publishing.

Whelan, Daniel J. and Jack Donnelly. 2007. "The West, economic and social rights, and the global human rights regime: Setting the record straight." *Human Rights Quarterly*, 29(4), 908–49. https://doi.org/10.1353/hrq.2007.0050.

Weller, Christian E. and Richard Figueroa. 2021. "Wealth Matters: The Black-White Wealth Gap before and during the Pandemic." *Center for American Progress*.

Whitmer, Benjamin. 2006. "'Torture chambers and rape rooms': What Abu Ghraib can tell Us about the American carceral system." *The New Centennial Review*, 6(1), 171–94.

WID. 2020. "Wealth inequality, USA, 1962–2020." *World Income Database*. https://wid.world/country/usa/.

World Economic Forum. 2021. "Global Gender Gap Report 2021: Insight Report." http://www3.weforum.org/docs/WEF_GGGR_2021.pdf.

World Health Organization. 2021a. "Infant Mortality Rate (Probability of Dying between Birth and Age 1 per 1000 Live Births)." https://www.who.int/data/gho/data/indicators/indicator-details/GHO/infant-mortality-rate-(probability-of-dying-between-birth-and-age-1-per-1000-live-births).

———. 2022. "Abortion Care Guidelines." https://www.who.int/publications/i/item/9789240039483.

———. 2021b. "Maternal Mortality Ratio (per 100,000 Live Births)." https://www.who.int/data/gho/data/indicators/indicator-details/GHO/maternal-mortality-ratio-(per-100-000-live-births).

World Population Review. 2021. "Happiest Countries in the World 2021." https://worldpopulationreview.com/country-rankings/happiest-countries-in-the-world.

Yin, Owen, Brett Wheatley and Brendan Tuytel. 2020. "How Unemployment Benefits Are Calculated by State." *Bench.* https://bench.co/blog/operations/unemployment-benefits-by-state/?blog=e6.

Ziegler, Mary. 2022. "Roe's Death Will Change American Democracy." New York Times, June 24, 2022. https://www.nytimes.com/2022/06/24/opinion/roe-v-wade-dobbs-democracy.html?pageType=LegacyCollection&collectionName=abortion-opinion&label=abortion-opinion&module=hub_Band&region=inline&template=storyline_band_recirc.

Zucman, G. (2016). "Wealth Inequality (State of the Union)." *Stanford Center on Poverty and Inequality.* https://www.homeworkgain.com/wp-content/uploads/edd/2019/10/20180321223352pathways_sotu_2016_wealth_inequality_3.pd.

6

EQUALITY, OPPORTUNITY, AND THE AMERICAN DREAM

Mitja Sardoč and Vladimir Prebilič

The Interpretation of the American Dream

In 1900, Sigmund Freud published *The Interpretation of Dreams*, a book that would come to define psychoanalysis as the 'science of the unconscious'. The interpretation of dreams, as Freud famously wrote in one of the most well-known lines from this book, is 'the royal road to a knowledge of the unconscious activities of the mind' (2010 [1900]: 604). As the 'most secure foundation of psychoanalysis' (1957: 33), Freud later pointed out in *Five Lectures on Psychoanalysis*, dreams have had a transformative effect on psychoanalysis as their use in interpreting our psychic life has metamorphosed psychoanalysis from a therapeutic method to a general theory of the mind. Interestingly enough, the analogy between Freud's use of dreams in clinical practice [alongside jokes, slips of tongue and other forms of everyday 'psychopathology'] with "dreams" as an ideal representation of a nation's ethos could not have been more telling. The most indicative embodiment of this assertion has been the idea of the American Dream.

As arguably the most recognizable national dream narrative and the US 'dominant national ideology' (Hochschild and Scovronick, 2003: x), as well as a trademark of US 'soft power' (Nye, 1990), the American Dream has represented a distilled version of basic American values and the single most important emancipatory ideal associated with the American 'way of life' and its popular culture.[1] As Jennifer L Hochschild emphasized in her book *Facing Up to the American Dream*, it represents 'a central ideology of Americans […], a defining characteristic of American culture' (Hochschild, 1995: xi). In fact, both in the US and abroad, the American Dream constitutes a symbol of progress and has been synonymous with hope in general. Moreover, throughout history, its progressive idealism has had a galvanizing influence on a number of emancipatory social projects, e.g. the Civil Rights movement. At the same time, its promise of upward social mobility [firmly grounded in the merit-based idea of equal opportunity] encapsulates best the idea of non-discrimination and fairness that stand at the very center of social phenomena as diverse as racial desegregation,[2] the 'war for talent', the New Green Deal, migrations, educational reforms, etc.

The voluminous literature on the American Dream in disciplines as diverse as sociology (Hauhart, 2016), political science (Ghosh, 2013; Hochschild, 1995; Jillson, 2016), the economy (Shaanan, 2010; Stiglitz, 2013), migration studies (Clark, 2003), history (Cullen, 2003; Ratner-Rosenhagen, 2019), advertising (Samuel, 2001), cultural studies (Lasch,

DOI: 10.4324/9781003326243-7

1996; Lawrence, 2012), linguistics (Fischer, 1973), sports (Lawrence, 2019), religious studies (D'Antonio, 2011), anthropology (Duncan, 2015), economics (Chetty, 2021), literary studies (Long, 1985), educational theory (DeVitis & Rich, 1996) as well as philosophy (Cannon, 2003; Peters, 2012; Sandel, 2020, Sardoč, 2016a, 2017), points out that the idea of the American Dream is far from simple or unproblematic. In fact, as Robert Hauhart emphasizes in his book *Seeking the American Dream*, '[i]t would be foolish, and counterproductive, to ignore the contributions that derive from history, literature, economics, anthropology, political science and journalism' (Hauhart, 2016: ix).

Yet, its 'standard' interpretation as a central element of American culture and an idealized 'metaphor of basic American values' is no longer straightforward, as the American Dream has also been associated with a wide range of ideas not everyone finds appealing. As an archetype of (material) success and consumerism in general, the American Dream has been subjected to a number of objections leading to the criticism that its promise of equal opportunity, progress, upward social mobility, and material prosperity for all has not been fulfilled. As the contributors to the joint report *Opportunity, Responsibility and Security: A Consensus Plan for Reducing Poverty and Restoring the American Dream* by two of the leading US think-thanks, i.e. Brookings Institution and the American Enterprise Institute (AEI) for Public Policy Research, have emphasized that the current state of affairs 'contradicts our country's founding ideals' (AEI/Brookings, 2015: 8).[3]

Nevertheless, despite a number of divergent approaches aiming to shed light on this complex [and controversial] social ideal, some of the recent interpretations over its alleged failure(s) have been disturbingly simplistic. In particular, much of contemporary scholarship on the American Dream focuses primarily [or even exclusively] on the promise of upward social mobility [as well as material prosperity, e.g. owning a house] associated with the idea of equality of opportunity. Interestingly enough, it is this promise of equality of opportunity that has started to figure as a burden in evaluating the vitality of the American Dream. Backed with indicators and other data on increasing economic inequality [compared to other democratic countries], some of the leading contemporary scholars (e.g. Chetty, 2021; Lemann, 2019; Markovits, 2019; Peters, 2012; Putnam, 2015; Sandel, 2020; Taussig, 2021) and public intellectuals (e.g. Chomsky, 2017) have questioned its emancipatory potential as well as its basic promise of upward social mobility and affluence.[4]

It is precisely this gap between its idealized image on one side and a set of indicators suggesting that the American dream has utterly failed that has given rise to a series of objections leading to the assertion it represents an empty or even a false promise. In fact, while its advocates champion it as some sort of a 'brilliant construction' (Hochschild, 1995: xi), its [many] critics depict it as nothing less than a "necessary illusion" (Lasch, 1996: 52). Nevertheless, the national dream narrative of the American Dream has served as a blueprint for global alternative political visions. Two examples stand out as particularly indicative. On the one hand, the European Dream has become an important generator of European integration (Rifkin, 2004). On the other hand, the Chinese Dream[5] has emerged as a leading national dream narrative in a 'post-American multi-polar world' (Peters, 2019: 110).

This chapter examines the intricate relationship between the American Dream and the meritocracy-based conception of equality of opportunity. In contrast to the 'data behind the words' approach championed by Richard Reeves (2014) in his analysis on equality of opportunity and the American Dream, this article takes the 'concepts behind the data' approach. The introductory part outlines the 'standard' interpretation of the American Dream as the most tangible materialization of the idea of equality of opportunity. The next section presents some distinctive aspects of equality of opportunity, in particular, the idea of opportunity as its key foundational characteristic. In particular, it focuses on the promise of the American Dream that is associated with the meritocracy-based conception of equality of opportunity. The next section examines some criticism that addresses the alleged failure of the American dream and its decreasing vitality. At the same time, a peculiar conception of fairness is brought to the forefront as a central legitimating idea of meritocratic (in)equality. The concluding section sets the stage for possible future research on the intricate relationship between these two ideas and the vitality of the American Dream itself.

Equality of Opportunity and the American Dream

Few, if any, of the concepts that are part of the American Dream's gravitational orbit of ideas have been more closely associated with it than that of equality of opportunity. Both historically and conceptually, equality of opportunity has arguably been the single most important building block of the 'standard' interpretation of the American Dream. As Richard V. Reeves emphasizes in his book *Saving Horatio Alger*,

> [m]any countries support the idea of meritocracy, but only in America is equality of opportunity a virtual national religion, reconciling individual liberty—the freedom to get ahead and "make something of yourself"—with societal equality. It is a philosophy of egalitarian individualism. The measure of American equality is not the income gap between the poor and the rich, but the chance to trade places.
>
> *Reeves, 2014*

In contrast to the hierarchical structure of 'old' class culture in Europe, best described by the parables of 'silver spoons' [and 'golden parachutes'] associated with 'old' aristocratic elites [based on largely inheritance], the idea of the American Dream and its promise has a distinctively meritocratic character (Sandel, 2020). Its promise of upward social mobility associated with the 'meritocratic equation' IQ + effort = *merit* has ultimately transformed the distribution of advantaged social positions and has had a lasting influence on the very idea of fairness itself. As a land of opportunity, Robert Merton accentuated in his article 'Social Structure and Anomie', America is perhaps best characterized by the 'ideology of open classes' (Merton, 1938: 679) and the formal absence of 'traditional' barriers including social class, gender roles, race, etc. The 'standard' interpretation of the American Dream, therefore, includes the following three characteristics, i.e. [*i*] freedom to pursue individual life goals; [*ii*] confidence that hard work will lead to economic security; and [*iii*] the expectation that things will be better in the future for oneself and one's children (Rank et al., 2016).

A clear example of how this promise is being viewed is perhaps most evident in one of the most eloquent contemporary examples of political rhetoric, i.e. the 2nd Inaugural Address by US President Barack Obama (delivered on January 21, 2013). As he pointed out, '[w]e are true to our creed when a little girl born into the bleakest poverty knows that she has the same chance to succeed as anybody else, because she is an American; she is free, and she is equal, not just in the eyes of God but also in our own' (Obama, 2013). Its ideological power, as Douglas Rae accentuates in his book *Equalities* is based

> in the wish and hope that the children of yesterday's losers may become tomorrow's winners, or, more exactly, in the belief that their birth-date prospects may become equal to those of other infants who are luckier in their choice of parents.
>
> *ibid.: 67*

This promise of upward social mobility premised on individual merit has actually become – as Lawrence Blum emphasizes – 'a deeply-held conception of the promise of American life' (Blum, 1988: 1) and perhaps the 'most distinctive and compelling element of our [American] national ideology' (Rae, 1983: 64). Interestingly enough, the centrality of equality of opportunity in the national dream narrative of the American Dream is actually nowhere more clearly stated than in James Truslow Adams' *The Epic of America*. Here Adams brings to the forefront the promise associated with the idea of equality of opportunity. As he emphasizes, the American Dream represents

> that dream of a land in which life should be better and richer and fuller for everyone, with opportunity for each according to ability or achievement. It is a difficult dream for the European upper classes to interpret adequately, and too many of us ourselves have grown weary and mistrustful of it. It is not a dream of motor cars and high wages merely, but a dream of social order in which each man and each woman shall be able to attain to the fullest stature of which they are innately capable, and be recognized by others for what they are, regardless of the fortuitous circumstances of birth or position.
> (Truslow Adams, 2012 [1931]: 317)

This promise, as Jennifer Hochschild accentuates, represents a 'promise that all Americans have a reasonable chance to achieve success as they define it—material or otherwise—through their own efforts, and to attain virtue and fulfillment through success' (Hochschild, 1995: xi). On this interpretation, an individual's success [largely] depends on his efforts or hard work. As Howard Schneiderman emphasizes,

> [f]rom the start, therefore, the American Dream was not about the elimination of social class distinctions, but for mobility through those ranks based on hard work. Indeed, any discussion of the American dream today still must hinge on the high value placed on work and achieving upward mobility through it.
> *Schneiderman, 2012: xiii*

An individual's success and his social mobility are therefore allegedly based exclusively on the merits of the individual and not on any of the morally arbitrary factors an individual may not have any influence over, e.g. gender, race, religion, socioeconomic status of the individual, one's talents,[6] inherited privileges or family background. As Michael Peters accentuates, 'American dreams emphasize a vision of a social order in which every individual – despite their social background – can succeed' (Peters, 2012: vii). In fact, several life stories attest to this fact including the writer Horatio Alger, the industrialist Andrew Carnegie, TV presenter Oprah Winfrey, media mogul David Geffen, US President Barack Obama, etc.[7]

In fact, the meritocracy-based conception of equal opportunities is based on the key assertion, as David Miller emphasizes, 'in which each person's chance to acquire positions of advantage and the rewards that go with them will depend entirely on his or her talent and effort' (Miller, 1999: 177). The distribution of advantaged social positions is based on the basis of individual merit and not on any of the morally arbitrary factors including race, religion, gender, socioeconomic status of the individual, etc. This is why the promise associated with the American Dream, as Robert Hauhart accentuates, represents the 'central motivating impulse in American life' (Hauhart, 2015: 74).

Despite a clear-cut message of this idea – depicted by Joshua Preiss as a fair race (2021) – a basic question comes to the forefront, i.e. when are individuals' opportunities being equal?

In order to answer this question, it is first necessary to provide an adequate response to a substantive question associated with equality of opportunity, i.e. 'what is an opportunity'. As Sven Ove Hansson emphasizes, discussions on equality of opportunity have often been 'hampered by insufficient attention to the very notion of opportunity itself' (Hansson, 2004: 315). Without further clarification of this concept and its basic characteristics, this question cannot adequately be addressed.

Opportunity and the American Dream[8]

Any conception of equality of opportunity, as Peter Westen emphasizes, consists of four basic elements, i.e. [*i*] agent or agents of equal opportunities, [*ii*] objective or objectives to which equal opportunities are directed, [*iii*] the relationship between the agent and the objective of equal opportunities, and [*iv*] obstacles to the realization of equal opportunities (Westen, 1997 [1985]: 837–838). The first element primarily brings together the individuals who are entitled to equal treatment, which implies – at least formally – the same conditions. The second aspect, as Peter Westen emphasizes, defines the objective of opportunities that can be 'a job, or an education, or medical care, or a political office, or land to settle, or housing, or a financial investment, or a military promotion, or a life of 'culture', or the development of natural ability or whatever' (Westen, 1997 [1985]: 838). The third element [the relationship between the agent and the objective of opportunities] is not yet a guarantee that the objective of equal opportunities will be achieved.

The concept of opportunity may therefore be defined in two separate ways, i.e. [*i*] as the absence of obstacles to the attainment of a particular objective [*negative justification*] and [*ii*] as the ability of an individual to attain a particular goal by using his efforts [*positive justification*]. An opportunity, as Peter Westen emphasizes, 'is a chance of an agent X, to choose to attain a goal, Y, Z without the hindrance of obstacle Z' (Westen, 1997 [1985]: 849) or – as Alan H. Goldman argues – 'the lack of some obstacle or obstacles to the attainment of some goal(s) or benefit(s)' (Goldman, 1987: 88). Having an opportunity, as Brian Barry claims, means that there 'there is some course of action lying within my power such that it will lead, if I choose to take it, to my doing or obtaining the thing in question' (Barry, 2005: 37).

At the same time, an opportunity has also been closely linked to the issue of a risk an individual is exposed to when aiming to achieve a particular goal.[9] It is the idea of the 'self-made man', as Christopher Lasch pointed out in *The Culture of Narcissism* as the 'archetypical embodiment of the American Dream' (Lasch, 1979: 52–53). In fact, as John Roemer emphasizes, the individual is actually being 'responsible for turning that access into actual advantage by the application of effort' (Roemer, 1998: 24). If an individual is therefore responsible for the outcome of the process of competing for advantaged social positions, then, it is necessary to ensure that only those factors an individual may be responsible for should be taken into account. Morally arbitrary factors such as gender, race, religion, ethnicity, socio-economic status, etc. should, therefore, not affect the process in which individuals compete for advantaged social positions.

The promise of the American Dream embedded in the 'standard' interpretation outlined above consists of a set of separate claims each representing a particular aspect of the 'ethics of success' (Sandel, 2020) associated with the American Dream, i.e.

1. each individual [irrespective of morally arbitrary factors associated with one's circumstances], e.g. gender, race, socioeconomic background, religious beliefs, etc., should have equal opportunities to achieve the desired goal [*assumption of non-discrimination*];

2. individuals' upward social mobility is the result of hard work and effort to succeed [*assumption of an individual's open future*];

3. an individual is solely responsible for the outcome of the process of competing for an advantaged social position and the associated transformation of an opportunity into an advantage [*the assumption of the instrumental nature of transformation*];

4. an individual's [material] success is the result of his effort and hard work and not of the factors he might not have influence over and would therefore not be responsible for [*the assumption of the voluntaristic nature of individuals' success*];

5. the greater an individual's effort, the lower the risk for the achievement of the objective of [*the assumption of proportionality of risk and success achieved*].[10]

These claims lead to the assertion that the American dream represents the best possible materialization of the idea of equality of opportunity and ultimately portrays the US as a land of opportunity. This promise of the American Dream has been encapsulated most eloquently in the opening paragraph of Cal Jillson's book *The American Dream in History, Politics and Fiction* (2016), where he accentuates that '[t]he grand promise of the American Dream has always been that those willing to learn, work, save, persevere, and play by the rules will have a better chance to grow and prosper in America than anywhere else on earth' (2016: ix).

As the promise of the American Dream sketched above makes clear, the idea of equality of opportunity is far from being either unquestionable or unproblematic. In fact, John Rawls emphasizes in *Justice as Fairness*, it as a 'difficult and not altogether clear idea' (Rawls, 2001: 43). A key issue to be pointed out is its relationship with inequality. In particular, it should be pointed out that neither the idea of equality of opportunity nor the American dream itself and inequality are not mutually exclusive. As Samuel Scheffler emphasizes, 'inequalities in the advantages that people enjoy are acceptable if they derive from the choices that people have voluntarily made, but that inequalities deriving from unchosen features of people's circumstances are unjust' (Scheffler, 2003: 5). This idea, as Shlomi Segall accentuates, is based on the assumption 'that is unfair for one person to be worse off than another due to reasons beyond her control' (Segall, 2008: 10). To stretch this interpretation further, a person can legitimately be required as Andrew Mason points out, 'to bear the costs (or allowed to enjoy the benefits) of those consequences of her behavior the production of which lies within her control but not those the production of which lies beyond it' (Mason, 2001b: 763). In contrast to an idealized portrayal of the American Dream, the only solid assumption different conceptions of equality of opportunity share in common, as Richard Arneson (2015) accentuates, is their rejection of fixed social relations, but not hierarchy itself.

It is precisely this aspect of the American Dream that represents the single most important challenge for its advocates as, over the last few decades, a number of indicators have shown that its vitality is faltering (Chetty, 2021; Krueger, 2015). This and a number of other pressing criticisms advanced by its critics have questioned not only its emancipatory and progressive potential (Lawrence, 2012) but have denigrated it as being either an empty ideal or even a false one.

Mind the [Opportunity] Gap: The American Dream in 'Crisis'

The crisis of the American Dream and its vitality is hardly any news. In fact, for more than two decades now scholars writing on it have identified a number of shortcomings that have put the American Dream in jeopardy. In particular, the American Dream and its promise of upward social mobility have come under considerable scrutiny. Interestingly enough, as in the case of the study of neoliberalism (O'Connor, 2010), the criticism of the American Dream has become some sort of a 'cottage industry'. Just a few weeks after Barack Obama's 2nd Inaugural Address as US President,[11] Joseph E. Stiglitz [the Nobel laureate in economics and professor at Columbia University] published an article in the *New York Times*[12] where he questioned the relevance of the idea of equality of opportunity by labeling it 'our national myth'. He pointed to a diminishing vertical upward social mobility as well as the deepening of the differences between those who have and those who have no chance of success and remain underprivileged. As he emphasizes,

> It's not that social mobility is impossible, but that the upwardly mobile American is becoming a statistical oddity. According to research from the Brookings Institution, only 58 percent of Americans born into the bottom fifth of income earners move out of that category, and just 6 percent born into the bottom fifth move into the top. Economic mobility in the United States is lower than in most of Europe and lower than in all of Scandinavia.
>
> *Stiglitz, 2013*

On this interpretation, part of the problem with the American Dream is largely attributable to rising inequality and lower intergenerational social mobility. As Paul Krugman wrote in an op-ed article published in the *New York Times,*

> although we still see ourselves as the land of opportunity, we actually have less intergenerational economic mobility than other advanced nations. That is, the chances that someone born into a low-income family will end up with high income, or vice versa, are significantly lower here than in Canada or Europe.
>
> *Krugman, 2012*

This gap between the idealized image of the American Dream and its emancipatory potential on the one hand, together with indicators and other data [including 'big data' (e.g. Chetty, 2021)] showing a diminishing intergenerational upward social mobility on the other, leads to the assertion that they might represent an empty or even a false promise. In order to explain this phenomenon, the economist Alan Krueger introduced a graphical representation labeled the 'Gatsby Curve' in order to represent the inverted correlation between intergenerational mobility and income inequality.[13] For both critics and those sympathetic to it, the American Dream has been under scrutiny for either not delivering what it purportedly needed to deliver or that it has nothing to deliver at all.

In order to fully comprehend the shortcomings of the existing criticism of the American Dream, a distinction needs to be made between two distinct forms of idealization of the American Dream, i.e. the [*i*] 'direct' idealization and the [*ii*] 'indirect' idealization. This is of particular importance as each of the two idealizations contributes very different types of legitimacy to the national dream narrative impetus. As Aaron M. Duncan emphasizes in *Gambling with the Myth of the American Dream*, 'the myth of the American Dream works to rationalize our class system, social structure, and culture' (Duncan, 2015: 1). The direct idealization uses a straightforward strategy of acknowledging that all is fine with the current status of American society and its national dream narrative. In contrast, the indirect idealization delivers a twofold message. On the one hand, it points out to a particular problem or challenge that the existing state of affairs over the American Dream is problematic and that it represents some sort of a deviation from a previous situation. On the other hand, while this message delivers a criticism of the phenomenon, its other [hidden] message is that there previously was a stage which we only need to return to. Most of the contemporary criticisms of the American Dream fall into this category. This 'indirect' idealization is, therefore, equally or even more ideological than the 'direct' one.

Conclusion: The Easy Rider dilemma

The crisis over the vitality of the American Dream explicated above has been complemented with a 'crisis' embedded in the scholarly work aiming to make sense of this phenomenon so central to the American way of life. The 'standard' interpretation over the American Dream as the 'central principle of American public philosophy' (Preiss, 2021: xi) is primarily [or even exclusively] targeting its faltering longevity. Parables such as the 'opportunity gap' (Putnam, 2015), the 'meritocracy trap' (Markovits, 2019), or the 'Great Gatsby Curve' (Krueger, 2015) [alongside a platitude of other slogans, metaphors, and thought-terminating clichés] portray a reductionist understanding of the American Dream and the idea of equality of opportunity it has been associated with. While indicators showing a decrease in upward social mobility rightly point to problems plaguing the vitality of the American Dream, this alone does not qualify as a sufficient element to pronounce its demise. In contrast, these objections and criticism rather point to a twofold problem with the 'standard' interpretation of the American Dream, i.e. [*i*] a change in the very perception of the American Dream and [*ii*] the shift of emphasis in the language of neoliberalization (Sardoč, 2020b).

On the one hand, the prevailing perception of the American Dream has been filtered through its 'standard' interpretation dominated by a central *substantive* question best epitomized by the title of Jennifer Hochschild's introductory chapter to *Facing up to the American Dream* ['What is the American Dream']. A good illustration of this paradigm comes from one of the most memorable scenes from *Easy Rider*, one of the flagship motion pictures of New Hollywood and the 1960s counterculture in general. In an iconic movie scene leading to the 'We made it, we blew it' argument, the two leading characters played by Peter Fonda and Dennis Hopper disagree over the very definition of success, one of the main characteristics of the American Dream [the 'Easy Rider' dilemma]. For the character portrayed by Dennis Hopper, the definition of 'making it' ['what it's all about man'] boils down to become rich and to retire in Florida. In contrast, Peter Fonda's character synoptic line ['We blew it'] provides a more enigmatic answer to what the 'ethics of success' (Sandel, 2020) associated with the American Dream might stand for.

While instructive enough, this question of what best characterizes a national dream narrative and its ethos somehow circumvents many of the issues that require further clarification. As Robert Hauhart pointed out, the American dream is supposed to be 'the source of the highest aspirations of Americans as well as the source of their most common and lowest shortcomings' (Hauhart, 2015: 75).[14] It, therefore, comes as no surprise that the main substantive question 'What is the American Dream' emanated in a range of alternative interpretations about the 'core meaning' of the American Dream (Rank et al., 2016) or its 'deep structure' (Ghosh, 2013). Nevertheless, despite much of its productivity, this approach – in large part – turns out to 'hit the target but misses the point'. Perhaps the central navigating question might be not a *substantive* one, i.e. 'What is the American, European or the Chinese Dream'. Instead, the question to be asked is more likely a *motivational* one, i.e. 'why is the American Dream actually important'? As Doron Taussig points out in his book *What We Mean by the American Dream*, '[o]ur belief in this mythology is supposed to help explain why we accept our position in an unequal society and take responsibility for our own lot in life' (Taussig, 2021: 5).

On the other hand, our perception of the American Dream has also been influenced by neoliberalism's resemanticization of egalitarian and progressive vocabulary. If the 'first-wave' neoliberalism associated with free-market fundamentalism evangelized by Margaret Thatcher and Ronald Reagan in the 1970s and 1980s has been advanced under the banner of privatization and deregulation, its most recent 'developmental stage' started to incorporate concepts and ideas previously outside its gravitational orbit, e.g. equality, justice, well-being, fairness, equality of opportunity, etc. This reappropriation of the progressive and emancipatory rhetoric has reshaped our understanding of social phenomena previously thought to be outside of the neoliberal purview including the American Dream.

While the credibility of the analyzes and the plethora of statistics supporting the thesis that the American dream does not work is by no means questionable, their conceptual nature is multifaceted and problematic, as they represent, as Jim Cullen pointed out, a 'complex idea, with many meanings [...] understood in different ways' (Cullen, 2003: 7). As Christopher Lasch pointed out in *The Revolt of the Elites and the Betrayal of Democracy*, 'the concept of social mobility embodies a rather recent and sadly impoverished understanding of the American dream' (Lasch, 1996: 50). This is [in a way] also confirmed by a number of different – and in some cases even contradictory – concepts that are part of its 'conceptual cartography', e.g. liberty, equality, social mobility, hard work, equality of opportunity, ideology, meritocracy, success, self-realization, responsibility, idealism, 'fair play', trust, risk, consumerism, individualism, honesty, optimism, and hope.

Ultimately, the idealism of the American dream best represented by the vision that each individual can achieve the set goal has been replaced by a dystopian picture of social Darwinism driven by the illusion of a common goal: material success. As Michael Sandel pointed out in *The Tyranny of Merit: What's Become of the Common Good?* (2020), meritocratic triumphalism and its 'ethics of success' associated with both the American Dream and equality of opportunity in general also has a 'dark side': In particular, the weaponization of college credentials, the practice of 'incentivizing people', populist discontent, helicopter parenting, and meritocratic hubris turns out to be a collateral damage arising out of governing by merit.

The analysis of the 'standard' interpretation of the American dream and its link with the idea of equality of opportunity provided in this chapter points in the direction of contextualizing each and every one of its elements in a much more in-depth manner. In fact, the vast majority of the existing analyses of the American Dream have been a way to simple and univocal. As Walter Fischer has emphasized in his 'classical' article 'Reaffirmation and Subversion of the American Dream', the American Dream is composed by two separate myths, i.e. [i] material myth and [ii] egalitarian moral myth (Fischer, 1973). It looks like both its advocates and its critics have been on autopilot while discussing the various complex issues associated with this social phenomenon. As Michael Sandel pointed out in *Democracy's Discontent*, the 'predicament of American democracy resides not only in the gap between our ideal and institutions, but also within the ideals themselves, and within the self-image our public life reflects' (Sandel, 1996: x).

Retrospectively, though, perhaps the weakness of the various analyses that have been offered regarding the American Dream's apparent promises of equal opportunity for all and a life filled with material abundance is that virtually all of the commentators have disregarded Freud's teaching. Freud knew that dreams were merely ephemeral vestiges of symbolic, subconscious, wish-fulfillment. The reality of social life is simply that the promises of equal opportunity for all; material abundance for all; and a life in a land which is "better and richer and fuller for every man [and woman]" is a vision that is unattainable. Although life is not, as Hobbes contended, "solitary, poore, nasty, brutish, and short", it is not possible to reconcile what we know about human history and the succession of wars, pogroms, genocides, and plagues that litter it, with unadulterated optimism. Rather, as Freud understood, we dream because our unconscious wishes to resolve a mental tension or conflict. Thus, the American Dream is a socially collective effort to resolve the irresolvable, not only within our minds but within society. Dreaming the Dream permits us to substitute hope in place of the grim realization that the embodiment of the American Dream may only entail bitter, futile struggle, not success. Believing in the Dream rescues us from despair; achieving reality, in a sense, does not matter.

Notes

1 For an in-depth analysis of the American Dream and its role in American popular culture, see Lawrence (2012).
2 As Howard Schneiderman has emphasized, there is a close connection between the American Dream and Martin Luther King's speech "I Have a Dream" (2012: xii).
3 The report is available at Brookings' webpage: https://www.brookings.edu/wp-content/uploads/2016/07/Full-Report.pdf
4 See, for example, Alan Krueger's article "The great utility of the Great Gatsby Curve" discussing the relationship between intergenerational mobility and income inequality in USA https://www.brookings.edu/blog/social-mobility-memos/2015/05/19/the-great-utility-of-the-great-gatsby-curve/
5 The voluminous literature in disciplines and areas of research as diverse as political theory (Wang, 2014), international relations (Do, 2015), Asian studies (Gow, 2017), Sinology (Koptseva, 2016), travel and tourism research (Weaver et al., 2015), American studies (Pena, 2015), communication studies (Zhong and Zhang, 2016), policy analysis (Kalha, 2015), critical discourse analysis (Boc, 2015), "soft power" (Servaes, 2016), education (Peters, 2019; Sardoč, 2020a), etc. is a testament to the growing importance of the Chinese Dream.
6 For a detailed presentation of the many tensions, problems, and challenges arising out of the intricate relationship between talents and distributive justice, see Sardoč and Deželan (2021).
7 As Alan Wolfe pointed out in his review of Robert Putnam's book *Our Kids*, life stories perform a didactical role: "[t]hey are there to make larger points and not because they are especially interesting in themselves" (2015).
8 For a detailed examination of the idea of opportunity, see Sardoč (2016b).
9 The American Dream has also been associated with risk and gambling in particular. In fact, on some interpretations, poker as a "form of gambling best exemplifies modern American culture". This link has already been emphasized by Jeremy Rifkin in his book *The European Dream* (2004: 28–29). For a detailed elaboration of this link, see Duncan (2015).
10 For an elaboration of this "scheme", see Sardoč (2016b).
11 The transcript of this Inaugural Address is available at the website https://obamawhitehouse.archives.gov/the-press-office/2013/01/21/inaugural-address-president-barack-obama
12 The article *Equal Opportunity, Our National Myth* is available at the *New York Times* website http://opinionator.blogs.nytimes.com/2013/02/16/equal-opportunity-our-national-myth/
13 For an informative presentation of the "Great Gatsby curve," see Krueger's article "The great utility of the Great Gatsby Curve" https://www.brookings.edu/blog/social-mobility-memos/2015/05/19/the-great-utility-of-the-great-gatsby-curve/
14 As Steven Messner and Richard Rosenfeld point out in their book *Crime and the American Dream*, "[h]igh crime rates are intrinsic to the basic cultural commitments and institutional arrangements of American society" and – relatedly – that "the American Dream itself and the normal social engendered by it are deeply implicated in the problem of crime" (Messner and Rosenfeld, 1994: 6).

References

Adams, J.T. (2012 [1931]). *The Epic of America*. New Brunswick: Transaction Publishers.
Arneson, R. (2015). Equality of Opportunity. *Stanford Encyclopedia of Philosophy*. Available at: https://plato.stanford.edu/entries/equal-opportunity/

Barry, B. (2005). *Why Social Justice Matters.* Cambridge: Polity Press.

Blum, L. (1988). Opportunity and Equality of Opportunity, *Public Affairs Quarterly*, 2(4), pp. 1–18.

Brooking Institution & AEI (2015). *Opportunity, Responsibility and Security: A Consensus Plan for Reducing Poverty and Restoring the American Dream.* Available at http://www.brookings.edu/research/reports2/2015/12/aei-brookings-poverty-and-opportunity

Boc, A. (2015). The Power of Language: Globalizing "the Chinese Dream." *Fudan Journal of the Humanities and Social Sciences*, 8(4), pp. 533–551.

Cannon, L. (2003). The Butterfly Effect and the Virtues of the *American Dream, Journal of Social Philosophy*, 34(4), pp. 545–555.

Chetty, R. (2021). Improving Equality of Opportunity: New Insights From Big Data, *Contemporary Economic Policy*, 39(1), pp. 7–41.

Chomsky, N. (2017). *Requiem for the American Dream: The 10 Principles of Concentration of Wealth & Power.* New York: Seven Stories Press.

Clark, W.A.V. (2003). *Immigrants and the American Dream: Remaking the Middle Class.* New York: Guilford Press.

Cullen, J. (2003). *The American Dream: A Short History of an Idea That Shaped a Nation.* Oxford: Oxford University Press.

D'Antonio, W. (2011). Religion and the American Dream. In: S.L. Hanson & J.K. White [eds.], *The American Dream in the 21st Century*, pp. 117–140. Philadelphia, PA: Temple University Press.

DeVitis, J.L. & Rich, J.M. (1996). *The Success Ethic, Education and the American Dream.* New York: SUNY.

Do, T.T. (2015). China's Rise and the "Chinese Dream" in International Relations Theory, *Global Change, Peace & Security*, 27(1), pp. 21–38.

Duncan, M.A. (2015). *Gambling with the Myth of the American Dream.* London: Routledge.

Fischer, W.R. (1973). Reaffirmation and Subversion of the American Dream, *Quarterly Journal of Speech*, 59(2), pp. 160–167.

Freud, S. (2010 [1900]). *The Interpretation of Dreams.* New York: Basic Books.

Freud, S. (1957 [1909]). *Five Lectures on Psycho-Analysis.* New York: W. W. Norton & Company.

Ghosh, C. (2013). *The Politics of the American Dream: Democratic Inclusion in Contemporary American Political Culture.* New York: Palgrave Macmillan.

Goldman, A. (1987). The Justification of Equal Opportunity, *Social Philosophy and Policy*, 5(1), pp. 88–103.

Gow, M. (2017). The Core Socialist Values of the Chinese Dream: Towards a Chinese Integral State, *Critical Asian Studies*, 49(1), pp. 92–116.

Hansson, S.O. (2004). What Are Opportunities and Why Should They Be Equal, *Social Choice and Welfare*, 22(2), pp. 305–316.

Hauhart, R.C. (2011). Exporting the American Dream: Global Implications, *International Journal of the Humanities*, 9(2), pp. 1–12.

Hauhart, R.C. (2015). American Sociology's Investigations of the American Dream: Retrospect and Prospect, *The American Sociologist*, 46(1), pp. 65–98.

Hauhart, Robert C. (2016). *Seeking the American Dream: A Sociological Inquiry.* New York: Palgrave Macmillan.

Hochschild, J.L. (1995). *Facing Up to the American Dream.* Princeton, NJ: Princeton University Press.

Hochschild, J.L. & Scovronick, N. (2003). *The American Dream and the Public Schools.* Oxford: Oxford University Press.

Jillson, C. (2016). *The American Dream: In History, Politics and Fiction.* Lawrence: The University of Kansas Press.

Kalha, R.S. (2015). An Assessment of the Chinese Dream: 2015, *Strategic Analysis*, 39(3), pp. 274–279.

Koptseva, N.P. (2016). "The Chinese Dream" Through the Mirror of Modern Social Research. *Journal of Siberian Federal University. Humanities and Social Sciences*, pp. 374–393. Available at https://core.ac.uk/download/pdf/38647286.pdf

Krueger, A.B. (2015). "The Great Utility of the Great Gatsby Curve," Social Mobility Memos [Brookings Institution], http://www.brookings.edu/blogs/social-mobility-memos/ posts/2015/05/19-utility-great-gatsby-curve-krueger (December 28, 2015).

Krugman, P. (2012). How Fares the Dream? *The New York Times* (January 15, 2012), http://www.nytimes.com/2012/01/16/opinion/krugman-how-fares-the-dream.html?_r=0 [October 6, 2015].

Lasch, C. (1979). *The Culture of Narcissism: American Life in an Age of Diminishing Expectations*. London: W.W. Norton & Company.

Lasch, C. (1996). *The Revolt of the Elites and the Betrayal of Democracy*. London: W.W. Norton & Company.

Lawrence, I. (2019). *Soccer and the American Dream*. London: Routledge.

Lawrence, S. (2012). *The American Dream: A Cultural History*. Syracuse, NY: Syracuse University Press.

Lemann, N. (2019). *Transaction Man: The Rise of the Deal and the Decline of the American Dream*. New York: Farrar, Straus and Giroux.

Long, E. (1985). *The American Dream and the Popular Novel*. London: Routledge.

Markovits, D. (2019). *The Meritocracy Trap: How America's Foundational Myth Feeds Inequality, Dismantles the Middle Class, and Devours the Elite*. New York: Penguin.

Mason, A. (2001b). Equality of Opportunity, Old and New, *Ethics*, 111(4), pp. 760–781.

Merton, R.K. (1938). Social Structure and Anomie, *American Sociological Review*, 3(5), pp. 672–682.

Messner, S.F. & Rosenfeld, R. (1994) *Crime and the American Dream*. Belmont, CA: Wadsworth.

Miller, D. (1999). *Principles of Social Justice*. Cambridge, MA: Harvard University Press.

Nye, Joseph S. Jr. (1990). Soft Power, *Foreign Policy*, 80, pp. 153–171.

Obama, B.H. (2013). Inaugural Address by President Barack Obama. Washington, DC: The White House/Office of the Press Secretary, http://www.whitehouse. gov/the-press-office/2013/01/21/inaugural-address-president-barack-obama [January, 23, 2016].

O'Connor, J. (2010). Marxism and the Three Movements of Neoliberalism, *Critical Sociology*, 36(5), pp. 691–715.

Pena, D.S. (2015). Comparing the Chinese Dream with the American Dream, *International Critical Thought*, 5(3), pp. 277–295.

Peters, M.A. (2012). *Obama and the End of the American Dream: Essays in Political and Economic Philosophy*. Boston, MA: Sense Publishers.

Peters, M.A. (2019). *The Chinese Dream: Educating the Future*. New York: Routledge.

Preiss, J. (2021). *Just Work for All: The American Dream in the 21st Century*. London: Routledge.

Putnam, R. (2015). *Our Kids: The American Dream in Crisis*. New York: Simon & Schuster.

Rae, D.W. (1983). *Equalities*. Cambridge, MA: Harvard University Press.

Rank, M, Hirschl, T. & Foster K. (2016). *Chasing the American Dream: Understanding What Shapes Our Fortunes*. Oxford: Oxford University Press.

Ratner-Rosenhagen, J. (2019). *The Ideas That Made American: A Brief History*. Oxford: Oxford University Press.

Rawls, J. (2001). *Justice as Fairness: A Restatement*. Cambridge, MA: Harvard University Press.

Reeves, R.V. (2014). *Saving Horatio Alger: Equality, Opportunity and the American Dream*. Washington: Brookings Institution Press.

Rifkin, J. (2004). *The European Dream: How Europe's Vision of the Future Is Quietly Eclipsing the American Dream*. New York: Penguin.

Roemer, J.E. (1998). *Equality of Opportunity*. Cambridge, MA: Harvard University Press.

Samuel, R.L. (2001). *Brought to You By: Postwar Television Advertising and the American Dream*. Austin, TX: University of Texas Press.

Sandel, M.J. (1996). *Democracy's Discontent: America in Search of a Public Philosophy*. Cambridge, MA: Harvard University Press.

Sandel, M.J. (2020). *The Tyranny of Merit: What's Become of the Common Good*. London: Allen Lane.

Sardoč, Mitja (2016a). Ameriške sanje: med idealom in ideologijo, *Teorija in praksa*, 53(6), pp. 1468–1483.

Sardoč, M. (2016b). Equality of Opportunity, Cultural Diversity and Claims for Fairness, *CEPS Journal: Center for Educational Policy Studies Journal*, 6(2), pp. 25–41.

Sardoč, Mitja (2017). Education and the American Dream, *Šolsko polje*, XXVIII(¾), pp. 5–10.

Sardoč, M. (2020a). The Chinese Dream and Its Future: Review Essay on Michael Peters Book *The Chinese Dream: Educating the Future*, *Educational Philosophy and Theory*, DOI: 10.1080/00131857.2020.1712673

Sardoč, M. & Deželan, T. (2021). Talents and Distributive Justice: Some Tensions, *Educational Philosophy and Theory*, 53(8), pp. 768–776.

Scheffler, S. (2003). What Is Egalitarianism?, *Philosophy and Public Affairs*, 31(1), pp. 5–39.

Schneiderman, H. (2012). James Truslow Adams and the American Dream. In: J.T. Adams, *The Epic of America*, pp. ix–xviii. New Brunswick: Transaction Publishers.

Segall, S. (2008). *Health, Luck and Justice*. Princeton, NJ: Princeton University Press.

Servaes, J. (2016). The Chinese Dream Shattered between Hard and Soft Power?, *Media, Culture & Society*, 38(3), 437–449.

Shaanan, J. (2010). *Economic Freedom and the American Dream*. New York: Palgrave Macmillan.

Stiglitz, J.E. (2013): Equal Opportunity, Our National Myth, *The New York Times*, http://opinionator. blogs.nytimes.com/2013/02/16/equal-opportunity-our-national-myth/ [March 7, 2014)].

Taussig, D. (2021). *What We Mean by the American Dream: Stories We Tell about Meritocracy*. Ithaca, NY: Cornell University Press.

Truslow A.J. (2012 [1931]). *The Epic of America*. London: Transaction Publishers.

Wang, Z. (2014). The Chinese Dream: Concept and Context, *Journal of Chinese Political Science*, 19(1), pp. 1–13.

Weaver, D., Becken, S., Ding, P., Mackerras, C., Perdue, R., Scott, N., & Wang, Y. (2015). Research Agenda for Tourism and the Chinese Dream: Dialogues and Open Doors, *Journal of Travel Research*, 54(5), 578–583.

Westen, P. (1997 [1985]). The Concept of Equal Opportunity. *Ethics*, 95(4), pp. 837–850..

Wolfe, A. (2015). Book Review: "Our Kids: The American Dream in Crisis" by Robert D. Putnam, *The Washington Post* (March 6, 2015). Available at https://www.seattletimes.com/entertainment/ books/class-divides-are-killing-the-american-dream-writes-robert-putnam-in-our-kids/

Zhong, L. & Zhang, J. (2016). Political Myth as Strategic Communication: Analysis of Chinese Dream's Rhetoric and English News Media's Interpretation, *International Journal of Strategic Communication*, 10(1), pp. 51–68.

7

WHAT "AMERICAN" DREAM?

Contemporary reflections

Melanie E.L. Bush

Section I: Historical Foundations – The Modern World-System

The emergence of coloniality included the development of world capitalism, nation-states, white supremacy/Euro-centered dominance, and particular forms of cis-heteronormative patriarchy. These systems converged to constitute the modern world system. The founding and rise of the U.S. as a hegemonic power was birthed of this process and brought about a new era entrenched in coloniality. These developments had profound global significance and material manifestation, laying the foundation for the structure of most all societies over the last six centuries through contemporary times. They provided the context for the emergence of the 20th-century concept known as the "American" Dream.[1]

The roots of the hierarchical system within which European hegemony is embedded and the "global designs" for domination upon which the system rests are rationalized by a series of myths. These include the notion of objectivist/universalist knowledges, an assertion that the decolonization of the modern world-system has been completed, and that developmentalism (along the lines of the model proposed by the U.S. in the 1950s and 1960s) is the path to a better life for all (Grosfoguel and Cervantes-Rodriguez 2002). These ideas are intertwined with each other, intrinsically tied to Eurocentric systems of knowledge creation and reproduction, and structurally embedded through the imposition of essentialized hierarchies, binaries, and divides. These foundational organizing myths have served to limit the imaginations of the oppressed and rendered their representations of ways of being, political options, and epistemologies invisible as if they never existed and do not currently endure (Grosfoguel and Cervantes-Rodriguez 2002).

These dominant and hegemonizing ideologies are deeply built into white world supremacy and constitute a commonsense and systemic reality deeply in need of interrogation, rupture, and transformation. They form the political, economic, and social historical foundation for the emergence of the rhetoric of an "American" dream despite the structural presets that continue to organize U.S. society along a path where upward mobility is less and less the reality, even for those groups who were provided temporary access. Of course, not everyone has the same relationship to "nation" within the U.S., and not everyone outside the U.S. is viewed through the same lens. This is painfully evident in longstanding discourses and practices related to inequalities within all institutions of society, immigration policies, and notions of belonging.

DOI: 10.4324/9781003326243-8

Coloniality, Americanity, and White Supremacy

"Nations" exist in a world scale system of inequality, ordered around the ideology of pan-European racism derived from the colonization of the Americas and subsequently the entire globe. During this period, the idea of race was invented to naturalize the power of Europeans and through enslavement, establish Africans as the core labor force in the "new world." This process involved the construction of a hierarchical social-economic-political system elevating Europeans above all. In this way, white world supremacy formed the structural and ideological bedrock of the modern world-system, capitalist world-economy, and the U.S. nation.

The founding principles that are asserted in much of the nation's mainstream historiography neither conform to the perspectives of the settlers (who themselves were not immigrants) nor to their practices, which were based on very clear principles of the inclusion of some and exclusion of others. These practices were not exceptions to the rule as is most often argued, rather exclusion is and has been the rule. It is systemic and systematic, as well as structurally, institutionally, materially, and ideologically embedded. Any notions of "'America' the beautiful," as a nation of immigrants who consciously forged a "New Eldorado"/"City on a Hill"/beacon of light to all in the world/magical land like no other that offered(s) opportunity to all those willing to work "hard enough" have always been a fabrication.

After the attack on the world trade center and other targets on September 11, 2001, Immanuel Wallerstein spoke at Brooklyn College referencing the title of a previous lecture: "America and the World: Today, Yesterday, and Tomorrow" and discussing God's blessings to "America" – in the past, liberty; in the present, prosperity; in the future, equality.

> Somehow, God had not distributed these blessings to everyone everywhere. I noted that Americans were very conscious of this unequal distribution of God's grace. I said that the United States had always defined itself, had always measured its blessings, by the yardstick of the world. We are better; we were better; we shall be better. Perhaps blessings that are universal are not considered true blessings. Perhaps we impose upon God the requirement that She save only a minority.
>
> *Wallerstein 2001*

This logic of inequality favoring a minority is reflective of the logic of our historical social system, the capitalist world-economy, an inherently polarizing social system. The capitalist/colonial world system facilitates this polarization by breaking the bonds of humanity between those in the "modern" centers and those located in parts of the globe inhabited by the racialized majority of humankind. This system enacts a similar dynamic within nations between different and among populations.

Scholars and militants from these "peripheral" zones and their allies in the first and second worlds[2] have long labored to explain this relationship between capitalism and inequality on every level. In the works of Marx and Engels in the 19th century, Lenin and DuBois in the early 20th century, Raul Prebisch and the Economic Commission on Latin American in the 1940s, Aime Cesaire and Frantz Fanon during the Bandung period, Immanuel Wallerstein, Samir Amin, Giovanni Arrighi, Anibal Quijano, and Andre Gunder Frank in the middle and late 20th century, the critical relationship of inequality to the modern world has been central. An early 1990s work of Quijano and Wallerstein provides an important analysis that explains the role of race (and white supremacy/Eurocentrism) in the capitalist/colonial world system, as well as the specific role that the founding of the U.S. played in consolidating the modern world and its systemic premises.

135

Quijano and Wallerstein (1992) argue that the creation of the geo-social entity called the Americas was the constitutive act of the modern world system in the long 16th century. Along with the destruction of the indigenous populations that attended the birth of the modern world-system, Americanity was associated with "modernity" and identified as the "new world." Four elements distinguished the Americas from the "old world": coloniality, ethnicity, racism, and the concept of newness itself (Quijano and Wallerstein 1992, 550). "Coloniality was essentially the creation of a set of states linked together within an interstate system in hierarchical layers" (Quijano and Wallerstein 1992, 550). This system "manifested itself in all domains-political, social, and not least of all cultural" (Quijano and Wallerstein 1992, 550). This hierarchy reproduced itself over time though there was always some mobility for a few. Coloniality was essential to the integration of the interstate system creating a ranking order, rules for interaction among states, and social relations within nation-states themselves.

Nationality and ethnicity emerged as building blocks of the modern world-system, and a communal identity that located groups within a given state. Quijano and Wallerstein argue that ethnicity was the inevitable consequence of coloniality as it served to delineate the social boundaries corresponding to the division of labor. This was used as justification for different forms of labor and control that came to exist within the Americas: slavery for Black Africans, various forms of cash crop labor arrangements for Native Americans, indentured labor for certain groups of European workers, and positions of power for others. While forms of labor control evolved with changes in the capitalist division of labor, the hierarchy has been a constant of the system. Given this, white settler populations were mindful of the specters of Black ex-slave republics as in Haiti and rural Amerindian claims to sovereignty as they viewed these movements for independence as upsetting to the ethnic-identified work hierarchy (Quijano and Wallerstein 1992, 551). This threat, in turn, was used as a disciplinary tool by elites to keep the general white population in line. This structural positioning was therefore critical to the maintenance of white elite's status and control.

Coloniality continued to develop in the form of a sociocultural hierarchical ranking of labor and control between Europeans and non-Europeans after the system of formal colonialism and slavery came to an end. Ethnicity came to be reinforced by a conscious and systematic racism theorized during the 19th century (Quijano and Wallerstein 1992, 552). The purpose was to culturally shore up an economic hierarchy, some of whose political guarantees were weakened in the post-1789 era of "popular sovereignty." In the 19th century, the U.S. was the first state in the world-system to enact a system of formal segregation, as well as the first to force Indigenous people onto reservations and bar whole populations such as the Chinese in the Exclusion Act of 1882. Quijano and Wallerstein argue that it was precisely its strong position within the world-economy that made this practice necessary. In the U.S., the upper stratum as a percentage of total population was growing much faster than any other country, providing opportunities for upward mobility for larger numbers. In such a situation, "informal constraints of ethnicity" were not up to the task of maintaining "workplace and social hierarchies" (Quijano and Wallerstein 1992, 551). In this way, formal racism (Black codes, Jim Crow, scientific racism, etc.) became a further contribution of Americanity to the world-system. Additionally, these developments were critical in the formalization of whiteness itself, including the history-making of "white people."[3]

Twentieth-Century Challenges

While initially functional, post-World War II, this system of formal racism was not compatible with U.S. social and geopolitical realities after the nation's ascension to a hegemonic position within the world-system. The U.S. that sought to separate and insulate itself from the affairs of Europe, operated on a different logic than one concerned about matters of world power. These circumstances created the opening for the African American-led civil rights movement to push for challenges to the Jim Crow system of de jure segregation. This fight was of enormous symbolic value in forcing the U.S. to end this obvious contradiction to its democratic pretensions, especially given its new mantle as the leader of the so-called "free world." However, most engaged in the fight for racial equality understood that there was another deeper layer to racial equality beyond the struggle against de jure segregation.

Outright discrimination as in the Jim Crow South was an obvious relic within a country that professed to represent a progressive global liberalism and presented itself to the world as an anti-colonial power distinct from colonial Europe. Wallerstein contended that the more enduring form in which racial privilege is maintained is not discrimination but the creation of de facto but informal privileged access to non-state institutions (education, occupation, housing, health care) through the operation of an apparent individual attribution of advantage. In this way, institutions abstract the totality of social factors that account for differential performance and hence widen rather than narrow existing inequalities (Wallerstein 1979). This process was very evident in the "whitening" of numerous populations during the late nineteenth and early part of the 20th century.

The social compacts of the core states during the period from 1945 to 1970 were based on the power of the working classes of the dominant ethnic strata. The workplace bargaining power of these labor forces and other sociopolitical dynamics required the expansion of the U.S. into economic spaces throughout the world-system. During the post-war period, the European working classes were quite powerful in relationship to their employing classes and states. Therefore, the U.S. and its Marshall Plan were needed to ensure social order in the Western European core states. The strength of its economic position also made it necessary that the U.S. expand widespread legal and illegal migration from non-European countries. The combination of the internally colonized populations of African descent, Mexican, Puerto Rican, Native American, and various Asian populations with the "new" immigrants created a phenomenon that came to be called by some observers "the third world within." Furthermore, the federal government recognizes 537 Indigenous tribes (not including those that are state-recognized or without political recognition), represents a clear example of nations within a nation and an ongoing colonial endeavor (Keeler 2022). Over the short run, these dynamics pushed large sections of the dominant white ethnic working class to the right, and over the longer term, it polarized the society in such a way that even the nationalism of the empire could not overcome the obvious weakening position of the social arrangements of subordination upon which the dominant strata depended.

This situation thus called for a more subtle practice of racism and ideological forms of discourse that reinforced but did not openly expose it. Racism took refuge in what seems to be its opposite, universalism and the concept of meritocracy (Quijano and Wallerstein 1992). For example, examination systems generally deemed "neutral" (e.g. the Graduate Record Examination (GRE), the Scholastic Achievement Test (SAT, the ACT, the Miller Analogies Test) within an ethnic hierarchy inevitably disproportionately favor the upper ethnic strata because of underlying inequalities at all levels. Capitalism's commandments are deeply embedded in the 20th-century U.S. psyche – all predicated on a deeply racial and genocidal foundation. These include for example: "greed is good, never show any empathy or compassion, the purpose of life is to profit …," etc. (haque 2019).

Consequently, racist attitudes appeared justified without needing to explicitly verbalize them. Racial coding became so routine that "When the official subject is presidential politics, taxes, welfare, crime, rights, or values … the real subject is Race" (Edsall and Edsall 1991). That an ethnic stratum that performs poorly was considered "inferior" appeared as an obvious fact. This was/is presumed to be simply statistical and, therefore, "verified" by "scientific" explanations for inequality. Corresponding to the rise of the culture of poverty explanations, the rise of these explanations for racial inequality was deemed as having nothing to do with racism. Hence, the possibility of arriving in a "post-racial" society with a deeply entrenched racial structure was presumed by some to be inevitable.

This appeared to be new not only because of the lack of critical history but also because of the way that the U.S. nation's racial commonsense was often echoed by social scientists and other scholars and even by the U.S. Supreme Court during the 20th century. An early example was the 1922 Supreme Court case of Ozawa v. United States and the 1923 – Supreme Court case of United States v. Thind.[4] The misuse of social science by self-interested protectors of white racial supremacy and privilege, though longstanding, caught fire during the 1960s, not coincidentally corresponding to the increase of power of marginalized communities as a result of the uprisings during this time. The nation had entered a turning point as the power of the racialized strata soared in the public sphere in contrast to its traditional position as the "losers" in a social and cultural system presented as the fount of opportunity. The challenge to the nation was not unlike that posed at the outset of the U.S. trajectory from settler colony to global hegemony. One hundred years later, the U.S. had become the hegemonic power in the world-system, and the stakes were even higher. This was exemplified in the example that W.E.B. DuBois had titled his 1935 masterwork, *Black Reconstruction of Democracy in America*. How presumptuous, some must have thought; in fact, the publisher changed the title to *Black Reconstruction in America* to indicate that in their view, the problem with U.S. society was Black people and not the structure as a whole.

This point is critically important as the struggle for equality has always been an issue not only for racialized groups but for all dominated groups and, indeed, all humanity. The politics of racial exclusion, as Dr. King so brilliantly explained, is a cover for the broader domination of the lower strata of a society often misleadingly referred to as the middle class rather than the working class. Likewise, the anthropologist Oscar Lewis' work on the devastating cultural ravages of capitalism upon the (all too human) impoverished victims of its inherently polarizing economic machine was revised by mainstream talking heads. They framed it as an explanation of why the "poor" are unable to succeed in a society where they assert that there is equal opportunity for all who are willing to work hard (or very, very hard for sub-minimum wages at sub-minimum wage jobs as Booker T. Washington argued for over 100 years prior).

During the high tide of the movement for racial equality and against racial discrimination, the seemingly subtle (to some) practice of racism became normative and omnipresent. *Everyday Forms of Whiteness: Understanding Race in a "Post-Racial" World*[5] (Bush 2011) sought precisely to expose the coded language that came to be used to disguise the racial animus of the dominant strata since it was now less respectable in "polite" company. As mentioned previously, it is evident that when some speak of the social implications of welfare and crime, they are referring to the issue of the "so-called" minority race.[6]

The reification and deification of newness is an additional element of Americanity that justifies inequality and should be viewed in the context of the misrepresentation of Lewis' concept of a "culture of poverty." This contributed to the rhetoric of meritocracy and led to the denial of the history and systemic legacies and contexts. "Modernity became the justification of economic success, but also its proof" (Quijano and Wallerstein 1992, 552). The circularity of this argument has continued to escape the attention of many. "The appearance of offering a way out of the inequalities of the present, the concept of 'newness' encrusted them and inserted their inevitability into the collective superego of the world-system" (Ibid.).

Desperately in Need of a Dream

The possibility of advancement thus became a part of the logic of the lower stratum inserted into these new conditions. However, the assumption of potential was much less present for the formerly enslaved and Jim Crowed racialized strata. Populations inhabiting a parallel universe operating according to different social principles developed their own perspectives in accordance with their own conditions. Condescending expressions of the more privileged social strata had hardened their hearts toward their less fortunate co-residents and dulled their social sensitivities, blaming individuals and communities for the fate established by systemically imposed structural inequalities. This exemplifies the ideology of white supremacy.

Given that white supremacy was the organizing principle central to both the capitalist world-system and the U.S. nation, these frameworks provide the historical context for our consideration of the ways that Americanity, nation, racism, and capitalism emerged and developed simultaneously. Falsely constructed borders and boundaries obfuscate the inherent interconnectedness of all humanity. While the concept of nationhood emerged in Europe, the founding and development of the U.S. nation embedded the idea that this way of organizing society makes sense. The centrality of white supremacy within the capitalist world-system and the U.S. national ideology meant that the demonization of African descended peoples and Indigenous civilizations were constitutive of the current world order and foundational to the stratification processes of the U.S. nation.

This essential tension in the "American" dream reflects the contradictions embedded in the core foundation of world capitalism, Americanity, racism, and nation. We have been led to believe these formations reflect "natural" rather than human-created arrangements and that they are to be assumed, protected, and defended at all costs. As such, they are the foundation upon which the idea of the "American" dream was built .... to support, reproduce and justify the vast inequalities of the modern colonial, capitalist, white supremacist, cis-heteronormative reign of the last 500 years.

Section II: Dream Matters

Just more than one century after its creation, the U.S. nation-state expanded to become a global power, with an established pattern of territorial and imperial conquest and expansion and by the mid-20th century, it was recognized as the hegemonic actor within the world-system. As such, the nation was challenged to reckon with how contradictions within its own borders reflected on its position as the world leader. The nation struggled with the question of how it was positioned and perceived in this new era of imperialism. Many of the anti-colonial struggles occurring around the globe were aligned with movements for social change among marginalized populations within its borders. How could the rhetoric of democracy be rationalized as imperial interventions around the globe intensified? How could the demands for justice, inclusion, and access be reconciled with the military interventions being engaged throughout the world and the use of violence – both structural and material within its own borders?

In this sociohistorical context, rhetoric of the existence of an "American" dream flourished. This idea emerged in the early 20th century as an assertion of aspiration for people in the U.S. and many around the globe and was considered accessible to all deemed worthy. In the early

1930s, James Truslow Adams sought to write a book about this emerging idea. He was told by the publisher, "that title won't work. No one will pay three dollars for a book about a dream" (Cullen 2003, 13). Though the book was published as *The Epic of America* in 1931, during the 1930s, the notion of an "'American' dream" became a central component of the image of "America" itself. The idea of upward mobility for all became a part of the nation's self-conception. This was different from the idea of freedom, which was limited to the resources at one's command, definitively shaped by one's positionality in the social hierarchy. This dream was considered reachable by anyone who tried hard enough despite the very significant inequalities that structured all aspects of U.S. society.

Several related clusters of beliefs reinforce(d) and reproduce(d) this mainstream discourse about rights, belonging, nation, and opportunity. The "American" dream was(is) considered to be achievable with hard work, and lack of effort (cultural sophistication or intelligence) is asserted as the cause of failure. Mainstream claims include(d) that "Americans" (only some, though) are superior beings in the global context; a "true" "American" is white, of European descent; and that we need inequality and competition so people will be motivated to work. It is worth noting the convergence of these ideas with capitalist values and ideology and how these serve corporate and dominant interests. Resistance or objection to these narratives has been considered anti-American, seditious, and ungrateful, asserted by those unwilling or unable to do the hard work to achieve upward mobility. Acknowledging the historical realities that have led to the betterment of living conditions in the U.S. (for some) in contrast to those of other people around the world is also outside the bounds of acceptable everyday conversation. Structural forces that shape social realities are rendered invisible.

Another aspect is that the story of the U.S. as a "nation of immigrants" masks the reality of this fabled liberal utopia, in actuality, born as a settler colony and developed into an imperial power. The idea of this nation as a "shining city on a hill" was part of the justifying ideology of the European conquest of the non-European world. The creation of the concept of "race" functioned to naturalize the conquest of so-called "inferior" peoples and was(is) viewed as simply a fact of life. Colonial hierarchies were explained as a consequence of the survival of the fittest, achieved by those with superior "science," music, and just about everything. Roxanne Dunbar Ortiz eloquent lays these lies to rest in *Not a Nation of Immigrants* (2021). The truth is that the U.S. of America was born of the theft of indigenous land, the capture and enslavement of Africans for labor, conquest of Mexican territory in the U.S., and imperial intervention in Cuba, the Philippines, and throughout what is arrogantly referred to (with little self-reflection) as the U.S. backyard. The geopolitical and geo-cultural elements of our social world are fundamental and not ancillary to the global stratification order as well as the political, economic, and social hierarchies within the U.S. Some assert this racial domination as a form of internal colonialism or internally colonized "third world within" not as a "colonial analogy," but part of the core reality of the modern capitalist world-system. The contradiction between the imagery and the rhetoric about the character of nation and the realities was part of the U.S. national psyche from inception. This predicament – of the rhetoric versus the reality – of equality/inequality in the U.S. has longstanding roots. How long could the romanticized imagery remain untarnished by the facts and unquestioned in mainstream discourse?

Particularly "American"?

Though the U.S. trajectory from settler colony to global hegemony fits well into the narrative of U.S. exceptionalism, the very concept of the "American" dream has implied that the dream of human possibility is not the dream of all humanity and not linked to ways that the nation's practices in the global arena restrict the possibilities of the rest of the world. With New Deal Liberalism, the U.S. began to elaborate the idea of democracy for the common people, though not all of them. The idea of race was at the center of its limitations both in the domestic and international arena. The emergence of the working class as a force with increasing strength during the 1930s and 1940s fundamentally altered these relations of force. Further and perhaps not counter-intuitively, the agency of some racialized populations was in the forefront of altering the relations of force between the dominant social strata and a diverse lower stratum with a geopolitical grasp that heightened their social power considerably.

Movements of the 1950s and 60s were often thought to be fighting for access to that dream. During that period, the economy was expanding and provided upward mobility for a portion of the U.S. population. This was most particularly true for European "ethnic" groups who were provided opportunities for achieving material stability through education and home ownership. This compounded the longstanding advantages given to European indentured servants and poor whites throughout history, even before the nation was formed such as in the aftermath of Bacon's Rebellion.[7] In the 20th century, this process consolidated the whitening of Europeans who immigrated to the U.S. from places like eastern and southern Europe. Books such as *How the Irish Became White* (Ignatiev 1995); *How the Jews Became White* (Brodkin 1998); *Are Italians White? How Race is Made in America* (Guglielmo and Salerno 2004) provide a full discussion of this process. Steinberg's *The Ethnic Myth: Race, Ethnicity, and Class in America* (2001) demystifies the process and reveals the way that discourse and structural factors provided the ideological and material foundation for the lies of meritocracy. The contradiction between the realities of race and racism and the rhetoric of equality is indeed at the core of the idea of "America" and the "American" dream.

Ethnicity as Proxy for Race and White Supremacy

Throughout the second half of the 20th century, the idea of the "American" dream as a legitimate and achievable goal was routinely asserted through all forms of media. These imaginaries conveyed the essence of what life in "this great country" is said to be about. The notion that immigrants can arrive penniless and, in time, get rich saturated everyday discourse. This concept has been a central pillar of the ideology of U.S. society (Hochschild 1995). For some, this upward mobility and "success" has been a reality. The post–World War II era of rapid industrial growth and U.S. hegemony around the globe brought much to many. This was especially true for European immigrant communities whose migration at the turn of the 20th century well-positioned them in the industrializing society to rise in positions of management and then later in the expanding economic boom post-World War II.

The assimilation and process of becoming "white," particularly for Jews, Irish, and Italians, meant surrendering identifying markers that distinguished them from the dominant. This appeared to be a small price for access and opportunity to realize the "American" dream as housing, education, and upward mobility became a reality through the Federal Housing Act Loans and mortgages, educational support through the GI Bill, affirmative action policies in the workplace (whether described as such or not) and other social programs. For African Americans, Latinos, Asians, and Native Americans, this dream was a much less common reality as discriminatory policies and practices were ongoing. After immigration laws changed in 1965, increasing numbers of people came to the U.S. just as deindustrialization began to occur. The most prominent explanations for why these groups were(are) not upwardly mobile drew increasingly from a culture-of-poverty framework as biological explanations for inequality were losing legitimacy. Asians faced another formulation along the lines of this same theme. The myth of Asians as a "model minority" was extremely detrimental to the very diverse communities included in this panethnic category. This rhetoric provided yet another way to suggest that the position of different groups within the racial economic and political hierarchies was due to the character of the groups themselves and not the historical circumstances of their experience in the U.S. In each of these cases, these narratives distort and disguise the true nature of the nation's structure.

The dynamics shaping mainstream discourse from the late 1960s to the mid-1970s were complex. Many groups and individuals were calling for a new vision of society based on social equality and justice for all and concern for the common good. This led to the characterization of this period as a "Second Reconstruction." The prevalence of the culture-of-poverty frame-work reflected a conservative influence that sought to command the parameters of thinking about the poor in an attempt to limit the power of a vision of society concerned with the common good, so well-articulated by many popular movements of this period (DiLeonardo 1999, 59; Steinberg 1999, 222). The ruling elite was clear about what was at stake should structural factors responsible for the unequal organization of society become revealed.[8] The image of the U.S. as the land of opportunity and locus of democracy epitomized would be vulnerable. As options expanded for white ethnics allowing for significant upward mobility, justifications were needed to explain persistent inequality evident in the experience of all other groups.

During the late 1960s, "momentum built within white ethnic neighborhoods to the extent that their concerns and grievances demanded the attention of the society at large" (Ryan 1973, 1). "Partly it [was] a consequence of the growing discontent among white ethnics with their socio-economic position in America, partly it was one facet of the broader movement toward self-definition on behalf of many groups within American society …. It is in part a reaction to the social and political upheavals of the 1960s compounded by the inflationary economic spirals which followed" (Ryan 1973, 1). The white ethnic position accepted the civil rights demand for outlawing discrimination, but not if it called for proactive or affirmative measures that they perceived to be threatening to their own mobility and access (Glazer and Moynihan 1963, 17; Omi and Winant 1994, 19). This perspective asserted that "through hard work, patience and delayed gratification, etc. Blacks could carve out their own rightful place in American society" (Omi and Winant 1994, 19), echoing the culture-of-poverty argument from the perspective of white panethnicity. Ethnic identification by whites was constituted in the form of "white backlash" against the social programs that were set up as part of or as a result of the Civil Rights Act (1964), Voters Rights Act (1965), Immigration Act (1965), War on Poverty, and the Welfare Rights and nationalist movements of the 1960s. White ethnics (partially funded by the government as Heritage Societies) asserted that they, too, suffered and should be the recipients of social programs.

Rather than the disappearance of ethnicity, there was a resurgence and a demand for the recognition and acceptance of white ethnic groups as a political force. It is ironic that, although the antipoverty and civil rights programs and policies were portrayed as benefiting Blacks and Latinos exclusively, in fact, many white ethnics (particularly women) also bene-fited. For example, 75 percent of students initially admitted through the Open Admission Policy in the City University of New York were white ethnics who were the first in their family to attend college (Ryan 1973, 164; Lavin, Alba, and Silberstein 1979, 69). Information such as this was muted in the public arena as the "new ethnicity" movement took strong stands against such programs and demanded resources for their own groups. Emphasis was placed on ethnicity as the primary classification for discussing groups as carriers of culture.

These ideas then influenced the public discourse about rights, equality, democracy, community self-definition, and resistance.

The concept of ethnicity was reinforced as another explanation for group differences during the 1970s. While previously employed in discussions about the process of assimilation, this notion had not been consolidated as an explanation for differences in social position between "white ethnics" and communities of color (Bush 2011). As mentioned in Section One, this marked the emergence of oblique coding of race in literature, media, and discourse, allowing racialized policies and practices to function without the bluntness of explicit language. After all, who would argue against upholding "standards" for education or measures to make our communities "safe" or disagree with the need for "family values"? (Bush 2011) Theoretical notions of the culture of poverty have remained a core part of public discourse. By the 1990s, this concept had been utilized in attacks on the public sector and debates about welfare and higher education. Issues of standards and merit have been raised without the language of the race yet implying cultural deficits of Black and Latino communities and implicitly presuming white superiority, though most often denied as the rationale.

It has been assumed that the "dream" revolves around the achievement of success in the forms of high income, a prestigious job, and economic security (presumed accessible to all) (Hochschild 1995, 15) and built into what it means to be "American." Consider President Bill Clinton's speech in 1993 to the Democratic Leadership Council: "The American dream that we were all raised on is a simple but powerful one—if you work hard and play by the rules, you should be given a chance to go as far as your God-given abilities will take you" (Hochschild 1995, 18). How ironic it is that the very system that systemically discriminates touts a lack of bias. "Ours is a society that routinely generates destitution—and then, perversely, relieves its conscience by vilifying the destitute" (Ehrenreich 2002, 9).

If people have an understanding of economic forces and how they influence politics, they may be more willing to understand race as a smokescreen for elites who manipulate whites into believing that Blacks are to blame. Having now lived through four years of the Trump presidency, a capital insurrection and expanding and ever more empowered white supremacist populous it is ever more evident that this ideological frame is just a more overt expression of what has been brewing since the 1960s, and in actuality since the nation's inception. There seems little doubt that the future holds a consolidation of these forces as the global elite attempt to maintain capitalism's stronghold by any means necessary. With over 74 million votes (46 percent of voters/57 percent of white men and 53 percent of white women/65 percent of white voters with some college or less) (Igielnik, Keeter, and Hartig 2021), this is no small minority of the population that support a racist, right-wing agenda that explicitly supports business and capital over concerns for working class well-being (Ibid.). Furthermore, "... 43% of the world's top 1 million websites are hosted in the United States" evidences the continuing hegemonic ideological role around the globe (Pingdom 2012; Pearson 2017).

Structural Implosion

It was one thing to promote this idea of endless possibility when the economy was expanding and another as the wealth and income gap began to significantly grow in the 1970s. Since that time, the skewed pattern of income distribution in the U.S. and worldwide has led to ongoing and massive increases in the income of the top 10 percent and especially the top 1 percent of the world's populations, yet a decline in real income of much of the rest of the world's populations. This trend has intensified over the last two decades, and to many people's surprises, even during the COVID pandemic. An article by *Bloomberg Businessweek* entitled,

"Covid Can't Stop Corporate Profits from Climbing to Record Highs," notes that tax cuts and government assistance to corporations provided a huge boost. "U.S. corporations pulled in more profits in the three months ended in September than ever before. Not just in dollar terms, something that happens frequently—but as a share of the economy" (Boesler, Deaux, and Dmitrieva 2021). They also note that after tax corporate profits amounted to 11 percent of the gross domestic product. Before 2010, they had never gone over 9 percent.

In 2011, the Occupy Movement's declaration that we are the 99 percent was an unprecedented rejection of the orthodoxy of 30 years that had led to an enormous increase in inequality. Making the point that the increase in inequality affected not only the racialized poor but the entire 99 percent resulted in a dramatic change in public discourse. The focus of public discussion previously tended to focus on the distinction between the Black and Latino residents of low-income segregated neighborhoods and the white working and middle classes residents of "close-knit," "hard-working" neighborhoods, which of course, were also segregated neighborhoods, though this was not always mentioned. The Occupy Movement language of the 1 percent versus the 99 percent seemed to surge into the public discourse with an unprecedented authority and became something of a new commonsense. This complicated the rhetoric of endless possibility because the light was shed on the reality of inequality and that for most people in the U.S., wages have stagnated since the 1970s.

As illustrated in the following charts, the periods 1948–1979 and 1979–2020 provide evidence that worker compensation rose along with productivity in the earlier period though diverged in the more recent years when productivity grew at a rate 3.5 times greater. "… the same set of policies that suppressed pay growth for the vast majority of workers over the last 40 years were also associated with a slowdown in overall economic growth. In short, economic growth became both slower and more radically unequal" (Economic Policy Institute 2021). Rather than go to workers, the economic growth went to the salaries of high paid workers, owners, and to profits. Taxes were cut on the very wealthy, raises in the federal minimum wage became rare and regulations that protected worker wages were dismantled (Ibid.).

The Economic Policy Institute summary of the Bureau of Labor Statistics and Bureau of Economic Analysis data provides evidence that there is "a disconnect between productivity and typical workers compensation" that occurred between 1948 and 2013. From 1948 to 1973, productivity went up 96.7 percent and hourly compensation, 91.3 percent. Between 1973 and 2013, productivity went up 74.4 percent, yet hourly compensation went up only 9.2 percent (Mishel, Gould, and Bivens 2015/Economic Policy Institute).

Finance was deregulated and unions were crushed. Productivity continued to climb, but wages stalled and declined. This pattern continued from 1979 onward. In 2020, CEO-worker pay ratios averaged 830 to 1 (Anderson and Pizzigati 2021, 1). The status of inequality in recent years is further elucidated in the fact that even in the one year between 2019 and 2020, average CEO pay at the 100 largest low-wage employers went from $12,074,288 to $13,936,558, yet median worker pay increased only $58, from $30,416 to $30,474 (Institute for Policy Studies, Executive Excess, Anderson and Wakamo 2021). Furthermore, during the pandemic, U.S. billionaire wealth has risen 70 percent, and corporate profits increase 50 percent (Ibid.).

The racial wealth gap also significantly widened. "According to Survey of Consumer Finances data, in 2019 the median Black family had $24,100 in wealth. This is just 12.7 percent of the $189,100 in wealth owned by the typical white family. The median Latino family, with $36,050, owns just 19.1 percent of the wealth of the median white family" (Institute for Policy Studies/Inequality.org 2019). Another dimension of this has been visible as the Covid-19 pandemic forced many workers to remote work though "… not everyone has the same ability to work from home. Pre-pandemic figures indicate that only 19.7 percent of Black and 16.2 percent of Latinx people work in jobs where they are able to telework, compared to 29.9 percent of White and 37.0 percent of Asian workers" (Ibid.) These disparities are also evident in significantly lower home ownership rates,[9] higher student debt, underrepresentation at the top level, and overrepresentation at lower levels of the income tiers. This is particularly evident in the higher levels of poverty among Black, Native American, and Latino women (Ibid.) The racial wealth divide has also significantly grown in the last several decades (Institute for Policy Studies/Inequality.org 2019).

The Crumbling of U.S. Exceptionalism

The wealth of the U.S. is most often explained as an outcome of being the "greatest country in the world," with more modernity, more technology, more efficiency, more liberty, more culture, and more democracy than anywhere else. This notion of cultural and technological superiority is deeply ingrained in the American psyche and provides the context for why a "dream" and the idea that upward mobility and material success are accessible to all would be considered exclusively "American."[10]

> We are more civilized than the rest of the world … We represent the highest aspirations of everyone …. We are the leader of the free world, because we are the freest country in the world, and others look to us for leadership, for holding high the banner of freedom, of civilization …
>
> *Wallerstein 2001*

However, the U.S.' decline as a hegemonic power looms large on the horizon. The substance of the "American" dream has been shaken, even among some who most vigorously defend its possibility. According to a very recent Pew Research survey among young people (18–29), only 10 percent say that the U.S. "stands above all other countries" (a decline from 27 percent in 2011) (Tyson 2014; Hartig 2021) and 55 percent of those who identify as Democrats and Democrat leaning independents say other countries are better (Hartig 2021).

The multiple political and economic crises signal a precarious era, made worse by the COVID pandemic and ruling class' determination to continue expanding profits. Increasing unemployment and greater numbers at soup kitchens, mutual aid networks and homeless shelters are just the beginning. While in 2019, over 11.1 percent of families in the U.S. faced food insecurity in 2018 that doubled in 2020 to almost 1 in 4 families (Schanzenbach and Pitts 2020, 1, 4). Furthermore, Black families are more than twice as likely to experience this (36 percent, 32 percent) as white families (18 percent) (Ibid, 3). These trends are compounded by the expanded privatization of all aspects of social services, to such an extent that schools, medical facilities, and policing, for example, have largely become domains for profit-bearing as opposed to being services delivered for the public good. Some "American" "dream" …

Section III: Conclusion – The Moral Exhaustion of "'America' the Beautiful"

The quandary has been how the imagery of the U.S. as a shining "city on a hill" co-exists with the reality of the nation's imperial history. How does the rhetoric of the U.S. as the land of opportunity be reconciled with a quarter of the nation's people being food insecure? These discourses are components of a logic of the nationalism of empire, deeply rooted in colonial presumptions about who is of value, used as a justification for imperial conquest, colonization, and exploitation. In the last several decades, increasing inequalities and the long struggles over racial justice have undermined support for the belief in a so-called "American" dream, which had become a symbol of the special character of the U.S.[11]

Simultaneously, a portion of the U.S. population, most specifically whites, has become even more convinced of the righteousness of white supremacy as a means to explain society's woes. *Everyday Forms of Whiteness: Understanding Race in a "Post-Racial" World* (Bush 2011, Chapter 6) provides a discussion of 14 mechanisms of this process. For example, the naturalization and mystification of poverty, wealth, and inequality; the naturalization of whiteness and American identity and the invisibility of race-dominance; rigid regulation of discourse; coding of language to camouflage the racial component of policy and actions; the use of fear and silences as means of control; the use of oppositional and dichotomous ways of thinking; the use of racialized narratives of invidious distinction; is the belief in ideals and apparent awareness of racial inequality, but a lack of willingness to actualize the ideals or acknowledge the consequences of not doing so; the segregation of most aspects of daily living and casual interaction between whites and people of color; "unwritten rules" that dictate the parameters for interaction between people from different groups; Social pressures supporting both individualism and competition function simultaneously; the illusive nature of race, expressed through ambiguities, ambivalences, and shifting borders; the way that resistance is stigmatized, marginalized, and racialized, with the ultimate message that things are the way they are because that's the way they should be and they won't and can't change; and that the historical and current tradition of struggle for human dignity and the common good – both in the U.S. and globally is kept almost entirely out of view.

The process of unraveling began to occur with the increasing social power of racial "minorities" during the 1960s and 1970s, leading to the moral exhaustion of the notion of "'America' the Beautiful." This conjuncture was not destiny but a familiar pattern in geopolitics sometimes difficult to recognize because of the premise of U.S. exceptionalism. Is an imperial nation the underbelly of the shining city on a hill? What is a city that shines only on parts of the hill and only at times?

The conservative backlash of the 1960s that led FBI Director J. Edgar Hoover to conclude that the nation was in the midst of a social revolution with the racial movement at its core was part of a broader counterinsurgency designed to turn the nation away from a commitment to the general welfare. The goal was to establish a focus on the social survival of the fittest, defined as those who had earned their positions because of their adherence to the work ethic, their superior cultural and family values, intelligence, biology, etc. The U.S. contention with the most dishonored sections of its population challenged the master narrative of democracy and equality for all and exposed the race, class, and gender inequality at the heart of the internal social order of the U.S. However, increasingly the conservative notion that social position should be based on individual performance was not new and increasingly could not only be attributed to conservatives.

These ideas are far more mainstream than many would like to believe. A 2015 Pew Research survey of 44 countries found that people in the U.S. much more than elsewhere disagreed that "Success in life is pretty much determined by forces outside our control" (U.S. 57 percent versus global median 38 percent) and believed that working hard is important to getting ahead in life (U.S. 73 percent versus the global median of 44 percent) (Gao 2015). This is quite notable given that income inequality has significantly risen in the last several decades (more so than in other G-7 countries), with the share held by middle-income falling from 32 percent to 17 percent (Horowitz, Igielnik, and Kochhar 2020). Further, the chance of upward mobility for middle income earners decreased about 20 percent since the early 1980s (Carr and Wiemers 2016).

As discussed earlier in this chapter, a key component of the "American" dream is the idea of meritocracy that has been deeply embedded in the narratives of the U.S. nation. The dramatic increase in the social power of the racialized and gendered lower strata, particularly significant in the midst of increasing economic, social, and political crises, gave many though not all cause to re-evaluate the meaning of this rhetoric. The continuing profit squeeze, labor strife exacerbated by transformations in the global labor force, and a geopolitical crisis caused by the continuing aftermath of the U.S. defeat in the war in Vietnam created an environment that increased vulnerability for the majority.

In this historical context, Malcolm X had argued that he did not see an American dream but an American nightmare and in doing so captured the "true meaning of 'our' creed," which was the possession of U.S. elites because of the nation's geopolitical and geo-cultural hegemony. Both Martin Luther King, Jr. and Malcolm X were increasingly able to articulate with exceptional clarity the scope of a dream for all humanity that could not be given by the United States of America but was the rights of all people. Malcolm was skeptical of the ability of the U.S. state to do anything other than what they had been doing. Dr. King wanted the U.S. to get on the right side of history for a change. King did not fear to appropriate the "American" dream as the legitimate right of Black people, though he did not hesitate to chastise the nation for failing to deliver on its promise. A year or so after the 1963 March on Washington, legislation had been passed which broke the back of Jim Crow and de jure segregation.

Malcolm X argued that Black people should have no illusions about being included in the American dream. He said just because kittens are born in an oven, you don't call them biscuits. You can't sit at the table and throw us a few crumbs from the table and call us Americans. Furthermore, Malcolm X argued you could not go to the criminal and ask for civil rights, you had to take the criminal to the world court and sue for denial of our human rights. Malcolm X was not rearticulating the "American" dream, he was transcending it. After 50 years, these conversations were prophetic – both in predicting the crises and the ideology and portions of the population that would hold them in check, urging moderation rather than full disclosure of the systemic forces headed toward catastrophic demise.

Tensions in the American Dream

After decades of struggle, the rampage of right-wing backlash across the land appeared to some to be defeated by the election of an African American as president of the U.S., which most thought was quite unlikely. Obama came to the fore with the racial neutralism of William Julius Wilson as a tactic, but as an heir to the moral power of the Black liberation struggle (civil rights movement), he had a silent appeal to the original sins of the European invaders whose conquest of the Americas cannot be denied. Obama was willing to do the work of the imperialist state as a matter of relations of force. His election was a sign of the times. The weakness of the U.S. elite, now derided as the 1 percent and their fear of losing racial and economic privileges drives their assault on the "American" dream as they hold tight to capitalism and empire. That is a signal of the weakness of these social strata and not their strength. Even the more privileged sectors of the workforce (e.g. in unions) are rising up to resist the elite's imposition of impossible demands for unreasonable compensation. In 2021 alone, there were over 300 strikes.[12] "Who else wants to shred democracy for the sake of…feeling 'great' again? Where else do people constantly, consistently vote against their own 'best interests'… their own happiness, prosperity, safety, stability … so much so, so predictably … that merely trying to point out that they act like fools has become a whole subject of national debate in itself? …

America and Britain are the only two places in the world where life expectancy, incomes, and savings are falling in tandem. Yet they're also 2 of the richest and most powerful countries in the world" (haque 2019).

The rhetoric of modernization that simply calls for the integration of the lower strata into the full benefits of society by self-improvement does not deal with the inherently polarizing nature of the historical system in which we have lived over the last 500 years. The whole world is rising in rebellion against the domination of the economic elites and the domination of the rich states of the pan-European world. Whether it is the more than 250 million Indian farmers who were on strike for almost a year against brutal laws that would have destroyed their livelihood or the rise of progressive politics in Latin America, it is evident that a new day is dawning. The colonial-capitalist system is in irrevocable decline. The forces at the top are determined to maintain it "by any means necessary," and = middle strata constituencies present only means for reform regardless of how temporary it may be through elections and small victories.[13] The centrality of the U.S. nation to the structure and organization of the world system of the last six centuries means that "American" society – and the core premises of the "American" dream are being exposed as fallacies built on social relations of coloniality and power.

Frantz Fanon, the psychiatrist from Martinique who was a theorist of the Algerian revolution, said that "every generation rises from relative obscurity and either fulfills its historic mission or betrays it." We are at a moment of historic rupture when the structures, institutions, and justifications of the system no longer make sense. The pre-imminent crisis in the capitalist world system will either generate a more or a less unequal world. At times of rupture such as this, what ordinary people do matters more than in times of stability (Wallerstein 2009). The place of the U.S. in the modern world is increasingly suspect as is the rhetoric of the "American" dream. An element of this is recognizing the role of ideology in providing justifications for highly racialized, gendered, and classed structures. Ultimately what is needed is an extensive "decolonizing the mind" process to make broadly accessible an understanding of how the modern world developed from the emergence of coloniality and the presumption of the universalism of Eurocentric ideas and capitalist political economy, opening spaces for a pluriversal understanding of the world, politics, economies, and social relations. That along with building the most forceful movement of all times.

Indeed to "end the racial nightmare" (Baldwin 1964, 141), "We should never forget that the agency of those social groups whose critical consciousness has been instilled in them by their own histories and struggles – not only as intellectuals and activists but as people – is absolutely central to building a system that is democratic, egalitarian and just" (Bush 2005, 89). The notion of the "American" dream has distorted and distracted for far too long. It is time for a dream that leaves no one hungry, houseless, and in harm's way. That is fully possible – the resources exist on earth to do so. However, the foundation of society would need to be rooted in values of justice, community, and truth that emanates from those most vulnerable. For only when they are free can we all be free, and true dreams will become realities.[14]

"Whether we turn to the declarations of the past, or to the professions of the present, the conduct of the nation seems equally hideous and revolting. America is false to the past, false to the present, and solemnly binds herself to be false to the future" (Douglass 1852).

Notes

1 Throughout this chapter, "American" will be put in quotes to signify that the equation of this label with being of the U.S. is not only inaccurate but it also represents a linguistic form of U.S. imperialism. There are 35 nations in the Americas.

2 Language that distinguishes parts of the globe in relation to colonial domination varies. For a period of time, the concept of first-second-third worlds was in use. World systems theorists reframed this as core/semi-periphery/periphery. Global north/global south is a more recent formulation as is majority/minority worlds.

3 Many thanks to Dr. Wende Marshal for this important point in her reading of a draft of this manuscript. Since the publication of Quijano and Wallerstein's article, significant writings about this process have emerged. See, for example, works listed in Toward a Bibliography of Critical Whiteness Studies edited by Tim Engles (2006) and many others since then, https://thekeep.eiu.edu/cgi/viewcontent.cgi?article=1050&context=eng_fac

4 For an informative review of these Supreme Court cases, see the well-known documentary, Race: The Power of an Illusion, Part III: The House We Live In https://www.racepowerofanillusion.org/episodes/three

5 Previously published as Breaking the Code of Good Intentions: Everyday Forms of Whiteness (Bush 2004).

6 Black and Brown people are in the majority globally; hence, language of "so-called" minority.

7 California Newsreel. 2003. RACE – The Power of an Illusion. http://newsreel.org/guides/race/whiteadv.htm Accessed December 27, 2021.

8 Gil Scott-Heron describes this period, "Civil rights, women's rights, gay rights; it's all wrong. Call in the cavalry to disrupt this perception of freedom gone wild. First one wants freedom, then the whole damn world wants freedom" (1981). "B-Movie." Reflections. https://genius.com/Gil-scott-heron-b-movie-lyrics).

9 A recent study by Zillow notes that Black mortgage applicants are 84 percent more likely to be denied than white borrowers. See https://www.zillow.com/research/black-denial-rate-hmda-2020-30510/

10 Note, however, there are some articulations of dreams attached to other nations. As a few examples, see https://this.deakin.edu.au/self-improvement/wild-and-free; https://www.foet.org/project/the-european-dream/; https://www.economist.com/briefing/2013/05/04/chasing-the-chinese-dream

11 An interesting recent study about current beliefs in the American Dream, conducted by an undergraduate student at Boston University can be found here: https://open.bu.edu/bitstream/handle/2144/34965/Cameron%20Adajian%20Honors%20Thesis.pdf;jsessionid=C25B3C9E37F4CA719D02E60C668B13F8?sequence=3

12 Cornell University. International Labor Relations School. Labor Action Tracker. https://striketracker.ilr.cornell.edu/ Accessed December 27, 2021.

13 For a very thoughtful analysis of this moment and the challenge of short-term wins versus long-term strategies, see Akuno, Kali, Brian Drolet, and Doug Norberg. 2021. "Shifting Focus: Organizing for Revolution, Not Crisis Avoidance." Navigating the Storm. November 1. https://navigatingthestorm.blogspot.com/2021/11/shifting-focus-organizing-for.html

14 "If Black women were free, it would mean that everyone else would have to be free since our freedom would necessitate the destruction of all the systems of oppression." Combahee River Collective statement, 1977. https://combaheerivercollective.weebly.com/the-combahee-river-collective-statement.html

References

Amin, Samir, and Edward Ousselin. 1997. "The Nation: An Enlightened or Fog-Shrouded Concept?" *Research in African Literatures*. Vol. 28, No. 4. Winter. 8–18. Bloomington, IN: Indiana University Press.

Anderson, Sarah, and Sam Pizzigati. 2021. "Executive Excess." Institute for Policy Studies. https://ips-dc.org/wp-content/uploads/2021/05/report-executive-excess-2021-PDF.pdf Accessed January 15, 2022.

Anderson, Sarah, and Brian Wakamo. 2021. "The Year in Inequality in 10 Charts." Inequality.org. December 15. https://inequality.org/great-divide/year-in-inequality-10-charts/ Accessed January 15, 2022.

Baldwin, James. 1964. *The Fire Next Time*. New York: Dell.

Boesler, Matthew, Joe Deaux and Katia Dmitrieva. 2021. "Fattest Profits since 1950 Debunk Wage-Inflation Story of CEOs." Bloomberg.com. November 30. https://www.bloomberg.com/news/articles/2021-11-30/fattest-profits-since-1950-debunk-inflation-story-spun-by-ceos Accessed November 30, 2021.

Brodkin, Karen. 1998. *How the Jews Became White Folks and What That Says about Race in America.* Piscataway, NJ: Rutgers University Press.

Bush, Melanie E.L. 2004. "Race, Ethnicity and Whiteness." *Sage Race Relations Abstracts (SRRA).* Louis Kushnick, Editor. Vol. 29, Nos. 3–4. August/December. 5–48. London.

———. 2011. *Everyday Forms of Whiteness: Understanding Race in a "Post-Racial" World.* Second Edition. Lanham, MD: Rowman and Littlefield Publishers, Inc. (initially published in 2004 as *Breaking the Code of Good Intentions: Everyday Forms of Whiteness*).

———. 2018. "United Statesians: The Nationalism of Empire." *Handbook of the Sociology of Racial and Ethnic Relations.* Second Edition. Pinar Batur and Joe R. Feagin, Editors. New York, NY: Springer Science and Business Media, Inc.

Bush, Roderick D. 1998. *We Are Not What We Seem: Black Nationalism and Class Struggle in the American Century.* New York: NYU Press.

———. 2005. "Reflections on Black Internationalism as Strategy." *Socialism and Democracy* 19, no. 2 (July): 82–90.

Bush, Melanie E.L., Rose Brewer, Robert Newby, Daniel Douglas and Loretta Chin, Editors. 2019. *Rod Bush: Lessons from a Radical Black Scholar on Liberation, Love and Justice.* Cambridge, MA: Okcir Publishing, Inc.

Bush, Melanie E.L. and Roderick D. Bush. 2015. *Tensions in the American Dream: Rhetoric, Reverie or Reality.* Philadelphia, PA: Temple University Press.

Carr, Michael D. and Emily E. Wiemers. 2016. "The Decline in Lifetime Earnings Mobility in the U.S.: Evidence from Survey-Linked Administrative Data." Washington Center for Equitable Growth. Working Paper Series. http://cdn.equitablegrowth.org/wp-content/uploads/2016/05/02160305/carr_wiemers_2016_earnings-mobility.pdf Accessed January 15, 2022.

Cornell University. International Labor Relations Labor Action Tracker. https://striketracker.ilr.cornell.edu/ Accessed January 15, 2022.

Cullen, Jim. 2003. *The American Dream: A Short History of an Idea That Shaped a Nation.* Oxford: Oxford University Press.

DiLeonardo, Micaela. 1999. "'Why Can't They Be Like Our Grandparents?' and Other Racial Fairy Tales." In *Without Justice for All: The New Liberalism and Our Retreat from Racial Equality.* Edited by Adolph Reed Jr, 29–64. Boulder, CO: Westview Press.

Douglass, Frederick. 1852. "Fifth of July" Speech. Knowledge for Freedom Seminar. Dickinson College. https://housedivided.dickinson.edu/sites/teagle/texts/frederick-douglass-fifth-of-july-speech-1852/ Accessed January 10, 2022.

Dunbar Ortiz, Roxanne. 2021. *Not "A Nation of Immigrants": Settler Colonialism, White Supremacy, and a History of Erasure and Exclusion.* Boston, MA: Beacon Press.

Economic Policy Institute. 2021. "The Productivity–Pay Gap." August. https://www.epi.org/productivity-pay-gap/

Edsall, Thomas Byrne and Mary D. Edsall. 1991. "When the Official Subject Is Presidential Politics, Taxes, Welfare, Crime, Rights, or Values ... the Real Subject Is Race." *The Atlantic.* May. http://www.theatlantic.com/past/politics/race/edsall.htm

Ehrenreich, Barbara. 2002. "Hobo Heaven." Review of *Down and Out, on the Road.* By Kenneth L. Husmer. *New York Times Book Review.* January 20.

Fanon, Franz. 1967. *Black Skin, White Masks.* New York: Grove Press.

Gao, George. 2015. "How Do Americans Stand Out from the Rest of the World?" Pew Research Center. March 12. https://www.pewresearch.org/fact-tank/2015/03/12/how-do-americans-stand-out-from-the-rest-of-the-world/ Accessed January 10, 2022.

Glazer, Nathan, and Daniel Patrick Moynihan. 1963. *Beyond the Melting Pot: The Negroes, Puerto Ricans, Jews, Italians, and Irish of New York City.* Cambridge: Massachusetts Institute of Technology.

Gonzalez, Juan. 2011. *Harvest of Empire: A History of Latinos in America.* Revised Edition. New York: Penguin Books. http://www.snagfilms.com/films/title/harvest_of_empire

Grosfoguel, Ramón. 2013. "The Structure of Knowledge in Westernized Universities Epistemic Racism/Sexism and the Four Genocides/Epistemicides of the Long 16th Century." *Human Architecture: Journal of the Sociology of Self-Knowledge* XI, no. 1 (Fall): 73–90.

Grosfoguel, Ramon, and Ana Margarita Cervantes-Rodriguez. 2002. "Unthinking Twentieth-Century Eurocentric Mythologies: Universalist Knowledges, Decolonization, and Developmentalism." In *The Modern/Colonial/Capitalist World-System in the Twentieth Century: Global Processes, Anti-systemic*

Movements, and the Geopolitics of Knowledge. Edited by Ramon Grosfoguel and Ana Margarita Cervantes-Rodriguez, xi–xxix. Westport, CT: Praeger.

Guglielmo, Jennifer and Salvatore Salerno. 2004. *Are Italians White? How Race Is Made in America.* New York: Routledge Publishing Inc.

haque, umair. 2019. "How Predatory Capitalism Made America the World's Dumbest Country." Eudaimonia.co. September 6. https://eand.co/how-capitalism-made-america-the-worlds-dumbest-country-ed33f15d1100 Accessed December 26, 2021.

Harney, Stefano, and Fred Moten. 2013. *The Undercommons: Fugitive Planning & Black Study.* Brooklyn, NY: Autonomedia.

Hartig, Hannah. 2021. Younger Americans Still More Likely Than Older Adults to Say There Are Other Countries Better Than the U.S. December 16. https://www.pewresearch.org/fact-tank/2021/12/16/younger-americans-still-more-likely-than-older-adults-to-say-there-are-other-countries-better-than-the-u-s/ Accessed December 26, 2021.

Hochschild, Jennifer L. 1995. *Facing Up to the American Dream: Race, Class, and the Soul of the Nation.* Princeton, NJ: Princeton University Press.

Horowitz, Juliana Menasce, Ruth Igielnik, and Rakesh Kochhar. 2020. "Trends in Income and Wealth Inequality." https://www.pewresearch.org/social-trends/2020/01/09/trends-in-income-and-wealth-inequality/ Accessed December 26, 2021.

Igielnik, Ruth, Scott Keeter, and Hannah Hartig. 2021. "Behind Biden's 2020 Victory." Pew Research Center. June 30. https://www.pewresearch.org/politics/2021/06/30/behind-bidens-2020-victory/ Accessed December 26, 2021.

Ignatiev, Noel. 1995. *How the Irish Became White.* New York: Routledge.

Institute for Policy Studies (IPS) and Inequality.org. 2019. Racial Wealth Divide Racial Economic Inequality Report. https://inequality.org/wp-content/uploads/2019/01/IPS_RWD-Report_FINAL-1.15.19.pdf Accessed December 26, 2021.

———. 2021. Racial Inequality. https://inequality.org/facts/racial-inequality/ referencing the Survey of Consumer Finances, Board of Governors of the Federal Reserve System. https://www.federalreserve.gov/econres/scf/dataviz/scf/chart/#series:Net_Worth;demographic:racecl4;population:all;units:median;range:1989,2019 Accessed December 26, 2021.

Keeler, Jacqueline. 2022. "Origin Stories." *Counterpunch.* January 9. https://www.counterpunch.org/2022/01/09/origin-stories/ Accessed January 9, 2022.

Kelley, Robin D. G. 2016. "Black Study, Black Struggle." Boston Review. March 7. http://bostonreview.net/forum/robin-d-g-kelley-black-study-black-struggle Accessed December 26, 2021.

King Jr, Martin Luther 1965. "Remaining Awake through a Great Revolution." Commencement Address. Oberlin College, Oberlin, Ohio, June.

Lavin, David E., Richard D. Alba, and Richard A. Silberstein. 1979. "Ethnic Groups in the City University of New York." *Harvard Educational Review* 49, no. 1 (February): 53–92.

Miller, Ben. 2021. A.B. Original's "Dumb Things": Decolonizing the Postcolonial Australian Dream. *a b Original: Journal of Indigenous Studies and First Nations and First Peoples' Cultures* 4. no. 1–2. Pennsylvania State University. University Park, PA. 103–123. https://scholarlypublishingcollective.org/psup/ab-original/article-abstract/4/1-2/103/288860/A-B-Original-s-Dumb-Things-Decolonizing-the?redirectedFrom=fulltext

Mishel, Lawrence, Elise Gould, and Josh Bivens 2015. "Wage Stagnation in Nine Charts." Economic Policy Institute. January 6. https://www.epi.org/publication/charting-wage-stagnation/

National Public Radio. 2020. "Food Insecurity in the U.S. By the Numbers." September 27. https://www.npr.org/2020/09/27/912486921/food-insecurity-in-the-u-s-by-the-numbers

Northwestern Institute for Policy Research. 2020. Rapid Report. June 10. https://www.ipr.northwestern.edu/documents/reports/ipr-rapid-research-reports-pulse-hh-data-10-june-2020.pdf

Omi, Michael, and Howard Winant. 1994. *Racial Formation in the United States.* New York: Routledge.

Oxfam. 2016. Briefing Paper 210. "An Economy for the 1%" Oxfam Great Britain for Oxfam International. 18 January.

Pearson, Tamara. 2017. "When the U.S. Pretends It's the Center of the Universe."Medium.com. March 18. https://medium.com/the-establishment/when-the-u-s-pretends-its-the-center-of-the-universe-f31cb5705976 Accessed December 26, 2021.

Pingdom. 2012. "The US Hosts 43% of the World's Top 1 Million Websites." Data and Analysis. July 2. https://www.pingdom.com/blog/united-states-hosts-43-percent-worlds-top-1-million-websites/ Accessed December 27, 2021.

Quijano, Anibal, and Wallerstein, Immanuel. 1992. "'Americanity' as a Concept, or the Americas in the Modern World-System." *Social Science Journal* 44, no. 4: 549–557.

Ryan, Joseph. 1973. *White Ethnics: Their Life in Working Class America.* Englewood Cliffs, NJ: Prentice-Hall.

Schanzenbach, Diane, and Abigail Pitts. 2020. "How Much Has Food Insecurity Risen? Evidence from the Census Household Pulse Survey Institute for Policy Research." Northwestern Institute for Policy Research. 2020. Rapid Report. June 10. https://www.ipr.northwestern.edu/documents/reports/ipr-rapid-research-reports-pulse-hh-data-10-june-2020.pdf Accessed December 27, 2021.

Schwalbe, Michael. 2002. "The Costs of American Privilege" *Counterpunch.* October 4. http://www.counterpunch.org/2002/10/04/the-costs-of-american-privilege/ Accessed December 27, 2021.

Silva, Christianna. 2020. "Food Insecurity in the U.S. by the Numbers." September 27. https://www.npr.org/2020/09/27/912486921/food-insecurity-in-the-u-s-by-the-numbers Accessed December 27, 2021.

Steinberg, Stephen. 1999. "Occupational Apartheid in America: Race, Labor Market Segmentation and Affirmative Action." *Without Justice for All: The New Liberalism and Our Retreat from Racial Equality.* Edited by Adolph Reed Jr., 215–234. Boulder, CO: Westview Press.

———. 2001. *The Ethnic Myth: Race, Ethnicity and Class in America.* Boston: Beacon Press.

Tyson, Alec. 2014. "Most Americans Think the U.S. Is Great, but Fewer Say It's the Greatest." Pew Research Center. July 2. https://www.pewresearch.org/fact-tank/2014/07/02/most-americans-think-the-u-s-is-great-but-fewer-say-its-the-greatest/ Accessed December 27, 2021.

Wallerstein, Immanuel. 1979. *The Capitalist World-Economy.* Boston, MA: Cambridge University Press.

———. 2001. "America and the World: The Twin Towers as Metaphor." December 5. https://iwallerstein.com/wp-content/uploads/docs/America-and-the%20World-The-Twin-Towers-as-Metaphor.pdf Accessed December 27, 2021.

———. 2009. "An American Dilemma of the 21st Century." Societies without Borders. http://societieswithoutborders.files.wordpress.com/2009/10/wallerstein1-1.pdf Accessed December 27, 2021.

8

ACHIEVING THE AMERICAN DREAM

How middle class blacks socialize their children to make it to the top

Karyn Lacy

Introduction

Horatio Alger, a fictional character introduced in the 19th century, helped to popularize a core tenet of the American Dream, that anyone can become rich no matter their origins since he seemed to rise from rags-to-riches through hard work. That's the version of the story that is told most often. But it isn't the full story. In reality, the character typically experienced good fortune, returning lost money he found and collecting the reward in one instance, or saving the child of a wealthy man from being run over by a streetcar in another, after which the rescued boy's father adopts him. Thus, it was Alger's altruism, coupled with his indisputable morality, not work ethic, propelling him from the bottom of the class ladder to the top. Put simply, possessing the values reinforced by the larger society contributed to Alger's success.

Alger's story is fiction, and for most people, so too is the American Dream. To be sure, the belief that everyone has the same chance of becoming economically successful is in a fixture in America. But climbing the class ladder has always been harder for some groups than others. For one thing, middle class people are far more likely than the poor to raise children who make it into the middle class too once adult, a process scholars call *social reproduction*. This is because people at and near the top of the class ladder control the majority of society's most desirable resources, which means they are most capable of hoarding resources and converting them into opportunities while denying others the same option (Bourdieu, 1984; Massey, 2007; Tilly, 1998). Most of the time, we think of this dynamic in terms of white people controlling a larger share of society's limited resources than black people (Benjamin, 2009; Feagin, 1991; Pager, 2003; Lacy, 2002, Royster, 2003) or the Black middle class gaining an advantage over the black poor (Lacy, 2007; Pattillo, 2007; Wilson, 1978), not a severely understudied dimension: upper middle class blacks creating more status-enhancing opportunities for their children than lower-status members of the Black middle class are capable of doing (Lacy, 2007, 2012).

Part of the mystique of the American Dream is that the precise steps required to make it to the top are invisible to those who have not already made it. It is not a matter of simply tracing an upwardly mobile person's steps. Although the ideology is commonplace, the American Dream is not for everyone. Capitalist societies are structured to prevent everyone from rising to the top.

DOI: 10.4324/9781003326243-9

Capitalism requires a cheap source of labor, a permanent working class. This means that the finer details on how to achieve a high status position and use it to your advantage circulate exclusively among the people who have made it. To understand how people achieve the American Dream, we need to focus not on those who are still actively chasing the Dream but on those who are living it.

In this chapter, I show that middle class blacks are not merely dreaming about their children becoming economically successful, they are actively socializing them to become members of America's black middle class. There is not a single path to achieving the American Dream. Some middle class blacks, feeling financially strapped, are concerned with maintaining their class position, leading to a focus on status maintenance. Through emphasizing hard work, spending conservatively, and requiring their children to buy luxuries with their own money, some middle class blacks are socializing their children to become members of what I call the *core* black middle class. The group just above them on the class ladder, free from financial constraints, focuses on achieving financial independence through work, spending liberally on the material items and experiences that make life more comfortable, and supplying their children with luxuries they believe someone in their class position should enjoy. In doing so, they are socializing their children to become members of what I call the *elite* black middle class when they grow up, that is, to reproduce the upper-class status that their parents have provided for them.

The Struggling Black Middle Class?

In the United States, many believe it is possible for children to become more successful than their parents. Seamless economic progress from one generation to the next ensures that the middle class is stable over time. Yet, the dominant narrative among scholars and journalists is that the black middle class is struggling, raising penetrating questions about the extent to which members will be able to pass on their class status to the next generation (Brown, 2016; Darity and Smith, 2021; Long and Dam, 2020; Perry and Romer, 2020; Petersen, 2021; Wenger and Zaber, 2021). The foreclosure crisis, the Great Recession, the covid pandemic, and the dramatic rise in CEO and other white-collar income have all contributed to the erosion of the black middle class in recent decades.

But studies proclaiming the decline of the black middle class are, more often than not, drawn from monolithic samples of *lower* middle class, that is, *working class* populations, not solidly middle class ones (Lacy, 2007, 2012). To properly understand whether the American Dream is sustainable for *middle class* black people, we need to distinguish between lower middle class blacks and those who sit above them on the class ladder. In *Blue-Chip Black*, I show that within the middle class, there are two groups: the *elite* black middle class and the *core* black middle class. The middle class lifestyles that blue-chip blacks hope to pass on to their children are distinguished in the first instance by income.

In contrast to scholars who define the black middle class as somewhere between two and four times the poverty level, a very low barometer for inclusion in the group, the *core* black middle class is actually middle class as they earn between $50,000 and $99,999 annually working in white-collar occupations that require a college degree. Members of the core black middle class feel a bit stretched financially, so they make an effort to stay on budget, prioritizing basics over luxuries. Just above the core on the class ladder, the *elite* black middle class, the most financially stable strata of the black middle class, earns more than $100,000 a year. In my discussion of both the core and the elite, I refer to *individual*, not household income. Among the core, each parent earns at least $50,000. Among the elite, each parent earns at least $100,000. Because they tend not to worry about money, the elite spend liberally on luxuries for their children, including backyard swimming pools, luxury cars, and private schooling.

Another distinction between the core and the elite is homeownership. It is common knowledge that black people are less likely than white people to own their own homes, whether they are middle class or working class. Less well-known is that a higher class status is associated with lower disparities in the black-white homeownership gap. About 80 percent of core middle class whites are homeowners, and 66 percent of core middle class blacks are, a difference of fourteen percentage points. Among the elite, the homeownership gap is smaller. About 90 percent of elite middle class white people own their homes while 80 percent of elite middle class blacks do. It stands to reason that the elite black middle class might be less likely to experience foreclosure than the core, the core less likely than the lower middle class (Lacy, 2007, 2012).

Finally, a residence in the suburbs is another factor distinguishing the elite from the core. The suburbs are stereotyped as havens for the white middle class, but the majority of America's black population is living in the suburbs too (Lacy, 2016). Members of the core black middle class are evenly distributed between the suburbs and urban areas: 46 percent in both communities. But elite middle class blacks live in the suburbs in higher numbers. Over 57 percent of elite middle class blacks call suburbia home. Only 39 percent of this group lives in the city (Lacy, 2007).

To be sure, some members of the black middle class are struggling to stay afloat. But the majority of those who are in danger of sliding back down the class ladder are not middle class to start with, not in the same way that core and elite middle class blacks are.

Maintaining and Reproducing the Black Middle Class

Blue-chip blacks cannot afford to leave to chance the possibility that their children will achieve the American Dream. They know that the next generation of middle class black people is at stake. Brad, a 40-year-old judge, revealed concerns about status reproduction that are shared by many middle class families. "The top priority for me," he explained, "is getting both of my sons through their educations, as far as they need to go … I will do everything that I can to help" them be successful, "whether that's through academics, setting up a business, or whatever." Brad's commitment to ensuring his children's future success shapes his current financial decisions. "I don't take a lot of chances," investing in the stock market or other options where the probability of losing money is as great as the chance of a windfall, Brad confessed. "For me, that's risky money" (Lacy, 2007). Like Brad, other *elite* middle class blacks are also willing to defer their own material gains in order to put their children on the right path to attaining a middle class lifestyle for themselves. Because they earn good money, elite middle class blacks do not worry about how to make ends meet, so spending lavishly on their children seems normal, the right thing to do. It is limiting their children's opportunities to get ahead that is unthinkable.

Members of the *core* middle class think differently than the elite about how to prepare their children to become middle class. Jasmine and her husband, Richard, for example, expect their sons to go to college too, but they plan to require their sons to contribute toward the cost of their tuition. Unwilling to jeopardize her retirement savings to educate her sons, Jasmine stressed, "I want money in the bank." She is critical of parents who deplete their savings to cover tuition at their children's private schools. Her husband is even more adamant that his sons should apply for scholarships or take out student loans. Richard told his oldest son, "I ain't using my retirement money! So *you* make it happen" (Lacy, 2007). Core middle class blacks, who feel more financially burdened than their elite counterparts, balance concerns about maintaining their middle class status with providing their children with the resources to secure a lifestyle as comfortable as the one their parents have provided for them.

Both the core and the elite are members of the black middle class, but the two groups of parents are socializing their children to think differently about the kinds of things that are standard practice for someone in their class position. These differences in worldview, what Bourdieu calls *habitus*, are rewarded differently in the larger society, putting one group on more solid footing than the other in terms of their ability to secure and leverage a middle class status. Made up of a set of internalized dispositions or preferences that are transmitted from one generation to the next, the habitus determines what is possible or improbable, and these expectations are converted into behavior which ultimately reproduces the existing class structure, inequalities and all (Swartz, 1997). In what follows, I identify variation in the components of a black middle class habitus across the two groups of middle class blacks: work ethic, spending responsibly, and sacrificing for their children.

How Work Matters

Core and elite middle class blacks both believe that hard work is a prerequisite to securing a middle class lifestyle. Still, there are notable differences in how the two groups interpret the concept of work ethic, which is so central to the American Dream ideology. The beliefs of core middle class blacks align closely with the working poor, all of whom see work as a *moral obligation* and criticize those who avoid committing to work, either by collecting welfare or opting to "just sit home and not do anything." Elite middle class blacks, on the other hand, see work as a *pathway to independence*, not a moral imperative. Noting the considerable effort it took to achieve economic success, "you work for it," and "we paid our dues," the elite expressed admiration for wealthy people because they need not work to maintain their luxurious lifestyles (Lacy, 2007).

Work as a Moral Obligation

Core middle class blacks socialize their children to believe that working is the only realistic way to achieve the American Dream. Terry, a married mother of two girls who works as a hospital administrator, explained that getting into the middle class and staying put requires motivation, discipline, and hard work. The people living in her middle class neighborhood, she observed, "work to stay here ... everybody goes to work. *This is your reward for going to work* ... You know how people say, 'You've arrived'? ... Nope, we go to work every day. If you do that, you can get here too." Terry suggests there's no mystery to achieving the American Dream. You just have to be willing to hustle.

Being productive citizens is an attribute highly valued by both the working poor and the core black middle class. Poor working residents of Harlem expressed resentment for their neighbors who chose not to work or to go out and look for work, feeling their laziness costs those who do elect to work. One worker complained, "I'm not knocking welfare, but I know people that are on it that can get up and work. There's nothing wrong with them ... I don't think it's right because that's my tax dollars going for somebody who is lazy" (Newman, 1999, 98). These low-skilled workers earn very little money working in minimum wage jobs, but that's not the point. What's important, from their perspective, is that they contribute to the economy, to the tax base, just like middle class people do.

Members of the core black middle class express a similar resentment toward able-bodied people who refuse to work. Like the working poor, they believe that welfare recipients fail to demonstrate a strong work ethic along with the discipline to hold down a job. In short, they feel welfare recipients gain access to more far more resources than they are entitled to. Audrey, a married mother and retired real estate agent indicated support for the 1996 federal Personal Responsibility and Work Reconciliation Act but worried the policy is not effective enough. "This welfare business," she said, "is not helping these people [the poor]. They're *expecting* it, we're not helping them to be responsible ... most of 'em are the ones that really should be out in the workplace."

Without referencing the 1996 policy, Alana, who is married with two teenage children, believes "everybody should work." The poor should not be allowed to collect government assistance without first performing some kind of work or public service. "There should be a work component attached to it ... you can do more than just sit home and collect a check ... if it's no more than requiring these people to go to the public library and put up some books – everybody can do something. I don't think they should get a free ride" (Lacy, 2007).

Work as a Pathway to Independence

While core middle class blacks believe no one should enjoy the good life unless they worked hard to achieve it, elite middle class blacks socialize their children to believe that work is one stop on the pathway to financial independence. Let me be clear: members of the elite middle class work hard too, but not because they agree with the core middle class that holding down a job is a way to earn respect as a productive citizen. Instead, they work, as Michael, a married father of three confessed, because "we got bills to pay ... you got to have some money coming in to pay the note (mortgage). Everybody out here has got to pay the house note." Echoing Michael, John explained, "I work now to pay for violin lessons for [his daughter], and for the house, and for my car [and] to be able to pay that mortgage."

What elite middle class blacks value is not the *moral* satisfaction of merely holding a job but the independence that working a high-status job bestows. Michael, a corporate manager, relishes that his job offers "freedom," meaning he can leave work to watch his children perform in a play or if, in the middle of the workday, his friends want to go fishing, "then I can say, 'Well, let me check my schedule,' and then we can go." Michael acknowledged, "You're going to have to work, but it's *how* you work and *how* you make your money" that matters.

Moreover, this affinity for financial independence is inextricably tied to a career choice in the discussions elite middle class blacks have with their children. A job at McDonald's is frequently invoked as the kind of low-skilled, dead-end work that the children should seek to avoid but could very well be their fate if they fail to plan their futures or refuse to be strategic about their career. Crystal, a stay-at-home mom who is married to Brad, remembers her husband telling their sons, "Listen, you can go to college ... get a good job, make a nice living, be able to go out to dinner, buy nice clothes. Or you can not do that—you have a choice—and have a little teeny apartment somewhere, take a bus, work at McDonald's. That's up to you, what you do." Michael is even more direct with his children. He shows them the monthly bills he and his wife must pay. "I told my oldest son, I said, "look at those people [working] at McDonald's. They working hard ... At the end of the day, if they work eight hours, they made what, forty-eight dollars? ... In a month they made a thousand dollars. Okay, this how much our house note is, okay? So you ain't living here [on that kind of salary]. You can't live [someplace like] here."

Elite middle class blacks do not miss an opportunity to assure their children that they need to think seriously about how they will reproduce the lifestyle they have enjoyed living in their parents' home. Even elementary school children are encouraged to pursue occupations that facilitate financial independence. When he was very young, Crystal's son told her, "Mommy, you know what I want to do when I grow up? I want to wash cars!" Her reaction was to steer him toward opening his own business, away from becoming a laborer: "That's fine," she responded, "but you want to *own* the car wash, and then you can wash cars anytime you want to, and when you don't feel like it, you don't have to." Becoming a boss over a worker means that their children will never be, as Philip, a married father of two daughters put it, "dependent upon other people" (Lacy, 2007).

Spending Responsibly

No purchase symbolizes harnessing the American Dream more than homeownership. Both core and elite middle class blacks believe owning a home distinguishes responsible consumers from spendthrifts. But that is where the similarities end. Core middle class blacks define "spending responsibly" the way that most Americans do, in the context of a budget that prioritizes basics over luxuries to minimize the feeling of being financially strapped. Free from financial constraints, elite middle class blacks spend more liberally than the core, purchasing necessities along with expensive luxuries that expose their children to the finer things in life. They define responsible spending as consumption that makes a comfortable life all the more comfortable, reflecting their membership in America's upper middle class.

Prioritizing Essentials

Core middle class blacks believe that a home should take priority over any other purchase. Engaging a critique popular in many black communities, they disparage black people who spend the bulk of their money on luxury cars while living in a rental property. Kevin, a high school football coach, observed, "These guys will get a loan for a car quicker than they get a loan for a house." And Terry admonished, "Don't complain that you live in the ghetto, when you're driving around in a Lexus." Respondents perceive choosing an expensive car over owning a home is the kind of irresponsible behavior that characterizes working-class black people's spending. They perceive the white middle class as more frugal than blacks. Terry describes a white physician who was devastated after his *20-year-old* car was stolen. According to Terry, he ranted, "How can I replace that car? It only cost me seven hundred fifty dollars. I pay [virtually] no insurance on it." Laughing as she recalled the conversation, Terry concluded that white people "prioritize things. They don't go buy the Mercedes first. They go buy their house."

Charlotte gained insight into the lifestyle of the upper class by shopping with her wealthy friend one day during their lunch hour. Charlotte needs to work to help make ends meet, but her friend Sarah is a trust fund recipient; she works because she is committed to educating youth. Charlotte recalled, "we go to Lord & Taylor and she walks up to the sales lady and says, 'I'd like some things for my daughter. I'd like a coat and something for play, something for dress.' The lady said, 'No problem.'" Then Sarah "said, 'Let's go,' and we went upstairs and had our yogurt." When they were done eating, they headed back down stairs to look at the clothing that the salesperson had selected. Sarah went through all the items, saying, "'I'll take this, this, this, and this. Wrap 'em up.' *She never looked at the price once!* The lady gave her 'bout five or six bags and she walked out the store." Although Sarah spent her lunch hour eating while the salesperson carefully selected clothing for her daughter, as Sarah exited the store, Charlotte laughingly recalled "She said, 'I *hate* to shop!' I said, 'yeah, I know what you mean!'".

Of course, Charlotte did *not* know what Sarah meant, at least not from personal experience. Her budget demands that she constantly "look at prices, comparing, waiting on sales, using coupons." Charlotte marveled that her wealthy friend Sarah could shop with no budget constraints whatsoever. "My girl never, ever looked [at the prices]. She said, 'I'll take that, that, that, that, that. Okay, that'll do her for a while.' And she put it in the bag, paid [the sales person] and went on." Charlotte remembers thinking at the time, "'Dag,' 'cause that's how you shop!'"

Charlotte is actually not poor, even though she insisted that middle class blacks are all "just one paycheck away from poverty." Others members of the core middle class are not really poor either, but they do worry about staying on budget or living with mounting debt. Terry and her husband are a young couple, in their early 30s, with a relatively new mortgage as first-time homeowners. "It's a constant, worrying about money is a constant," she lamented. "You get a mortgage and it's early on, like I said, third year ... you gotta have this [mortgage] money no matter what—furnace goes out, car breaks down–you gotta have that money ... you have to budget." And Kevin determined that if it came to it, "I ain't too proud to work two jobs. I got to provide. My wife and I joke that everybody else got an *investment* portfolio, we got a *debt* portfolio. So we goin be in debt ... you always worry about it, but you juggle stuff." Feeling financially strapped, core middle class blacks focus on maintaining their place in the middle class while socializing their children to make it into the middle class and avoid slipping back down the class ladder (Lacy, 2007).

Purchasing Comfort

Elite middle class blacks do not believe spending responsibly means doing without luxuries. Like the core, the elite middle class believe in homeownership, but they see buying a home as a natural thing for people in their class position to do, something that they will teach their children to do automatically, like going to college after high school. They can be critical of renters, arguing, as Brad does, that "to be responsible, you have to have ownership," a preference he acquired from his grandfather and his mother. Unlike Brad, Michelle was not socialized to privilege homeownership above renting. She grew up working-class in New York, an expensive, congested city where renting an apartment is not unusual. "I didn't know anybody who owned a house," Michelle recalls. "I knew people who had apartments ... I didn't invest anything. It was just shop [and] have a nice place." And after graduating from college, Michelle did have a nice apartment, which she shared with a roommate. She reflects, "I was never a homeowner, so I was *way* out of my league ... I would put so-o-o much money into having a fabulous apartment ... I should have bought property ... I should have bought *something*." Instead, she and her roommate "had a *beautiful* apartment ... It had a pool, a club-house ... Never once did it occur to us, 'We should buy a house.'" Michelle takes comfort in knowing that her children know better, they are being socialized to focus on investments and are unlikely to make the same mistakes that she did. "A lot of the things that you choose in life are based on your exposure and your knowledge, and the more that my daughters can be exposed, the more they'll know what their choices are as opposed to picking something ... because you didn't know to pick something else."

Elite middle class blacks are financially stable and, therefore, do not worry constantly about money or how to make ends meet. Not having to focus on budgeting leaves them free to concentrate on exposing their children to a preferred lifestyle. Most of the material things that they want, they buy. As Lydia explained, "It could be as simple as going to the grocery store and being able to buy whatever you want." Not having to budget is a reassurance for the elite middle class that they have achieved the American Dream. "It's the kind of *mental security* that you can get things that you want ... I mean, you can't get *everything*. I can't go out and buy a boat and have three Mercedes in the driveway. But generally, I can have the things that make my life comfortable."

Shopping is another indicator distinguishing the elite black middle class from the core. Brad tried to convince his wife, Crystal, to go shopping for brand new clothes. She did not want to. Crystal had gained weight after each of her pregnancies, and she told her husband, "I don't want to spend a lot of money [on clothes] until I lose weight." After an extended discussion, Crystal finally agreed to go shopping for fashionable clothing. She remembered Brad "took me to Nordstrom, 'cause I, I am very cheap [she smiles sheepishly]. Except for my children and for him. If I like it, and I know they'll like it, I would buy it. But for me, I could not see spending the money ... I had never shopped at Nordstrom or no store like that." Brad saw things differently and wanted her to have well-made clothing. "So we went into this department looking for large sizes, and I started finding things that I liked, and that I thought looked nice ... So now [she laughs], I've been shopping [there] since then. I don't shop no place else now!" Of course, core middle class blacks shop too, often at upscale stores like Nordstrom. But it's *the way* Crystal shops that aligns her with wealthy people like Charlotte's friend Sarah and separates her from the core middle class. Crystal told me, "I met a [sales]girl who works there, Jennifer, and she brings in things that she thinks I'll like." Just as Sarah did, Crystal relies on a personal shopper to sort through the many racks of clothing, pulling out items that might appeal to her tastes, as opposed to spending hours looking through the racks for just the right outfit on her own (Lacy, 2007).

Sacrificing for Your Children

The core and the elite differ not only with respect to perceptions of work and spending but also in terms of the kinds of sacrifices they are willing to make to provide their children with the advantages associated with their class position. Core middle class blacks require their children to purchase luxury items with their own money. Elite middle class blacks willingly buy these items for their children.

Necessities

In fact, core middle class blacks do buy their children many of the toys and material items they ask for, but they draw the line at luxury items such as designer tennis shoes or cars for teenagers when they turn sixteen. They believe these items are inessential for a middle class lifestyle. Then too, they feel the items are far too expensive, especially for a child. Shelley's seven-year-old son, Eric, wants to wear the Jordan tennis shoes he sees his friends wearing. Shelley doesn't mind his high-end taste, but she is unwilling to spend the money to fulfill his desire for the shoes. She did allow Eric to buy the shoes with his birthday money since he wanted them so badly. As Shelley explains, the shoe purchase was a teaching moment. "The shoes were small, they were maybe fifty dollars. Fifty dollars is a lot, I think, to pay for children's shoes ... once you give [the sales clerk] that money, that money's gone. So, don't say, he looked at the [sales]guy like, 'Okay, I gave you my money, where is my change?!'" Laughing, Shelley said she told her son, "You don't have any more money. You spent your money on those shoes because that's what you wanted." Her son was "disappointed for a few minutes, but then he realized what the lesson was. The lesson was if you want something that costs one hundred dollars or fifty dollars, *you* have to buy it."

Luxuries

While their children are members of the household, elite middle class blacks are willing to sacrifice their own desires for their children's benefit. They spend conservatively on themselves, allocating the bulk of their resources for their children's needs. John and his wife have one daughter. "It's so much of a challenge to get her grown up ... I wish I didn't have to spend so much money," he sighs. "I wish I could save more money. I wish I could do other things with my money. But I can't. And the thought crosses my mind, and just as quickly as it comes, it goes, because that's just the way it is." By sacrificing their own desires, elite middle class parents help their children to develop a taste for the finer things in life, a commitment that is not undertaken haphazardly: taste is the basis for the kind of cultural distinctiveness that underlies social privilege in America. Philip would like to do other things with his money too. "I'd like to have a bigger house," he tells me. "I'd like to have a Mercedes, I'd like to have a boat. I'd like to have ... a winter home in the Caribbean." Like John, Philip knows that he can't have these things right now. "What is important?" he asks rhetorically. "Your kids are important, so you give them priority over everything else."

A common priority for the elite middle class is purchasing a car for their teenage children once they are old enough to drive. The elite want their children to have luxuries denied to them by their parents when they were growing up. But a new car is also a response to the dictates of suburban culture. Greg, a married father of two, told me that most of the teens do not take the bus to the local high school. They drive themselves to school. In luxury cars. "Drive up to the high school sometime," he suggested. The "kids pull up in Lexuses ... BMWs ... Mercedes." I ask if he means the kids or their teachers. "The kids," he says. "Parking lot *full*. Parking lot *full* ... Once they get to a certain age, it's not cool to ride the [school [bus anymore." Greg is surprisingly tolerant of the teens' preference for their own car. In fact, when his daughter was accepted into an accelerated program for high school students at the University of Maryland, he felt pressured to buy her a car. "She said, 'Dad, I need a car.'" In the absence of her own car to drive to campus quickly, his daughter feared she would fail the course. So, Greg indulged her, but he bought an American-made compact car, not the foreign or luxury cars coveted by so many suburban teens. Brad, who you will recall only buys himself a car every ten years, bought his teenage son a brand new car.

Brad's son did not ask for a car. He received a car because Brad determined that "when he was sixteen, we needed another car" so that his son could drive himself wherever he wanted to go as opposed to waiting for his parents to take him or come home in one of their cars. A belief that parents should provide children with an abundance of material expressions of status – whether they request these items or not – is common among the elite black middle class. John grew up in the core middle class. His parents saw no good reason to spend $12 on the Converse tennis shoes that other kids were wearing when they could pay three dollars instead for a pair of generic tennis shoes at Kmart. Wearing the inexpensive shoes, John felt less than, and that feeling of unworthiness motivates him to provide only the best for his daughter. As he explained, black parents reason, "Well, white people have it. Why shouldn't my kid have it? ... Why should their kid have hundred-fifty dollar tennis shoes and mind shouldn't? ... And now that I can do it, or struggle to do it ... hell yeah! I'm gonna do it ... because that's what they're supposed to get."

Still, there is a limit to the elite black middle class' generosity. They are determined to put their children firmly on the path to success. "They've got to be educated," Michael said, referring to his three children. "I owe them that much." But once their children have completed college, elite middle class blacks consider their work done, and the children are on their own. "They must become independent," Michael added. His wife, Lydia, agrees with him: "They've got to go out and make their own way ... it's like giving up their wings ... I want them to be able to take care of themselves and to live comfortable lives." Brad shares this view, saying, "My sons ... know that their ability to be supported by this family is limited ...

When they have families, they are responsible for that family, and whatever they need to do to prepare for that, they should do."

Michelle and her husband, whose daughters attend private school, have a limit too. Michelle tells me, "I've spent most of my working years investing in their educations. We don't second-guess that, we just do it. I think that's what we're supposed to do." But when her children graduate from college, she says her priorities will shift. "The money that I'm dropping for private school and for this house, I want to be able to reel back in and put into my retirement" (Lacy, 2007).

Conclusion

Middle class parents passing their class position on to their children is a central component of the American Dream. The prevailing view is that the black middle class is less likely to achieve this goal because the group's status is so unstable. The foreclosure crisis, the Great Recession, and the covid pandemic destabilized the black middle class, proponents of this view argue, to such an extent that the group is endanger of becoming extinct.

In this chapter, I show that this dominant narrative is typically based on analysis of the experiences of the lower middle class or working class, not the middle class blacks positioned higher up on the class ladder. By exploring the parental socialization practices of *core* middle class and *elite* middle class blacks, who are not in any real danger of falling out of the middle class, we can understand how middle class blacks seek to ensure that their children will take their rightful place in the black middle class once adult.

The processes by which middle class people engage in status reproduction are often frustratingly invisible to groups below them on the class ladder. I show that these middle class parents are demystifying the process of achieving the American Dream for their children. They socialize their children into specific beliefs about what it means to be middle class along three dimensions: the importance of work, spending responsibly, and sacrificing for your children.

It is important to note that core middle class and elite middle class blacks do not socialize their children to think about being middle class in the same way. In Bourdieu's terminology, the two groups of parents are invested in different versions of the *habitus* associated with the middle class and socialize their children to adopt their respective beliefs and preferences. Elite middle class blacks, supremely secure in their status near the very top of the class ladder, teach their children that work is not valuable in and of itself. Instead, work is a pathway to becoming financially independent. These parents spend lavishly on their children, teaching them that the finer things in life are within reach and that they are entitled to these material items and opportunities. And elite middle class blacks sacrifice their own desires until their children graduate from college, at which point they redirect resources for their own use. Core middle class blacks teach their children that work is a moral obligation. Holding down a job demonstrates to the world that you are a responsible citizen. Feeling financially strapped, core middle class blacks spend conservatively on their children, providing them with necessities, not luxuries. These parents allow their children to have luxuries occasionally, but they require the children to purchase these items with their own money.

Americans tend to believe that working hard is the key to achieving the American Dream (Hochschild, 1996). But this kind of success is not merely a matter of working hard. It is also about acquiring the right habitus, beliefs, and preferences that encourage middle class people to believe that they are entitled to society's most coveted resources and an insider's knowledge on how to obtain them. Elite middle class blacks are better positioned than those below them on the class ladder to crack this code.

References

Benjamin, Rich. 2009. *Searching for Whitopia: An Improbable Journey to the Heart of White America.* New York: Hyperion.

Bourdieu, Pierre. 1984. *Distinction: A Social Critique of the Judgment of Taste.* Cambridge: Harvard University Press.

Brown, Steven. 2016. *The Stalled, Struggling Black Middle Class.* Washington, DC: The Urban Institute.

Darity, William and Imari Smith, 2021. "A Subaltern Middle Class: The Case of the Missing 'Black Bourgeoisie' in America." *Contemporary Economic Policy* 39:494–502.

Feagin, Joe. 1991. "The Continuing Significance of Race: Antiblack Discrimination in Public Spaces." *American Sociological Review* 100:750–80.

Hochschild, Jennifer. 1996. *Facing Up to the American Dream: Race, Class, and the Soul of the Nation.* Princeton, NJ: Princeton University Press.

Lacy, Karyn. 2002. "'A Part of the Neighborhood?': Negotiating Race in American Suburbs." *International Journal of Sociology and Public Policy* 22:39–74.

Lacy, Karyn. 2007. *Blue-Chip Black: Race, Class, and Status in the New Black Middle Class.* Berkeley, CA: University of California Press.

Lacy, Karyn. 2012. "All's Fair? The Foreclosure Crisis and Middle-Class Black (In)Stability." *American Behavioral Scientist* 56:1565–80.

Lacy, Karyn. 2016. "The New Sociology of Suburbs: A Research Agenda for Analysis of Emerging Trends." *Annual Review of Sociology* 42:369–84.

Long, Heather and Andrew Van Dam. 2020. "The Black-White Economic Divide Is as Wide as It Was in 1968." *Washington Post*, June 4, 1920.

Massey, Douglas. 2007. *Categorically Unequal: The American Stratification System.* New York: Russell Sage Foundation.

Newman, Katherine. 1999. *No Shame in My Game: The Working Poor in the Inner City.* New York: Knopf.

Pager, Devah. 2003. "The Mark of a Criminal Record." *American Journal of Sociology* 108:937–75.

Pattillo, Mary. 2007. *Black on the Block: The Politics of Race and Class in the City.* Chicago: University of Chicago Press.

Perry, Andrew and Carl Romer. 2020. *The Black Middle Class Needs Political Attention, Too.* Washington, DC: The Brookings Institution.

Petersen, Anne Helen. "The Mirage of the Black Middle Class." *Vox.* January 26, 2021.

Royster, Deirdre. 2003. *Race and the Invisible Hand: How White Networks Exclude Black Men from Blue-Collar Jobs.* Berkeley, CA: University of California Press.

Swartz, David. 1997. *Culture and Power: The Sociology of Pierre Bourdieu.* Chicago: University of Chicago Press.

Tilly, Charles. 1998. *Durable Inequality.* Berkeley, CA: University of California Press.

Wenger, Jeffrey and Melanie Zaber. 2021. "Most Americans Consider Themselves Middle Class. But Are They?" The RAND Blog.

Wilson, William. 1978. *The Declining Significance of Race.* Chicago: University of Chicago Press.

PART II

Contemporary Issues in American Dream Studies

9

WHAT (AMERICAN) DREAMS ARE MADE OF

Disney's fairy tale narratives

Tracey Mollet

On April 30, 2021, Disneyland theme park reopened after a record 412 days of closure, following the effects of the COVID-19 global pandemic. While many of the other theme parks had been sporadically open throughout the previous year, Disneyland's persistent closure was hugely significant and troubling to the American people in a time of considerable upheaval. Indeed, Disneyland had been closed only a handful of times since its historic opening in 1955; once for a national day of mourning after President John F. Kennedy was assassinated in 1963 and following the attacks of September 11, 2001 (Pallotta 2020). Writing as the closure was announced on March 14, 2020, *Los Angeles Times* journalist Todd Martens reflected that "Disneyland has been able to fight through whatever ails our country's national consciousness, even as it so often directly reflects it" (2020, n.p.). It seems, then, that in a time of international crisis, the American people relied upon the presence and durability of Disneyland and, most importantly, the fairy tale narratives that permeate its fantastical lands. The Walt Disney Company is unquestionably an important cultural fixture on the landscape of contemporary entertainment and as Mittermeier reminds us, the park itself "has become shorthand for excitement, fairy tale endings, (American) dream (s) come true" (2020, 1). The Disney brand and the fairy tale narratives at its heart encompass a range of entertainment experiences from theatrical feature films, streaming services, cruise ships, stage musicals, and retail outlets. It is deeply ingrained within the American consciousness as a signification of *the* dream come true. It functions as part of a national myth, acting as "a comfort blanket for the nation" (Wills 2017, 72). In a time of deep social and cultural dislocation, Disney "[made] the world seem simpler and more comfortable for us to inhabit" (Campbell and Kean 1997, 9). It is a "willing sponsor of the American Dream and uses its fairy tales to uphold its mythical dimensions" (Mollet 2020, 6). In short, the Disney fairy tale is a fantastical manifestation of the American Dream.

The similarities between the American Dream and the Disney fairy tale, however, do not start and end with their stabilizing impact on the American people during a time of turmoil. Both narratives were born in the 1930s. Coined in 1931 by James Truslow Adams in *The Epic of America*, the essence of the term was a "dream of social order in which each man and each woman shall be able to attain the fullest stature of which they are innately capable" (1931, 214–215). It was a dream of limitless personal opportunity in which it "makes no difference who you are" and that ultimately, in America, "anything your heart desires will come to you", as iterated in the Walt Disney Company's undisputed "theme" song "When You Wish Upon a Star" (Harline and Washington 1940). During the Great Depression, in which breadlines, high unemployment and foreclosures were endemic, the American Dream flourished, providing stability and hope for the future. As Van Elteren suggests, "It was in the context of mainstream Americanism of the 1930s that the vision of the American Dream became articulated [...] not in what its citizens are at a certain point, but in who they shall become" (2006, 81). Central to this vision was the belief that despite all obstacles, Americans would eventually triumph and live happily ever after, as indicated in the optimistic narratives of 1930s musicals such as *42nd Street* (Bacon 1933a) and *Footlight Parade* (Bacon 1933b) and in the journeys of animated characters such as Mickey Mouse, Donald Duck and Porky Pig (Mollet 2017). One such narrative was especially significant in underlining the intrinsic connection between the Disney fairy tale and the American Dream. *The Three Little Pigs* (Gillett 1933) immediately resonated with the American people as the short's central song, "Who's Afraid of the Big Bad Wolf?" became a confident rallying cry for people's feelings about the Depression, following the election of Franklin Delano Roosevelt to the presidency. Indeed, as I have argued elsewhere, *The Three Little Pigs* was:

> the first time that the American people had placed themselves within the fairy tale world and identified themselves in the position of fantasy characters, crystallising the connection between Disney's colourful fairy tale world and the harsh realities of their everyday lives.
>
> *Mollet 2020, 5*

Following the success of this short subject, and due to Walt Disney's own long-held fascination with fairy tales, the Walt Disney Studios achieved enormous success with their animated adaptation of *Snow White and the Seven Dwarfs* (Hand et al. 1937), beginning a relationship with the fairy tale that would last through the 20th century and beyond.

The longevity and continued cultural resonance of the Disney fairy tale are evident through the studio's numerous successful productions, including but not limited to *Cinderella* (Geronimi et al. 1950), *Sleeping Beauty* (Geronimi 1959), *The Little Mermaid* (Clements and Musker 1989), *Beauty and the Beast* (Trousdale and Wise 1991), and *The Princess and the Frog* (Clements and Musker 2009). The studio reached further heights of success with its 50th animated feature, *Tangled* (Greno and Howard 2010), and it is impossible to ignore the phenomenal impact of *Frozen* (Buck and Lee 2013). The significance (and profitability) of these fairy tales was sufficient for the Walt Disney Studios to parody their fairy tale creations through the critically acclaimed *Enchanted* (Lima 2007) and to expand their fairy tale world into live action television shows such as *Once Upon a Time* (Horowitz and Kitsis 2011–2018) and theatrical reboots such as *Maleficent* (Stromberg 2014), *Cinderella* (Branagh 2015), and *Beauty and the Beast* (Condon 2017). I would argue that such resilience underlines that the Disney fairy tale is a flexible narrative that reflects "changing tastes and attitudes in American culture" (Teverson 2013, 141). The same can be said for the American Dream. Much like Disney's fairy tales, the American Dream is upheld by powerful imagery and discourse, attempting to define America's national ethos at any one moment in time. It is also inherently nostalgic in its reach – as it permits a longing for home, but this is a home that never truly was: a fantasy existing only *once upon a time* (Campbell and Kean 1997; Boym 2001). Samuel has argued that this myth proves its resilience through its "adaptive behavior" (2012, 4). As mentioned above, it was founded on a premise of collectivism and equal opportunity, transforming into a desire for upward social mobility and wealth toward the end of the century. Sands (2018) has underlined that, indeed, the economic dimension of the Dream, the "riches" of the Horatio Alger "rags to riches" narrative that underpins America's national myth was very much tied to consumerism. It was a journey of self-empowerment for the working and middle classes that was "made for Hollywood" (7).

The American Dream and fairy tales have powered both the institution and productions of Hollywood since its inception. The American Dream assured that *anyone* could become a star, including Walt Disney himself, who acted as a living proof that the dream could be achieved. Indeed, Sternheimer confirms that American culture provides "continuous examples that the American Dream of rising from the bottom of the economic ladder is real" (2011, 6). On screen, fairy tale endings of happily ever after are built into the classical narrative story-telling structure that Hollywood is so known for (Bordwell, Staiger and Thompson 1986). Its enormous filmography is dominated by fairy tales, including mainstream hits such as *Pretty Woman* (Marshall 1990) and *Shrek* (Adamson and Jenson 2001), cult classics such as *The Princess Bride* (Reiner 1987), and niche tween fare such as *A Cinderella Story: If The Shoe Fits* (Johnston 2016). While these films are specifically *fairy tale* inspired narratives, Hollywood films often perpetuate the myth of the United States as a site for the achievement of a happily ever after through their "sense of national mission and idealism" (Schuck and Wilson 2008, 629). They Americanize themes such as happiness, romance, individualism, and heroism, weaving these ideals into the fabric of their narratives. This allows such texts to assume a shared understanding of and desire for the American Dream among *all* audiences, facilitating an aspiration for its attainment (Campbell et al. 2004; Arnold 2013). Or as Restad so bluntly argues, "The operating idea here is that in every foreigner, there is an American waiting to get out" (2015, 236). Furthermore, thanks to the overwhelming dominance of American movies (and more specifically, Disney movies) at the global box office, both the American Dream and the Disney fairy tale have become central to academic debates surrounding globalization and American exceptionalism. At different points in their history, both narratives have been accused of conservatism, class prejudice, and racism. While scholars such as Schickel (1986), Bryne and McQuillan (1999), and Wasko (2001) have been deeply critical of Disney fairy tales for their conservatism and heteronormativity, Giroux has more widely argued that Disney's narratives "aggressively rewrite the historical and collective identity of the American past" (1995, 4). Similarly, accusations have been held against the American Dream. Jenkins et al. (2020) underline that Donald Trump's presidential campaign activated a toxic white privilege as the "true" essence of the American Dream, lost in the 1980s, as Trump claimed to "make America great again" (Kimmel 2017; Churchwell 2018).

This chapter seeks to further conceptualize the relationship between the American Dream and the Disney fairy tale, charting changes throughout their histories and the way in which they each transform their focus, tone, and character, depending on the significant shifts within American society.

"We'll Be Happy Forever, I Know" – Nostalgic Fantasies in the 1930s and 1950s

Disney's first princess, Snow White, emerged at a pivotal moment of the Great Depression. While the first few years of Roosevelt's presidency were marked with success through the projects guided by the National Recovery Act and the Works Progress Administration, in 1936, concern was arising in the Treasury as to how much FDR's New Deal was costing Americans (Romasco 1983). This concern was justified, given that the United States fell into further recession between September 1937 and June 1938 (Bernstein 1987). America's national myth was crumbling and in need of further validation. The American Dream in the

1930s, powered by Roosevelt's New Deal, was marked with a "communitarian ethic" that envisaged the country working together as a collective (Parrish 1992, 409). When the Wall Street Crash had prompted widespread bank failures, unemployment, and homelessness, it seemed more important than ever that emphasis was placed on the potential of the common man. Adams' American Dream places significant importance on equality of opportunity – the chance for Americans to develop their capacities for success without limitations. The nature and location of this success are also of interest here. Roosevelt put much stead in the importance of farmlands to rejuvenate America's economy, as shown by the schemes enacted through the Agricultural Adjustment Administration. In other words, the key to America's future lay within its past: a nostalgic embrace of the rural idyll. To achieve this desirable vision, Americans had to *work hard* and *have hope* (Deszcz 2002, my emphasis). This also draws attention to the values of the public during times of crisis. One of the bestselling books of the 1930s was Dale Carnegie's *How to Win Friends and Influence People*, which placed importance upon the character of individuals.

While the post-war period did witness a significant transformation in the economic fortunes of the American people, with a period of unprecedented affluence, there are significant similarities in the cultural foundations of the American Dream in the 1930s and the 1950s. Each decade contained a wish and hope for more. In the case of the 1930s, Americans wished to escape from the clutches of economic depression, whereas in the 1950s, there was a widespread desire for a return to normalcy following the social and cultural upheavals of the war. This was both a literal and figurative infusion of the American Dream's nostalgic spirit: stability was to be found in the gender roles of the pre-war period and in the physical structure of the home. As Samuel confirms, "the home became the bedrock of the Dream" in these years, facilitated by the National Housing Act of 1949 (2012, 6; Pach Jr and Richardson 1991).

The Disney fairy tales of the 1930s and 1950s serve to reinforce these notions of the American Dream. *Snow White and the Seven Dwarfs, Cinderella,* and *Sleeping Beauty* built their narratives toward the happily ever after of marriage for their princesses. Research on the representation of these Disney heroines has been vast, with substantial criticisms of their perceived passivity (England et al. 2011; Stover 2013; Whelan 2014) and the way in which these heroines are primed for marriage from the beginning of their narratives (Bradford 2012). While it cannot be denied that these fairy tales have a domestic focus (Snow White cleans and cooks for the dwarfs, Cinderella is a slave in her own home and Aurora dreams of meeting her prince), these princesses provided an identifiable touchstone for Americans, during the attempted reaffirmation of America's national myth.

One of the most important ways in which Disney princesses engage with the American Dream is through their desire for freedom or relief from their current setting. While these princesses effectively move from one domestic setting to another, each of their journeys is positioned as desirable as they move from "rags to riches". Snow White is first seen scrubbing the floor of the castle courtyard while her jealous stepmother looks on. Like Cinderella, she is dressed in rags but hopes for a better time when her faith in her dreams will be rewarded. All of Disney's princesses are kind and good and never lose hope in the value of their dreams, no matter what the circumstances and their faith is rewarded: such is the promise of belief in the American Dream. As noted previously, when Snow White is faced with frightening trees that transform into monsters and river logs that resemble crocodiles, she is terrified and loses faith, but soon realizes that her fear was unwarranted, as the sweet woodland creatures lead her to the dwarfs' cottage (Mollet 2013). Similarly, in *Cinderella*, when the stepsisters rip the heroine's dress to shreds, she is on the cusp of losing hope, sobbing, "I can't believe, not anymore!" when the fairy godmother appears, ready to reward her faith.

As these heroines are positioned as trapped at the beginning of their narratives, they "appear as Americans without the freedom to choose and with barriers to their eventual upward mobility" (Mollet 2020, 42). These barriers largely take the form of older women who prize material wealth over hard work and are jealous of the beauty and sweet dispositions of these younger princesses. The heroines' journeys are therefore worthy, and their destinations familiar to Americans. Their happily ever afters were a nostalgic return to the way it was perceived things were supposed to be, with women finding stability and comfort in a *romantic* partnership. Snow White and Aurora both spend a substantial amount of time living in rural cottages situated in the middle of idyllic forests, providing the nostalgic setting for their journeys to happily ever after. However, much like the American Dream in this era, these narratives simultaneously embrace both the past and the future. In *Cinderella* and *Sleeping Beauty*, fathers appear anti-progressive in their outlook as they view the marriage of their sons and daughters as a basis for the rearing of children. In the former film, when the prince appears disinterested in his prospective brides, the king cries, "There must be one who would make a suitable mother!" When the Grand Duke questions his intentions, he mutters, "A suitable wife". Prince Phillip, in the latter film, berates his father for rejecting his decision to marry the peasant girl, Briar Rose (who is obviously Princess Aurora in disguise). Furthermore, Aurora is noted as turning sixteen during the film's narrative, on the cusp of a new era for America. Many scholars have noted that as *Sleeping Beauty* was released in 1959, it was attempting to speak to a "changing generation" (Stover 2013, 3) on the cusp of the sexual revolution of the 1960s. Aurora is desperate to be treated as an adult, and thus her journey toward marriage with Phillip is framed as a desire for freedom from the restraints of childhood. This situates the young princes and princesses of the future as forward thinking by basing marriage upon a foundation of *love* and not *children* and constitutes a partial rejection of the values that underpinned the post-war return to normalcy.

Each of these fairy tales also draws particular attention to the triumph of the underdog – the extraordinary actions of the common man. I have noted elsewhere that the dwarfs in *Snow White and the Seven Dwarfs* take center stage and overshadow Snow White's prince as the heroes of this story (Mollet 2019b). The dwarfs are representative of hard-working Americans (of all mentalities), central to Roosevelt's conceptions of the American Dream in the 1930s, and indicative of the men from all walks of life who fought together to defend America's values in the Second World War. The dwarfs work hard and are an integral part of Snow White's happily ever after, as they chase the wicked queen up the mountain where she eventually meets her downfall. However, the extraordinary actions of scrappy underdog characters are also evident in *Cinderella* and *Sleeping Beauty*. In *Cinderella*, the mice work tirelessly to help Cinderella achieve her happily ever after, locating a sash and beads for her first attempt at a dress for the ball and, most importantly, to locate the key to Cinderella's attic when she is imprisoned by her stepmother, Lady Tremaine. The fairies in *Sleeping Beauty* also fulfill this function, particularly the lovable character of Merryweather, who sees the evil Maleficent as her personal foe. The fairies are integral to Philip's escape from captivity, clear his pathway through the thorny forest, and place a spell on his sword to ensure its success in striking Maleficent when she transforms into a dragon.

"I Want Adventure in the Great, Wide Somewhere" – Consumerist Desires and Globalization in the Renaissance Era

Following *Sleeping Beauty*, the Walt Disney Company did not return to its fairy tale roots until the release of *The Little Mermaid* in 1989, kickstarting not only a period of growth for America but for the Company itself, in what is largely lauded as the "Renaissance era" of Disney's animated feature productions (Davis 2006; Pallant 2011; Mollet 2020). Disney's growth in this era was undoubtedly facilitated by the policies of the previous decade. Historians are generally in agreement that the neoliberal economic policies of President Reagan completely transformed American life. Reagan believed that America's needs were best served by deregulation and government spending cuts. Between 1980 and 1987, government spending on social welfare decreased from 28 percent to 22 percent (Livingston 2010). This was accompanied by a rise in consumer culture as spending habits increased and the forging of American conglomerates became a permanent fixture of the international economic landscape: in short, the United States became a globalized power (Hesmondhalgh 2003). Teen markets became of particular value during this era, with the rise of popular shows such as *Buffy the Vampire Slayer* (Whedon 1997–2003) and films such as *Clueless* (Heckerling 1995), which target this demographic through excessive intertextuality, popular music, and clothing (Wee 2008). While the consequences of Reagan's policies are still being felt today, Schaller (1992) argues that in the late 1980s and 1990s, these measures funded a substantial economic recovery for the United States.

Reagan's ideologies also prompted further changes in the nature of the American Dream. This era rejected the communitarian ethic of Roosevelt's presidency – the individual now had to take responsibility for their own path to achieving the American Dream. Furthermore, Reagan's claims to "make America great again" invoked a nostalgia for the 1950s and the values that accompanied this decade. Reagan won support from the middle classes as he favored a return to the nuclear family, a restoration of domesticity for women, and athleticism for men (Wood 1986). This disregard for the advances of second wave feminism in the 1960s and 1970s manifests in what scholars have termed "post-feminism" (Faludi 1991; McRobbie 1991; Tasker and Negra 2007). It underlines that feminism is a fight that has effectively been won and that women should have the choice to follow their own path, whether that be a life raising children in the home or one that centers around a career, both or neither. As such narratives are integral to the nature of the journey toward "happily ever after", these concerns are inherent in the American Dream in this era and surface in the narratives of Disney's fairy tales. In the previous section, I underlined the ways in which the American Dream is an amalgamation of nostalgia and progress, evidencing its adaptability in times of social upheaval. This is evident in the way in which men's proposed "happily ever afters" changed in this period. Reagan advocated a return to traditionalism, evidenced by popular treatises such as *Iron John* (Bly 1990) and movies such as *The Terminator* (Cameron 1984) and *Die Hard* (McTiernan 1988). This is also confirmed by the positions of Disney's 1950s princes, who have just returned from war and are expected to marry. However, the "new man" of the 1990s, as confirmed by Jeffords (1995), was expected to quash his hyper-masculine tendencies and become a sensitive, worthy partner of 1990s heroines, evident in films such as *Pretty Woman* (1990) and *10 Things I Hate About You* (Junger 1999).

These cultural shifts provided rejuvenated models for social action for the American people. Furthermore, the general global reach of the United States during the 1980s and 1990s, including the Walt Disney Company who notably opened EuroDisney in 1992, seemed to confirm the tenets of American exceptionalism. American people were "endowed with a unique mission", and they could hope to "change the world without changing [themselves]" (Restad 2015, 14, 228). Indeed, such global aspirations shape the dreams of Ariel and Belle, princesses of the European fairy tales of this era, *The Little Mermaid* and *Beauty and the Beast*. These heroines are still as good natured as their predecessors and still desire relief from their current setting, maintaining this intrinsic connection to the American Dream. However, the desires of Disney's first three princesses were framed in terms of romance, whereas Ariel and Belle want different things. Reagan's policies of deregulation and marketization led to a consumer boom founded upon the notion of choice. These heroines are young women who *consume*; they buy, they read and they collect, and by doing so, they scope out their place in the world and pre-empt the endings to their own fairy tales, ensuring their achievement of the American Dream (Livingston 2010). Their dreams also have a geographical dimension absent from the princesses of the 1930s and 1950s. Ariel wants to be a part of another world and thus dreams far beyond the life she currently has. Belle dreams of "adventure in the great wide somewhere" – global aspirations that puzzle the lowly, narrow-minded villagers in her provincial town but that resonate with the reach of America's national myth in this era. Byrne and McQuillan (1999) have argued that *Beauty and the Beast* is indicative of Disney's cultural ambitions in Europe during this era, with the installation of EuroDisney. In this reading, an Americanized Belle is fated to change things for the better in the Beast's castle (to be read as France). However, this is not really borne out in the film's narrative, as Belle already seems to fit among the enchanted objects of the castle and it is the *Beast* and not her, that needs to transform to break the spell and activate the happily ever after.

Under Belle's tutelage, Jeffords notes that the Beast transforms into the "considerate, loving and self-sacrificing man of the 1990s", discovering his inner American (1995, 67). He even gives Belle a library, with more *choice* of books than she could ever have hoped for. Prince Eric, too, offers such "riches" to Ariel when she trades her voice to the sea witch, Ursula, to join the human world. Ariel is excited by the offerings of a life on the land and is shown to enjoy dancing and shopping with Eric in his kingdom. While Eric does not undergo a trans-formation in his value system, he is significantly different from the princes of the 1930s and 1950s. When his aide, Grimsby presents him with a statue of himself dressed in traditional prince-like armor (complete with sword and shield), he is less than impressed, preferring to dream about the day when he will meet the woman he loves. Brode has argued that Eric envisages his happily ever after when he "[marries] happily, and without hesitation when he meets a woman who impresses him as an individual" (2005, 185). Much like Prince Adam (the Beast), he embodies the spirit of male leads in 1990s movies. Disney's endorsement of male sensitivity to ensure the happily ever after is made clearer once we consider the character of Gaston.

Gaston is, of course, the embodiment of the hyper-masculine ideal. He is shown to be dated in his outlook, specifically his views on women, which Belle warns are "positively primeval". He hunts, spits, drinks beer, and enjoys the company of petite blonde women who fawn over his every move. In the 1950s, perhaps his plans for his and Belle's nuptials may have been framed as part of the American Dream of domesticity. However, here we see another shift in the character of the national myth. As well as his views on women, his general obses-sion with his appearance ally him with the villainesses of 1930s and 1950s Disney fairy tales. Much like the Wicked Queen from *Snow White and the Seven Dwarfs*, Gaston enjoys looking at himself in the mirror to ensure the perfection of his appearance. His value system is thus associated with an anti-American outlook which prizes superficiality, material wealth, and trophies. His anger at being snubbed by Belle on their supposed wedding day also echoes Maleficent's upset over her lack of invitation to Aurora's christening in *Sleeping Beauty*. Ursula also shares this un-American ideological outlook. When luring Ariel into making a deal for human legs to pursue Eric, the sea witch tries to convince the young princess that she should place value in her appearance to try and secure her prince. Do Rozario (2004) convincingly claims that Ursula is the last of Disney's femme fatales, the famous villainesses that permeated film noirs narratives. When considering that Ursula is also a tyrant who imprisons those who do not obey her orders, the ideological position of Ariel and Eric as "good" Americans becomes clearer. At the close of the film, the hero and heroine manage to vanquish this threat to American ideals, and only then can the happily ever after be achieved.

"A Place Where There Are No Happily Ever Afters" – Post 9/11 Disney Fairy Tales

The events of September 11, 2001 had a substantial impact on American cultural identity (Halliwell and Morley 2008; Kellner 2009; Prince 2009). With the brunt of the attacks being in New York City, it seemed as though the target was the American Dream itself. New York had long been viewed as emblematic of the United States and its ideology, a "gateway to a land of opportunity for European immigrants [hoping] to start a new life" (Mollet 2020, 75). It was also iconic within wider American culture; a "vast city, recreated from half remembered fragments of films, TV dramas, popular music and advertising images" (Campbell and Kean 1997, 176). The events of 9/11 and the agenda of President George W. Bush set in motion a chain of events that would ultimately lead the United States to war in the Middle East and into a spotlight of criticism throughout the globe. Widespread disillusionment with America's involvement in these conflicts led to a flurry of support for presidential candidate Barack Obama and a sense of alienation from President Bush. Nowhere was this change in the tide more evident than in the handling of the devastation left by Hurricane Katrina in New Orleans in 2005, which led to the deaths of over 1200 people and $108 billion of property damage (Gibbens 2019). Katrina's victims were mostly African American and low-income earners, and thousands lost the foundation of their connection to the American Dream: their homes (Schuck and Wilson 2008; White and Hanson 2011). The market crash of 2008 widened the homeownership crisis as millions found that they could no longer afford their mortgages. More than 7 million jobs were lost, and 10 million Americans are believed to have lost their homes: many of them African Americans who had been specifically targeted for cheap mortgages by Wells Fargo (Picchi 2018). The time had come for the Dream to adapt once more. Barack Obama was elected to the presidency in 2008, heading up a new *inclusive* version of America's national myth, a "different America", which acknowledged and worked to reduce the substantial differences in opportunities offered to African Americans in comparison to white people (Pease 2009, 208; Kimmage 2011). Comparisons with FDR are not amiss here, as "like Roosevelt before him, Obama had to summon the nation from the sloughs of despair" (Hanson and White 2011, 5). America had to be underlined as the place where dreams could still come true.

While it may seem that fairy tales and the fantastic had no place in a world of apocalyptic nightmare, tragedy, and war, in fact, such narratives flourished in the first decade of the 21st century, evidenced by the success of the *Harry Potter* series (2001–2011), Peter Jackson's *Lord of the Rings* trilogy (2001–2003), and the *Shrek* franchise (2001–2010).[1] These narratives offered comfort in a time of crisis and attempted to rejuvenate belief in the American Dream and a happily ever after. As Pershing and Gablehouse have argued, they reinvigorated social conservatism and the hegemonic order through their escapist fantasy and familiarity as adaptations and parodies (2010). Popular culture was also dominated by "rags to riches" narratives fronted by teenagers, such as *A Cinderella Story* (Rosman 2004), *Another Cinderella Story* (Santostefano 2008), *A Cinderella Story: Once Upon a Song* (Santostefano 2011), and even Disney's own ABC series *Once Upon a Time* (2011–2018). These narratives all situate their fairy tales within America itself, and the dreams of their young protagonists are all *American* in nature, for example, Sam in *A Cinderella Story* wants to attend Princeton University, and Mary Santiago in *Another Cinderella Story* dreams of enrolling in a dance college in Manhattan.

This is taken further in *Once Upon a Time,* where protagonist Emma Swann finds her happily ever after in the distinctly American locale of Storybrooke. Storybrooke is positioned as the suburban idyll, lined with white picket fences, large houses, and a small-town high street. Most importantly, Storybrooke is the home of fairy tale characters who live their lives with significant material comforts, regardless of their level of income. No one suffers financial hardship while living in Storybrooke, further constructing the image of America as a magical fantasyland where dreams come true and where social inequalities are non-existent. These narratives and their locations thus served to underline that happily ever afters were still possible and that the United States was the place where they could and *should* occur. Building on from this, the events of the first decade of the 21st century thus make it more significant that Disney's first two fairy tale narratives of the new millennium take place explicitly in America and, moreover, in the poignant locations of New York and New Orleans.

Enchanted (2007) functions as both nostalgic homage and parody of the Disney fairy tale. Its heroine, Giselle, is, at first, as regressive as mid-20th century princesses Cinderella and Sleeping Beauty. She is kind, gentle, and most importantly, she has a dream that she will find her true love, Edward, and live happily ever after. When she is banished to New York (and the fairy tale is transformed into a live action narrative), the evil Queen Narissa sniggers that she has sent Giselle to "a place where there are no happily ever afters". Giselle proceeds to emerge from a steam grate in Times Square, New York, and meet divorce attorney Robert, who teaches her how relationships *should* work in the "real world", discarding her fairy tale outlook. However, Robert soon falls in love with Giselle, and *their* fairy tale narrative believably comes to light within New York. Regarding the American Dream, what is of interest here is how the story highlights the supposed magic of consumerism inherent in America's national myth. When Robert's daughter, Morgan, and Giselle go shopping for a dress for an upcoming ball, Morgan pulls out her father's credit card, declaring it "better than a fairy godmother". This underlines the fact that, indeed, magical transformations can take place in the real world, but the Manhattan-based shopping and makeover montages that accompany their excursions set their fairy tale narrative exclusively in New York.

It also seems of note that Times Square, the iconic stage of America's cultural power, functions as the magical gateway into the animated fairy tale world of Andalasia. It acts as a porous membrane allowing Giselle's fairy tale magic to spread throughout the city. What is more, the people of New York are receptive to her value system. Her belief in happily ever afters makes her the perfect American citizen and she is delighted with what America can offer her as a former princess. The film even closes with her starting her own business: Andalasia Fashions. More widely, the film highlights the inherent compatibility between the American Dream and the Disney fairy tale. Disney's animated characters are at home in New York, and "real life" Americans are more than happy to immerse themselves in Disney's magic. *Enchanted* underlines that "while there is a hidden fairy tale character inside every American, there is also an American within every fairy tale character" (Mollet 2020, 87), and thus the American Dream is married to the Disney fairy tale, given new life, significantly in the city of New York.

Just as 9/11 adds emotional poignancy to *Enchanted*'s setting of Manhattan, the devastation left by Hurricane Katrina and the election of Barack Obama to the presidency underline the importance of *The Princess and the Frog*'s setting of New Orleans, and heroine Tiana's cultural significance as the first African American Disney princess (Lester 2010). It is also of note here that in the wake of the economic crash of 2008, we see the resurgence of the "triumph of the underdog" narrative inherent in the American Dream of the 1930s during the Great Depression. Tiana works exceptionally hard as a waitress, saving against all odds to open her own restaurant. Her entrepreneurial spirit and modernity illuminate the opportunism inherent in the American Dream. As Mitchell-Smith has argued, she is positioned as a "modern girl in conflict with an ancient and repressive regime" (2012, 210), and much like dreamers Belle and Ariel, she *wants* more than what she currently has. Framed in a window against the night sky, Tiana is told by her father that she should not just rely upon wishing on stars ("that old star will only get you part of the way"); she needs to rely on herself – the spirit of individualism inherent in Reagan's self-reliant conception of the American Dream – still prevalent in the 21st century neoliberal United States economy.

Scholars have been somewhat critical of *The Princess and the Frog* and its presentation of race, especially considering that Tiana is rendered as a frog for much of the film and that the obstacles she faces in achieving her dream could easily be put down to gender, rather than skin color (Barnes 2009; Moffitt 2019). The film could be construed as color-blind, as Turner asserts, "Audiences must simultaneously see her blackness and overlook it in favor of her character and her desire to access the American Dream" (2013, 84). Despite President Obama's acknowledgment of significant structural inequalities in the United States that could prevent the upward mobility of an African American woman such as Tiana, the film engages with a post-race mentality, whereby anything is possible as long as "your heart is in your dream" (Harline and Washington 1940). This is also quite troubling considering the film essentially practices what Fjellman (1992) has termed "Distory" – a "Disneyfication" of history, ignoring what Tiana's reality would have been under the significant constraints of the Jim Crow laws of the 1920s.

However, what is perhaps more important to note here is the overall positioning of race within the narrative. Tiana's dreaming, charisma, work ethic, and inherent goodness are the embodiment of the perfect American citizen. Moreover, her color and disposition are particularly marked when she is placed alongside the hyperbolic character of Charlotte: a spoiled, blonde, *white* "princess" more in league with romantic dreamers such as Cinderella and Snow White. The film also celebrates African American culture with overwhelmingly positive images of African American communities, jazz music, and delicious food. Much like Obama's ambitions for an inclusive America, Tiana seeks to unify the city, which she achieves with her restaurant at the close of the film. Much like New York in *Enchanted*, New Orleans functions as a microcosm of America: a place where the American Dream is alive and well and where Disney fairy tales can end in happily ever after.

An Act of True Love – The Power of Women and Inclusivity in the Age of #MeToo and President Trump

When Donald Trump was elected to the presidency in 2016, the American Dream shifted once more. Claiming that Obama's election had somehow crushed the original spirit of America's national myth, he pronounced that the American Dream was dead but promised to revive it (Churchwell 2018, 1). To do this, he evoked nostalgia for Reagan's 1980 presidential campaign, which promised an end to big government and a return to "traditional" family values. This was the dream of the working- and middle class *white* man, who could and *should* expect the promises of America. Trump's rhetoric relied upon a divisive "us versus them" strategy, "pitting immigrants' dreams *against* American values" (Jenkins et al. 2020, 4, emphasis added). Of particular interest to this discussion is his position as a rich, white male who had been accused of sexual harassment and misconduct on a significant number of occasions (Carpenter 2019) and who, during his presidency, presided over significant reductions in women's reproductive rights (Andaya 2019). His disposition chimes with that of

Harvey Weinstein: a wealthy white man in a position of power who was arrested and charged with rape in 2018.

Such ideals and actions are illuminating when placed alongside the significant evolution of the #MeToo movement. On October 15, 2017, following US actor Alyssa Milano's tweet sharing her experiences of sexual harassment, "within just 24 hours, 12 million Facebook posts using the hashtag were written or shared, and within 48 hours, the hashtag had been shared nearly a million times on Twitter" (Lawton 2017). The movement's significant resonance throughout the globe activated what Boyle has termed a "networked feminism", made possible by the prevalence of social media in our everyday lives (2019, 3). Indeed, this feminism was global in its reach and has contributed significantly toward the general popularity of feminism in the 21st century (Banet-Weiser 2018). Feminist activism over the last few decades has also chimed with consistent calls for a more inclusive America when considering LGBTQ rights. Gay pride merchandise flourished in the late 1990s, and following Bill Clinton's announcement that June was "Gay Pride" month in 1999 and 2000, this pronouncement was also echoed by Obama between 2009 and 2016.

These cultural shifts have significantly impacted the shape and character of the Disney fairy tale. With recent princess films such as *Brave* (Andrews and Chapman 2012), *Frozen*, and *Moana* (Clements and Musker 2016), the company has attempted to revise the princess figure as a feminist icon, pulling narratives away from the romantic focus of *Cinderella* and *Sleeping Beauty* and toward activist girlhood. This transformation was a conscious move by the company, as Disney animator Mark Henn shared with MTV News in 2015 that the company had decided to create "more powerful, self-aware princess characters that continued to inspire generations of girls" (Henn cited in Mallory 2017, 10). What is of note here for a discussion of the American Dream is the way in which these films show an explicit *disengagement* with the white male privilege inherent in Trump's conception of the United States' national myth. By contrast, Disney's princess films have attempted to foreground female relationships in their films of the last decade. *Frozen* centers around the friendship between two sisters, *Maleficent* focuses on the mother-daughter relationship between Maleficent herself and the princess, Aurora and *Moana*'s titular heroine is inspired to seek adventure by her quirky grandmother. By placing such dynamics as the focal point of their narratives, it is hard to ignore Disney's *deviation* from Trump's popular, toxic, conservative, and exclusive rendering of the American Dream.

In *Frozen,* Anna takes the role of the "dreaming" princess, who is desperate for freedom following years of captivity while she and her sister, Elsa, mourned the loss of their parents and sought to protect the kingdom from Elsa's destructive ice powers. Anna's obsession with finding a man, however, proves to be her downfall, as she is manipulated by Prince Hans into believing that he has fallen in love with her when he simply seeks more power and influence for himself (Hackett 2020). Furthermore, while Anna does find love with the simple ice seller, Kristoff, their dynamic is largely insignificant to the story, as the narrative foregrounds the importance of her relationship with her sister. *Frozen* enacts a significant change in its fairy tale conclusion by transforming its "true love's kiss" into "an act of true love", whereby Anna sacrifices her life to save her sister. Such a dynamic is also echoed in the narrative of *Maleficent.* Many of Disney's most recent live action reboots echo the adaptability and revisability of the American Dream. Acknowledging the problematic rendering of female characters in its early productions, these films enact what I have termed a "contingent nostalgia" (Mollet 2019a). They look back nostalgically upon their original animated counterparts but seek to "correct" their more problematic ideological outlooks. In this film, a reenactment of the traditional fairy tale, *Sleeping Beauty,* "true love's kiss" is changed. Maleficent, a villain in Disney's animated film, is remade as a feminist heroine who watches over the Princess Aurora as she grows into a young woman and becomes a deeply significant figure and role model in her life. "True love's kiss" is shared between "mother" and daughter and is shown to be far more powerful than the love shared between Prince Philip and the young princess. Furthermore, the film leaves no doubt over its villain: the power-hungry King Stefan, consumed in his quest for power and vengeance. Not only does the film suggest that Stefan is of a working-class background, showing the potential toxicity and entitlement of some working-class men (and who largely populate the alt-right political movement that voted for Trump), but the film also notes Stefan's treatment of Maleficent. As young lovers, the pair spend the night together, but Stefan drugs Maleficent and cuts off her wings, which reads explicitly as a harrowing rape narrative (Schwabe 2019). Positioned as villains in these fairy tales, entitled white men, who have a disregard for women's rights, are not granted their happily ever afters and are, therefore, excluded from Disney's conception of the American Dream.

While excluding these figures from the promises of a happy ending, Disney's fairy tales have become much more *inclusive* over the past few decades, which again shows the discrepancy between *their* American Dream narrative and that of Donald Trump and his supporters. While the "triumph of the underdog" has always been an important part of the American Dream narrative, it resurfaces in this era in a different form. In the original conceptions of the Disney fairy tale, the underdog was an inherently good character who fought many personal battles and emerged as a hero or heroine, such as the dwarfs in *Snow White*. In the 21st century, the underdog can be a thief but become a hero (such as Flynn Ryder in *Tangled*); they can be of a humble background and become a prince (such as Kristoff in *Frozen*), or can even be allied with a villain and then realize their true identity (such as Captain Hook and Regina, the Wicked Queen in *Once Upon a Time,* or Lefou in Condon's *Beauty and the Beast*). Lefou's characterization is of particular interest, as he is the first openly gay character in a Disney fairy tale. Throughout the narrative of *Beauty and the Beast*, he fantasizes over being with Gaston but eventually realizes that he needs to break away from such a toxic relationship and find happiness. He is even shown dancing at Belle and the Beast's wedding with another man. It seems, then, that Disney fairy tales endorse a more liberal and inclusive version of the American Dream enacted by Barack Obama as they reject the binary othering inherent in Trump's politics and show that *anyone*, providing their intentions are good, can have access to the Dream and the Disney happily ever after.

Conclusion

In this chapter, I have shown that there is an inherent connection between the American Dream and the Disney fairy tale. Each of these narratives shifts with significant changes in American society. Certain elements of the Dream are foregrounded in the fairy tale at certain points within history, while others remain dormant until activated by economic and social upheaval.

From their beginnings in the 1930s, the Dream and the fairy tale are communitarian in nature, domestic in focus, and it is claimed that those who are hard-working, good, and patient can reap its rewards. They embrace nostalgia for America's past as a basis for the future but show a willingness to *adapt* to show progression and accommodation for likely changes in America's social structure. Moving toward the end of the 20th century, the "rags to riches" narrative once fundamental to the American Dream all but disappears from Disney's fairy tales. It appeared that America was already blessed with the riches it needed, facilitated by Reagan's free market economy. It is, however, replaced by a fundamental need for its characters to realize their inner Americans through an embrace of a progressive gender outlook, global aspirations, and liberation for those trapped by a dated un-American value system. With the events of 9/11, Hurricane Katrina, the market crash of 2008, and the election of Barack Obama, the cultural fabric of American society was changed irrevocably. The American Dream needed reviving through the simplicity of happily ever after found within Disney's fairy tales, which situated their narratives in locations that had undergone significant turmoil and crisis in the first decade of the 21st century. In the wake of widespread unemployment, the "rags to riches" narrative returned to the Disney fairy tale, as the American Dream once again had to incorporate that Americans could emerge from poverty and homelessness as long as they had faith. Furthermore, Obama's election to the presidency had opened the American Dream to African Americans. Disney's happily ever after evolved into a more inclusive space, where race, class, and background were of no object and where anyone could achieve anything if they worked hard and believed their dream would come true. Lastly, over the past decade, Disney's fairy tales have shown a new inclusivity and have positioned themselves *against* the white masculine entitlement of President Trump's rendering of the American Dream. They foreground positive female relationships, reject toxic masculinity, and celebrate the American citizen that wishes to transform their life and circumstances through their revival of the "triumph of the underdog" narrative.

In essence, at the heart of all of Disney's fairy tale narratives are three key American attributes central to the American Dream. Firstly, they all feature a good natured, but the restless character that desires to escape from their current situation. They dream of a new life, which is intrinsically tied to American notions of freedom from oppression and a yearning for opportunity. These characters have defining American characteristics such as restlessness and a desire for flight (Mauk and Oakland 2005; Duncan and Goddard 2009; Samuel 2012). The narrative character of this new life, however, is deeply connected to historical context. Secondly, these fairy tales all celebrate the "triumph of the underdog" so central to the American Dream, particularly in times of economic uncertainty. In both the Great Depression and during a long-awaited period of post-war stability, Disney's fairy tales reassured the American people that the common man could and *should* be successful. This narrative also importantly resurfaces in Disney's *Princess and the Frog* following the financial crisis of 2008. Thirdly, Disney's fairy tales all contain a *form* of the "rags to riches" storyline. While all of Disney's fairy tales do conclude with a "royal" happily ever after centered around a castle, not all Disney princesses are born into royalty (Davis 2006), underlining the centrality of this transformation. However, such "riches" are incidental to the Disney fairy tale and are never the main desire of the narrative's protagonist. This subtle change underlines that to achieve the American Dream, citizens need to learn to "want the national order they already have" (Pease 2009, 4). Or, as I have argued in my previous work, "In order for the hero or heroine within the fairy tale to achieve their happily ever after, they must embrace their inner American" (2020, 168). As a result, these stories conclude with their protagonists finding "home" at the point of their happily ever after, which is psychologically, socially, and often, geographically, American in nature. Through exploring such areas, I have shown that throughout their complex histories, the American Dream and the Disney fairy tale reinforce one another, changing their focus and tone depending on social, political, and cultural circumstances.

Note

1 With reference to the *Harry Potter*, *Lord of the Rings*, and *Shrek* film franchises, I have provided only a source reference to the initial film in each series, although my comments extend to the series as a whole and their general themes of fantasy and magic.

References

Adams, James Truslow. 1931. *The Epic of America*. New York: Simon Publications.

Adamson, Andrew, and Vicky Jenson. 2001. *Shrek*. Film. United States.

Andaya, Elise. 2019. "I'm Building a Wall around My Uterus": Abortion Politics and the Politics of Othering in Trump's America. *Cultural Anthropology* 34 (1): 10–17.

Andrews, Mark, and Brenda Chapman. 2012. *Brave*. Film. United States: Pixar Studios.

Arnold, Gordon B. 2013. *Projecting the End of the American Dream: Hollywood's Visions of US Decline*. Santa Barbara: Praeger.

Bacon, Lloyd. 1933a. *42nd Street*. Film. United States: Warner Brothers.

———. 1933b. *Footlight Parade*. Film. United States: Warner Brothers.

Banet-Weiser, Sarah. 2018. *Empowered: Popular Feminism and Popular Misogyny*. Durham: Duke University Press.

Barnes, Brookes. 2009. Her Prince Has Come. Critics, Too. *The New York Times*, May 29. Accessed May 6, 2021.

Bernstein, Michael A. 1987. *The Great Depression: Delayed Recovery and Economic Change in America, 1929–1939*. New York: Cambridge University Press.

Bly, Robert. 1990. *Iron John: A Book about Men*. Cambridge, MA: DaCapo Press.

Bordwell, David, Janet Staiger, and Kristin Thompson. 1986. *The Classical Hollywood Cinema: Film Style and Mode of Production to 1960*. New York: Columbia University Press.

Boyle, Karen. 2019. *#MeToo, Weinstein and Feminism*. London: Palgrave Macmillan.

Boym, Svetlana. 2001. *The Future of Nostalgia*. New York: Basic Books.

Bradford, Clare. 2012. "Where Happily Ever After Happens Every Day": The Medievalisms of Disney's Princesses. In *The Disney Middle Ages: A Fairy Tale and Fantasy Past*, eds. Tison Pugh and Susan Aronstein, 171–188. New York: Palgrave Macmillan.

Branagh, Kenneth. 2015. *Cinderella*. Film. United States: Walt Disney Pictures.

Brode, Douglas. 2005. *Multiculturalism and the Mouse: Race and Sex in Disney Entertainment*. Austin, Texas: University of Texas Press.

Bryne, Eleanor, and Martin McQuillan. 1999. *Deconstructing Disney*. London: Pluto Press.

Buck, Chris, and Jennifer Lee. 2013. *Frozen*. Film. United States: Walt Disney Pictures.

Cameron, James. 1984. *The Terminator*. Film. United States: Orion Pictures.

Campbell, Neil, Jude Davies, and George McKay. 2004. Introduction. In *Issues in Americanisation and Culture*, eds. Neil Campbell, Jude Davies, and George McKay, 1–40. Edinburgh: Edinburgh University Press.

Campbell, Neil, and Alasdair Kean. 1997. *American Cultural Studies: An Introduction to American Culture*. London: Routledge.

Carpenter, Amanda. 2019. Trump's Treatment of Women Was His Original Abuse of Power. *Time*. 30 October. Available at: https://www.time.com/5714064/trump-abuse-of-power-women. Accessed May 6, 2021.

Churchwell, Sarah. 2018. *Behold America: A History of America First and the American Dream*. New York: Bloomsbury.

Clements, Ron, and John Musker. 1989. *The Little Mermaid*. Film. United States: Walt Disney Pictures.

———. 2009. *The Princess and the Frog*. Film. United States: Walt Disney Pictures.

———. 2016. *Moana*. Film. United States: Walt Disney Pictures.

Columbus, Christopher. 2001. *Harry Potter and the Philosopher's Stone*. Film. United States: Warner Brothers Pictures.

Condon, Bill. 2017. *Beauty and the Beast*. Film. United States: Walt Disney Pictures.

Davis, Amy M. 2006. *Good Girls and Wicked Witches: Women in Disney's Feature Animation*. London: John Libbey Publishing.

Deszcz, Justyna. 2002. Beyond the Disney Spell, or Escape into Pantoland. *Folklore* 113 (1): 83–90.

Do Rozario, Rebecca-Anne C. 2004. The Princess and the Magic Kingdom: Beyond Nostalgia, the Function of the Disney Princess. *Women's Studies in Communication* 27 (1): 34–59.

Duncan, Russell, and Joseph Goddard. 2009. *Contemporary America*. London: Palgrave Macmillan.

England, Dawn Elizabeth, Lara Descartes, and Melissa A. Collier-Meek. 2011. Gender Role Portrayal and the Disney Princesses. *Sex Roles* 64 (7–8): 555–567.

Faludi, Susan. 1991. *Backlash: The Undeclared War against American Women*. New York: Crown Publishing Group.

Fjellman, Stephen. 1992. *Vinyl Leaves: Walt Disney World and America*. New York: Avalon Publishing.

Geronimi, Clyde. 1959. *Sleeping Beauty*. Film. United States: Walt Disney Pictures.

Geronimi, Clyde, Hamilton Luske, and Wilfred Jackson. 1950. *Cinderella*. Film. United States: Walt Disney Pictures.

Gibbens, Sarah. 2019. Hurricane Katrina: Explained. *National Geographic*. https://www. nationalgeographic.com/environment/natural-disasters/reference/hurricane-katrina/. Accessed April 30, 2020.

Gillett, Burt. 1933. *The Three Little Pigs*. Film. United States: Walt Disney Studios.

Giroux, Henry. 1995. Memory and Pedagogy in "The Wonderful World of Disney": Beyond the Politics of Innocence. In *From Mouse to Mermaid: The Politics of Film, Gender and Culture*, eds. Elizabeth Bell, Lynda Haas, and Laura Sells, 43–71. Bloomington, IN: University of Indiana Press.

Greno, Nathan, and Bryon Howard. 2010. *Tangled*. Film. United States: Walt Disney Pictures.

Hackett, Susanne R. 2020. "Let It Go" as Radical Mantra: Subverting the Princess Narrative in Frozen. In *Recasting the Disney Princess in an Era of New Media and Social Movements*, ed. Shearon Roberts, 211–223. Lanham, MD: Lexington.

Halliwell, Martin, and Catherine Morley, eds. 2008. *American Thought and Culture in the 21st Century*. Edinburgh: Edinburgh University Press.

Hand, David, Wilfred Jackson, Ben Sharpsteen, and William Cottrell. 1937. *Snow White and the Seven Dwarfs*. Film. United States: Walt Disney Pictures.

Harline, Leigh, and Ned Washington. 1940. When You Wish Upon A Star. *Pinocchio: Original Soundtrack*. Performed by Cliff Edwards. United States: EMI.

Heckerling, Amy. 1995. *Clueless*. Film. United States: Paramount Pictures.

Hesmondhalgh, David. 2003. *The Cultural Industries*. Los Angeles: SAGE.

Horowitz, Adam, and Edward Kitsis. 2011–2018. *Once Upon a Time*. TV. United States: ABC.

Jackson, Peter. 2001. *The Lord of the Rings: The Fellowship of the Ring*. Film. United States: New Line Cinema.

Jeffords, Susan. 1995. The Curse of Masculinity – Disney's Beauty and the Beast. In *From Mouse to Mermaid: The Politics of Film, Gender and Culture*, eds. Elizabeth Bell, Lynda Haas, and Laura Sells, 161–172. Bloomington, IN: University of Indiana Press.

Jenkins, Henry, Gabriel Peters-Lazaro, and Sangita Shrestova. 2020. *Popular Culture and the Civic Imagination*. New York: New York University Press.

Johnston, Michelle. 2016. *A Cinderella Story: If the Shoe Fits*. DVD. United States: Warner Home Video.

Junger, Gil. 1999. *10 Things I Hate about You*. Film. United States: Touchstone Pictures.

Kellner, Douglas M. 2009. *Cinema Wars: Hollywood Film and Politics in the Bush-Cheney Era*. Oxford: Wiley-Blackwell.

Kimmage, Michael C. 2011. The Politics of the American Dream: 1980 to 2008. In *The American Dream in the 21st Century*, eds. Kenneth White and Sandra L. Hanson, 27–40. Philadelphia, PA: Temple University Press.

Kimmel, Martin. 2017. *Angry White Men: American Masculinity at the End of an Era*. New York: Nation Books.

Lawton, Georgina. 2017. #MeToo Is Here to Stay. We Must Challenge All Men about Sexual Harassment. *The Guardian*. 28 October. Available at: https://www.theguardian.com/lifeandstyle/2017/oct/28/ metoo-hashtag-sexual-harrassment-violence-challenge-campaign-women-men/ AccessedMay7, 2021.

Lester, Neal A. 2010. Disney's *The Princess and the Frog*: The Pride, the Pressure, and the Politics of Being a First. *Journal of American Culture* 33 (4): 294–308.

Lima, Kevin. 2007. *Enchanted*. Film. United States: Walt Disney Pictures.

Livingston, James. 2010. *The World Turned Inside Out: American Thought and Culture at the End of the Twentieth Century*. Lanham, MD: Rowman & Littlefield Publishers.

Mallory, Marie. 2017. "The Power of a Princess: Examining the Role of the Disney Princess in the Lives of Adolescent Girls", PhD thesis, Virginia Beach: Regent University.

Marshall, Gary. 1990. *Pretty Woman*. Film. United States: Touchstone Pictures.

Martens, Todd. 2020. "Coronavirus Fallout: Why Closing Disneyland Is Such a Blow to American Optimism". *Los Angeles Times*, 14 March. Available at: https://www.latimes.com/entertainment-arts/story/2020-03-14/disneyland-coronavirus-closure-reflects-america-mood Accessed May 6, 2021.

Mauk, David, and John Oakland. 2005. *American Civilisation: An Introduction*. Abingdon: Routledge.

McRobbie, Angela, ed. 1991. *Feminism and Youth Culture: From Jackie to Just Seventeen*. London: Macmillan.

McTiernan, John. 1988. *Die Hard*. Film. United States: 20th Century Fox.

Mitchell-Smith, Ilan. 2012. The United Princesses of America: Ethnic Diversity and Cultural Purity in Disney's Medieval Past. In *The Disney Middle Ages: A Fairy Tale and Fantasy Past*, eds. Tison Pugh and Susan Aronstein, 209–224. New York: Palgrave Macmillan.

Mittermeier, Sabrina. 2020. *A Cultural History of the Disneyland Theme Parks*. Bristol: Intellect.

Moffitt, Kimberly R. 2019. Scripting the Way for the 21st-Century Disney Princess in the Princess and the Frog. *Women's Studies in Communication* 42 (4): 471–489.

Mollet, Tracey. 2013. With a Smile and a Song: Walt Disney and the Birth of the American Fairy Tale. *Marvels and Tales: Journal of Fairy Tale Studies* 27 (1): 109–124.

———. 2017. *Cartoons in Hard Times: The Animated Shorts of Disney and Warner Brothers in Depression and War 1933–1945*. New York: Bloomsbury Academic.

———. 2019a. Demogorgons, Death Stars and Difference: Masculinity and Geek Culture. Stranger Things. *Refractory: Journal of Entertainment Media*, 31, 2019. Available at: https://refractoryjournal.net/demogorgons-death-stars-and-difference-masculinity-and-geek-culture-in-stranger-things/

———. 2019b. The American Dream: Walt Disney's Fairy Tales. In *The Fairy Tale World*, ed. Andrew Teverson, 221–231. London: Routledge.

———. 2020. *A Cultural History of the Disney Fairy Tale: Once Upon an American Dream*. London: Palgrave Macmillan.

Once Upon A Time. 2011–2018. TV. United States: ABC.

Pach, Chester J., Jr, and Elmo Richardson. 1991. *The Presidency of Dwight D. Eisenhower*. Lawrence, Kansas: Kansas University Press.

Pallant, Chris. 2011. *Demystifying Disney: A History of Disney Feature Animation*. London: Bloomsbury Academic.

Pallotta, Frank. 2020. "Disneyland Closes because of the Coronavirus Outbreak". *CNN*, 12 March. Available at: http://edition.cnn.com/2020/03/12/media/disneyland-close-coronavirus/index.html. Accessed May 7, 2021.

Parrish, Michael. 1992. *Anxious Decades: America in Prosperity and Depression 1920–1941*. New York: W.W. Norton.

Pease, Donald E. 2009. *The New American Exceptionalism*. Minneapolis, MN: University of Minnesota Press.

Pershing, Linda, and Lisa Gablehouse. 2010. Disney's Enchanted: Patriarchal Backlash and Nostalgia in a Fairy Tale Film. In *Fairy Tale Films: Visions of Ambiguity*, eds. Pauline Greenhill and Sidney Eve Matrix, 137–156. Boulder, CO: University of Colorado Press.

Picchi, Aimee. 2018. 5 Groups Still Recovering from the Financial Crisis. *CBS News*, 14 September. https://www.cbsnews.com/news/5-groups-still-recovering-from-the-financial-crisis. Accessed May 06, 2021.

Prince, Stephen. 2009. *Firestorm: American Film in the Age of Terrorism*. New York: Columbia University Press.

Reiner, Rob. 1987. *The Princess Bride*. Film. United States: 20th Century Fox.

Restad, Hilde. 2015. *American Exceptionalism: An Idea That Made a Nation and Remade the World*. New York: Routledge.

Romasco, Albert U. 1983. *The Politics of Recovery*. New York: Oxford University Press.

Rosman, Mark. 2004. *A Cinderella Story*. Film. United States: Warner Brothers Pictures.

Samuel, Lawrence R. 2012. *The American Dream: A Cultural History*. Syracuse, NY: Syracuse University Press.

Sands, Zach. 2018. *Film Comedy and the American Dream*. New York: Routledge.

Santostefano, Damon. 2008. *Another Cinderella Story*. Film. United States: Warner Premiere.

———. 2011. *A Cinderella Story*: Once Upon a Song. Film. United States: Warner Premiere.

Schaller, Michael. 1992. *Reckoning with Reagan: America and Its President*. Oxford: Oxford University Press.

Schickel, Richard. 1986. *The Disney Version: The Life, Times, Art, and Commerce of Walt Disney*. New York: Simon and Schuster.

Schuck, Peter H., and James Q. Wilson. 2008. *Understanding America: The Anatomy of an Exceptional Nation*. Philadelphia, PA: Public Affairs.

Schwabe, Claudia. 2019. *Craving Supernatural Creatures: German Fairy Tale Figures in American Pop Culture*. Detroit, MI: Wayne State University Press.

Sternheimer, Karen. 2011. *American Dream: Stardom and Social Mobility*. New York: Routledge.

Stover, Cassandra. 2013. Damsels and Heroines: The Conundrum of the Post-Feminist Disney Princess. *LUX* 2 (1): 1–10.

Stromberg, Robert. 2014. *Maleficent*. Film. United States: Walt Disney Pictures.

Tasker, Yvonne, and Diane Negra, eds. 2007. *Interrogating Postfeminism: Gender and the Politics of Popular Culture*. Durham: Duke University Press.

Teverson, Andrew. 2013. *Fairy Tale*. Abingdon: Routledge.

Trousdale, Gary, and Kirk Wise. 1991. *Beauty and the Beast*. Film. United States: Walt Disney Pictures.

Turner, Sarah E. 2013. Blackness, Bayous and Gumbo: Encoding and Decoding Race in a Colorblind World. In *Diversity in Disney Films: Critical Essays on Race, Ethnicity, Gender, Sexuality and Disability*, ed. Johnson Cheu, 83–98. Jefferson, NC: McFarland & Co.

Van Elteren, Mel. 2006. *Americanism and Americanisation: Domestic and Global Influence*. Jefferson, NC: McFarland.

Wasko, Janet. 2001. *Understanding Disney: The Manufacture of Fantasy*. 1st ed. Cambridge: Polity Press.

Wee, Valerie. 2008. Teen Television and the WB Television Network. In *Watching Teen TV: Essays in Programming and Fandom*, eds. Sharon M. Ross and L.E. Stein, 43–60. London: McFarland and Co.

Whedon, Joss. 1997–2003. *Buffy the Vampire Slayer*. TV. 20th Television.

White, Kenneth, and Sandra L. Hanson. 2011. *The American Dream in the 21st Century*. Philadelphia, PA: Temple University Press.

Whelan, Bridget. 2014. Power to the Princess: Disney and the Creation of the Twentieth Century Princess Narrative. In *Kidding Around: The Child in Film and Media*, ed. Alexander N. Rowe, 167–192. New York: Bloomsbury Academic.

Wills, John. 2017. *Disney Culture*. New Brunswick: Rutgers University Press.

Wood, Robin. 1986. *Hollywood from Vietnam to Reagan*. New York: Columbia University Press.

10

HOW FREE-MARKET FAMILY POLICY CRUSHED THE AMERICAN DREAM

Maxine Eichner

Every country has myths that capture the identity and ambition of its citizens. The myth of national purpose to which Americans have long subscribed is known as the "American Dream." The writer James Truslow Adams, who coined that term in 1931, made the point that the American myth isn't built on the simple idea that citizens can compete for the right to obtain material comforts. Instead, it envisions something more: a "social order" that allows Americans to attain "the fullest stature of which they are innately capable," regardless of where or to whom they are born, and that gives them the opportunity for a "better and richer and fuller" life. In short, the Dream postulates a society that enables Americans to lead good lives.

Recently, however, Americans have had the increasing sense that the country has gone off the rails. Where exactly it has gone astray is a matter of some debate. This essay argues that a significant part of the problem stems from the damage economic forces have been wreaking on American families. The American Dream promises a social order that supports Americans in leading flourishing lives. Flourishing lives, though, require strong family bonds; without the caretaking, human development, and affiliation that family relationships provide, the well-being and happiness of adults and children founder.[1] Yet, in the last five decades, U.S. policymakers have proceeded based on the false premise that families do their best when they are forced to compete in the free market. In regulating based on this view, they have created economic conditions hostile to the development and functioning of strong, stable families.[2] And as the well-being of U.S. families has crumbled, so has the well-being and happiness of Americans declined. Americans' recognition that the existing social order stymies rather than supports their desires to lead rich, full lives—a rent in the social scaffolding caused by the undermining of families' well-being—underlies their sense that the American Dream has gone badly wrong.

In the past several decades, economic pressures have taken a significant toll on U.S. families up and down the economic ladder. These pressures, to be sure, create problems that look very different for families of different classes. Low-income families, and particularly poor families, clearly have it worst of all.[3] Uncertain job prospects and low wages mean that many adults in this group won't ever form the stable partnerships they badly want. Because of this, a rising number of their children are born to unmarried parents, and most children from families toward the bottom of the income ladder will, at some point, be raised by single mothers. On top of that, low-income families' budgets are so tight that parents are constantly stressed about

DOI: 10.4324/9781003326243-12

how to make ends meet, which harms their ability to parent. To make matters still worse, these parents have little chance of giving their children even the basics they need to have a solid start in life.

Take the situation of Wanda Johnson, a single mother from Charlotte, North Carolina.[4] Her son, Deonte, was born when she was 18 and yet to graduate high school. Because she couldn't afford to pay for daycare and the waitlist for childcare assistance was years long, she couldn't continue her job as a cashier or finish high school. That meant her only income was a monthly welfare check of $236, which left her family in deep poverty. The meager check wouldn't allow her to afford even the smallest apartment. She and her son wound up living with which-ever relatives would have them in a series of overcrowded homes during most of Deonte's first five years. At one time, they shared a three-bedroom, one-bathroom house along with six other people. Wanda and Deonte slept in a den along with her grandmother because the bedrooms were full. At another time, they lived in a small home, again with six other people, with Wanda and Deonte sharing a twin bed in a room that also served as a passthrough. These situations were lousy, particularly for Deonte. The homes hadn't been childproofed, so he had little freedom to roam or play in his first years. He was repeatedly bullied by an older child in one, verbally abused and overdisciplined by an adult in another, and was raised in houses that reeked of tobacco and in which someone was screaming morning to night. But Wanda had no other way to put a roof over their heads.

At one point, Wanda found their situation so intolerable that the two moved out of the overcrowded, unpleasant house they were living in. When she couldn't find a new place to live, Child Protective Services took Deonte away and put him in foster care for an entire year before Wanda got him back. The only good thing to have come out of it was that Deonte was elevated to the top of the long waitlist for childcare subsidies because he was in foster care. He was allowed to keep the subsidy on his return to Wanda, which mean that, with his daycare paid for, Wanda could finally work full-time—at least when she could find full-time work. Working at a minimum-wage job with no welfare benefits by then, though, still meant living below the poverty line in overcrowded homes with many others. The difficulty of their situ-ation kept Wanda on edge all the time, which made her a harsher parent to Deonte than she wanted to be. And Wanda stayed up late at night worrying about how to get Deonte the many things he needed. She could usually put food on the table, but when it occasionally ran out, she'd need to make a trip to the food bank during its sporadic weekend hours so she wouldn't miss work. There was no money for extras—not the recreational sports teams Deonte badly wanted to join (she couldn't afford the fees and gear) and not the birthday parties he saw other kids having. On top of all this, Wanda herself was, and is, lonely. She put all her energy and resources toward raising Deonte and is now raising a younger son, Trevor, by herself. She never found the stable, responsible man she was looking for to be her partner (Eichner 2020).

Middle-income families don't often face the same struggles that low-income families do just to put food on the table (although rising financial insecurity means that an increasing number sometimes do) or to ensure decent conditions at home for their kids.[5] But they're still economically stressed. Most young couples with kids have fewer savings than parents did in the past because their basic expenses are much higher today. They're also often burdened with high mortgage payments, education loans, and out-of-pocket healthcare costs. What's left over from entry-level salaries isn't close to enough to give their kids what they need to thrive, particularly when it comes to good preschools and prekindergartens. On top of this, the cost of quality daycare is so high, and combining work with parenting and managing a household is so tough, that many mothers (and, increasingly, some fathers) wind up leaving their jobs to care for their kids, making family finances even tighter. And economic struggles mean that far more middle-income adults aren't marrying at all and, even when they do, are divorcing more often.

Annette Simmons, a married mother in Kansas City of two preschool-aged girls, Chloe and Sarah, lives with these pressures every day. Her husband, Bob, earns about $58,000 a year including fringe benefits as a biologist with a non-profit institute. Annette was a cook at local restaurants before she had kids. Even though she enjoyed her job, she didn't go back to work after she had her first child because good daycare would have cost as much as she earned, and daycare for two kids would have cost far more.

But staying home has required scrimping, saving, and virtually constant financial worry. Before the girls were born, Bob and Annette bought a modest house with a little help from their parents. Once they had kids, between paying the mortgage, paying back Bob's college loans, and meeting the out-of-pocket medical expenses from complications during Annette's pregnancies and C-sections, they wound up with thousands of dollars of credit-card debt. They have been digging their way out of that financial hole ever since, but it has meant a bare-bones life—no paid babysitters to give them a break or a night out, no vacations, and constant efforts to pare down costs. To help make ends meet, Annette has been babysitting two other children for a few hours Monday through Friday, earning another $150 or so a week. She doesn't know how much longer her family can afford to have her stay home with the girls, and she worries about it all the time. On the other hand, she doesn't know what she'll do when she goes back to work since they can't afford good daycare on her cook's wages. And on their budget, paying for prekindergarten when the girls are ready will be out of reach, let alone paying tuition when they're ready for college (Eichner 2020).

Finally, high-income families have all the money they need to support their families (although it may not always feel that way to them).[6] But the long hours demanded by their jobs, combined with the many hours they put in to make sure that their kids will be economically stable when they grow up, often make life a grinding slog. Their stress and exhaustion are aggravated by technology: these parents are never completely off-the-clock and are always checking for texts and emails from work, even at home. Meeting all these demands leaves them overwhelmed.

Amira Patel knows something about feeling overwhelmed.[7] She is a junior partner at a large Washington, DC law firm, where she represents workers in employment matters. Her husband works in public policy. They have two sons, one seven and the other four.

Amira gave birth to her first child while she was a senior associate at the firm. Professionals are the group most likely to get paid leave in the United States, where market power dictates benefits. Amira's firm's policy was generous even by the standards of U.S. professionals— 12 weeks of paid maternity leave—although that's less than a quarter of the leave available to all families with a new child in some European countries. She turned out to need those twelve weeks, plus six weeks of paid sick leave that she had banked and another six weeks of unpaid leave due to pregnancy complications and a very difficult childbirth and recovery. Even then, when she returned to work at the time her son was six months old, she still wasn't feeling well as a result of symptoms of postpartum depression.

Once she returned to work, though, she had to resume the schedule expected of the firm's litigators. On the plus side, the hours weren't exceptionally long by the standards of American professionals—on average 50–60 hours a week—and she was allowed to work from home one and sometimes two days a week. But her hours fluctuated tremendously: some weeks she worked 65 or 70 hours; some she needed to work 80 hours to meet pressing deadlines. That meant that she was constantly exhausted from lack of sleep, and she saw her son far less than she wanted. Her exhaustion grew after her second child was born and he took a long time to start sleeping through the night. Amira was getting between five and six hours sleep a night and being woken up at 3 a.m. every morning to boot—all while working long hours at her job. Her grueling work schedule meant she missed dinner with her kids three or four nights a week. She had little time to take care of herself. Looking after her own health and well-being fit nowhere into her life.

Amira says she worries about the long-term effects on her body of her years of constant stress combining work and raising young children. During some periods, her stress levels were so high that it felt like she was in a constant state of borderline panic attacks. Recently, she's been trying to exercise regularly and meditate to keep the stress under control. But of course, that takes time, which has to come out of somewhere. "You're constantly robbing Peter to pay Paul," she says of her life. In the last months, she's also been trying to work a schedule in which she gets to the office by 6:30 or 7 a.m. Although it means that she doesn't see her kids in the morning, this schedule lets her make it home for dinner with her family two or three weeknight evenings a week. The nights she misses dinner, she works until late in the evening, often putting in a 14-hour workday, and gets home after her husband and the boys are in bed.

Amira says she and her husband outsource far more than they'd like to save any time they can. They had nannies for their kids' first years. They get groceries delivered when they don't have time to shop. They have also pared their lives down significantly to make the time they need for family and work. Still, Amira has a continual sense of having too many balls up in the air, with one of them about to drop at any moment. The result is that she constantly feels like she's doing neither her paid work nor her parenting well.

Amira's a partner at her law firm now—couldn't she just work fewer hours and take a pay cut? Not with her job, she says. Although her firm is more reasonable than most, in the hard-charging world of American law firms, there's only so far you can buck the dominant culture of long work hours, which is almost totally unresponsive to the needs of families. The result, she says, is that "we make it all work at great personal expense."

Why not quit and work someplace with fewer hours? Amira says that she and her husband ask themselves the same question at least once a week. But she loves her job and the people she represents and thinks, in some small way, she's serving the cause of justice in the world. She just wishes the costs of doing a job like hers weren't so high. Despite this, she recognizes how privileged her family's situation is compared with many American families. She and her husband have jobs that mean that they don't have to worry about how to feed their kids, whether they can afford good caretaking, or about where their next paycheck will come from. But that doesn't make the acute tradeoffs between work and family she has been forced to make any easier (Eichner 2020).

The struggles that low-, middle-, and high-income American families are having today look very different, but they are all manifestations of the same problem: the increasingly large toll that market forces have been taking on families during the past several decades. The harm inflicted on U.S. families, however, was not inevitable. Instead, the defeat of American families by market forces was the product of a long-term failure of American public policy to safeguard families from the negative effects of the free market.

U.S. Free-Market Family Policy

All contemporary Western democracies recognize that families play a vital role in our individual and collective well-being. A wealth of research demonstrates that children need strong family relationships and the caretaking and human development they provide to build the stable foundation that will enable them to become sound adults (Bowlby 1951; Howard et al. 2011;

National Scientific Council on the Developing Child 2009). Family relationships are also central to most adults' life plans and moral commitments, as well as to their happiness and well-being (Waldinger 2016). It is through these relationships that much of the caretaking that adults need, particularly as they grow older, are delivered (Smith 2004). In addition, families play a key role in knitting adults into the social fabric of the community (Case and Deaton 2017).

In the last five decades, countries have chosen between two very different policy regimes when it comes to ensuring that families have the conditions they need to thrive. The first policy regime, most closely associated with the United States, I will call "free-market family policy."[8] The view that underlies it is that families do better when they get what they need privately through markets. If markets are strong, this theory has it, then every family will get a big enough slice of the pie to privately satisfy its needs. In this model, it is the job of workers to bargain with employers privately over how much they'll work and when. Parents use paychecks and savings to purchase the goods and services their children need to do their best. Finally, parents pay for or personally provide the caretaking and other circumstances their members need to do their best.

Free-market family policy stands in stark contrast to the policy regime most other wealthy democracies have adopted, which I will call "pro-family policy." This policy model considers the market to be an important tool for ensuring that families get the resources they need to thrive, but it doesn't trust the market to do this on its own. Instead, pro-family policy seeks to regulate markets to make them better able to support families. Further, it insulates family life from many market pressures and actively supports getting families what they need to succeed. In this model, the government helps people harmonize work and family. It also helps provide families with children both the economic resources and conditions they need to raise their kids well. In this way, pro-family policy treats the imperative that families have the circumstances they need as a joint responsibility of both families *and* government.

Pro-family policies can take a number of forms. Some reduce market inequality and insecurity in ways that improve families' well-being, for example, through laws setting a relatively high minimum wage or protecting collective bargaining. Others "decommodify" services that benefit families, for example providing high-quality daycare for young children regardless of their family's income. Still, others come from the state acting in its role as "traffic cop" to ensure that the market stays in its lane when it comes to paid work. These include laws that guarantee workers adequate time with their families by, for example, establishing the maximum number of hours employees can be made to work, requiring employers to give workers paid vacation and holiday time, and allowing reduced work hours for parents of young kids. Countries with pro-family policy also regularly give cash to families with children to ensure that their needs are consistently met even when parents' market earnings are inconsistent or inadequate.

The distinctions I make between free-market and pro-family policy are between ideal types; no countries are perfect exemplars of either of these policies. However, the United States comes closer than any other wealthy country to having a system of pure free-market family policy. It provides no paid parental family leave, no mandated vacation or holiday leave, no child benefits (although child benefits were one of the temporary measures taken in the extraordinary conditions of the COVID epidemic), few parents receive financial aid for childcare or preschool, and it has no strong limits on weekly work hours (Eichner 2020). In contrast, most wealthy Western European democracies have adopted all or almost all of these measures over the last decades (Eichner 2020; Gornick and Meyers 2003).[9] Finland is one of the countries whose policies fall particularly close to the pro-family policy end of the spectrum.

Free-Market Family Policy and the U.S. Economy

Free-market family policy leaves families to their own devices when it comes to arranging the resources and services they need. If families cannot get what they need privately, which largely means through earnings from work, they are out of luck. This means that economic trends beyond families' control can have a big impact on the ways that families function and on their ability to provide for their members. Unfortunately, two major economic trends in the past five decades, in the form of rising economic inequality and insecurity, have made both of these far more difficult for U.S. families. Scholars have already shown that these economic trends were the product of a related set of government actions and inactions (Hacker and Pierson 2010), which I have elsewhere linked to the rise of free-market family policy (Eichner 2021). The remainder of this essay will focus on how these economic shifts, in combination with contemporary free-market family policy, have degraded both the stability of U.S. families and their abilities to support their members effectively.

America's Skyrocketing Economic Inequality

Between 1973 and 2015, even as earnings among the top fifth of workers skyrocketed, the hourly wages of the two-thirds of men without college diplomas dropped 18 percent in real dollars (Binder and Bound 2019, 2). Further, the drop in the real value of the minimum wage in these decades and the large increase in the number of low-wage service jobs in our economy means that far more jobs don't pay nearly enough to support a family. Almost a third of those in the workforce today make less than $12 an hour, and few in these low-wage jobs receive benefits (Economic Policy Institute and Oxfam Am. 2016, 4–5, 12). Many of these workers have children, and no matter how hard or long they work, they simply won't earn enough to get their kids what they need to do their best (Economic Policy Institute 2021).

It is true that, in these decades, real household income grew, even in the bottom fifth of households (Hacker and Pierson 2010, 21–25; Wolff 2017, 13). Yet this growth largely comes from two factors: (1) women's increased hours of paid work (Mishel et al. 2012, 36–38, 123–126; Warren and Tyagi 2003) and (2) increased Medicare and Social Security benefits for middle- and low-income senior citizens during this era (Mishel et al. 2012, 123–126). Neither of these is much help for families raising children. The birth of a child usually causes at least one parent to cut back on paid work; insofar as both parents remain in paid work, most will have to pay the high cost of daycare (Laughlin 2011; Stanczyk 2016, 33–34; Warren and Tyagi 2003). And most Medicare and Social Security benefits go to families further along in life than families with young children.

Disparities in families' wealth have also mushroomed in these decades. Today, families in the top 1 percent now hold roughly twice as much wealth as those in the entire bottom 90 percent (Bricker 2017; Congressional Budget Office 2016; Wolff 2017, 9). The drop in net worth of households headed by adults younger than 35—the families most likely to have young kids—has been particularly steep. In 1984, the median net worth of these younger households was $11,500 in constant dollars; in 2009, it was $3,500 (Fry et al. 2011, 1). Some of this drop comes from the decreased real wages of men without college degrees between those decades, as well as the decrease in real wages of entry-level jobs (Autor and Wasserman 2013, Fig. 2). The ballooning of two types of costs in recent decades—housing and college—also plays a major role. Buying a house and going to college are milestones in life often associated with responsible adulthood (Warren and Tyagi 2003). Attaining them, though, can deplete families' assets for two decades or longer, a period during which most will have young kids to support (Hiltonsmith 2013, 10).

This decrease in the wealth of young adults makes it tough for most young families to get their kids off to the best start possible. The average wealth of $3,500 that most young households have is generally tied up in a house or a car. But even if that wealth were liquid and available, it would be almost completely depleted by the $3,400 average out-of-pocket fees that hospitals charge for a baby's delivery—and that's the cost for parents with health insurance (Declercq et al. 2013, 46). That means most parents will have to scramble even to buy basics like diapers, formula, and baby food.

The economic situation is even tougher for African American and Hispanic families. The income gap between the median Black and white household has lingered at about 60 percent for decades (Daly, Hobijn, and Pedtke 2017, 2–3; Wilson 2020). That's partly because unemployment rates of Black workers have remained roughly double those of white workers since 1970 for workers at every level of education and during both boom and bust economies (Desilver 2013; Fairlie and Sundstrom 1999, 255). And even when Black workers find jobs, they are paid far less than white workers (Wilson and Rodgers III 2016). This is due in some part to the fact that fewer Black families can afford to pay the high costs of college tuition (which is reduced or free in pro-family policy countries), and in some part because of persistent racism (Bertrand and Mullainathan 2004; Cainer et al. 2017, 23; Daly, Hobijn, and Pedtke 2017, 3; Wilson 2015). The median Hispanic household, meanwhile, earns only 74 percent of the median white household earned (Wilson 2020).

Families headed by single mothers must also deal with the gender income gap. Women as a group make 82 cents for every dollar men make (Bleiweis 2020). For Black women, that figure drops to 62 cents for every dollar men make (2020). While pro-family policy countries like Finland increase child-benefit checks for families headed by single parents to ensure that they can dependably support their children, no such subsidies are paid under U.S. free-market family policy.

Economic Insecurity

The other economic trend that has significantly undercut families' ability is the steep rise in economic insecurity in the past five decades (Dahl, DeLeire, and Schwabish 2011; Dynan, Elmendorf, and Sichel 2012; Gottschalk and Moffitt 2009; Hardy 2016; Hardy and Ziliak 2013; Ziliak, Hardy, and Bollinger 2011). Much of this increased insecurity comes from private companies offloading risks they had once assumed onto American workers and their families. Employers who need work done are more likely to hire temporary employees or independent contractors than in the past and more likely to lay workers off when business is slow, leading to fewer workers having steady, full-time jobs with benefits ((Hacker 2006 68–69, 71; Katz and Krueger 2016; Morduch and Schneider 2013, 1, 3; NPR and Marist 2018; U.S. Government Accountability Office 2015, 15–16). Employers have also moved to scheduling systems that shift employee staffing based on customer demand, which maximize employer profits but at the cost of erratic schedules and paychecks for employees (Golden 2015, 1; Morduch and Schneider 2013, 3). Companies are also less likely to provide health insurance than in the past and, when they do, to pass on more costs to employees through higher deductibles and less generous terms (Claxton 2017, 8, 106; Mishel, Bivens, Gould, and Shierholz 2012, 200, Table 4.10; Schoen 2015, 4, 6). The result is that, with or without coverage, one serious illness or significant chronic medical condition can destroy a family's budget (Jacoby and Holman 2014, 56–60).

It is not just poor households that are affected by this rising insecurity: 94 percent of Americans whose earnings are between 100 and 150 percent *above* the poverty line fall below that line for at least one month per year. Among all Americans, more than one-third—roughly 98 million people—were officially poor for at least two months between 2009 and 2012 (Morduch and Schneider 2017, 159). And many who don't fall below the poverty line are just one emergency away from that fate. In 2017, four in ten Americans reported that they wouldn't be able to cover an unexpected expense of $400 (Board of Governors of the Federal Reserve System, Federal Reserve Board, Division of Consumer and Community Affairs 2018, 21). Even hourly workers with middle-class incomes commonly have shifts in income of 30 percent per month (Cohen 2017). Families of color bear the brunt of this insecurity: nearly two-thirds of African American families and half of Hispanic families live in a household with moderate or high levels of economic insecurity (Hacker 2011, 27; Hacker and Pierson 2010, 21–22; Jones, Cox, and Navarro-River 2014). These increases in inequality and insecurity mean that far fewer families today can reliably support themselves and provide the conditions that serve their members best than families could five decades ago.

Free-Market Family Policy in an Unequal, Insecure Economy

While countries with pro-family policy use public spending and direct provision to decrease inequality and insecurity, no such relief is provided to American families under free-market family policy. Figure 10.1 demonstrates the difference between pro-family and free-market policies on public spending for children in graphic detail. Overall for children ages 0 to 5, the average level of Finland's public spending on family benefits in 2017, per child, including spending on family programs like parental leave, child benefits, daycare, and tax expenditures, clustered somewhere around $10,000 a year, calculated in purchasing power parity (PPP) adjusted dollars. Most of that amount was for cash benefits in the first year, transitioning to large amounts spent for childcare after that. This stream of public funding is intended to make sure that children's needs are consistently met, taking into account the fact that parents' market earnings can sometimes be inconsistent and inadequate. Public funding is meant to ensure that all children have a "floor" of economic support even when parents hit hard economic times, and, at other times, the "ceiling" of children's economic support is increased beyond what their parents alone could pay. In contrast, the average level of U.S. public spending per child—much of it from tax breaks—was far lower. U.S. public spending bumped up a little when kids reach ages three and four because of the limited amount of public funds spent on childcare programs like Head Start and prekindergarten at these ages. It bumped up still more when children reach kindergarten at age five because our public spending on education kicks in. But by that age, it is often too late for children to make up for what they didn't get in earlier years.

The Effect of Free-Market Family Policy

Americans still believe in strong marriages and stable families, and they continue to put family at the top of their list of priorities in life. Yet, in the last five decades, despite the fact that the gross domestic product of the U.S. economy has increased three times over, a yawning gap has opened up between Americans' desires and lived reality. This is true with respect to the basic structure of families, as the United States now leads the world in family *instability*—a prize that no country hopes to win (Cherlin 2009, 25). And it is also true with respect to how

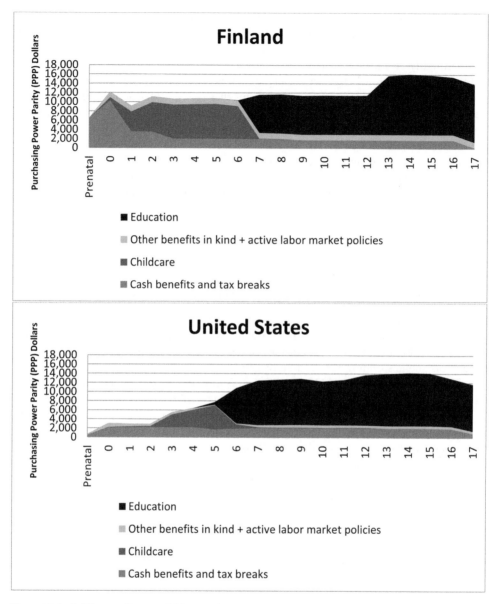

Figure 10.1 Public spending on children and youth by age, the United States and Finland.

Source: OECD (2017c).

Note: Spending includes tax breaks for families with children, cash transfers (family allowance), paid maternity and paternity and parental leaves, institutionalized early childhood care, and education.

families function, as parents and others with heavy caregiving responsibilities are constantly overwhelmed trying to balance their work and family lives. The combination of the current economic conditions in tandem with free-market family policy has eroded Americans' ability to have thriving family lives, as well as to raise strong, solid children. In turn, this has caused the well-being and happiness of both children and adults to plummet.

Family Structure and Stability

In contrast to citizens of other countries, Americans still deeply believe in the institution of marriage. Those who marry believe that their marriage will last forever (Cherlin 2009, 25). And most of those who haven't been married would like to be (Parker and Stepler 2017). Under free-market family policy, though, these beliefs no longer become a reality for many Americans. Marriage rates have declined precipitously since the 1970s (Social Indicators of Marital Wellbeing 2009). Among those couples who marry, after just five years, more than one-fifth are either separated or divorced (Bramlett and Mosher 2002, 17). Cohabiting relationships, which are on the rise, are even less stable than marriages. Almost half of those couples break up within five years, and the breakup rates appear to be increasing (14; Cherlin 2009, 16–17; Guzzo 2014, 833–834; Manning 2015). The instability of these relationships means that one in five children born to married parents will see their parents separate or divorce by the time they reach age twelve. Almost half of all children born to cohabiting parents will see the same (DeRose, Lyons-Amos, Wilcox, and Huarcaya 2017, 11, Fig. 1; Kennedy and Bumpass 2008, 1685).

The instability of American families is concentrated among the less educated, including those without bachelor's degrees. Men and women with bachelor's degrees are far more likely to marry than their less-educated counterparts. Meanwhile, couples with less education are more likely to cohabit without marrying (Cohen 2018, 1; Wilcox and Marquardt 2010, 39–40). This disparity is driven by the increased economic inequality and insecurity in the United States. Younger Americans up and down the economic ladder want to be married. Yet the way that marriage is perceived has changed over time. As sociologist Andrew Cherlin describes it, in the mid-20th century, marriage was considered a "cornerstone" of adult life, the first step toward adulthood (Cherlin 2014). Today, though marriage has become the last step, the "capstone" of adult life—something that young adults do only after having acquired other incidents of adult life, including a stable job. While less-educated Americans, like their better-educated peers, want to be married, the rising U.S. economic inequality and insecurity mean that poor and working-class Americans never achieve the stability they believe should attend marriage. So their better educated peers marry, but they do not (Edin and Kefalas 2005).

Large disparities have arisen with respect to births outside of marriage. In 2016, 62 percent of all births to women without a high school degree occurred outside of marriage. The same was true for only 10 percent of births to women with college degrees (Wildsmith, Manlove, and Cook 2018). Here, too, the disparities are driven by economics. The once-strict cultural prohibition on having a child outside of marriage has weakened across Americans generally. How unmarried young people respond to this less stringent prohibition on non-marital births, though, is heavily influenced by their economic prospects. Those who are college-bound generally wait until they are married to have children because having a child would cause them to miss out on education, job advancement, or a relationship that might lead to marriage. Yet less-educated youth today have far smaller odds of achieving any of these and, therefore, less incentive to put having children off. What is more, humans are built to seek meaning in their lives, and the economic conditions fostered by free-market family policy have foreclosed those with less education seeking meaning in either jobs or marital roles. As sociologists, Kathryn Edin and Maria Kefalas put it, "While middle-class teens and twenty-somethings anticipate completing college and embarking on careers, their lower-class counterparts can only dream of such glories." Lacking a realistic shot at a stable job and stable marriage, "[v]isions of shared children stand in vivid, living color against a monochromatic backdrop of otherwise dismal prospects" (Edin and Kefalas 2005**)**.

Even when less-educated U.S. couples marry, they often cycle through a pattern of divorce, remarriage, and blended families that sociologist Andrew Cherlin has dubbed the "marriage-go-round" (Cherlin 2009). Here, too, free-market economics is a central driver as husbands' insecure jobs, and wages create significant family stress that keeps wives in the workplace, which in turns increases work-family conflict (Carbone and Cahn 2014).

The growth in family instability toward the bottom of the economic ladder has created a huge divide in the family structures in which American kids are raised. If you were a child in the early 1980s, it didn't much matter which side of the tracks your family lived on: you were very likely to be raised by both your parents (Pew Research Center 2015b, 15; Putnam 2015). Today all that has changed. Eight in ten fourteen-year-old girls whose mothers are college graduates live with both parents. The same is true for only five in ten girls whose mothers haven't graduated from high school (Wilcox and Marquardt 2010, 25–26).

The stability of U.S. families stacks up poorly compared to that of other countries. Our divorce rates rank among the highest across wealthy nations (OECD 2018a, 4). For U.S. children born to married parents, approximately 25 percent will see their parents break up by the time they're twelve, compared with less than 15 percent in Norway and France and less than 10 percent in Belgium (DeRose, Lyons-Amos, Wilcox, and Huarcaya 2017, 11–12, Fig. 1). And while couples in other countries have more children outside of marriage, their cohabiting relationships are also far more stable than our own (11–13; Cherlin 2009, 17–18; OECD 2011, 27, Fig. 1.6). Compared with the almost half of American children born to cohabitating parents who will see their parents' union dissolve by age twelve, only about one in five children will see the same in France, Norway, and Belgium. And children in these other countries will experience far fewer familial transitions on average than U.S. children (DeRose, Lyons-Amos, Wilcox, and Huarcaya 2017, 11–13). In fact, Sweden's relationships generally are so much more stable than U.S. relationships that a set of *unmarried parents* in Sweden is more likely to stay together than a set of *married parents* in the United States (Cherlin 2009, 3, 18; Heuveline, Timberlake, and Furstenberg 2003, 57). Overall, more than 21 percent of kids aged zero to five in the United States live with just their mother, the highest rate by far of any member nation in the Organisation for Economic Co-operation and Development (OECD), a group of 38 wealthy nations. By comparison, this value is 8 percent in Finland and 10 percent in France (OECD 2018b, 3).

Work–Family Conflict

Free-market family policy, and the high levels of inequality and insecurity it has fostered, have also taken a large toll on the ways that American families function. The high number of hours that U.S. employees are expected to work means that American parents are stretched thin and stressed out by the conflicting demands of home and paid work. U.S. workers work on average 1,767 hours per year—far more than workers in any other wealthy country (OECD 2021). Two-earner families spend a combined average of 83 hours a week at their jobs—*twice* as many hours as American families worked in the 1960s and significantly more than their peers in any other wealthy country (Medalia and Jacobs 2008). Our absence of work-family reconciliation policies is partially responsible for workers' long hours (Eichner 2020). So are the country's high levels of economic inequality and insecurity, which, as Harvard economist Richard Freeman describes, act as both a carrot and a stick to push Americans to work long hours:

> The carrot is that Americans who work hard have a better chance of being promoted, moving up in the wide distribution of earnings, and experiencing substantial earnings

increases. The stick is that Americans who lose their jobs suffer greatly because the United States has a minimal safety net for the unemployed.

Freeman 2007

When these high hours of paid work are added to the unpaid workload in middle-class families where both parents work full time, the total hours of paid and unpaid work is a stunning 135 hours a week—close to ten hours a day, seven days a week for each parent. And that workload increases for single parents (Bianchi, Robinson, and Milkie 2006, 55, Table 3.4, 118, Fig. 6.1).

The result is that more than half of American parents find it difficult to balance work and family life, and more than a third always feel rushed, even just to do the things they have to do (Bianchi, Robinson, and Milkie 2006; Parker and Wang 2013, 19; Pew Research Center 2015a, 2, 7–8; Schulte 2014). In one study, zero percent (*not* a typo) of mothers said they often had time to spare, and just 5 percent of fathers said the same (Boushey 2016; Schulte 2014, 25). To compensate, working parents empty out the other areas of their life besides work and children. Today's parents are far less likely than parents were two generations ago to spend time together with their spouses eating, socializing with friends, or working on projects around the house (Amato, Booth, Johnson, and Rogers 2007, 67; Milkie, Raley, and Bianchi 2009). Sleep goes by the wayside—employed mothers get three fewer hours a week than those who don't work for pay. Another casualty is leisure time. Employed mothers have nine fewer hours of free time a week than women who don't work for pay (Bianchi and Wight 2010, 35–36). Most full-time working mothers report that they have too little free time for themselves. Most married fathers say the same (Bianchi, Robinson, and Milkie 2006, 135; Bianchi and Wight 2010, 40).

One of the many tolls this system takes is on the happiness of Americans. A recent study compared the "happiness gap" between parents and non-parents (in other words, it calculated how much happier non-parents are than parents in a particular country) in twenty-two countries. The researchers found that our nation's happiness gap was by far the largest of all the countries considered—meaning that parents in the United States were less happy than non-parents to a greater degree than parents in any other wealthy country. In eight of the countries surveyed, parents actually reported being happier than non-parents (Glass, Simon, and Andersson 2016, 907, Table 3). What was the key difference between countries with smaller or non-existent gaps and countries like ours with large happiness gaps? The presence or absence of pro-family policies, which improved parents' happiness without reducing that of non-parents. Given that more than eight in ten Americans will become parents during their lives, the drain on happiness that accompanies U.S. parenting will eventually drag most Americans down with it.

The Well-Being of U.S. Children

No factor has a bigger effect on children's well-being than the quality of their family relationships. Given families' battered state in the United States, it should come as no surprise that children are doing far less well than in other countries. On the measure of children's own sense of satisfaction with their lives, you might think the United States would top the scale given the nation's great wealth. But when children from developed countries are ranked on life satisfaction, U.S. children fall below the average. One recent United Nations study of 27 industrialized countries ranked our country tied for fifteenth along with seven other countries, including the Slovak Republic and the Czech Republic. That put the United States below not only wealthy countries like Sweden, the Netherlands, and Spain but also far poorer countries like Estonia and Slovenia (OECD 2015, 174, Fig. 4.32; 2017a, 39, Fig. III.1.1; UNICEF 2013, 39, Fig. 6.0).

When children are less able to get what they need in material support and caretaking in their early years, a failure is much more likely under free-market family policy than under pro-family policy, they do less well academically. It should therefore come as no surprise that American children's academic achievement is stunningly mediocre compared with kids' performance in other wealthy countries (Esping-Andersen 2009, 115–116). The United States ranked fortieth on the mathematics portion of the Programme for International Student Assessment (PISA), a test administered to fifteen-year-olds worldwide in 2015 (OECD 2016, 177). That's well below the average of our peers in OECD countries. We were also beaten by much poorer countries, including Vietnam, Russia, the Czech Republic, Portugal, Spain, Latvia, Malta, and Lithuania, as a partial list.

The Well-Being of U.S. Adults

While families don't play the same formative role for adults that they do for children, solid family ties, whether in a family of birth or of choice, are still critical to the well-being and happiness of adults. As Robert Waldinger, director of the Harvard Study of Adult Development, which tracked over 700 men over time, summed up the study's conclusion:

> The clearest message that we get from this 75-year study is this: Good relationships keep us happier and healthier. Period. . . . We've learned . . . that social connections are really good for us, and that loneliness kills. It turns out that people who are more socially connected to family, to friends, to community, are happier, they're physically healthier, and they live longer than people who are less well connected.
>
> *Waldinger 2016*

By creating economic circumstances hostile to sound family relationships, free-market family policy has caused indices relating to American adults' well-being to plummet. When it comes to happiness, among the citizens of 38 developed countries compared in one recent study, Americans reported that they were less satisfied with their lives than adults in fourteen other countries. That puts us far behind countries much less wealthy than our own (OECD 2017b).

Americans' poor showing on happiness measures is unsurprising given the close link between life satisfaction and strong family bonds. As the founder of scientific research on happiness, Richard Layard, put it, "family relationships. . . are more important than any other single factor affecting our happiness" (Layard 2005, 61). The instability free-market family policy has induced in marital and cohabiting relationships plays a significant role in Americans' discontent with their lives—divorce, separation, and never marrying top the list of factors that negatively affect happiness (Layard 2005). So does this policy's contributing to the massive work-family conflict that American parents face, as the "happiness gap" study described above shows (Glass, Simon, Andersson 2016, 907, Table 3).

The recent work of two Princeton economists, Anne Case, and Angus Deaton, helps clarify the relationship between economics, families, and the despair many Americans feel today. In 2015, Case and Deaton noticed that U.S. death rates had increased significantly in one particular group: middle-aged whites with no more than a high school education—the group that used to be identified as the "white working class." That increase was especially shocking given that death rates had decreased in every other age group, every other racial and ethnic group, and every other wealthy country during those years (Case and Deaton 2015, 2017; Stein et al. 2017). When Case and Deaton sought the source for the increase in death rates among this group, they discovered that it came from a growing number of suicides, drug overdoses, and alcohol-related diseases, which they came to call "deaths of despair." They surmised that shrinking economic opportunities for less-educated white Americans have caused a cascade of changes, including changes in family life, that have contributed to patterns of risky behavior that cause early death. In their words:

> These changes left people with less structure when they came to choose their careers, their religion, and the nature of their family lives. When such choices succeed, they are liberating; when they fail, the individual can only hold him or herself responsible. In the worst cases of failure, this is a . . . recipe for suicide. We can see this as . . . a loss of the structures that provide meaning to life.
>
> *Case and Deaton 2017, 39*

Key among the structures that lend stability and impart meaning to people's lives is the family. And in America today, free-market family policy has left the nation's families embattled.

Conclusion

Free-market family policy is crushing the health and stability of U.S. families. It's time to replace this system with one that actively partners with families to support the circumstances that families need to do their best. The health of families, the well-being and happiness of American adults, and the future of our children depend on it.

Notes

1 Because a wide range of long-term relationships foster the well-being, caretaking, and human development that humans need to flourish, I use the term "family" expansively to apply to all long-term relationships in which caretaking occurs.

2 Of course, markets are never truly "free" since no market could exist without significant government involvement, including laws that establish a stable currency, enforce property rights, and back contracts with the force of law. I will use the term "free market," as it is usually used, to mean markets that are not regulated with non-market goals in mind, like promoting fairness, good family lives, or other social welfare goals, not to mean that markets are not regulated at all.

3 I use the term "low-income families" to describe families whose earnings are less than twice the poverty level, or about $42,000 in 2018 for a family of three. (The 2018 poverty level for a family of three was $20,780.) By "poor families," I mean those at the federal poverty level or below.

4 I conducted all the interviews described in this chapter, but used pseudonyms to preserve their immunity. For more information about the interviews, see Eichner (2020, 227, n. 4).

5 I use the term "middle-income families" to describe families with earnings that fall between 2 and 6.5 times the federal poverty level, or about $42,000 to $135,000 for a family of three in 2018.

6 I use the term "high-income families" for those with incomes more than 6.5 times the federal poverty level, which in 2018 was roughly $135,000 or more for a family of three.

7 Interview with author.

8 I develop the contrasts between what I call "free-market family policy" and "pro-family policy" in more detail in my book, *The Free-Market Family: How the Market Crushed the American Dream (and How It Can Be Restored)* (2020). I discuss the ideological shifts that led to free-market family policy in a later article, *The Road to Free-Market Family Policy* (2021).

9 My typology is based on one that sociologist Gøsta Esping-Andersen laid out in *The Three Worlds of Welfare Capitalism* (1990). The model I call "free-market family policy" is based on Esping-Andersen's "liberal" welfare state model. Meanwhile, "pro-family policy" is loosely based on his "social democratic" model (Esping-Andersen 1990, 26–28). As scholars have recognized (e.g. Gornick and Meyers 2003, Orloff 2006, Esping-Andersen 2009), even the countries that Esping-Andersen labeled as "corporatist" in his original typology have moved closer to the social democratic model when it comes to supporting children and families.

References

Amato, Paul, Alan Booth, David Johnson, and Stacy Rogers. 2007. *Alone Together: How Marriage in America Is Changing.* Cambridge, MA: Harvard University Press.

Autor, David and Melanie Wasserman. 2013. "Wayward Sons: The Emerging Gender Gap in Labor Markets and Education." *Third Way*: 1–64. https://thirdway.imgix.net/downloads/wayward-sons-the-emerging-gender-gap-in-labor-markets-and-education/Third_Way_Report_-_NEXT_Wayward_Sons-The_Emerging_Gender_Gap_in_Labor_Markets_and_Education.pdf.

Bertrand, Marianne and Sendhil Mullainathan. 2004. "Are Emily and Greg More Employable Than Lakisha and Jamal? A Field Experiment on Labor Market Discrimination. American." *American Economic Review* 94, no. 4: 991–1013.

Bianchi, Suzanne, John Robinson, and Melissa Milkie. 2006. *Changing Rhythms of American Family Life.* New York: Russell Sage Foundation.

Bianchi, Suzanne and Vanessa Wight. 2010. "The Long Reach of the Job: Employment and Time for Family Life." In *Workplace Flexibility: Realigning 20th-Century Jobs for a 21st-Century Workforce*, edited by Kathleen Christensen and Barbara Schneider, 17–42. Ithaca, NY: Cornell University Press.

Binder, Ariel J. and John Bound. 2019. "The Declining Labor Market Prospects of Less-Educated Men." *Journal of Economic Perspective* 33, no. 2 (Spring): 163–190. doi:10.1257/jep.33.2.163.

Bleiweis, Robin. 2020. "Quick Facts About the Gender Wage Gap." Center for American Progress, March 24, 2020. https://www.americanprogress.org/article/quick-facts-gender-wage-gap/.

Board of Governors of the Federal Reserve System, Federal Reserve Board, Division of Consumer and Community Affairs. 2018. *Report on the Economic Well-Being of U.S. Households in 2017.* Washington, DC: Board of Governors of the Federal Reserve.

Boushey, Heather. 2016. *Finding Time: The Economics of Work-Life Conflict.* Cambridge, MA: Harvard University Press.

Bowlby, John. 1951. *Maternal Care and Mental Health.* Geneva: World Health Organization.

Bramlett, Matthew D. and William D. Mosher. 2002. "Cohabitation, Marriage, Divorce, and Remarriage in the United States." *Vital and Health Statistics* 23, no. 22. https://www.cdc.gov/nchs/data/series/sr_23/sr23_022.pdf.

Bricker, Jesse. 2017. "Changes in U.S. Family Finances from 2013 to 2016: Evidence from the Survey of Consumer Finances." *Federal Reserve Bulletin* 103: 1–42. https://www.federalreserve.gov/publications/files/scf17.pdf.

Cainer, Tomaz, Tyler Radler, David Ratner, and Ivan Vidangos. 2017. *Racial Gaps in Labor Market Outcomes in the Last Four Decades and Over the Business Cycle.* Finance and Economics Discussion Series. Washington, DC: Federal Reserve Board. https://www.federalreserve.gov/econres/feds/files/2017071pap.pdf

Carbone, June and Naomi Cahn. 2014. *Marriage Markets: How Inequality Is Remaking the American Family.* New York: Oxford University Press.

Case, Anne and Angus Deaton. 2015. "Rising Morbidity and Mortality in Midlife among White, Non-Hispanic Americans in the 21st Century." *PNAS* 112, no. 49: 15078–15083. https://www.pnas.org/content/pnas/112/49/15078.full.pdf.

Case, Anne and Angus Deaton. 2017. "Mortality and Morbidity in the 21st Century." https://www.brookings.edu/wp-content/uploads/2017/08/casetextsp17bpea.pdf.

Centers for Disease Control and Prevention. 2017. "QuickStats: Suicide Rates, for Teens Aged 15–19 Years, by Sex: United States, 1975–2015." *Morbidity and Mortality Weekly Report* 66, no. 30: 816. https://www.cdc.gov/mmwr/volumes/66/wr/mm6630a6.htm#suggestedcitation.

Cherlin, Andrew J. 2009. *The Marriage-Go-Round: The State of Marriage and the Family in America Today.* New York: Alfred A. Knopf.

Cherlin, Andrew J. 2014. *Labor's Love Lost: The Rise and Fall of the Working-Class Family in America.* New York: Russell Sage Foundation.

Claxton, Gary, Rae, Matthew, Long, Michelle, Damico, Anthony, Foster, Gregory, and Whitmore, Heidi. 2017. Employer Health Benefits: 2017 Annual Survy. Henry J. Kaiser Family Foundation and Health Reserch & Educational Trust. http://files.kff.org/attatment/Report-Employer-Health-Benefits-Annual-Survey-2017.

Cohen, Patricia. 2017. "Steady Jobs, with Pay and Hours That Are Anything But." *New York Times*, May 31, 2017. https://www.nytimes.com/2017/05/31/business/economy/volatile-income-economy-jobs.html.

Cohen, Philip N. 2018. "The Coming Divorce Decline." *SocArXiv.* https://osf.io/preprints/socarxiv/h2sk6/.

Congressional Budget Office. 2016. *Trends in Family Wealth, 1987 to 2013.* Washington, DC: Congressional Budget Office. https://www.cbo.gov/sites/default/files/114th-congress-2015-2016/reports/51846-familywealth.pdf.

Dahl, Molly, Thomas DeLeire, and Jonathan A. Schwabish. 2011. "Estimates of Year-to-Year Variability in Worker Earnings and in Household Incomes from Administrative, Survey, and Matched Data." *Journal of Human Resources* 46, no. 4: 750–774.

Daly, Mary C., Bart Hobijn, and Joseph H. Pedtke. 2017. *Disappointing Facts about the Black-White Wage Gap.* Federal Reserve Bank of San Francisco: 1–5. https://www.frbsf.org/economic-research/files/el2017-26.pdf.

Declercq, Eugene R., Carol Sakala, Maureen P. Corry, Sandra Applebaum, and Ariel Herrlich. 2013. *Listening to Mothers III: New Mothers Speak Out.* Childbirth Connection. https://www.nationalpartnership.org/our-work/resources/health-care/maternity/listening-to-mothers-iii-new-mothers-speak-out-2013.pdf.

DeRose, Laurie, Mark Lyons-Amos, W. Bradford Wilcox, and Gloria Huarcaya. 2017. "The Cohabitation-Go-Round: Cohabitation and Family Across the Globe." In Social Trends Institute, *World Family Map 2017, Mapping Family Change and Child Well-Being Outcomes.* http://worldfamilymap.ifstudies.org/2017/files/WFM-2017-FullReport.pdf#page=36&zoom=auto,-99,307.

Desilver, Drew. 2013. "Black Unemployment Rate Is Consistently Twice That of Whites." *Pew Research Center,* August 21, 2013. https://www.pewresearch.org/fact-tank/2013/08/21/through-good-times-and-bad-black-unemployment-is-consistently-double-that-of-whites/.

Dynan, Karen E., Douglas W. Elmendorf, and Daniel E. Sichel. 2012. "The Evolution of Household Income Volatility." *The B.E. Journal of Economic Analysis & Policy* 12, no. 2: 1–41.

Economic Policy Institute. 2021. *Fact Sheet: Why the U.S. Needs a $15 Minimum Wage.* Fact Sheet. https://www.epi.org/publication/why-america-needs-a-15-minimum-wage/.

Economic Policy Institute and Oxfam Am. 2016. "Few Rewards: An Agenda to Give America's Working Poor a Raise." https://s3.amazonaws.com/oxfam-us/www/static/media/files/Few_Rewards_Report_2016_web.pdf.

Edin, Kathryn and Kefalas, Maria. 2005. *Promises I Can Keep: Why Poor Women Put Motherhood Before Marriage.* Berkeley, CA: University of California Press.

Eichner, Maxine. 2020. *The Free-Market Family: How the Market Crushed the American Dream (and How It Can Be Restored).* Oxford: Oxford Press.

Eichner, Maxine. 2021. "The Road to Free-Market Family Policy." *Journal of Law and Political Economy* 1: 239.

Esping-Andersen, Gøsta. 2009. *The Incomplete Revolution: Adapting Welfare States to Women's New Roles.* Cambridge: Polity Press.

Fairlie, Robert W. and William A. Sundstrom. 1999. "The Emergency, Persistence, and Recent Widening of the Racial Unemployment Gap." *Industrial and Labor Relations Review* 52, no. 2: 252–270.

Freeman, Richard. 2007. *America Works: The Exceptional U.S. Labor Market.* New York: Russell Sage Foundation.

Fry, Richard, D'Vera Cohn, Gretchen Livingston, and Paul Taylor. 2011. *The Old Prosper Relative to the Young: The Rising Age Gap in Economic Well-Being.* Pew Research Center: Washington, D.C., 1–38. https://www.pewresearch.org/wp-content/uploads/sites/3/2011/11/WealthReportFINAL.pdf.

Glass, Jennifer, Robin W. Simon, and Matthew A. Andersson. 2016. "Parenthood and Happiness: Effects of Work-Family Reconciliation Policies in 22 OECD Countries." *American Journal of Sociology* 122, no. 3: 886–929.

Golden, Lonnie. 2015. "Irregular Work Scheduling and Its Consequences." *Economic Policy Institute*, April 9, 2015. https://www.epi.org/publication/irregular-work-scheduling-and-its-consequences/.

Gornick, Janet, and Marcia Meyers. 2003. *Families That Work: Policies for Reconciling Parenthood and Employment*. New York: Russell Sage Foundation.

Gottschalk, Peter, and Robert Moffitt. 2009. "The Rising Instability of U.S. Earnings." *Journal of Economic Perspectives* 23, no. 4 (Fall): 3–24.

Guzzo, Karen Benjamin. 2014. "Trends in Cohabitation Outcomes: Compositional Changes and Engagement among Never-Married Young Adults." *Journal of Marriage and Family* 76, no. 4: 826–842.

Hacker, Jacob. 2006. *The Great Risk Shift: The Assault on American Jobs, Families, Health Care, and Retirement and How You Can Fight Back*. New York: Oxford University Press.

Hacker, Jacob. 2011. "Understanding Economic Insecurity: The Downward Spiral of the Middle Class." *Communities & Banking* 22: 25–28.

Hacker, Jacob, and Paul Pierson. 2010. *Winner-Take-All Politics: How Washington Made the Rich Richer—and Turned Its Back on the Middle Class*. New York: Simon & Schuster.

Hardy, Bradley. 2016. "Addressing Income Volatility in the United States: Flexible Policy Solutions for Changing Economic Circumstances." *Washington Center for Equitable Growth*, October 31, 2016. https://equitablegrowth.org/addressing-income-volatility-in-the-united-states-flexible-policy-solutions-for-changing-economic-circumstances/.

Hardy, Bradley and James Ziliak. 2013. "Decomposing Trends in Income Volatility: The 'Wild Ride' at the Top and Bottom." *Economic Inquiry* 52, no. 1: 459–476.

Heuveline, Patrick, Jeffrey M. Timberlake, and Frank G. Furstenberg. 2003. "Shifting Childrearing to Single Mothers: Results from 17 Western Countries." *Population and Development Review* 29, no. 1: 47–71.

Hiltonsmith, Robert. 2013. *At What Cost? How Student Debt Reduces Lifetime Wealth*. Demos. https://www.demos.org/sites/default/files/publications/AtWhatCost.pdf.

Howard, Kimberly, Martin, Anne, Berlin, Lisa, and Brooks-Gunne, Jeanne. 2011. "Early Mother-Child Separation, Parenting, and Child Well-Being in Early Head Start Families." *Attachment and Human Development* 13, no. 1: 5–26.

Jacoby, Melissa and Mirya Holman. 2014. "Financial Fragility, Medical Problems and the Bankruptcy System." In *Living and Working in the Shadow of Economic Fragility*, edited by Marion Crain and Michael Sherraden, 53–69. New York: Oxford University Press.

Jones, Robert P., Daniel Cox, and Juhem Navarro-Rivera. 2014. Economic Insecurity, Rising Inequality, and Doubts about the Future: Findings from the 2014 American Values Survey. *Public Religion Research Institute*. https://www.prri.org/wp-content/uploads/2.

Katz, Lawrence and Alan B. Krueger. 2016. *The Rise and Nature of Alternative Work Arrangements in the United States, 1995–2015*. National Bureau of Economic Research Working Paper No. 22667. https://www.nber.org/system/files/working_papers/w22667/w22667.pdf.

Kennedy, Sheela and Larry Bumpass. 2008. "Cohabitation and Children's Living Arrangements: New Estimates from the United States." *Demographic Research* 19, no. 47: 1663–1692.

Laughlin, Lynda. 2011. *Maternity Leave and Employment Patterns of First-Time Mothers: 1961–2008*. Current Population Report No. P70-128. US Census Bureau. https://www.census.gov/prod/2011pubs/p70-128.pdf.

Layard, Richard. 2005. *Happiness: Lessons from a New Science*. New York: Penguin Press.

Manning, Wendy. 2015. "Cohabitation and Child Wellbeing." *Future Child* 25, no. 2: 51–66.

Medalia, Carla and Jacobs, Jerry. 2008. "Working Time for Married Couples in 28 Countries." In *The Long Work Hours Culture: Causes, Consequences, and Choices*, edited by Ronald Burke and Cary Cooper. Bingley: Emerald Group.

Milkie, Melissa, Sara B. Raley, and Suzanne M. Bianchi. 2009. "Taking on the Second Shift: Time Allocations and Time Pressures of U.S. Parents with Preschoolers." *Social Forces* 88, no. 2: 487–517.

Mishel, Lawrence, Josh Bivens, Elise Gould, and Heidi Shierholz. 2012. *The State of Working America, 12th Edition*. 12th ed. Ithaca, NY: Cornell University Press.

Morduch, Jonathan and Rachel Schneider. 2013. "Spikes and Dips: How Income Uncertainty Affects Households." *US Financial Diaries*, 2013. https://static1.squarespace.com/static/53d008ede4b0833aa2ab2eb9/t/53d6e12ae4b0907fe7bedf6f/1410469662568/issue1-spikes.pdf.

Morduch, Jonathan, and Rachel Schneider. 2017. *The Financial Diaries: How American Families Cope in a World of Uncertainty*. Princeton, NJ: Princeton University Press.

National Scientific Council on the Developing Child. 2009. "Young Children Develop in an Environment of Relationships." *National Scientific Council on the Developing Child Working Paper Series*. Working Paper No. 1. Harvard Center on the Developing Child.

NPR and Marist, NPR/Marist Poll January 2018: Picture of Work. *NPR and Marist*, January 22, 2018. https://maristpoll.marist.edu/nprmarist-poll-results-january-2018-picture-of-work/.

OECD. 2011. *Doing Better for Families*. OECD Publishing. https://www.oecd.org/els/soc/47701118.pdf.

OECD. 2015. *How's Life? 2015: Measuring Well-Being*. Paris: OECD Publishing. https://read.oecd-ilibrary.org/economics/how-s-life-2015_how_life-2015-en#page1.

OECD. 2016. *PISA 2015 Results (Volume I): Excellence and Equity in Education*. Paris: OECD Publishing.

OECD. 2017a. *PISA 2015 Results (Volume III): Students' Well-Being*. Paris: OECD Publishing. https://www.oecd-ilibrary.org/education/pisa-2015-results-volume-iii_9789264273856-en.

OECD. 2017b. "Life Satisfaction." *OECD Better Life Index*. Last visited October 13, 2017. http://www.oecdbetterlifeindex.org/topics/life-satisfaction.

OECD. 2017c. *P.F1.6: Public Spending by Age of Children*. http://www.oecd.org/els/family/PF1_6_Public_spending_by_age_children.xlsx.

OECD. 2018a. *SF3.1: Marriage and Divorce Rates*. OECD Family Database. https://www.oecd.org/els/family/SF_3_1_Marriage_and_divorce_rates.pdf.

OECD. 2018b. *SF1.3: Further Information on the Living Arrangements of Children*. OECD Family Database. https://www.oecd.org/els/soc/SF_1_3_Living-arrangements-children.pdf.

OECD. 2021. *Hours Worked*. https://data.oecd.org/emp/hours-worked.htm.

Orloff, Ann Shola. 2006. "From Maternalism to 'Employment for All': State Policies to Promote Women's Employment Across the Affluent Democracies." In *The State After Statism: New State Activities in the Age of Liberalization*, edited by Jonah Levy. Cambridge, MA: Harvard University Press.

Parker, Kim and Renee Stepler. 2017. "As U.S. Marriage Rate Hovers at 50%, Education Gap in Marital Status Widens." *Pew Research Center*, September 14, 2017. https://www.pewresearch.org/fact-tank/2017/09/14/as-u-s-marriage-rate-hovers-at-50-education-gap-in-marital-status-widens/

Parker, Kim and Wendy Wang. 2013. "Balancing Work and Family Life." In *Modern Parenthood: Roles of Moms and Dads Converge as They Balance Work and Family*. Washington, DC: Pew Research Center. https://www.pewresearch.org/social-trends/wp-content/uploads/sites/3/2013/03/FINAL_modern_parenthood_03-2013.pdf

Pew Research Center. 2015a. Raising Kids and Running a Household: How Working Parents Share the Load. *Pew Research Center*. https://assets.pewresearch.org/wp-content/uploads/sites/3/2015/11/2015-11-04_working-parents_FINAL.pdf.

Pew Research Center. 2015b. "Parenting in America: Outlook, Worries, Aspirations Are Strongly Linked to Financial Situation." *Pew Research Center*. https://www.pewresearch.org/wp-content/uploads/sites/3/2015/12/2015-12-17_parenting-in-america_FINAL.pdf.

Putnam, Robert. 2015. *Our Kids: The American Dream in Crisis*. New York: Simon & Schuster.

Schoen, Cathy, Radley, David, and Collins, Sara R. 2015. State Trends in the Cost of Employer Health Insurance Coverage, 2003-2013. Commonwealth Fund. https;//www.commonwealthfund.org/sites/default/files/documents/___media_files_publications_issue_brief_2015_jan_1798_schoen_state_trends_20003_2013.pdf.

Schulte, Brigid. 2014. *Overwhelmed: Work, Love, and Play When No One Has the Time*. New York: Sarah Crichton Books.

Smith, Peggy. 2004. "Elder Care, Gender, and Work: The Work-Family Issue of the 21st Century." *Berkeley Journal of Employment and Labor Law* 25(2): 351–400.

Social Indicators of Marital Wellbeing. 2009. *State of Our Unions*. http://stateofourunions.org/2009/si-marriage.php.

Stancyzk, Alexandra B. 2016. "The Dynamics of Household Economic Circumstances Around a Birth." *Washington Center for Equitable Growth Working Paper Series*: 1–67. http://cdn.equitablegrowth.org/wp-content/uploads/2016/09/30112707/10042016-WP-income-volatility-around-birth.pdf.

Stein, Elizabeth M., Keith P. Gennuso, Donna C. Ugboaja, and Patrick L. Remington. 2017. "The Epidemic of Despair among White Americans: Trends in the Leading Causes of Premature Death, 1999–2015." *American Journal of Public Health* 107, no. 10: 1541–1547.

UNICEF. 2013. *Child Well-Being in Rich Countries: A Comparative Overview*. Florence: UNICEF Office of Research. https://www.unicef-irc.org/publications/pdf/rc11_eng.pdf.

U.S. Government Accountability Office. 2015. *Contingent Workforce: Size, Characteristics, Earnings and Benefits.* Washington, DC: Government Accountability Office. https://www.gao.gov/assets/670/669899.pdf.

Waldinger, Robert. 2016. "What Makes a Good Life? Lessons From the Longest Study on Happiness." *TEDx*, January 25. https://www.youtube.com/watch?v=8KkKuTCFvzI.

Warren, Elizabeth and Amelia Warren Tyagi. 2003. *The Two-Income Trap.* New York: Basic Books.

Wilcox, William Bradford and Elizabeth Marquardt. 2010. *When Marriage Disappears: The New Middle America.* The National Marriage Project and the Institute for American Values. http://stateofourunions.org/2010/SOOU2010.pdf.

Wildsmith, Elizabeth, Jennifer Manlove, and Elizabeth Cook. 2018. "Dramatic Increase in the Proportion of Births Outside of Marriage in the United States from 1990 to 2016." *Child Trends*, August 8, 2018. https://www.childtrends.org/publications/dramatic-increase-in-percentage-of-births-outside-marriage-among-whites-hispanics-and-women-with-higher-education-levels.

Wilson, Valerie. 2015. "Black Unemployment Is Significantly Higher Than White Unemployment Regardless of Educational Attainment." *Economic Policy Institute*, December 17, 2015. https://www.epi.org/publication/black-unemployment-educational-attainment/.

Wilson, Valerie. 2020. "Racial Disparities in Income and Poverty Remain Largely Unchanged Amid Strong Income Growth in 2019." *Economic Policy Institute*, September 16, 2020. https://www.epi.org/blog/racial-disparities-in-income-and-poverty-remain-largely-unchanged-amid-strong-income-growth-in-2019/.

Wilson, Valerie and William M. Rodgers III. 2016. "Black-White Wage Gaps Expand with Rising Wage Inequality." *Economic Policy Institute*, September 19, 2016. https://files.epi.org/pdf/101972.pdf.

Wolff, Edward N. 2017. "Household Wealth Trends in the United States, 1962 to 2016: Has Middle Class Wealth Recovered?" *National Bureau of Economic Research Working Paper No. 24085*: 1–75. https://www.nber.org/system/files/working_papers/w24085/w24085.pdf.

Ziliak, James P., Bradley Hardy, and Christopher Bollinger. 2011. "Earnings Volatility in America: Evidence from Matched CPS." *Labour Economics* 18: 742–754.

PART III

Migration and the Immigrant American Dream

11

TWENTY-FIRST-CENTURY AFRICAN IMMIGRANT VIEW OF THE AMERICAN DREAM

Challenges and opportunities

Enock Ariga Marindi and Robert C. Hauhart

A principal global trend over the past three centuries, and one of the most notable effects of increasing globalization, is the migration of people from one country, and one continent, to another (Defoort and Rogers 2008). These movements have seen parents give birth to children whose childhoods (and perhaps adulthoods) are spent in cultures and countries other than their own. Such is the case of African immigrant families to the United States.

A Short History of African Immigration to the United States

African migration to the United States started with the forced migration imposed on West Africans through the Transatlantic Slave Trade beginning in 1619. Those early involuntary migrants who were enslaved, and their progeny over multiple generations, now constitute the overwhelming majority of black Americans who we deem "African Americans." According to the latest census figures, black and/or African Americans number approximately 41.1 million persons, or about 12.4 percent of the U.S. population (U.S. Census 2020).

Congress banned the African slave trade in 1807 (Kolawole 2017). Since that time, African migration to the United States has been exclusively voluntary, although severely inhibited up until 1865 by the possibility of enslavement of blacks who immigrated to the United States and lived or traveled in the South prior to issuance of the Emancipation Proclamation (1863). Yet voluntary African migration to the United States is only one segment of the broader migration of black individuals from multiple regions of the world to the United States. For example, one estimate suggests that one out of three black immigrants to the United States is from either Jamaica or Haiti (Boundless 2021). Other Caribbean countries, including notably Trinidad and Tobago and the Dominican Republic, as well as Brazil, have contributed significant numbers to the non-African black immigrant population to the United States since the 1960s (Boundless 2021).

African immigration to the United States in the nineteenth and early twentieth centuries was negligible. While some of the earliest voluntary African migration to the United States took place in the nineteenth century from the Cape Verde Islands to New Bedford, Massachusetts, where African men settled to work as seamen in the commercial whaling industry (Kolawole 2017, 379), the numerical totals were small. African immigration to the

DOI: 10.4324/9781003326243-14

United States in the early twentieth century was inhibited by the nationality quota system adopted by the Immigration Act of 1924. Briefly, the Act allotted visas based on the percentage of Americans who traced their ancestry to a particular country. This approach allotted the highest percentage of visas to countries from the northern and western European countries, while restricting the numbers from southern and eastern European countries, and severely limiting (if not refusing[1]) quotas to those seeking to migrate from most other countries in the world, including those in Africa. Since most African nations were under European colonial rule at this time, the United States only recognized four African countries in 1924 (Egypt, South Africa, Liberia, and Ethiopia) and awarded only a minimal assignment of 100 visas each to these countries and a handful of European African protectorates (381).

The Immigration and Nationality Act of 1965 constituted a significant change to this approach. Rather than basing immigration quotas on national origin, the revised immigration act allowed immigration to the United States based on existing family connections and professional qualifications, thereby prioritizing family reunification and occupational skills. This change in the law inspired a growth in black migration to the United States, including those from African countries. Prior to 1965, African migrants to the United States made up approximately one percent of the total immigrant population (Kolawole 2017, 383). By way of comparison, Africans now constitute approximately 3.9 percent of immigrants to the United States according to 2010 estimates (McCabe 2011).

The latter half of the twentieth century also saw changes in law that expanded African migration. The 1980 Refugee Act's Federal Refugee Resettlement Program broadened admission to the United States among those forced to flee their homeland and migrate (Refugee Act of 1980). Among other countries whose citizens were able to qualify for refugee status, one can note those from the African countries of Liberia, Somalia, Sudan, Eritrea, and Ethiopia (Kolawole 2017, 383). The Immigration Act of 1990, and particularly the Diversity Visa Program, which was added to it in 1994, also facilitated the expansion of African migration to the United States. This program provided 55,000 immigrant visas to citizens of countries and regions that have been historically underrepresented under U.S. immigration laws (383).

African Migration in the Context of Global Migration

The twenty-first century has witnessed massive migration from the African continent to both Europe and, to a lesser degree, to the United States (Hassène Kassar, et al. 2014). There are various ways to measure African immigration to the United States. As one example, the Migration Policy Institute (2019) reports that there is a total of 2.4 million African immigrants in the United States with more than two million originating from sub-Saharan Africa (Echeverria-Estrada and Batalova 2019). The greatest numbers of African immigrants to the United States have arrived since 2000. One apt comparison, citing Department of Homeland Security figures, notes that over the four decades from 1960 to 1999, 583,594 immigrants arrived in the United States from African countries. In the single decade between 2000 and 2010, the number of African immigrants to the United States rose to 857,988 (Arthur, Takougang, and Owusu 2012, xi–xii).

As many writers and scholars have made clear, recent African immigration generally, and to the United States in particular, is part of a "new diaspora" that can be measured over only a few decades (Okpewho and Nzegwu 2009, 9–14). While some portion of African immigration to the United States in recent decades has arisen from refugees seeking asylum from countries such as South Sudan and Ethiopia, the climate of insecurity has not been the principal cause. Rather, most African immigrants during this period have come to the

United States primarily seeking a better life through voluntary expatriation. As Okpewho (2009, 10) reflects regarding those Africans who leave their homeland,

> If conditions deteriorate to such an extent that you can no longer guarantee to your-
> self and your family the basic needs of life: ... who, under these conditions, would
> resist the urge to seek employment outside the country just so the family can at least
> survive?

Over and above mere survival, many writers and commentators have remarked upon the poor social and infrastructure services available in many African countries even as we slog further into the twenty-first century. It is rather too easy to enumerate them: power grids and electrical service; land, water, and in-country air transportation; and health services, identify only the most obvious. Addressing the power outages that plague many African countries for many hours daily alone would alleviate harsh conditions and make life immeasurably more livable by enabling Africans to read during more hours; work uninterrupted with longer internet access; and share and experience culture at all hours of the day and night. Voluntary migration affords African families unique challenges, but also provide unprecedented oppor-tunities, whether socially, financially, and/or spiritually, simply based on better access to rou-tine infrastructure upgrades and improved social services of all kinds. As Okpewho queries, who wouldn't seek out such opportunities when the local conditions in Africa's homelands have not improved over those decades earlier, and in many instances, have deteriorated?

The aftermath of the period of African colonization brought many cultural changes to the continent, even as it plunged a number of African countries into internal dissension, pollical authoritarianism, and civil war. As but one example, Africans began looking beyond their home towns, home countries, and the continent for "the fulfillment of unmet needs at home" (Arthur, Takougang, and Owusu 2012, 1). As Arthur and his colleagues recite, faced with economic deprivation, "outmigration from Africa (particularly to the advanced nations of the western hemisphere) provide[d] the best option to improve upon one's economic status and standard of living" (2). Scholars of the African diaspora generally speak of "three waves" of African migration: first, through students supported by their home countries in the 1950s; second, as a consequence of the many African countries that were embroiled in social, eco-nomic, and political conflict beginning in the mid-1970s; and third, since the millennia, which has become the most robust outmigration of the three. International migration during this most recent period is "seen as panacea" for the structural economic imbalances at home. In short, it is the lure of a better life and escape from economic destitution in Africa that is "the driving force behind this mass migration" (4). Indeed, some scholars of the new African diaspora have compared this migratory trend since 2000 with "the transcontinental migration of Europeans to North American during the nineteenth and twentieth centuries" (4).

The motivations that inspire Africans who emigrate from their home countries to choose the United States, as compared to Europe or other countries in the world, appear to be widely shared. As Arthur et al. (2012) summarize it in the subtitle to their book, they are "searching for promised lands" Ette (2012, 111–122), limiting his examination of the motiv-ations Nigerians express for coming to the United States, to a handful of major themes. They are quite representative of the motivations expressed throughout the African immigrant lit-erature more generally.

Many Nigerians, along with many other Africans including the lead author, come to the United States to acquire an American higher education (112–113). As we will hear in more detail from the lead author's interview research in St. Paul, some Africans – including the

Nigerians Ette interviewed – see education as the "springboard" to success. These African students are highly motivated to do whatever it takes to complete their curriculums and acquire their degrees.

According to Ette, a second common motivation, especially for women, is to come to the United States to join a husband who has already immigrated to America (113). Ette reports that it is less common for Nigerian men to immigrate to America to join a wife or female who is already in the United States, perhaps one studying for an advanced degree (113).

While many Nigerians came to the United States during a time that the Nigerian economy was doing well, Nigeria has suffered economic downturns since then. In the 1980s, though, the Nigerian economy floundered. As our preliminary remarks have already suggested, Nigerians joined many from other African nations in seeking to avoid hardship and unemployment (115). Like elites from other African nations, even those Nigerians with advanced degrees and professional careers would often become immigrants on this basis. As Ette (2012, 116) relates, "Bob came to escape poverty. He had studied in the United States and returned to Nigeria to teach at a college there. He discovered that his salary did not allow him to buy the basic necessities, so he planned to return to the United States despite his expired visa."

Finally, as with many African political expatriates and refugees since, some Nigerians either chose to stay in the United States after they were already here or joined those newly choosing to leave a less stable Nigeria. Kinte mentioned his reason for not returning by saying, "There were so many coups and counter-coups. The country was not safe, and life was hard I heard" (117). Others that Ette interviewed echoed this sentiment.

While African immigrants to the United States have expressed motivations other than these four, these are the predominant explanations given by African immigrants regardless of country of origin. Motivations may, of course, change after African immigrants arrive, as did those of several respondents Ette (2012) interviewed. Thus, it is important to distinguish between the reasons for coming and the reasons for staying.

Economic Opportunity Here and There

First, it is true there are many opportunities in the United States compared to many countries (perhaps most) in twenty-first-century Africa. Certainly, that statement is true with respect to the lower, and even the middle, classes. Arguably, however, one can only live a comfortable life anywhere in the world. Yet to do so, one must undergo a positive mental shift, as well as a geographic shift, that will inspire one to accept, and be ready to overcome, whatever cultural barriers and attendant frustrations a new country and culture impose. Many of the Africans who have had an opportunity to live and work in America, including the lead author, didn't know there would also be many special challenges in the United States. Many African immigrants seem to think, wrongly, that American life is perfect without visualizing the many difficulties they would face in their (American) dream destination.

As one example, little is told to new immigrants concerning the working ethics in America as contrasted to those in Africa. The duration of time one spends at work is often the basis for comparison, and compensation, in employment in the United States. In most African countries, it does not matter whether an employee attends work or not, provided that one is on the payroll. There, employees are paid one's full salary at the end of the month, regardless. In the mind of African immigrants, the American dream entails a land of plenty that promises higher returns compared to the African immigrant's motherland. Africans who emigrate to the United States often do not comprehend that admission to the American dream is conditional. Such thoughts of a better life led many Africans to abandon relatively well-paying jobs in their home country with vividly envisioned, but unrealizable, prospects of even a better working life in the United States. Little do they know, that in many cases their hopes will perish due to non-attainability.

The disjunction between life for many Africans in their home country and the United States is three-fold. First, while income can be very low in African countries for the great majority of the population, expenses have also been historically low, particularly outside of major urban centers. Second, income in the United States for African migrants – except for the highly educated who are employed in professional and technical fields – can be significantly lower than migrants' expectations. Correspondingly, and third, expenses in urban centers in the United States can be much higher than anticipated by many.

This form of disappointment or mismatch between fantasies of what the American dream is before coming to America and the reality of the United States has led many African immigrants to live with bitterness, and anger untold. The American dream is often envisioned as an embodiment of opportunities or a platform where every individual can attain anything that he/she needs. African immigrants to the United States routinely expect good education, job opportunities, good medical attention, improved security, good housing, respect of human rights, and many other benefits through hard work, persistence, and discipline. This definition of the American dream owes a great deal to the work of historian James Truslow Adams (1878–1949) in his book entitled *The Epic of America*, who beautifully argues,

> But there has been also the American Dream, the dream of a land in which life should be better and richer and fuller for every man, with opportunity for each according to his ability or achievement ... It is a difficult dream for the European upper classes to interpret adequately, and too many of us ourselves have grown weary and mistrustful of it. It is not a dream of motor cars and high wages merely, but a dream of a social order in which each man and each woman shall be able to attain to the fullest statute of which they are innately capable, and be recognized by others for what they are, regardless of the fortuitous circumstances of birth or position. No, the American dream that has lured tens of millions of all nations to our shores in the past century has not been a dream of merely material plenty, although that has doubtless counted heavily. It has been much more than that. It has been a dream of being able to grow to the fullest development as man and woman, unhampered by the barriers which had slowly been erected in older civilizations, unrepressed by social orders which had developed for the benefit of classes rather than for the simple human being of any and every class. And that dream has been realized more fully in actual life here than anywhere else, though very imperfectly even among ourselves.
>
> *Adams 1933, 317–318*

Still, it is worth noting how Adams minimizes, rather than exalts, the purely economic definition of the goals of the American dream. Indeed, Adams' definition can be read as emphasizing the spiritual and personal development goals of the American dream over and above all other goals. Many African immigrants to the United States are lured by, and concentrate their expectations on, the economic (and related educational and occupational) advantages that they hope to accrue.

The United States as a nation provides many equal opportunities for economic advancement. A person from any quarter of the world who steps into this country, possessing literally nothing except a valid dream, is able to rise to succeed economically, socially, and otherwise, sometimes to the pinnacle of society, through his/her hard work and determination.

Arthur et al. (2012, 13) cite several sources to the effect that many immigrants to the United States put in more hours of hard work and willingly undertake the dirty dangerous and difficult jobs that most Americans avoid. As Takougang and Tidjani (2012, 117–134) document, African small business owners in the Cincinnati, Ohio have prospered by embracing business sectors that are labor intensive, including the retail grocery business, neighborhood auto repair shops, gas stations, taxi cab licenses, restaurants, and other examples of small retail outlets. The small business owners they interviewed were largely successful due to two factors. First, these African small business owners relied on family members to work in, and support, their businesses. This business approach creates family cohesion and keeps costs low, a time-honored method employed by generations of immigrants to the United States. Second, African small business owners also tended to save and reinvest profits in their enterprises, all the while sending remittances home (also see: Kaba 2009, 117). According to Takougang and Tidjani (2012, 128), "all indications are that these businesses are a realization of the American dream …" Such upward economic mobility, however modest, provided these small business owners not only the means to live, but offered social and political mobility that would then guarantee the individual and his family enjoyment of freedoms of liberty and equality beyond the experience of living in their parent countries. There are many accounts of immigrants to the United States who have prospered in this way. African communities in the United States have, in this regard, trod the well-traveled path of many prior immigrant communities in the United States.

Defining the American Dream as Upward Economic Mobility

This American dream is often defined as a guarantee of upward mobility for everyone regardless of his/her place of origin, creed, color, or religious persuasion. It is the notion of a guarantee, or promise, or entitlement that can prove pernicious. In advancing this idea of the American dream as the goal of upward mobility, Hochschild (1995) opines that the American dream has to do with arising from humble beginnings and seemingly with little possibility for success. Yet, the United States, conceived as the land of opportunity, holds out the promise – as an exceptional country that has lured hundreds of millions to its shores – of offering unique conditions for those who will work hard to eventually succeed. Upon such a foundation, it is not unrealistic to believe the United States will guarantee one the ability to move upward toward the attainment of his/her dream of increased financial security due, in part, from the modest success sought. There are constraints and limitations that disrupt the routine expectation of successful upward mobility though. Hochschild observes that the middle-class black Americans of the late twentieth century, who were enjoying the success achieved by the faith of their parents in the American dream, were not able to motivate young African Americans to look for that success, even as they have lost the faith of succeeding due to racial discrimination by the white population (Hochschild 1995). In short, the relative strides made by one generation may not translate into further success for the succeeding generation.

Although there is potential, and even a degree of promise at the heart of the American dream, the attainment of better economic circumstances is not guaranteed. Rather, there is an invitation to devote one's ingenuity, skill, and effort toward the goal of increased economic security. With this "upward mobility" definition of the American dream, therefore, an individual has a choice on how to use the resources that he or she has acquired: one can use those resources to pay the bills and enjoy life as best one can, without further thought toward one's future; yet another person will opt to save enough money to invest, whether in education or entrepreneurial micro-capitalism, to realize further his or her dream. Ben Franklin

(1895) urged that the little money one gets can help make a significant change in one's life if invested wisely. This understanding, however, is contrary to the approach some African immigrants to the United States envision and pursue. The freedom to succeed economically that the United States offers cannot be detached from the possibility of failure, as many cautionary texts, including Fitzgerald's *The Great Gatsby* (2004), advise. The notion that there is no guarantee of achieving the American Dream strikes some who hasten to America's shore as something of a surprise.

It is these differing conceptions of the meaning of the American dream that is most crucial to comprehend in examining migrant Africans' experiences in the United States. On the one hand, one can emigrate from one's African homeland and work to get by. On the other hand, one can aspire to more but one will need to strictly apply oneself to the task of achieving it. Consequently, those who invest in education, can go to school, improve their knowledge, skills, and attitude, and – in some cases – prosper. Here is an excerpt of the tale of African immigrants as told by one respondent interviewed during research in the African community of St. Paul, Minnesota.

> It depends on the individual and what he wants to do. If you want to get a job here, it is not as hard to get it as compared to where we came from. Because here you don't have to make (a strict) choice. You can do any job and get money. And the money you get, you can use it to pay the bills and not just to wait to save enough money to realize your dream. The little money you get can help you change your life. Another thing, those who want to go school, actually can be able to go school in this country than in the country where we came from. So it depends from one individual to another and how one wants your life to be. From where we came, even when you don't work (if employed) you can get your salary at the end of the month. But in this place you have to get disciplined.
>
> *Marindi 2018, 89*

Many of the African immigrants who have had this good experience have used education to translate into better pay and an improved quality of life. The question still becomes for many: is the American dream attainable by the African immigrant or is it like chasing wind? The answer to this question depends to whom the question is directed. By and large, many African immigrants feel that it is attainable, but only if the dreamer is willing to adjust his or her expectations to the realities that emerge in his or her pursuit of the American dream. What this means is that the dreamer who dreamt that one day he/she would own a very good house, may have a house but perhaps one that doesn't perfectly fit the dreams he or she imagined; nevertheless, she/he will still have a house. If one dreamt that one would be able to drive a good car, one might be able to drive a car, even though it may not have met the model of his or her expectation. Nonetheless, one is still driving, as this discussant puts it:

> When I arrived here, there are some dreams I had to adjust. Because what I knew before coming over here is different from what I got here. I thought that I will just get here and get a job and start earning just like that. When I arrived here I realized that my going to school didn't count. You have to go through a process to prove to them that you went to school and their system is different. I spent 5 years trying to study how to get to their system and eventually I did. But that is something that I didn't know before I came to America. I would say, if one is patient, one can achieve the dream but again you have to define your dream. Sometimes you have to adjust

or make some adjustments to your dream. The reason why I say this is because there are things that we saw on TV about America which got into our heads such as I will get a big nice house, a good car, and maybe a boat. But you realize, well those things are there, but then, you can't afford them. The reason being sometimes the money you have may not be able to afford all those things. Overall, I would say, if one is patient over time, putting in hard work, I think it is achievable. You have to put hard work to get that money.

Marindi 2018, 90

In sum, most African immigrants still view the United States of America as a sure bet for upward mobility, economically and socially. Despite the challenges that they may face, most of the interview subjects expressed a determined willingness to adjust their dreams to situations that may come their way. African immigrants, as many observers of African communities in the United States attest, are determined to make sure that they are successful in their dreams (Arthur and Owusu 2012, 308).

As the interview respondent, above, suggests a major adjustment that African immigrants must address in their pursuit for the American dream is the question regarding education. Most African immigrants sooner or later realize that their previous schooling in Africa doesn't count for so much in America. The idea of going through a process to prove that one actually went to school, qualified, and graduated with knowledge of their field is disheartening for many African immigrants to the United States. The lead author knows of so many physicians who while they were in Africa acquired a master's degree in medicine and surgery from reputable African universities and then gained a working knowledge and experience of over ten years. Yet, these qualified health care providers will not be allowed to practice in the United States until they complete tutorage for over an additional two years under a supervisor who has fewer, or perhaps equal, qualifications! Perhaps one may argue that the education system is different and the tropical diseases in Africa may be different from the health needs in America but, as an African, it strikes one as manifestly unjust, indeed as outrageous, for one to train further for two to four years to qualify to work independently in a field where one has both educational credentials and experience. It is bureaucratic and monopolistic barriers like these that confront African immigrants to the United States in the twenty-first century.

One consequence is there are those who feel that the American dream is a mirage too good to be grasped. These thoughts are premised on the fact that when one compares his/her life, back in Africa and what he/she goes through here in America, one is only left to cast a dark shadow on the attainability of the American dream. Based on the lead author's interview study in St. Paul, their view may represent a significant number of African immigrants who may not have the courage to voice their opinion confidently in the open. Some of these recent immigrants might be among those who have come to America with expectations that there are free things in America, only to realize that living in the United States now means simply existing from paycheck to paycheck. In essence, immigrants' attitude with respect to the achievability of the American dream tends to differentiate among respondents based upon the attitude expressed. Our presupposition is that, the stronger the urge of pursuing the American dream (in case it is narrowly defined to mean, good life and more money), the less time the pursuant will think negatively about his/her state and the more commitment the person will demonstrate toward achieving upward economic mobility. We deem this to be true because belief in the American dream is perhaps one of the more critical elements that make the dream a self-fulfilling prophecy. While a positive, optimistic attitude toward achieving one's goal is not the sole prerequisite to success in a venture, the obverse is often a powerful deterrent to maintaining an effective goal orientation sustainably. Moreover, there is an easy alternative for those who experience the United States as a treadmill to nowhere rather than a stairway one may ascend to a comfortable life. Expatriate African immigrants to the United States can, of course, repatriate themselves to their homeland, thus further dividing immigrant Africans into ardent believers in the American dream and disenchanted voyagers, who have come, experienced, and left.

Misconceptions of the American Dream

Many Africans tend to think that the grass is greener in parts of Europe and America than in their home country. As we have described, there are certainly reasons to believe that basic physical infrastructure, social services, and health services will be better, assuming the ability to pay in a country like the United States. In fact, some make dangerous journeys across deserts and seas in an attempt to try and cross the borders to reach their dream destinations in these economically and technologically advanced countries (Beauchemin, et al. 2020). In their mind, African immigrants' thoughts are often occupied with dreams of the good life: more money, higher quality services, good educational opportunities, and a higher level of security. Beauchemin, et al. argue that, "Migrants who chose new destinations (Ghanaians to the Netherlands, Congolese to the UK, Senegalese to Spain and Italy) share the following common traits: their destination choice is more frequently driven by work opportunities, they engaged much more frequently in an unauthorized migration, and they are less inclined to return to their home country" (Beauchemin et al. 2020). In interviews conducted among prospective migrants studying in Uganda in September, 2021, many felt that the United States offered a great opportunity for better education and job opportunities. Anitah, a Rwandan, and a prospective immigrant commented,

> It is my dream that one day I will get an opportunity to emigrate to America to study and work. It is my desire to get the American Education since all those who studied in America once they came back to Africa they get better jobs and earn respect and recognition in the society. I want to be among such.

In the same vein, Goldanayo Silversea, a Kenyatta University Student pursuing a bachelor's degree in microbiology said,

> I want to go to America to expand my ability in the business and education, to improve myself and my family financially and definitely think of a business opportunity that will help the people around me as well as my country. America is a superpower and all those who have been there speak well of the country as a place where you can enjoy your freedoms as well as get a job that can guarantee you change the prospects of your family especially those of us who come from a poor family backgrounds.

By and large, these would-be immigrant Africans who share the attitudes of many immigrant populations: those who emigrate self-select as do those who remain in their home country. In this regard, young people studying for university degrees are among those most likely to leave their African homelands: they are young, ambitious, and educated as compared to their African peers who have not graduated university, or even high school.

Regardless of educational level, however, all African immigrants' assumptions are shaped to a degree by the mental pictures distributed by the global media, especially European and

American television programs and Hollywood movies that often portray both Europe and America as blissful and bountiful destinations. Africans, especially those who have been exposed to Christian religious influences, often conceive of European countries and the United States as a type of Canaan portrayed in the Bible: as a land that flows with milk and honey. These media portrayals – especially of the United States – as the epitome of goodness naturally fail to show the whole, complex picture of the American way of life. This is especially true with respect to the economically competitive nature of twenty-first-century neoliberal capitalism. This other side of the United States, where people juggle between two part-time jobs and school, or where one works two or even sometimes three jobs to make ends meet, is often obscured by the rosy visions that immigrants often mistakenly conceive. Here is an excerpt from an interview from research in St. Paul that makes the point well:

> I think while I was in Kenya, my American dream was shaped with what I was seeing in the media and people who had been here before. Whenever they came back to Africa and the projects they did, gave us a good impression that there are good things here in America. They build good houses and some would come within a span of a year, and he is driving a car and given that, in Kenya not many people would afford to drive a car then- it appeared that whenever one came to America then, it would became very easy for him/her to do some of the things which are hard to do back in Africa. And the images we used to see on TV about comfortable life in America, people living a good life, made us yearn for that life as well. And getting here I may not deny there are many opportunities compared to back in Africa. And you can be able to live a comfortable life. But the only thing we didn't know is that, there are also special challenges here. I know we thought that there will only be good American life had many challenges we would face. You know the working ethics here are little bit different from the ones in Kenya. The duration of time you spend at work is what you will be paid for. And then as for me, who came to America with young children, the American dream became a nightmare! Children became disobedient and I found myself unable to control them. This sometimes became scary.
>
> *Marindi 2018, 87*

We cannot wholly blame the illusions of African immigrants to the United States as they dream of the American way of life purely based on the sources available to them. Some of their erstwhile dreams are as a result of the letters and works of those who have been to America, worked hard, and saved a few dollars for development back home with plans to return. Immigrants who have made small amounts of savings in U.S. dollars often dream of building good houses or driving personal cars that few people can afford to drive in their country of origin. While these letters may exaggerate their actual success, and downplay the difficulties of their experience, friends and family back in their home country have little context in which to evaluate these accounts of life in the United States they receive. Moreover, it is a well-known psychological principle that people tend to hear and believe reports that are consistent with either what one already believes or what one wants to believe. Given conditions in many African countries for the bulk of their citizens, one would certainly expect many to hold wish-filled hopes for a better life. If one could not reasonably envision achieving that better life in one's own homeland, it should not be unexpected that one might transfer those hopes and dreams to a distant land portrayed as paradise on earth on television, in the movies, and through the other visual media so easily accessible today. This, then, are the means whereby some African migrants' hopes are built up beyond any reasonable likelihood they can be fulfilled, whether in Europe or the United States. Still, desperation will drive many to emigrate and hope, whether rational or delusional, based on what others have told them.

The American Dream and Family Values

Another major challenge in the pursuit of the American dream is the place of, and the import-ance of, the family to an African immigrant. In African culture, the child belongs to the society and therefore the upbringing of a child in the moral sense is a collective work of the society (Clinton 1996). This is in stark contrast to the American family system where the onus of bringing up a child entirely lies on the parents. The importance of the family as a basic unit and driving force that motivates the African immigrants to seek ways to improve the state (and the estate) of their families both here in America and back in their African Homeland can't be overlooked. Many African immigrants are up to the task of doing two to three work shifts a day in order to make their families live a decent life, whether in America or back in Africa where they come from. Yet in Africa families would normally benefit from a degree – and perhaps a substantial degree – of child care support to facilitate complicated and time-consuming parental work schedules. This corporate responsibility is engrained in the African culture where communalism is the mode of life. The community becomes the custodian of an individual whereby societal norms dictate that one must at all times subscribe to the com-munity ideals. For example, the idea that a child belongs to the community in Africa is not merely a matter of rhetoric. Rather, if the upbringing of a child is the responsibility of every member of the community then arrangements will be in place, or will be instituted for the welfare of the child and community, in Africa. In contrast, where the American values dictate that a parent or parents are solely responsible for his, her, or their child, child care will simply devolve into one more onerous obligation to carry out virtually alone.

Bringing up a child by an African immigrant family in America is a hard job since by trad-ition, one parent has to primarily keep a keen eye on the child, and his or her development, until he or she is 18 or 21, unless there are cultural others who can serve in the parents' place. This scenario has made most immigrant families seek to employ the services of a nanny to care for younger children, who is probably "imported" specifically for that task from Africa. This affords an African family couple the space for them to engage in employment knowing that there is an African adult responsible for the youngest children back in their home. This model mimics the village setting in many African nations, where other adults in the com-munity provide supervision and care. To some African immigrants, this responsibility is seen as an impediment to the attainment of their American dreams, whether one member of the couple provides child supervision or a nanny is employed.

The family therefore can support the realization of one's dreams or can ruin the prospects of fulfilling them, especially when the extended family back in Africa sees an immigrant dreamer as an automated machine that provides money and other resources needed to take care of all other family members who have remained behind. As we took occasion to observe earlier, remittances from expatriated Africans constitute a major source of funds, both for family members who remain in Africa and for the economics of their respective homelands (Okome 2012, 208–212). The extended family also still forms an important part of their com-munity connectedness and cultural identity. This idea is well expressed in the words of one of the discussants from research in St. Paul:

> **C4:** My family is very important. But what is my American dream when I came to America at this age? My dream was that my family, especially my wife and children

may have all they need. We brought our children here so that they can have the American education and prosper. That was our dream me and my wife. Had it been that I had no children, there is no way I could have come to America. Because the job I had was enough to give me a good life and guaranteed me good retirement benefits which were ok. But since I knew the conditions in Kenya were not conducive with the change of governments, I said to myself, let me take my children to America so that I can realize the dreams of my children in America. My dream of seeing my children progressing and prospering is still what I am praying for. And I can say that the Lord is good. Despite ups and downs of this country, our children are sometimes doing things which are not good but still I can say we are together. We are still pursuing this American dream. And my dream is that my children achieve something. That was my dream when I was coming here. I did not come here to go school. I came here specifically for my children to go school and that is what I pray for my children every day every night. Soon and very soon I may realize that dream.

Marindi 2018, 92

Other challenges with respect to child care in the United States include the non-existence of community spirit in bringing up children akin to that found in Africa. Paid child care can be rudimentary, essentially bureaucratic, and – at worst – unfeeling in the United States. Where a child belongs to the community in African culture, it is arguably more attentive, supportive, and embracing of community values (Amos 2013). In underscoring this point, Degbey (2012) argues that it is within the extended family set up where "social and moral norms and safeguards both material and spiritual customs and traditions as well as providing a variety of role models preparing the way for adulthood" (Degbey 2012, cited and quoted in Amos 2013). Amos (2013) beautifully advances the role of an extended family in child upbringing when she writes, "The uniqueness of this system with regards to parenting in our traditional African communities is that the responsibility in taking care of the child is not only to the biological parents. This is shared by all in the extended family. This is buttressed by the African proverb on parenting which says that, 'a single hand cannot nurse a child.' This implies that although the mother has the responsibility of taking care of the child, the responsibility is being shared by all."

Raising Children in an African Immigrant American Community in the Land of Plenty

In the realm of American social life, the children of African immigrants are raised in an environment that neither embraces fully the culture of their parents, nor embraces fully the culture in which they are raised, due to the amalgamation of cultures that surround them. This dual culture effect is often further enhanced for African immigrants to the United States due to movements back and forth from one locality to another. On the positive side, these children have an opportunity to learn other people's cultures – in addition to a sort of standard American culture – and adopt ways to live together with each other harmoniously. In the financial sphere, the parents often find themselves in a rat race in order to meet the bills – including for paid child care – and thus afford to live a good life in the United States, regardless of educational and occupational attainment.

In the realm of spirituality, children of African immigrant families face a diversity of religious beliefs and traditions that may have been less likely to be part of their experience had their immigrant families remained in their home country. From Mormons to Muslims, from

Anglicans to Baptists, from Pentecostals to Lutherans, and from Catholics to Seventh Day Adventists, African immigrant families may have little experience with these (mostly) western religious traditions before arriving in the United States. Correspondingly, even in the small pocket of an African immigrant community in the United States, immigrants may have trouble connecting with traditional African religious sources, doctrines, or practices since these differ widely due to culture and country of origin. These varied religious encounters leave African immigrants often confused about which traditions to embrace – especially in the absence of proper guidance from parents and elder family members, which African culture encourages them to honor, respect, and consult. Children in such families can become "casualties" of multicultural immersion, lost in the economic rat race being run by their parents but without any separate moral or spiritual tradition to guide them. Like many immigrants to a new land and culture, these African immigrant children find that they belong neither here nor there.

Thus, African immigrants to the United States experience many of the same culturally dislocating experiences that immigrants from other non-English speaking cultures experience (Pike and Crocker 2020). When less time is dedicated by parents to child-rearing, the church, and the community, the effort to nurture children holistically, that is physically, mentally, spiritually, and socially, can fail. Children may be unable to develop a connection to any religious, moral, or spiritual tradition. African immigrants to the United States, immersed in a culture that is predominantly Christian, may face difficulty in conveying some connection to that broad tradition to their children. Like many other immigrant groups, the "second generation" may be drawn ineluctably to the many cultural diversions offered by the contemporary United States and the twenty-first-century ease of communication via the internet. The importance of developing a spiritual tradition, recognizing the presence of God in their lives, and other cultural particularities for shaping religious faith, or specifically Christian discipleship, may well fade into the background. These African immigrant children – like the children of other immigrant groups who have gone before them – may be left in the dark, scrambling for the comfort, belonging, and nurture that the presence of their parents and a shared religious tradition would have offered. Yet it is a fact of life that none "wants to be wondering through trials without a sense of belonging and purpose" (Yust 2004). It is a spiritual dilemma that an African immigrant separated from his/her religious tradition of origin cannot easily solve.

Opportunities for African Immigrant Families in the United States

African immigrants in the United States may deride many experiences of their new homeland as less than a home full of opportunities and potentialities. As we have discussed, and as our interviews in St. Paul have reflected, their actual experiences are mixed. By and large, we can say African immigrants' stay in America may still be a gateway to better social and economic improvement. The United States can provide a chance for immigrants to work hard and long hours enough to guarantee upward social and economic mobility, but American culture often does so at a cost. With enabling environments, African immigrants have come up with business enterprises that they would have not managed to start back in their African homelands. For example, there is a television program aired on Kenyan airwaves dubbed, "Daring Abroad." The show features Kenyans excelling in business and entrepreneurships abroad in other countries. In one of the episodes aired, the narrator, one Alex Chamwada, tells a story of four Kenyans who own over 300 trucks doing freight business across the United States under the business name Seagate Holdings. Alex Kalundu, Michael Njenga,

Herbert Langat, and Bernard Langat immigrated to the United States as students but ended up identifying a business opportunity in trucking and logistic freight services in the spirit of the American dream. By doing so, they created over 300 job opportunities for Americans as well as offering a mentorship program for graduates in the community (CHAMS MEDIA TV 2019). Another example of an African immigrant who has embraced the American dream in the line of business, is Kevin Onyona. Based in Virginia, Onyona ventured into restaurant business under the business name "Swahili Village Restaurants." He described plans to set up over 50 restaurants across America (CHAMS MEDIA TV 2021). Individual success stories, of course, do not in and of themselves demonstrate the American dream is a viable model for all immigrants. Indeed, this Kenyan television show may end up doing more damage than good since viewers may mistakenly see themselves as able to emulate these African entrepreneurs' successes.

There are other tangible advantages that African immigrants to the United States can obtain even as upward economic mobility eludes them. The availability of quality medical care and insurance has enabled African immigrants improve and prolong their life as compared to when they were back in Africa. The quick medical evacuation in instances of emergency is something that African immigrants don't take for granted. Quality health care has improved their birth rates by reducing infant mortality rates as compared to those found in their African countries (Martinez et al. 2015; Omenka et al. 2020).

The respect of rule of law has meant that justice is afforded to those who seek it in corridors of justice without fearing political interference in the United States as is often the case in many African countries (Ssensikombi 2017). However, African immigrants need to adhere to the spirit and letter of the law to receive its benefits. The danger exists that American immigrants will cry foul when the large arm of the law catches up with those who do not fully adopt law-abiding behavior. African and Caribbean immigrants to the United States face a complicated status vis-à-vis the American justice system, however. This is due to the fact that black pigmentation is a significant marker and often a salient fact with respect to American police and other representatives of the criminal justice system. African and Caribbean blacks often arrive without a full appreciation of what blackness connotes in the context of historical American racism. As Africans or Caribbean blacks, often from predominantly black nations, these immigrants are unprepared for enacting and accepting a devalued status solely based on skin color (Arthur 2009, 2017–2020). Given the inherent biases that inform parts of American society, black African and Caribbean immigrants can experience discriminatory treatment by the police and other elements of the American justice system. As Americans full well know, college campuses are not representative of the treatment one may receive on urban streets in the United States. Immigrants may need to learn to navigate both society and the justice system in their new land.

Conclusion

Overall there are contrasting challenges between what the American dream looked like in the mind of an African immigrants before and after they settled in America. Now that they have seen the reality of the American dream, African immigrants must translate their dreams into reality. They have to work hard and spend long hours to improve their lives and ensure a better future. In order for their children to enjoy a quality education, the parents have to intentionally invest in their education. In terms of freedom and justice, like other immigrant populations, African must realize that both concepts require respect for individual choices as well as a strict observance of the law of the land.

Note

1 The 1924 Act instituted a total ban on Asian immigration to the United States (Kolawole 2017, 380, 383). The 1965 Act eliminated this ban.

References

Adams, James Truslow. 1933. *The Epic of America*. Boston, MA: Little, Brown, and Co.

Amos, P.M. 2013. "Parenting and Culture – Evidence from Some African Communities." In Maria Lucia Seidl-De-Moura, Ed., *Parenting in South American and African Contexts*. https://www. intechopen.com/books/3440. Retrieved November 14, 2021. https://www.intechopen.com/ chapters/45760; https://doi.org/10.5772/56967.

Arthur, John A. 2009. "Immigrants and the American System of Justice: Perspectives of African and Caribbean Blacks." In Okpewho and Nzegwu, Eds., *The New African Diaspora*. Bloomington, IN: Indiana University Press.

Arthur, John A., Joseph Takougang, and Thomas Owusu, Eds. 2012. *Africans in Global Migration: Searching for Promised Lands*. Lanham: Lexington Books.

Arthur, John A. and Thomas Owusu. 2012. "Africans in Global Migration: Still Searching for Promised Lands." In Arthus, Takougang, and Owusu, Eds., *Africans in Global Migration: Searching for Promised Lands*. Lanham: Lexington Books.

Beauchemin, Cris, Marie-Laurence Flahaux, and Bruno Schoumaker. 2020. "Three Sub-Saharan Migration Systems in Times of Policy Restriction." *Comparative Migration Studies* 8(1): 19. https:// doi.org/10.1186/s40878-020-0174-y.

Boundless 2021. "Where Black Immigrant Come From." https://www.boundless.com/research/ black-immigrants-in-the-united-states-status-challenges-and-impacts/ Retrieved November 3, 2021.

CHAMS MEDIA TV. 2021. *Daring Abroad Sn3 Ep1: Towards 50 Restaurants in 50 US Cities – Kevin Onyona's Journey Begins*. Accessed August 12, 2021. https://www.youtube.com/watch?v=rblKJY6b0Pc.

CHAMS MEDIA TV. 2019. *From 3 to 300 Trucks : The Four Kenyans Excelling in Trucking in U.S.A.* Accessed August 12, 2021. https://www.youtube.com/watch?v=VhX3rUBEfAI&t=84s.

Clinton, Hillary. 1996. *It Takes a Village: And Other Lessons Children Teach Us*. New York: Simon and Shuster.

Defoort Cécily and Godfrey Rogers. 2008. "Long-Term Trends in International Migration: An Analysis of the Six Main Receiving Countries." *Population* 63(2): 285–317. DOI: 10.3917/popu.802.0317. https://www.cairn-int.info/journal-population-2008-2-page-285.htm.

Degbey, D.L. 2012. "African Family Structure." Cited and quoted in Amos, P.M. (2013). "Parenting and Culture – Evidence from Some African Communities." In Maria Lucia Seidl-De-Moura, Ed., *Parenting in South American and African Contexts*. https://www.intechopen.com/ books/3440 Retrieved 11/14/21. https://www.intechopen.com/chapters/45760; https://doi. org/10.5772/56967.

Echeverria-Estrada, Carlos and Jeanne Batalova. 2019. *Sub-Saharan African Immigrants in the United States*. Washington, DC: Migration Policy Institute. https://www.migrationpolicy.org/article/ sub-saharan-african-immigrants-united-states-2018. Retrieved November 3, 2021.

Emancipation Proclamation. January 1, 1863. Presidential Proclamations, 1791–1991; Record Group 11; General Records of the United States Government; National Archives.

Ette, Ezekiel Umo. 2012. Nigerian immigrants in the United States: Race, Identity, and Acculturation. Lanham, Md: Lexington Book.

Fitzgerald, F. Scott. 2004. *The Great Gatsby*. New York: Scribner.

Franklin, Benjamin. 1895. *An Autobiography*. Philadelphia, PA: Henry Artemis Company.

Hassène Kassar, Diaa Marzouk, Wagida A. Anwar, Chérifa Lakhoua, Kari Hemminki, and Meriem Khyatti. August 2014. "Emigration flows from North Africa to Europe." *European Journal of Public Health* 24(suppl_1): 2–5. https://doi.org/10.1093/eurpub/cku105.

Hochschild, Jennifer L. 1995. *Facing Up to the American Dream: Race, Class, and the Soul of the Nation*. Princeton, NJ: Princeton University Press.

Immigration Act of 1924. Pub. L. No. 68-139, 43 Stat. 153 (1924).

Immigration Act of 1990. Pub. L. 101-649, 104 Stat. 4978 (1990).

Immigration and Nationality Act of 1965. Pub. L. No. 89-236, 79 Stat. 911 (1965).

Kaba, Amadu Jacky. 2009. "African's Migration Brain Drain: Factors Contributing to the Mass Emigration of Africa's Elite to the West." In Isidore Okpewho and Nkiru Nzegwu, Eds., *The New African Diaspora*. Bloomington, IN: Indiana University Press.

Kolawole, Bolatito. 2017. "African Immigrants, Intersectionality, and the Increasing Need for Visibility in the Current Immigration Debate." *Columbia Journal of Race and Law* 7(2): 373–409.

Marindi, Enock Ariga. 2018. *Living the American Dream: Faith Formation and The Missio Dei Dilemma among Seventh Day Adventist African American Immigrant Families*. Unpublished Master's Degree Thesis. St. Paul: Luther Seminary.

Martinez, Omar et al. 2015. "Evaluating the Impact of Immigration Policies on Health Status among Undocumented Immigrants: A Systematic Review." *Journal of Immigrant and Minority Health* 17(3): 947–970. https://doi.org/10.1007/s10903-013-9968-4

McCabe, Kristen. 2011. "African Immigrants in the United States in 2009." Washington, DC: Migration Policy Institute. https://www.migrationpolicy.org/article/african-immigrants-united-states-2009. Retrieved November 3, 2021.

Okome, Mojúbáolú Olúfúnké. 2012. "African Immigrant Relationship with Homeland Countries." In John A. Arthur, Jospeh Takougang, and Thomas Owusu, Eds., *Africans in Global Migration: Searching for Promised Lands*. Lanham: Lexington Books, 199–224.

Okpewho, Isidore. 2009. "Introduction: Can We "Go Home Again"?." In Isidore Okpewho and Nkiru Nzegwu, Eds., *The New African Diaspora*. Bloomington, IN: Indiana University Press.

Okpewho, Isidore and Nkiru Nzegwu. 2009. *The New African Diaspora*. Bloomington, IN: Indiana University Press.

Omenka, Ogbonnaya I et al. January 8, 2020. "Understanding the Healthcare Experiences and Needs of African Immigrants in the United States: A Scoping Review." *BMC Public Health* 20(1): 27. https://doi.org/10.1186/s12889-019-8127-9

Pike, Ivy L. and Rebecca M. Crocker. October 2020. "'My Own Corner of Loneliness:' Social Isolation and Place among Mexican Immigrants in Arizona and Turkana Pastoralists of Kenya." *Transcultural Psychiatry* 57(5): 661–672. https://doi.org/10.1177/1363461520938286.

Refugee Act of 1980. Pub. L. 96-212, 94 Stat. 102 (1980).

Ssensikombi, Alexander. May 28, 2017. The Independence of the Judiciary: An Assessment of the Reality of the Constitutional Doctrine in Uganda. Available at SSRN: https://ssrn.com/abstract=2984300 or http://dx.doi.org/10.2139/ssrn.2984300.

Takougang, Joseph and Bassirou Tidjani. 2012. "Making In-Roads: African Immigrants and Business Opportunities in the United States." In John A. Arthur, Joseph Takougang, and Thomas Owusu, Eds., *Africans in Global Migration: Searching for Promised Lands*. Lanham: Lexington Books, 117–134.

U.S. Census. 2020. https://www.census.gov/library/stories/2021/08/improved-race-ethnicity-measures-reveal-united-states-population-much-more-multiracial.html#:~:text=In%202020%2C%20the%20Black%20or,million%20and%2012.6%25%20in%202010. Retrieved November 3, 2021.

Yust, Karen-Marie. 2004. *Real Kids, Real Faith: Practices for Nurturing Children's Spiritual Lives*. San Francisco, CA: Jossey-Bass, xx.

12

THE BOYS FROM LITTLE MEXICO REDUX

Dreaming the immigrant dream

Steve Wilson

Woodburn Now

July 2021 US Census Estimates

Oregon: Population 4,217, 737. 13.4 percent Latino.

Woodburn, Oregon: Population 26,273. 56.8 percent Latino

I drove south from bicycle-riding, gluten-freeing, micro-brewing Portland to the Woodburn Premium Outlets, one of those ubiquitous American freeway shopping malls, then a little further east into downtown Woodburn, a few square blocks of very distinct businesses: Zapateria El Jalicience, El Mercadito, Club Saludable Celular, La Morenita Tortillas, several of the best taquerias in the state, and the town zocalo, the public square that is part of nearly every village in Mexico.

From the zocalo, I could glimpse the lights of the high school soccer pitch where the Woodburn Bulldogs, locally called Los Perros, were taking on a team from the southern end of the Willamette Valley. The game had already started by the time I climbed into the stands and the overhead lights glared down on the pitch like a constellation of tiny moons. The evening was cold and a handful of fans were scattered throughout the bleachers, bundled in jackets and masked.

Woodburn, wearing blue, was playing a possession game, patiently protecting the ball and making short, crisp passes. On the field and in the stands, shouts rang out in Spanish. The players seemed unhurried, even languid, but the ball sped from foot to foot. I glanced at the scoreboard: 1-0, Woodburn.

For the last ten years, Los Perros boys varsity soccer team had dominated Oregon high school athletics. Beginning with its first state championship in 2010, Los Perros followed up with wins in 2011 and 2012, then four straight from 2016 to 2019. That's seven championships in ten years. In 2019, the Woodburn girls team won its first state championship as well. COVID-19 had disrupted the 2020 season, pushing it into the spring of 2021 when I visited. The Oregon State Athletic Association would eventually cancel the state's championship tournament, potentially placing an asterisk next to Woodburn's string of first-place finishes.

DOI: 10.4324/9781003326243-15

2021 would also mark a move from the 4A league to 5A, meaning that Woodburn High School (WHS) would face teams from larger schools, schools with a bigger student body from which to draw their student athletes. Could the Bulldogs continue to win against better competition? Coach Leroy Sanchez, a WHS graduate and one-time varsity soccer player, seemed confident.

"We have moved up in classification before," he said. "It gives us a good opportunity to measure ourselves against the best teams in the state."

Talking after the game, Sanchez, also the school social worker, gave me the kind of coach speech that a more cynical person might suspect isn't entirely genuine: the outcome of the games isn't important; what really matters is fostering teamwork and helping young men to grow up; winning games is a side effect of learning hard work—that kind of thing. But you get the sense that Sanchez means it.

Sanchez was a student on the Woodburn team when they went to the 3A championship in 1998 and lost. When he began to work at WHS, Sanchez found a second job as an assistant coach, years later becoming the head coach and eventually winning the Northwest Region Coach of the Year for the 2018–2019 season.

Sanchez had left Woodburn to get his Master's in Social Work at Portland State University and as a college-educated, bright, bilingual young man, he could have moved just about anywhere. But he chose to return to Woodburn because he wanted to improve life for the next generation of kids growing up in Oregon's only majority-minority city.

Sanchez came back partly out of a sense of responsibility to his family, who still live in town, but also because he wanted to be part of Woodburn's future, a future in which the town's population is increasingly like him, straddling the Latinx and Anglo worlds and perhaps finding a way to blur the edges. He returned because he believes in the school system, with its focus on promoting bilingualism for everybody. He returned because it's home.

After speaking with Sanchez, I talked to several graduating seniors as they made their way out to the parking lot. One wanted to go into IT. One wanted to go into Business Administration. One was interested in Sports Management. They were tall and fit and exuded confidence that the next stage in their journey would go as smoothly as the last few years.

I asked them what happened in the second half of the game when the opposing team, West Albany, scored twice in ten minutes.

"They wanted it more," one said. There were some shrugs and laughter as if the game's outcome didn't matter. Was this a buy-in to Coach Sanchez's belief that playing the right way is more important than winning? Or was this indifference—the result of a strange season during a strange year—or worse, disrespect of what lay before them?

Woodburn Then

July 2005 US Census Estimates

Oregon: Population 3,641, 56. 9.9 percent Latino

Woodburn, Oregon: Population 22,160. 54.4 percent Latino.

Back in 2005, I followed the Woodburn Bulldogs through their fall soccer season, attending games and practices, interviewing the players, the coaches, school administrators, and parents, and I turned the experience into a book: *The Boys from Little Mexico: A Season Chasing the American Dream.*

I called the boys Carlos, Angel, and Octavio. Most of the teenagers who made up the 2005WHS varsity soccer team got fictional names to protect them from the facts of their birth, the movement of their parents, and their legal status. Half of the team was made of kids who had arrived in the United States when they were too young to choose, stuck in the No Man's Dreamers Land: American by culture and Mexican by birth.

In 2005, the WHS varsity soccer team had never won a championship, and the high school was graduating only 70 percent of its students. The handful of students who went on to college was mostly from the school's white minority. There were rumblings that the state might take over the school and the principal and administrators were scrambling to come up with something new, something that hadn't been tried before, to turn things around quickly.

What I saw off the field, in terms of the dominant culture accepting those young men, their educational success, and their professional futures, was mirrored neatly on the soccer pitch. By some measures, the Woodburn Bulldogs were successful: the year I followed the team marked 20 straight years of making the playoffs, an Oregon state record for a major team sport. But the team had never won a state championship and despite the community passion for and knowledge of soccer that was probably unrivaled in Oregon, Los Perros were losing to teams simply because players on those teams had the advantage of wealth and training. Most of the Bulldogs couldn't afford to join premier club teams and learn from expensive private coaches. Most of them didn't have parents with the flexibility to travel across the state or into other states to club tournaments. Many of them had to work to help support their families or look after younger siblings when school was finished.

Off the field, these same disadvantages limited the Bulldogs' job opportunities, academic feats, college choices, and career training. Life improved in many ways for the people who moved to Woodburn from Mexico and Central America, but the children of those immigrants didn't always experience the same rise in financial or social standing. And those first-generation high school students could see the obstacles with an unrelenting clarity.

The adults associated with the 2005 Bulldogs, like then Coach Mike Flannigan, also a Language Arts teacher, saw something disturbing when they looked closely at their students. To Flannigan, it seemed as if his players internalized the obstacles the outside world was presenting. Coach Flannigan was so concerned about the mental state of his student athletes that on the first day of practice, he gathered his team in a classroom and gave them a handout titled "Characteristics of the Mentally Tough Competitor."

Mike had created the handout early in his coaching career to address what he considered a major hurdle to athletic success: his team's mental state. He had seen it over and over on the field and in the classroom. His teams had talent but lacked confidence. In one memorable playoff game, tied at the end of regulation, the Bulldogs' best two players missed their penalty kicks—missed the goal entirely. In the classroom, Coach Flannigan's sophomore students every year showed him during preparations for the state's mandatory reading and writing tests that they expected to fail.

Mike thought he understood why. His students had no history of success. They had few positive role models. They grew up in homes with poorly educated parents who spoke little English. Some of them didn't have permission to be in the country. Most were poor. By the time they got to high school they had figured out that the future of Latinx students in America did not include wealth or fame. In the classroom, they stopped trying. On the field, they wilted when they were behind and fell to pieces when they lost.

A newspaper reporter once pointed this out to Coach Flannigan, saying that of all the high school teams he covered, only Woodburn's soccer players wept when their season was over. Mike knew exactly what he meant. Losing a playoff game demolished his players. They fell to the grass, unashamedly sobbing; their heads and shoulders drooped; they looked as if they had lost a family member.

The members of the 2005 team had a name for this. They called it The Woodburn Curse. For years players talked about the Woodburn curse—making it to the playoffs only to be beaten by the team that won the championship. Making it to the championship but losing to the refs. Making it to the playoffs. Losing.

The curse struck in 2005 in the second round of the state playoffs when Woodburn lost an away game amid pelting rain and collapsing players. Over the course of the game, Coach Flannigan felt his team give up and knew that he had failed them. Not because of the final score but because he was unable to give his boys confidence. It was all their expectations, he thought. They fall behind and think, "Shit, we're going to lose this and then we're not going to win the state championship and I'm not going to go to college. I'm going to be picking berries for the rest of my life."

Miguel

One of the students on Coach Flannigan's 2005 team was sophomore Miguel Arellano, who in 2020 was working at Oregon State University (OSU). An intelligent and intense father of two daughters. Miguel's job as OSU's Basic Needs Navigator places him at the junction of education and social welfare, helping poverty-level OSU students figure out our country's complex social services network.

Like many others in Woodburn, Miguel's parents had traveled from Mexico looking for an opportunity to work, which they found in the fields and agricultural infrastructure of the Willamette Valley. In the summer before the 2005 season, when the team had informal practices, Miguel was one of many students who were often late to evening practices due to long hours at nearby farms.

Miguel also attended WHS during a turbulent time. Bogged down for years with low graduation rates, struggling with a large number of English Language Learners and with the children of migrants who didn't always make it through a school year in one location, the high school had gambled on the Bill and Melinda Gates Foundation's Small Schools education reform project.

The project's guidelines required WHS to switch from a single comprehensive high school of about 1,200 students to four specialized small schools of about 400 students each. The transition was complex, requiring physical changes to the buildings as well as re-training the habits of students and teachers.

Miguel was one of the students caught in the middle: his first two years at WHS were at the comprehensive high school. He spent his second two years at WEBBS, the Wellness, Business, and Sports School.

When we talked during the 2005 season, Miguel planned to go to college and become a parole officer. But when he arrived at OSU, Miguel selected a program in Human Services, returning to get his Master's in Education.

"I wanted to help people," Miguel said. "I thought through probation and criminal justice I could help, but I changed my mind and thought, 'where can I address the root causes of crime?' I decided that I wanted to address education as a pathway for economic stability and critical thinking skills."

Miguel thought that he was prepared for college. His grades were excellent. He had a full scholarship. But his first year at OSU turned out to be an endless lesson in how he didn't belong. Miguel seemed to do everything differently than the other (almost all white) students: different expectations, different cultural references, and different ways of working with others. For a while, Miguel was lost.

"I would be put into group projects and try to participate and I would be ignored," he said. "I would try to be collaborative and people would say, 'No, you do this.' They'd give me insignificant things. There's a cultural mismatch. My world view and values were so different than that of the dominant culture. People's privilege and classism spewed out during class projects."

Miguel didn't know how to breach the gap between his upbringing and that of his white college classmates. Part of his identity had been formed working summers and weekends in farms and nurseries alongside his parents, but that seemed to be foreign to his classmates. Part of his identity had been formed by playing soccer for a club team that couldn't afford interstate travel; Miguel had to sell cans to afford soccer jerseys. His classmates? Not so much.

"It made me doubt myself. Do I belong here? Am I smart enough? You start questioning yourself, doubting yourself," Miguel said. "You wonder, 'How do I connect with others?'"

The first of his friends and family to go to college, Miguel had nobody to turn to for help and considered dropping out. Then he found OSU's Cultural Resource Center and the Centro Cultural César Chávez, which offer support to campus Latinx students. He began taking smaller classes with other minority students and his engagement changed. He had found a community.

But he wishes that WHS had better prepared him for college. Not academically but culturally.

"It would have been great to learn about the cultural clash you are about to experience," Miguel said. "And to learn some language about how to cope with it."

"You grow up being othered and knowing you're marginalized. You get messages as a farmworker and as the child of farmworkers. It's amplified in white spaces. These conversations could be had with high school students. What does it mean to be poor and working class in high school versus when you are in college at a privileged place?"

After graduation, married and now a father, Miguel moved around a bit: big city Portland (too much traffic) and small-town Albany (too many Confederate flags), before returning to Corvallis to accept a job at OSU. He feels comfortable in Corvallis, a small city surrounded by farmland, he's pleased with the dual-language immersion programs available through the public schools, and he's motivated by his job helping low-income and homeless students, some of them the children of farmworkers like himself.

"If your basic needs are not secure it's harder to focus on studies," Miguel said.

Miguel was fortunate not to need much assistance himself, having secured a full scholarship. Nevertheless, his mother always worried that he didn't have enough and packed him meals to take home whenever he came to visit, even though he received three meals a day at the dorm.

Today, Miguel sees how his education has already created distance between himself and his peers. "I don't have to worry about the basics," Miguel said. "That sets me apart from my friends to some extent. But I don't see myself as better. My brother's an electrician and makes much more money that I do. I still have to navigate everything as a first generation professional. I'm the only person of color in my office."

Miguel pointed out that he is fortunate to work indoors, have a 401k, a flexible schedule, and a degree of job security that his parents may never achieve. And not just his parents. Many of Miguel's friends work at unskilled jobs. But, like many who are the first in their family to go to college, Miguel is very aware of the ways that his degree has set him apart.

"Being the first means also how do I navigate back home?" Miguel said. "I was always self-aware when I went back to Woodburn to visit from college. I didn't want to make people feel like I was better than them."

I asked Miguel if he thought there was a ceiling above which Latinos could not go. He said there is, perhaps, a thinner, higher ceiling than before but an ever-present one. And he worries about how young Latinx graduates will cope with the wealth gap and the debt created by a university degree.

"I feel that the way wealth works, and with education creating so much debt, your degree doesn't have the same market value as it did 40 or 50 years ago," he said. "So, you have to wonder if college is worth it. More students are graduating but their education is worth less."

Miguel's thoughts echo widely studied patterns of immigrants. According to the Pew Research Center and the Economic Policy Institute, immigrants typically earn less than US-born workers and never catch up ("Generation Differences," Mora). Their children, less encumbered with language, education, and cultural differences, usually earn similar amounts to multi-generation American peers. However, the long-term wealth of established families (things like family businesses, real estate holdings, and inheritance) can take generations to establish. With rising college costs—a 25 percent increase over the last decade—and rising student debt, building that wealth is becoming more difficult. Thinking about the students he helps and the next generation of his family, Miguel worries that this is a trend that will continue.

"Generational wealth and-long term compound interest has helped white families for a long time. We're starting from way behind. How can we hope to catch up?" Miguel paused. "The American Dream is less of a reality now."

Despite his concerns, Miguel is hopeful for positive change in the United States.

"When I was in high school I would wake up at 6 am in the summer to go work in the field," he said. "I didn't like it. But I got through that by looking toward the future. So, I'm optimistic and hopeful that the country can heal and get better. But I'm not naïve."

Trump

On May 26, 2017, a mentally disturbed white man named Jeremy Christian began haranguing two teenage black Muslim girls on Portland's MAX light rail. Three men stood up to defend the girls and Christian slashed at them with a pocketknife, killing two of the men before being subdued.

The incident became national news as an example of the increase of racially-motivated attacks in the country, gaining even more attention when then-president Donald Trump seemed to ignore the attack for days, causing TV journalist Dan Rather to write an open letter to Trump, encouraging him to address the incident.

As the father of two brown-skinned daughters, the Jeremy Christian MAX attack smacked Miguel's optimism in the mouth.

"I had hopeless days for their future. The stabbing was a local version of the national rhetoric."

It was far from the only racially motivated incident that troubled Miguel. He recalled taking his family to a Red Robin's for dinner, where he saw a large chalk wall inside the restaurant lobby. The chalk wall was a blank canvas on which customers could draw and write messages. As his daughters picked up shards of chalk to begin their own drawings, Miguel saw a large mural of Donald Trump and next to it, the words "Build the Wall Go Home."

Miguel directed his daughters' attention elsewhere, distracting them from the mural until they were seated. Before leaving the restaurant, he quickly erased the image and words. He moved out of Albany soon after to return to Corvallis.

"It was way more apparent there," Miguel said. "This community doesn't want you."

Others agree with Miguel. Two recent WHS graduates, one of whom had been a student during the Trump presidency, said that fellow students, even the American-born children of Latinx immigrants, taunted those without legal documents, and at high school, the question of nationality, always delicate, became a topic to be feared.

Miguel pointed out that although anti-Latinx racism may have peaked during Trump's presidency, his departure hasn't been followed by more acceptance. Miguel still has undocumented family members and he worries about how the post-Trump world will affect them. He worries that they aren't safe. In most places outside of Woodburn, he experiences a low-level anxiety about how he is viewed by others. "There's always the feeling that you don't belong," he said.

"It always comes from institutions, "Miguel said. "You don't belong. You can't get the Oregon Health Plan. You can't get DMV ID or licensure. The fear was highlighted because of Trump. I realize now how thankful I am that my parents landed in Woodburn and not Lake Oswego [a white suburb of Portland]. Then I would have had to navigate the white world from a young age. At least in Woodburn my culture is normal."

Kaylee and Michael Vasquez

Miguel's experience with university life was echoed by nearly every other Woodburn grad I spoke with, both those who had graduated decades ago and those who are still at the university. As a person, they felt unprepared for the college experience. But it was never the academics that felt untenable, it was the shift in cultural surroundings.

Kaylee and Michael Vasquez, siblings who both graduated from WHS and matriculated with full scholarships to the University of Oregon U of O), described their experiences using language eerily similar to Miguel's.

Michael, a handsome young man with a broad smile, graduated from U of O with a degree in Political Science. His freshman year at the university was a struggle, he said. He was uncomfortable joining groups and was surprised by how many of his fellow students had gone to private schools or had private tutors. With so few Latinx students at the university, Michael instead found common ground with first-generation white college students from Oregon's poor, rural communities.

"College was an eye opener," Michael said. "Everything I knew was wrong. We were raised to learn math and writing but academics at a university is much different. Culturally, I didn't feel like I fit in. How do you have a conversation with somebody whose life is so different?"

The other Woodburn students at U of O struggled as well. Out of the 12 WHS students that started college with Michael, only four graduated with him. Those who dropped out said that college wasn't for them. But to Michael, the problem wasn't a mismatch between the students' goals and university life, the problem was that Woodburn's students didn't know how to navigate the world outside of their hometown.

"We need to be better at coping with the reality of what is outside of Woodburn," Michael said. "Our high school kids aren't being prepared. It's a [cultural] bubble. Money wasn't the problem. They had scholarships. It was cultural."

I asked Michael what he meant. Was it the experience of being a racial minority on a mostly white campus? Did he encounter overt racism? Michael said no, it wasn't so simple. The discomfort came from assumptions being made about reference points, about values, about history, and those assumptions were built into the fabric of the classroom experience.

"You're taught from a white perspective," Michael said. "But us Latinos don't understand it. We didn't live it. Teachers need to be more culturally competent."

The dissonance Michael experienced fed into an anger already simmering under the surface. It wasn't an anger toward Anglo culture or Republicans or the America he grew up in. It was an anger aimed at his hometown. During his time at college, Michael was seriously pissed off at Woodburn and at WHS. Pissed off enough that he planned to move away when he graduated and find some other town where he might fit in.

Part of Michael's anger might have come from the way he was handled at WHS. When moving from middle to high school in Woodburn, students are asked to rank the small schools into which they want to be placed. Michael ended up in his last choice, Ace, the "International Studies" small school, the school into which many immigrant kids are placed and which puts more emphasis on language instruction than other subjects. But for Michael, born in the US, fluent in English, and part of the WHS varsity wrestling squad, being placed in Ace felt like Harry Potter being sorted into Hufflepuff. His friends were in WEBBS and the other small schools. Why was he polishing English skills that were as good as his instructor's?

After lobbying for a shift to another school, Michael was moved, but the experience clung to him like a cold wet shirt. If the entire point of the small school experiment was to make students feel seen and heard and part of a community, it failed Michael Vasquez. He took that feeling of being failed with him, carried it in his pocket, all the way through graduation and all the way through college.

Michael might have followed through on his plan to leave town and never look back. But COVID happened. When Michael graduated from college in the summer of 2020, instead of launching into a career as he had expected, Michael was sitting at home sending out resumes to a world that wasn't hiring anybody except delivery drivers. Instead of a job, Michael took an unpaid internship at the Oregon State Legislature, where he found himself inspired to move into politics. He began volunteering at Oregon's farmworker's union, Pineros y Campesinos Unidos del Noroeste (PCUN), which is based in downtown Woodburn. The volunteer work turned into a job as PCUN's Digital and National Campaigns Organizer. Michael said that the anger against WHS still simmers, but his job helped him to try and turn the emotion into action.

"My dad used to say don't run away from your problems; face them."

The job helped to do that. But it wasn't enough. He wanted to change the town. So, in 2021, Michael ran for an open position on the Woodburn School Board.

"I always felt that there was something missing," Michael said. "School wasn't preparing you for the real world. But people kept celebrating it, saying that we've got a great graduation rate, great bilingual program. But when you graduate and move on, you see the difference."

Michael's experience at WHS and U of O showed him a gap between how the school was preparing students and how they needed to be prepared.

"I started talking to coaches and mentors. I wanted something but I didn't know what it was. So, I thought, prepare yourself, get training, return to make it a better place."

At 23, Michael was the youngest person ever to run for office in Woodburn, and not surprisingly, he lost. That hasn't stopped him from making plans to change WHS. He wants the school to encourage graduates to return and discuss their experiences, to teach financial literacy and business skills, as well as practical skills like buying a car and renting an apartment—things that the mostly white, middle-class teachers might assume students will learn from their parents.

"There's so much potential in Woodburn but we can't tap into it," Michael said. "I want to change that."

Michael's younger sister, Kaylee, who played on the WHS girls soccer team, echoed her brother's desire to lead Woodburn in a new direction. For Kaylee, the focus is on building relationships.

Kaylee was in high school when she first realized the importance of networking. She had landed a medical internship at Oregon Health Sciences University (OHSU), a large teaching and research hospital in Portland. There were very few people who looked like Kaylee at OHSU (unless you counted the patients).

"The moment I started my internship I felt that I didn't belong," she said. Kaylee went looking for a Latina doctor to act as a mentor, and she found nobody.

The experience sparked an idea in Kaylee—she would grow up to be the mentor to young Latinas that she wanted for herself.

"I want to be the person to help younger people, to say this is how you do it."

Kaylee graduated from WHS with a full scholarship to the University of Oregon. But, while U of O is only an hour south of Woodburn, it can still feel far away. Kaylee insists that the only reason she is able to attend is that her family is small—one brother conveniently four years older—so while he was at college, she was at home, and when she went to college he came back.

"Kids from Latinx homes—we still have to help our parents," Kaylee said. "We value loyalty and family over everything, rather than personal growth. So how do you leave home to go to college if you still need to help take care of the younger kids in your house?"

Kaylee credits her brother as the trailblazer who helped chart a course through college waters and credits her parents both with the foresight to clearly seethe American path to success and for their ability to adapt to the American system and foster independence in herself and Michael.

"Usually it's a collective idea of family," Kaylee said, "But my parents pushed us to go to college. They would say, 'We came here for you to have a better life.' My dad would come home from working in the field in his dirty clothes to go to meetings about how to write college applications."

"My parents always said we had to go to a four-year university or join the military," Kaylee added, so early in her high school career, she began looking at universities and working toward a career in medicine.

Along with the Latinx family obligations, Kaylee worries about the mentoring gap holding back Latinx students from accessing the kind of informal cultural and professional guidance that many white students get from their friends and family.

"We need mentorship programs connecting students who graduated from WHS and are in college with students who want to go to college," she said. "We also need mentors who went to really good schools, not just the local community college."

Kaylee can feel torn between loyalty to WHS and her desire to smooth the paths of younger students. She sees that Woodburn has made positive changes but argues that it isn't enough.

"Woodburn High for a long time has been all about the graduation rate. We now have one of the highest rates in the state. But where do we go from here?"

Her answer is to raise expectations, especially when it comes to preparing for college. Kaylee's experience at WHS was that students are expected to attend community colleges or a state college if the student is an academic standout. The colleges that she dreamed of, like Harvard, Johns Hopkins, or her ideal, Stanford medical school, were never mentioned.

There are also no classes that address the life changes new college freshman are about to experience.

Kaylee said that the lack of familiarity with Oregon's dominant white culture means that a lot of students fail to launch. "You leave but you feel unprepared so you return to Woodburn where it's comfortable," she said.

She felt that her teachers, when approached, worked hard to help her, but they had limited resources themselves. Some stayed after school to help her with college applications and the letters of recommendation. But they were busy, sometimes overwhelmed with classwork. (One side effect of the small school system is that while the total population of the "school" diminishes, class sizes increase.)

Kaylee had the advantage when she first started at U of O and was feeling lost of two people: her brother, and Michelle Torres, a Woodburn grad just a few years older than Kaylee. Torres, who received a golf scholarship to U of O, is also interested in a medical career. Having Michelle at the university as a trailblazer gave Kaylee confidence that she's not sure she would have ever felt on her own.

Today, halfway through her undergrad career, Kaylee sees a future in which she returns to Woodburn to make it better. More specifically, she envisions developing a program that provides low-cost or free health care to agricultural workers in Woodburn and the surrounding area in clinics staffed by Latinx employees. "I want to get to a place where I can offer free health care."

The idea of running clinics wasn't her first focus, as she enjoys medical research. But she kept thinking about the narrative Michael had of Woodburn not living up to its possibilities and her father's emphasis on fixing the problems that you see.

"Michael and I struggled coming back and helping," Kaylee said. "We were stuck thinking that the town hadn't prepared us to succeed, and that made us resentful. But as I got older I thought, if we don't come back and help, who will?"

"The change has to happen and since we're fortunate, we have the tools, we need to use them. We don't have the privilege of not looking back like white communities do."

Woodburn High School

The feelings expressed by Michael and Kaylee were ones that I had heard in 2005 from Miguel Salinas, a retired teacher and principal of Woodburn's elementary schools, who worried that Woodburn is becoming an ethnically isolated community.

"Which is a problem if [the kids] want to succeed outside of Woodburn," he said.

Salinas has argued for decades that Woodburn needs to put resources into forms of education outside of academics, such as mentoring, and has insisted that Latinx in Woodburn and the United States will not rise as a group until Latinx citizens begin to view education as a means of accessing power.

But Salinas felt that his ideas fell on deaf ears, partly because the local population in Woodburn doesn't demand change. When he would meet with the Woodburn School Board and describe the changes he thought were necessary, the board members would reply that he was the only one asking for such change.

"They said to me, 'the phones are not ringing.' Without external stimulation, you are dependent on the goodwill of the people within the institution who have no motivation to change."

Was the school board right? Or were they missing another cultural clue? Did they understand the way their students' parents thought about high school? Or were they making assumptions based on their own upbringing and culture?

In 2006, the Chalkboard Project, a non-profit organization aiming to improve Oregon schools, surveyed low-income parents across Oregon. As reported in the Portland newspaper The Skanner, the survey found some interesting and some surprising results: Latinx parents volunteered an average of three days a year at their children's school while white parents volunteered 30 days. On the other hand, nearly a third of Latinx parents helped their kids with homework five days a week and a little more than 10 percent of white parents did the same ("Minority Parents").

The findings demonstrated some distinctly different cultural expectations. White families often view schoolwork as the individual responsibility of the student and school administration as within the family's and community's sphere of influence. But Latinx parents view schoolwork as part of a family responsibility and school administration as a task left to the experts at the school.

When the Woodburn School Board told Salinas that parents were not demanding change, it did not mean that the parents didn't want change or might not have welcomed change. It meant that the parents didn't feel it was their role to advocate for change. The parents weren't demonstrating disinterest; they were being respectful.

There also may be very different expectations of involvement with upper grade students between Latinx and Anglo communities. According to the survey, by the time kids made it to high school, many Latinx parents seemed to feel that the children were old enough to take care of themselves. Coaches saw this on the soccer field. In elementary and middle school, Latinx parents showed up to watch games and signed their kids up for club teams. By high school, those same parents stopped going to games and their kids stopped playing club sports. Anglo parents never seemed to stop being involved.

One Latina Woodburn student told me that, in her and her friends' households, parents had a large part in helping children with homework during elementary school. "But when you are older, when you're in high school, it becomes your responsibility."

Some of this might be traced back to the institutional role of schools in different countries. In Mexico, schoolteachers are given a wide degree of authority and autonomy in their treatment of children and a large percentage of the population is poorly educated. What US school administrators expect—the busy parent who wants to know exactly how Sally and Johnny spend their days and what teachers are going to do to improve their kids' grades —was not what the parents of WHS students felt comfortable asking about—much less demanding.

As former Woodburn High principal Laura Lanka said: "In Mexico, [parents] would never let their kids stay out late, never let them get away with what they do here. But here the child and parents become totally mixed up. The kid can speak English, the parents can't. They have to rely on their child to do all this stuff for them. It's a total mix-up and the kids begins to not respect the parent. I saw it all the time in my office when a child would be so disrespectful to their parents. It was just a surprise. The parent would say to me, 'In America, you just allow these things to happen.'"

"The perception that many of our kids' parents have is that this country is out of control. This country doesn't make their kids do homework ... I would always be sort of in shock when they would say the United States is so easy, high school is so easy. I would be sitting there thinking, 'Your child is flunking. How can you tell me that high school is so easy?'"

"I think what they were saying is that in Mexico, the school would have laid the law down. The teachers in Mexico would have laid the law down. As parents, they lay the law down about social things. But for them, everything is mixed up in this country."

Another ex-teacher, Jose Romero, said something similar.

"Sometimes parents write themselves off as the generation that is lost so the next generation won't be lost. White parents won't put up with any mistreatment of their children. They will demand a meeting with the principal and the teacher and call the board member that they know from the Rotary Club. But Mexican parents don't want to make waves, so they will ignore it, tell their kids to suck it up."

Romero pointed out that it can be difficult for immigrant parents to be involved for other reasons as well.

"They can be ashamed of themselves and of their appearance," he said. "They don't want to come to parent teacher meetings. They only have one car, so who is going to take care of the kids? They don't have time to do those things. Especially if you are working at a factory and have no control over leaving in the middle of the day."

For all the ways in which WHS might be failing students, or at least not bringing out their full potential, the school is currently seen as a very good school. When I was hovering around the soccer pitch in 2005, WHS had one of the state's lowest graduation rates and few of its Latinx students went to four-year universities.

Fifteen years later, on the waning edge of the global COVID-19 pandemic, Woodburn is both the same and very different. Still the Latinx cultural center of the state, Woodburn (both the town and the high school) is bigger and both the city and the school have become more sophisticated.

In fact, WHS looks like a surprising success. High school graduation rates have soared to 89 percent, now among some of the highest rates in the state. Every year, increasing numbers of WHS grads attend college, both two- and four-year, and the school's bilingual program has become a model other school districts emulate.

The academic achievements are especially notable when you consider how quickly the changes took place. In less than ten years, the high school went from one of the worst to one of the best in the state.

How much of Woodburn's academic success stems from the switch to the small school model is hard to calculate. The small schools movement has had mixed results nationally, and Woodburn has experienced its own struggles as students compete for the most desired small schools, which creates at least an impression of a lack of educational equity between some of the small schools.

Nationally, one of the difficulties that small schools have experienced is the physical separation of students, and intermingling students from the various small schools might be one reason why the community effect hasn't taken place at some high schools. Woodburn has worked hard to maintain physical separation and may have benefitted from those changes.

But small schools at WHS may be coming to an end, or at least may need to be put through some changes. Students have reported not being able to go to their school of choice, having frustration that they couldn't take courses from other schools, bemoaned a lack of college prep and job training courses, and pointed to a lack of equal representation in the populations of the different schools ("High School 2.0"). There also appears to be cultural differences between the schools and a stereotype of each school shared by all students.

It's possible that the small schools model has served its purpose in Woodburn and as the town matures and Latinx students are increasingly second- and third-generation Americans, there is no longer a need to separate students into smaller cohorts. This remains to be seen. But one clear success and one that many people agree has had a great impact on graduation rates, is the school's language instruction.

AT WHS, bilingual education is available for all students—not uncommon in schools nowadays—but the path Woodburn uses to achieve bilingualism is unusual. Here's how it's explained by the Oregon School Board Association:

> Parents can choose one of three paths for students: English and Spanish; English and Russian; or just English. About 80 percent of students enter one of the dual-language tracks, including those who only speak English. Core classes are taught in Spanish or Russian by bilingual teachers. Students develop fundamental numeracy and literacy

in Spanish or Russian while they are learning English. The approach keeps students from developing academic gaps as they learn English (Arnold).

Bilingual instruction begins in kindergarten. Each year, as the students move up a grade, the percentage of instruction in Spanish or Russian lessens and the percentage of instruction in English increases. By fifth grade, most students are proficient in two languages and are receiving equal class time in each. By middle school, core subjects are taught in English. After that, students can voluntarily continue language instruction in Spanish or Russian.

While one positive side effect of this plan is that most of Woodburn's students are now functionally bilingual, the ongoing, adaptive language instruction also has allowed schools to keep teaching subject matter, which ultimately bolstered graduation rates. Small schools or not, it could be that all Woodburn students needed was to understand what they were being taught.

Mike and Carlos

A month after speaking with Michael and Kaylee, I drove to Wilsonville to meet Carlos Pehr and Mike Flannigan for coffee.

When I first met Carlos, he was a high school junior and Woodburn's star goalkeeper, one of the kids on the team that everybody expected to land an athletic scholarship. Today, burly, bearded, outgoing Carlos is in his 30s, the branch manager of a bank, the father of three boys, and the coach of Newberg High School's varsity soccer team, one of Woodburn's regular league competitors. His ex-coach, Mike Flannigan, quit the Woodburn team in 2008 and now helps out with Woodburn's golf team. Mike, long haired, with a charming lopsided smile, still teaches Language Arts at the WEBBS small school.

For different reasons, both Carlos and Mike were leaders of the 2005 team, and both had surprising parallels in their lives that always made me lump the two together. Separated by 20 years, Mike and Carlos both were children when they moved to Woodburn to live with new families; both found friends and community through soccer; both remain passionate fans of English Premier League teams.

Carlos was five years old when social workers from the state's child protective services took him away from his mother for the first time. He was ten when they took him away the second and final time and placed him in the first of several foster families. After several families and several years, Carlos moved in with the coach of his club soccer team, a man whose strategy for raising boys was to keep them busy and make sure that their friends all came to his house.

Mike moved to Woodburn when he was 10 to live with his uncle, who later adopted him. Mike found friends through club soccer and was part of the Woodburn varsity team in the 1980s (coached by his uncle) when it began its extraordinary run of post-season appearances. Back then, the town hadn't received the big influx of immigrants that would turn the high school into a majority Latino institution and the team was half Anglo, half Latino.

As we sat down and caught up on personal histories, I asked Mike and Carlos what they thought about WHS today. Was the school doing all it needed to prepare kids for college? Was WHS perhaps selling the kids short, not encouraging them to reach for universities? Mike and Carlos both rejected this idea. Mike said that lots of students ask for his help applying for college, and Carlos expressed confidence in the school's counselors. Instead, Carlos said, parents are focused on the wrong measures of success.

"I see it all the time [as a coach at Newberg]," he said. "We have team meetings and these parents show up wanting to know why their kid isn't getting more playing time or getting more skill improvement. None of these kids are going to be professional soccer players. The parents should be more focused on pushing their kids to get better grades."

He smiled.

"My kids are going to play soccer, club soccer, school soccer, and they are going to use that to get a scholarship. They're not going to be professional soccer players."

Carlos leans on his own experience when making this statement. When he graduated high school, Carlos was accepted to George Fox University, a private Quaker college in Newberg with a Division 3 soccer team. At the time, Carlos believed that he was going to turn pro and didn't focus his energy on academics, despite the pressure around him to do so.

"The kids around me, they were going to the library to study and I was out trying to find people to kick a ball around," he said.

When his young wife told him that she was pregnant, Carlos quit school. Although dropping out was humiliating at the time, Carlos now sees leaving college as the beginning of his current success. Not only did he let go of unrealistic hopes for a future in the English Premier League, he also landed a job at a bank and learned how to manage his money.

With his warm, outgoing personality, Carlos thrived in a business built on relationships. He no longer plays soccer, but he is deeply involved in coaching high school and club and harbors dreams of one day coaching college. While Carlos disagrees with Michael, Miguel, and Kaylee about the role WHS should play in college preparation, he did agree that when he graduated from WHS, he had no idea of what to expect.

"[Woodburn's Latinx students] are told they need to go to college but they graduate without any real idea of what that means," he said, shaking his head. "They aren't prepared for the discipline, the academic focus."

Sitting across the table from Carlos, Mike Flannigan sipped his coffee and said that he noticed a big difference in the preparation level of students whose families have been in the US for decades and those whose parents are new arrivals. His comment reminded me of something he had said years ago.

"I had a student whose grade was marked down on a state test because he had never heard of a country club. He's from a farm in Michoacan [Mexico]! Why in the world should we expect him to hear of a country club?"

In 2005, one of Mike Flannigan's biggest worries about his students was an apparent willingness to give up and to assume that the world was stacked against them. When his team lost in the 2004 playoffs to a highly questionable call, Mike spent weeks angrily replaying the incident and feeling that something had been stolen from his team. He worried that the defeat would break some of his kids, cause them to quit pushing forward, either in sports or academics; he worried that they would take the experience as proof that in the game of life, the cards really were stacked against them.

Today, at least for most of his students, it seemed to Mike that they were less inclined to assume failure but might be just as unprepared for the reality of what to expect after high school.

"I don't know if it's the school's responsibility," he said. "I wish I saw more parent participation in parent-teacher meetings and college prep."

Carlos nodded his head. Whatever the reality of WHS's ability to prepare its students for college, the school had done a great job of expanding its influence on sports teams in the area. As the coach of a nearby high school, Carlos is one of many extending Woodburn's history of ex-players coaching across the state. Woodburn's neighboring agricultural community, Gervais, has a high school team helmed by Martin Maldonado, one of Carlos's friends and a member of the 2005 Los Perros squad. Another, older Woodburn player, Scott Enyart, coached at nearby Canby High School and was the director of the Oregon Youth Soccer Association.

There is an ex-Woodburn coachnow at the helm of a premier club in Florida. Luis Del Rio, who led the Bulldogs to their first championship, moved on to Del Rio coach at a nearby four-year college. Former Woodburn players are on the staff at the Portland Timbers Youth Academy, Salem Capitals FC, the Tualatin Hills United Soccer Club, and other local club teams in Oregon. Andrea Whiteman, the coach of the 2019 girls soccer team, Woodburn's first female team to win a state soccer championship, coaches at Nike's Sports Campus.

Everardo Castro, who graduated from Woodburn in 1986, coached one of the first all Latinx club soccer teams in the state. For several years, his team dominated the state tournaments, their closest competitor being another all-Latinx team from another Willamette Valley town. "We'd go to a tournament, "Castro said, "and it would always end up with us two at the finals. One of us would win and then the other would win."

Carlos Pehr's term as the head coach at Newberg High School probably won't be his last. The rumor that Leroy Sanchez is considering leaving his WHS coaching job is well known in Oregon high school circles. For somebody who loves soccer like Carlos, there might not be a better high school coaching job in the state. Currently living in Wilsonville, Carlos and his family recently purchased property in Woodburn and are waiting for the construction of their house to be finished. Another Bulldog coming home.

COVID

Increased Latinx college enrollment and graduation has been one of the bright spots in American higher education for two decades: college enrollment by Latinx students nearly doubled from 2000 to 2017, making it the fastest-growing group by ethnicity ("The Condition").

The COVID-19 pandemic stopped that progress abruptly. According to a 2020 survey, the global pandemic caused Latinx college students to postpone or quit college at twice the rate of white Americans ("Public Viewpoint"). Raul Prudencio, a 2019 WHS graduate and member of the championship soccer team, was one of them.

"When Covid hit [our courses at Chemeketa Community College] went online," said Raul. "I was okay with online school for a few months. I had one class on Zoom and the others were online but not interactive. Then it got really difficult and I didn't feel like I was learning anything."

Raul quit college and started working a landscaping job with his uncle, followed by a second job at a retail store at the nearby mall. When the pandemic caused that store to close, Raul found a job at Home Depot. At WHS, Raul had attended the Arts and Communication Academy, the small school dedicated to liberal arts studies. His photography attracted the attention of private arts colleges in Portland, Seattle, San Francisco, and New York, although only the college in Portland offered a scholarship, enough to cover about half of his tuition.

"My parents were supportive but they wanted me to get a practical job. My sister went to [Portland Community College] to get a job as a medical assistant. I started thinking about going to school for a dental assistant job, or maybe a trade school."

Raul sidestepped the arts college and started taking classes at Chemeketa Community College in September 2021. He quit before the end of his first year. Raul explained his decision by pointing out the differences between Latinx and Anglo families' perceptions of the purpose of higher education, the pursuit of individual personal growth and achievement versus gaining practical employment skills. One of his classmates, an Anglo, is currently attending the same art school in Portland that offered Raul a partial scholarship. But Raul has already put art school behind him.

"Most of my friends put family needs into consideration," he said. "I don't want to disappoint my parents. And if you're not going to school, you have to work."

A 2021 publication by the National Student Clearinghouse Research Center put Raul's experience into context: "The Latinx persistence and retention rates declined the steepest of all four groups examined in the 2019 cohort. Compared with last year, Latinx students saw a 3.2 pp drop in their persistence rate while White, Asian, and Black students' rates all declined by less than half of that ('Persistence and Retention')."

This decline in college attendance by Latinx students was true across all types of colleges and was higher at the community college level, where many students already were walking the thin line between education, work, family, and poverty. COVID may have been the impetus for the loss of Latinx students, but it isn't the only sword looming overhead. Latinx educational attainment is still fragile, a gently inflating balloon that can be burst at any time.

Kevin Vasquez, who graduated two years before Raul, had his chance at college but left months before the start of the pandemic because of the overwhelming feeling that he didn't belong. Vasquez had graduated from WHS in 2017, hoping to earn an athletic scholarship. But none was offered. The local four-year colleges with soccer teams were all Division 3 schools, meaning they were unable to offer financial help based solely on sports prowess.

"These school only offer academic scholarships and I didn't have the grades," he said. For a while, he wasn't sure if he would be able to attend a university. His family couldn't afford to pay for college without significant help. Ultimately, he applied to Portland State University, taking advantage of Four Years Free, a program designed to cover all tuition costs for applicants who receive Pell grants. Four Years Free pays the difference between tuition and the financial aid received by the student.

Kevin moved into an apartment with a friend from Woodburn and two strangers, a black PSU student from Louisiana and an older white man not attending college. The conflict with the white man started immediately.

"He didn't like us," Kevin said. "He didn't like me and [my friend from WHS] because we were Latinos and he didn't like the other guy because he was black."

With parents unable to help pay for food and lodging, Kevin took a part-time job on campus. The money helped, but it wasn't enough. Kevin struggled with feeling like an outsider, often being the only Latinx student in a classroom. The monetary struggles, the conflict with his roommate, and the isolation ultimately became too much to bear. Halfway into his second year at PSU, Kevin quit and moved back home. His friend from Woodburn dropped out soon after.

The struggles of students like Kevin are common, although colleges and universities have been very slow to adapt. Natalia Alvarez wrote about the need for changes in a post on EAB (formerly the Education Advisory Board). She identified three distinct structural changes that needed to be implemented: reduce barriers to access and success, foster belonging and Latinx representation, and increase the use of technology to increase access to faculty, staff, and resources.

These solutions include adapting existing resources such as tutoring and advising centers to include longer hours and remote access, using apps and case management systems to identify early the students who might need extra help, and perhaps most importantly, increase the percentage of Latinx staff and teachers to help build a sense of belonging. One of Alvarez's contacts was quoted like this: "These students feel that these schools weren't built for students like them, and we've been too slow as an industry to facilitate meaningful change (Alvarez)."

Jorge

Jorge Flores grew up in a small village near the hill city of Irapuato, Mexico. A natural athlete and the child of impoverished farmers, Jorge completed his mandatory education, which in Mexico ends at 8th grade. Unable to afford to go to high school, Jorge moved in with an uncle and began working out with a soccer academy associated with the Mexican soccer team Club Atlas. Before too long, though, Jorge injured his knee and had to return home, where he faced a complete lack of future: no sports, no school, and no jobs.

In 2005, Jorge was a temperamental star on the Woodburn team, a hard-driven perfectionist who had walked across the desert into Arizona with an uncle just a few years earlier. Undocumented but ambitious, Jorge charmed me with a description of wooing his high school girlfriend—now his wife—by writing her a formal letter introducing himself and stating his honorable intentions.

Jorge filled many pages in *The Boys from Little Mexico* (using the aka Octavio) because he epitomized so much of what I saw as the benefits of Latinx culture spreading into the less-diverse American states. Jorge came and stayed in America with the blessing of his family because, at 14, he was already running out of options in Mexico. Too poor to afford college and not quite skilled enough to be a professional soccer player, Jorge worked hard to learn English during the day and worked hard painting and tending to local vineyards on the weekends. The opposite of the stereotyped lazy immigrant, Jorge was hard-working and ambitious.

But his move to America happened almost by accident.

Jorge had planned to come to El Norte for a few months, just enough time to see his father, who had been away from home for years. Jorge stayed at his uncle Ricardo's house, where his father also lived, spending time with them in the evenings and wandering around Woodburn during the day when his father and uncle were at work.

Then, one day that summer, uncle Ricardo pulled Jorge aside for a serious talk.

"Listen," Ricardo said. "You could stay here, not be like us. Look at us, your father and me, we work hard for little money. You are smart. In this country, the way ahead is through education. You could stay here and study, get an education here, maybe go to college, so you don't have to work hard labor all day the way that we do. Here we have opportunity, and if you don't try to be different, you'll be the same and me and your father."

Jorge was surprised and had to take time to reevaluate everything. He had said goodbye to his family, but a temporary goodbye. He planned to return to Mexico with his father in the fall. His father was still planning to go home and wasn't sure if he would ever return. With the difficulty and expense of crossing the border, Jorge knew he might not see his mother or his siblings for years. At fourteen, Jorge was facing the biggest decision of his life.

Jorge thought of all the things he would have to leave behind: family, friends, a girlfriend, his tryout at the Club Atlas academy. Staying in America meant leaving behind all the external parts of his identity. If he stayed, could he ever really go back?

Another part of him wondered if he really wanted to go back. He wondered if returning home after seeing so many new ways of life would leave him hungry and unfulfilled. It was like his brief time training with Atlas—seeing how the professional athletes lived, running on the perfectly groomed, lush, green fields in enormous stadiums, visiting other cities, then returning to his little village with its scruffy schoolyard dirt pitch.

A few years earlier, back in Mexico, Jorge and his father had made a similar decision about whether Jorge should try out for Club Atlas or go to high school and maybe college. Jorge wanted to go to high school and college, but there was no money. His father offered to sell some of the family acreages, to sell their tractor, to go all in, essentially, on a bet that Jorge would do well academically and come back to help his family along.

The gesture was tremendously moving to Jorge but, he felt, too risky. Staying in America was also risky, in a different way.

They continued to talk about it and Jorge continued to be torn. Then his uncle and aunt told him that they had signed him up to attend Woodburn High. Almost as an afterthought, Ricardo said that they had also signed him up for the high school soccer team.

"They have a soccer team?" Jorge asked, intrigued.

"Yes, they're very good."

That was enough. Jorge decided to stay.

While Jorge was a good student, made friends, worked under the table, and was generally a responsible hard-working kid, the sense of uncertainty that he felt at 14 never really left. When Jorge was preparing to graduate from WHS, he faced a new question: how would he succeed without legal papers?

The question made him wonder if he should return to Mexico, even though returning almost certainly meant a life of poverty and possible violence. He almost wished that he had never come to the US because what had started as an adventure had awakened in him all the possibilities of the future, as well as the knowledge that he may never be allowed to chase those dreams. In the US, everybody who was successful, and many who weren't, went to college. They studied and became teachers, scholars, and architects. He wanted that badly. But sometimes, it seemed unrealistic. The undocumented didn't get what they wanted. America was such a strange country. American culture seemed to both welcome him and reject him.

Despite the documentation problems, Jorge secured a scholarship to nearby Chemeketa Community College, where he played on the school soccer team and received an Associate degree, all while working full time. He played on Chemeketa's soccer team all the way to the regional championship in 2008, where they were finally stopped.

It took almost a decade, but Jorge went on to three different four-year schools and ended up with a Master's Degree in Education. During that decade, Jorge was able to get Dreamer status. He married his girlfriend, an American citizen, returned to Mexico to apply for legal residency, and, working as a housepainter, paid his own way through college. Three years ago, Jorge started teaching Spanish at WHS.

"My experience in college is that other students doubt your skills and talent until you demonstrate otherwise," he told me. "At Corban College, for example, where there were very few Latinos, I had to show them that I was on the same level as them. A lot of that comes from imperfect English. So, what do you do to show that we're that same? Even though we sound different; we're the same. I always tell my students—you need to show you're not different. We have more similarities than differences."

Jorge's story, one that validates the American ideal of self-determination and hard work, is one that he leans on a lot in class in his endless efforts to inspire.

"Kids tell me they aren't going to college," he said. "They say their family isn't supportive or their family wants them to do x or y, or it's too expensive. I say, 'I'm here to help you.' I sometimes tell them my own experience. That's my secret weapon with students."

Jorge is also another voice suggesting that changes need to be made at WHS.

"I think we should have more tools for students to go to college or to go into the trades or to run a business," he said. "Seniors should make field trips. We should be connecting high school students to college students over a longer period."

He also pointed out that white teachers don't understand just how intertwined are the family lives of Latinos. I agreed. In my own family, white and college-educated, part of the measure of success for kids after high school was that they leave home and never come back. I wondered if most of the white teachers grew up with similar assumptions about college. But for many Latinx families that kind of independence and separation is not sought after, an attitude that mostly-white high school teachers might not understand.

"They don't realize how much of an impact there is on a family when one of the kids leaves," Jorge said patiently. "But Steve, It's our culture."

Home Is North of the Wall

We like to talk about the Latinx community in America with shorthand references to distinct groups, regions, or moments in time: Little Havana, Nuyoricans, Tejanos, Zoot Suit Riots, Dreamers. In Oregon and other historically Anglo states, the presence of Latinx communities has often been an afterthought, if they are thought about at all. But even in Oregon, Latinx presence and participation in American life has a long history.

Like many towns in America, Woodburn's story began with World War II, when Americans shipped overseas created a shortage of agricultural laborers. As part of the now infamous Bracero Program, single Mexican men traveled by bus from places like Oaxaca and Michoacan to the US border, where they were sprayed with DDT before being shipped north. Typically, the Braceros lived in tents supplied with folding cots and blankets and sometimes with wood stoves. These workers had their pay docked for petty or non-existent offenses, received no health care, and worked long hours in unsafe conditions. Lee G. Williams, the US Department of Labor officer in charge of the program, was once quoted in the Dallas Morning News describing the Bracero Program as a system of "legalized slavery (Kuempel)." The Bracero Program in Oregon ended after the war, but it set in motion a human migration to the Willamette Valley that continues today. Michael McGlade, a professor of geography at Western Oregon University, believes that well over half the field laborers in the Willamette Valley today can trace their migration back to someone recruited from the Bracero era.

That's a long history for a state as young as Oregon.

Woodburn's Latinx population increased in the 1960s; many of the newcomers were Mexican Americans from Texas. Mexican nationals began coming to Woodburn in larger numbers in the 1980s after the collapse of the Mexican economy, helping to spur Ronald Reagan's immigration reform laws, which offered amnesty to undocumented immigrants who could prove five years of continuous residence in the United States. Those individuals turned Woodburn into Oregon's largest Latinx-majority town. Similar events spread immigrants into other areas of the United States far from the border states, sparking triple-digit growth in parts of the country where Spanish speakers used to be rare: South Carolina, Alabama, Wisconsin, Iowa.

Latinx population growth now counts for over half of all US population growth over the past decade, and the Latinx portion of the country is closing in on 20 percent (Jensen). One in five Americans will soon have Latinx heritage. And in Woodburn over half of the population is already Latinx ("Quick Facts"). And yet, despite an almost 80-year Latinx foothold in Woodburn, the town is still adapting to their presence. Even in Woodburn, positions of power are still primarily in the hands of Anglos.

Michael Vasquez learned this lesson when he was six years old. "I was in first grade," he said, "And somebody asked my teacher what you needed to become president. And she said that to be President of the United States you need to be tall, rich, and white."

In Woodburn, the mayor is white, as are four of the six city council members. The Police Chief is white. The City Administrator, City Attorney, Recorder—all Anglos. However, change is coming. Half of the Woodburn District School Board is Latinx. The Superintendent is Latinx. Principals, teachers, counselors: Latinx. A couple of years ago, Woodburn elected State Representative Teresa Alonzo Leon, the state's first elected immigrant Latina lawmaker. The town is beginning to represent itself.

In the 16 years since I first visited Woodburn, many changes have come to the town and the high school. But an essential struggle remains, described by everybody I spoke with and repeated in towns across the country. The Latinx community continues to be viewed by many as outside of America and Latinx are viewed as outside of the communal American self-identity that is expressed in our stories, on our TV shows, through our assumptions and myths, and inherent beliefs. Latinx kids growing up in America, with as much claim to a birthright as the bluest blood Yankee with ties going back to the Mayflower, don't get to assume that their story is understood. Built into the institutions that educate these kids are ideas about their value, their future, and their family life that don't match the life experience of the Latinx kids. No wonder they want to see change in their schools. The students and graduates of WHS are ready to be part of our national identity, equals, and leaders, even if the world around them continues to balk at the necessary embrace.

On my first outing with the 2005 WHS soccer team, I traveled with Los Perros to a day at the beach, a preseason bonding session. Early that day, when some of the kids were kicking a ball around on the sand, a blonde young man approached, lingering nearby, clearly interested in joining the informal game. When one of the Woodburn students passed him the ball, Coach Flannigan wheeled on me and said intently, "You see! These are good kids!" Sometimes it seems to me that all of Woodburn is jumping up and down, pointing at Miguel and Carlos and Kaylee and shouting, "You see!"

Today I still see a group clamoring for full equality, a demand that attention must be paid. But today, the people making noise are not just the Coach Flannigans of the world, the well-meaning shepherds hovering around their flock. Today, the people demanding change are those who desire it most; and, most importantly, those who finally feel that they have the ability to affect that change from within: Michael Vasquez, fueled by anger that a previous generation might not have felt capable of either admitting or acting on; Kaylee Vasquez, charting a course to not only help her parents' peers but also to make the trip easier for the next prospective Latina doctor; Carlos Pehr, returning home with a plan to guide his kids to a successful future, and with the resources to do so.

Miguel Arellano, whose profession allows him to throw a net under those students most likely to slip off the edge, has thought long and hard about the role of his generation of new professionals and of his complex identity as immigrant, Latino, professional, American, husband, and father, and he distilled the turmoil into a question about the way he and the dominant American culture impact each other.

"What risks come of *not* being othered?" He wondered. "Does it mean that I've assimilated into white culture? If so, then that's bad. But if I can have an impact on the dominant culture, if that culture changes, then it's good."

When Miguel took his daughters to a family dinner at Red Robin and was confronted with the anti-immigration slogan on the restaurant's chalkboard—*Build the Wall Go Home*—he saw what the writer intended, an assumption that he and his family can't claim an American identity. But for Miguel and millions like him, Woodburn and other small towns are home and have been for generations. Woodburn is on this side of the wall.

It's trite to point out that change is slow, especially when discussing immigration when change necessarily takes place generation by generation. Yet we continually overlook the generational effect of immigrants, so much so that less than 20 years ago, commentators regularly opined that Latinx immigrants, unlike previous immigrant groups, would never assimilate into American society. In a popular 2004 book titled "Who Are We? The Challenge to America's Identity," political scientist Samuel Huntington wrote: "There is no American dream. There is only the American dream created by an Anglo-Protestant society. Mexican-Americans will share in that dream and in that society only if they dream in English (Huntington)." Huntington believed both that the American identity was successful only if it remained static, attached to its earliest roots, and that people born in the United States to Latinx immigrant parents would somehow find it more valuable to cling to their parents' identities than to create their own. He was wrong, of course. Wrong that the communal American identity is static and wrong that the children of Mexican immigrants would not learn English, celebrate Thanksgiving, and climb the corporate ladder just like those of us whose ancestors came over from Denmark and Scotland.

Huntington's thesis arose from fear, a fear that used a rational and logical explanation to cover up the essential truth that those of us living in the dominant culture of a country often feel uncomfortable sharing the table with people we used to look down upon. But this generation of Latinx Americans and those that follow will not allow themselves to be treated as secondary citizens. Miguel is right: he and his peers can change our American culture, and it's good.

References

Alvarez Diaz, Natalia. 2020. "What I learned about Latinx student success from 8 Hispanic-Serving Institutions." *EAB*. https://eab.com/insights/blogs/student-success/latinx-hispanic-student-success/

Arnold, Jake. "Woodburn's dual-language programs promote academic success." *Oregon School Board Association*. January 31, 2018. www.osba.org/News-Center/Announcements/2018-01-31_Woodburn_2.aspx

Barton, Rhonda. "Creating believers." *Northwest Education Magazine*. Spring 2006. educationnorthwest.org/sites/default/files/11-3.pdf

"The Big Picture on Oregon's Small Schools." *Oregon Small Schools Initiative*. November 2010. https://orbusinesscouncil.org/docs/archive/BigPictureonSmallSchools.pdf

"The Condition of Education." *National Center for Education Statistics*. May 2019. https://nces.ed.gov/pubs2019/2019144.pdf

"Generational Differences." *Pew Research Center*. March 19, 2004. www.pewresearch.org/hispanic/2004/03/19/generational-differences/

"High School 2.0 Task Force to identify strengths and gaps at WHS." *Woodburn School District*. November 7, 2020. www.woodburnsd.org/apps/news/article/1333985

Huntington, Samuel. 2005. *Who Are We? The Challenges to America's National Identity*. Simon and Schuster.

Jensen, Eric, Jones, Nicholas, Rabe, Megan, Pratt, Beverly, Medina, Lauren, Orozco, Kimberly, Spell, Lindsay. "2020 U.S. population more racially and ethnically diverse than measured in 2010." *United States Census Bureau*. August 12, 2021. www.census.gov/library/stories/2021/08/2020-united-states-population-more-racially-ethnically-diverse-than-2010.html

Krogstad, Jens Manuel, Lopez, Mark Hugo. "Coronavirus economic downturn has hit Latinos especially hard." *Pew Research Center*. August 4, 2020. https://www.pewresearch.org/hispanic/2020/08/04/coronavirus-economic-downturn-has-hit-latinos-especially-hard/

Kuempel, George, Swindle, Howard. "Ex-chief recalls bracero 'slavery'." *Dallas Morning News*. April 30, 1980. https://library.ucsd.edu/dc/object/bb3072990k/_1.pdf

Mora, Marie T., Dávila, Alberto. "The Hispanic–white wage gap has remained wide and relatively steady." *Economic Policy Institute*. July 2, 2018. www.epi.org/publication/the-hispanic-white-wage-gap-has-remained-wide-and-relatively-steady-examining-hispanic-white-gaps-in-wages-unemployment-labor-force-participation-and-education-by-gender-immigrant/

"Persistence and retention: Fall 2019 beginning cohort." *National Student Clearinghouse Research Center.* July 2021. https://nscresearchcenter.org/wp-content/uploads/PersistenceRetention2021.pdf

"Oregon." *U.S. Census.* https://data.census.gov/cedsci/profile?g=0400000US41

"Quick facts Woodburn City Oregon." *U.S. Census.* 2020. https://www.census.gov/quickfacts/fact/table/woodburncityoregon/PST045219

"Minority parents uncomfortable at school." *The Skanner.* February 22, 2006. https://www.theskanner.com/news/northwest/367-minority-parents-uncomfortable-at-school-2006-02-23

Public viewpoint: Education—disruption, enrollment, and advice." *Strada Center For Consumer Insights.*" May 20, 2020. https://www.stradaeducation.org/wp-content/uploads/2020/05/Public-Viewpoint-Charts-Week-8.pdf

Wilson, Steve. 2010. *The Boys from Little Mexico: A Season Chasing the American Dream.* Boston, MA: Beacon Press.

PART IV

Marginalized Americans and the American Dream

13

INCORPORATION AND DISRUPTION

What fictional narratives reveal about the realities of the American Dream

Elda María Román

One of the common associations of the American Dream is that of upward mobility. The belief goes that through hard work, one can reach financial security or exceed it. There is also the hope that the rise will be continual, with each generation doing better than the preceding one.[1] Despite how difficult this actually is,[2] biographical and fictional narratives about upward mobility remain a popular genre. This is a genre that includes "rises" of various kinds: educational trajectories, political memoirs, business successes, triumphant stories about athletes, adaptations of the Cinderella tale, as well as crime dramas, underground and white collar. Coming in many forms, they might offer lessons on how to overcome adversity, appealing to audiences seeking inspiration as well as entertainment. They can also be escapist, offering a relationship to a fantasy that is comforting even if the outcome remains out of reach, a relationship that can seem cruel in its optimism.[3] No matter the reason consumed, these narratives are laden with values, communicating messages about society and its structures. Moreover, because they move between socio-economic contexts, they are important cultural sites to understand for how they reflect and shape ideas about hierarchies and group boundaries.

As narratives about structures—hierarchical and bounded—upward mobility narratives have a lot to tell us about race and class. In what follows, I demonstrate how ethnic upward mobility narratives employ certain narrative strategies to demarcate the boundaries of the American Dream and various responses to those boundaries. Socio-economic mobility is impeded for many, but severe gaps in health, education, and wealth exist between white Americans and non-white Americans. Most ethnic upward mobility narratives deal with these disparities in how they feature characters moving through different contexts—inequalities become apparent through contrast. In grounding their stories through particular characters, they also grapple with the individualist component of the American Dream. If one of the key tenets of the American Dream is about "being able to live out our individual biographies to their fullest extent" (Rank et al. 2014, 2), these narratives often probe the question: what is the relationship between the individual and the group? As narratives that foreground this question, they, therefore, offer ethical scenarios by which to think about the collective story of the US itself: regardless of one's background, what is one's relationship within and between groups, especially if we take into account histories of stratification and exclusion? Do people

DOI: 10.4324/9781003326243-17

uphold existing power dynamics or challenge them? Given that individualism is so celebrated in American culture, narratives about collective gains have not had as much appeal. Yet, we are also in a historical moment where the American Dream and America itself are vitally in need of collectivist visions.

In my book, *Race and Upward Mobility* (Román 2017), which examines African American and Mexican American literature, television, and film from 1940s to 2000s, I discussed how writers depict racial and class conflicts through certain plot lines and characters. Specifically, I identified four character types that often appear in ethnic upward mobility narratives: *status seekers, gatekeepers, mediators,* and *conflicted artists*. I argued that these figures serve as allegorical pathways of social incorporation, meaning that they dramatize the ways people identify within, between, and against groups. Groups can be coded as, for example, working class/ middle class, poor/rich, non-white/white, immigrant/assimilated, employees/employers, and so on. Whatever the particular groups are, there are implicit and explicit messages that socio-economic conditions have led to the formation and maintenance of these groups. In this essay, through an analysis of the 2018 film *Sorry to Bother You* along with other cultural examples, I add to my book's arguments by highlighting that these character types serve as allegorical pathways of incorporation *as well as* disruption, meaning they exemplify how individuals and collectives reinforce and/or destabilize group dynamics and their accompanying value systems.

Dreams of Incorporation

Sorry to Bother You centers on an individual's upward mobility narrative but does so in order to emphasize the necessity of collectivist working-class politics. A Marxist workplace satire, this film was written and directed by activist-artist Boots Riley. Its protagonist, Cassius Green (Lakeith Stanfield), is a young Black male who begins working at a telemarketing company named Regal View. He struggles to make sales until advised by a coworker (Danny Glover) to use a "white voice," which entails "sounding like you don't have a care." Once Cassius adopts this tactic, he quickly becomes a top seller and is excited at the thought of becoming a "Power Caller," the lucrative telemarketing position at their parent company Worryfree. Cassius, meanwhile, is witnessing two unfolding protests: he sees news reports about demonstrations against Worryfree and hears charges the company is using slave labor. His coworkers are also organizing against Regal View for better pay, a cause that the apolitical Cash halfheartedly supports. His lukewarm commitment to them is tested once he receives an offer from Worryfree to become a Power Caller. In a pivotal moment in the middle of the film, he crosses his former coworkers' picket line to start in his new position. In depicting individual vs. group interests, the film exemplifies how these narratives, even though following the stories of individual characters, are often concerned with issues related to groups of people more broadly. Ethnic upward mobility narratives like *Sorry to Bother You* are able to evoke broader patterns through their use of character types, specifically ones related to race and class.

Cassius, for example, fits the characteristics of the *status seeker*. The status seeker allegorizes the desire for dominant group membership. When writers construct narratives featuring these characters, they accentuate social as well as economic barriers between groups. They do so by, for example, exploring the relationship as well as the disconnect between class and status. As Max Weber (1946) distinguished, class indicates one's position in an economic hierarchy, while status refers to one's position in a social hierarchy. Consider one of the most famous narratives about the American Dream, F. Scott Fitzgerald's *The Great Gatsby* ([1925] 1995); this novel reads as an ethnic upward mobility narrative and one featuring a status seeker. Jay

Gatsby's intense desire for and pursuit of Daisy Buchanan takes on another valence once we realize that along the way to amassing wealth, Gatsby changed his name—he was originally James Gatz—and cut ties with his past. The novel has been read as a story about a Jewish man passing as non-Jewish in order to be accepted by the "old money" white Anglo Saxon set of which Daisy is part. In order words, it was not enough for Gatsby to rise in class. In the face of anti-Semitism, which the novel also indicates through the characterization and perception of his business associate, Meyer Wolfsheim, Gatsby sought to change his status in order to seem a viable partner to Daisy. In Gatsby's idealization of Daisy and the value system for which she stands, the novel constructs a character working within and not against existing class and racial hierarchies.

Sorry to Bother You plays with the extent to which Cash can "pass" in portraying his use of the "white voice," which sounds like a comedic, eerie voiceover dubbing (the voice belongs to actor David Cross). Like Gatsby, Cassius's status seeking reveals the conditions and value systems under which he believes he can achieve success. The advice Cash receives to speak differently underscores the implicit criteria for success in that he starts assimilating to accommodate power differentials—adopting a voice that is racially coded as more credible in order to make more sales. The most explicit criteria for doing well at his workplace is the mandate the telemarketers receive to "S.T.T.S," meaning to "Stick to the script" when speaking to customers. Barring improvisation, imagination, and doing things differently, this rule given to sell goods is one that correlates to how the status quo is maintained generally. These criteria are just the start, however, because once Cassius assimilates and sticks to the status quo, he is a step away from accepting the work that comes from being a Power Caller, which entails selling slave labor and weapons of mass destruction.

Cassius is so determined to step into a higher status and more resourced job position and the film makes clear why he is trying so hard to indeed be "worry free," in visually demonstrating the spatialization of wealth and resources through Cassius's living and workspaces. Before Cassius becomes a Power Caller, he is living precariously. He lives in his uncle's garage and is behind in rent for the space. His uncle himself is several months behind in mortgage payments and is in danger of losing his house. Private homeownership is so integral to the mythos of the American Dream, a mythos that has gotten exported globally (Hauhart 2016). Yet this mythos belies the reality of exclusion policies like redlining and discriminatory FHA practices, which prevented Black Americans from buying homes in certain areas or buying homes at all. Even when home ownership is attained, Black Americans are more likely to lose their homes during economic recessions, as revealed during the subprime mortgage crisis of 2006.

Cassius' house-adjacent living space meant for a vehicle captures not only his own lack of mobility and lack of private home ownership but also his lack of privacy. Cash has little control over his space, as illustrated when, during an intimate moment with his girlfriend at the beginning of the film, the garage door opens and exposes them to the street and public taunting ensues. It is played as a comedic moment, but it taps into the broader phenomenon of how historically privacy has been afforded along the lines of class as well as race, revealing or not revealing who can erect boundaries to keep out the public eye and surveillance. This theme is echoed when Cassius sees an ad for Worryfree's cost reduction shelters, which are small living quarters for workers that look like jail cells, spaces conceptualized to break down the divide between work and home in order to extract more time and labor from workers. The Power Suite, where the higher ups work at Worryfree, is, in contrast, reached through an ascent in an elevator requiring an elaborate security code and is removed from oversight or regulation.

Like his living situation, Cassius's workplace reinforces the sense of a lack of privacy and a sense of stasis. He works as a telemarketer in a cubicle office layout where supervisors can keep an eye on employees. Yet, Cassius is hopeful that he will rise up. Telemarketing offers the appeal of potential white-collar work (the first time Cassius uses his "white voice," he is actually wearing a white collar) in the sense that it is work done in an office setting and is not manual labor (he is not one of the workers at the Worryfree factories). However, the telemarketing job does not pay much, which is why the workers are Regal View are trying to organize a union. In his cultural history of the office workplace, Nikil Saval writes about the in-betweenness of office workers, which is applicable in the portrayal of Cassius. As "neither of the working-class nor of the elite holders of capital," writes Saval, "White-collar workers rarely knew where they were, whom they should identify with. It was an enduring dilemma, rooted in what might be called a class *un*consciousness" (2014, 28). Cassius is part of the working class, but his lack of class consciousness is emphasized by his role as a salesman; he sells encyclopedias, among other items, so he is selling compendiums of knowledge but is unaware himself of the larger conditions under which he works. Moreover, his potential to identify with the working-class coalition organizing around him gets interrupted when he is offered the Power Caller position.

As a build up to this decisive moment—will he or will he not take the job and cross the picket line—the first half of the film moves Cassius toward incorporation. It portrays Cassius as a status seeker, someone who just wants to join a hierarchical and bounded structure, not change it, putting him in conflict with those who do want change. This dynamic plays out in the confrontation that Cassius has with his friend Salvador the morning he starts as a Power Caller. His friends and coworkers are outside protesting the workplace; they see Cassius appear, who declares he is a Power Caller now, "Trying to get paid." Salvador says they are all trying to get paid but as a team. "Are you on the team?" Salvador asks. Cassius relays that his uncle is about to lose his house, to which his friend responds: "Cash, I'm sorry about your uncle, man, but that don't mean sell out." Cash declares, "I'm not selling y'all out. My success has nothing to do with you, alright?" Here this scene exemplifies how ethnic upward mobility narratives often critique a status seeker's desire for self-gain and recognition at the expense of the collective. Cassius does not realize that his success at Worryfree is indeed intertwined with his coworkers' fates, for his rise and inclusion at the company is dependent on their lack thereof.

Since criteria for inclusion can entail limiting or barring others from accessing the same resources, status seekers may correlate with or have a conflict with *gatekeepers*. Gatekeepers police group boundaries. They can be characters who police boundaries as a result of their vocation and/or they have internalized values by which certain people are seen as more worthy of inclusion and, as a result, try to keep others out. These are significant character types because the bounded nature of any group leads to gatekeepers; these characters, therefore, enable creatives and audiences to explore the traits and values which groups use to demarcate boundaries and the means by which they are enforced. To return to *The Great Gatsby*, Tom Buchanan, married to Gatsby's love interest, Daisy, is the narrative's gatekeeper. We get a sense of Tom's views during a meeting between him, Daisy, and Nick Carraway, the novel's narrator and Daisy's cousin. Nick relays:

> "Civilization is going to pieces," broke out Tom violently. "I've gotten to be a terrible pessimist about things. Have you read 'The Rise of the Coloured Empires' by this man Goddard?"

"Why, no," I answered, rather surprised by his tone.

"Well, it's a fine book and everybody ought to read it. The idea is if we don't look out the white race will be—will be utterly submerged. It's all scientific stuff; it's been proved."

...

"Well, these books are all scientific," insisted Tom, glancing at [Daisy] impatiently. "This fellow has worked out the whole thing. It's up to us who are the dominant race to watch out or these other races will have control of things." (17)

Here Fitzgerald alludes to two actual white supremacist books, *The Rising Tide of Color* (1920) by Lothrop Stoddard and *The Passing of the Great Race* (1916) by Madison Grant. Tom Buchanan is the novel's device for depicting the ideology of white supremacy among the elite echelon to which Gatsby aspires. Even though Tom is a fictional character, he vocalizes the kind of racism and xenophobia which led to actual gatekeeping immigration policies like the Immigration Act of 1924.

As I write this essay in 2020, there has been a resurgence of the white power movement in the US and continued attempts to bar non-white groups from full enfranchisement. In light of the 2010 census, demographers predicted that the country would be majority non-white by the middle of the 21st century. This has shaken some Americans, who fear that racial hierarchies will be overturned. For many, the rise of the Black Lives Matter Movement has added to this fear. Intense political polarization, a worsening economy, the effects of climate change, as well as a global pandemic in 2020 also contributed to the sense that resources are scarce. These feelings, whether manifesting in nostalgia for a time past or rage at a coming future, can now be more quickly and widely disseminated (and manipulated) because of social media. Social media enables white power organizations to recruit more easily and the 2016 election gave them an ally and credibility in the White House. The Trump administration attempted gatekeeping policies to stop what pundits and writers have described as the "browning of America."[4] These policies add to the US's history of past successful efforts to socially engineer society into ethnoracial groups with disproportionate representation and unequal access to resources. The idea that the American Dream is available to anyone rests on not knowing the extent of concerted efforts to bar entry, incorporation, and access.

Desiring Disruption

Does the pursuit of one's American Dream entail barring others from accessing theirs? Will a character side with or against power? Even though *Sorry to Bother* You does not explicitly deal with fears of changing racial demographics, it does deal with fears toward protest and insurgency. As such, this film, which moved its protagonist toward incorporation in the first half, dramatizes a character enacting disruption in the second. It does so by first exploring the extent to which Cassius accommodates to dominant value systems. Worryfree's CEO Steve Lift offers him a highly lucrative position when he shows him a promotional video illuminating that Worryfree's profit-making plan entails turning more workers into Equisapiens, workers who are part human, part horse as a result of, as the video boasts, a "chemical change to make humans stronger, more obedient, more durable, and therefore more efficient and profitable."

Until this moment, Cassius' status has been dependent on the labor that he has not been able to see. It has been hidden from him as well as from the film viewer. The only time we see Worryfree factory employees working is through the promotional video portrayed in Claymation, emphasizing an attempt to downplay dehumanizing conditions. The hiddenness of these laborers correlates with the phenomenon of the "disappearing [factory] worker" that occurred over the course of the 20th century in popular culture, news media, and scholarship (Freeman 2018, 244). From the late nineteenth to the middle of the 20th century, factories and their workers in the US and abroad were held up as signs of progress in the process of modernizing people and nations. Yet, they were always sites of labor exploitation. Factories originated in English and US textile mills and employed child laborers and depended on the enslavement of Africans to pick cotton in the Americas. In their modern form, they continue the practice of extracting surplus value from workers enduring "long hours, low pay, and harsh conditions" in the US and throughout the world (Freeman, 315). So rather than being celebrated, factories and their working conditions are now hidden from most consumers, especially as manufacturers outsource labor to other countries in search of lower production costs.

The start of Cash's reconsideration of his role at Worryfree occurs when he inadvertently discovers actual Equisapiens at Steve Lift's home, screaming in pain and asking for help. Lift still makes him watch the rest of the Claymation promotional video and to consider his offer:

LIFT: Now, the proposal I want to make you is this. That is the future of labor. OK?

> They're bigger. They're stronger. They hopefully gripe a lot less. And also, soon, I'm gonna have millions of them. They're gonna form their own society. They'll probably form their own culture. Then maybe they want to organize. Maybe they want to rebel. And that's why we need someone on the inside who represents Worryfree's needs. Someone they can relate to.

CASSIUS: To manage it. For fucking horse people.
LIFT: No, no. The Equisapien Martin Luther King, Jr. But one that we create. One that we control.
CASSIUS: So you want to create a false leader for these fucking horse people. But at the same time, he works for you?
LIFT: Yeah. Keeps shit simple.

Cassius recognizes that Worryfree wants him to serve as a gatekeeper so that conflicts never get severe enough to disrupt the company's capital accumulation. Chang Rae Lee's novel *Native Speaker* (1995) also centralizes this scenario, though with a difference. In contrast to the film, which builds up to this proposal, the novel begins with a protagonist already working to stifle political unrest. Its protagonist is Henry Park, a young Korean American whose working-class immigrant father worked long hours and sacrificed so his son could have a better life. And by some measures, Henry does: he went to college, lives in the suburbs, and has a stable job. However, that job entails spying on other ethnic peoples and those threatening to capital. He narrates that he works for an intelligence agency that is hired by "multinational corporations, bureaus of foreign governments, individuals of resource and connection. We provided them with information about people working against their vested interests" (18). The trajectory of the novel leads Henry to confront himself and his work, admitting "My ugly immigrant's truth … is that I have exploited my own, and those others who can be exploited" (318). Cassius, too, has a moment of reconsideration of his work as he hears what Lift expects of him. Crucially, he understands that his gatekeeping would not be through force; rather, it would be through his role as a placating mediator.

Mediators exemplify ways of working between groups. In ethnic upward mobility narratives, the intentions and outcomes of what mediators do can vary. Given their experiences of moving within and between groups, they may work on behalf of power or against it. For example, at the beginning of the TV sitcom series *George Lopez* show (ABC, 2002–2007), Mexican American actor and comedian George Lopez plays a factory employee who, after years of working on the assembly line, is promoted to management. The question driving the pilot and the rest of the series is: will he side with the workers or with management? He often sides with the workers and, in the series finale, joins others in a protest to keep the factory from closing and relocating in search of cheaper costs. As a sitcom, the show fulfills expectations that conflicts will be resolved harmoniously; it also centralizes George's stance in a heroic light. In contrast, consider Lynn Nottage's Pulitzer Prize winning play about factory workers and deindustrialization, *Sweat* ([2015] 2017). It also features a ground-floor employee, Cynthia, a Black female, who is promoted to management. She faces accusations that she has sold out when she carries out orders to stop workers from organizing against wage reductions. Explaining to a friend that she tried to negotiate on behalf of the workers: "I explained, I fought, I begged" (78), she laments that it did not matter because the real wielders of power made her lock out her former coworkers to prevent them from entering the plant. She asks, "I wonder if they gave me this job on purpose. Pin a target on me so they can stay in their air-conditioned offices. Do you know what it feels like, to say to the people you've worked with for years that they're not welcome anymore?" (78). In showing the limits to Cynthia's ability to do anything to change working conditions, the play offers a more realistic depiction of the compromised position ethnic intermediaries are in when there is still such an asymmetry of power relations.

When Cassius refuses to be a gatekeeper and a mediator for corporate interests, he exemplifies another narrative strategy that ethnic upward mobility narratives employ to highlight inequalities in that they present ethical scenarios by which characters switch allegiances once they gain awareness of power dynamics. Cassius is so disturbed at seeing Equisapiens who yell out in pain that he tries to disseminate news about them—his first attempt at disruption. He calls a news outlet, to no avail. Then he goes on a popular entertainment show, "I got the S#*@ Kicked Out of Me," where he allows himself to be beat up in exchange for showing a video made by the Equisapiens. There are many narratives that show an individual coming to consciousness and/or coming to the conclusion that they need to speak out and raise awareness. This film dismisses that as an easy resolution. Cassius thinks that sounding the alarm and providing evidence of Worryfree's exploitation will catalyze people to call their congressional representatives. However, Worryfree's stocks actually go up. His former coworker and organizer friend Squeeze explains, "Most people that saw you on that screen knew calling their congressman wasn't gonna to do shit. If you get shown a problem, but have no idea how to control it, then you just decide to get used to the problem." Squeeze's response points to how people learn to live with things that seem insuperable. The failure of Cassius's attempt to catalyze action also points to the limits of individual action.

Notably, the film spans out to show how other characters are responding to the conflicts. While Cassius exhibits traits of three of the character types appearing in ethnic upward mobility narratives, his fiancé Detroit stands in for the fourth, the *conflicted artist*. At one point, she wavers between being drawn romantically to Squeeze, the committed political organizer, and getting back with Cassius, even though he has betrayed the group. Artists are also mediating figures, and because they stand in for representation itself, they can be conflicted about their interpretation and/or ways to represent. To return to *The Great Gatsby* one final time, Nick Carraway is both in the finance world and a writer (he wrote "solemn and obvious editorials" (8) back in college, and he tells the whole story of Gatsby). In other words, he is of the society to which Gatsby aspires, but also has a conflicted relationship with that society, as well as with Gatsby, which comes out in his storytelling. For instance, his dismissal of Gatsby's conspicuous consumption and extravagance reveals his mores stemming from his "old money" background. Yet his fascination with and sympathy for Gatsby, as well as his critique of the Buchanans and himself at the end of the novel ("perhaps we possessed some deficiency in common" (184)), reveals how much Gatsby has affected him.

An updated version of this influential novel along with *Sorry to Bother You* have bearing on ways to understand how artist figures can be employed to critique the effects of race and capitalism. In a contemporary adaptation of *The Great Gatsby*, *Bodega Dreams* (2000) by Ernesto Quiñonez, the Carraway figure (mediator and artist) is Julio, a young Ecuadorian and Puerto Rican artist who is known for painting murals. He is also torn about his allegiances, given that he and his wife aspire to leave their Spanish Harlem neighborhood in search of a better life, yet he is increasingly pulled into staying and fighting for his neighborhood in the face of gentrification by linking up with Willie Bodega, a former Young Lords activist turned real estate developer. Bodega is the Gatsby figure in that he is driven by unrequited love—he wants to win back a former girlfriend—but he is also driven by his love for his Puerto Rican community and wants to ensure that there are homes, economic opportunities, and cultural institutions available so that community members can have upward mobility while staying in their neighborhood. Like Gatsby, he also engages in criminalized activity in order to accumulate wealth, which is what makes Julio ambivalent about joining his cause. The novel is an exploration of some of the political strategies taken in light of the backlash against socialist attempts to fight for socio-economic change in the 1960s and 70s. The former socialist activist is now a capitalist, trying to, as the Jay Z song (2017) goes, to "buy the neighborhood." Bodega stands in for an outcome of neoliberal ideology in that private efforts (i.e. social entrepreneurship and philanthropy) get seen as more viable than collective organizing or efforts undertaken by the state. Thus, Julio remains conflicted about the means that Bodega takes to help the community while sympathetic to his goals.

Significantly, Julio in *Bodega Dreams* and Detroit in *Sorry to Bother You* are associated with making art outside of formal art institutions. In another example of how the US is spatialized along the lines of race and class, the art world and funding sources for art production remain largely white and exclusionary. A study of 18 Major US Museums found that as of 2019 "85% of artists are white and 87% are men" (Topaz et al. 2019). Another study from 2015 found that 77.6 percent of working artists are white (Jahoda et al. 2014). Significantly, the film depicts Detroit creating art in and outside of institutions. She has a gallery exhibit about capitalism's exploitation of Africa but is also producing guerilla street art to raise awareness about Worryfree's exploitive labor practices. The fact that her consciousness-raising art making is still dependent on funding sources is, however, still a tension that Cassius brings up. When Detroit argues with Cassius about his willingness to work for Worryfree and sell slave labor, he dismisses the organizing efforts against Worryfree as ineffectual and also adds, "You ain't gonna do shit neither by selling art to fucking rich people." Riley has revealed that all the characters are aspects of himself as an organizer: "I think that Detroit represents that conflict within me, whether art is really doing anything, whether it's effective, all the hypocrisy around it. Also, add some hope, because what she's trying to do is paint a vision that people can do something about this" (Fuchs 2018). The film is self-reflexive here about the role of art, ultimately conveying that political action needs lots of different strategies in multiple forms and contexts.

Romantic unions in narratives can serve allegorical functions and it is unsurprising that the formally apathetic Cassius ends up reuniting with Detroit, the figure who stood for disruption all along. At the end of the film, Cassius also acts as a mediator on behalf of the workers: he takes his knowledge of having been on the inside of Worryfree to help those organizing on the outside. There are still protests, and this time Cassius strategizes with others to bar employees from crossing the picket line. Their protest seems to be working until the police show up and start brutalizing protestors. Cassius has been able to secure communication with the Equisapiens inside the company, however, and at a pivotal moment, they come and help turn the tide in the protestors' favor.

The final scenes reiterate the temptation toward and rejection of complacency. A penultimate ending shows Cassius and Salvador talking about the newly formed union at Regal View. It is a win for their workplace. Even Cassius's living space has changed a bit. While he still lives in his uncle's garage, the space is now decorated reminiscent of the apartment he had when he was a Power Caller. "I couldn't come back to the exact same thing after all that, right?" he tells Detroit. Right after, he starts screaming and realizes he is turning into an Equisapien. The next and real final scene shows him and other Equisapiens barging into Steve Lifts house, disrupting his privacy after announcing themselves on his security camera. Leshu Torchin (2019) sums up that the ending "refuses containment and control. It's time to disturb everything, Riley seems to say at last: borders, capitalism, and how to think about rights" (36). That Cassius only becomes insurgent after his physical transformation perhaps suggests the difficulty of identifying completely with the oppressed unless one is in their situation. Yet narratives can facilitate the process of identification. They can also make situations that previously seemed unimaginable seem more possible and even necessary. As George Lipsitz has argued, culture can both be a form of politics and a "rehearsal for politics, trying out values and beliefs permissible in art but forbidden in social life" (Lipsitz 1990).

The appeal of incorporation and of individual upward mobility still has seductive narrative pull, so it would take many narratives, and in different forms, to expand how people imagine the attainment of the American Dream. *Sorry to Bother You* takes the appeal of the traditional upward mobility narrative—rising up as a result of hard work—to highlight the hierarchy of power and oppression that often does not get portrayed. Its use of the four character types allows viewers to more clearly "see" boundaries as characters move up and down hierarchies (Cassius literally moves up to the Power Suite in an elevator) and into new group contexts (Cassius changes workplaces as well as living situations). The character types also enable viewers to see when inclusion in itself does not do anything to change power dynamics. These narratives can prompt viewers to consider why characters opt for certain choices in particular scenarios, but it is important to understand that these individuals make choices as a result of systems already in place, such as race and capitalism, that inform what is seen as possible or imaginable in any given moment. Yet, what is seen as possible can change over time. Fiction participates in shifting boundaries on the imagination, and narratives like *Sorry to Bother You* insist on breaking down and breaking through for the many over the few.

Notes

1 Books by Hochschild (1996), Rank et al. (2014), and Putnam (2015), for example, examine the association of the American Dream in relation to perceptions of and attainment of upward mobility.
2 See Hout (2019), Hout 2018, and Chetty et al. (2016).
3 Affect theorist Lauren Berlant argues that "cruel optimism exists when something you desire is actually an obstacle to your flourishing. It might involve food, or a kind of love; it might be a fantasy of the good life, or a political project … These kinds of optimistic relation are not inherently cruel.

They become cruel only when the object that draws your attachment actively impedes the aim that brought you to it initially" (2011, 1).

4 Among these has been the intensification of deportations by Immigration and Customs Enforcement (ICE), the separation of and detention of families at the border, the Executive Order in 2017 seeking to halt travel from Islamic countries, and efforts to put a citizenship question on the 2020 census.

References

Berlant, Lauren. 2011. *Cruel Optimism*. Durham, NC: Duke University Press.

Chetty, Raj, David Grusky, Maximilian Hell, Nathaniel Hendren, Robert Manduca, Jimmy Narang. 2016. *The Fading American Dream: Trends in Absolute Income Mobility Since 1940*. Cambridge, MA: National Bureau of Economic Research.

Fitzgerald, F. Scott. [1925]1995. *The Great Gatsby*. New York: Simon and Schuster, Inc.

Freeman, Joshua B. 2018. *Behemoth: A History of the Factory and the Making of the Modern World*. New York: W.W. Norton & Company.

Fuchs, Cynthia. 2018. "Act It Out: Interview with Boots Riley of 'Sorry to Bother You'." *PopMatters*, July 23.

Hauhart, Robert C. 2016. *Seeking the American Dream: A Sociological Inquiry*. New York: Palgrave Macmillan.

Hochschild, Jennifer. 1996. *Facing Up to the American Dream*. Princeton, NJ: Princeton University Press.

Hout, Michael. 2018. "Americans' Occupational Status Reflects the Status of Both of Their Parents." *Proceedings of the National Academy of Sciences*. 115 (38): 9527–9532.

——— 2019. "State of the Union 2019: Social Mobility." *Pathways*. Stanford Center on Poverty and Inequality. 29–32.

Jahoda, Susan, Blair Murphy, Vicky Virgin, and Caroline Woolard. 2014. "Artists Report Back: A National Study on the Lives of Arts Graduates and Working Artists," BFAMFAPhD.com, http://bfamfaphd.com/#artists-report-back.

Lee, Chang Rae. 1995. *Native Son*. New York: Riverhead Books.

Lipsitz, George. 1990. *Time Passages: Collective Memory and American Popular Culture*. Minneapolis, MN: University of Minnesota Press.

Nottage, Lynn. [2015] 2017. *Sweat*. New York: Theatre Communications Group.

Putnam, Robert. 2015. *Our Kids: The American Dream in Crisis*. New York: Simon and Schuster.

Quiñonez, Ernesto. 2000. *Bodega Dreams*. New York: Vintage Books.

Rank, Mark Robert, Thomas A. Hirschl, Kirk A. Foster. 2014. *Chasing the American Dream: Understanding What Shapes Our Fortunes*. New York: Oxford.

Román, Elda María. 2017. *Race and Upward Mobility: Seeking, Gatekeeping, and Other Class Strategies in Postwar America*. Stanford, CA: Stanford University Press.

Saval, Nikil. 2014. *Cubed: A Secret History of the Workplace*. New York: Doubleday.

Topaz, C. M., B. Klingenberg, D. Turek, B. Heggeseth, P. E. Harris, J. C. Blackwood, et al. 2019. "Diversity of Artists in Major U.S. Museums." *PLoS ONE* 14 (3): e0212852. https://doi.org/10.1371/journal.pone.0212852

Torchin, Leshu. 2019. "Alienated Labor's Hybrid Subjects: Sorry to Bother You and the Tradition of the Economic Rights Film." *Film Quarterly*. 72 (4): 29–37.

Weber, Max. 1946. "Class, Party, Status," in *From Max Weber: Essays in Sociology*, ed. H. Gerth and C. Wright Mills. New York: Oxford University Press: 180–195.

Filmography

George Lopez. First broadcast March 27, 2002, by ABC.

Sorry to Bother You. 2018. Directed by Boots Riley. Cinereach.

Discography

Jay-Z. 2017. "The Story of OJ." *4.44.*

14

THE AMERICAN DREAM AND MUSLIM AMERICANS

(Im)possibilities and realities of pursuing the dream

Arshia Anwer

The idea of the American Dream has been studied and understood differently by different scholars and groups in American society. It is an ethos incorporating hope, opportunity, and inspiration; and garners a sense of national identity and belonging in the United States. In its simplest sense, the idea of the American Dream is understood as the way by which people can have an effect on their lives through individual endeavor and work toward achieving "success" (Hochschild, 1995). It is the idea that, with effort, one has a reasonable chance at achieving a good life.

Perhaps the most popular account of the American Dream was articulated by John Truslow Adams (1931), who described it as the concept through which "life should be made richer and fuller for everyone and opportunity [should remain] open to all" (308). Adams believed that this was uniquely possible in the United States, where people were free of social order or class, a land arguably different from where they had migrated. He goes on to say that the American Dream provides that "each man and each woman shall be able to attain to the fullest stature of which they are innately capable, and be recognized by others for what they are, regardless of the fortuitous circumstances of birth or position" (415). In this "New World," people could hope for upward social mobility through honest, hard work.

The ideal of the American Dream has been invoked and referenced multiple times at landmark moments in American history – very famously by Martin Luther King Jr. (1963) in his "I Have a Dream" speech in which he called for an equal possibility of attainment of the American Dream by *all* Americans, regardless of race. Eleanor Roosevelt (1961), in an essay where she delineated the American way of life from that of other nation states, characterized it as "not merely … a hope and an aspiration, but as a way of life, which we can come ever closer to attaining in its ideal form if we keep shining and unsullied our purpose and our belief in its essential value." And more recently, it was referenced by Barack Hussein Obama (2006) in his autobiography, *The Audacity of Hope: Thoughts on Reclaiming the American Dream*, where he linked the dream to the idea of hope of its achievement for all.

While the American Dream has been invoked and studied by multiple scholars and writers, the idea remains elusive and ambiguous. What exactly does a "richer and fuller" life mean? What are the aspirational contours, normative values, and hope-filled suggestions inherent in the idea of the American Dream? And what are the indicators through which one can say

DOI: 10.4324/9781003326243-18

that one has, in fact, achieved the dream? Cullen (2003) believes it is the very undefinable characteristic of the idea that gives it a "mythic power" (7) that grips the nation. Even the poorest, most marginalized Americans often come to believe that they, too, can benefit from the ambiguous but powerful promise of the American Dream (Duina, 2018).

Cullen (2003), in *The American Dream: A Short History of an Idea that Shaped a Nation*, sees the American Dream, not as one idea but as several, including the search for religious freedom that brought the early Pilgrims to the shore of North America, and the thirst for political freedom that followed it; or the drive for upward social mobility in the early nation, the aspiration toward equality during the first half of the twentieth century, or the idea of home ownership in later periods. Cullen traces the evolution of the idea of the American Dream to a present-day desire for personal success, embodied in the attainment of affluence, fame, and fortune exemplified by the Hollywood way of life. In its broadest interpretation, Cullen states, the American Dream "appears to mean that in the United States anything is possible if you want it badly enough" (5).

While the American Dream can be understood in its many and varied conceptions, it is also important to understand the foundations on which the idea rests and the various antecedents and ideals it is based on. It is also necessary to understand perhaps not so much what the dream is and promises but who the dreamers are. Thus, it becomes essential to understand the underlying and foundational aspects of the American Dream narrative that can have an effect on the attainment of the dream for minorities in general and Muslim Americans in particular.

The Ideological Foundations of the American Dream

The origins of the American Dream ethos can be traced back to the birth of the American nation. When it was codified into the Declaration of Independence, that "We hold these truths to be self-evident, that all men are created equal, that they are endowed by their Creator with certain unalienable Rights [including] Life, Liberty and the pursuit of Happiness" ("Declaration of Independence," 1776) the newly declared Americans stated a particular ideology through which life should be lived. Here, close examination is merited toward three issues: First, were all men truly understood as being created equal by the writers of the declaration? Second, does the mention of a "Creator" indicate an underlying inclination toward a particular faith-based perspective? And third, the importance of unalienable rights being understood as "life, liberty, and the pursuit of happiness."

The declaration that all men were considered equal at the time of the founding of the United States can now, of course, be understood as essentially untruthful. As the Constitution makes clear, that lofty sentiment applied only to *some* men on the basis of race, ethnicity, or nationality while excluding other men and all women. This has been recognized by the struggles the American people had to undergo to fight for their equal rights, whether in the Civil War, the Emancipation Proclamation, and the Civil Rights movement ("The Civil Rights Act of 1964 and the Equal Employment Opportunity Commission," 1964), or procuring the right for women to vote ("The 19th Amendment," 1919), or the granting of citizenship rights to Native Americans ("Indian Citizenship Act 1924"). Even citizenship and immigration restrictions (O'Brien, 2003) of this newly established nation were part of the notion of who would be included in, or excluded from, the expansively-stated "all men."

Early colonists and settlers in colonial America predominantly migrated to the New World in search of economic prosperity or to flee religious constraints. This land afforded them the idea of freedom and independence, and this set of circumstances also fostered in them "the quality and drive inherent in individualism" (Hauhart, 2016, 1). The idea of Americanism, from the beginning, has been underscored by what Perry Miller (1938) calls "the New England Mind," by which he means thinking that is influenced by Protestantism and a plain-speaking style of word and deed. The Protestant work ethic (Weber, 1905/2002) determines political, social, and economic activity as part of religiosity, particularly of the Protestant faith, and encourages the pursuit of worldly goods and monetary profit. Of course, the understanding of hard work and the resultant success is individualistic in nature. The idea of "pulling yourself up by your bootstraps," i.e. by doing hard work and fulfilling one's duties, one will be rewarded by economic prosperity, was coded into the language and ethos of Americanism. While the ideological origins of the United States *seem* to privilege the notion of religious liberty, the nation has a very strong Protestant ideological foundation (Kosmin and Lachman, 1993) which was ultimately transformed into an overall normatively Christian ideal during the early twentieth century (Kruse, 2015). This reliance on Christianity continues to pervade American public discourse and is reaffirmed in political and state symbolism ("H. Rept. 107-659"). The pervasiveness and centrality of symbolic Christianity (Straughn and Feld, 2010) often leave little space for other religious discourses and identities, including Judaism (Cohen, 1992), to flourish in the public sphere.

The other part of the American Dream ideology is its reliance on American exceptionalism and its belief in the doctrine of the Unites States' manifest destiny (Pratt, 1927). This narrative was important, at first, to persuade the earliest migrant and settler communities in the United States to colonize the farthest reaches of this new land, but also as a way of divorcing the new nation from the autocratic societies of Old Europe. Then later, this very narrative was instrumental in persuading citizens that the United States was destined to play a part in various wars that were fought in the name of bringing the American way of life and ideology to the rest of the world (Coles, 2002).

Perhaps the idea of the American Dream is most apparent in the phrase "life, liberty, and the pursuit of happiness," acknowledged as unalienable rights in the Declaration of Independence of the United States. In this phrase lies the idea of freedom, agency, and the ability of individuals to be able to pursue their dreams and achieve success – however they may define that success; and *that* seems to be the crux of the idea of the American Dream.

While there are multiple ways the idea of the American Dream can be understood, in its most common sense, it is understood as the idea of economic prosperity and upward social mobility (Cullen, 2003; Bush and Bush, 2015). As we understand the idea of the American Dream a little better, there are still multiple issues to consider while determining if everyone has equal access to the opportunity for economic prosperity and upward social mobility. For instance, Hauhart (2016) examines the access and attainment of the American Dream for understudied populations like the homeless. Similarly, Hochschild (1995) discusses structural barriers that can, and do, prevent minorities from access to and attainment of the American Dream. The American Dream seems to be accessible to people who are considered normatively American, and this conception, as we've seen above, has historically excluded multiple groups based on race and ethnicity, religious beliefs, socioeconomic status, and gender. Ultimately, the question for this essay becomes not whether Muslim Americans can dream but whether their American Dream can be realized. The American Dream embodies hope and possibility, but there are so many different factors that contribute to achieving the promised potential.

American Dreams for American Muslims

Muslim Americans are not a homogenous group. Curtis (2009), in *Muslims in America: A Short History,* states that "Muslim America, like the rest of the country, is often divided along lines of race, class, and ethnicity" (5). GhaneaBassiri (2010), in *A History of Islam in America: From the New World to the New World Order,* declares that Muslims in America "arguably comprise the most diverse Muslim population in any single country in the world" (2). Muslims have migrated, forcibly or voluntarily, from multiple regions and countries of the world, bringing their cultural and religious practices and beliefs with them. In addition to this, Muslims in America have also established new religious movements, like the Nation of Islam, that borrow from multiple faith traditions in the world.

The Pew Research Center, in its most recent report on Muslims in America ("Demographic Portrait of Muslim Americans," 2017), estimates that there are 3.45 million Muslims in America, comprised of 2.15 million adults and 1.3 million children. The survey finds that 82% of Muslims living in the United States are citizens, with 42% born in the United States and 40% who were born abroad and have become naturalized U.S. citizens. It is also worth noting that 58% of Muslims in the United States are first-generation Americans, which points to a significant immigration pattern in the latter half of the twentieth century. About a quarter (24%) of the U.S. Muslim population is indigenous Muslims, i.e. they are from families who have been present in the United States for three or more generations.

Apart from being diverse in terms of citizenship and settler status, Muslim Americans are also racially diverse. The Pew Research Center report states that "a plurality (41%) are white, a category that includes those who describe their race as Arab, Middle Eastern, Persian/ Iranian or in a variety of other ways" (para 12). This classification of Middle Eastern and North African Muslims as "white" will be discussed further on. About three-in-ten Muslim Americans are Asian (28%), including those from South Asia, while 20% are black, 8% are Hispanic, and the rest (3%) identify with another race or multiple races.

In short, there is a comprehensive diversity of political, social, cultural, racial and ethnic, and national origins of Muslims in America. While there is no one Muslim experience or one understanding of Muslims in America, we can still reach some understanding about the political, social, and economic opportunities available to Muslims in America with respect to the prospects for realization of their American Dream.

Muslims have been present in the Americas from the time the first Europeans landed on her shores,[1] about the sixteenth century onwards, and were present throughout the colonial period. The early presence of Muslims on the North American continent can be attributed to the transatlantic slave trade that had been in effect since before the institution of the United States as an independent nation. As scholars have documented, slaves were brought to North America from the Islamic regions of North and West Africa (Curtis, 2009). Even during the early colonial period, Muslims were thought of as anti-Christian or the exotic "Other" (Marr, 2006; Beydoun, 2016) – their lived experience was not considered "American." Islam certainly did not flourish during this time within this population due to the harsh conditions of slavery and slaves' total lack of control of their religious practices. As one example, punishment was meted out for practicing Islam in some cases (Diouf, 1998). In the later stages of the American enslavement of Africans,[2] the forced separation of slave families played a role in these early Muslims' inability to pass on their African and Islamic heritage. Consequently, Islam as a religious way of life mostly died out in North America by the time of the Civil War (Haddad, 1993).

The history of Islam in the United States from the Civil War to the early twentieth century is largely synonymous with the history of African Americans in America, characterized by large scale racial violence and persecution. The internal migration of African Americans from the South to the North during this time is a significant factor in the story of indigenous Muslim Americans as well (Curtis, 2009). The internal migration freed African Americans from southern Reconstruction, placed them in urban centers and provided them with a broader outlook of the world through their inclusion in the military and role in fighting in the World Wars. These factors proved to be a fertile ground for a growing Muslim American conscience and a religious identity that was not bound to Middle Eastern or even early African Islam. Organizations like the Garvey Movement, the Moorish Science Temple of America, and the Nation of Islam grew out of the idea that "nearly a century after the Civil War, black Americans still remained outside of America's national narrative" (GhaneaBassiri, 2010, 228) These movements were based on an anti-imperial opposition to Western thought and Christianity, and an effort to erase the inferior coding of African Americans as slaves. Thus, these religious movements focused on African American pride and self-help while tying adherents to a uniquely African American-born notion of Islam (Turner, 2003). Leaders of American Muslim movements of this period tied the ideologies of self-determination and individualism, hallmarks of the American collective consciousness, to the religious identity of Islam in the African American community. Here then, is the first inkling of Muslim Americans trying to reach for the ideals embodied in the American Dream.

The period following the American Civil War to the end of World War II saw the beginning of voluntary Arab Muslim immigration into the United States. Immigrants during the earlier part of this period were uneducated laborers who found work in factories or mines in the United States (Haddad and Lummis, 1987). Arab Muslim immigrants established mosques in the areas where they settled in order to primarily preserve the cultural values of the Islamic way of life (Leonard, 2003). The Arab Muslim population, the only substantial immigrant group of Muslims to America during this period, even though economically not as well off as European landowners and businessmen, was different from African American Muslims who had earlier been forcibly brought to the nation as slaves. Leonard finds that Middle Easterners were initially considered "white" while demarcating their racial status in the census during this time. However, this categorization was overturned in 1910, when the Census Bureau re-defined them as Asiatic and not "free, white" people. This decision was then appealed and again reversed in 1923. The racial coding becomes significant as access to the American Dream has been markedly divided along racial lines throughout the history of the United States. Thus, the racial identity of Arab Muslims has been contested, and their social place and status as Americans has historically been associated with their affinity and identity in relation to "white" Europeans.

The Immigration Act of 1924 ("The Immigration Act of 1924 (The Johnson-Reed Act)," 1924) and its 1965 revision ("Immigrations and Nationality Act of 1965") again affected the Muslim community in the United States, leading to a dramatic growth of immigrants from various Muslim countries since the 1960s in response to the demands in the labor market and changes in immigration laws (Haddad, 1993). This period of migration saw people from South Asia (India, Pakistan, Bangladesh, and Afghanistan) and Eastern Europe join the primarily Arab Muslim American immigrant population in the United States. The majority of Muslim immigrants during this time were graduates and professionals, coming into the country to fill higher level positions in multiple industries. These Muslim immigrants, however, came at a time when there was increasing racial segregation in the United States, and this impacted their role and integration into the larger American community (Curtis, 2009). While this relatively new immigrant community was economically at par with the American middle class, where for the first time, Muslim Americans' American Dream could begin to truly blossom, they still faced cultural and societal alienation due to common American attitudes toward Muslims (Haddad, 1993).

It was during the 1970s that the indigenous African American form of Islam came in contact with the Islam that was practiced by newly arrived Middle Eastern and South Asian

Muslims. The indigenous African American version of Islam had emerged after the American Civil War to reclaim racial identity as much as it had to foster religious identity. Middle Eastern and South Asian Muslims were initially considered "white," as was described earlier, and were not affected by the racial Othering faced by indigenous African American Muslims. The coming together of these different facets of Islam promoted the confluence of different practices and conceptions of the religion into a more mainstream and orthodox form of Sunni Islam that could trace its origins to its birth in the Middle East.

Still, Sherman Jackson (2003, 2005) argues that African Americans' recognition of Sunni orthodox Islam has always been uneasy and not fully accepted. Islam was not just a religious order but also a sociopolitical and activist charge through which African American Muslims could realize their potential, free from the oppression, ostracism, and enslavement they experienced in the United States. The traditional practice of "true" Islam imported by the new Middle Eastern and South Asian immigrants did not offer them this understanding or sense of community. The identification that African American Muslims have with their racial community, rather than their purely religious ones, is supported by the Pew Research Center report that states, "American-born black Muslims are more likely than other U.S. Muslims to say it has become harder in recent years to be Muslim in the United States. Nearly all American-born black Muslims (96%) say that there is a lot of discrimination against Muslims in America, almost identical to the share who say that there is a lot of discrimination against black people in the U.S. (94%)" ("Demographic Portrait of Muslim Americans," 2017, sidebar: "A closer look at U.S.-born black Muslims").

The fact is that throughout the history of Islam in America, Muslim Americans have never enjoyed integration or acceptance from the white American elite (Haddad and Esposito, 1998; Beydoun, 2016). The impact of the terrorist attack and events of 9/11/2001 has shaken the Muslim American community, as it has the United States and the world. But for Muslim Americans, what is worse is that the terrorist attack and its aftermath have fostered a return of Islamophobia (Beydoun, 2016; Kraut, 2020), which had always inherently been present in the United States, where Islam had been Othered as foreign and hostile (Haddad, 1993; Beydoun, 2016). With 9/11, the attitude of many Americans toward Muslims hardened. The resultant increase in discrimination, along with ensuing global upheaval, has taken a heavy toll on the lives and lived experiences of Muslim Americans (Cainkar, 2009; Sides and Gross, 2013; Beydoun, 2016; Kraut, 2020). Added to this, most recently, Donald Trump's presidency has been a cause of concern for most Muslim Americans, with many Muslim Americans reporting discrimination against them. They state that being Muslim has become more difficult in the United States ("U.S. Muslim Americans Concerned about Their Place in Society, but Continue to Believe in the American Dream," 2017). The experience of U.S. Muslims is corroborated by a 2017 Pew Research study that reports an increase in anti-Muslim assaults in 2016 and 2017, exceeding even 2001 levels ("Assaults against Muslims in U.S. Surpass 2001 Level," 2017).

Muslim Americans in the United States today are a diverse and heterogeneous group. This still generally means exclusion from the normative white, male, European, and Christian ideal of the American elite regardless of national origin. For particular Muslims, like African Americans, it comes with added issues of racial discrimination and oppression. The structural barriers for upward social mobility and cultural assimilation of American Muslims, in certain cases, prove to be detriments to their achievement of the American Dream.

Assessing economic achievement and upward social mobility among Muslim Americans, the Pew Research Center report states that Muslim Americans, in general, have similar levels of education compared to Americans overall but report lower incomes ("Demographic

Portrait of Muslim Americans," 2017). Fewer than half of adult Muslim Americans (44%) report fulltime employment. Twenty-nine percent of Muslim Americans are underemployed, compared to only 12% of the larger American population. Muslim Americans are as likely to have incomes of $100,000 or higher as compared to Americans in general (24% of Muslims and 23% of Americans). However, the disparity is evident in the lower socioeconomic strata. Forty percent of Muslim households have a household income of less than $30,000, compared to 32% of the general U.S. population. Thirty five percent of Muslims fall under the middle range, i.e. between $30,000 and $99,000, compared to 45% of all Americans. These results can be understood as reflecting possible discrimination based on perceived racial characteristics as well as the experience of new immigrants to any country, including the United States.

Muslim African Americans, for a long time, were not free to pursue economic success in the United States. Freedom from slavery has been a relatively recent attainment when compared to their presence on the continent, and even then, after starting their "pursuit of happiness" late compared to white Americans, Muslim African Americans have been hindered by social and systemic barriers. GhaneaBassiri (2010) states that "while Anglo-American Protestants' experiences of America's political freedoms, scientific advancements, and economic power at the turn of the twentieth century led them to triumphantly celebrate the accomplishments," indigenous Muslim Americans' experiences of the same were "coupled with experiences of racism, religious bigotry, and economic hardship" (183). Hochschild (1995) and Beydoun (2016) point out that poverty and unemployment among African Americans remain disproportionately high even today when compared to the larger U.S. population, an assertion supported by the Pew Research Center survey (2017) shared above.

In the case of home ownership, one of Cullen's (2003) markers of the attainment of the American Dream, Muslim Americans again perform considerably worse than the general American population – 37% of Muslim Americans own their homes, as compared to 57% of the overall American population. Muslim Americans tend to be much younger than U.S. Americans overall (the median age of Muslim Americans is 35, as compared to the median age of the U.S. population as a whole, which is 47 ("Demographic Portrait of Muslim Americans," 2017), which could account for some of the differences in income and home ownership. But then, America's history of segregation of African Americans and exclusionary zoning also played a large role in Muslim Americans' dream of home ownership.

Immigrant Muslim Americans, especially the Arab and South Asian populations, fare relatively better in economic terms, as they tend to be more educated than their indigenous brethren and voluntarily migrated to the United States in pursuit of economic and other opportunities. Curtis (2009) states that the majority of Muslims who entered the United States after immigration laws relaxed in the 1960s had higher levels of educational attainment and were professionals who came to the United States to work in skilled worker positions. The immigrant story has always been tied to the American Dream, and Muslim American immigrants have also understood that "like other immigrants, they must work hard to achieve the dream in a country where racial/ethnic minorities still face a glass ceiling and other forms of institutionalized discrimination in their careers and thus have limited upward mobility" (Wang, 2014, 84). Even among immigrant Muslim American populations, Somali, Iraqi, and Bangladeshi immigrants, in particular, are more likely to be at or below the poverty line in large numbers (Beydoun, 2016). Arab Americans, on the other hand, have shown a keen entrepreneurial spirit and enjoyed relative economic success (Boosahda, 2003; Beydoun, 2016). It is the South Asian Muslims, though, who are perceived as achieving a higher socio-economic status as compared to Arab Muslims and African American Muslims. However, this perception might not be a reality, as most of the studies done in this area are of the South

Asian community as a whole, and other religious denominations within the community fare better than Muslim South Asian Americans economically (Wang, 2014; Beydoun, 2016).

On the whole, Muslims in the United States generally fall into the broad middle class and achieve better financial success than Muslims elsewhere in the world (Wang, 2014). However, while Muslim Americans continue to achieve a moderate degree of economic success, there are divisions among racial lines in how they are able to attain the American Dream when it comes to economic advancement. Generationally, Muslim Americans show upward economic mobility, but overall, there is also a disproportionately larger percentage of Muslim Americans who are poor and remain so for a longer time than the larger American population (Beydoun, 2016).

The political realization of Muslim Americans' American Dream carries with it notions of citizenship, immigration, political activity and representation, the United States government's use of surveillance and perceived discrimination against the Muslim American population in recent times, and the United States' foreign policy in relation to Muslim Americans' affiliation to other nations. In some cases, like political representation, Muslim Americans have increasingly been politically active in their local and regional communities, and very recently at the national level as well. But Muslim Americans' relationship with citizenship, immigration, foreign policy issues, and their association with law enforcement has been complicated.

Muslim Americans have always faced issues with the procurement of citizenship in America. In its most famous instance, the Naturalization Act of 1790 ("Naturalization Bill, March 4, 1790," 1790) denied citizenship to African Americans, limiting access to only "free white persons," i.e. the white immigrants of Western Europe. This law was not amended by Congress until 1870 when it allowed citizenship to African Americans and persons of African descent. Similar laws were passed at various times to limit immigration and naturalization for South Asians, Arabs, and other Muslim Americans. Citizenship and immigration laws continued to be imposed by local officials to include and exclude various indigenous and immigrant Muslim Americans until the turn of the twentieth century, but non-African Muslim Americans fought these laws "by arguing that they should be considered white ... In other words, they did not challenge the racism and bigotry involved in the conflation of whiteness, Protestantism, and progress; rather, they argued for their inclusion within this matrix" (GhaneaBassiri, 2010, 153). This practice of non-African American Muslims demarcating themselves as white continues to date as seen in the 2017 Pew Research Center report, where Arab and Middle Eastern Muslims were counted as white. Immigration and citizenship requirements have continued to change, as shown by The Immigrations Act of 1924 and its revision in 1965 mentioned earlier.

Most recently, one instance of the changing of laws was the Trump administration's Executive Order 13769 ("Protecting the Nation from Foreign Terrorist Entry into the United States," 2017), popularly known as the "Muslim ban," which suspended the entry of refugees and revoked visas of people from Iran, Iraq, Libya, Somalia, Sudan, Syria, and Yemen. The relationship between Donald Trump and Muslim Americans has been fraught, especially after Trump's statement during his 2016 presidential campaign that he would seek a "total and complete shutdown of Muslims entering the United States" (Taylor, 2015), followed by his 2017 executive order blocking travel from seven Muslim-majority countries.

The Pew Research Center report also reports that "U.S. Muslims are somewhat mistrustful of law enforcement officials and skeptical of government sting operations" ("U.S. Muslim Americans Concerned about Their Place in Society, but Continue to Believe in the American Dream," 2017). Three out of ten Muslim Americans believe innocent Muslims that pose no real threat have been arrested by law enforcement officials. Muslim Americans' relationship with law enforcement seems to be both a racial and religious issue. One, owing to the significant portion of African American Muslims in the United States, police brutality and disproportionate incarceration is a systemic racial issue (Hochschild, 1995; Beydoun, 2016). And two, after 9/11, Muslim Americans have reported both higher levels of discrimination from the general populace as well as higher levels of surveillance from airport officials and law enforcement officials ("U.S. Muslim Americans Concerned about Their Place in Society, but Continue to Believe in the American Dream," 2017).

As a large immigrant population, Muslim Americans have historically felt a distinct disconnect between their former national identities and American foreign policy "given the U.S. government's interference in the global political structure in the Middle East and other Muslim countries" (Wang, 2014, 133). American foreign policy in favor of Israel, the United States' ally in the Middle East, or the nation's presence and wars in Iraq and Afghanistan, or its foreign policy relationships with the other Middle Eastern States – all of these have been causes for some consternation for immigrant Muslim Americans. Haddad (1993) writes that Islam was considered a threat to the American way of life and equated with radical terrorism, fanaticism, and extremism even before 9/11. The political views and other disenfranchisements detailed above have perhaps led to a larger political consciousness and urge to have political representation of Muslim Americans in recent times.

Political activity and representation in political spaces by American Muslims have traditionally not been at par with their presence in the nation (Johnson, 1993; Schoettmer, 2015), but it is slowly growing, led by Arab Muslim Americans in mostly local and regional contexts (Venkatraman, 2020). Other groups of Muslim Americans have organized into religious political institutions – like the Chicago-based League of Voters led by Indo-Pakistani Muslims – to lobby for foreign policy, aid, or realize other policies that affect them. The younger generation of American Muslims has also started to organize itself into various bodies to have a voice in public affairs, join in civic discourse, or otherwise influence politics in their communities (Wang, 2014). An increasing number of these bodies tend to be affiliated with religious institutions or mosques (Jamal, 2005). Religious institutions have always served to mobilize people politically, to build in them a sense of civic duty, political ability, and knowledge of political decisions that can affect them. Religious institutions have served those functions in Muslim American communities, right from organizations like the Moorish Science Temple of America and the Nation of Islam to present-day local mosques.

On a national scale, Keith Ellison was the first Muslim to be elected to Congress in 2007 from Minnesota's 5th congressional district ("Thomas Jefferson's Copy of the Koran to Be Used in Congressional Swearing-in Ceremony," 2007). In 2019, two Muslim women, Rashida Tlaib ("About | Representative Rashida Tlaib") and Ilhan Omar ("About | Representative Ilhan Omar") made history by being the first Muslim women to be elected to Congress. An unprecedented number of Muslim Americans, around 100, ran for political office in 2018, and more than half of these candidates won their local, state, and congressional races. In 2020, the number of Muslim candidates competing for political office increased to around 110 ("Muslim Candidates Again Make History in 2020," 2020). Even as political representation increased, Muslim American candidates were still coded as the racial, gendered, and religious Other in media representations (Anwer and Kern-Stone, 2019). The growth of Muslim Americans running for political office is attributed to an increased civic conscience in response to the above-mentioned immigration laws, anti-Muslim sentiment, discrimination, and disenfranchisement faced after 9/11 (Salem, 2010; Schoettmer, 2015). One of the core facets of the American Dream is agency and autonomy, and it is through political representation that Muslim Americans can make the changes that are important for their communities.

The cultural or social aspect of the American Dream is perhaps the one that lies at the heart of what makes the dream a successful idea people are willing to believe in. The notion that the American Dream promotes a sense of identity or belonging is a very potent one. The American Dream, at its very core, is an idea that requires faith and hope. It fosters a sense of oneness in the land of opportunity, and the constructed mythos can both bind people together or be the cause for Othering for people who do not have the opportunity to achieve the American Dream. As mentioned earlier, understanding the many facets of the American Dream can be achieved through examining who the dreamer is, but it can also be considered through who is telling the story of the American Dream.

In *Tensions in the American Dream: Rhetoric, Reverie, or Reality*, Bush and Bush (2015) state that the American Dream is essentially the white man's story:

> [the] tale of American (European, white) success had enormous implications worldwide. European colonialism racialized and gendered the economic structure throughout the globe. This was justified in similar terms, as those in positions of wealth and power were presumed to be in their social positions due to their inherent superiority and worthiness. The idea that upward mobility is not just possible but limitless provided just the rationale to garner loyalty to ideological rules and principles of capitalism and white supremacy. This justification implied that those who succeed are worthy, while those who do not succeed are not worthy or deserving. (95)

An uncritical understanding of the achievement of the American Dream does not account for cultural, structural, and systemic barriers faced by minority and immigrant groups in the United States. Muslims Americans are both religious and racial minorities and are largely made up of immigrants. Where one is positioned in the social hierarchy in a community plays a significant role in how accessible the American Dream is to them.

As we have seen, the earliest ideological foundations of the United States of America and racial subjugation have played a significant role in hindering upward social mobility for certain races and classes of people. Hochschild (1995) states that the inspirational seduction of the American Dream is such that people who were able to relate to it and achieve it turned it into a norm for every individual. The "all men are [created] equal" mythos is deeply ingrained… and lives on. She writes:

> White men, especially European immigrants able to ride the wave of the Industrial Revolution (and to benefit from the absence of competition from the rest of the population) to comfort or even prosperity, are the epitomizing demonstration of America as the bountiful state of nature. Those who do not fit the model disappear from the collective self-portrait. Thus, the irony is doubled: not only has the ideal of universal participation been denied to most Americans, but also the very fact of its denial has itself been denied in our national self-image. (26)

In this sociocultural environment, immigrant and racially disadvantaged Muslims who live amidst a normatively white, Christian culture that is often hostile to people of other races and religions do feel alienated and Othered. This sense of alienation and Othering is not just a perception. A January 2016 Pew Research Center survey ("Republicans Prefer Blunt Talk about Islamic Extremism, Democrats Favor Caution," 2016) reports that Americans have reservations about Muslims and the role of Islam in American society. A quarter of the survey respondents said that they feel at least half or more of Muslims in America are anti-American. In a recent poll ("How the U.S. General Public Views Muslims and Islam," 2017), fully half (50%) of Americans say that Islam is not part of mainstream American society and 44% state that Islam and democracy are not compatible.

Eighty percent of Americans say that there is a lot or some discrimination against Muslims in America today ("Discrimination in Society," 2021). Muslim Americans' experiences with discrimination uphold their feeling of alienation. Muslim Americans whose appearance identifies them as Muslim are more likely to face harassment or discrimination, with 38% of Muslims and 49% of Muslim women saying that there is typically something that identifies them as Muslim in their appearance or clothing ("Identity, Assimilation and Community," 2017). Sixty-four percent of the Muslims who *look* Muslim face the types of discrimination asked about in the survey. Muslim American respondents said that discrimination and persecution are the most pressing issues for them in the United States, and these issues were fueled by misconceptions about Islam and Muslims by the rest of American society. They stated that misconceptions include statements about Muslim extremists in other countries, misconceptions and stereotyping about Islam among the U.S. public, and Trump's attitudes and policies toward Muslims ("U.S. Muslim Americans Concerned about Their Place in Society, but Continue to Believe in the American Dream," 2017).

Media coverage of Muslims also has a large part to play in the misconceptions about Islam in the wider U.S. society, as mass media are an important source of furthering ideologies in society. Research about media representations of Muslims (Ahmed and Matthes, 2017; Anwer and Kern-Stone, 2019) finds that Muslims are generally negatively portrayed, and Islam is framed as a terrorist or violent religion. Additionally, "The West" and "Islam" are portrayed as polar opposites. According to Beydoun (2016), this portrayal predates the foundation of the United States and is tied to the tropes of Orientalism, which "positions Islam and Muslims as a subordinate civilization, geopolitical antithesis, and ever-looming threat" (1481). In recent research, Islam has been portrayed in the media as "a monolithic, homogenized, or sexist religion" (Ahmed and Matthes, 2017, 222) which we have seen even in the Muslim American community, is not the case, let alone worldwide. Muslims in popular media are often portrayed negatively, coded as "heartless, brutal, uncivilized, religious fanatics, militants, terrorists, or as societal problems" (222). Islam is presented not through the voices and lived experiences of Muslims but through the white man's gaze. Muslims agree, with a majority (60%) stating that they believe media coverage of Muslims is unfair ("U.S. Muslim Americans Concerned about Their Place in Society, but Continue to Believe in the American Dream," 2017).

In such a bleak societal landscape replete with racial and religious Othering, Muslim Americans would seem to be further away from seeing themselves as participants in the narrative of the American Dream. However, the allure of the American Dream is based on the fact that it offers hope for betterment, and the hope of the disadvantaged, immigrants, and Black Muslim Americans, often has to be audacious. Accordingly, a large majority (70%) of Muslim Americans report that they continue to have faith in the American Dream, that by working hard, they can achieve success ("U.S. Muslim Americans Concerned about Their Place in Society, but Continue to Believe in the American Dream," 2017). Most interestingly, the Pew Research Center survey found that Muslim Americans are more likely than the general U.S. population to say that most people who work hard can succeed.

This points to the exceptional seduction of the American Dream, for at its core, it is an ideological construct. The power of the dream lies in its ability to persuade people to *aspire* to it. Hauhart (2016) concurs that the American Dream, while seemingly about an ambiguous understanding of "success," is also at its heart about psychological satisfaction and finding a purpose in living. Muslim Americans, as we have seen, fall short of actualizing the fullest measure of their capabilities due to multiple barriers and are not recognized by others as belonging to the American ethos and, by extension, the realization of the American Dream, but they have not stopped believing in the dream.

The Muslim community in the United States is a diverse one. Muslim Americans are divided through racial and ethnic origins, citizenship and immigrant status, socioeconomic class and cultural differences, and sometimes even religious differences are the norm. In such a case, it is difficult to definitely determine whether Muslim Americans, as a group, have access to and achieve the American Dream. Nevertheless, as we have seen, there are certain ways in which we can understand their engagement with it. In terms of economic achievement, Arab Muslim Americans and South Asian Muslim Americans are perceived to perform better than African American Muslims and, by and large, seem to be at par with the American middle class. However, Muslim Americans, on the whole, tend to also inhabit the lower end of the economic spectrum and are underemployed or unemployed at disproportionate rates.

When it comes to political and civic issues, Muslim Americans have historically been targeted by harsh immigration and segregation policies. They have faced discrimination and have a fraught relationship with law enforcement officials, particularly after the 9/11 terrorist attacks. They remain interested in U.S. foreign policy, especially as it concerns the Middle East and other Muslim majority nations, and are increasingly joining political or civic discourse and representation in the United States. This increased interest in political and civic matters is evident in the number of Muslim Americans who ran for political office in recent elections.

Finally, socially and culturally, Muslim Americans overwhelmingly feel alienated in mainstream American society. They face discrimination and misconceptions by Americans about themselves and their faith and search for a sense of belonging. However, amidst the impacts of racism, classism, and Islamophobia in the United States that hampers Muslim Americans' access to and achievement of the American Dream in a lot of respects, they still are able to keep the faith and believe in the dream in their own pursuit of happiness.

Notes

1 There have been accounts of the earlier presence of Muslims in the Americas (see Leo Wiener, *Africa and the Discovery of America* (Philadelphia, PA: Innes, 1922), Ivan Van Sertima, *They Came before Columbus* (New York: Random House, 1922), and Sulayman S. Nyang, *Islam in the United States of America* (Chicago, IL: ABC International Group, 1999)), but these accounts are generally discounted as not being based on substantiated evidence or historical writings.
2 I do not write "African Americans" only because slaves did not enjoy citizenship rights at that time.

References

"About | Representative Ilhan Omar." United States House of Representatives. Accessed July 16, 2020. https://omar.house.gov/about.

"About | Representative Rashida Tlaib." United States House of Representatives. Accessed July 16, 2020. https://tlaib.house.gov/about.

Adams, James Truslow. *The Epic of America*. New York: Routledge, 1931/2017.

Ahmed, Saifuddin and Jörg Matthes. "Media Representation of Muslims and Islam from 2000 to 2015: A Meta-Analysis." *The International Communication Gazette* 79, no. 3 (2017): 219–244. doi: 10.1177/1748048516656305.

Anwer, Arshia and Rebecca Kern-Stone. "Running while Muslim: Media Representations of Muslim-Americans in U.S. Politics." In *Gender, Race, and Social Identity in American Politics: The Past and* the *Future of Political Access*, edited by Lori L. Montalbano, 131–154. Lanham, MD: Rowman and Littlefield, 2019.

"Assaults against Muslims in U.S. Surpass 2001 Level." Pew Research Center, 2017. Accessed on June 1, 2021. https://www.pewresearch.org/fact-tank/2017/11/15/assaults-against-muslims-in-u-s-surpass-2001-level/.

Beydoun, Khaled, A. "Between Indigence, Islamophobia, and Erasure: Poor and Muslim in War on Terror America." *California Law Review* 104, no. 6 (December 2016): 1463–1502. doi: 10.15779/Z38S56B.

Boosahda, Elizabeth. *Arab-American Faces and Voices: The Origins of an Immigrant Community*. Austin, TX: University of Texas Press, 2003.

Bush, Melanie L. and Roderick D. Bush. *Tensions in the American Dream: Rhetoric, Reverie, or Reality*. Philadelphia, PA: Temple University Press, 2015.

Cainkar, Louise A. *Homeland Insecurity: The Arab American and Muslim Experience After 9/11*. New York: Russell Sage Foundation, 2009.

Cohen, Naomi W. *Jews in Christian America: The Pursuit of Religious Equality*. New York: Oxford University Press, 1992.

Coles, Roberta L. "Manifest Destiny Adapted for 1990s' War Discourse: Mission and Destiny Intertwined." *Sociology of Religion* 63, no. 4 (Winter 2002): 403–426. Accessed May 26, 2020. https://www.jstor.org/stable/3712300.

Cullen, Jim. *The American Dream: A Short History of an Idea that Shaped a Nation*. New York: Oxford University Press, 2003.

Curtis IV, Edward E. *Muslims in America: A Short History*. New York: Oxford University Press, 2009.

"Declaration of Independence: A Transcription." National Archives, 1776. Last reviewed on July 24, 2020. https://www.archives.gov/founding-docs/declaration-transcript.

"Demographic Portrait of Muslim Americans." Pew Research Center, 2017. Accessed on July 12, 2020. https://www.pewforum.org/2017/07/26/demographic-portrait-of-muslim-americans/.

Diouf, Sylviane. *Servants of Allah: African Muslims Enslaved in the Americas*. New York: New York University Press, 1998.

"Discrimination in Society." Pew Research Center, 2021. Accessed on June 1, 2021. https://www.pewresearch.org/global/2021/05/05/3-discrimination-in-society/.

Duina, Francesco. *Broke and Patriotic: Why Poor Americans Love Their Country*. Redwood City, CA: Stanford University Press, 2018.

GhaneaBassiri, Kambiz. *A History of Islam in America: From the New World to the New World Order*. New York: Cambridge University Press, 2010.

"H. Rept. 107-659 – To Reaffirm the Reference to One Nation Under God in the Pledge of Allegiance." Accessed June 5, 2020. https://www.congress.gov/congressional-report/107th-congress/house-report/659/1.

Haddad, Yvonne Yazbeck (Ed.). *The Muslims of America*. New York: Oxford University Press, 1993.

Haddad, Yvonne Yazbeck and Adair T. Lummis. *Islamic Values in the United States: A Comparative Study*. New York: Oxford University Press, 1987.

Haddad, Yvonne Yazbeck and John L. Esposito (Eds.). *Muslims on the Americanization Path?* Atlanta, GA: Scholars Press, 1998.

Hauhart, Robert C. *Seeking the American Dream: A Sociological Enquiry*. New York: Palgrave Macmillan, 2016.

Hochschild, Jennifer L. *Facing Up to the American Dream: Race, Class, and the Soul of the Nation*. Princeton, NJ: Princeton University Press, 1995.

"How the U.S. General Public Views Muslims and Islam." Pew Research Center, July 26, 2017. Accessed July 20, 2020. https://www.pewforum.org/2017/07/26/how-the-u-s-general-public-views-muslims-and-islam/.

"Identity, Assimilation and Community." Pew Research Center, July 26, 2017. Accessed July 20, 2020. https://www.pewforum.org/2017/07/26/identity-assimilation-and-community/.

"Immigrations and Nationality Act of 1965." United States House of Representatives Archives. Accessed July 4, 2020. https://history.house.gov/Historical-Highlights/1951-2000/Immigration-and-Nationality-Act-of-1965/.

"Indian Citizenship Act 1924." National Archives. Accessed May 25, 2020. https://www.archives.gov/files/historical-docs/doc-content/images/indian-citizenship-act-1924.pdf.

Jackson, Sherman A. "Black Orientalism: Its Genesis, Aims and Significance for American Islam." In *Muslims in the United States*, edited by Philippa Strum and Danielle Tarantolo, Washington, DC: Woodrow Wilson International Center for Scholars, 2003.

Jackson, Sherman A. *Islam and the Blackamerican: Looking toward the Third Resurrection*. Oxford University Press, New York, 2005.

Jamal, Amaney. "The Political Participation and Engagement of Muslim Americans: Mosque Involvement and Group Consciousness." *American Politics Research* 33, no. 4 (July 2005): 521–544. doi: 10.1177/1532673X04271385.

Johnson, Steve A. "Political Activity of Muslims in America." In *The Muslims of America*, edited by Yvonne Yazbeck Haddad, 111–124. New York: Oxford University Press, 1993.

King, Jr., Martin Luther. "I Have a Dream." American Rhetoric. 1963. Accessed on May 25, 2020. https://www.americanrhetoric.com/speeches/mlkihaveadream.htm.

Kosmin Barry A. and Seymour P. Lachman. *One Nation Under God: Religion in Contemporary American Society*. New York: Crown Publishers, 1993.

Kraut, Julia Rose. *Threat of Dissent: A History of Ideological Exclusion and Deportation in the United States*. Cambridge, MA: Harvard University Press, 2020.

Kruse, Kevin M. *One Nation Under God: How Corporate America Invented Christian America*. New York: Basic Books, 2015.

Leonard, Karen Isaksen. *Muslims in the United States: The State of Research*. New York: Russell Sage Foundation, 2003.

Marr, Timothy. *The Cultural Roots of American Islamicism*. New York: Cambridge University Press, 2006.

Miller, Perry and Thomas H. Johnson. *The Puritans: A Sourcebook of Their Writings*. New York: American Book Co., 1938.

"Muslim Candidates Again Make History in 2020." Jetpac, 2020. Accessed on June 1, 2021. https://www.jet-pac.com/muslim-candidates-again-make-history-in-2020/.

"Naturalization Bill, March 4, 1790." U.S. Capitol Visitor Center, 1790. Accessed on July 12, 2020. https://www.visitthecapitol.gov/exhibitions/artifact/h-r-40-naturalization-bill-march-4-1790.

O'Brien, Gerald V. "Indigestible Food, Conquering Hordes, and Waste Materials: Metaphors of Immigrants and the Early Immigration Restriction Debate in the United States." *Metaphor & Symbol* 18, no. 1 (January 2003): 33–47. doi: 10.1207/S15327868MS1801_3.

Obama, Barack. *The Audacity of Hope: Thoughts on Reclaiming the American Dream*. New York: Three Rivers Press, 2006.

Pratt, Julius W. "The Origin of 'Manifest Destiny'." *The American Historical Review* 32, no. 4 (1927): 795–798. Accessed May 25, 2020. https://www.jstor.org/stable/1837859.

"Protecting the Nation from Foreign Terrorist Entry into the United States." Federal Register, National Archives, 2017. Accessed July 16, 2020. https://www.federalregister.gov/documents/2017/02/01/2017-02281/protecting-the-nation-from-foreign-terrorist-entry-into-the-united-states.

"Republicans Prefer Blunt Talk about Islamic Extremism, Democrats Favor Caution." Pew Research Center, February 3, 2016. Accessed July 20, 2020. https://www.pewforum.org/2016/02/03/republicans-prefer-blunt-talk-about-islamic-extremism-democrats-favor-caution/.

Roosevelt, Eleanor. "What Has Happened to the American Dream?" *The Atlantic*, April 1961 Issue. Accessed May 25, 2020. https://www.theatlantic.com/magazine/archive/1961/04/eleanor-roosevelts-american-dream/306023/.

Salem, Ola. "Why Muslim Americans Are Running for Office in Record Numbers." *Al Jazeera*, August 6, 2010. Accessed on July 16, 2020. https://www.aljazeera.com/news/2018/08/muslim-americans-running-office-record-numbers-180805140505236.html.

Schoettmer, Patrick. "Mobilization and the Masjid: Muslim Political Engagement in Post-9/11 America." *Politics, Groups, and Identities* 3, no. 2 (2015): 255–273. doi: 10.1080/21565503.2015.1029497.

Sides, John, and Kimberly Gross. "Stereotypes of Muslims and Support for the War on Terror." *The Journal of Politics* 75, no. 3 (2013): 583–98. Accessed June 1, 2021. doi: 10.1017/s0022381613000388.

Straughn, Jeremy Brooke and Scott L. Feld. "America as a 'Christian Nation'? Understanding Religious Boundaries of National Identity in the United States." *Sociology of Religion* 71, no. 3 (Fall 2010): 280–306. Accessed June 5, 2020. https://www.jstor.org/stable/40961206.

Taylor, Jessica. "Trump Calls for 'Total and Complete Shutdown of Muslims Entering' U.S." *NPR*, December 7, 2015. Accessed July 16, 2020. https://www.npr.org/2015/12/07/458836388/trump-calls-for-total-and-complete-shutdown-of-muslims-entering-u-s.

"The 19th Amendment." National Archives, 1919. Last reviewed on May 14, 2020. https://www. archives.gov/exhibits/featured-documents/amendment-19.

"The Civil Rights Act of 1964 and the Equal Employment Opportunity Commission." National Archives, 1964. Last reviewed on April 25, 2018. https://www.archives.gov/education/lessons/ civil-rights-act.

"The Immigration Act of 1924 (The Johnson-Reed Act)." Office of the Historian, 1924. Accessed July 4, 2020. https://history.state.gov/milestones/1921-1936/immigration-act.

"Thomas Jefferson's Copy of the Koran to Be Used in Congressional Swearing-in Ceremony." Library of Congress, 2007. Accessed July 16, 2020. https://www.loc.gov/item/prn-07-001/.

Turner, Richard Brent. *Islam in the African-American Experience*, 2nd ed. Bloomington, IN: Indiana University Press, 2003.

"U.S. Muslim Americans Concerned about Their Place in Society, but Continue to Believe in the American Dream." Pew Research Center, 2017. Accessed on July 15, 2020. https://www. pewforum.org/2017/07/26/findings-from-pew-research-centers-2017-survey-of-us-muslims/.

Venkatraman, Sakshi. "Muslims in the U.S. Are More Politically Engaged Than Ever, Study Finds." *NBC News*, October 28, 2020. Accessed June 1, 2021. https://www.nbcnews.com/news/ asian-america/muslims-u-s-are-more-politically-engaged-ever-study-finds-n1244879.

Wang, Yuting. *Between Islam and the American Dream: An Immigrant Muslim Community in Post-9/11 America*. New York: Routledge, 2014.

Weber, Max. *The Protestant Work Ethic and the Spirit of Capitalism*. New York: Penguin Books, 1905/2002.

15

GAY NEIGHBORHOODS

Reimagining the traditional conception of the American Dream

Theodore Greene

On November 8, 1977, Harvey Milk made history as the first openly gay elected official in the United States. His fourth campaign for public office proved the charm. In 1973, the former financial advisor-turned-hippie ran for City Supervisor of San Francisco in a virtually grassroots campaign without money, staff, or the backing of the conservative gay political establishment. Despite garnering significant attention for his fiery, flamboyant political speeches and a culturally liberal platform that included legalizing marijuana, Milk finished tenth in a field of 32 candidates. When Milk ran two years later, he opted for a more conservative presentation, cutting his hair, wearing three-piece suits, and swearing off marijuana and bathhouses. He managed to gain the support of several unions in San Francisco yet finished seventh in a field of six incumbents, all of whom recaptured their seats. When he ran for California State Assembly in 1976, he lost by less than 4,000 votes in a tight race. Yet, by the time he ran for City Supervisor in 1977, a referendum would tip the scales in Milk's favor. In 1976, San Franciscans voted to restructure the supervisor elections to elect supervisors from neighborhood districts instead of a citywide election. Instead of running in a citywide election, Harvey Milk became Supervisor of the newly created District Five, which included the Castro, a gay neighborhood he had helped transform into a political force.

Milk moved to San Francisco in 1972 and opened a camera shop with his lover on Castro Street. A "decaying Irish neighborhood with two gay bars catering Hippies from the Haight" (Fitzgerald 1986, 43), the Castro first catered to gay men involved in the countercultural movement. As gay men "invaded" the Castro (Shilts 1982), the Castro would become a destination for gay men in the 1970s. Milk became central in this transformation. When the Teamsters waged a strike against Beer distributors who refused to sign a union contract, Milk helped organize a successful boycott in the Castro, canvassing the local gay bars to dissuade them from selling the beer. When the Eureka Valley Business Association attempted to prevent two gay men from obtaining a business license for their antique shop, Milk helped organize the Castro Village Association, the first association of predominately gay businesses in the country. Believing that gay people should patronize gay businesses, Milk organized the Castro Street Festival in 1974 to attract more customers to the area (Shilts 1982, 90).

His visibility and efforts to organize politically paid off. Despite his losses in 1973 and 1975, his strong showing in the Castro demonstrated the political power of the local gay community. His camera shop soon became a hub for political organizing in the area, and he soon

DOI: 10.4324/9781003326243-19

developed the reputation as "The Mayor of Castro Street." Based out of his camera shop, Milk mobilized San Francisco against the successful passage of California's Proposition 6 in 1978, which would have legalized the firing of gay teachers and open supporters of gay rights (Clendinen and Nagourney 1999, 388–89). By the end of the decade, the Castro had anchored such a strong voting bloc that politicians believed in the impossibility of winning an election in San Francisco without courting the "gay vote" (Castells 1983; Castells and Murphy 1982; Clendinen and Nagourney 1999).

Yet before his assassination in 1978, Harvey Milk also worried about the changes threatening the "community" he created. As gay men purchased and renovated homes in the Castro, real estate prices soared. By 1976, houses sold for five times their value in 1972, forcing working- and middle-class gay men to seek affordable housing in surrounding neighborhoods (Boyd 2011; Fitzgerald 1986, 59; Israels 1979). The "small businesses" that Milk represented had made way for upscale shops that now included "an expensive home furnishings shop, a wine- and quiche café, a card and gift shop … two men's clothing stores … and boutique shops …" (Fitzgerald 1986, 59). The rent on Milk's camera shop had tripled in 1977, ultimately forcing him to move his camera shop off Castro Street "into a cubbyhole on Market Street." His famous camera shop "was quickly occupied by a boutique selling Waterford crystal" (Fitzgerald 1986, 59). Local gay bars began discriminating against women, effeminate gay men, and African Americans, reinforcing an image of gay identity that privileged white, athletic, masculine, cisgender, middle-class men.

Even the politics that Milk championed had shifted among his constituents. As his opponent for the 1977 Supervisor Race garnered significant support by describing himself as a "professional man who happens to be gay," Milk derided the gay "Uncle Toms," who privileged social acceptance at the cost of protecting the gay community. "We don't want sympathetic liberals," he told *The New York Times*. "We want gays to represent gays … I represent the gay street people – the 14-year-old runaway from San Antonio. We have to make up for hundreds of years of persecution. We have to give hope to that poor runaway in San Antonio. They go to bars because their churches are hostile. They need hope. A piece of the pie! Gay for Gay!" (Gold 1977, 17). Despite his many successes, Milk also became a casualty of them, as the Castro blossomed from a grassroots community championing liberal causes to a thriving middle- and upper-middle-class community populated by white gay professionals representing a politics of gay respectability.

Both Harvey Milk and the Castro District represent the paradoxes of the American Dream that motivate this chapter. The Castro became a model for the emergence and development of gay neighborhoods in American cities throughout the twentieth and twenty-first centuries. Emerging out of the ruins of poor, abandoned, and marginalized communities, gay neighborhoods have gained legitimacy as the fulfillment of the American Dream. A central strategy for "coming out" in the wake of the 1969 Stonewall Riots, gay neighborhoods have evolved from "fringe areas" that celebrate and anchor the free expression of sexual and gender-variant identities to fashionable residential and cultural districts that attract hip, monied cosmopolitans in search of authentic experiences in the post-industrial city (Brown-Saracino 2004, 2007; Florida 2003; Ghaziani 2014; Hess and Bitterman 2021; Knopp 1997; Orne 2017; Zukin 1987). Scholars have attributed gay neighborhoods to the growing political and sociocultural acceptance of LGBTQ citizens,[1] providing safe spaces for heterosexuals to experience and understand firsthand the issues that impact the lives of sexual minorities (Brodyn and Ghaziani 2018; Doan and Higgins 2011; Florida 2003). Gay men have become so closely associated with revitalizing decaying urban neighborhoods that municipalities have developed urban redevelopment strategies around attracting LGBTQ residents and businesses.

Modeling the successful revitalization of a nearby suburb, city officials in Detroit once attempted to attract gay residents into its decaying downtown area by authorizing LGBTQ-friendly initiatives, including an extension of benefits to same-sex couples of city employees (Robertson 2003).

The very question about the future of iconic gay neighborhoods like the Castro reflects the fulfillment of the American Dream. Challenging prevailing assumptions of homosexuality as "deviant," early scholars established how gay neighborhoods conformed with cultural enclaves (Castells and Murphy 1982; Lauria and Knopp 1985; Levine 1979; Murray 1979). These days, popular and academic scholars assume the declining salience of gay neighborhoods as the culminating "vision" of LGBTQ citizens to assimilate into the mainstream. The demographic and institutional "straightening" of iconic gay neighborhoods, alongside the visible presence of same-sex couples in suburban and rural areas, reveal LGBTQ residents as "regular people" with the same hopes and dreams as their heterosexual counterparts. The ubiquity of rainbow flags and equality stickers adorning downtown businesses and municipal buildings reveal the broad incorporation of LGBTQ culture. And the decreasing reliance on gay neighborhoods for safety and protection by new generations of LGBTQ citizens highlights the diminishing role of sexuality as a defining feature of one's identity. On paper, academic and popular predictions over the "demise" of iconic gay neighborhoods epitomize the political and economic promise of the American Dream.

This chapter complicates that version. Aligning gay neighborhoods alongside more traditional urban communities erases a diversity of urban geographies that LGBTQ citizens have created in their pursuit of the American Dream. Tracing these geographies over the twentieth and twenty-first centuries, this chapter exposes how various LGBTQ communities have drawn on the enterprising, innovative, and revolutionary spirit of the American Dream to create visible, vibrant subcultures that encourage diverse expressions of sexuality and gender. Often existing in the shadows of the dominant (i.e. white, heteronormative, middle-class) culture, these geographies often relied on appropriating and reimagining existing spaces to pursue the freedom and opportunity promised through the American Dream. In the face of persecution, policing, and sexual exploitation, these communities nevertheless persisted, seeking recognition through place-making practices often legible as immoral, illegal, and illicit to outsiders. And yet, they allowed the sexual communities that emerged from these spaces to challenge and redefine notions of entitlement, ownership, and, ultimately, what it means to be a citizen.

Remapping the American Landscape

The April 13, 1888, edition of *The Washington Post* featured a story of a police raid in Washington, DC. The previous evening, a police lieutenant observed "strange-looking Females" entering a residence on the corner of 12th and F Streets NW for a "supper and dance." When the police entered the home, they discovered fifteen Black men dressed as women in "rich material … made in the latest fashions" seated in a "handsomely furnished room" around a "luxurious supper" (*The Washington Post* 1888, 3). While the party guests jumped out of windows and stripped naked to evade arrest, one of the guests stood their ground. William Dorsey Swann, "a big Negro … dressed in a gorgeous dress of cream-colored satin" and "bursting with rage," rushed toward the police to prevent their further entry into the room (*The Washington Post* 1888, 3). A brawl ensued for several minutes, after which the police arrested Swann and about a dozen guests from the party.

Born into slavery, William Dorsey Swann distinguished himself as the self-proclaimed "queen" of Washington DC's Black drag ball scene in the late-nineteenth century. When few protections existed for homosexuals, Swann created the "House of Swann," comprising Black male domestic workers and employees of the federal government who would hold drag balls in private residences throughout the city. Despite the threats of police raids, having their lives exposed in the local papers, and facing ostracism from the families and community, Swann and his friends continued hosting and participating in "drag dances." When sentenced to jail time in 1896 for holding a drag ball, Swann petitioned President Grover Cleveland for a pardon. While the president denied his request, the petition reflected the first time an American took legal action to defend the right for homosexuals to gather (Cherry 2021).

Not all the gay men and lesbians who participated in the gay worlds of the late-nineteenth and early-twentieth centuries possessed Swann's revolutionary spirit. Yet, the geographies that gay men and women created in the late-nineteenth and early-twentieth centuries reflected the ingenuity and imagination that animates the American Dream. In the absence of opportunities to explore their sexual and gendered identities, gay men and women created their own, reimagining existing public and private spaces for their own use. Public parks, theaters, and restrooms transformed into nighttime spaces for discreet sexual encounters. Gay men also refashioned city bridges, beaches, and storefront windows into meeting places. Starkly contrasting their daytime uses, the gay worlds emerging from these spaces fostered a "highly sophisticated system of subcultural codes – codes of dress, speech, and style – that enabled [gay men] to recognize one another and carry on intimate conversations whose coded meanings were unintelligible to potentially people around them" (Chauncey 1994, 4).

Many gay worlds existed concurrently with a space's more mainstream use. Historians Elizabeth Lapovsky Kennedy and Madeline D. Davis (1997) explore how lesbians in Buffalo, New York developed strategies to meet each other within straight bars. While not exclusively for their use, lesbians referred to these spaces as "lesbian bars" to reflect the patrons' sense of safety to meet other queer women. In his controversial study of anonymous sex in public restrooms, sociologist Laud Humphreys (1975) revealed an extensive social world governed by unspoken rules and roles that ordered the practices taking place there. Accessing the sexual world of the "tearoom" depended on knowing how to position yourself within the space, interact with the other participants, and what to do when an outsider (or a police officer) enters.

For white gay men and lesbians, the same qualities of urban life that early scholars contributed to the "loss" of community facilitated the production and flowering of these alternate geographies. The sense of anonymity arising out of the size, density, and heterogeneity within cities (Wirth 1938) afforded a certain degree of freedom for white gay men and women to construct lives and distinct underground subcultures independent from their families, careers, and mainstream cultural conventions.[2] "The complexity of the city's social and spatial organization," writes historian George Chauncey, "made it possible for gay men to construct the multiple identities necessary for them to participate in the gay world without losing the privileges of the straight: assuming one identity at work, another in leisure; one identity before biological kin, another with gay friends"(1994, 133–34). Gay white men enjoyed greater freedom to participate in gay social worlds at a distance from the straight worlds they created. In the 1920s, many gay white men in New York and Chicago ventured into the Black gay worlds of Harlem and Bronzeville, respectively, where they could more freely express their gay identities.

Anonymous, brief contact also proved vital in the persistence of certain gay worlds, such as cruising areas in parks, public bathrooms, literary societies, and YMCAs. The anonymous nature of these spaces enables imagining community built around one's investment to place. In his diaries, Jeb Alexander shows how cruising in the parks of Washington, DC, "was nearly a nightly ritual each spring and summer during the early 1920s" (Beemyn 1997, 20). Although not too successful in picking up men, Alexander would continue going, fearing "that [he was] missing something if he did not go every night" (c.f., Beemyn 1997, 20). While cruising areas may create opportunities to build social networks, gay men "could recognize that they were not the 'only one' and begin to develop a network of like-minded friends, and perhaps belong to a sense of belonging to the larger community"(Beemyn 1997, 19).

Episodic in nature, these gay worlds were both fleeting and lasting. Existing in the shadow of the dominant culture, many gay worlds cultivated communities at that moment, rising and falling as the place production also shifted from "straight" to "gay." Gay men and lesbians fostered restricted relationships limited to the places and the times they were together. Anthropologist Esther Newton (1997) describes how, between the 1930s and 1960s, Cherry Grove became a weekend escape for upper-middle and upper-class white lesbians who could not live openly in New York City. Many of the platonic, sexual, and romantic relationships developed among these women were primarily limited to the weekends and summers when they could spend in that "magical place" (Newton 1997, 147). At the same time, the daily and nightly reproduction of queer places facilitated continuity that supported and maintained vibrant gay subcultures over time. Certain commercial establishments earned reputations well beyond the immediate communities they supported. For example, in Washington, DC, during the 1930s and 1940s, "daytime patrons" knew when to finish their meals before downtown restaurants transitioned into nightly gay gather spots. Hotel guests also knew which nights to avoid the hotel bars unless they wanted to face being labeled homosexual (Beemyn 2015).

The anonymity of cruising areas in cities did not keep them hidden from visitors and newcomers to the gay world. In his gay life in Chicago during the early twentieth century, historian David K. Johnson (1997, 97) describes how "Harold," a high school student with an "active social life with a bohemian crowd that favored 'smoking, nightclubs, and beer flats,'" easily stumbled upon a gay world during his first encounter. "Harold discovered the fairies he was intent on meeting not in some dark alley or obscure tavern but in the doorway of the Wrigley building – one of the most central, well-lit, public locations in all of Chicago"(Johnson 1997, 101). In large cities, hidden gathering places had a reputation well beyond city limits. Johnson describes how "Jimmy" corresponded with men from Michigan, Indiana, and Maryland, who were quite familiar with Chicago's cruising areas. Describing the reputation of Lafayette Park outside the White House, historian Genny Beemyn describes "[t]he extent to which Lafayette Square was renowned as a cruising location was that one of the men had heard about the park while he was in the Virgin Islands" (2004, 157). Gay novels also fueled readers' imagination about the city's covert gay gatherings paces. Reading a series of gay novels sparked "Harold's" imagination and fueled his motivation to "meet some of these so-called fairies" (Johnson 1997, 97). Lafayette Square particularly benefitted from references in print media. "Gay novels published in the 1930s made reference to the park as a meeting place for homosexuals" (Johnson 2004, 47).

While racial segregation prevented Black gay men and lesbians from participating in many white gay establishments during the early twentieth century, they created parallel gay worlds that refashioned existing commercial and cultural institutions to foster community. In addition to the restaurants, speakeasies, and nightclubs that allowed gay men and lesbians opportunities to dance, Black gays and lesbians gathered at private house parties, where they could dance and socialize without fear of harassment by authorities and disapproving neighbors (Beemyn 2015; Kennedy and Davis 1997). Drag balls and festivals also provided spaces for gay Black men to explore their sexual and gender identities. At times including Black professionals, these festivals challenged sexual mores of the era, centering lavish displays of gender expression and unapologetically celebrating sex. Describing one "drag dance" in Washington, DC, neurologist Charles H. Lewis expresses outrage over the fact that many of these men, "lasciviously dressed in womanly attire … and deport[ing] themselves as women" occupied positions as either domestic employees for some of Washington's elite families or as "subordinate" professionals working for the government (Hughes 1893, 731–732). Neurologist Charles Rosse (1892, 802) also depicts one such orgy of "phallic worship," whereby a "big buck with a turgescent penis decorated with gaily colored ribbons" stood in the center of a room while admirers touched and kissed it.

In contrast to white gay men who could escape their local worlds, Black gay men and lesbians often encountered relatives, neighbors, and coworkers during their nightly rounds. However, despite the disapproval by elite members of Black society, Black gay men and lesbians often had to navigate their presence in shops and churches. This also resulted in bolder expressions of gender and sexual identity that surpassed their white counterparts. Historian Allen Drexel describes how black female impersonators endured harassment and threats of violence to perform a version of male homosexuality publicly. "As the most visible figures in male homosexual culture," Drexel explains, "they were persistent, flamboyant, public transgressors of an otherwise apparently 'natural' and uniform heterosexual regime" (1997, 122).

Both the Great Depression and the repeal of Prohibition fundamentally reshaped gay worlds in cities, as local, state, and federal authorities developed a variety of laws and practices to eradicate public expressions of homosexual life and culture (Chauncey 1994; D'Emilio 1983; Heap 2009). As a result, gay patrons and bar owners faced considerable risks by assembling in bars. "While many [gay] men patronized bars," writes Chauncey, "others were unwilling to do so, at least during crackdowns, for fear of being caught in a raid, which might result in being arrested or at least being forced to divulge their names and places of employment" (Chauncey 1994, 348–349). Few gay men and lesbians assumed the risk of owning a bar. Many bars that catered to gay clientele had ties to the criminal underworld, who cared less about their patrons than they did making profits. Regardless of ownership, these bars survived through creative branding. In Washington, DC, many of the "gay bars" branded themselves as restaurants, requiring men to be seated to purchase drinks (Beemyn 2015). Owners classified The Stonewall Inn as a "private bottle club," where patrons had to sign their "names" in a book to gain entry (although patrons almost exclusively used pseudonyms) (Carter 2004; D'Emilio 1983; Duberman 1993). While these bars did not provide ideal conditions to assemble, they nevertheless developed reputations as gay bars through the presence and participation of their patrons. As anchoring institutions for gay communities, these bars served various functions that offered a sense of social and institutional completeness for their gay patrons. "A particular gay bar," observes sociologist Nancy Achilles, "may serve as a loan office, restaurant, message reception center, telephone exchange, and so forth" (1967, 175).

Additionally, gay bars offered not only environments that facilitated social interaction, but these spaces also offered patrons a "third space" (Oldenberg 1989), which offered protection from family, residential, and career-based networks. Elizabeth Lapovsky Kennedy and Madeline D. Davis (1997) argue that many working-class lesbians in Buffalo preferred socializing in bars than drawing attention to themselves by socializing in or near their local communities. Despite the various threats to their physical safety, white working-class lesbians relied on bars for community building. "Although the entertainment bars were not gay space in the sense that gays and lesbians could not be open about who they were," they write, "they did provide a space where lesbians were comfortable and could have a good time without having to fear being ridiculed or harassed" (Kennedy and Davis 1997, 37). Gay bars in mid-century also possessed a supra-spatial quality. As state agencies forced the closure of gay establishments, new ones would open in their place where the same customs and traditions would continue. "When a bar closes," writes Achilles, "its patrons shift their activities else-where. In the new bar, the same music comes out of the jukebox, the same bartenders mix drinks, the same faces appear, and the conversation repeats the same pattern" (1967, 182). In the face of legal and economic obstacles, gay nightlife persisted because patrons carried over the cultural representations and practices associated with their communities from one site to the next.

Because gay men and lesbians did not enjoy the visibility and freedom to live their lives openly in the late-nineteenth and early-twentieth centuries, scholars easily dismiss these gay worlds as "fragile," lying under the radar of the heteronormative culture. However, these worlds also expose qualities embodying the spirit of the American Dream. In the face of a hostile culture, gay men and lesbians persisted, deploying creative strategies to take ownership over spaces to create and foster communities that supported the safe exploration of sexuality and gender. While indeed "scattered gay spaces" (Forsyth 2001; Ghaziani 2014), they also reflected complex geographies where gay men and women navigated anti-gay hostility within the dominant culture and mitigated the isolation often associated with the pre-Stonewall era.

Stonewall, Gay Neighborhoods, and the Remaking of Local Citizenship

When police detectives started toward the Stonewall Inn in the late evening of June 27, 1969, "they must have expected it to be a routine raid"(D'Emilio 1983, 231).[3] In the midst of a mayoral campaign, the Stonewall Inn provided an easy target. Once a restaurant hastily transformed into a gay bar after a fire, the Stonewall conspicuously stood on Christopher Street in Greenwich Village, quite unconventional for gay bars during this era. The bar circumvented the State Liquor Authority by branding itself as a private bottle club, serving watered-down, overpriced drinks without a license and with alcohol almost exclusively supplied by the Mafia, which owned and operated this bar. It had no fire exits and no running water behind the bar. The toilet overran constantly. In fact, its unhygienic practice for cleaning glasses had resulted in several hepatitis outbreaks among Stonewall's customers (Carter 2004, 80). Yet despite these conditions, the Stonewall attracted a broad cross-section of gay and lesbian patrons, including the most marginalized contingents of the gay community: male hustlers, drag queens, transsexuals, and homeless street youth, many of whom were non-white. Police raids on the Stonewall were common (the police raided the bar a few nights before); however, as the Mafia paid off the police regularly, the bar typically reopened the following evening.

Therefore, when the new commanding officer of the Sixth Precinct set out to raid the Stonewall on the fateful Friday night, he organized carefully to ensure that this raid would permanently close the bar. That night, after raiding the bar, a city inspector would cite the bar's infractions. A federal agent from the Bureau of Alcohol, Tobacco, and Firearms would identify himself and gather liquor samples for testing. Pine "had no doubt the Stonewall Inn was watering down its liquor, which was a violation of federal law … Maybe if he hit the Stonewall Inn often enough and hard enough, he just might succeed in shutting it down for good" (Carter 2004, 131).

That evening, things did not go as planned. As the police moved through the club, customers resisted. Many refused to show identification to the police. Transvestites refused to go into the bathrooms for a police examination. As the cops continued to push patrons outside, a crowd formed on the street, jeering at police officers as they began loading prisoners into the paddy wagon – first, the Mafia employees, followed by the non-Mafia employees. The crowd out-side grew increasingly angry as they began taking stock of the injustices they had routinely endured at the hands of the police. "The gay men who stood outside the Stonewall talked about the destruction of their lovers' lane[4] as well as about how many of their other clubs had been raided in recent weeks: the Snake Pit, the Checkerboard, and the Sewer. Now not only had the Stonewall Inn been hit twice in one week, but also tonight's raid had come on a Friday night and at the evening's peak" (Carter 2004, 143).

Two incidents incited the riot. "The first hostile act outside the club occurred when a police officer shoved one of the transvestites, who turned and smacked the officer over the head with her purse. The cop clubbed her, and a wave of anger passed through the crowd, which immediately showered the police with boos and catcalls, followed by a cry to turn the paddy wagon over" (Carter 2004, 148). Yet the crowd erupted after the police threw a lesbian patron who resisted arrest into a police car. Lucian Truscott IV of *The Village Voice* reported:

> [T]he scene became explosive. Limp wrists were forgotten. Beer cans and bottles were heaved at the windows and a rain of coins descended on the cops ... Almost by signal the crowd erupted into cobblestone and bottle heaving ... From nowhere came an uprooted parking meter – used as a 'battering ram' on the Stonewall door. I heard several cries of "let's get some gas," but the blaze of flame which soon appeared in the window of the Stonewall was still a shock.
>
> *1969, 18*

The police retreated into the bar and barricaded themselves "as all kinds of objects continued to crash around the police" (Carter 2004, 157). Police reinforcement arrived to liberate the trapped officers as the violence escalated. Protesters openly mocked the police as they attempted to quell and dissipate the crowd into the night. The rioting went into the night; by 4 am Saturday, the police managed to clear the streets and restore order. "By the time the last cop was off the street Saturday morning, a sign was going up announcing that the Stonewall would reopen that night. It did" (Teal 1971, 20).

Riots would continue around the Stonewall over the next several nights. On Saturday, as people stopped by to inspect the wreckage, several slogans appeared in chalk on the walls encouraging support for gay power. That evening, many of the rioters returned, along with onlookers and tourists who supported the protests. Speeches and chants intensified: "Liberate Christopher Street!" and "Christopher Street belongs to the queens" (Carter 2004, 183)! "Hand-holding, kissing, and posing accented each of the cheers with a homosexual liberation that had appeared only fleetingly on the street before" (Truscott IV 1969, 18). Eventually, the crowd spilled onto the street, prompting the decision to block Christopher Street from ongoing traffic. "When an occasional car did try to bulldoze its way in, the crowd quickly surrounded it, rocking it back and forth so vigorously that the occupants soon proved more than happy to be allowed to retreat" (Duberman 1993, 204). Protesters started fires in trashcans and threw bottles at the approaching police officers, attempting to quell the demonstration. As protesters overwhelmed the police, NYPD's Tactical Police Force arrived on the scene for the second night to clear the street. Once again, the street fights and police chases continued throughout the night and into the early morning.

The Stonewall Riots offer a valuable lens for examining how sexuality has reconfigured notions of community and citizenship in industrial and post-industrial American cities. In the decades since the uprising, scholars have focused mainly on its lingering impact – either as the "spark" that ignited the contemporary gay rights movement (Bérubé 1990; Duberman 1993; Faderman 1991; Ghaziani 2008) or as "a repeated and cherished *movement myth* [that] neither [offers] an accurate description nor a compelling explanation of the origins of gay liberation"(Armstrong 2002, 63). However, the Stonewall Riots also reveal the deep attachment and sense of ownership LGBTQ people felt toward a bar that legally did not belong to them. Far from ideal, the bar still "offered its patrons [four] crucial things: space, security, ... freedom," and a sense of continuity that comes with the bar's longevity in the area. "Through the power of music and dance, the club fused these elements to create amongst most of its regular customers a sense of gay community and thus a loyalty to the Stonewall Inn" (Carter 2004, 88). As the state denied gays and lesbians the rights to visibility in and access to the community, Stonewall patrons defended the only sense of community they had – and in doing so, articulated their legitimate claims of participation as members of a visible gay community. That sense of ownership extended well outside the bar. John O'Brien recounts to David Carter that "when [the police] tried to clear the streets is when people resented it, [be]cause it came down to 'Whose streets are these? They are our streets. And you cops are not from this area; this is our area. It's gay people's streets' (2004, 178). Compared to urban riots that preceded and followed them, the Stonewall Riots represented a unique milestone in American History in which the demands for state recognition are inextricably linked to the appropriation of space and the production of its meaning.

Central to the gay liberation movement that burgeoned after the Stonewall Riots in 1969 was the need to create visible gay communities, which required gay men and lesbians to officially come out of the closet and live their lives in the open. "Publicly declaring one's homosexuality," writes Jeffrey Escoffier, "was the decisive innovation of the post-Stonewall gay and lesbian movement. This 'coming out' strategy demonstrated a sizeable group of people engaged in primarily homosexual behavior" (1998, 209). The new gay liberation movement also accelerated the development of gay neighborhoods in American cities, made possible by a unique alignment of political, demographic, and ecological opportunities. Gay neighborhoods not only emerge out of the vision of self-governance. They also benefited from the deindustrialization and residential deconcentration of cities, resulting from both the outmigration of white working- and middle-class families to the suburbs and race riots of the 1960s, which left many urban communities in extreme disrepair (Armstrong 2002; Clendinen and Nagourney 1999; Lauria and Knopp 1985).

While the Stonewall Riots accelerated the emergence of gay neighborhoods in the 1970s, "the gay movement developed the *idea* of building a gay neighborhood before the *reality* of the gay neighborhood was achieved" (Armstrong 2002, 116, emphasis in original). Homophile activists in the 1950s and 1960s intensely debated creating segregated gay spaces. While many believed in integrating with heterosexuals or avoiding public exposure entirely, others saw value in developing a visible presence by creating gay-specific institutions and organizations. As gay liberationists built upon the momentum of the Stonewall Riots, many, like Carl Wittman, envisioned a separate, self-governing territory from a homophobic mainstream American society:

> To be a free territory, we must govern ourselves, set up our own institutions, defend ourselves, and improve our lives. The emergence of gay liberation communes and our own paper is a good start. The talk about a gay liberation coffee shop-dance hall should be followed through. Rural retreats, political action offices, food cooperatives, a free school, unalienated bars and after hours [sic] places – they must be developed if we are to have even the shadow of a "free territory."
>
> *Wittman 1970*

Wittman's vision of a "free territory" differed from the existing areas he characterized as ghettos.[5] "[They are] ghetto[s] rather than free territor[ies]," he writes, "because [they are] still theirs. Straight cops patrol us, straight legislators make our laws, straight employers keep us in line, straight money exploits us" (Wittman 1970).

Although gay neighborhoods did not achieve Wittman's utopian vision, they represented a distinct departure from the gay worlds that flourished in the previous era. "While homosexual bars and commercial establishments were clustered together in specific neighborhoods of most major urban areas in the United States in the twentieth century, [gay neighborhoods like] the Castro took this spatial segregation to a new level" (Armstrong 2002, 116). Territories developing in cities like San Francisco, Los Angeles, Chicago, and New York combined gay-owned and operated institutions with a visible residential concentration to create a protected and stable space to foster community building and politically mobilize residents as a voting bloc (Castells 1983; Escoffier 1998). This spatial concentration forms the basis on which scholars will define community in gay neighborhoods. "When gays are spatially scattered," says Henry Britt in an interview with Manuel Castells, "they are not gay because they are invisible" (Castells 1983, 138).

Early scholars contributed to the political project of gay neighborhoods, strategically conceptualizing the gay community around a quasi-ethnic identity to "strengthen the notion that gays and lesbians function like an oppressed minority" (Davis 1995, 286). Stephen Murray (1979) shows how the institutional infrastructure of gay communities resembled those found in ethnic enclaves. Challenging earlier assumptions that no gay "community" exists, Murray argues that, despite the absence of primary kinship ties, Toronto's gay territories have the characteristics of ethnic communities: distinctive gay area, institutional completeness, shared culture and history, and collective consciousness to mobilize politically. Similarly, Martin P. Levine (1979) follows similar processes of deduction to compare gay territories to Park and Wirth's definitions of urban ghettoes: culture area, social segregation, and institutional and residential concentration. Relying mainly on secondary information, spot maps, and "informal ethnography" of main streets and thoroughfares, Levine argues how various gay territories in his study represent different stages of community development.

Promoting gay neighborhoods as "liberation zones," Manuel Castells defines the gay community through the collective efficacy of residents, whose efforts to consciously create a distinct and visible residential community are essentially indistinguishable from the creation of a gay movement in San Francisco (Castells and Murphy 1982, 238; Castells 1983, 157).[6] To advance their political interests, Castells argues, gays needed "a spatially defined community for a long period, where culture and power can be reformulated in a process of experimental social interaction and active political mobilization" (Castells and Murphy 1982, 189). Gay settlers represented "moral refugees," who intentionally located in the Castro at significant economic and personal risk (Castells 1983, 161). Legal repression, social prejudice, and the threat of violence restricted their ability to create social networks, find sexual partners, and lead visible, uninhibited lives. Bars provided one of the few venues where social networks developed, but socializing in these spaces also carried risk, as they were under close surveillance. The cultural revolts of the 1960s created opportunities for gays to expand their space – from the bars to specific neighborhoods and from the neighborhood to "larger areas of the city that became, by the mid-1970s, gay free communes" (Castells 1983, 145). For Castells, gay people deliberately constructed gay ghettoes as a means of political and physical protection and to create a distinct culture that would enable them to live openly gay lives.

The gay neighborhoods conceptualized by Murray, Levine, and Castells depend almost entirely on conforming gay neighborhoods to traditional sociological processes of residential citizenship. However, these connections are somewhat misleading. While a residential concentration is an important indicator of a gay community, not all who claimed community membership in gay neighborhoods like the Castro were residents of the area. While the Castro emerged as the political and commercial heart of San Francisco's gay community, "the Castro ghetto grew and expanded dramatically in all adjacent areas ... reach[ing] the Dolores Corridor on the border with Latino Mission District" (Castells 1983, 156). As housing prices increased in neighborhoods like the Castro, forcing out original residents (Boyd 2011; Israels 1979), accessibility to the Castro institutions became equally crucial to maintaining community ties than residential ties.

Furthermore, these studies underestimate the persistent role of gay institutions in building and fostering notions of community. Levine, for example, acknowledges that the character of gay neighborhoods changes depending on the time of day:

> Relatively quiet on weekday mornings and afternoons, bars and streets are crowded at nights and on weekends, because participation in the gay world, for homosexual males, occurs after normal working hours ... At such times, the areas are flooded with residents as well as with gay men from surrounding neighborhoods who travel in to participate in the local gay scene.
>
> *Levine 1979, 372*

While both Levine (1979) and Murray (1979, 168) acknowledge that residential outsiders participate in the cultural and commercial life of gay neighborhoods, none investigates how these forms of participation evince alternate claims of community identification and membership. As gay culture and politics consolidated in gay neighborhoods, participation in local institutions provided consumers with a panoply of shared cultural experiences that could facilitate heightened investment in the sense of community in gay neighborhoods (Armstrong 2002).

Gay bars have played a central role in the movement toward LGBTQ equality, bringing together a diversity of gay constituents[7] and concentrating political organization, consciousness-raising, and mobilization within gay neighborhoods. For example, in San Francisco, bar patrons proved decisive in the McGovern presidential campaign in 1972. In one night of canvassing, the Alice B. Toklas Democratic club obtained one-third of the northern California signatures necessary to place George McGovern on the primary ballot (Shilts 1982, 63). While Castro certainly concentrated much of the gay voting bloc, the power of gays in San Francisco became such that "no mayor can afford to risk openly opposing gays in the election" (Castells 1983, 139). Randy Shilts, in his article about Castro, describes how local and state politicians go to gay bars during election years, "ready to give smiles and handshakes to all takers" ([1982] 1994, 155). In Washington, DC, Marion Barry successfully challenged the Black electoral establishment by courting the gay white vote in bars. Therefore, protecting gay bars was also essential to gay electoral politics. "Gay politics in San Francisco, as in LA and New York had been formed almost entirely in reaction to the continuing crackdown by authorities on gay bars and gay male sexuality" (Clendinen and Nagourney 1999, 150).

Scholars studying the formation of gay neighborhoods engaged in a political project that simultaneously positioned gay communities as oppressed minorities who accomplished the American Dream through property ownership. However, in defining gay neighborhoods through their residential dimension, scholars largely overlook the key dimensions of community building that distinguished the formation of gay neighborhoods. Access to gay social, cultural, and political institutions proved vital in claiming communities in gay neighborhoods seeking residence within their borders. As gentrification priced-out gay men and lesbians from iconic gay neighborhoods, many created alternate paths of citizenship and belonging that connected them to visible LGBTQ communities. Ultimately, the emergence of gay neighborhoods in the 1970s and 1980s is not the culmination of a distinct project of gay identity building. Instead, "gay community" emanates from the convergence of a combination of residential and non-residential actors whose visions of the community depend upon one's participation in the cultural, political, economic, and sexual life of gay neighborhoods.

Yet not all LGBTQ citizens can pursue this version of the American Dream. Racial and economic segregation often excluded queer women and communities of color from participating in iconic gay neighborhoods. The exact economic, legal, and sociopolitical mechanisms that shaped racial segregation in cities equally worked to exclude LBQ women and queer communities of color from the housing markets in iconic gay neighborhoods. Discriminatory housing and commercial practices made it particularly difficult for Black gays and lesbians to participate in the life of the gay neighborhood. In his pointed critique of geographer Lawrence Knopp's (1997) exploration of the Marigny as a gay neighborhood, Charles Nero (2005) highlights how the racially exclusive hiring practices of the University of New Orleans in the 1960s, which hired many of the early settlers in Marigny, played a pivotal role in the racial homogeneity of the gay neighborhood. "Racially segregated workplaces," Nero notes, "made it highly unlikely that middle-class black and white gay males would create" the kind of informal networks that made gentrification in Marigny possible (2005, 232). Additionally, various examples of "velvet rope racism" (Buford May 2018) persist in gay bars and nightlife, further limiting the participation of LGBTQ communities of color in iconic gay neighborhoods. Yet these barriers have not prevented these marginalized communities from pursuing a different American Dream. Developing alternate geographies that rely on and challenge gay neighborhoods, underrepresented LGBTQ have challenged their erasure from a movement that has primarily equated success with achieving white, middle-class, heteronormative respectability.

Reimagining Gay Neighborhoods and Communities in the "Post-Gay" Era

In the last two decades, popular and scholarly attention to gay neighborhoods often centers on factors contributing to their disappearance or declining salience. A 1994 *New York Times* article describes how "predominately gay neighborhoods have arisen in a dozen major cities over the last two decades, at once bolstering sagging tax bases, pumping thousands of dollars into the economy, and sometimes making tired neighborhoods safer and more attractive to heterosexuals" (De Witt 1994). Driven by the successful transformation of neighborhoods like Greenwich Village and Chelsea in New York, Dupont Circle in Washington, DC, Boystown in Chicago, Montrose in Houston, and Capitol Hill in Seattle, gay men (and, to a lesser extent, lesbians) increasingly became influential economic actors, who transformed dilapidated urban neighborhoods into trendy and economically viable enclaves. As more gay residents select out of iconic gay neighborhoods and heterosexuals continue selecting them, gay neighborhoods also transform into sexually diverse spaces, losing their culture, political, and social distinctiveness.

This understanding coincided with a growing tolerance for LGBTQ citizens, signaling shifts in the direction of the gay and lesbian movement. In the 1990s, queer scholars began challenging the political strategy of gays and lesbians segregating in discrete gay neighborhoods, problematizing gay ghettos as "another sort of closet" (Davis 1995; Escoffier 1998; Kinsman 1995). Gary Kinsman (1995) notes that the gay ghetto is "both a playground and a concentration camp. While it provides people a place to meet and to explore and develop aspects of their lives and sexuality, it can also separate people from the rest of the population in a much larger closet that can be isolated and maintained" (412). As gay identity and politics shifted toward the mainstream, activists stressed that achieving full equality under the law meant exposing the ordinariness of LGBTQ Americans and their families. In addition to census data that reveal the presence of same-sex couples in 99.3 percent of all counties in the United States (Gates 2007; Gates and Ost 2004), various studies have depicted the lives of LGBTQ communities in suburban (Brekhus 2003), small towns (Brown-Saracino 2017), and rural areas (Blotcher 2002; Stone 2018). In highlighting the spatial diversity of LGBTQ populations throughout the country, scholars reveal communities who consciously reject – to varying degrees – lifestyles they associate with living in gay-specific urban spaces.

Finally, scholars have raised the alarm on the disappearance of gay bars and nightlife in the United States, which have proven central to mobilizing LGBTQ communities throughout the twentieth century (Mattson 2020b; Renninger 2018; Savage, Lavietes, and Anarte 2020; Usher and Morrison 2010). Sociologist Greggor Mattson (2020a) notes a 37 percent decline in gay bar listings in the United States from 2007 to 2019, with the most significant periods of the decline occurring between 2012 and 2017 (18.6 percent decline) and 2017 and 2019 (14.4 percent). These trends are most acute among venues serving specific LGBTQ subcultures. From 2007 to 2019, lesbian bar listings decreased by nearly 52 percent, while "cruisy" bars, serving men engaging in various forms of sex on the premises, declined by nearly 60 percent. Nearly 60 percent of bars supporting LGBTQ communities of color have also shut down (Mattson 2020a). Scholars have largely attributed these closures to the rise of geospatial dating apps, which have supplanted many of the functions of gay bars for LGBTQ communities, including mobilizing communities around important sociocultural and political issues.

Amin Ghaziani (2010, 65) connects these factors to the transition of gay neighborhoods into a post-gay era, "which impacts these gay neighborhoods by potentially unraveling them and rendering them 'passé.'" The absorption of gay, lesbian, bisexual, and transgender people into the mainstream, Ghaziani argues, has diminished the imperative for sexual minorities to seek safety and a sense of community in discrete gay neighborhoods. "The assimilation of American gays [into the straight mainstream] has generated feelings of acceptance, integration, and safety, which is reversing an earlier propensity of lesbians and gay men to concentrate in discrete urban enclaves" (Ghaziani 2010, 65). The implications are twofold. First, he argues that assimilation results in an "overextension of the gay residential imagination," which involves the expansion of the "spatial position of homosexuality from the specific streets of a gay enclave to an entire city itself" (2010, 65).

Yet the diminishing material culture of iconic gay neighborhoods has not erased their symbolic culture. Iconic gay neighborhoods persist in the imagination of LGBTQ citizens as safe spaces to publicly express their gendered and sexual identities. For many, gay neighborhoods are spaces where they can display public affection with their partner, where they can feel comfortable walking down the street in heels next to a straight couple enjoying their bunch. Moreover, as gay bars and nightclubs have decreased significantly over the last two decades, LGBTQ subcultures draw on the remaining institutions to create fleeting but recurrent places to sustain their ties to the local area. Theme nights like "Retro Night," "Jai-Ho," "Latino Night," and "Ladies Night" constitute time-contingent, segmented social orders (Suttles 1968), where culture and community flourish and ebb at the moment, only to regenerate when the time comes around for the event to happen again. Following the tragic shooting at Pulse Nightclub in 2016, LGBTQ communities around the world reactivated spaces in iconic gay neighborhoods as sites of collective mourning. From the Castro in San Francisco to the Stonewall Inn in New York City, LGBTQ citizens held vigils, created makeshift memorials, and gave passionate speeches about the need to preserve queer safe spaces. While indeed fleeting, these geographies reinforce the value of gay neighborhoods as sites of community support and mobilization.

While popular perceptions of Black homophobia within the "iconic ghetto" (Anderson 2012) often render them invisible, Black sexual minorities created and fostered vibrant and variably visible communities throughout the twentieth and twenty-first centuries. Due to segregation, many Black LGBTQ people have lived out their sexual lives within their families and friends (Beemyn 2015; Cabello 2012b, 2012a; Drexel 1997; Heap 2009). Black queer culture often mirrors certain spatial practices associated with Black urban life, relying on "interaction and meaning to transform spaces into places, however ephemeral they may be" (Hunter et al. 2016, 12). Private house parties, nightclubs, cookouts, and drag balls remain essential sites for fostering Black LGBTQ communities. These places lack the spatial stability scholars have assigned to queer institutional anchors in iconic gay neighborhoods. Nevertheless, these communities marshal their available resources to carve out spaces where they are visible to one another and where they can leverage economic opportunities that mitigate the effects of poverty and hypersegregation (Hunter 2010). As their white neighbors might misrecognize these spatialized logics as "closeted," being "invisible in plain sight" represent strategies of resilience, belonging, and resistance for queer communities of color, particularly as urban revitalization threatens their displacement.

Equally, the singular scholarly focus on gay neighborhoods also ignores the creative strategies that lesbians, bisexuals, and queer women use to create spatial communities. Scholars have long noted the fleeting nature of queer women's geographies, arguing that, unlike gay men, LBQ women lack the territorial aspirations to create distinct "lesbian" neighborhoods (Castells 1983; Lauria and Knopp 1985). Feminist scholars like Bonnie Morris note the increasing diversification and fragmentation of LBQ communities, which results in spatially diffuse gathering places for queer women to congregate (Morris 2016). Exploring the disappearing geographies of lesbian feminists, Morris argues that this diffusion has resulted in the absorption of lesbian culture into the mainstream and a loss of a distinctive lesbian culture that once mobilized and fostered political and sociocultural communities. In a recent study of lesbian, bisexual, and queer women in four small cities, sociologist Japonica Brown-Saracino (2017) describes the role of location in shaping the various communities that these women created. While the liberal political culture of Ithaca allows LBQ women to downplay their sexual identities and assimilate into the community, San Luis Obispo's conservative climate necessitates queer women to project their "lesbian" identities as static and central to their political and communal lives. Brown-Saracino even exposes intergenerational differences within LBQ communities. In Greenfield, Massachusetts, she discovered that while older generations of LBQ women held on to communities that centered a distinctly "lesbian" identity, newer generations downplayed their sexuality to integrate themselves into sexually diverse communities.

While LBQ women have not laid the kinds of spatial claims as gay men, it would be a mistake to argue that LBQ women have not developed distinct geographies to support and foster community. Critiquing the "myth of neighborhood liberation," geographer Jen Jack Gieseking (2020) describes how queer women and transgender, non-conforming people create distinct geographies unbounded to property ownership and neighborhood boundaries. As lesbian and queer neighborhoods in New York City fell victim to gentrification, queer women nevertheless created overlapping geographies of fleeting and fragmented spaces where they could find each other and foster community. Elaborating the metaphor of constellations, Gieseking challenges us to rethink what it means to claim ownership over the spaces that signify community.

Even as scholars question the importance of iconic gay neighborhoods in the lives of LGBTQ communities, they nevertheless remain valuable as sites that support the safe exploration of sexual and gender identity. My research on "queer street families" (Greene 2018) explores queer youth of color create and foster communities in Chicago's Boystown by reproducing "street corner" culture indigenous to their communities. In recent years, iconic gay neighborhood areas have increasingly become popular destinations among Black and Latinx LGBTQ queer youth, who travel for hours to participate in a community they believe will support their gender and sexual identities. Escaping the violence and homophobia within their local communities, these youths receive a hostile reception from local community members. They endure racial profiling and discrimination from business owners who find their presence undermining business. Many are too young or lack the economic resources to patronize gay bars and restaurants. Some, rejected by their families, resort to participating in the local sexual economy, picking up the same white gay men who publicly label them as menaces to community safety. As the overwhelmingly commercial focus of gay institutional anchors renders spaces in the gayborhood inaccessible to them, these youths develop a public relational order that mirrors the "codes of the street" governing street families in inner cities (Anderson 1994). At times, these youths use violence to mediate internal conflicts and external threats; as a result, residents, including gay white men, criticize their presence as a threat to public safety. Nevertheless, these youths defend their right to the neighborhood, drawing on their spatial practices as legitimate forms of local community participation. Combining the symbolic culture of gay neighborhoods with street corner practices, these youths make the gay neighborhood socioculturally relevant to them and, in so doing, reinforce the role of gay neighborhoods as spaces where gender and sexual identities are affirmed and supported.

Conclusion

On paper, the evolution of gay neighborhoods over the twentieth and twentieth-first centuries epitomizes the promises of the American Dream. A significant outgrowth of the contemporary gay rights movement, iconic gay neighborhoods like San Francisco's Castro Village and Greenwich Village in New York redirected conventional approaches to achieve a radical vision. The economic and cultural consolidation of queer life in these areas enabled LGBTQ people the opportunity to live their lives freely and safely in the open. Additionally, gay neighborhoods fostered a radical, public sexual culture that challenged the historically accepted heteronormative values of family and morality embedded in the traditional American Dream. This newfound visibility also consolidated political power, transforming the LGBTQ community into a powerful force in more progressive cities. Over time, as these neighborhoods flourished, they would not only contribute to broad social and political acceptance for LGBTQ citizens. Gay neighborhoods would also spark the revitalization of decaying urban centers at the end of the twentieth century.

This story, however, offers an incomplete picture. While some scholars and activists champion the declining salience of gay neighborhoods as the achievement of the American Dream, others have called attention to a diversity of LGBTQ communities and geographies that persist throughout cities. Some communities continue to rely on these areas as spaces of community, freedom, and empowerment, while others create and foster geographies beyond iconic gayborhoods. Nevertheless, the persistence of LGBTQ geographies in cities, both within and outside of iconic gay neighborhoods, represents new citizenship claims that legitimate their rights to recognition while also critiquing the assimilation of gay life into the mainstream. While misrecognized or disregarded, these ephemeral, unconventional forms of placemaking reflect the radical, expansive potential of the American Dream on which iconic gay neighborhoods emerged and evolved. Gay neighborhoods represent a small period of American LGBTQ history, where sexual minorities would evoke the revolutionary spirit of the American Dream to create geographies that would render each other visible and foster communities that supported their unique subcultures. These geographies persisted against moral and legal codes that placed the lives of their participants in peril. As gay neighborhoods displaced and excluded various LGBTQ populations, alternate geographies emerged that would render these citizens visible and give them a sense of ownership over the spaces and places they occupied. And while these forms of placemaking might not always succeed, it is the persistence and resilience of these communities to embrace and express their sexual and gender identities with pride that inspire LGBTQ Americans to continue pursuing the American Dream on their terms.

Notes

1 LGBTQ refers to lesbian, gay, bisexual, transgender, and queer communities. In recent years, the acronym has expanded to incorporate various gender non-conforming, asexual, questioning, two-spirit, and same-gender loving communities. However, for the sake of legibility, this chapter uses LGBTQ as a shorthand with the Q functioning as an (admittedly imprecise) stand-in for the diverse communities not included in the LGBTQ umbrella.
2 Highlighting the anonymous qualities of urban life is not to suggest that gay men and women were anonymous to or isolated from each other. "Although the anonymity of the city was important because it helped make possible for gay men to live double lives," writes George Chauncey, "it's only a starting point. It will prove more useful to focus on the ways gay men utilized the complexity of urban society to build an alternative gay social order" (1994, 133).
3 The description of the Stonewall Riots in this chapter is based on the following sources: Carter, David. 2004. *Stonewall: The Riots That Sparked the Gay Revolution*. New York: St. Martin's Press; D'Emilio, John. 1983b. *Sexual Politics, Sexual Communities: The Making of a Homosexual Minority in the United States 1940–1970*. Chicago: University of Chicago Press; Duberman, Martin. 1993. *Stonewall*. New York: Penguin Books; Humphreys, Laud. 1972. *Out of the Closets: The Sociology of Homosexual Liberation*. Englewood Cliffs: Prentice-Hall; Teal, Donn. 1971. *The Gay Militants*. New York: Stein and Day; Truscott IV, Lucian. 1969. "Gay Power Comes to Sheridan Square." *The Village Voice*, July 3, 1969, pp. 1, 18.
4 The "lovers lane" refers to Kew Gardens, a public park and convenient trysting place for gay men in Queens. In late-June 1969, a group of neighborhood vigilantes cut down the trees in Kew Gardens. Several citizens reported the park's destruction to the police, "only to see the police cars drive, up, and an officer get out and chat with the vigilantes, then leave without taking any action" (Carter 2004, 123).
5 The use of the term "ghetto" in this chapter will reflect the array of positive and negative associations that scholars and activists used to describe gay neighborhoods. Although none of the negative definitions associate "ghetto" as places for the involuntary segregation of racial, ethnic, or other minorities (often marked by extreme or concentrated poverty) (Gans 2008; Wilson 1987), Wittman's use of the ghetto does describe the sense of powerlessness and lack of agency that gays experience in places marked for gay consumption. Later uses will define ghetto in terms of "a collective closet," evoking the spatial, political, and commercial isolation of gay neighborhoods (Escoffier 1998; Davis 1995; Kinsman 1995).
6 See also Hunter (1975) for a discussion on how the conscious creation of "ideological communities" can also function as part of a broader sociopolitical movement.
7 I do not wish to minimize here the experiences of discrimination queer communities of color faced during this period in gay neighborhoods. Evidence shows that gay black men were often the victims of discriminatory and exclusionary practices in the 1970s white gay bar circuit, such as the practice of having to show multiple forms of identification for entrance (Armstrong 2002; Clendinen and Nagourney 1999; DeMarco [1983] 1999).

References

Achilles, Nancy. 1967. "The Development of the Homosexual Bar as an Institution." In *Social Perspectives in Lesbian and Gay Studies*, edited by Peter M. Nardi and Beth E. Schneider, 175–82. London: Routledge.

Anderson, Elijah. 1994. "The Code of the Streets." *Atlantic Monthly* 273: 80–94.

———. 2012. "The Iconic Ghetto." *The ANNALS of the American Academy of Political and Social Science* 642: 8–24.

Armstrong, Elizabeth. 2002. *Forging Gay Identities: Organizing Sexuality in San Francisco, 1950–1994.* Chicago: The University of Chicago Press.

Beemyn, Genny. 1997. "A Queer Capital: Lesbian, Gay, and Bisexual Life in Washington, DC 1890–1955." Dissertation, Iowa City: The University of Iowa.

———. 2004. "The Geography of Same-Sex Desire: Cruising Men in Washington, DC in the Nineteenth and Early Twentieth Century." *Left History* 9 (2): 141–59.

———. 2015. *A Queer Capital: A History of Gay Life in Washington, DC.* New York: Routledge.

Bérubé, Allan. 1990. *Coming Out Under Fire: The History of Gay Men and Women in World War II.* New York: Free Press.

Blotcher, Jay. 2002. "Gay Voices in Rural America." *The Advocate,* December 24, 2002.

Boyd, Nan Alamilla. 2011. "San Francisco's Castro District: From Liberation to Tourist Destination." *Journal of Tourism and Cultural Change* 9 (3): 237–48.

Brekhus, Wayne. 2003. *Peacocks, Chameleons, and Centaurs: Gay Suburbia and the Grammar of Social Identity.* Chicago: University of Chicago Press.

Brodyn, Adriana, and Amin Ghaziani. 2018. "Performative Progressiveness: Accounting for New Forms of Inequality in the Gayborhood." *City & Community* 17 (2): 307–29.

Brown-Saracino, Japonica. 2004. "Social Preservationists and the Quest for Authentic Community." *City & Community* 3 (2): 135–56.

———. 2007. "Virtuous Marginality: Social Preservationists and the Selection of the Old-Timer." *Theory and Society* 36 (5): 437–68.

———. 2017. *How Places Make Us: Novel LBQ Identities in Four Small Cities.* Chicago: University of Chicago Press.

Buford May, Ruben. 2018. "Velvet Rope Racism: Racial Paranoia, and Cultural Scripts: Alleged Dress Code Discrimination in Urban Nightlife, 2000–2014." *City & Community* 17 (1): 44–64.

Cabello, Tristan. 2012a. "Being Black and Queer in 1940s Bronzeville: Race, Class, and Queer Black Chicago, 1940–1950." Windy City Times. February 29. https://www.windycitytimes.com/lgbt/Queer-Bronzeville-African-American-LGBTs-on-Chicagos-South-Side-1900-1985/36389.html.

———. 2012b. "The Emergence of African-American Queer Cultures on Chicago's South Side, 1920–1940." Windy City Times. March 13. https://www.windycitytimes.com/lgbt/Queer-Bronzeville/36615.html.

Carter, David. 2004. *Stonewall: The Riots That Sparked the Gay Revolution.* New York: St. Martin's Press.

Castells, Manuel. 1983. *The City and the Grassroots.* Berkeley, CA: University of California Press.

Castells, Manuel, and Karen Murphy. 1982. "Cultural Identity and Urban Structure: The Spatial Organization of San Francisco's 'Gay Community'." In *Urbanism Under Capitalism,* edited by Norman Fainstein and Susan Fainstein, 237–59. Beverly Hills, CA: Sage.

Chauncey, George. 1994. *Gay New York: Gender, Urban Culture, and the Making of the Homosexual.* New York: Basic Books.

Cherry, Kittredge. 2021. "William Dorsey Swann: Ex-Slave Fought for Queer Freedom in 1880s as America's First Drag Queen." *QSpirit,* 2021, April 21 edition. https://qspirit.net/william-dorsey-swann-queer/.

Clendinen, Dudley, and Adam Nagourney. 1999. *Out for Good: The Struggle to Build a Gay Rights Movement in America.* New York: Simon & Schuster.

Davis, Tim. 1995. "The Diversity of Queer Politics and the Redefinition of Sexual Identity and Community in Urban Spaces." In *Mapping Desire: Geographies of Sexualities,* edited by David Bell and Gill Valentine, 284–303. London: Routledge.

DeMarco, Joe. [1983] 1999. "Gay Racism." In *Black Men/Whitemen: Afro-American Gay Life and Culture,* edited by M. J. Smith, 109–18. San Francisco: Gay Sunshine Press.

De Witt, Karen. 1994. "Gay Presence Leading a Revival in Many Urban Neighborhoods." *The New York Times,* September 5, 1994. http://www.nyt.com.

D'Emilio, John. 1983. *Sexual Politics, Sexual Communities: The Making of a Homosexual Minority in the United States 1940–1970.* Chicago: University of Chicago Press.

Doan, Petra L., and Harrison Higgins. 2011. "The Demise of Queer Space? Resurgent Gentrification and the Assimilation of LGBTQ Neighborhoods." *Journal of Planning Education and Research* 31 (6): 6–25.

Drexel, Allen. 1997. "Before Paris Burned: Race, Class, and Male Homosexuality on the Chicago South Side, 1935–1960." In *Creating a Place for Ourselves: Lesbian, Gay, and Bisexual Community Histories*, edited by Genny Beemyn, 119–44. New York: Routledge.

Duberman, Martin. 1993. *Stonewall*. New York: Penguin Books.

Escoffier, Jeffrey. 1998. *American Homo: Community and Perversity*. Berkeley, CA: University of California Press.

Faderman, Lillian. 1991. *Odd Girls and Twilight Lovers: A History of Lesbian Life in Twentieth-Century America*. New York: Penguin.

Fitzgerald, Frances. 1986. *Cities on a Hill*. New York: Simon and Schuster.

Florida, Richard. 2003. "Cities and the Creative Class." *City & Community* 2 (1): 3–19.

Forsyth, Ann. 2001. "Sexuality and Space: Nonconformist Populations and Planning Practice." *Journal of Planning Literature* 15 (3): 339–58.

Gans, Herbert. 2008. "Involuntary Segregation and the *Ghetto*: Disconnecting Process and Place." *City & Community* 7 (4): 353–57.

Gates, Gary J. 2007. *Geographic Trends Among Same-Sex Couples in the U.S. Census and the American Community Survey*. Los Angeles: The Williams Institute.

Gates, Gary J., and Jason Ost. 2004. "Getting Us Where We Live." *The Gay and Lesbian Review*, 11: 19–22.

Ghaziani, Amin. 2008. *The Dividends of Dissent: How Conflict and Culture Work in Lesbian and Gay Marches on Washington*. Chicago: University of Chicago Press.

———. 2010. "There Goes the Gayborhood?" *Contexts* 9 (3): 64–66.

———. 2014. *There Goes the Gayborhood?* Princeton, NJ: Princeton University Press.

Gieseking, Jen Jack. 2020. *A Queer New York: Geographies of Lesbians, Dykes and Queers*. New York: New York University Press.

Gold, Herbert. 1977. "A Walk on San Francisco's Gay Side," *The New York Times*, November 6 edition, 17.

Greene, Theodore. 2018. "Queer Street Families: Place-Making and Community among LGBTQ Youth of Color in Iconic Gay Neighborhoods." In *Queer Families and Relationships After Marriage Equality*, edited by Michael Yarborough, Angela Jones, and Joseph Nicholas DeFilippis, 168–81. New York: Routledge.

Heap, Chad. 2009. *Slumming: Sexual and Racial Encounters in American Nightlife, 1885–1940*. Historical Studies of Urban America. Chicago: University of Chicago Press.

Hess, Daniel Baldwin, and Alex Bitterman. 2021. "Who Are the People in Your Gayborhood? Understanding Population Change and Cultural Shifts in LGBTQ Neighborhoods." In *The Life and Afterlife of Gay Neighborhoods: Renaissance and Resurgence*, edited by Daniel Baldwin Hess and Alex Bitterman. New York: Springer International Publishing. https://doi.org/10.1007/978-3-030-66073-4.

Hughes, Charles H. 1893. "Postscript to Paper on 'Erotopathia,' – An Organization of Colored Erotopaths." *The Alienist and Neurologist* 14 (4): 731–32.

Humphreys, Laud. 1975. *Tearoom Trade: Impersonal Sex in Public Places*. London and New York: Routledge.

Hunter, Albert. 1975. "The Loss of Community: An Empirical Test through Replication." *American Sociological Review* 40 (5): 537–52.

Hunter, Marcus Anthony. 2010. "The Nightly Round: Space, Social Capital, and Urban Black Nightlife." *City & Community* 9 (2): 165–86.

Hunter, Marcus Anthony, Mary Pattillo, Zandria F. Robinson, and Keeanga-Yamahtta Taylor. 2016. "Black Placemaking: Celebration, Play, and Poetry." *Theory, Culture, and Society*, 33 (7–8): 1–26.

Israels, David. 1979. "Castro St's Casualties, Dilemmas of Gay Success." *The Berkeley Barb*, March 1, 1979.

Johnson, David K. 1997. "The Kids of Fairytown: Gay Male Culture on Chicago's Near North Side in the 1930s." In *Creating a Place for Ourselves: Lesbian, Gay, and Bisexual Community Histories*, edited by Genny Beemyn, 97–118. New York: Routledge.

———. 2004. *The Lavender Scare: The Cold War Persecution of Gays and Lesbians in the Federal Government*. Chicago: University of Chicago Press.

Kennedy, Elizabeth Lapovsky, and Madeline D. Davis. 1997. "I Could Hardly Wait to Get Back to That Bar: Lesbian Bar Culture in Buffalo in the 1930s and 1940s." In *Creating a Place for Ourselves: Lesbian, Gay, and Bisexual Community Histories*, edited by Genny Beemyn, 27–72. New York: Routledge.

Kinsman, Gary. 1995. "Men Loving Men: The Challenge of Gay Liberation." In *Men's Lives: Third Edition*, edited by Michael S. Kimmel and Michael A. Messner, 481–96. Boston, MA: Allyn and Bacon.

Knopp, Lawrence. 1997. "Gentrification and Gay Neighborhood Formation in New Orleans: A Case Study." In *Homo Economics: Capitalism, Community, and Lesbian and Gay Life*, edited by Amy Gluckman and Betsy Reed, 45–63. New York: Routledge.

Lauria, Mickey, and Lawrence Knopp. 1985. "Toward an Analysis of the Role of Gay Communities in the Urban Renaissance." *Urban Geography* 6 (2): 152–69.

Levine, Martin P. 1979. "Gay Ghetto." *Journal of Homosexuality* 4 (4): 363–77.

Mattson, Greggor. 2020a. "Are Gay Bars Closing? Using Business Listings to Infer Rates of Gay Bar Closure in the United States, 1977–2019." *Socius* 5 (1–2). https://doi.org/10.177/2378023119894832.

———. 2020b. "Shuttered by the Coronavirus, Many Gay Bars – Already Struggling – Are Now on Life Support." *Slate*, 2020, May 01 edition. https://slate.com/human-interest/2020/05/gay-bars-struggling-reopen-coronavirus.html.

Morris, Bonnie. 2016. *The Disappearing L: Erasure of Lesbian Spaces and Cultures*. Albany, NY: State University of New York Press.

Murray, Stephen O. 1979. "The Institutional Elaboration of a Quasi-Ethnic Community." *International Review of Modern Sociology* 9 (July): 165–77.

Nero, Charles I. 2005. "Why Are the Gay Ghettos White?" In *Black Queer Studies: A Critical Anthology*, edited by E. Patrick Johnson and Mae G. Henderson, 228–45. Durham: Duke University Press.

Newton, Esther. 1997. "The 'Fun Gay Ladies': Lesbians in Cherry Grove, 1936–1960." In *Creating a Place for Ourselves: Lesbian, Gay, and Bisexual Community Histories*, edited by Genny Beemyn, 146–64. New York: Routledge.

Oldenberg, Ray. 1989. *The Great Good Place: Cafés, Coffee Shops, Community Centers, Beauty Parlors, General Stores, Hangouts, And How They Get Us Through the Day*. New York: Paragon House.

Orne, Jason. 2017. *Boystown: Sex and Community in Chicago*. Chicago: University of Chicago Press.

Renninger, Bryce. 2018. "Grindr Killed the Gay Bar, and Other Attempts to Blame Social Technologies for Urban Development: A Democratic Approach to Popular Technologies and Queer Sociality." *Journal of Homosexuality* 66 (September): 1–20. https://doi.org/10.1080/00918369.2018.1514205.

Robertson, Tatsha. 2003. "Finding Hope in Gay Enclaves in Detroit and Suburb Say Such Neighborhoods Can Rejuvenate the City." *The Boston Globe*, January 15, 2003, Third edition, sec. National/Foreign.

Rosse, Irving. 1892. "Sexual Hypochondriasis and the Perversion of the Genetic Instinct." *The Journal of Nervous and Mental Diseases* XVII (1): 795–811.

Savage, Rachel, Matthew Lavietes, and Enrique Anarte. 2020. "'We'll Die': Gay Bars Worldwide Scramble to Avert Coronavirus Collapse." *Reuters*, 2020, May 13 edition. https://www.reuters.com/article/us-health-coronavirus-LGBTQ-nightlife-trf-idUSKBN22P1Z5.

Shilts, Randy. 1982. *The Mayor of Castro Street: The Life and Times of Harvey Milk*. New York: St. Martin's Press.

Stone, Amy L. 2018. "The Geography of Research on LGBTQ Life: Why Sociologists Should Study the South, Rural Queers, and Ordinary Cities." *Sociology Compass* 12 (11). https://doi-org./10.1111/soc4.12638.

Suttles, Gerald D. 1968. *The Social Order of the Slums: Ethnicity and Territory in the Inner City*. Chicago: University of Chicago Press.

Teal, Donn. 1971. *The Gay Militants*. New York: Stein and Day.

The Washington Post. 1888. "A Negro Dive Raided: Thirteen Black Men Dressed as Women Surprised," 1888, April 13 edition.

Truscott IV, Lucian. 1969. "Gay Power Comes to Sheridan Square." *The Village Voice*, July 3, 1969.

Usher, Nikki, and Eleanor Morrison. 2010. "The Demise of the Gay Enclave, Communication Infrastructure Theory, and the Transformation of Gay Public Space." In *LGBTQ Identity and Online New Media*, edited by Christopher Pullen and Margaret Cooper, 271–87. New York: Routledge.

Wilson, William Julius. 1987. *The Truly Disadvantaged: The Inner City, the Underclass, and Public Policy*. Chicago: University of Chicago Press.

Wirth, Louis. 1938. "Urbanism as a Way of Life." *American Journal of Sociology* 44 (1): 1–24.

Wittman, Carl. 1970. "Refugees from Amerika: A Gay Manifesto." ttps://www.historyisaweapon.com/defcon1/wittmanmanifesto.html.

Zukin, Sharon. 1987. "Gentrification: Culture and Capital in the Urban Core." *The Annual Review of Sociology* 13: 129–47.

16

THE AMERICAN DREAM

Rhetoric of opportunity and reality of exclusion

Joan Maya Mazelis

The American dream that we were all raised on is a simple but powerful one—if you work hard and play by the rules, you should be given a chance to go as far as your God-given ability will take you. This American ideology that each individual is responsible for his or her life outcomes is the expressed belief of the vast majority of Americans, rich and poor.

President Bill Clinton[1]

The founding creed of the United States of America, which asserts our rights to Life, Liberty, and the Pursuit of Happiness, inspired the formulation of these human rights. Our government signed the UDHR [Universal Declaration of Human Rights] in 1948; its full implementation would mean that our country would be living out the true meaning of its creed. This American Dream is possible because our country is the richest and most powerful in the world.

The Poor People's Economic Human Rights Campaign[2]

The American Dream is widely seen in the way President Clinton articulated it in the 1990s: success awarded to those who work hard, with personal responsibility paramount and external barriers absent. The Poor People's Economic Human Rights Campaign (PPEHRC) is an organization of and for poor people. It was spearheaded in the 1990s by the Kensington Welfare Rights Union (KWRU), which poor antipoverty activists founded in 1991. The quotation PPEHRC used in their mission statement of the familiar words from the Declaration of Independence connects founding beliefs in life, liberty, and the pursuit of happiness to the American Dream. Their statement suggests that the meaning of the American Dream is deeply tied to our notions of full citizenship rights and the ideals underlying the United States. PPEHRC members are poor people who often feel invisible and marginalized, but even to them, the American Dream symbolizes a hopeful promise. Life, liberty, and the pursuit of happiness are, to them, emblematic of our society's commitment to the American Dream.[3]

The American Dream has been defined in varied ways. It can focus on individual success or a utopian societal ideal; it can be characterized by material wealth and financial well-being or it can be possible to fulfill with non-material achievements. John Truslow Adams defined it as "that dream of a land in which life should be better and richer and fuller for every man, with opportunity for each according to his ability or achievement" (2001, 404).[4] Robert Merton

DOI: 10.4324/9781003326243-20

noted that in the United States, we value and emphasize "the accumulation of wealth as a symbol of success" (1938, 675), prizing material success above everything else—for everyone in society, regardless of their socioeconomic position and how realistic that aim might be. Adams's definition does not preclude the domination of this economic motive, but it also includes a broader understanding, the hope of a better and freer life. It is not only about an individual's personal material success, but also about whether everyone has access and opportunities to reach their own highest possible achievement. Similarly, Jennifer Hochschild described the American Dream as "the promise that all Americans have a reasonable chance to achieve success as they define it—material or otherwise—through their own efforts, and to attain virtue and fulfillment through success" (Hochschild 1995, xvii).

In our society, the American Dream has come to be generally understood as the notion that individual effort and persistence will allow people to achieve whatever their talents promise. The American Dream of a better life earned through meritocratic achievement is a broadly desired and promised goal. This is the "Dream" in the American Dream—ownership and material success, with increased freedom and happiness secondary effects rather than goals in and of themselves. But what of the "American" piece of the Dream? Being American is about being a citizen and the citizenship rights Americans possess. For example, the right to vote, which I will discuss more below, is one symbol of being American. The notion that one must be American to have access to the Dream is used to bar those seen as not American from what would give them access to the Dream—one obvious example is the resistance to giving citizenship and its accompanying rights to the group of US-born children of non-citizens, aptly named "Dreamers." As reflected in the excerpt from the Poor People's Economic Human Rights Campaign's mission statement above, the rights of American citizens to "life, liberty, and the pursuit of happiness" represent the very nature of who we say we are as Americans. And our commitment to citizenship rights is just as fundamental as our commitment to the promise of achieving the Dream.

Cal Jillson draws particular attention to the substitution of "life, liberty, and the pursuit of happiness" as fundamental rights in place of what he identifies as philosopher John Locke's original identification of life, liberty, and property. Jillson argues that while founders like Jefferson certainly recognized the importance of property as support for "security, independence, and autonomy," the substitution of "pursuit of happiness" evokes the idealism, egalitarianism, and desire for citizens to not only *survive* materially but to *thrive* (Jillson 2004, 58). Despite the intentional broadening of this statement of rights to be more aspirational, we frequently dispense with "happiness" to focus on property when we think about the American Dream. Even leaders tasked with helping to fulfill the foundational goals of the United States have neglected the focus on the pursuit of happiness, emphasizing the protection of property instead.[5]

Citizenship, Ownership, and Individualism

In 1950, British sociologist T.H. Marshall described three kinds of rights as the components of citizenship: civil, political, and social rights. Civil rights include freedom of speech and religion and the rights of people to marry, own property, live where they choose, and to equal justice under the law. Political rights include the rights to participate in elections and to run for office. Social rights are embodied in the welfare state, through which government organizations provide material benefits for individuals who are unable to adequately support themselves through employment. I will discuss citizenship rights—the *American* piece of the American Dream—through the examples of housing, voting, and welfare, detailing how each relates to the American Dream's ideals of *individualism* and *ownership*.

The achievement Americans hope to attain by virtue of their hard work—the *Dream* piece—often centers on *ownership* in some form: land, property like an owned home, or some other form of wealth. And it is undeniable that owning assets creates cumulative advantages and broadens opportunities (Oliver and Shapiro 2006). The widespread rhetoric and understanding of the American Dream cast it as both an inspiration to individuals and achievable for all, so long as they work hard (Hochschild 1995). The focus on the *individual* is crucial.

Individualism has a long history in United States society. American individualism's roots are strong and deep, dating back to the writings of Benjamin Franklin (Bellah et al. 1985; Franklin 2005). In *The Protestant Ethic and the Spirit of Capitalism*, Max Weber draws on Franklin's work in describing the foundation of capitalism in the United States: people perceived material success, he argued, as a sign of predestination for heaven and eternal salvation (Weber 1905). In this we also see the American ideal of wealth through ownership, which, like individualism, is a key facet of the American Dream.

Individualism promises that personal effort is effective and that the pursuit and fulfillment of the American Dream is equally accessible to all. Most Americans believe that openness and opportunity do indeed largely characterize American society, and they believe in the American Dream (Lareau 2003; McCoy 2015; Putnam 2015). In my own research on two unrelated projects—one on people living in poverty, including members of the Poor People's Economic Human Rights Campaign, and one on student loan debt—I found that interviewees generally demonstrated this faith in the American Dream. In research I conducted in the early 2000s, I found people in poverty who held fast to the tradition of individualism and believed working hard could bring a better life (Mazelis 2017). My more recent in-depth interviews with new college graduates (from 2016 to the present) have reflected that same faith as they looked toward their futures.

And yet, though the American Dream is ostensibly about *opportunity and openness*, and this perception of it is broadly believed, I argue that in reality, the Dream is predicated on *exclusion*. Rhetorical idealism aside, Jillson notes the longstanding exclusionary nature of the American Dream as experienced in reality, referring to ours as "a society born in hierarchy and exclusion" (2004, 1).[6] While exclusion has been a persistent factor, Jillson qualifies this, stating that, "Over time, the right to dream the American Dream has been opened, at least formally, to new and increasingly diverse groups" (2004, 11). Jillson focuses on fading exclusion and increasing inclusiveness over the centuries, whereas I focus on the way in which new *restrictions* have served to continue *exclusion* even as more obvious barriers appeared to recede. Further, the shift away from exclusion has sometimes been an inclusion that is predatory[7] rather than one that furthers equity. At times, "practices that were intended to facilitate inclusion reinforced existing patterns of inequality and discrimination" (Taylor 2019, 18).

In this chapter, I will discuss individualism and ownership as key tenets of the American Dream, and I will contrast the rhetoric of opportunity and openness with the reality that the Dream is exclusionary. This is not only because of practices that further inequality and perpetuate disadvantage, as I will discuss below. The American Dream has been *built* on a premise of exclusion, particularly an exclusion founded on a racial hierarchy, and this exclusion is an intended feature of our society. The American Dream is simply not open to everyone—not to the poor, to those who live paycheck to paycheck, or to those who may never qualify for a mortgage. These "unsuccessful" unfortunates are blamed for failing to achieve the American Dream; "perhaps they made the wrong choices" many people muse. But the American Dream is *meant* to be exclusionary—as homeownership has been—to be classist and racist, to celebrate the rich and demonize the poor.

The achievement of goals in the name of the American Dream is accepted as personally earned—but some have had opportunities to achieve while others have not. In many ways, achieving the American Dream *requires* that others do not. We tell ourselves a zero-sum story that privileges individual achievement and fosters division and exclusion (McGhee 2021). A picket fence surrounding a suburban house symbolizes privacy and separation from excluded others (Fishman 1987; Morton 2002; Redbook 1957). How can one be a member of an exclusive residential community without that community keeping others out? Black people have been frequently and intentionally kept out. Hierarchy is fundamental to the American Dream's persistence, and real-estate practices such as redlining and racially restrictive covenants are examples of the systemic racism that has sustained this exclusive hierarchy (Hirsch 1983; Massey and Denton 1993; McGhee 2021; Oliver and Shapiro 2006). Understanding the American Dream's basis in exclusion is key to a comprehensive understanding of its operation both in the past and in contemporary life.

Attainment of the American Dream, so often measured by ownership of property and material wealth, requires money and so prioritizes capitalism and monetary gain. Exclusion, then, is about excluding poor people, Whites included, as well as Black people and other people of color. Yet poor Whites' exclusion encourages the rage some White people feel when they perceive people of color as beginning to gain access to *their* American Dream while they remain excluded based on class. It has fed their anxious grasping "to make sure that America was theirs" (Tavernise 2021). Feelings of abandonment and fear among White people affirm the earlier pattern that Jillson posits, asserting that, by the middle of the twentieth century, "Most Americans were comfortable ... with opening rights and opportunities to Americans that previously had been excluded. But as the number of claims expanded and the groups with claims proliferated ... White Americans ... withdrew into a sullen determination to defend their possessions and privileges" (2004, 197). This continued when, as Heather McGhee states, many White Americans felt they were "getting left behind" during the first Obama administration—the first instance of a Black person fully accessing the political right to secure the presidency—even though White dominance in US society continued (2021, 5). As McGhee argues, "The zero-sum idea that white people are now suffering due to gains among people of color has taken on the features of myth: it lies, but it says so much" (2021, 15). Racial exclusion is at the core of the exclusion that characterizes the American Dream.

The American Dream, Personal Effort, and Shared Mythology

The idea of the American Dream is enduring and powerful: work hard and play by the rules, and you will achieve success. Fundamentally, it claims that all Americans have the chance to achieve their goals, provided they have the necessary dedication and persistence (Hacker and Pierson 2010; Hochschild 1995; Lareau 2003). That equal chance to achieve goals is based on a notion of openness and opportunity that denies the existence of structural barriers and systemic disadvantages. It prioritizes agency over structure as it claims that free will is unfettered, always (if exercised "correctly") leading to the accomplishment of personal goals—meaning that it is all under individual control (Esping-Anderson 1990; Lareau 2003; Stiglitz 2012).

Persistence and individual effort are at the heart of the American Dream, something it shares with the concept of the popularly accepted *achievement ideology*, "the reigning social perspective that sees American society as open and fair and full of opportunity. In this view, success is based on merit, and economic inequality is due to differences in ambition and ability. . . . The American Dream is held out as a genuine prospect for anyone with the drive to achieve it" (Macleod 2008, 3). The achievement ideology is only about people as individuals, how they behave, and what they think—not about the structure that surrounds and helps shape people's lives. When we focus on people's adherence to the achievement ideology—do they believe in it or are they skeptical of its promises?—and how this perspective can improve or hurt their chances for success and mobility, we reinforce the primacy of the individual by focusing only on what those individuals believe while neglecting the ways in which the social structure informs their beliefs and circumscribes their ability to make the Dream a reality. The achievement ideology has varied and complicated consequences. Believing in it has some positive effects, providing motivation even when confronted with powerful structural barriers of discrimination. "It can give us a reason to get up in the morning, to live to fight another day, to have hope" (Mazelis 2017, 32). For those not born into immense wealth, hard work is likely a necessary element to achieve survival, even if not sufficient to achieve material success. Yet, the effects of believing in the American Dream are not all positive.

The Dream promises that if people rely on their own talents and skills, their reward is material success—and getting credit for that success in their own and others' eyes. This, of course, leads people, even those inhibited by structural disadvantage, to blame themselves anytime they fail (Edin and Shaefer 2015; Fader 2013; Hansen 2005; Hochschild 1995; Kluegel and Smith 1986; Lareau 2003; Macleod 2008; Mazelis 2017).

Hochschild described four tenets of the American Dream: (1) everyone may pursue their dream; (2) one may reasonably anticipate success—it's not guaranteed, but there's a good chance; (3) talent and hard work lead to success; and (4) success is associated with virtue. Americans tend to "believe that this country is fundamentally *open*. They assume that society is best understood as a collection of individuals. They believe that people who demonstrate hard work, effort, and talent are likely to achieve upward mobility" (Lareau 2003, 235). As stated above, Hochschild notes that the American Dream is open to interpretation but that it is "susceptible to having the open-ended definition of success, which can equally include salvation or writing the great American novel, narrowed to wealth, job status, or power" (Hochschild 1995, 35–36). But when it "reduces an array of values to single thin one" (Hochschild 1995, 36), it guarantees most people will fail. The notion that in our free and open society, effort will lead to success—individual material success—has proven to be powerful and enduring. Hochschild notes, "Not all Americans can achieve their dreams no matter how hard they try. But the American Dream obscures those structural facts under a cloak of individual agency, thus giving people unjustified hopes and unwarranted feelings of failure" (1995, 259). When things work out, they can confidently take credit, but when the Dream disappoints, strivers are left to wonder what they did wrong. But even if the belief in the American Dream can bring benefits of individual confidence and hope that could outweigh the disadvantages of disappointment and self-blame, it would not absolve the Dream of its exclusionary nature.

Inequality has been rising for decades, pushing the American Dream farther and farther out of reach. Yet as Jennifer Silva (2013) points out, growing inequality seems to increase some people's commitment to the notion that hard work will lead to success. She notes that her working-class research participants are the kind of "young people who would benefit most from social safety nets and solidarity with similarly disadvantaged others," but they "cling so fiercely to ideals and practices of untrammeled individualism and self-reliance, not only as the way things are but also as the way they should be" (Silva 2013, 109). Silva's research participants, like mine and many others', consider opportunity for economic mobility to be widely available and, therefore, inequality to be expected and just, a manifestation of individual failures rather than structural barriers (Domínguez 2011; Kluegel and Smith 1986; Mazelis 2017; Wilson 1996). Inequalities, and their own struggles, do not cause their faith in the Dream to falter.

Findings from interviews I conducted with a group of graduating college seniors for a project on student loan debt demonstrate the pervasiveness and power of belief in the American Dream. In qualitative in-depth interviews conducted almost annually between 2016 and 2022, participants have shared their perspectives about success, happiness, and the American Dream. Findings suggest that the American Dream generally shapes their understandings of their family trajectories as well as their aspirations for their own futures.

Noah,[8] a 25-year-old Black man and son of West Indian immigrants, was still living with his parents to save money three years after graduating college. "I just want to have my own home. I think that's the next big step," he said. When I asked him what he thought it meant to be an adult, he first suggested "taking responsibility for yourself and being accountable for your actions," but added that home ownership is "part of the Dream, I guess. The American Dream." In his first interview, as he approached graduation, 22-year-old PJ referenced the American Dream in relation to his South Asian immigrant parents, who both worked menial jobs in the past but had since attained jobs that provided relative financial stability. He explained to me, "That's actually the American Dream. You start off with nothing and then you just go up." Their relative success felt like the American Dream to PJ and provided him with a sense of hope that that the American Dream is attainable. Like Noah, PJ was living with his parents to save money and pay off his student loans so that he could launch into the fully independent adulthood he imagined in his future. Both men are US citizens, sons of immigrants, who strongly believed in the American Dream.

Four years after college graduation, participants also shared their definitions of success; they saw it as something individual: individual goals and completing and achieving those goals through their individual effort. Jennifer (26, White) told me success means that you have "accomplished what you wanted" and everything you "have worked for." Alice (26, Black) explained, "I would define success as completing your goals that you want to accomplish." Jason (33, White) said, "when you've set a goal and you achieve the goal that you've set." The notion of success as not necessarily about material success, but as goals subjectively and personally defined, fits with Adams's definition of the American Dream. All of these participants believed in their own ability to set goals and attain those goals. None of them acknowledged that structural factors may largely influence who achieves their goals.

Participants in this student loan debt study have at least one foot in the middle class in that all of them hold a Bachelor's degree. But their belief in the American Dream echoes the opinions I heard when I interviewed people living in poverty in Philadelphia over a decade earlier. Those interviewees also shared their thoughts on the importance of their own individual effort and persistence to achieve their goals. Kim, like Noah and Alice, is Black. But, unlike Noah and Alice—22 and approaching college graduation when I first interviewed them—Kim was 44 years old, unemployed, and studying for her GED when we spoke. Still, she demonstrated that these ideas do not belong only to one generation or only to college graduates. Kim told me what she would say to people who are struggling: "Get up and get a job. Or try to get a training or something like that there to better themselves . . . It starts with you. Everything starts with you.. . you have to want it or get up and get it. It's not gonna come to you. It starts with you. You can't get nothing if you don't go for it." Her advice centered on personal actions to achieve goals.

When I asked Tina, a 29-year-old White military veteran, what people who are struggling to survive should do, her advice was similar to Kim's: "I think they should work hard and try to get themselves together the best way that they know how and try to, you know, just pull themselves out of the situation that they're in, as hard as it is. As hard as it is, I found that it can be done. It's hard. I'm not going to say that it's not hard, but I think it can be done." She added, "It doesn't just happen; you have to make it happen, you have to push yourself, you know. Life is all about hard work."

At the time of our interview, Tina was living with her infant daughter in a single room in a rooming house, sharing a bathroom down the hall with other tenants she didn't know. Their fathers had custody of her two older children, a consequence of her time away in military training camp and then necessitated by her lack of funds and space. She was discharged when she became pregnant with her youngest child. Tina imagined her future, telling me that she wanted to "be a chef and get that job that I want and own that restaurant that I want and have everything that I feel like I deserve, you know. I think that I deserve it. I think that I worked hard enough to where I think I deserve, I think I should have what I want." Tina's faith in the American Dream—that hard work leads people to "deserve" to get ahead—mirrored her beliefs about what people who are struggling should do. Recognizing that it is an uphill battle didn't stop Tina from believing that anything is possible with hard work. Considering her own situation, Tina believed she had "worked hard enough" and should be rewarded. She didn't want to admit or perhaps did not fully realize that upward mobility might simply be impossible for some people, particularly by "just pulling themselves out of the situation that they're in."

Karen, a Black woman in her 40s who was unemployed at the time of her interview, expressed the same kind of faith that people can pull themselves out of poverty. She told me that she believed things would work out for her because "If you think beneath your level, that's where you're gonna stay.. . you've got to have great expectations in life. And you have to go for them, you know, you have to reach for them … Things are not just gonna, just, land in your lap. You have to, you know, you have to work and plan." These women I interviewed all strongly believed in the power of people's own efforts to escape poverty and achieve their goals. But individuals' optimistic faith in the American Dream does not mean its promises become reality. For the women from my poverty research who I quoted above, their economic precarity persisted—regardless of their shared, deeply held conviction in a sure path to fulfilled promises of the American Dream.

False Pretense: Glimmers of Awareness of the Dream's Elusiveness

Not all of the people I spoke to believed in the American Dream. In 2021, Flo, a White college graduate in the student debt study, frankly offered, "the American Dream is some bullshit propaganda, you know, that was sold to people. I don't even buy it at all. There's no American Dream." She added, "Pick yourself up by your bootstraps, right? Work hard, get to the top. This endless rat race, the invisible ladder—there's no ladder. You can work so hard and you're not gonna make it, and it comes down to who you know and your social circle more than anything else." A married homeowner, Flo referred to the American Dream as including owning your own house. She noted, "I don't own a thing. The bank owns my house. If I don't pay the mortgage, I will not be able to stay. Even if I owned it, no loans. I would still owe taxes on the land. You know, so you don't own anything, ever." While, by some measures, Flo has attained the American Dream, she retained skepticism about it as something possible and worthy to attain.

Paloma, a 28-year-old Latina activist in the Poor People's Economic Human Rights Campaign, explained to me that it is simply untrue that all people can escape poverty and achieve material success:

> Some people do struggle and get out of [poverty], but I think that people help them along the way … If they really analyze their life, somebody helped them, opened

some door to get somewhere. And other people are just born lucky. I think the majority of the people who are well off are born lucky. It's very few that actually like pull themselves up by their bootstraps and become rich overnight.

Paloma's reasoning echoes the words of Martin Luther King, Jr., who said, "It is all right to tell a man to lift himself by his own bootstraps, but it is a cruel jest to say to a bootless man that he ought to lift himself by his own bootstraps" (King 1968).[9]

James, a Black man in his thirties, had a perspective similar to Paloma's, one that centered on what he identified as false promises. Like Paloma, he was also an activist in PPEHRC. He told me: "They give you this false, this false pretense that you can become a millionaire. And have everybody working towards this illusion. . . . They have like, you know, dead-end jobs and penitentiary and the grave and all these things waiting for you instead of the American Dream." Even though James saw the American Dream as elusive, he explained to me why other poor people continued to believe in the American Dream and therefore blamed themselves for their poverty:

> When you got parents and everybody teaching you, you got to get good grades. . . . You got to go to college. You got to be the best. You got to work hard. When people tell you all those different things and then you're going to be successful you going to have . . . [a] piece of paper saying that you graduated from a good university. And you have a job that pays a real good salary where you are able to buy a house and pay for a car and take vacations and have money for school for your kids, then you're successful. Anything less than that, you are a failure. And so when your parents are telling you, these are all the things that your grandparents and everybody telling you . . . they're all around you. These are the things that you got to do to be a success and then you don't meet any of those things, boom, you're going to automatically think it's yourself, you're a failure. It's you.

The American Dream promises people credit for achieving it and blame when they don't, even though the system is *designed,* through means of exclusion, restrictions, and predatory inclusion, to make it impossible for many to achieve it regardless of how hard they work. The American Dream celebrates individual achievement as people are assumed to hold personal responsibility for their successes and failures. Virtually everyone wants to achieve the Dream and takes credit if they do, so the implication is that those who do not achieve it have failed. But beyond self-blame for failures, the notion of the individually achieved American Dream also obscures the social structure, particularly in terms of politics and policy, and ignores the reality of exclusion—exclusion shaped in large part by the racial hierarchy in the United States.

Rights to and Exclusion from the American Dream

The American Dream is undoubtedly, unavoidably, rooted in racial exclusion. This "Dream" is one of material success. But we must also engage with the "American" part of this term, and we can do so by considering the philosophical rights to life, liberty, and the pursuit of happiness in terms of the legally codified citizenship rights mentioned above: civil, political, and social rights. I will discuss an example of each type of right and its connection to ownership and to exclusion. Each of the three types of citizenship rights is assumed to be universal in the United States today, yet from the nation's beginning, entire categories of people have been excluded, and restrictions have continued to limit full access.

The American Dream, and the rights that provide access to the Dream, are about owning. But an entire group of Americans is descended from Africans who were kidnapped and enslaved and could not own property—as they themselves were legally designated property. Their enslavement enabled those who enslaved them to establish their own pieces of the American Dream on land forcibly taken from Indigenous people. The American Dream has therefore been built on stolen labor and stolen land. After the abolition of slavery, institutions of power dominated by White people found new ways to make it nearly impossible for descendants of enslaved people to attain the American Dream—through policies that required and encouraged racial discrimination in housing, the disinvestment and defunding of cities, and killing Black business owners.[10] Unequal access to the Dream continues, through the contemporary defunding of public education, mass incarceration, felon disenfranchisement, and the school to prison pipeline (Alexander 2010; Brophy 2002; Hill 2019; Jackson 1985; Manza and Uggen 2008; Massey and Denton 1993; McGhee 2021; Oliver and Shapiro 2006; Zucchino 2020).

The importance of property and ownership to the American Dream is perhaps most obvious in considering the role of housing and the housing discrimination against Black people that has been a pervasive violation of civil rights in the United States. But in reality, ownership also matters for voting (one example of political rights), for welfare eligibility (one mechanism to ensure social rights), and for much more. Each of these examples of rights has roots in ownership and in racial exclusion.

Housing

Housing is central to the myth of the American Dream. Where and how we live is an organizing aspect of our lives. And civil rights are fundamental to housing, as they are what allow us access to own property and to live where we choose. Black Americans, however, were constitutionally denied these civil rights, and even after the passage of the Fourteenth Amendment, civil rights for Black Americans existed in name only (Giddens et al. 2021, 419).

There are powerful mechanisms that allow some to own dwellings and land and to benefit from the cumulative advantages this ownership bestows, while others do not have this same access to ownership and face cumulative disadvantages as a result (Oliver and Shapiro 2006). Most Americans who have significant wealth have it in the value of a home, and parental wealth inherited by subsequent generations often comes through owned homes passed along to the next generation (Glantz and Martinez 2018; Shapiro, Meschede, and Osoro 2013; Taylor 2019). But, while the civil right to own a home is available to all, the history of residential segregation makes for disparate access to this right. And homes in Black neighborhoods typically have not appreciated in value as much as those in White neighborhoods, in part because systemic racism feeds the subjective nature of home values (McCabe 2017; Taylor 2019). This is one reason homeownership, when Black people obtain it, rarely produces the financial benefits it provides to their White counterparts (Taylor 2019).

One main advantage home ownership provides is the mortgage interest tax deduction, which helps make home ownership a key way to accumulate wealth. In the first few years of mortgages, the largest part of monthly payments goes to interest; the mortgage interest tax deduction allows homeowners to subtract a large portion of the money they spend on housing from their taxable income (Schuetz 2019). Homeowners also build equity over time they can pass on in the form of inherited wealth to the next generation. Meanwhile, renters unable to assemble a down payment or qualify for a mortgage get no tax break for rent paid and build no equity to pass along. Because they were initially excluded from the right to property ownership, and have more recently been excluded from access to valuable home ownership options, Black Americans have been systematically denied the access to the American Dream that homeownership can afford.

For hundreds of years, America formally excluded certain people from the right to buy a home. But as formal *exclusion* became illegal, there was a shift to the implementation of *restrictions*. In the middle of the twentieth century, the Federal Housing Authority's rules ensured mortgages went to those purchasing single-family homes in the suburbs. However, racially restrictive covenants kept Black Americans out of those suburbs and redlining effectively prevented them from getting mortgages (Jackson 1985; Massey and Denton 1993; McGhee 2021; Taylor 2019). Racially restrictive covenants were contracts that applied to geographic areas. If a majority of residents in the area voted for the covenant, no one in the area was permitted to rent or sell to Black Americans. Racially restrictive covenants spread widely throughout the United States from early in the twentieth century until the US Supreme Court declared them unenforceable in 1948 (Massey and Denton 1993). Meanwhile, the practice of redlining also had powerful and enduring effects. Its roots were in a rating system the Home Owners' Loan Corporation developed to assess credit risks for potential loans. Those neighborhoods in the highest risk category were designated undesirable and colored in red on maps. Black neighborhoods were always colored in red and, therefore, continually denied mortgage funds (Blumgart 2017; Jackson 1985; Massey and Denton 1993; Taylor 2019).[11] Although the Community Reinvestment Act outlawed redlining in the 1970s, discrimination in lending, in credit rating processes, and in steering potential homebuyers to neighborhoods where homes are less likely to appreciate in value continues unabated (Glantz and Martinez 2018).

As formal practices of *restriction* like racially restrictive covenants and redlining became illegal, Black people's exclusion from homeownership took on a more covert form— "predatory inclusion" (Taylor 2019). Barriers that represented exclusion were removed, but inclusion happened only nominally and with little benefit to Black people. In fact, their legal inclusion allowed lenders to prey on Black Americans, taking advantage of their desire for homeownership, "a cornerstone of the American Dream," and sometimes nearly coercing them into homeownership that deepened their poverty (Taylor 2019, 169). FHA employees, real estate brokers, and appraisers cooperated to sell the homes. They would often tell potential buyers that no rentals were available and steer them to dilapidated homes for purchase, in the hopes that Black buyers would default—and that after foreclosure, brokers could resell to other unsuspecting buyers. Though brokers often dishonestly secured higher rates than a dwelling's condition warranted, mortgages were insured by FHA, which strengthened buyers' comfort and assurance that purchasing was a wise decision. They targeted poor Black women in particular—and then blamed them as foolish for falling prey to the allure of homeownership when they could not afford to keep or repair their properties! Even though they were assured their budgets would allow them to pay monthly mortgage payments, many women did not have the funds to cover the unanticipated costs of maintaining homes already in disrepair (Taylor 2019). Once *excluded*, now Black people were included in ways that depleted their resources, leaving them in debt and poverty, while profits for White individuals and institutions increased. As a result, the American Dream drifted further and further out of reach (McGhee 2021).

These continued *restrictions* accomplished what legal *exclusion* no longer could, and predatory inclusion helped to both reserve the American Dream for Whites who inherit wealth and deny it to Black people, even many of those who become homeowners. Discrimination is ubiquitous. Housing audits across the United States have demonstrated that landlords and realtors call back White rental applicants and offer them apartments more often than they do Black rental applicants who are similarly economically situated; Black applicants are charged credit check fees while White applicants are not (Massey and Lundy 2001).

Despite persisting obstacles to homeownership for Black Americans today, they may be even more likely to believe in the American Dream than are White Americans (McCabe 2017). But access and barriers to the American Dream are shaped, in part, by owning a home, "a commodity ... promoted as the fulfillment and meaning of citizenship" (Taylor 2019, 262). Black people's *exclusion*, the rampant *restrictions* they face, and their predatory inclusion in the housing market have kept them from attaining the full value of the commodity of an owned home, and therefore, full citizenship.

Voting

Political rights are part of how we understand citizenship, just as civil rights are. The main way we exercise our political rights is with the right to vote. While the US constitution initially excluded Black people from the civil right to own property, it also excluded anyone besides "white, male, Protestant, property holders" from the political right to vote (Jillson 2004, 8; see also Klinghoffer and Elkis 1992). Originally, this stemmed from the notion that "only those owning sufficient land to give them a stake in the future stability and prosperity of the society should be allowed to participate in the governance of the society" (Jillson 2004, 63). Ownership became officially defined as a prerequisite to freedom, which "drew a sharp line between citizens and mere inhabitants" (2004, 75).

While Black people were disallowed from ownership and therefore the vote, the majority of White men who were too poor to own property were also barred from full access to the American Dream, as they were unable to participate fully in the new democracy (McGhee 2021). Enslaved Black Americans' designation as property was the most severe mechanism of their exclusion—beyond exclusion from access to citizenship rights and to the American Dream, it was exclusion fundamentally from being recognized as fully human. "Slaves were denied all but the thinnest legal existence. They could hold property only as the master allowed, and they could not legally marry, inherit, sue in court ... Free blacks could not vote or hold office, testify against a white man in court, serve in the militia, or marry across racial boundaries. Like a single white woman, free blacks had a cramped and restricted legal personality" (Jillson 2004, 46), in effect excluding many people from the legal definition of "people" and thereby from the American Dream.

Disenfranchisement affected groups beyond White men without property and enslaved people. Women did not gain the right to vote until the Nineteenth Amendment was ratified in 1920; and not until the passage of the Voting Rights Act of 1965 was racial discrimination in voting prohibited (Giddens et al. 2021). Before 1965, "A complicated array of rules and practices, including literacy tests, poll taxes, white primaries, and grandfather clauses kept blacks, other minorities, and the poor generally from registering and voting in elections. Specifically, the Voting Rights Act of 1965 prohibited literacy tests and other practices deemed to have a discriminatory impact" (Jillson 2004, 222). Without the right to vote, citizenship remained incomplete for these groups, rendering the American Dream inaccessible.

In voting, as with housing, first came formal *exclusion*—depriving people of the right to vote based on ascribed characteristics. But when legal progress removed that ability— when legal requirements stated that all have a right to vote—there was a shift to *restrict* what law had made available. Formal exclusion ended, but obstacles remained in the form of restrictions; the poll tax and literacy test accomplished aims of *restriction* when categorical *exclusion* was no longer possible, and the grandfather clause targeted the restrictions to exempt poor White Americans from the obstacles placed in front of Black Americans (Zucchino 2020).

As David Zucchino details in his book, *Wilmington's Lie: The Murderous Coup of 1898 and the Rise of White Supremacy*, the poll tax barred poor Black people from exercising their right to vote while the literacy test required would-be voters to clear an incredibly difficult bar, such as reciting from memory the Preamble to the Constitution. But when it became clear that both the poll tax and literacy test would prevent many poor White people from voting, White supremacists enacted variations of the grandfather clause in several states to effectively exempt White voters from the poll tax and literacy test if they, their fathers, or grandfathers had voted before Reconstruction (Zucchino 2020). It allowed White men to vote regardless of wealth and education, while preserving racial exclusion.

In 2021, we no longer have the poll tax, literacy test, or grandfather clause—which the Voting Rights Act of 1965 finally eliminated—but voting rights continue to be suppressed. In 2013, the US Supreme Court eliminated the preclearance requirement that had required certain jurisdictions with a history of voter suppression to prove that any new voting restrictions did not have a discriminatory effect, paving the way for new voting restrictions (McGhee 2021; Zucchino 2020). As of this writing, an effort renewed in intensity and broadened in scope is underway to restrict voting rights. *The Washington Post* reported:

> Multiple scholars and historians said the proposed restrictions would amount to the most dramatic curtailment of ballot access since the late-19th century, when Southern states effectively reversed the 15th Amendment's prohibition on denying the vote based on race by enacting poll taxes, literacy tests and other restrictions that disenfranchised virtually all Black men.
>
> It took many more decades for Congress to prohibit such laws and broadly enshrine voting rights with the passage of the Voting Rights Act of 1965 and other anti-discrimination laws. Voting rights advocates say the avalanche of proposed restrictions flowing through state legislatures this year could undo much of that progress.
>
> *Gardner, Rabinowitz, and Stevens 2021*

We now face pushes for voters to show photo identification, calls for removals of drop boxes, and renewed efforts to cement obstacles to early and mail voting. Aligned with a history of racialized suppression, this wave of changes disproportionately affects voters who are poor and voters who are Black (Dade 2012; McGhee 2021). And while the masses are held back through complicated restrictions, full exclusions remain for some, as modern felon disenfranchisement disproportionately affects Black Americans (Manza and Uggen 2008).

The stated motivation behind recent moves to make voting more difficult is rooting out electoral fraud (Wines 2021). The efforts at excluding people from the electorate in the name of eliminating fraud that is non-existent are certainly motivated by officials' desire to win elections through curtailing the voting rights of those who would vote against them (Wines 2021). This onslaught of obstacles to voting would accomplish the full exclusion of some, including many Black Americans. Once again, they face barriers to the full exercise of their political rights and, therefore, others' recognition of their status as Americans with full access to the American Dream.

Welfare

The shift from categorical *exclusion*—from access to rights and thereby to the American Dream—to targeted *restrictions* are demonstrated in the denials of the civil right to own property and the political right to vote. In this section, I discuss how the American Dream was deferred for some groups, first through their formal exclusion from social rights and subsequently through targeted restrictions that hindered access to these rights. Social rights represent the welfare state's promises to provide for those unable to support themselves. But since the inception of the programs, rules restricting eligibility for welfare, unemployment benefits, and social security have made these promises empty for many—particularly low-income Black Americans (Jillson 2004).

The New Deal of the 1930s federalized and expanded various social insurance programs but had exclusionary consequences for those already marginalized by stunted access to housing and the vote. New Deal programs were transformative for some of the lowest-earning workers (McGhee 2021), but "The social insurance components of the program [the Social Security Act of 1935], principally social security and unemployment compensation, excluded workers in agriculture, domestic service, and low-paying jobs, which meant that most blacks remained outside the system" (Jillson 2004, 194).

Welfare, in the form of cash assistance from the government to poor families, began as state mothers' aid programs to help support widows and their children, becoming federalized in the 1930s as Aid to Dependent Children and soon renamed to Aid to Families with Dependent Children (Katz 1996). Much as with property ownership and voting, exclusion was initially categorical but soon gave way to restrictions that accomplished the same aims. Women of color were systematically excluded from receiving welfare benefits; "man in the house" and housekeeping rules were implemented to exclude Black women from benefit eligibility (Brown 1999; Katznelson 2005; Lieberman 2001; Mink 1995; Neubeck and Cazenave 2001). These rules could have hypothetically been applied to White women as well, but they were not. Rather, they were tools caseworkers implemented to restrict welfare eligibility and exclude Black women. Women of color did not begin to receive welfare benefits they were legally entitled to until the 1960s, a change achieved in part through the efforts of the national welfare rights movement (Kornbluh 2007; Nadasen 2005; Piven and Cloward 1979, 1993).

The ebbing of Black women's exclusion garnered backlash among Whites; the notion of paying "undeserving" poor women—Black women—to stay home and care for their children was an anathema, even as many people believed it was best for (White) children if their (White) mothers could be home with them. Linking the perception of welfare to the racialized image of the undeserving poor fueled welfare opposition. Although Whites benefitted equally from welfare benefits, "the idea of a Black person getting for free what white people had to work for—helped sink white support for all government" (McGhee 2021, 33). New methods to limit welfare through other restrictions arose (Gilens 1999; Katz 1989; Quadagno 1994). As McGhee argues, non-wealthy White Americans tend to withdraw support for programs that would benefit themselves because of racism (2021). She states that when welfare supports are withdrawn, Black people get hurt first and worst, but White people get hurt as well. So welfare cuts meant that White people lost out on these resources too.

As public support evaporated, policymakers reduced welfare benefits and made it more difficult to apply for, receive, and maintain benefits, through the use of obscure rules, sanctions, and stigma. By the time the 1996 "welfare reform" eliminated Aid to Families with Dependent Children and replaced it with Temporary Assistance for Needy Families, the shame welfare receipt represented was pervasive, enrollment was already declining, and the promise of social rights that provide access to a minimum standard of living was absent for the poor.

The degradation of welfare for the past several decades has rendered benefits "so stigmatized that people whose lives would be transformed by them don't even want them" (McGhee 2021, 59). Aside from the social barrier of stigma, long-term policies make those with assets—like savings in a bank account—ineligible for assistance (Hamilton, Wingrove, and Woodford 2019). Such policies prevent those in need from accessing assistance while also working outside the home for pay, making the American Dream of financial independence, self-sufficiency, and property ownership all the more inaccessible to them. This furthers the American Dream's exclusionary aims, and while poor White Americans are also bereft of the help they need, it is systemic racism that has consistently fueled the increasingly restrictive marginalization that characterizes welfare.

Beyond Civil, Political, and Social Rights: Education

Pursuing advanced education is widely accepted as a strategy to achieve upward mobility—to achieve the American Dream. "Like land in the nineteenth century, education by the mid-twentieth century had become the foundation for individual aspiration and the pathway to the American Dream" (Jillson 2004, 222). And while exclusion from civil, political, and social rights is in the past, its legacy of contemporary restrictions keeps Black Americans from fully accessing the Dream. Higher education simultaneously symbolizes opportunity and a path to fulfillment of the American Dream, yet its funding structure over the past several decades has meant more exclusion than opportunity.

When college students were mostly White men, college costs were far lower than they are now, and government aid was largely in the form of grants students were not required to repay.[1213] As McGhee notes, "When the public meant 'white,' public colleges thrived" (McGhee 2021, 42). However, college funding changed as the composition of student bodies changed; as women and people of color began to be able to attend college in large numbers and did so, public funding declined. As Federal funds were diverted to prisons and jails (McGhee 2021), rising college costs pushed students to finance their own educations with mounting student loans.

An increasingly diverse group of college students is shouldering an increased burden, but this burden falls unequally: "Black students on average wind up paying more for college through interest-bearing student loans over their lifetimes because they don't have the passed-down wealth that even poorer white students often have" (McGhee 2021, 14–15). Lack of intergenerational wealth due to exclusions in the arena of homeownership creates additional burdens for Black students in the arena of education.

The student debt crisis has yielded recent calls for student loan forgiveness, or cancellation, as a means to further racial equity. Zewde and Hamilton (2021) have proposed student debt cancellation as a mechanism to reduce wealth inequality by race. Noting that "the aggregate amount of student debt is more than triple its level just 13 years ago," Hamilton and Zewde (2020) point out that Black students have more student debt than White students do, and that those higher debt burdens are in part a result of the racial wealth gap (which is rooted in slavery, restrictions in access to property, and homeownership obstacles). As of this writing, the chances for student loan cancellation are unclear, but debt continues to grow.

Of course, students made a choice to take on debt precisely to forge an avenue to their own achievement of the American Dream, but their access to higher education through crushing debt is strikingly similar to the predatory inclusion Taylor documented in housing. If we believe in individualism, why wouldn't we believe that people should take out loans as individuals, bearing the brunt of the risk debt entails, in the hopes of obtaining a piece of the proverbial pie? Those I first interviewed as they approached college graduation espoused belief in the American Dream and saw student loans as a path to it. Noah explained that he felt he had no choice: "You have to go to school for basically anything nowadays, so I had to go, so I have a career." Similarly, PJ said, "I know how important education is" and "my mom and dad, they always used to tell me to be successful you need a really good education. To be something."

And yet, returns to college degrees are unequal (Zewde and Hamilton 2021), and their value seems to be shrinking in an ever-more-competitive labor market, even as those degrees seem more necessary than ever. The focus on individual persistence may sound like empowerment on the road to mobility, but structural obstacles persist and the contemporary system smacks of predatory inclusion; for college students, the high cost coupled with declining public investment means they take on what can become crushing student loan debt. College education must be paid for by individuals and their families; those without sufficient wealth take on individualized burdens of debt they may never be able to repay.

How well does the current college funding system work to position people to achieve the American Dream? Many students learn that after taking on immense debt for an undergraduate degree, they will need to double down on that investment and take on more debt for a post-graduate degree, a Master's in something to help set them apart from others, so that they might attain a job that will pay enough to repay the loans, to buy a house, to put their own children through college. This highlights the cyclical nature of the exponentially increasing need to take on more as an individual—more debt, more risk, more education— to meet an ever-more distant goal, always just out of reach, to achieve an elusive, mythic, idealized future.

McGhee includes a story in her book that exemplifies the intended goal and reality of exclusion that characterizes societal orientations toward the American Dream: the Dream is for some people, but not for others, and particularly not for Black Americans. In the 1920s and 1930s, public swimming pools were built all over the country, but they were restricted— Black Americans were excluded from using them. As legal challenges began to open pools to Black people, sometimes White people stopped using them. Sometimes public officials created private corporations to run the pools—and maintain their Whites-only status. And sometimes, they drained the pools and paved them over (McGhee 2021).

The story of what happened to America's public pools is emblematic of the shift to targeted *restriction* when categorical *exclusion* is no longer legally possible.[14] Just as filling pools and paving them over, ceasing construction of public housing, and slashing welfare spending demonstrate a commitment to exclusion, so too does depriving colleges of needed funding rather than letting expanded access reach new communities. Indeed, McGhee refers to it as "the story of how America drained the pool of our public college system" (McGhee 2021, 44).[15]

Conclusion

Fundamentally, self-interest, greed, fear, and racism lie at the heart of the exclusion that characterizes the American Dream. Its deep roots in racial subordination and hierarchy make the mechanisms of exclusion abundantly clear. Confronted with Black Americans who manage to claw their way to a semblance of the American Dream in the face of immense barriers, those with power to wield have found ways to quash any success. They have used legal exclusions and restrictions to prevent Black Americans from exercising basic civil, political, and social rights; they have used violence to silence them and strip them of their resources.[16] Is it possible that any Dream based on personal wealth must be exclusionary and unjust?

To make the American Dream a reality that is inclusive, and a reality worth attaining, we should increase access to asset-building opportunities that offer mobility, such as homeownership, but we should also remove obstacles—including ones to enforce racial subordination—that we as a society have installed. This would help to dismantle exclusion and allow ownership to spread. Still, this American Dream would still be rooted in individualism and ownership. Can we think more creatively and holistically about what else the Dream can be?

Cal Jillson notes that in recent decades, some have begun to reject the view of success as wealth and status. He states:

> As work became more abstract, fulfillment and satisfaction became things one sought in one's free time to achieve a balanced life in which work did not overwhelm family, leisure, and pleasure …. would an American Dream that stretched beyond the material to the psychological and philosophical, that promised Americans a certain quality of life beyond abundance, still be the American Dream?
>
> *Jillson 2004, 214*

I think it needs to be. And so do some of those I interviewed for my research. Flo, the married homeowner with student debt who is skeptical of the American Dream as commonly understood, described what she would want the Dream to be, something more equitable and accessible. She mentioned term limits for politicians, gender equality in pay, and "no racist systems" because, as it stands now, to her "America is like this poster child of equality but it couldn't be further from the truth." She added, "We need to think big picture, and more collectively with everybody in the world, not just, there's these imaginary borders of America, this is all we care about."

I agree with Flo that we can aim for a more inclusive Dream. What is of value to dream about that does not involve individualistic material goals? Does it have to be about owning? Can the American Dream be based on something other than building personal wealth? What about a collective American Dream to use our enormous resources to take care of each other—within and beyond our borders—to push scientific innovation to aid in environmental recuperation and pandemic prevention, to provide medical care that reduces illness and promotes good health, to create excellent educational opportunities for all, to ensure all have adequate housing and a living wage? That might be an American Dream worth striving for, as individuals and as a society, one that realizes the full potential of the values we claim to hold dear.

Notes

1 This is from a 1993 speech to the Democratic Leadership Council, quoted in Hochschild (1995,18).
2 From the Poor People's Economic Human Rights Campaign's online mission statement. Retrieved from an earlier version of their website, economichumanrights.org. Current organization website: poorpeoplesarmy.com.
3 Mentions in this essay of "our society" refer to United States society and "we" to its members.
4 As a dream of a just society, Jillson states that it symbolizes "an America that offers citizens and immigrants a better chance to thrive and prosper than any other nation on earth" (2004, xii) and "a shimmering vision of a fruitful country open to all who come, learn, work, save, invest, and play by the rules" (7). Jillson also offers a more individual-focused view of the American Dream as "a fair chance to succeed in open competition with fellow citizens for the good things of life" (2004,

xi) and the notion that "education, hard work, and a little luck will lead to success" (2004, xiii). These varied definitions within one author's work demonstrate the American Dream's ambiguity and flexibility.

5 President Lyndon Baines Johnson said America was founded "to protect and foster the life, liberty, and property of its people" (Jillson 2004, 211). President Franklin D. Roosevelt was more pointed when he asserted that access to the American Dream depends in part on the opportunity to make money. Jillson quotes him thus: "'Liberty requires opportunity to make a living—a living decent according to the standard of the time, a living that gives man not only enough to live by, but something to live for.' Without the opportunity to make a living, 'life was no longer free; liberty no longer real; men could no longer follow the pursuit of happiness'" (Jillson 2004, 178).

6 Jillson cautions: "we deceive ourselves if we imagine that American history has been an unambiguously uplifting story of opportunity, competition, and widespread success. Truth requires that we remember, acknowledge, and explain the fact that full, free, and unquestioned membership in the American society has always been more readily available to white men of a certain level of wealth and status than to others. For most of American history, some poor white men and virtually all women, blacks, American Indians, Asians, and others were barred from effective pursuit of the American Dream" (Jillson 2004, xii–xiii). In describing life in 1830–1860, he notes that "the federal government also stood against the inclusion of free blacks in American life. Blacks were barred from voting in the western territories ... [and] from taking up land in the West ... the United States Supreme Court, in the *Dred Scott* case, held that blacks, whether slave or free, could not be citizens" (Jillson 2004, 111).

7 Taylor describes "predatory inclusion" through the example of the discontinuation of formal government practices like "redlining, instead turning to new policies that encouraged low-income African Americans to become homeowners in the 1970s . . . granting access to conventional real estate practices and mortgage financing, but on more expensive and comparatively unequal terms" (Taylor 2019, 5). Predatory inclusion can also be seen in the widely accepted practice of offering large educational loans to low-income students for college attendance. The opportunity to attain promises of the American Dream—such as homeownership and college degrees—is afforded to historically disadvantaged groups, but the hidden risks and costs can render their inclusion predatory.

8 All participant names are pseudonyms chosen by the participants.

9 In her quotation above, Flo also mentioned the notion of nonexistent bootstraps; the phrase is well-known and has evocative and enduring power for many people, including some research participants in my study.

10 See, for example, Brophy (2002) on the Tulsa, Oklahoma massacre and Zucchino (2020) on the Wilmington, North Carolina coup.

11 Mortgage benefits in the GI Bill also helped White Americans far more than people of color because of housing discrimination (McGhee 2021).

12 The GI Bill of 1944 paid for college for hundreds of thousands of veterans, but few Black veterans benefited, and those who did were funneled mostly to segregated vocational schools (McGhee 2021).

13 "In 1981 Pell grants, which students do not have to repay, covered up to 98 percent of tuition at a public four-year college. However, in the past two decades, tuition charges have increased far faster than Pell grant authorizations. Today, the annual maximum Pell grant covers only about half of tuition at public four-year colleges. The college-funding gap has been covered by loan programs, which place a heavy burden on the poor, and by politically popular tuition tax rebate programs for which the poor may not qualify" (Jillson 2004, 281).

14 We saw the same pattern in public housing construction that McGhee describes with public pools. In the 1960s, tenants filed a lawsuit charging the Chicago Housing Authority (CHA) and the U.S. Department of Housing and Urban Development with discrimination—housing projects were almost exclusively in Black neighborhoods, and Black people were not allowed to enter the few in White neighborhoods. The CHA was ordered to build the next 700 units in White areas as part of the court ruling in the tenants' favor to desegregate public housing, but instead of doing so, it simply halted all public housing construction (Hirsch 1983; Massey and Denton 1993, 190). Years later, a federal court required the desegregation of public housing in Chicago, but it only granted a small number of rent subsidy vouchers to Black families to allow them to move into less segregated neighborhoods (Massey and Denton 1993). The rhetoric of openness and opportunity was preserved; technically, legally, a path was open—but in actuality, a path blocked at every turn offers no way through to the promised destination.

15 This applies to primary and secondary education as well. "Increasingly, public education has been hollowed out by the way that racism drains the pool in America: public goods are seen as worthy of investment only so long as the public is seen as good" (McGhee 2021, 179). In addition, houses in higher-rated school districts are more expensive, pricing out people of color and White people who can't afford them. But it also means that the homes they can afford are valued at lower amounts and therefore have less capacity to build wealth for their owners.

16 When that violence has been brought to bear as a means of excluding Black Americans, we as a society either pretend such instances never occurred by excising them from history's lessons, or we rename them "race riots," implying spontaneous conflicts with both Black and White instigators equally to blame. In reality, events like the Tulsa massacre and the Wilmington Coup—both sometimes referred to as riots—were about destroying the wealth of Black communities, in effect to exclude them from the American Dream.

References

Adams, James Truslow. *The Epic of America*. Boston, MA: Little, Brown & Co., 1931. Reprint, Safety Harbor, FL: Simon Publications, 2001.

Alexander, Michelle. *The New Jim Crow: Mass Incarceration in the Age of Colorblindness*. New York: The New Press, 2010.

Bellah, Robert N., Richard Madsen, William M. Sullivan, Ann Swidler, and Steven M. Tipton. *Habits of the Heart: Individualism and Commitment in American Life*. Berkeley, CA: University of California Press, 1985.

Blumgart, Jake. "How Redlining Segregated Philadelphia." *Next City*, December 8, 2017. https://nextcity.org.

Brophy, Alfred L. *Reconstructing the Dreamland: The Tulsa Race Riot of 1921, Race Reparations, and Reconciliation*. New York: Oxford University Press, 2002.

Brown, Michael K. *Race, Money, and the American Welfare State*. Ithaca, NY: Cornell University Press, 1999.

Dade, Corey. "Why New Photo ID Laws Mean Some Won't Vote." *NPR*, January 28, 2012. https://www.npr.org.

Domínguez, Silvia. *Getting Ahead: Social Mobility, Public Housing, and Immigrant Social Networks*. New York: NYU Press, 2011.

Edin, Kathryn J., and H. Luke Shaefer. *$2.00 a Day: Living on Almost Nothing in America*. Boston, MA: Houghton Mifflin Harcourt, 2015.

Esping-Anderson, G. *The Three Worlds of Welfare Capitalism*. Princeton, NJ: Princeton University Press, 1990.

Fader, Jamie J. *Falling Back: Incarceration and Transitions to Adulthood among Urban Youth*. New Brunswick: Rutgers University Press, 2013.

Fishman, Robert. *Bourgeois Utopias: The Rise and Fall of Suburbia*. New York: Basic Books, 1987.

Franklin, Benjamin. *Benjamin Franklin: Autobiography, Poor Richard: Autobiography, Poor Richard, and Later Writings*, edited by J.A. Leo Lemay. New York: Library of America, 2005.

Gardner, Amy, Kate Rabinowitz, and Harry Stevens. "How GOP-backed voting measures could create hurdles for tens of millions of voters." *Washington Post*, March 11, 2021. https://www.washingtonpost.com.

Giddens, Anthony, Mitchell Duneier, Richard P. Appelbaum, and Deborah Carr. *Essentials of Sociology, 8th edition*. New York: W.W. Norton & Company, 2021.

Gilens, Martin. *Why Americans Hate Welfare: Race, Media and the Politics of Antipoverty Strategy*. Chicago: University of Chicago Press, 1999.

Glantz, Aaron, and Emmanuel Martinez. "Kept Out: For people of color, banks are shutting the door to homeownership." *Reveal*, February 15, 2018. https://revealnews.org.

Hacker, Jacob S., and Paul Pierson. *Winner-Take-All Politics: How Washington Made the Rich Richer—and Turned Its Back on the Middle Class*. New York: Simon & Schuster, 2010.

Hamilton, Leah, Twila Wingrove, and Kati Woodford. "Does generous welfare policy encourage dependence? TANF asset limits and duration of program participation." *Journal of Children and Poverty* 25, no. 2 (2019): 101–113.

Hamilton, Darrick and Naomi Zewde. "The coronavirus recession is an opportunity to cancel all U.S. student loan debt." *Washington Center for Equitable Growth*, June 24, 2020. https://equitablegrowth.org.

Hansen, Karen V. *Not-So-Nuclear Families: Class, Gender, and Networks of Care.* New Brunswick, NJ: Rutgers University Press, 2005.

Hill, Leah. "Disturbing Disparities: Black girls and the school-to-prison pipeline." *Fordham Law Review Online* 87, Article 11 (2018): 58–63. https://ir.lawnet.fordham.edu/flro/vol87/iss1/11.

Hirsch, Arnold. *Making the Second Ghetto: Race and Housing in Chicago, 1940–1960.* Cambridge: Cambridge University Press, 1983.

Hochschild, Jennifer L. *Facing Up to the American Dream: Race, Class, and the Soul of the Nation.* Princeton, NJ: Princeton University Press, 1995.

Jackson, Kenneth T. *The Crabgrass Frontier: The Suburbanization of the United States.* New York: Oxford University Press, 1985.

Jillson, Cal. *Pursuing the American Dream: Opportunity & Exclusion Over Four Centuries.* Lawrence, KS: University Press of Kansas, 2004.

Katz, Michael B. *The Undeserving Poor: From the War on Poverty to the War on Welfare.* New York: Pantheon Books, 1989.

Katz, Michael B. *In the Shadow of the Poorhouse: A Social History of Welfare in America, Tenth Anniversary Edition, Revised and Updated.* New York: Basic Books, 1996.

Katznelson, Ira. *When Affirmative Action Was White: An Untold History of Racial Inequality in Twentieth-Century America.* New York: Norton, 2005.

King, Martin Luther, Jr. "The Hammer of Justice." Delivered at Ohio Northern University, Ada, Ohio, on January 11, 1968. https://www.onu.edu/mlk/mlk-speech-transcript.

Klinghoffer, Judith Apter, and Lois Elkis. "'The petticoat electors': Women's Suffrage in New Jersey, 1776–1807." *Journal of the Early Republic* 12, no. 2 (1992): 159–193.

Kluegel, James R., and Eliot R. Smith. *Beliefs about Inequality: Americans' Views of What Is and What Ought to Be.* New York: Aldine de Gruyter, 1986.

Kornbluh, Felicia. *The Battle for Welfare Rights: Politics and Poverty in Modern America.* Philadelphia, PA: University of Pennsylvania Press, 2007.

Lareau, Annette. *Unequal Childhoods: Class, Race, and Family Life.* Berkeley, CA: University of California Press, 2003.

Lieberman, Robert C. *Shifting the Color Line: Race and the American Welfare State.* Cambridge, MA: Harvard University Press, 2001.

Macleod, Jay. *Ain't No Makin' It: Aspirations and Attainment in a Low-Income Neighborhood.* 3rd edition. Boulder, CO: Westview Press, 2008.

Manza, Jeff and Christopher Uggen. *Locked Out: Felon Disenfranchisement and American Democracy.* New York: Oxford University Press, 2008.

Marshall, Thomas Humphrey. *Citizenship and Social Class and Other Essays.* Cambridge, England: Cambridge University Press, 1950.

Massey, Douglas S., and Nancy A. Denton. *American Apartheid: Segregation and the Making of the Underclass.* Cambridge, MA: Harvard University Press, 1993.

Massey, Douglas S., and Garvey Lundy. "Use of Black English and racial discrimination in urban housing markets: New methods and findings." *Urban Affairs Review* 36, no. 4 (2001): 452–469.

Mazelis, Joan Maya. *Surviving Poverty: Creating Sustainable Ties among the Poor.* New York: New York University Press, 2017.

McCabe, Caitlin. "For minorities, there's still inequality in the housing market." *Philadelphia Inquirer,* November 17, 2017. https://www.inquirer.com.

McCoy, Sean. "The American Dream is suffering, but Americans are satisfied: 15 Charts." *Atlantic,* July 1, 2015. www.theatlantic.com.

McGhee, Heather. *The Sum of Us: What Racism Costs Everyone and How We Can Prosper Together.* New York: One World, 2021.

Merton, Robert K. "Social Structure and Anomie." *American Sociological Review* 3, no. 5 (1938): 672–682.

Mink, Gwendolyn. *The Wages of Motherhood: Inequality in the Welfare State, 1917–1942.* Ithaca, NY: Cornell University Press, 1995.

Morton, Marian. "The suburban ideal and suburban realities: Cleveland Heights, Ohio, 1860–2001." *Journal of Urban History* 28, no. 5 (2002): 671–698.

Nadasen, Premilla. *Welfare Warriors: The Welfare Rights Movement in the United States.* New York: Routledge, 2005.

Neubeck, Kenneth J., and Noel A. Cazenave. *Welfare Racism: Playing the Race Card Against America's Poor.* New York: Routledge, 2001.

Oliver, Melvin L. and Thomas M. Shapiro. *Black Wealth/White Wealth: A New Perspective on Racial Inequality, Tenth-Anniversary Edition*. New York: Routledge, 2006.

Piven, Frances Fox, and Richard A. Cloward. *Poor People's Movements: Why They Succeed, How They Fail*. New York: Vintage, 1979.

Piven, Frances Fox, and Richard A. Cloward. *Regulating the Poor: The Functions of Public Welfare*. New York: Vintage, 1993.

Poor People's Economic Human Rights Campaign. Retrieved August 4, 2015, http://economichumanrights.org/, http://economichumanrights.org/mission-statement.

Putnam, Robert D. *Our Kids: The American Dream in Crisis*. New York: Simon & Schuster, 2015.

Quadagno, Jill. *The Color of Welfare: How Racism Undermined the War on Poverty*. New York: Oxford, 1994.

Redbook. "In The Suburbs." 1957. https://www.youtube.com/watch?v=QFk5y5C82tk

Schuetz, Jenny. "Renting the American Dream: Why homeownership shouldn't be a prerequisite for middle-class financial security." *The Brookings Institution*, February 13, 2019. Washington, DC. https://www.brookings.edu.

Shapiro, Thomas, Tatjana Meschede, and Sam Osoro. "The roots of the widening racial wealth gap: Explaining the Black-White economic divide." Research and Policy Brief. Institute on Assets and Social Policy, 2013. http://iasp.brandeis.edu/pdfs/Author/shapiro-thomas-m/racialwealthgapbrief.pdf

Silva, Jennifer M. *Coming Up Short: Working-Class Adulthood in an Age of Uncertainty*. New York: Oxford University Press, 2013.

Stiglitz, Joseph E. *The Price of Inequality*. New York: W. W. Norton, 2012.

Tavernise, Sabrina. "The officers danced at a Black Lives Matter rally. Then they stormed the capitol." *New York Times*, March 8, 2021. https://www.nytimes.com.

Taylor, Keeanga-Yamahtta. *Race for Profit: How Banks and the Real Estate Industry Undermined Black Homeownership*. Chapel Hill, NC: UNC Press, 2019.

Weber, Max. *The Protestant Ethic and the Spirit of Capitalism*. Translated by Talcott Parsons, 1930 [1992, 2001]. New York: Routledge, 1905.

Wilson, William Julius. *When Work Disappears: The World of the New Urban Poor*. New York: Vintage Books, 1996.

Wines, Michael. "In statehouses, stolen-election myth fuels a G.O.P. drive to rewrite rules." *New York Times*, February 27, 2021. https://www.nytimes.com.

Zewde, Naomi and Darrick Hamilton. "What canceling student debt would do for the racial wealth gap." *The New York Times*. February 1, 2021. https://www.nytimes.com.

Zucchino, David. *Wilmington's Lie: The Murderous Coup of 1898 and the Rise of White Supremacy*. New York: Atlantic Monthly Press, 2020.

PART V

The American Dream Goes Global?

17

"GOOD LIVING" AND IMMIGRANTS IN THE LITERATURE OF ALEKSANDAR HEMON

Toward the Humble Dream[1]

Iva Kosmos

Aleksandar Hemon, a Bosnian-American writer, appears in profiles published in the mass media as the epitome of the American Dream. The young author came to Chicago in 1992 as a refugee from war-torn Bosnia without a good knowledge of English. He struggled through hard physical and intellectual work, from menial jobs to persistent attempts to master a new language. Slowly, he became a published author. Then, in 2004, he landed a MacArthur Genius Grant and, in 2008, a nomination for the National Book Award for fiction. To share the most recent news, he became engaged as a professor of creative writing at Princeton. Is there better proof that hard work pays off in the land of equal opportunities? Hemon's literary work, as well as his public persona, cannot escape reflecting the story of the American Dream. However, in his fiction and memoirs, the author offers us a much more complex picture of this cultural imaginary, firstly deconstructing the neat story of upward mobility and success and then reinventing the values, aspirations, and goals of immigrants' dreams, creating the alternative vision of a "good living" in America, which I name here the Humble Dream.

It is interesting that among scholarly research into Hemon's prose, there is insufficient insight into the author's treatment of American cultural codes and narratives, although all of his novels, essays, and stories include the immigrant experience of the American reality. Scholars have studied Hemon's work through paradigms of immigrant displacement (Beganović 2009; Matthes and Williams 2013), nostalgia, melancholy (Beganović 2009), fragmented cultural identity (Bošković 2008; Miočević 2013), and the experience of dispossession (Vervaet 2017). Hemon is also seen as a writer who integrates his native Yugoslav culture into global cultural streams (Vervaet 2016) and resists the usual stereotypes of Eastern Europe (Luca 2020) while contributing to the international "understanding of the background and consequences of the war in Balkans in the 1990s" (Raudvere 2017, 180). Bosnian background and displacement are surely central to Hemon's work; however, it seems that the American cultural elements of his work have been somewhat neglected. Hemon is writing and publishing in the American context for an American audience since his first book; this inevitably brings him in communication with American cultural codes and myths. This chapter is thus trying to raise awareness with respect

DOI: 10.4324/9781003326243-22

to American elements in Hemon's writing and to contribute to the understanding of Hemon as an active member of the American literary field, creatively integrating and reflecting American cultural codes, including the American Dream, in his writing.

This chapter is composed of four parts. First, I present Hemon's literary attempts at deconstructing the fantasy of success by juxtaposing the celebratory narrative of the American Dream against a depiction of immigrants' realities. In the second part, I treat insight into the stereotype of immigrants as the embodiment of the American Dream, which Hemon uses to examine the effects of this cultural figure on the communicative interaction between immigrants and native-born Americans. Xenophobic aspects of the conventional immigrant myth and the American Dream are revealed in the third part. Finally, I treat Hemon's vision of "good living" in North America in light of his narrative and temporal reinvention of the immigrant Dream and the American Dream in general.

Celebratory Narrative of the American Dream versus Immigrant Reality

Since his debut, short story collection, *The Question of Bruno* from 2000, Hemon has published seven books in English, both fiction and non-fiction, all of them addressing the immigrant experience in North America. Literary characters reflect the author's life path, as most of his leading characters come from Bosnia and the former Yugoslavia. Each portrays different stages in an immigrant's life: there are newcomers, then integrated and settled immigrants. We will first turn our attention to Hemon's stories on freshly arrived immigrants, which serve as a special vehicle to inspect contradictions in the myth of the American Dream, especially its postulates of equal opportunities and upward mobility. The narrative of the American Dream, as expressed in rags to riches stories, naturalizes the low social position of the immigrant, as it frames the low paid jobs as (good) opportunities that will naturally lead upward if combined with hard work and diligence. Hemon does not simply negate the existence of an opportunity or the Dream in general but questions its nature. He offers a more complex picture of social reality by using a simple and effective strategy: juxtaposing the celebratory narrative of the American Dream with bleak immigrant realities.

This technique has a special place in Hemon's first works, including the story "Blind Jozef Pronek & Dead Souls" from his first collection and a novel *Nowhere Man* (2002), in which he employs an autofictional protagonist Jozef Pronek. Pronek is a newcomer from Bosnia trying to navigate his new surroundings. He tries to find a job, a place to live, and a human companion while undergoing the trauma of watching his birthplace, Sarajevo, disappear in flames. In his everyday encounters with different Americans, Pronek constantly listens to phrases and assurances based on the American cultural narratives. Right on his arrival, on his first domestic plane ride, he is assured by a fellow traveler that he is at the best place to be.

> "What do you think of America? Isn't it the greatest country on earth?"
> "I'm afraid I don't know yet. I just arrived."
> "It's great. People are great. Freedom, all that. Best in the world."
> *Hemon 2001, 143*

The line of reassurances continues in his later encounters. Pronek's friend's father tells him: "I'm sure you'll do fine if you stay here. This is the greatest country in the world, you just have to work hard" (Hemon 2001, 178). His friend's mother goes in the same line: "I know you're a hard worker […]. It is people like you who built this great country for us" (Hemon 2001, 195). In the story "Blind Jozef Pronek & Dead Souls," even the narrator joins this

American chorus. The narrator, in the first-person plural, is cast in the role of a representative of the American nation and addresses the reader as a fellow American who needs guidance to understand the foreign protagonist. When Pronek finally finds a job, the narrator enthusiastically exclaims: "Oh what a lucky break for our immigrant" (Hemon 2001, 195). Hemon does not moralize or offer comments on the American chorus, and rather, he lets the contrast between the lighthearted reassurances and immigrant reality speak for itself. A "lucky break" thus actually means that Pronek is about to join a cleaning service and become a bathroom cleaner, "the shit boy." Pronek's stories present a line of low paid jobs, always exhausting, sometimes humiliating, often dangerous, meaningless, and/or boring: a garbage cleaner and a fast food clerk, a waiter, a parking assistant, a kitchen equipment salesman (asked to laugh more to please customers), a deliverer of subpoenas, the seller of newspaper subscriptions, a canvasser for Greenpeace. Vivid descriptions use smell, tactile, and visual perceptions to evoke the discomfort, filth, and repetitiveness of the work. Each of the characters' jobs stands in stark contrast to the bright tone and atmosphere of the American Dream rhetoric they are forced to endure. Here is Pronek as a garbage cleaner in a fast-food restaurant:

> They would push the cart on to an altar-like lift, hook up the axis of the cart, then raise it to the edge of the container. One of them would push a red button that would make the altar flip over and empty out the cart. Often, the cart would just maliciously drop in, and they would have to enter the supreme garbage bin, which would groan with pleasure. They would have to lift the cart above their heads, up to their knees in rotting food, and midwife it out of the bin, as a mixture of mayo, Dijon mustard, vinegar, gumbo and reduced-fat chili crawled down their forearms. They would wash the garbage remnants out of the cart, wash their hands (EMPLOYEES MUST WASH THEIR HANDS, the sign over the sink said), never being able to wash thin lines of dirt out of the furrows of their palms.
>
> *Hemon 2001, 185*

The "opportunity" in the American Dream logically leads to a promise of a prosperous future. Hochschild explains this as one of the tenets of the American Dream. The fabled "opportunity" depends on the actual resources and not an insignificant measure of luck. However, the close link between anticipation and expectation presents a formal chance for success as a "significant likelihood" for realization of one's dreams (Hochschild 1995, 27). Hemon explores this further by questioning the nature of opportunities at hand. What if there are plenty of opportunities but not leading where the dramaturgical structure of the Dream sets them to go, promising that there is always a way to the top? What if there is no way to the top, or if the waiting period is extended to the never-ending future? This perspective reveals "opportunity" as a narrative cover for exploiting the working force of the United States' lower classes and immigrants.

Along with the nature of opportunity in the American Dream, Hemon also inspects closely the notion of fairness and self-responsibility for the failure, based on the assumption that the system rewards those who "follow the rules of the game." Hemon does not simply negate this system of promised reward but questions the nature of the rules. In whose favor are the "rules of the game" created and for whom are they working? Pronek's "fast-food career" is embedded in the promise of fairness and upward mobility, as the manager, offering the low paycheck, assures him: "We can offer you five, and maybe later you can work your way up. Here everyone has a fair chance" (Hemon 2001, 182). However, in this episode, Pronek is dismissed from his work for not following the rules exactly as his subservient role commands. When the customer demands from Pronek to replace his sandwich, which mistakenly contains

iceberg lettuce instead of romaine lettuce, Pronek questions his demand and offends the customer by asking: "What's difference?" The customer then demands to see a manager, who
fires Pronek. Hemon presents this situation from different viewpoints. A narrator describes
the customer's behavior from the point of righteous demand for the service that Pronek
should, but did not, deliver: "But the man, naturally, did not give up, for he demanded – and
rightly so – full and responsible service for his hard-earned money" (Hemon 2001, 189).
On the other side, Hemon adds nuances and social complexities to this formal approach to
fairness. He portrays Pronek's exhaustion over exploitative and repetitive physical work as a
relevant factor for the reader's consideration. Then, too, there are nuances of the communication, which show the customer's condescending approach and his exercise of the symbolic,
but ultimately quite real, power over someone of a lower working position. The customer
is addressing Pronek from a position of entitlement, inviting Pronek initially in a seemingly
polite manner: "Young man, would you please come here!" (Hemon 2001, 188). Then he
interrogates Pronek in a patronizing manner: "This is iceberg lettuce. What do you have to
say about that?" (Hemon 2001, 189). Upon hearing Pronek's answer, the customer raises his
voice, clearly expressing disbelief, and, finally, dismisses him over his verbal incompetence
and impertinence by pushing away his tray "with resolve" and asking: "May I talk to someone
who can speak English, please?" (Hemon 2001, 189). In this context, Pronek's questioning of
the customer appears as an impulsive refusal to submit to yet another act of social submission.
In the end, his small act of defiance is not tolerated, and Pronek is clearly shown his place.
Hemon shows what the myth hides: the narrative demand of hard work and following rules
of the game – of offering "full and responsible service" – is hiding the context of bad working
conditions, exploitation, and unequal treatment.

On top of working conditions, Hemon also explores meager living conditions and the
immigrant's isolation, cultural confusion, exclusion, and loneliness, all of which add another
un-stated price tag on the American Dream package. With his early work, Hemon does not
directly negate the American Dream but uncovers the part of social reality that the Dream
hides. What is presented as opportunity is uncovered as simultaneously a veil for exploitation.
What is offered as bright future is, to the contrary, a line of never-ending, exploitative jobs.
What is presented as fairness and just the common sense, neutral "rules of the game" is also
really a tool for disciplining the subjects involved in performing exploitative jobs. Hemon's
literature reveals the double nature of the Dream; in this regard, Hemon's work is a literary
counterpart to the work done by sociologists and other skeptical scholars of the American
Dream, who claim that the celebration of successful stories is posed to hide the reality of
social inequality and exploitation of cheap labor (Behdad 2005; Hochschild 1995). However,
Hemon's work also adds some insights into the functions of the Dream that have not been
widely researched within the existing scholarship.

Immigrant as the Projection Screen for the American Dream

The American Dream, with its ideas of equality of opportunity and upward mobility, is an
important part of the myth of immigrant America, which casts the immigrant in the positive role of a diligent worker making his way up toward success. It is an upbeat tale that, had
it not appeared independently of mainstream American movies and television shows, would
seem ready-made for Hollywood treatment. Hemon adds a specific observation on how this
idealized narrative and the figure of the honorable, striving immigrant impact the communication between immigrants and native-born Americans. Before we proceed further, though,
let us briefly look into the American cultural imagining of immigrants.

We can generally say that different nations construct themselves in a relation of difference toward the cultural, racial, or ethnic Other, which is often negatively portrayed in order for natives to establish themselves as their positive counterparts. However, what is characteristic of American relations to immigrants, is a specific interplay between xenophilia and xenophobia, between classical imagining of the foreigner as a social scapegoat and the foreigner in the exactly opposite role of "the agent of national re-enchantment that might rescue the regime from corruption and return it to its first principles" (Behdad 2005; Honig 2001, 74). In this same line, the American immigrant also becomes the champion of the American Dream that has long since lost its luster and allure for Americans. Honig explains that the figure of immigrant rejuvenator serves to convince the Americans that their ideals still exist and to reconcile the inner contradictions of American democracy, which is making its promises of upward mobility within a social structure that structurally disables them. The ideologically useful example in this regard is the figure of the economically successful immigrant, which "reassure[s] workers of the possibility of upward mobility in an economy that rarely delivers on that promise, while also disciplining native-born poor, domestic minorities, and unsuccessful foreign laborers into believing that the economy fairly rewards dedication and hard work" (Honig 2001, 74).[2] In other words, the immigrant reassures the masses that the main staples of the American Dream are still standing firm. What Hemon adds to these insights is how the American Dream and the idealized immigrant figure affect the interaction between native-born Americans and immigrants.

Hemon's immigrants are often faced with confident and brisk evaluations of their own circumstances and characters. Their American peers are always under the impression that they are very sure about who they are. In doing so, they are leaning on the well-known cultural narratives of the American Dream and the myth of immigrant America. The Dream is projected onto the immigrant figure, and the American interlocutors demand the immigrant to fit his or her story to the myth, as they are unable to perceive them beyond that narrative pattern. Having such a simple strong belief in the American Dream narrative, Americans are forced to disregard the actual immigrant and his peculiar story, thus avoiding any compulsion to directly engage with the person in front of them. Even more, Hemon's immigrants are very well aware of Americans' cultural expectations of them, and in order to navigate the American cultural landscape, they forge and adapt their identities to American expectations. A good example is the story "Good Living" from Hemon's fourth book, the short story collection *Love and Obstacles* (2009). Predicting what Americans seek to see from him, Hemon's hero readily stages his story as the embodiment of the American Dream:

> Back in the days of the war in Bosnia, I was surviving in Chicago by selling magazine subscriptions door-to-door. My employers thought that my Bosnian accent, clearly manufactured in the nether area of 'other cultures,' was quirky, and therefore stimulant to the shopping instincts of suburban Americans. I was desperate at the time, what with the war and displacement, so I shamelessly exploited any smidgen of pity I could detect in lonely housewives and grumpy retirees whose doors I knocked at. Many of them were excited by my very presence at their doorstep, as I was living evidence of the American dream: here I was, overcoming adverse circumstances in a new country, much like the forebears of the future subscriber, presently signing the check and wistfully relating the saga of the ancestral transition to America.
>
> *Hemon 2009, chap. 4*

Meeting the local priest, the immigrant hero continues his act and confirms the expectations on his previous suffering in the old land and current aspirations in the new homeland:

> "Have you lost anyone close to you in the war? Anyone you loved?"
> "Some," I said, and lowered my head, suggesting intense soul pain.
> "It must have been hard for you."
> "It hasn't been easy."
> Abruptly he turned his head toward the dark door in the back of the room and yelled: "Michael! Michael! Come here and see someone who is really suffering. Come and meet an actual human being".
>
> *Hemon 2009, chap. 4*

The narrative quickly turns to the quarrel between the local priest and Michael, presumably his lover. Both characters are accusing each other of moral corruption; at the same time, the immigrant hero is addressed as the moral figure, "an actual human being." The priest does not know anything about the actual person in front of him, but he refers to the xenophilic stereotype of the morally upright immigrant – struggling to overcome his modest circumstances and climb the social ladder. In the end, the priest buys some newspapers, and the immigrant hero continues to navigate the neighborhood sharing news on the magazines the priest had bought and rumors on the fight he had with "his young friend" – finally having a success in selling. The story ends in the optimistic feelings of the narrator's satisfaction: Hemon's immigrant hero navigated the cultural landscape of America and made a small step toward possible prosperity:

> It was by far my best day as a magazine salesman. At the end of the shift, waiting to be picked up by the turf manager, I watched the flickering TV lights in the windows and the sparkling stars up in the sky, and I thought: I could live here. I could live here forever. This is a good place for me.
>
> *Hemon 2009, chap. 4*

This light and optimistic ending is, of course, ambivalent. It does not only reveal the humble nature of the immigrant's economic achievements and professional prospects, but also the disregard of the actual immigrant experience and the pressure to adapt to expectations in order to communicate and be recognized in American society. The story reveals the relationship between Americans and immigrants as non-dialogical, and the American Dream appears as a tool to homogenize and silence immigrants from voicing their actual experiences. The Dream re-inscribes American cultural narratives onto immigrants and thus disables American characters from entering the space of actual communication in which two disparate voices could actually meet.

The same logic is employed with already integrated immigrants, which have to an extent, climbed the ladder, gone through the first phase of testing their endurance in the capitalist economy, and gathered some fruits of their "hard work." However, for the integrated immigrant, the bar has been raised, as he needs to prove himself against the figure of idealized super-citizen, which demands excellence in different areas of American life. Above all, the assimilated immigrant must show demonstrated attainment of material success and social recognition, but also conventional involvement in a family, community, and civic life. The super-citizen figure, explains Honig, additionally consolidates and legitimizes the belief in the possibility of the system to deliver on its promises. In this regard, the super-citizen is "an object of identification" and "the screen into which we project our idealized selves" (Honig 2001, 77). By working harder than Americans do, he or she manages to have it all, "even though these very goods are experienced by the rest of us as contradictory or elusive" (Honig 2001, 78). If the figure of super-citizen comforts Americans, it is nothing near as comforting for Hemon's immigrants. They find it impossible to embody the ideal that is projected on them while not finding other ways to communicate themselves beyond the narrative of super-success. Thus, the super-citizen figure also functions as a rhetorical vehicle that mutes immigrants' actual experiences.

Vladimir Brik, the central hero of the novel *The Lazarus Project* (2008), is an integrated Bosnian American with an American wife and some humble successes as a writer. He knows that he is not a failure, but he is also aware that his achievements do not perfectly match the super-citizen model. Consequently, he rationally chooses to perform the narrative of the American Dream in order to profit from its symbolic value. However, in his knowledgeable, clever reasoning on how to manipulate cultural codes, his true self remains half-hidden in front of his American compatriots, including his wife, and the authentic communication between the two is disabled.

> The party inquisitors were often given to gushing over the neatness of my immigrant story; many would recall an ancestor who came to America and followed the same narrative trajectory: displacement, travails, redemption, success. I couldn't bring myself to tell them that I had lost my teaching job and that I was pretty much supported by Mary. She liked the narrative trajectory too, for her people also had a history of displacement and replacement, though I was pretty sure that she was disappointed that my success stage seemed to have been suspended. Still, she mailed the column clips to her parents in Pittsburgh, who obediently put them up on their fridge; she suggested that I was greatly talented and would one day write a great book.
>
> *Hemon 2008a, 32*

Although both the American Dream, the immigrant myth, and the super-citizen figure portray the immigrants in mostly a positive light, they are also oppressive inasmuch as they demand total adaptation to the foreseen role. Hemon suggests that immigrants need to embody a figure of idealized citizen in order to be regarded at all and made visible to their American peers. In this way, the optimistic and positively envisioned, idealized figure of immigrants disables the authentic communication and interaction since almost no one, or only very rare individuals, actually fit the role that is demanded. As a consequence, immigrants are either invisible to their American peers, or they perform a script for them, adapting their biography to the prescribed scenario, one that does not actually reflect their lived experience.

The American Dream as Hiding the Continuity of Nativism and Xenophobia

In what is likely his best-known novel, *The Lazarus Project*, Hemon turns to those immigrants that did not manage to confirm the expectations and promises of the Dream and were thus erased from the collective cultural memory. With it, he also joins a wider debate on whether oppression toward immigrants and minorities in the United States is a matter of individual incidents or is a continuous practice based on structural racial and ethnic inequality. By addressing immigrant stories in two parallel, historical storylines that continuously refer to, reflect, and engage with each other, Hemon clearly confirms the latter.

The Lazarus Projects focuses on the aforementioned Brik, a semi-successful writer, and columnist, trying to prove himself in front of his American wife, family, and acquaintances. Brik discovers a peculiar story of Lazarus Averbuch, a historical character,[3] a young Ukrainian Jew at the turn of the century that has been killed by a Chicago police officer shortly after his arrival in the US amidst unclear circumstances. Lazarus' story strongly attracts Brik, and he decides to write a book based on it – which could bring him one step closer to becoming an established novelist, thus reaching the symbolic and material goals required by the Dream. In order to conduct research for the book, he departs for a field trip in Eastern Europe with his photographer friend Rora, trying to trace Lazarus' previous life.

While the first story takes place at the turn of the 21st century, the second story line arises in 1908 and departs from the moment Lazarus was killed. This latter narrative recreates the historic Chicago and follows the consequences that Lazarus' death brings to his impoverished sister Olga, striving to prove her brother's innocence. The story also traces the experiences of Lazarus' friends and fellows, who are routinely interrogated and beaten by the police, and finally, to the wider community of Eastern European Jews, who are publicly cast in the role of evildoers. Lazarus' death is accompanied by a wave of moral panic, created by media coverage and police investigation, alarming Chicagoans on the possible danger of the anarchist movement, ostensibly brought by the foreigners. Lazarus becomes a public scapegoat, an embodiment of the evil "anarchist," although no one has clear proof of his intentions or previous engagement with anti-democratic deeds. Hemon portrays different kinds of violence over immigrants, from structural everyday violence caused by legislative requirements and poor working and dire living conditions, to the more severe violence practiced by the state apparatus and police. However, where *The Lazarus Project* centers most and succeeds best is to reveal the formation of discursive violence. The novel closely follows the production of the rhetoric against anarchism, which turns Eastern European Jews into "anarchist" enemies of the American nation. Hemon reveals how narratives are created, disseminated, and then collectively accepted as a reality. The discourse is produced mainly by the media of that time – newspapers, supported by corrupted police work – while being quickly picked up and reproduced by the ordinary citizen.

Hemon uses the genre of historical metafiction in order to combine historical data with fictional elements (Hutcheon 2004). While considering the historical facts, the mission of the novel is to fill up the voids of the historically unknown. *The Lazarus Project* thus includes historical accounts but also imagines what could or might have happened and experiments with potentiality: different versions of the same event are placed together, side by side, testifying that none of them is a direct reflection of the historical reality, but each differing account is simply a textual attempt to capture the same history from a different viewpoint. For example, newspaper articles and police reports are juxtaposed with immigrants' accounts and the narrator's third person voice, adding another testimony to what is viewed as a provisional story. The textual juxtaposition of different versions of events questions the authoritative sounding narratives produced by the media and police. In this regard, it is obvious that media and police present immigrants as terrorists – or with the name of that time: anarchists – while the alternative voices show them as victims of brutal, unsanctioned violence founded on deep prejudices. On top of it, Hemon's inclusion of other discourses typical of that time, such as eugenics, racial stereotypes, and slurs (e.g. kike), serves to additionally highlight the general attitude toward immigrants embodied in the narrative used against Lazarus.

The central episode of the novel – a clash between Lazarus and a police officer, Shippy, in which the former is killed – is illustrative of Hemon's approach. The narrator follows Lazarus on his way to Shippy's home, describing his path and his impressions, although not discovering the motives for his visit. When both men meet, the narrative incorporates another voice: reporting in third-person by journalist Miller, which is marked in italics. It is clear that the narrator's and Miller's versions do not match and that we have two juxtaposed "truths." It is also obvious that everyone else, taking part in this episode and in the novel, form and transform the story according to their own beliefs and benefits.

"He handed me an envelope with my name and address on it," Chief Shippy will tell Mr. Miller. *"I did not wait to examine the envelope any further. The thought struck me like a streak of lightning that the man was up to no good. He looked to me like an anarchist. I grabbed his arms and, forcing them behind his back, called to my wife: 'Mother! Mother!'"*

Mother Shippy comes rushing in with all the natural force *Mother* implies. She is stout and strong, with a large head; in her haste she nearly tumbles. Her husband is holding the hands of *a Sicilian or a Jew,* and, in horror, she presses the palm of her hand on her chest and gasps with a boom. "Search his pockets," Chief Shippy orders. Mother pats the young man's pockets, her hands trembling, his sour smell making her stomach churn up. The young man fidgets and tries to wrestle away, grunting like a sinewy beast. "I think he has a pistol," Mother vociferates. Chief Shippy drops the stranger's hands and quickly draws his revolver. Mother dodges and wobbles toward a tapestry that featured – William P. Miller does not fail to note – *Saint George killing a squirming dragon.*

Chief Shippy's driver, Foley, who has just arrived to drive him to City Hall, runs up the front stairs, alarmed by the sound of scuffle, pulling out his revolver, while Henry, Chief Shippy's son *(on leave from the Culver Military Academy),* surges downstairs from his bedroom in his pajamas, clutching a shiny, blunt saber. The young man wiggles out of Shippy's grasp, steps away for a long instant – Foley opening the door with a gun in his hand, Henry stumbling down the stairs, Mother peeking from behind the dragon – and then lunges at him. Without thinking, Chief Shippy shoots at the young man; blood gushes so hard that the burst of redness blinds Foley, who, being well trained and aware of Chief Shippy's dislike of drafts, is slamming the door shut behind him. Startled by Foley, Chief Shippy shoots at him, too, and then, sensing a body rushing towards him, wheels around like an experienced gunfighter and shoots at Henry. *The vile foreigner shot at Foley, shattering his wrist, and then at Henry, the bullet piercing his lung.* Consequently, more bullets are fired by Shippy and Foley, seven of which hit the young man, his blood and brains spurting and splattering on the walls and on the floor. *Throughout the struggle,* William P. Miller writes, *the anarchist had not uttered a syllable. He fought on doggedly with that cruel mouth shut tight and the eyes colored with determination terrible to behold. He died without a curse, supplication, or prayer.*

Hemon 2008a, 9

From the following example, it becomes clear that there is no clear indication that Lazarus has shot a gun nor was he armed, although he is defined as an assailant by both police and media. We can say that Lazarus is thus created as an anarchist and assassin by the media and police accounts. Lazarus' story line parallels Brik's story line, placed at the turn of the century; after 9/11, amidst a social climate that creates a comparable discourse on terrorism. By this, Hemon implicitly suggests historic symmetry exists between the two narratives. In Brik's story line, Hemon never directly inspects media and discursive politics of the 21st century; rather, he only offers glimpses into social and political changes, including the surge of nativism and preparation for the upcoming War on Terror. Although the comment on the George W. Bush era is rare, events he subtly references are vivid and present in the American collective imagination, even if not directly evoked. So, by juxtaposing the War on Terror, which resonates in the cultural imagination of his readership, with the War on anarchism, on which he gives extensive details, Hemon is implicitly suggesting a correlation between the two. By this, he is doing two things. First, by showing the textual production of the discourse of anarchism, he invites the reader to question whether the discourse on terrorism might also be (co)created by mass media, police, and other conventional institutions. Second, while paralleling two discourses as reflections of one another and not as a historical deflection from an otherwise "hospitable nation" (Behdad 2005) he presents them as a continuation of historical Othering of immigrants. Hemon himself explained that he purposefully chose the story of Lazarus Averbuch as representative of the stories that do not fit the American Dream and are consistently concealed and erased.

> I have always been bothered by the American dream mythology. It is inherently assimilationist and it entirely denies all the exploitation, injustice, and loss that immigrants experienced upon arrival here. [...] Immigrants had to forget about what they left behind and pass through all this hardship – as though an unlivable wage were a way to teach them how to be American – and finally become human by virtue of becoming American. Those who could not, did not, or would not adjust and accept the conditions of being American have been eliminated from the story of the American dream. [...] That's what happened to Lazarus; he did not and does not fit into the story of the American dream.
>
> *Hemon 2008b*

Thus, Hemon's notions on the *long duree* of exclusion and injustice should be read as part of wider debates on continuity and discontinuity of such discourses and practices in American society. While some are seeing xenophobia as irregularly appearing due to periodic power change or as a result of economic problems (compare Honig 2001, 75; Behdad 2005, chap. 4), others see it as belonging to a longer line of historical exclusion of immigrants and nativism, concealed by the myth of a benignly hospitable and welcoming nation (Behdad 2005; Denvir 2020; Honig 2001). In this debate, Hemon clearly stands in line with the argument of the continuity of xenophobia, scapegoating, and nativism.[45]

Hemon's prose on newly arrived immigrants highlights the unfairness and exploitative nature of the existing system, while his historical novel *The Lazarus Project* underlines the historical nativism and systemic oppression that has been built deeply into the American experience, arguably since the nation's inception. In this regard, Hemon's work is a literary counterpart to sociological criticism of the American Dream. In the next section, I will briefly outline sociological inquiry of the Dream and highlight one of its main problems, and that is (unintentional) reduction of the Dream to its material aspect. I will then show how Hemon overcomes the conventional definition of the Dream and envisions "good living" in America beyond its material aspect.

What Is It All for?

Robert C. Hauhart (2016), offering a historical overview of different sociological studies of the American Dream, says that inequality of opportunity has been hailed as the main challenge of this idea. Different sociological studies point to the fact that US citizens start their pursuits from radically different social positions, some of them disproportionally better equipped by economic, cultural, and social capital, while the social system (e.g. education and housing policies) systematically restrains people at their current social position (Hauhart 2016, Hanson and White 2011). These aspects of the Dream have been recognized at least since 1938 and Merton's influential article on social structure and anomie (Merton 1938). Merton recognizes the cultural pressure for "monetary accumulation" and inequality of opportunity but adds another element to the equation: the ideology of egalitarianism. While other cultures might have "differential class symbols of achievement" (Merton 1938, 681) America believes that everyone can and should achieve what is defined as the desirable goal for all. This specific combination leads to anti-social behavior, which is another term for crime:

> It is only when a system of cultural values extols, virtually above all else, certain *common* symbols of success for *the population at large* while its social structure rigorously restricts or completely eliminates access to approved modes of acquiring these symbols *for a considerable part of the same population*, that antisocial behavior ensues on a considerable scale.
>
> *Merton 1938, 680*

On top of anti-social behavior, this specific cultural combination strengthens the radical competitiveness and brings out other social and psychological dysfunctions, such as "exaggerated anxieties, hostilities, neuroses" (Merton 1938, 680). As Merton already partly shows, the inequality of opportunity is not the only challenge to the Dream. Speaking from the contemporary perspective, Hauhart continues to argue that the idea of the American Dream faces an even bigger ideological challenge. The conventional economic conception of the American Dream is ideologically empty and, apart from material success, does not provide any place for "discussions of the need, or means of achieving, mankind's psychic satisfaction" (Hauhart 2016, 270). In other words, the crucial problem of the conception of the (material) American Dream is not (only) that it cannot be attained by many, but that even when it is attained, it does not provide directions for a meaningful life and fulfillment of social, spiritual, cognitive, moral, and other human needs. In other words, the Dream – as it is often conceptualized – reduces humanity to its economic dimension, thus leaving the other dimensions painfully unaddressed and unrealized.

Historically speaking, material success is not the only aspect of different versions of the American Dream (Cullen 2004). The current problem is, says Hauhart, that the economic definition is backed up also by the methodology of (sociological) research: researchers have tended to focus on middle class families while neglecting the rest of society, and while taking surveys, they have often defined the American Dram in monetary terms thus already preconditioning answers and reflections about monetary success (Hauhart 2016, 199–200). In this regard, the material definition of the Dream becomes the "self-fulfilling prophecy" (Hauhart 2016, 252). Too often, sociologists and others fail to consider other aspects of the Dream, as though other dimensions of a good life do not, or cannot, exist in the society. In the conclusion to his book, Hauhart addresses this ideological blind spot by re-posing the rarely asked question: "What is it all for?" In his words, if those who write about the American Dream cannot entertain the question, there is little hope for the future of the concept, especially as Hauhart's own research and other data he refers to shows that "some Americans, whether among the privileged or poor, have simply had enough of the American Dream fantasy" (Hauhart 2016, 270).

Research on the perceptions of the American Dream by the famous poll maker John Zogby seems to confirm the need for an ideological remake of the Dream. Thus, research suggests that a diverse group of Americans, most prominently but not exclusively the younger generation of so-called millennials, are slowly changing the understanding of the Dream toward the spiritual and less materialistic aspirations (D'Antonio 2011; Hanson 2011; Zogby 2011). In Zogby's words, these "spiritual secularist" Americans differ from the "traditional materialist" in terms of what they seek and what they believe it is possible to achieve. They identify with the statement that American Dream is possible to achieve "through spiritual fulfillment rather than material success" (Zogby 2011, 107) and demonstrate "an acceptance of a world with limits and a longing for simpler life" (Zogby 2011, 108), dedicated to family, hobbies or volunteer work. Zogby explains that parts of this new attitude are the adaptation to a re-emergent economic scarcity, but for a majority, and especially for younger, it is a formative stance, meaning that they do not wish to join the "rat race" (Zogby 2011, 108).

How does Hemon's work play into this need to re-imagine the American Dream beyond its material aspect? I will argue that this is Hemon's most important contribution to the idea of the American Dream. Lazarus' story might be a negation of the American Dream, but there are also Pronek, Brik, and other Eastern European immigrant characters that continue to live and find their ways in the society.[6] With time they slowly navigate new surroundings, find jobs, master cultural skills, and move to better neighborhoods. Finally, Hemon offers biographical accounts about himself, living in Chicago, and his family in Canada. Their stories offer a certain insight into an immigrant life in North America, not only from the perspective of the impossible promises of the Dream, but from the perspective of what is possible. And as the title of one of his stories suggests, his immigrant characters seem able to find some sort of "good living" in North America. In this way, Hemon not only deconstructs the conventional Dream but also re-constructs and reinvents the Dream – not in a way to strengthen its conventional ideological staples but to offer a different version of what a good life might be about. A "good living," as he names it in one of his stories, does not require material abundance and prosperity. It includes financial stability but also finding a social network and a community, making a connection with the physical space that surrounds you, and attaining a sense of purpose and satisfaction in your everyday work. For immigrants, this usually means finding ways to reconcile your old life and habits with your new economic, social, and linguistic surroundings. I name Hemon's version of the Dream the "Humble Dream" so as to contrast it with the conventional, materialist vision of the American Dream described in previous sections.

Hemon's Humble Dream, as I call it, or "good living," in the author's words, does not negate the material aspect, which is obvious from stories on immigrant newcomers who struggle with exploitative work, racial and ethnic exclusion, and a myriad of other problems. But, when Hemon's heroes manage to pass the first phase of an immigrant's life on the social bottom and acquire some financial stability, in terms of having decent housing and a steady income, the money chase disappears from their aspiration. I need to pause here in order not to reduce social inequalities and universalize the described material position. I recognize that "decent" housing and "steady" income might mean very different things for different groups of people – in Hemon's prose, that mostly means reaching a middle-class status. I also recognize that the middle class is an unreachable position for a sizable segment of American citizens and that not "worrying about money" is a position of privilege. However, these arguments lead us back to the issue of inequality, and while I recognize its importance, I still want to highlight Hemon's contribution that goes beyond the issue of inequality and concerns different qualities and re-ordering of the narrative structure of the Dream.

Immigrants' "Good Living" in America

The immigrant's version of the American Dream starts with an immigrant's arrival into the promised land. It obscures his or her past in favor of the future, which is reduced to a one-direction highway that confines rich and poor Americans alike to the never-ending pursuit of material success. Contrary to that, Hemon's characters envision different goals and have adopted a different temporal, non-linear logic. In Hemon's Humble Dream, the past matters, and the conventional narrative structure is turned upside down. Past and present are intertwined, as immigrants do not exist without their pre-immigrant past. In Hemon's work, temporal and spatial realities of "before" and "after," the old and new homeland, Sarajevo and Chicago, are constantly intertwined – they exist together, indivisible. Immigrants live both "there" and "here," "now," and "then," while two cultural spaces, Bosnian and American, overlap. This overlapping fundamentally influences their Dreams. Characters do not only remember the past but transpose their past to the present and the future, as their past rituals, values, habits, and aspirations define what they will seek in the new land. By recreating past rituals that served to bring purpose in their past, everyday existence, Hemon and his characters find meaning in their American life.

The best and most detailed examples of the Humble Dream are Hemon's autobiographical memoirs on his and his parents' adaptation to their American life. These also show how different paths can serve to reach the same goal, as he and his parents belong to different generations and spatio-temporal realities that influenced the strategies each used to find purpose in everyday life. In spite of different approaches, both Hemon and his parents are centered at finding a community and domesticating the foreign landscape into a space they can call their home. As Hemon writes in his biographical *Book of My Lives* (2013), he employs walking the streets of Chicago as the best method to do both. By walking, he joins his psychical space to the physical space and attaches personal meaning to the otherwise anonymous landscape. This is a strategy from his past, as he lived in Sarajevo, where rich social life evolves on the streets, parks, playgrounds, cafes (kafanas), walking promenades, and other public premises, as is characteristic of the organization of space in Eastern and Southern Europe. He learned in Sarajevo that by walking, you also connect to people who regularly inhabit the space and become part of the human city network. However, in his walking episodes, Hemon also learns to accept that Chicago is different and that it "was built not for people to come together but for them to be safely apart" (Hemon 2013, chap. 10). He continues to walk but learns how to adapt and do it differently, accepting that his Chicago experience is unavoidably different than the Sarajevan one. Instead of claiming the whole city as his own, he anchors his aspirations in the particular neighborhood:

> Little by little, people in Edgewater began to recognize me; I started greeting them on the street. Over time, I acquired a barber and a butcher and a movie theater and a coffee shop with a steady set of colorful characters—which were, as I'd learned in Sarajevo, the necessary knots in any personal urban network. I discovered that the process of transforming an American city into a space you could call your own required starting in a particular neighborhood. Soon I began to claim Edgewater as mine; I became a local. It was there that I understood what Nelson Algren meant when he wrote that loving Chicago was like loving a woman with a broken nose—I fell in love with the broken noses of Edgewater.
>
> *Hemon 2013, chap. 10*

Hemon's Chicago story is a story of "hard work" and success. The author makes sure to underline that he did not acquire his new connections by chance but with a persistent and continuous effort to find people, connect with them, merge with space, and domesticate the anonymous landscape into "home." Finally, he succeeds:

> [I] realized that my immigrant interior had begun to merge with the American exterior. Large parts of Chicago had entered me and settled there; I fully owned those parts now. I saw Chicago through the eyes of Sarajevo and the two cities now created a complicated internal landscape in which stories could be generated.
>
> *Hemon 2013, chap. 10*

Strategies on how one should acquire meaning in everyday life differ, but a common denominator remains the same. In his columns on his life-long admiration of soccer, which is gathered in an unpretentious and relatively unknown e-book, *The Matters of Life, Death and More* (Hemon 2014), Hemon writes about finding a colorful social network of people to play soccer with. This is another version of the same goal: engaging with people over a shared ritual, claiming the space, and inscribing your own story into the city.

While Hemon's Humble Dream evolves around building a social life in public space, the generation of his parents offers yet another approach. In his most recent book, the autobiographical *My Parents: An Introduction* (2019), Hemon lovingly writes about Mama and Tata, who immigrated to Canada around the same time as he left Bosnia, both in their fifties. With this book, Hemon is again violating the narrative rules of the American Dream, which should start with an immigrant arrival and then continue with the pursuit of the Dream. Contrary to that, *My Parents* is divided into chapters focusing on important topics of his parents life' – space, food, marriage, and music, among others, which are constantly alternating between here and there, before and after. As a consequence, the book has a lot more to do with socialist Yugoslavia than North America, as the Hemons were shaped in, and simultaneously embody, Yugoslav social structure, ideology, values, habits, and beliefs (even though Yugoslavia no longer exists). The practice of settling in is, as in their son's case, crucially connected to their Yugoslav past. They find community among other members of their migrant family, but that is not enough. They need to find meaning in their everyday work, and that offers insight into another specific tactic they bring from their previous life: they diligently work on construction and creation of things and food they could easily buy but prefer to make themselves.

The big endeavor of the Hemons resonates with one feature of the conventional vision of the American Dream: to acquire a homeownership. However, in their version of the Dream, it is not only important to own the space but to transform it and adapt it to their needs. Whatever they make is endowed with meaning and value in the process. Tata, the passionate beekeeper and an engineer by profession, constructs pieces of furniture and house equipment, adds a chimney to the house, places a wood-burning stove in the basement, builds an outdoor seating set, and self-makes hives and frames for beekeeping. Mama keeps up the household, supervises the garden, and preserves the vegetables to be used through the winter. Hemon insightfully observes that his parents were raised in post-war socialist Yugoslavia, which was literally a land under construction, with low purchase power and "few goodies to get" on the market (Hemon 2019, 69), which made their generation experts at DIY production. However, there is even more to their practice than an old habit of how to escape scarcity through ingenuity. Hemon writes about the deeper meaning of their work as giving his parents space for independence and creativity: "Over the years they've lived there, they've undertaken a number of projects that transformed the space into a domain for their self-(re)actualization (Hemon 2019, 73)". And then:

> The domain that my parents have built for themselves is possessed of perfect human sovereignty. In it they do and create things that allow them to be themselves, to fashion who they are; this is where they have agency, a bubble outside of which they are reduced to passivity inflicted by history. Their house, the Barn, and the backyard are the places where they're not refugees. Time they could not regain, but space they could, and so they did.
>
> *Hemon 2019, 79*

Hemon equalizes the value and effect of their manual labor with his intellectual work: "Though I have little interest in the actual work of beekeeping, as I've never cared about doing manual work, I fully endorse its ideological value, its rich field of meaning. I can identify with my father's striving to find and protect a domain in which he can practice agency with dignity and some form of sovereignty. What beekeeping is for him, literature is to me" (Hemon 2019, 62–63).

It is not only about labor as a physical or economic activity but about performing it and understanding it in a specific way, which explains why Hemon repeatedly uses the concept of "agency." I would like to additionally argue that this conception of work is also something that is transferred from their Yugoslav pasts. A history of Yugoslav socialism cultivated the idea of non-alienated labor, which has its roots in Marx's philosophy, but was specifically envisioned, thought of, and practiced. Thinkers and politicians in post-war Yugoslavia entertained an avant-garde idea of overcoming the difference between the manual and intellectual work, and labor and art. They reasoned that all kinds of work, including manual labor, could be endowed with noble meaning if done by the people for the people: organized and practiced by active citizens for the benefits of their own communities.[7] This idea later grew into a political, economic, and governing principle of "self-management," which envisioned active citizens as self-organizers who shaped the economy, municipal government, and cultural organizations, having diverse social and economic effects.[8] Evaluation of the implementation of self-management is a matter of lively debate in Yugoslav studies; and while this is no place to depart into these, we can suppose that the idea of labor as a space for practicing agency, creativity, and solidarity strongly impacted Yugoslavia's past. Consequently, this idea impacted Hemon's parents' experience and, finally, by Hemon's writing, found its way to American literature and the American Dream.

In both his and his parent's version of what I call the Humble Dream, Hemon connects some crucial elements of the American Dream with cultural elements he brings from his previous cultural background. As in the original conception of the Dream, the focus is on agency, self-actualization, diligence, and work, on being active in getting what you want. On the other side, all of this activity and work is not invested in material success but in achievements of domesticating your physical space, creating a place where you can feel at home, and finding and co-creating a community. Hemon is introducing goals and values, which are changing the quality and the structure of the Dream. We could say that Hemon "socializes"[9] the American Dream by importing specific cultural habits and strategies from his past, inseparable from the cultural context of socialist Yugoslavia and its underpinning values.

On the other side, it is not only the American Dream that is changed in this process. Yugoslav socialist ideas – such as active citizenship, self-management, and labor as a space for practicing agency – were imagined as a collective practice to build a better society, both a personal and political endeavor. Practiced in the American context, they are placed in the sphere of privacy and individual attempts at finding a meaning, as, to repeat Hemon's words, his parents' work creates "a bubble outside of which they are reduced to passivity inflicted by history" (Hemon 2019, 79). The Humble Dream is not trying to change the world but is inspecting the pockets of everyday freedom, where people can exercise agency, creativity, and connection.

Although Hemon's Humble Dream does not include a strategy to revolutionize the world, it implies a different vision of American society. The conventional version of the Dream most often discussed is built on the vertical vision of society that is consonant with late capitalism; this is due, in part as well, to its individualistic character arising from the historical prominence of individualism in American life. If the goal of the Dream is an individual success, and there are not enough resources for all to prosper, then it is a logical consequence that some, or a lot of the members of American society, must be left behind. Or, as Merton realized in 1938: "The pressure of such an order is upon outdoing one's competitors" (Merton 1938, 681). We can suppose that solidarity and collective prosperity, as a topic in such an order remain in the background (more on individualistic character of the Dream in Hochschild 1995, 35–37). The underlying quality of the Humble Dream is a horizontal vision of society: everybody is invited to participate. Envisioned heroes are not super-people but ordinary citizens who can dream together and have much better chances of acquiring their respective Humble Dreams. It is a non-competitive, inclusive vision of the Dream in which society does not need to leave anyone behind in order to achieve success. We can suppose that it is quite the contrary, the more dreamers there are, better is the Dream, as there are more people to form networks, share everyday life with, and enjoy the good life.

Can this collective Humble Dream pose an answer to the ideological emptiness of the current version of the conventional American Dream, addressed by Hauhart (2016) and pointed at by Zogby's research? The problem could be that Hemon's immigrants use the past as a source for their strategies to find meaning in everyday life. Where will native-born American find the inspiration to reinvigorate the Dream? I do not think this is a crucial problem, as Hemon shows that there is no universal strategy to employ. What remains of importance is a changed structure of the Dream so that is about creating connections with people and space. And this could be approached in different ways, finding inspiration in migrant or non-migrant stories and histories. While this could sound as diminishing the importance of the American Dream, it is also liberating, as it opens the door to look everywhere, socialist Yugoslavia and beyond, to finally address that question: What is it all for?

Notes

1 The author acknowledges the financial support from the Slovenian Research Agency research programme Historical Interpretations of the 20th Century (P6-0347).
2 Following this line of argumentation, Honig names four types of idealized immigrants, confirming different versions of American society. Aa already mentioned, economic immigrant confirms the capitalist version of the society. "The communitarian immigrant" reconciles the promise of communal living in the economic context that disables it by insisting on the mobile labor force. "Patriarchal immigrant" rejuvenates traditional family values and conceptions of traditional femininity and masculinity; while "liberal consenting immigrant" willingly and enthusiastically chooses the US as its homeland, which "addresses the need of a disaffected citizenry to experience its regime as choiceworthy" (Honig 2001, 74–75).
3 After the end of the novel, Hemon lists several historical works, he has built his narrative on. *The Lazarus Project* also includes historical photographs of Lazarus, attained from the Chicago Historical Society and photographs taken by Hemon's friend Velimor Božović, with whom he made a trip around

Eastern Europe. More on Hemon's approach to autobiographical writing and the role of photographs which are contributing to the novel's fusion between factual and fictional in Ward 2011.

4 The Lazarus Project, published in 2008, ghostly predicts another debate on the continuity or discontinuity of police violence against national and racial minorities, which has (re)captured the American attention in last years; the debate on the police violence toward the unarmed non-whites. Hemon's work, which inspects the historical story of a policeman killing an unarmed immigrant in a "self-defense" stands as the argument in favor of continuity of police violence. For a better understanding of Hemon's story, we should also remember that Eastern Europeans and Jews were not considered as "white" and hence represented a racial Other at the beginning of the 20th century.

5 Behdad argues that both hospitality and xenophobia toward immigrants are crucial ideas for the establishment of American national character; this is why he names American relations toward immigrants "ambivalent hospitality" (Behdad 2005).

6 They are, admittedly, in a different position than Lazarus, considering their racial status; while old-stock immigrants thought of southern and Eastern Europeans as a different and undesirable race as late as 1920s (Hochschild 1995, 243), they are today presented as "white," and as such better positioned, as they do not represent a racial other, but "only" a cultural other.

7 Andrea Matošević offers valuable insight into the concept of labor that goes beyond mere productivity and becomes a practice of creativity and solidarity. He inspects these ideas through the Yugoslav phenomena of shock labor and Youth Work Actions. The majority of his writing is in Croatian, however, some insight is available in English (Matošević, 2018). Yugoslav idea of overcoming the difference between intellectual and manual labor has roots in Yugoslav People's Liberation Struggle during World War Two, which had a strong cultural and artistic character; cultural activity thus merged with armed battle and other types of labor, all becoming equal tools in aspiring for social revolution and liberation from fascism (Kirn 2020).

8 It is important not to confuse the Yugoslav idea of self-management with a socialist planned economy, which was practiced in the Soviet Union and Eastern bloc allies. Yugoslavia separated from the Eastern bloc in 1948 and since then aimed at creating its own version of socialism, self-management policies included. More on self-management in (Kirn 2019; Musić 2011; Suvin 2016; Unkovski-Korica 2016).

9 This term is a collegial nod to Stijn Vervaet, who claims that Hemon and Dubravka Ugrešić, two post-Yugoslav authors, are "worlding" post-Yugoslav literature by including the literary and cultural legacy of the former Yugoslavia in the imaginary space of world literature. In the process, both post-Yugoslav literature and world literature are changed: the local literature enters the global space, while world literature is de-centralized from its Western-oriented perceptions (Vervaet 2016).

References

Beganović, Davor. 2009. *Poetika melankolije: na tragovima suvremene bosansko-hercegovačke književnosti.* Sarajevo: Rabic.

Behdad, Ali. 2005. *A Forgetful Nation: On Immigration and Cultural Identity in the United States.* Duke University Press. Kindle.

Bošković, Aleksandar. 2008. "Identitet, egzil i rod u prozi Aleksandra Hemona." In *Teorije i politike roda: rodni identiteti u književnostima jugoistočne Evrope,* edited by Tatjana Rosić, 253–270. Beograd: Institut za književnost i umetnost.

Cullen, Jim. 2004. *The American Dream: A Short History of an Idea That Shaped a Nation.* New York: Oxford University Press.

D'Antonio, William. 2011. "Religion and the American Dream." In *The American Dream in the 21st Century,* edited by Sandra L. Hanson and John Kenneth White, 117–140. Philadelphia, PA: Temple University Press.

Denvir, Daniel. 2020. *All-American Nativism: How the Bipartisan War on Immigrants Explains Politics as We Know It.* London; New York: Verso Books.

Hanson, Sandra L. 2011. "Whose Dream? Gender and the American Dream." In *The American Dream in the 21st Century,* edited by Sandra L. Hanson and John Kenneth White, 77–103. Philadelphia, PA: Temple University Press.

Hanson, Sandra L., and John Kenneth White, eds. 2011. *The American Dream in the 21st Century.* Philadelphia, PA: Temple University Press.

Hauhart, Robert C. 2016. *Seeking the American Dream: A Sociological Inquiry*. New York: Palgrave Macmillan.

Hemon, Aleksandar. 2001. *The Question of Bruno*. London: Picador.

———. 2008a. *The Lazarus Project*. New York: Riverhead Books.

———. 2008b. "Aleksandar Hemon: Interview." By Deborah Baker. Bomb Magazine. https://bombmagazine.org/articles/aleksandar-hemon-1/

———. 2009. *Love and Obstacles*. New York: Riverhead Books. Epub.

———. 2013. *The Book of My Lives*. New York: Farraf, Straus and Giroux. Epub.

———. 2014. *The Matters of Life, Death, and More: Writing on Soccer*. New York: Farrar, Straus and Giroux. Kindle.

———. 2019. *My Parents*. New York: Farrar, Straus and Giroux.

Hochschild, Jennifer L. 1995. *Facing Up to the American Dream: Race, Class, and the Soul of the Nation*. Princeton, NJ: Princeton University Press.

Honig, Bonnie. 2001. *Democracy and the Foreigner*. Princeton, NJ and Oxford: Princeton University Press.

Hutcheon, Linda. 2004. *A Poetics of Postmodernism: History, Theory, Fiction*. New York and London: Taylor&Francis e-Library.

Kirn, Gal. 2019. *Partisan Ruptures: Self-Management, Market Reform and the Spectre of Socialist Yugoslavia*. London: Pluto Press.

———. 2020. *The Partisan Counter-Archive*. Berlin; Boston, MA: De Gruyter.

Luca, Ioana. 2020. "The Transnational Matrix of Post-Communist Spaces." In *Eastern Europe Unmapped: Beyond Borders and Peripheries*, edited by Irene Kacandes and Yuliya Komska, 151–171. New York: Berghahn Books.

Matošević, Andrea. 2018. "Mediators in the Making of the Socialist Man's New Nature during Youth Labour Actions in Yugoslavia. Utopia, Dialectics and Time." *Südost-Forschungen. Internationale Zeitschrift Für Geschichte, Kultur und Landeskunde Südosteuropas* 76 (1): 64–81.

Matthes, Frauke, and David Williams. 2013. "Displacement, Self-(Re)Construction, and Writing the Bosnian War: Aleksandar Hemon and Saša Stanišić." *Comparative Critical Studies* 10 (1): 27–45.

Merton, Robert K. 1938. "Social Structure and Anomie." *American Sociological Review* 3 (5): 672–682.

Miočević, Ljubica. 2013. "'What's Difference?': On Language and Identity in the Writings of Aleksandar Hemon." In *Languages of Exile. Migration and Multilingualism in Twentieth-Century Literature*, edited by Axel Englund and Anders Olsson, 55–79. Oxford: Peter Lang.

Music, Goran. 2011. "Workers' Self-Management as State Paradigm." In *Ours to Master and to Own: Worker's Control from the Commune to the Present*, edited by Immannuel Ness and Dario Azzellini, 172–190. Chicago: Haymarket Books.

Raudvere, Catharina. 2017. "Experience and Expression: Aleksandar Hemon, Fiction, and (Dis)Placement." In *Contested Memories and the Demands of the Past: History Cultures in the Modern Muslim World*, 179–194. Islam and Nationalism. London: Palgrave MacMillan.

Suvin, Darko. 2016. *Splendour, Misery, and Possibilities: An X-Ray of Socialist Yugoslavia*. Leiden; Boston, MA: Brill.

Unkovski-Korica, Vladimir. 2016. *The Economic Struggle for Power in Tito's Yugoslavia: From World War Two to Non-Alignment*. London; New York: I.B. Tauris.

Vervaet, Stijn. 2016. "Ugresic, Hemon and the Paradoxes of Literary Cosmopolitanis: Or How to 'World' (Post-) Yugoslav Literature in the Age of Globalization." In *Komparativna književnost: teorija, tumačenja, perspektive. Encompassing Comparative Literature: Theory, Interpretation, Perspectives*, edited by Adrijana Marčetić, Zorica Bečanović-Nikolić and Vesna Elez, 161–169. Beograd: Filološki fakultet Univerziteta u Beogradu.

———. 2017. "Cosmopolitan Counter-Narratives of Dispossession: Migration, Memory, and Metanarration in the Work of Aleksandar Hemon." In *Claiming the Dispossession*, 224–246. Leiden; Boston, MA: Brill.

Ward, Wendy. 2011. "Does Autobiography Matter?: Fictions of the Self in Aleksandar Hemon's the Lazarus Project." *Brno Studies in English* 37 (2): 185–199.

Zogby, John. 2011. "Want Meets Necessity in the New American Dream." In *The American Dream in the 21st Century*, edited by Sandra L. Hanson and John Kenneth White, 105–116. Philadelphia, PA: Temple University Press.

PART VI

Sustainability and the American Dream

18

A DREAM DEFERRED

Professional projects as racial projects in US medicine

LaTonya J. Trotter

Introduction

There is more than one way to tell the story of the American Dream. The most popular version celebrates those who have reached the highest levels of wealth, fame, and power. But in the quiet of bedrooms and kitchens, many a parent has prescribed an alternate path to their children: earn a credential and enter a profession. This version may not lead to the top of the social hierarchy, but it does narrate a road to the comfortable middle. The medical profession has come to exemplify this version of the American Dream: reaching it may not be easy, but it is achievable and the rewards are certain.

The foundation of this certainty is the promise of a meritocracy. Medicine would appear to be the living embodiment of a "by one's own bootstraps" ideology in that the markers of success are clearly identified and individually attained. Historically, medicine was one of the first US occupations where the returns to training and merit mattered more than class and capital. Today, a reliance on quantitative criteria like standardized test scores and a uniform residency matching process make the strength of this promise even more pronounced. However, when we shift our focus from the achievements of individuals and look more closely at the group, we see that the historical work of raising the profession's collective status included more than ideologies of merit; they deployed those of race and gender.

This essay will explore the American Dream as a racial project through a historically grounded investigation of US medicine. It is well known that medicine upheld exclusionary barriers to Black people and white women until the latter third of the 20th century. What is less widely considered is how the status achieved by the profession *required* those barriers. For professional medicine, rescuing the medical arts from the province of "every old woman, savage Indian, or Guinea Negro,"[1] required transforming the physician into an icon of elite white masculinity. In this essay, I suggest that these exclusionary practices were not simply artifacts of a less progressive time. Rather, I argue that an investment in gendered forms of whiteness was at the core of medicine's battle for legitimacy, status, and economic rewards.[2]

DOI: 10.4324/9781003326243-24

Professionalization as a Racial Project

By the middle of the 20th century, to become a professional was synonymous with "having made it." While this accomplishment is often viewed as an individual achievement, the literature on the professions reveals it equally as a group level one (Abbott 1988; Freidson 1970; Larson 1979). Professionalization describes the set of processes through which an occupation accrues the rewards associated with "professional" rather than other forms of labor. In addition to generally receiving higher wages and inhabiting a higher social status, professionals are accorded the right to autonomously determine the content and scope of their work, as well as the right to regulate and police their own members. The strategies that occupations employ to secure these prerequisites were first conceptualized as "professional projects" by Magali Larson (Larson 1979). Her conceptual framework was in contrast to prevailing scholarship of the time, which asserted that "true" professions were defined by intrinsic characteristics and their inherent value to society. As she and others shifted the field's focus to conflict, later scholars were able to consider the ways in which "becoming a profession" was a political, historically contingent achievement.

While there are several occupations that we recognize as professions, American medicine remains the iconic case of a successful professional project.[3] It is exemplary, in part, because of the distance it has traveled. At the beginning of the 20th century, being a physician was a fairly humble way to make a living. By the 1950s, it had become synonymous with high status and income. The success with which physicians transformed their collective fortunes was so striking that the case has become a veritable playbook for aspiring professions. But the case is also a useful lens through which to consider what is often overlooked in scholarly evaluations of professionalization: racism.

In most of the scholarly literature, the strategies used to gain professional legitimacy are implicitly understood as race neutral. This is not to say that racism's impact has been ignored. It is fairly commonplace for professional actors to accept responsibility for past racist acts. For example, the American Medical Association (AMA) has openly acknowledged that predominately white medical schools barred prospective Black students from professional training for the greater part of the 20th century and that the AMA itself refused membership to Black physicians until the 1960s, which effectively blocked their path to licensure in most states (Baker et al. 2008, 2009; Haynes 2005). While acknowledging past sins is a laudable act, the function of racism in these accounts remains problematic. It appears either as the biased acts of individuals or as simply a part of the social background that medicine inhabited. In either telling, racism is positioned outside the strategic aims of the profession. However, scholars who study how racism structures US society have given us good reason to question such colorblind theorizing. Racism is not the product of individual prejudice; it is the routine accomplishment of a racialized social structure (Bell 1992; Bonilla-Silva 2013; Mills 1997; Omi and Winant 1994). The work that this structure effects is to legitimatize anti-black oppression while obscuring the privilege of whiteness. Therefore, as exhorted by Eduardo Bonilla-Silva, the task of inequality scholars is not simply to identify the vestiges of racist ideology but to uncover the wide range of "mechanisms responsible for the reproduction of racial privilege in a society" (Bonilla-Silva 2013, 9).

If professionalization is understood as the successful use of political strategies to legitimate unequal rewards, we should consider the ways in which professional projects are racial projects. The concept of racial projects is part of Omi and Winant's larger framework of racial formation. Racial formation describes the historically contingent processes through which racial categories—and the social meaning accorded them—are "created, inhabited, transformed, and destroyed" (Omi and Winant 1994, 55). At the core of racial formation theory is the assertion that racial categories are not mere proxies for class, nation, or ethnic-cultural groups but rather that race is a "*fundamental* axis of social organization in the US" that is actively reproduced within its institutions (Omi and Winant 1994, 13). Racial projects serve as the building blocks of racial formation by tying racial categories to the social organization of symbolic and material resources (Omi and Winant 1994, 56). Racial projects legitimize the exclusion of racialized groups from society's resources while obscuring the dominant group's hoarding of them.

Racial projects are also intrinsically gendered. One of the critiques of Omi and Winant's original articulation of racial formation is that it treats race and gender as separate axes of inequality. However, Black feminist scholars have theoretically and empirically demonstrated that racial categories are inherently gendered (Crenshaw 1989; Davis 1983; The Combahee River Collective 1983). A failure to employ an intersectional perspective not only risks overlooking the experiences of particular people but actively obscures how a racialized social order is reproduced. Feminist scholars have more generally critiqued the assumed gender neutrality of theories about work, workers, and the workplace. These scholars have demonstrated that the resources available to even craft professional projects should be understood as gendered, as socially recognized men and women have differential access to material resources, audiences for their claims, and legitimating logics (Bourgeault 2006; Witz 1990, 1992). More broadly, scholars have argued that gender is, itself, constitutive of notions of the ideal worker (Moen and Roehling 2005) and is interwoven throughout workplace logics and routines in ways that actively produce gendered workers (Acker 1990; Pierce 1996; Trotter 2017).

The broader literature on racial inequality has similarly questioned race-neutral theorizing about the labor market. For Black workers, there are racialized hurdles to entering higher paid forms of work, as well as hurdles to career advancement within them (Collins 1989; Maume 1999; Rivera 2012; Royster 2003). This essay is particularly indebted to work by Victor Ray, Adia Harvey Wingfield, and Melissa Wooten, who collectively theorize and empirically show how organizational level processes actively produce racialized workers and perpetuate racial inequality (Wooten and Couloute 2017; Ray 2019; Wingfield 2010; 2019; Wooten 2006).

In this essay, I build on these insights to reevaluate the race-neutral assumptions of professionalization. I invoke racial formation to demonstrate that professional projects are racial projects and to suggest that we should consider professionalization as one of the labor market mechanisms through which racial privilege is built and maintained. Specifically, I show how medicine's bid for cultural authority was grounded in embodying a hegemonic, elite white masculinity. I end the essay by considering how this embodiment of professional status remains a contemporary hurdle for racial equality, both in professional medicine and within the larger world of work it inhabits.

In the Absence of Medical Authority

At the dawn of the 20th century, medicine was an economically uncertain, hard scrabble way to make a living.[4] The key problem for physicians was that potential patients were unwilling to accord them any special ownership over curative practices. In part, this was due to the absence of a codified regime of education and licensing. Although the colonies had medical schools as early as the 1760s, without a system of accreditation, many were little more than diploma mills. Moreover, attending one would not be a consistently applied legal requirement for practice until the 20th century. As a consequence, most medical training happened through a non-standard program of self-study, individually-secured apprenticeships, and, for some, a few lectures at a for-profit medical school. While there were periodic efforts to regulate the education and practice of physicians throughout the 1800s, until the 20th century, there were few restrictions on who could hang out a shingle and profess their skill at doctoring.

There were also open questions about what physicians who *had* secured training knew. From the vantage point of the present, we know that most of the interventionist medicine prior to the 20th century was ineffective at best; harmful at worst. But even without the benefit of hindsight, prospective patients could directly observe that access to a physician did not necessarily produce better outcomes. To muddy the waters further, physicians themselves waged public, internecine wars between "schools" of medical thought. When even physicians questioned one another's skill, it was difficult for the public to put much trust in the occupation as a whole.

With little curative authority invested in the occupation itself, physicians cultivated sources of authority from outside of it. Leveraging class resources was the most certain path to curative authority, but it was a fairly narrow one. By the mid-1700s, there was a small group of elite physicians in port cities such as New York, Philadelphia, and Baltimore. However, their elite status was only tenuously related to their chosen profession. Most had pre-existing access to land or capital, which they used to obtain medical training in continental Europe. Upon their return, they were able to use this training to bolster their status claims. Few aspiring physicians, however, had the resources to take this route. Moreover, given the collective status of practicing physicians, most men with class resources would not have chosen such a humble aspiration.

And a humble aspiration it was assumed to be. The majority of physicians had to live on the small fees and in-kind payments of laboring families, not only suffering low incomes but the indignity—if they chose to feel it—of attending to those with a low social status.[5] The conditions of the work itself marked physicians as genteel members of the servant class. At a time when most health care happened at home, physicians "came when called." Those with a high status, urban clientele felt their servitude less keenly, but the power in the physician-patient relationship was squarely in the hands of the patient. There were, however, resources other than class that individuals used to establish a legitimate if more tenuous claim to healer status. These resources opened the door for white women as well as working class white men to assert their membership in the profession.

Medical Work as Domestic Practice

Well into the 20th century, "nursing the sick" was a woman's duty to family and community (Reverby 1987). While a good deal of that duty would today be understood as nursing work, much of it fell into the category of curative medicine. In the rural landscapes where most people lived, there was a vibrant tradition of domestic or lay medicine. There were male practitioners of lay medicine, but its most common practitioners were women (Spruill 1998; Tannenbaum 2019). To be sure, most women employed their curative knowledge outside of the paid labor market. However, more than a few white women parlayed these skills into paying work. In the colonial era, it was common to see newspaper advertisements of white women selling their skills in the treatment of specific conditions like "ringworm, scald heads, piles, [and] worms" (Blanton 1931, as found in Starr 1984, 39). In some parts of what became the US, medical work was done exclusively by women until the early 19th century (Kett 1968).

The association of medical work with domestic work was not based solely on assumptions of feminine sensibilities; it was an acknowledgment of the expertise women actively cultivated through the acquisition of oral tradition, experience, and the consumption of written medical advice.[6] Moreover, the title "doctoress" or "doctor woman" had a specific meaning. Even without the distinctions of degrees, paying patients distinguished between the women who nursed the sick, those who practiced midwifery, and those that performed medical work (Tannenbaum 2019). The inaccessibility of trained male physicians explains much of this reliance on women for medical care. However, it is notable that during the colonial era, white women without formal training were more likely to do this work than untutored white men. This gender difference was grounded in the prevailing belief that women had a natural affinity for—and practiced skill in—preventive medicine and sick care (Spruill 1998, 267–9).

As the colonies became a country and rural outposts became towns and cities, male physicians became more numerous and available for hire. As a result, the demand for women who doctored began to wane (Tannenbaum 2019). However, womanhood endured as a source of curative authority longer than many men would have liked. The unregulated nature of medical education and practice made it possible for women to maintain a foothold in medicine until the 20th century. It was not until the late 18th century that US states began their first experiments with licensing regimes for medical practice. Even then, the criteria were generally lax enough that few white applicants were kept out of the profession. In many cases, a diploma from a medical school was the primary criterium. But medical education, too, was unregulated. If one had the ability to pay the matriculation fee, one could find a school that would accept it. This was almost as true for white women as it was for white men.

Throughout the 19th century, some medical schools accepted white female students without much fanfare. Most such schools fell into the "irregular" category—a term that identified their dedication to botanical or sectarian forms of medicine. However, even some "regular" allopathic schools opened their doors to white women (Brown 1979; Haynes 2005; Starr 1984). While the majority of such schools only permitted a few women to sit in on carefully selected lectures, in 1893, there were 18 allopathic medical schools where women made up between 10 to 31% of regularly enrolled students (Walsh 1979, 193). There were also several women-only medical schools that successfully graduated female physicians (Walsh 1979).

To be clear, there were few opportunities for women to economically support themselves as educated physicians. The necessary time and fees for medical school were difficult to find for the working-class women who had once functioned as lay doctresses, while those with the class resources to acquire medical training found that working for wages clashed with the prescription of domestic seclusion for "respectable" women. Still, white women were more than token members of the profession. In 1900, women may have only accounted for 5.6% of all practicing physicians, but in bustling port cities like Boston, that percentage rose to as high as 18% (Walsh 1979, 186).

As long as the doors to medical schools were open to white women, they continued to enter the profession. While the rising influence of the women's movement may have inspired individual women to do so, most of the publicly circulated arguments for training female physicians did not represent new or radical claims but were grounded in older, conservative ones: to protect the modesty of female patients and as an expression of the traditional tie between womanhood, domestic work, and curative authority (Blake 1965; Walsh 1979). White female physicians were not fully welcomed by their male colleagues, but this displeasure was ameliorated by state legislatures that refused to grant medical men the power to exclude them and by the patients who continued to seek their services.

Alternative Sources of Curative Authority for White Men

White men did not have a gendered claim to medical expertise, but they had other sources of legitimacy. Throughout the 19th century, claims to Indigenous knowledge were leveraged by rural and non-elite white men as a source of curative knowledge.[7] Just as white settlers learned from Indigenous agricultural practices, so too did they benefit from Indigenous knowledge of bodily treatments. Manuscripts and letters authored by European settlers from 1600 to 1700s frequently referenced the cures that "Indian doctors" effected (Starr 1984, 48–49; Vogel 1970, 36–110). To be sure, most Indigenous healers did not receive payment for or otherwise "make a living" from this healing work. Commodifying medicinal knowledge was not a normative practice in Indigenous communities. Nor did Indigenous healers actively compete with white physicians; except in moments of desperation, European settlers were generally unwilling to seek such expertise (Vogel 1970, 123). But white settlers *were* willing to engage in the cultural work—and cultural theft—necessary to symbolically and materially relocate Indigenous medicinal practices to the toolkit of white men.

Many a white herbalist, irregular physician, and patent medicine salesman either claimed Indigenous heritage or attested they had learned their curative secrets "from an Indian medicine man."[8] Some were outright charlatans who knowingly purveyed false cures, such as the fictional rituals and concocted elixirs popularized by the traveling "Indian Medicine Shows" of the 1800s (Vogel 1970, 141). Others invoked an indigenous tie to add credibility to less illusory skills, such as that of "bone-setting" fractures or the application of herbal lore. Regardless of their intentions or efficacy, the imprimatur of "Indian medicine" was an alternative resource for white men without the benefits of class to legitimize their medical work.

For others, the specific appeal to Indigenous knowledge was transformed into a more general appeal to "natural knowledge." In some cases, this transformation was a wholesale whitewashing of Indigenous practices. For example, the use of sweat lodges by some Indigenous peoples is believed to be one source of inspiration of the liberal therapeutic use of steam by some irregular white physicians (Vogel 1970, 132). But for others, the existence of Indigenous curative knowledge was treated less as a well of expertise than as proof that "anyone" could divine curative knowledge through careful attention to nature (Vogel 1970, 133). This line of thought developed alongside the populism of the Jacksonian era and became the basis of one of the most popular medical sects of the period: Thomsonian medicine. Its founder, Samuel Thomson, a farmer who was rumored to be illiterate, believed that every man had a God-given right to be his own physician (Berman 1951). However, in selling a patented botanical medicine system and then training people in it, what he actually developed was a way for any white person, man or woman, to claim legitimacy as a medical provider. The model of "patenting natural cures" was one that many a medical sect employed, albeit with much less success than the Thomsonians.

A Segregated Place for Black Physicians

For Black providers, neither womanhood nor lay medicinal practices served as sources of legitimacy in the physician labor market. The ideal of benevolent womanhood and the logic of separate spheres that grounded it were explicitly reserved for white women (Davis 1983). During and after slavery, Black women's work was too valuable to the maintenance of racial capitalism to leave them to labor—materially or imaginatively—in domestic seclusion. And although Black communities, too, had a living tradition of lay "root doctors," neither African-ness nor Blackness represented a source of curative legitimacy for evaluating white audiences in the same way as Indigenousness.[9]

Black physicians may not have been seen as wielding a unique source of curative authority, but after Emancipation, the hardening and propagation of a segregated health care system did legitimate a limited but stable production of Black physicians (Byrd and Clayton 2015, 355). The provision of rudimentary medical care for Black people was considered a necessary evil in order to keep infectious diseases from spreading to white communities. However, white physicians could not always be relied upon to do so. In the antebellum south, white physicians did a brisk business doing the bidding of plantation owners in treating the enslaved. But in the north and in the post-Civil War south, white physicians who treated Black patients risked being considered "the lowest of the low."[10] As simply "being a doctor" provided no particular social cachet, there was a direct relationship between the status of one's patients and the status of the treating physician. Therefore, the limited production of Black physicians was seen as an important social good in which white religious groups, philanthropic organizations, and the federal government were willing to invest.

This investment, however, would take the form of building separate Black educational institutions rather than integrating white ones. Between 1870 and 1907, at least 14 medical schools or departments of medicine were established to educate Black physicians (Harley 2006, 1425).[11] A few white medical schools in the north could also be said to have trained Black physicians, but this should not be understood as a sign of racial integration. Most of this institutional magnanimity consisted of allowing one or two Black students to attend lectures. Few Black students were treated equally as enrolled students, and even fewer were allowed to graduate (Byrd and Clayton 2015, 387–88). Accordingly, most Black physicians of the time were educated in segregated schools with unequal resources.

Those who were able to finish their training faced additional hurdles to practice. Most were denied hospital privileges and refused membership into local professional organizations—which was increasingly becoming necessary to practice as a part of the nascent licensing movement. As a consequence, many Black physicians "cross-trained" in another profession—such as pharmacy or dentistry—in order to make a living (Byrd and Clayton 2015, 384, 404). Yet, in ways not always appreciated by contemporary observers, the inability of white physicians to categorically exclude Black people from their ranks through enforced educational and licensing regimes meant that Black men and women could and did claim a portion of the medical labor market, even though that portion was segregated and unequal.

As American medicine moved into the 20th century, few would call it diverse. However, it was demonstrably more diverse—by race, class, and gender—than it would be just a few decades later. When authority was not vested in the profession and had to be "won" by individuals, there existed a more flexible set of resources to legitimate one's practice. The accessibility of these resources opened medicine to a much wider demographic than prevailing narratives might predict. To be sure, elite white men held the reins of power within society at large; however, this power gave them *neither an exclusive nor superior claim* to curative authority. Encountering and engaging the services of a white doctress or a white male irregular was a possibility that Americans accepted throughout the 19th century. Black physicians were a small proportion of the medical workforce, but their presence was not an anomaly. They often became pillars of service and entrepreneurship in Black communities. In some quarters, they treated white as well as Black patients (Morais 1967).

This state of affairs would change along with the emergence of a distinctly professional authority. Many students of the professions are familiar with the political strategies that medicine used to establish this authority. However, it is equally important to account for how medicine came to be seen as the rightful vessel for such power. In order to be given the mantle of authority, medicine first had to be seen as deserving of it. Materially, it did so through reforming and regulating medical education and licensing. But this material reform had a symbolic counterpart. In order to be seen as a class apart, physicians had to *embody* legitimate authority. This symbolic transformation would require a fairly radical demographic shift.

Constructing an Elite, White, Medical Man

In some ways, the move to homogenize the profession along racial, class, and gender lines was a reflection of what medicine had always wanted. Throughout the 19th century, elite white practitioners chafed at having to share the title of "doctor" with those they did not feel deserved it. This disapprobation usually took the form of standing up against "quackery." Their stated concern was patient safety, but physicians were not above resorting to racialized and gendered language to define the boundaries of unsafe medicine. We can see this most clearly in the documented conversations of professional advocates after a majority of states repealed laws that licensed physicians in the 1830s. As medical societies debated what to do, they centered on the need to distinguish themselves from a wide variety of "quacks."

In the published proceedings of the 1844, 1845, and 1846 meetings of the Medical Society of New York, we can access physician responses from around the country to the changed legal environment. While many physicians expressed ambivalence about whether licensing laws harmed the profession or not, some had strong opinions. Dr. Logan, a physician from South Carolina, shared a pointed response, proclaiming that the repeal of laws in his state "allowed every old woman, savage Indian, or Guinea Negro, that chose to start up and call themselves doctors, surgeons, or apothecaries, 'to rise, kill, and slay,'" (Appendix IV. Report of a Committee on the Subject of Medical Legislation, to the Monroe County Medical Society, Rochester, November 9, 1842 1846). For Dr. Logan, quackery was embodied by a clear set of social characteristics. In this, he was not alone. Pairing accusations of quackery with language disparaging women and racialized people was an often used strategy in public debates (Haynes 2005). Sometimes the rhetorical arrow went the other way. Rather than denigrating Black and white female providers directly, physicians would use the appellation of quackery to refuse allowing them membership in local and state medical societies. Neither race nor gender was the official cause of their exclusion, but rather their alleged support of quackery (Baker et al. 2009; Haynes 2005).

This is not to say that medicine's anxiety only existed in racialized and gendered terms. It was widely known that neither white doctresses nor providers of color existed in large enough numbers to be a material threat to white male physicians. However, such language was used not just to disparage these groups but to delegitimize the irregular, white male practitioners who were, in fact, a considerable economic threat. An 1845 address made by the president of the Herkimer County Medical Society that was included as part of the New York medical society's official proceedings used such an approach. At one point, the president enumerated all manner of quacks, starting with "all grades from *her* [emphasis in the original] who scrupulously adheres to 'yarb and root' teas and him who deals in vapor baths, lobelia and cayenne pepper glisters, and who most religiously eschews the use of all minerals whatever, through a long list of cancer doctors, Indian doctors, German doctors, Hydropathists, to him who practices after the algebraic principle ..." (Green 1846, 97–98). This list ended with a rousing condemnation of all modes of quackery for their lack of basis in science. But there were clearly certain modalities whose derogation seemed to be defined by *who* they were as much as what they did. Their inclusion in such lists served to stigmatize the entire group.

Appeals to class were a related part of this strategy. In the same 1845 address, the society's president noted that medicine had become a haven for "wayward youth too idle to labor and many times after having been dismissed from the shop of the mechanic, or many of them in succession, as too intractable to learn," (Green 1846, 99). More tellingly, he paraphrased an unnamed French writer to which he attributed the following statement: "the legal profession is the only aristocracy of this country." After comparing the professions of law and medicine, his point was plainly stated: medicine was just as deserving a member of the "American aristocracy" as the legal profession (Green 1846, 99). That they were not was a direct result of medicine's infiltration by those who were collectively unfit to be members of an emerging group of occupational elites.

White male physicians had a great deal of status anxiety about their profession. This anxiety manifested as a desire to uproot quackery from their midst. But their rhetorical strategies belied a set of symbolic enemies who seemed to be just as consequential as their material competitors: white women, Black people, and working-class white men. However, as much as medicine wanted to excise these undesirable groups, the profession had little power to do so. This state of affairs would change, fairly dramatically, with the words and influence of Abraham Flexner.

New Institutions for the Physician to Come

In 1909, Abraham Flexner, former teacher and critic of the American educational system, was commissioned by the Carnegie Foundation to undertake an in-person survey of every medical school in the US and Canada. The resulting 1910 report is famous for solidifying the educational and licensing reforms that would establish physician control over medical work. His reforms would roil the medical world—but not because they were particularly controversial. In substance, the profession agreed with these reforms. Primarily because they had already thought of them (Brown 1979, 135–52). For decades, medical journals had printed calls for similar measures. Four years before Flexner's work, the AMA's own Committee of Medical Education had completed a similar survey that had concluded with almost identical recommendations (Brown 1979, 135, 140). Not only were medical reformers supportive of these changes, but so were rank-and-file providers. Practicing physicians only needed the realities of their own economic precarity to understand that if the profession could not control the number of physicians being created, they would never be able to set the price for their labor. And if they could not define what constituted medical expertise, they would forever be in competition with "hordes upon hordes of quacks."[12] The power to do so, however, had largely eluded them.

Before Flexner, medical reformers had the most success with licensing laws. They were able to stop and reverse the 1830s movement to repeal medical licensing legislation. By the 1880s, more states than not had reinstated some form of licensing. Still, most state boards relied heavily on the medical diploma as the primary criterium for a license to practice. As a consequence, they often made little distinction between an applicant with a rigorous, state of the art education abroad and one who paid the requisite fee of a thinly veiled diploma mill. An 1883 editorial in the *Philadelphia Medical Times* critiqued the impact of existing laws by noting that "instead of elevating the profession above irregulars and charlatans, [such laws have] degraded the regular practitioner to the level of any one who can register under the act, however unworthy he may be to be in the ranks of the medical profession" (*Philadelphia Medical Times* 1883).[13]

Physician education would have to be substantially reformed before licensing regimes would substantially change medical practice. However, there were hurdles to doing so, both within and without the profession. Throughout the 19th century, US medical education was primarily a for-profit endeavor that existed outside the higher education system. When Flexner issued his report, only 50 out of 155 medical schools were operated by universities (Brown 1979, 169). As a consequence, the prevailing business model was to keep enrollment high and fees low. High enrollment was achieved through low entrance requirements and an almost 100% graduation rate. There was little incentive for the operators of these schools to raise standards on their own; doing so would inevitably attract fewer paying students.

The for-profit model not only disincentivized raising standards for entry and graduation, but it also made it nearly impossible to update the curriculum. In England and continental Europe, advances in pathology, bacteriology, and physiology had already begun to reshape medical education and practice. But these advances, and their incorporation into medicine, required significant financial support from the state. America's self-funded, for-profit schools struggled to make this shift. Student fees could pay for the space and the time of a part-time lecturer, but they could not fund the building of laboratories nor support the employment of academic and lab-based faculty. Even schools associated with colleges and universities struggled to make these kinds of investments. Most were run by religious organizations or local municipalities, which, although a source of financial stability, lacked the capacity to be overly generous with their economic support (Brown 1979). The need for funding partially explains why Flexner's survey initially received support from reformers, physicians, and medical school operators alike. Many saw this is as one plank in a larger strategy to enact "an active organized propaganda for money in medical education" that would secure "state aid and private endowment."[14] Without a deep-pocketed source of support, the profession understood that all the editorializing in the world could not change the quality of medical education.

Although the desires of the profession and Flexner's prescriptions seemed to be in sync, his report would trouble practicing physicians and reformers alike. The source of their discontent was not with the report's recommendations but in its execution. The Flexner report was not simply a policy statement, it included a public, school-by-school assessment with specific recommendations for either reform or closure. Out of 155 schools surveyed, Flexner assessed that only 35 were worth saving. Regarding those he recommended closing, he had little good to say. Although the AMA had suggested similar reforms, it had chosen not to publicly disparage the alumni, students, and owners of US medical schools (Starr 1984; Weiss and Miller 2010). But Flexner, it seemed, was focused more on the profession than its professionals. By depicting the state of medical education as irredeemable, he set the rhetorical grounds for dismantling its existing institutions. Medicine's advocates wanted resources in order to raise the status of the profession's *current* occupants. Instead, Flexner's reforms would funnel investment in the profession's *future* members while expelling those who he felt should be left firmly in the past.

First, Flexner's reforms would fundamentally alter the class character of the profession. According to Flexner, medical schools were filled with "low-grade material" (Flexner 1910, 14). For him, the "crude boy or the jaded clerk" who responded to an "alluring advertisement or announcement" had neither the right educational preparation nor calling for the profession (Flexner 1910, 19). To fix this problem, Flexner pushed for two years of college to become a uniform prerequisite for medical school. It is hard to overestimate the impact of this change. In 1910, only 19% of 15- to 18-year-olds were enrolled in high school, and only 9% of 18-year-olds had managed to graduate (Goldin 2008, 195). In this context, making any amount of college a prerequisite quickly transformed medical work from a humble to a rarified aspiration and would fundamentally alter the class character of the profession. What medical reformers had struggled to achieve for half a century, Flexner's words achieved in less than a decade. By 1914, all US medical schools required one year of college; by 1918, they required two (Weiss and Miller 2010, 555).

The Flexner Report reforms would not just alter the class background of the students themselves but that of the schools that trained them. The move toward a scientific vision of medicine meant that medical students needed to be trained in the laboratory sciences. Students would also need hospitals for residency training, a need most easily addressed by investing in school-affiliated hospitals. As the profession had hoped, Flexner agreed that outside funding from philanthropists and state coffers was needed to make these capital investments. However, Flexner's directive was more specific than to simply fund medical schools. In addition to publicly naming schools that were poor investments, he advised wealthy individuals, religious organizations, and philanthropic foundations to *only* give to medical schools integrated into the country's emerging university system, and that could demonstrate their dedication to a science-oriented rather than a practice-oriented curriculum.

Flexner's directives would almost immediately spur private investment in medical schools. By 1920, the Carnegie Foundation alone had newly appropriated 15 million dollars for the nation's medical schools (Brown 1979, 155). This new source of funding not only resulted in medical schooling's incorporation into the university system but would set the stage for its positioning within the emerging elite strata of that system. With "fewer and better" as Flexner's guiding principle, most of this support went to a handful of large, private universities. Eventually, some of this philanthropic largesse would go to public universities; however, none of this windfall was granted to a single for-profit school (Brown 1979). With the stroke of his pen, Flexner dismantled the entire for-profit industry and replaced it with the university-based system we have today.

In truth, there had been little to recommend the for-profit system. But the impact of this change would go beyond technical improvements in instruction. It would put professional medicine in service to elite interests. The for-profit regime of medical education may not have advanced the profession's desire for status, but it did help it retain its independence: every school balanced its own accounts, and every physician made their own career. Once large capital investments became an operating necessity, medicine had to answer to those who held the purse strings. The vast majority of these new investments would come from philanthropic organizations run by robber baron capitalists. Through targeted giving, a handful of private citizens were able to purchase the right to shape medical education, and thus the future of the profession, around their economic and political interests (Brown 1979).

Standardizing Exclusion by Race and Gender

One could argue that these transformations in the class character of physicians and their institutions were an unintended consequence of these reforms. It is more difficult to explain away their impact on the medical careers of women and Black men. Flexner's decision to only support schools dedicated to "scientific medicine" effected the closing of irregular schools, as well as some schools that simply offered irregular lectures. Unfortunately, these were also the schools most likely to accept Black people and white women as students. Moreover, his reforms and the rhetorical devices he used to support them had an outsized impact on schools specifically dedicated to training white women and Black people as physicians.

Flexner's survey included the seven Black medical schools operating at the time. In a section of the report dedicated specifically to these institutions, he summarily dismissed the notion that the US should even try to train enough Black physicians to serve the Black population. In Flexner's view, white physicians would and should continue to treat most Black patients. However, in alignment with philanthropic organizations and the Federal government, he believed there was a necessary place for Black physicians to serve "humbly and devotedly" in public health, playing an "important part in the sanitation and civilization of the whole nation" by ensuring that the Black population did not become a reservoir of infectious disease that might harm the white population (Flexner 1910, 180).

Although the rewards of specialization had not yet reached American medicine, it was clear that Flexner was invoking a stratified hierarchy within the profession, where Black physicians would be relegated to the kind of low status medical work that white physicians had no interest in pursuing—and which was all that Black patients deserved. He recommended that five of the seven Black schools be closed, advising that they were "in no position to make any contribution of value" to the education of Black physicians (Flexner 1910, 180). Meharry Medical College and Howard University's Medical School were the only Black medical schools that would survive Flexner's culling.

The closing of and disinvestment in Black medical schools would drastically reduce the educational opportunities of aspiring Black physicians for almost a century. Although Flexner thought there was a role for Black physicians, he was pointedly silent on the almost universal policy of white medical schools' exclusion of Black students. Moreover, his assertion that Black physicians should only receive basic training would temper the amount of state and philanthropic investment that even the two remaining Black schools would receive. Some might counter that, despite the racist rhetoric in which it was packaged, Flexner's application of a single standard to Black medical schools appeared to be race-neutral or even somewhat lenient toward these institutions (Miller and Weiss 2012). There was little question that these schools, like most of their white counterparts, were struggling to provide a science-based education. But this veneer of neutrality breaks down when considering the larger context.

Less than 50 years removed from the nation's Civil War, it was the height of absurdity to ask that medical schools with a mission to train Black doctors suddenly require two years of college preparation. Moreover, there were alternative models already in existence that dealt practically and appropriately with the racial gap in educational opportunity. Prior to 1910, most Black medical schools allowed matriculated students to shore up their missing education through direct tutoring or through simultaneous enrollment in college (Byrd and Clayton 2015). If your priority was creating Black physicians to serve Black patients, this graduated approach was a more reasonable one. Flexner's recommendation to close most Black schools, as well as his silence on the racism of white schools, communicated a different set of priorities.

Flexner's words would also play a central role in pushing women out of the profession. Flexner was certainly no supporter of gender equality. He firmly believed that women ought to leave medicine to men. Yet he did not advocate barring women from medical education because he believed that women's innate preferences would take care of the matter in short order. He did, however, argue that there was no reason to support women-only medical schools. While not every medical school accepted female students, white women could enroll in 91 of the 155 schools he surveyed (Redford 2020). Based on this evidence, he saw no reason to support women-only schools on principle. Furthermore, he did not assess that there was much worth keeping in those currently in existence. When applying the same standard by which he had measured all other medical schools, he determined that none of the three women-only schools he surveyed could "be sufficiently strengthened without an enormous outlay" of economic investment—an investment that seemed unnecessary since women could attend co-educational institutions if they cared to do so (Flexner 1910, 179).

Again, Flexner failed to take the larger context into account. Women's seeming preference for irregular schools was often more practical than ideological. White women may have had a stable presence in regular medical schools, but their status was contentious and precarious. At regular schools, they were routinely denied residency appointments, were openly harassed by male students and were often denied lab space and materials by male faculty and students (Moldow 1987, 39). At several such schools, male students engaged in formal protest against female students on the grounds that it would "cheapen" their own degrees (Moldow 1987).

Until the Flexner report, these protests were usually unsuccessful; schools that depended on student fees usually found suitable rationales for accepting women's money as well as men's. However, the rising importance of philanthropy and the end of institutional reliance on student fees left little reason for these schools to continue allowing women to enroll. In dismantling the for-profit medical school industry, closing irregular schools, and arguing for the closure of women-only medical schools, Flexner would effectively end women's enrollment in most medical schools for half a century.

The expulsion of Black people and white women from medicine was not simply the result of ideology but of the institutionalization of physician power. That medicine finally had the ability to exclude women and Black people from its ranks was a direct consequence of that power. Some feminist scholars of the professions have argued that the resources that elite white male physicians used in their professionalization project—access to the institutional machinery of higher education, foundation money, and state legislatures—were not available as strategic resources to occupations in which women were predominant (Bourgeault 2006; Witz 1990). However, these resources were also unavailable to most practicing physicians at the dawn of the 20th century. Medicine's newfound power would *not* be in the hands of practicing physicians but in those of philanthropic foundations and, eventually, those of the new institutions they would help to create.

The change that Flexner heralded was less about winning economic and cultural power for those already inhabiting the profession than it was about reforming the profession to make it fit for its rightful heirs. The reforms crystallized by Flexner gave medicine both the power and the institutional machinery to transform not only physician training but the demographic composition of the profession. That these new physicians should be white and male was in accordance with the desires of the medical establishment. But that they would also be from "the higher classes" and be compelled to serve elite interests would turn out to be a devil's bargain for most of the men who currently called themselves physicians. The price for investing in an ideal of elite white masculinity would be their own expulsion from the profession.

The racialized, gendered forms of institutional exclusion that medicine erected in the late 19th and early 20th century was not an unintended consequence of medical reform; it was part of its intended effect. Transforming medicine into the exclusive province of elite white men, while not the purpose of its professionalization project, came to ground the key rhetorical and institutional mechanisms for its achievement. However, power—professional or otherwise—is a force that needs an object. The second pillar of medicine's racial project was in using its reconstitution as a scientific medicine to reposition the elite white male expert in asymmetrical relationships to new objects of expertise. Black bodies would become the "clinical material" through which this new medical man would hone that expertise, while white women would become the pliant patients who would become subject to it. The racialized, gendered character of these objects would resonate with the era of racial repression that followed Reconstruction and the rollback of white women's advancement that had occurred in the Gilded Age.

Reincorporation as Objects of Expertise

A well-known, if generally unspoken, aspect of medicine's scientific turn was its insatiable need for bodies. Physicians and anatomists were infamous for robbing graves under cover of night to meet the need for dead ones. When medical schools began incorporating human dissection into training, medical students too began to clamor for access to this scarce resource. What is less well-known is how much of that demand was met by the enslavement of Black people. In her book *Medical Apartheid*, medical ethicist Harriet Washington uncovered the deep connections between slavery and the ambitions of the medical profession (Washington 2008). Prior to the Civil War, plantation doctors actively sought the dead bodies of the enslaved to meet their need for bodies. They would post public advertisements offering to either take or even pay for these cadavers. Many of these bodies would serve as dissection material for medical students. When for-profit medical schools still had to actively sell their wares to fee-paying students, southern schools would boast about their robust supply of corpses (Washington 2008).

Slavery not only supplied medicine with the bodies of the dead but those of the living. Plantation physicians would often pay for the food and material upkeep of the enslaved in exchange for free reign to perform brutal experiments on their minds and bodies. Some physicians resorted to buying their own slaves expressly for that purpose. Medical schools had a hand in this practice; they would turn to plantation infirmaries to supply students with sick people whose diseases could be observed and whose bodies could be practiced on without consent. At a time when most health care still happened at home and when physicians had little authority over patients, the enslaved were the most reliable source of clinical material for both training and knowledge production (Washington 2008).

The Civil War did not mark the end of this practice but signaled its escalation. The slow but inexorable transformation of medicine into a science increased its need for bodies. As a result, the southern tradition of using Black people as subjects of experimentation became a national one. The institution of slavery may have ended, but practices of reenslavement—such as the convict leasing system, Jim Crow laws, and the absence of legal and police protection from terroristic violence—left Black communities vulnerable to medical exploitation. For example, Black people became the un-consenting subjects of radiation experiments as part of the Manhattan project, while Black prisoners were subjected to unregulated medical experimentation from the 1940s through the 1970s (Washington 2008). More routinely, medically underserved Black communities that were forced to turn to academic medical centers for "free care" became sources of everyday practice and experimentation by medical students, attendings, and clinical investigators.

When Black bodies became highly valued as clinical material, not only were Black physicians seen as unnecessary by the white medical establishment, they were a hindrance. The rightful clinical material for the professional medical man was a coerced Black subject. The words of Thomas Murrell, a physician who would eventually advise the investigators of the infamous Tuskegee Syphilis Study, articulated the sentiment of white medicine quite well when he wrote this in a 1910 JAMA article: "The future of the Negro lies more in the research laboratory than in the schools … When diseased, he should be registered and forced to take treatment before he offers his diseased mind and body on the altar of academic and professional education" (Murrell 1910, 849; Washington 2008). Murrell's imagined future could only come to pass because of a scarcity of Black physicians. Black patients had to be forced to accept the care of white physicians in order to remain available for practice and experimentation. The forced extraction of knowledge from Black bodies *required* the absence of Black physicians.

Medicine not only needed a subject from which to extract knowledge, but it also required a subordinate subject for its ministrations. It would find that subject in middle-class white women. Women had long been regarded as "the weaker sex" in western thought. However, by the middle of the 19th century, physicians began to postulate scientific rather than religious explanations for women's supposed congenital weakness (Carroll Smith-Rosenberg 1972; Ehrenreich and English 2011). Whether centered on the ovaries or the uterus, these explanations collectively conceptualized women's reproductive organs and capacities as a source of physical debility and mental instability. To be a woman, according to medical experts, was to live a life of chronic illness.

Although such theories were popular in both lay and medical circles, for most of the 19th century, they did not directly impact the care of most women. As a practical matter, they did not apply to the Black or working-class white women whose labor was needed in agricultural fields, the industrial factory floor, or in domestic service. Theories of female invalidism were only applied to women whose fathers or husbands could support their lack of economic activity as well as pay their doctor's bills (Ehrenreich and English 2011). But more crucially, routine care by a trained physician was not commonplace for women of any class. Before the acceptance of medical authority, the 19th-century male physician had to cajole his white female patients (and the men who were seen as their guardians) to accept his treatments. Competition from lay and irregular health care providers meant that he might not have been consulted at all. Without professional authority, medical theories about inherent female debility would be limited in their impact on the care that most women received.

Moreover, the Gilded Age seemed to signal an end to broader social beliefs in female incompetence. The weaker sex began to test its strength through organizing for women's suffrage and entering public life as social reformers, nurses, lawyers, and physicians (Moldow 1987, 5–15). Because womanhood remained a socially legitimate source of curative authority, medicine was a popular choice among women with access to advanced education. However, as the doors for women began to open, a concerted male backlash fought to keep them closed. Theories of female invalidism became a key resource for men hoping to banish women from the medical profession as well as most of public life. For medical men, these theories invalidated women's claims to curative authority by questioning their physical and emotional ability to withstand the new rigors of science-based education. But the impact of these theories outside the profession was just as significant.

Medicine's emerging authority enabled them to apply their "scientific" explanations of gender inequality to a much broader population of women. As physician care—and submission to medical authority—became a regular part of American life, so did medicine's view of women as chronically ill. Flexner-era reforms did the work of expelling middle- and upper-class white women from medicine. But its emerging professional power helped it to craft a new role for such women in the exam room. Appropriately classed white women would become medicine's idealized patients: constitutionally frail, mentally unstable, and subordinate to the white male expert (Ehrenreich and English 2011). The characteristics that made white women good patients would render them unsuitable as medical professionals.

Conclusion

At the dawn of the 20th century, the typical American physician was a lightly educated, lower middle class white man. He was deeply concerned with the practical challenges of his profession: an oversupply of competitors and its unfortunate effects on his status and income. Inside the profession, he competed for patients with irregularly trained–or sometimes untrained– "quacks," doctresses, practitioners of "Indian medicine", and Black physicians. The lowly status of his competitors only served to highlight his own precarious economic and social position. Outside the profession, he competed for authority with prospective patients, who, even when seeking his services, felt empowered to evaluate and often dismiss his judgment. Battered on all sides, he was supremely conscious of his profession's humble position on the social ladder.

By the 1950s, the American physician was a different man altogether. A highly educated member of the upper middle class, his authority inside the exam room was unquestioned, and his status outside of it was self-evident. This storied ascent is about as classic a rags-to-riches tale as one can get. Medicine not only achieved the American Dream as a group, but joining the profession would become one of several vehicles for the sons of elite white men to secure this dream for themselves. How professional medicine achieved this feat is usually understood as a political achievement, with a focus on how it won the support of state legislatures and philanthropists. However, attention to the cultural tools used to legitimate that support is equally important (Abbott 1988). Certainly, tying itself to the rising star of science was a key part of how medicine cemented its cultural authority. But so was imbricating itself within the racial and gender order that emerged after Reconstruction. American medicine's bid for elite status required the literal remaking of the physician's body into "the right kind of body" to possess and wield power. Those with the wrong social bodies were systematically excluded. Their exclusion was not happenstance but was part and parcel of medicine's professional project.

Reconceptualizing professional projects as racial projects is important not just for understanding the past but for understanding the enduring nature of racial and gender stratification in the medical workplace. While current processes of exclusion are not as explicit as they once were, their impact remains starkly visible in who does and does not enter medicine. In 1910, when Flexner released his report, Black physicians represented 2.6% of the physician workforce (Byrd and Clayton 2015, 125). Partly as a result of the reforms enumerated in that report, it took almost 100 years to exceed that benchmark (Baker et al. 2008). The most recent figures estimate that the percentage of US physicians who identify as Black has reached its all-time high of 5% (Ly 2021).

Although modest progress is still progress, it should not be attributed to changes within the profession. The predominately white institutions that make up professional medicine have done little to nothing to achieve this improvement. The existence of Black physicians at the turn of the 20th century was the result of extraordinary individual effort and the herculean institutional work of Black medical schools that persisted within a hostile and discriminatory context. Almost a quarter into the 21st century, little has changed. Today's Historically Black College and University (HBCU) medical schools have an outsized role in producing Black physicians (Butler 2011). Recent statistics suggest that four HBCU medical schools are directly responsible for producing 1 out of every 5 Black medical school graduates (Campbell et al. 2020). Moreover, if you consider the role of the 84 undergraduate degree granting HBCUs in educating Black medical school applicants, HBCUs are collectively responsible for educating 80% of all Black medical and dentistry degree holders (Johnson et al. 2017). What these statistics make clear is that the enduring presence of Black physicians is almost entirely the result of underfunded Black educational institutions and not the white institutions that reproduce the larger profession.[15] Despite medicine's *mea culpa* for past wrongs, there is little empirical evidence of a commitment to change.

As the historical record suggests, this lack of progress cannot be explained by the unmoored, racist beliefs of randomly-placed individuals. The more likely explanation is in medicine's investment in whiteness. It earned the prerequisites of professional power, in part, through its commitment to becoming a preserve of elite white masculinity. To abandon that project would be to lose its claim to the perks of professional status. Indeed, in the 21st century, a common set of forces seem to be behind both the lowered status of medicine and rising numbers of women and people of color entering the profession. Medicine as a whole is no longer dominated by white men, but the highest paying specialties, positions, and work locations remain so. Racial and gender stratification within the profession has meant that this version of the American Dream is more attainable for some more than others.

Reconceptualizing professionalization as a racial project also helps to explain why we should not expect diversity workshops and "the problem with the pipeline" conversations to make much of a difference. Fifty years after the US civil rights movement, such interventions have produced almost no impact on the production of Black physicians. This reconceptualization also calls into question the broader work of stratification researchers who prescribe the acquisition of educational credentials as the key to the American Dream. Such individual-level advice requires one to cultivate a studied "racial ignorance" of anti-Blackness as a constitutive framework for the American Dream.

A focus on individual acquisition of credentials is insufficient to counter the hurdles that racialized groups face in achieving the American Dream because this dream has never been an individual endeavor. Despite our ways of telling the story, group uplift—and group-level oppression—have always been a core part of this dream. The dreams of some have usually required the deferred dreams of others. Recentering the role of racial projects helps us to understand how seemingly meritocratic ladders of social mobility are just as likely to be vehicles of racial formation as racial uplift—actively legitimating unequal rewards rather than diminishing them. As a consequence, the solution to inequality will not be found in shaping the choices of Black or white individuals but in disrupting the racial projects of white institutions.

Notes

1 These are the words of Dr Logan from South Carolina, as contained in Appendix IV of the *Transactions of the Medical Society of the State of New York,* 1844. They were a part of his response to the effects of South Carolina's annulment of medical licensure requirements in 1838.

2 I am using the phrase "investment in whiteness," as articulated by George Lipsitz (2018).

3 The singularity of American medicine has also made it a locus of critique. Many have questioned its utility as a benchmark by which to measure or understand other occupations, as no other group has matched its rise or stability within the system of professions. Criticisms aside, its function as the paradigmatic case of professionalization means that other occupations are compared to its trajectory, explicitly or implicitly.

4 In summarizing US medicine's professional history and its transformation in status, I am relaying what has become a widely accepted account based on the following foundational works: Starr (1984), Brown (1979), and Byrd and Clayton (2015).

5 Many of the physicians residing in established towns and cities on the east coast *did* feel the indignities of serving the white working class. However, we also have evidence that those who served in rural locations felt a kinship with their patients that cultivated a sense of belonging and pride (see Chapter 3 of Pickard and Buley 1946).

6 Medical guides and "Receipt Books" of medicinal recipes were popular with the lay public well until the end of the 19th century (Leong and Pennell 2007). These books provided more than general advice; they served as technical manuals for domestic practitioners. One example was Dr William Buchan's *Domestic Medicine Or a Treatise on the Prevention and Cure of Diseases by Regimen and Simple Medicines*. Its 55 chapters covered the causes, symptomology, and treatment of specific disorders, including an appendix of medicinal recipes. It was so popular that 142 editions were issued over a 100-year period (Rosenberg 1983).

7 We can see parallels in contemporary society. Many white "alternative" practitioner markets their expertise through attestations of having learned from "Indigenous shamans" from South and Central America.

8 Whether these men had a lineage that contained native persons is hard to discern. However, the historical record suggests that these men were not claimed as citizens of any Indigenous nation and that they lived their lives socially as white men (Vogel 1970).

9 The answer to the "why" of this difference is complicated and beyond the scope of this essay. But part of the answer can be found in the different value of Native and Black peoples within a settler

colonialist framework. Under settler colonialism, Native people's value lay in eradication to legit- imate land confiscation, while Black people's value lay in their reproduction as a source of cheap labor. As a result, Native culture can be valued—but only to the extent that actual Native people do not exist, while Blackness has to be constantly devalued in order to render invisible the immense value of their labor to capitalist production (Glenn 2015).

10 Of course, given how difficult it was for many white physicians to make a living, some consented to do so. In fact, some white physicians took advantage of Black physicians' inability to secure hospital privileges and actively stole Black patients from them (Byrd and Clayton 2015).

11 The designation of "Black schools" or departments is somewhat misleading. Historically Black educational institutions were (and still are) open to students of any race or ethnicity. Howard University's first cohort of medical students famously contained a white man from Brooklyn (Byrd and Clayton 2015, 388). That white students did not apply for enrollment was a function of their choices rather than the institutional practices of Black schools.

12 These were the words of physician L. Green in his address to the Herkimer County Medical Society. As reprinted in Article VII, page 99 in the *Transactions of the Medical Society of the State of New York*, Volume 6, 1844, 1845, 1846. J. Munsell, Albany NY, 1846.

13 This opinion piece was written in reference to New York Laws, ch. 513, p. 723, and Pennsylvania Laws 1881, no. 78. n. 72.

14 These words were part of a speech that Dr. Arthur Dean Bevan, chairman of the AMA's Council on Medical Education, delivered at the 1907 AMA conference (Brown 1979, 142).

15 Predominately white educational institutions do not identify as "white" institutions. However, I have purposefully chosen to identify them as such. Given their demonstrated investment in repro- ducing a predominately white student body, a race-neutral appellation is not only inaccurate, but it would also be an act of obfuscation of the role that white supremacist logics play in contemporary US institutions.

References

Abbott, Andrew. 1988. *The System of Professions: An Essay on the Division of Expert Labor.* 1st ed. Chicago, IL: University of Chicago Press.

Acker, Joan. 1990. "Hierarchies, Jobs, Bodies: A Theory of Gendered Organizations." *Gender & Society* 4 (2): 139–58.

"Appendix IV. Report of a Committee on the Subject of Medical Legislation, to the Monroe County Medical Society, Rochester, November 9, 1842." 1846. In *Transactions of the Medical Society of the State of New York*, 1844, 1845, 1846, 6:37–53. J. Munsel: Albany, NY.

Baker, Robert B., Harriet Washington, Ololade Olakanmi, Todd Savitt, Elizabeth Jacobs, Eddie Hoover, and Matthew Wynia. 2008. "African American Physicians and Organized Medicine, 1846–1968: Origins of a Racial Divide." *JAMA : The Journal of the American Medical Association* 300 (August): 306–13. https://doi.org/10.1001/jama.300.3.306.

Baker, Robert B., Harriet A. Washington, Ololade Olakanmi, Todd L. Savitt, Elizabeth A. Jacobs, Eddie Hoover, and Matthew K. Wynia. 2009. "Creating a Segregated Medical Profession: African American Physicians and Organized Medicine, 1846–1910." *Journal of the National Medical Association* 101 (6): 501–12. https://doi.org/10.1016/S0027-9684(15)30935-4.

Bell, Derrick. 1992. *Faces at the Bottom of the Well: The Permanence of Racism.* New York: Basic Books.

Berman, Alex. 1951. "The Thomsonian Movement and Its Relation to American Pharmacy and Medicine." *Bulletin of the History of Medicine* 25 (5): 405–28.

Blake, John B. 1965. "'The Fielding H. Garrison Lecture': Women and Medicine in Ante-Bellum America." *Bulletin of the History of Medicine* 39 (January): 99–123.

Blanton, Wyndham Bolling. 1931. *Medicine in Virginia in the Eighteenth Century.* 1st ed. Richmond, VA: Garrett & Massie, incorporated.

Bonilla-Silva, Eduardo. 2013. *Racism without Racists: Color-Blind Racism and the Persistence of Racial Inequality in America.* 4th ed. Lanham, MD: Rowman & Littlefield Publishers.

Bourgeault, Ivy Lynn. 2006. *Push!: The Struggle for Midwifery in Ontario.* Montreal: McGill-Queen's University Press.

Brown, E. Richard. 1979. *Rockefeller Medicine Men: Medicine and Capitalism in America.* Berkeley, CA: University of California Press.

Butler, Barbara Marie. 2011. "Shifting Patterns in the Premedical Education of African Americans and the Role of the HBCU." *Journal of African American Studies* 15 (4): 541–56. https://doi.org/10.1007/s12111-010-9135-0.

Byrd, W. Michael, and Linda A. Clayton. 2015. *An American Health Dilemma: Race, Medicine, and Health Care in the United States 1900–2000*. New York: Routledge. https://doi.org/10.4324/9780203950784.

Campbell, Kendall M., Irma Corral, Jhojana L. Infante Linares, and Dmitry Tumin. 2020. "Projected Estimates of African American Medical Graduates of Closed Historically Black Medical Schools." *JAMA Network Open* 3 (8): e2015220. https://doi.org/10.1001/jamanetworkopen.2020.15220.

Collins, Sharon M. 1989. "The Marginalization of Black Executives." *Social Problems* 36 (4): 317–31. https://doi.org/10.2307/800818.

Crenshaw, Kimberle. 1989. "Demarginalizing the Intersection of Race and Sex: A Black Feminist Critique of Antidiscrimination Doctrine, Feminist Theory and Antiracist Politics." *University of Chicago Legal Forum* 1989: 139.

Davis, Angela Yvonne. 1983. *Women, Race, and Class*. New York: Vintage Books.

Ehrenreich, Barbara, and Deirdre English. 2011. *Complaints & Disorders*. 2nd ed. New York: The Feminist Press at CUNY.

Flexner, Abraham. 1910. "Medical Education in the United States and Canada: A Report to the Carnegie Foundation for the Advancement of Teaching." Bulletin 4. New York, NY: The Carnegie Foundation for the Advancement of Teaching. http://archive.carnegiefoundation.org/publications/pdfs/elibrary/Carnegie_Flexner_Report.pdf.

Freidson, Eliot. 1970. *Professional Dominance: The Social Structure of Medical Care*. Piscataway, NJ: Aldine de Gruyter.

Glenn, Evelyn Nakano. 2015. "Settler Colonialism as Structure: A Framework for Comparative Studies of U.S. Race and Gender Formation." *Sociology of Race and Ethnicity* 1 (1): 52–72. https://doi.org/10.1177/2332649214560440.

Goldin, Claudia Dale. 2008. *The Race between Education and Technology*. Cambridge, MA: The Belknap Press of Harvard University Press.

Green, L. 1846. "Article VII. Address Delivered before the Herkimer County Medical Society." In *Transactions of the Medical Society of the State of New York, 1844, 1845, 1846*, 6:37–53. J. Munsel: Albany, NY.

Harley, Earl H. 2006. "The Forgotten History of Defunct Black Medical Schools in the 19th and 20th Centuries and the Impact of the Flexner Report." *Journal of the National Medical Association* 98 (9): 1425–29.

Haynes, Douglas M. 2005. "Policing the Social Boundaries of the American Medical Association, 1847–70." *Journal of the History of Medicine and Allied Sciences* 60 (2): 170–95. https://doi.org/10.1093/jhmas/jri022.

Johnson, Glenn S., Vance Gray, Lolita D. Gray, N. Latrice Richardson, Shirley A. Rainey-Brown, Kimberly L. Triplett, and Luisa E. Bowman. 2017. "Historically Black Colleges and Universities (HBCUs) in the Twenty First Century: An Exploratory Case Study Analysis of Their Mission." *Race, Gender & Class* 24 (3–4): 44–67.

Kett, Joseph F. 1968. *The Formation of the American Medical Profession; the Role of Institutions, 1780–1860*. Yale Studies in the History of Science and Medicine 3. New Haven, CT: Yale University Press.

Larson, Magali Sarfatti. 1979. *The Rise of Professionalism: A Sociological Analysis*. Berkeley, CA: University of California Press.

Leong, Elaine, and Sara Pennell. 2007. "Recipe Collections and the Currency of Medical Knowledge in the Early Modern 'Medical Marketplace'." In *Medicine and the Market in England and Its Colonies, c. 1450–c. 1850*, edited by Mark S. R. Jenner and Patrick Wallis, 133–52. London: Palgrave Macmillan UK. https://doi.org/10.1057/9780230591462_7.

Lipsitz, George. 2018. *The Possessive Investment in Whiteness: How White People Profit from Identity Politics*. Philadelphia, PA: Temple University Press.

Ly, Dan P. 2021. "Historical Trends in the Representativeness and Incomes of Black Physicians, 1900–2018." *Journal of General Internal Medicine*, April. https://doi.org/10.1007/s11606-021-06745-1.

Maume, David J. 1999. "Glass Ceilings and Glass Escalators: Occupational Segregation and Race and Sex Differences in Managerial Promotions." *Work and Occupations* 26 (4): 483–509. https://doi.org/10.1177/0730888499026004005.

Miller, L. E., and R. M. Weiss. 2012. "Revisiting Black Medical School Extinctions in the Flexner Era." *Journal of the History of Medicine and Allied Sciences* 67 (2): 217–43. https://doi.org/10.1093/jhmas/jrq084.

Mills, Charles W. 1997. *The Racial Contract.* Ithaca, NY: Cornell University Press.

Moen, Phyllis, and Patricia Roehling. 2005. *The Career Mystique: Cracks in the American Dream.* Lanham, MD: Rowman & Littlefield.

Moldow, Gloria. 1987. *Women Doctors in Gilded-Age Washington: Race, Gender, and Professionalization.* Champaign, IL: University of Illinois Press.

Morais, Herbert M. 1967. *The History of the Negro in Medicine.* 1st ed. The International Library of Negro Life and History. New York: Publishers Co.

Murrell, Thomas W. 1910. "Syphilis and the American Negro: A Medico-Sociologic Study." *Journal of the American Medical Association* LIV (11): 846–49. https://doi.org/10.1001/jama.1910.92550370001001c.

Omi, Michael, and Howard Winant. 1994. *Racial Formation in the United States: From the 1960s to the 1990s.* 2nd ed. New York: Routledge.

Philadelphia Medical Times. 1883. "Registration Laws and Their Operation Philadelphia Medical Times, XIII (July 14, 1883)," July 14, 1883, XIII ed.

Pickard, Madge Evelyn, and Roscoe Carlyle Buley. 1946 *The Midwest Pioneer, His Ills, Cures, and Doctors.* New York: Henry Schuman.

Pierce, Jennifer L. 1996. *Gender Trials: Emotional Lives in Contemporary Law Firms.* 2nd ed. Berkeley, CA: University of California Press.

Ray, Victor. 2019. "A Theory of Racialized Organizations." *American Sociological Review* 84 (1): 26–53. https://doi.org/10.1177/0003122418822335.

Redford, Gabrielle. 2020. "AAMC Renames Prestigious Abraham Flexner Award in Light of Racist and Sexist Writings." *AAMC News,* November 17, 2020. https://www.aamc.org/news-insights/aamc-renames-prestigious-abraham-flexner-award-light-racist-and-sexist-writings.

Reverby, Susan. 1987. "A Caring Dilemma: Womanhood and Nursing in Historical Perspective." *Nursing Research* 36 (1): 5–11.

Rivera, Lauren A. 2012. "Hiring as Cultural Matching: The Case of Elite Professional Service Firms." *American Sociological Review* 77 (6): 999–1022. https://doi.org/10.1177/0003122412463213.

Rosenberg, Charles E. 1983. "Medical Text and Social Context: Explaining William Buchan's 'Domestic Medicine'." *Bulletin of the History of Medicine* 57 (1): 22–42.

Royster, Deirdre A. 2003. *Race and the Invisible Hand: How White Networks Exclude Black Men from Blue-Collar Jobs.* 1st ed. Berkeley, CA: University of California Press.

Smith-Rosenberg, Carroll. 1972. "The Hysterical Woman: Sex Roles and Role Conflict in 19th-Century America." *Social Research* 39 (4): 652–78.

Spruill, Julia Cherry. 1998. *Women's Life and Work in the Southern Colonies.* New York: W. W. Norton & Company.

Starr, Paul. 1984. *The Social Transformation of American Medicine: The Rise of a Sovereign Profession and the Making of a Vast Industry.* New York: Basic Books.

Tannenbaum, Rebecca J. 2019. *The Healer's Calling: Women and Medicine in Early New England.* Ithaca, NY: Cornell University Press. http://ebookcentral.proquest.com/lib/washington/detail.action?docID=5965079.

The Combahee River Collective. 1983. "The Combahee River Collective Statement." *Home Girls: A Black Feminist Anthology* 1: 264–74.

Trotter, LaTonya J. 2017. "Making a Career: Reproducing Gender within a Predominately Female Profession." *Gender & Society* 31 (4): 503–25. https://doi.org/10.1177/0891243217716115.

Vogel, Virgil J. 1970. *American Indian Medicine.* 1st ed. Norman, OK: University of Oklahoma Press.

Walsh, Mary Roth. 1979. *Doctors Wanted: No Women Need Apply: Sexual Barriers in the Medical Profession, 1835–1975.* New Haven, CT: Yale University Press.

Washington, Harriet A. 2008. *Medical Apartheid: The Dark History of Medical Experimentation on Black Americans from Colonial Times to the Present.* Illustrated edition. New York: Anchor.

Weiss, Richard M., and Lynn E. Miller. 2010. "The Social Transformation of American Medical Education: Class, Status, and Party Influences on Occupational Closure, 1902–1919." *The Sociological Quarterly* 51 (4): 550–75.

Wingfield, Adia Harvey. 2010. "Are Some Emotions Marked 'Whites Only'? Racialized Feeling Rules in Professional Workplaces." *Social Problems* 57 (2): 251–68. https://doi.org/10.1525/sp.2010.57.2.251.

———. 2019. *Flatlining: Race, Work, and Health Care in the New Economy.* 1st ed. Oakland, CA: University of California Press.

Witz, Anne. 1990. "Patriarchy and Professions: The Gendered Politics of Occupational Closure." *Sociology* 24 (4): 675–90. https://doi.org/10.1177/0038038590024004007.
———. 1992. *Professions and Patriarchy.* New York: Routledge.
Wooten, Melissa E. 2006. "Soapbox : Editorial Essays: Race and Strategic Organization." *Strategic Organization* 4 (2): 191–99. https://doi.org/10.1177/1476127006064068.
Wooten, Melissa E., and Lucius Couloute. 2017. "The Production of Racial Inequality within and among Organizations." *Sociology Compass* 11 (1): e12446. https://doi.org/10.1111/soc4.12446.

19

STATUS MAINTENANCE, MOBILITY, AND THE PERSISTENCE OF CLASS BARRIERS TO ACHIEVING THE AMERICAN DREAM

Robert C. Hauhart

Two questions have dominated studies of the American Dream since the concept was developed in print by James Truslow Adams in his popular history of the United States, *The Epic of America*, in 1931. First, since one common conception of the American dream is premised on achieving economic success, often defined as intergenerational economic mobility, sociologists, journalists, and others have routinely questioned whether upward economic mobility is still viable in a given era within the United States or, whether, to the contrary, the conditions, and therefore the opportunity, for upward economic mobility have disappeared. Second, when the answer to the first question has been a tentative acknowledgment that conditions in the United States have changed, and the likelihood of upward economic mobility in a particular era has been reduced or virtually disappeared altogether, the question turns to whether or not, then current economic barriers can be eliminated, thereby reinvigorating economic opportunity and reestablishing conditions for achieving the American dream. A great deal of ink has been spilled attempting to answer these questions up to and including the present day. I would like to suggest that both of these questions have produced more confusion than enlightenment, largely because they begin from incorrect premises about the structure of United States society and graft on to the American dream expectations that are at variance with firmly established American institutions and social structure.

Social Structural Foundations and the American Dream

The principal problem with framing the two questions in the manner set forth above is that the questions disregard the nature of U.S. society and the way in which established institutions operate. In essence, the questions fail because they treat economic mobility and economic aspirations as paramount and reductively dominant in all realms within U.S. society. More importantly, numerous studies of class in the twentieth and twenty-first century United States have rather consistently answered the question as to whether upward mobility from one class to another is a likely outcome; for most members of any class breakdown, it is not.

DOI: 10.4324/9781003326243-25

It is true that the language of economics – or, more precisely, rhetoric about and references to making money (and/or making *more* money) – are a routinely common mode of linguistic expression and an often-voiced, sought after expression of desire within American culture. This explains, in part, why Adams' conception of the American dream, which was not principally about materialism or economic mobility, has so often been reframed and reduced to a dream of upward economic mobility. (A related factor is our penchant for converting aspirations that are intangible – Adams' (1933, 317) "dream of a social order in which each man and each woman shall be able to attain the fullest nature of which they are innately capable" – into a quantifiable exercise, in this case, one of economic calculation and comparison.) A close reading of that portion of Adams' (1933, 316–27) text in *The Epic of America* where he addresses the American Dream indisputably shows that Adams was not evoking an American dream conceived solely on the basis of economic (material) success and upward economic mobility (Hauhart 2016, 67–72). The idea that the American dream is principally concerned with economic success (Merton 1938) and/or intergenerational upward economic mobility (Hochschild 1995) arises from the work of others.[1]

This conversion, albeit well-intended and certainly not without its reasons, has had the unintended effect of introducing confusion into our discussions of the American dream. Indeed, the primary reason that ever since the publication of Adams' book, the definition of the American dream has been re-focused on economic success is due to the influence, or the towering influence, of these prominent writers. The consequence is that we have had to busy ourselves recording, calculating, and re-calculating just what are the present economic circumstances among Americans of various social ranks and then attempting to forecast whether or not Americans of a certain rank are able to "move up" economically in each era or, alternatively, are reduced to remaining economically stagnant (if not headed economically downward).[2]

None of this is to say money does not matter. I would be among the last to suggest such a conclusion. Rather, though, it is to say that focusing on economics – or, more bluntly put, achieving success in "making money" – has a tendency to let us misunderstand how one "makes money" within society and how money relates to social status. Focusing on income or wealth exclusively then confuses the sort of evidence we seek to answer questions about success and mobility within U.S. society. Promoting a single focus on economic success as the *sine qua non* of the American dream distorts our perspective of the phenomenon. Arguably, to understand in a practical, tangible way how one achieves monetary success or achieves upward mobility, often not the same thing, one needs to examine U.S. social structure and its intersection with U.S. culture.

Money and Status

A fundamental misunderstanding for many of those who advocate for adopting a pecuniary definition of the American dream, whether the short-term version that equates success with ready and quick cash or the long-term version which envisions building a financial legacy which can then be passed on inter-generationally, is a failure to distinguish economic success from other forms of success, which we may denominate collectively as social success. A related failure is to not fully appreciate just how one acquires money, what it is money does, and what it can buy. This is due to the fact that in the United States, money is often accorded a commanding priority – what Sandel (2012, 6) terms "market triumphalism." As Sandel recites, before enumerating a lengthy list of things and services one may acquire with money, "There are some things money can't buy, but these days not that many" (3). A substantial portion of Sandel's 245-page book thereafter consists of numerous reports of unusual ways in which corporations, partnerships, and individuals have tried to make money and equally unusual ways in which those same entities have spent money. Sandel's discussion illustrates well that our culture's obsession with money can itself become an obsession for scholars, too, who have, among other things, modified Adams' original meaning of the American dream to adapt it to our money-driven cultural discourse.

This failure to distinguish monetary success from social success leads directly to our willingness to reduce the term "mobility" to mean "upward economic mobility," therefore disavowing the need to discuss social mobility as an independent yet related form of mobility worthy of analysis. Moreover, the focus on economics, economic success, and upward economic mobility spuriously make it appear that economics and money are somehow separable from, and can be achieved without reference to, the constraints of the existing social structure and established institutions. Nothing, of course, could be further from the truth. Indeed, it is the existing social structure and its established institutions that predominantly allocate money in the form of income, thereby conferring and supporting economic success, whether in the short term or long term. Many economic thinkers proceed as though it is only markets that matter, but with respect to the distribution of "life chances," including the opportunity to make more or less money from society, Max Weber convincingly demonstrated long ago that it is class boundaries, and the position(s) one holds within a class, that allocate life chances within society. Thus, we need to examine social classes in the contemporary United States and the positions that grow out of class membership, with their corresponding possibilities to profit therefrom, to understand even upward economic mobility. Recent studies of the working, lower, middle, and upper middle classes in United States society have confirmed Weber's understanding of the powerfully dominant role of class membership in stratifying the distribution of social benefits, including money.

Weber's (Gerth and Mills 1946, 181) definition of class is based solely on whether a given group of people find themselves in the same – or, effectively, the same – market situation; that is, class *is* fundamentally a function of economics but *not* simply a function of access to actual capital, as it would have been in the hey-day of late nineteenth-century capitalism. Indeed, one can argue, as Bourdieu (1986, 243) and others have persuasively argued, that while financial capital can go a long way toward extending one's ability to act effectively in one's own self-interest, the possession of what he and others have termed "cultural capital" or "social capital," can do likewise, and can themselves be converted into economic capital. Class, therefore, in contemporary terms, remains economically based so long as one understands economics behaviorally as a means whereby an individual can deploy his or her capital, whether financial, human, or social to achieve earthly ends.

Members of a similar class, therefore, share economic interests according to Weber (183), but he recognizes that the concept of economic class interest is not entirely amenable to clear boundaries and so is "an ambiguous one" (183). While conceding that members of a class "share a factual direction of interests following with a certain probability from the class situation for a certain 'average' of those people subjected to the class situation," Weber (183) is clear that one cannot extend the explanatory value of the concept much further. As he notes, although "the class situation and other circumstances [for multiple individuals] remain[ing] the same, the direction in which the individual worker, …, is likely to pursue his interests may vary widely, …" (183). Fortunately, in the end this matters very little, for membership in a class pre-ordains to a substantial extent the range of options one is offered in the life sphere and the nature, and forms, of capital one has in one's possession. In short, if one possesses money but does not possess "cultural capital," one cannot deploy cultural capital in seeking future benefits and opportunities when that is the form of capital needed.. While one could support this contention with reference to eloquent expressions from Weber, Bourdieu

(1986), Bourdieu and Passeron (1977), and others, the most compelling evidence may be found in detailed ethnographic works, particularly those works which arise from embedded observations of the working class and poor in contemporary U.S. society.

Class-Based Limitations on Mobility

Over the last several decades, American anthropologists and sociologists have conducted a number of comprehensive ethnographic studies of the working class and poor youth in the United States. Cumulatively, these field work studies have developed for us a relatively complete picture of the barriers and limitations that working class and poor youth face in seeking mobility. If one defines the American dream as achieving some combination of upward economic mobility and upward social mobility, these studies suggest that many more working class and poor youth succumb to the limitations they bring to the effort, and the barriers they face, than succeed. Moreover, the studies suggest that little has changed over decades, so while the working class and poor youth often still believe that the achievement of a better way of life is possible in the United States, more recent reports from the field commonly echo the fundamental social facts reported in earlier investigations.

Ain't No Makin' It

Jay MacLeod's intensive participant observation in the pseudonymous Clarendon Heights low-income housing development, located in a highly urbanized, northeastern U.S. city, is unique among many such studies because he was able to follow up his initial 1983 fieldwork twice: with re-interviews of most of his principal respondents in the summer of 1991 and again in 2006–7. Notably, the return to his field site was facilitated by the fact, as MacLeod ruefully notes, because "[M]ost [of his interview subjects] still lived nearby or were in prison ..." (2009, xii). This is a rather salient social fact since the United States is a highly mobile society, yet historically it is members of the middle and upper middle classes who more often move from one community, city, or region to another. Jennifer Silva, among others, re-confirmed this general trend in the double-edged title of her most recent book, *We're Still Here* (2019) – referencing both geography and class location. What MacLeod found in his initial study, and confirmed twice, is that class location acts in many ways as either a barrier or alternately an advantage, to economic and social mobility.

MacLeod's study group consisted of two peer groups of male teenagers who lived in Clarendon Heights: one predominantly white (the Hallway Hangers) and one "almost exclusively" black (the Brothers) (6). In his initial field work, MacLeod draws a clear distinction between the two groups' attitudes toward education. The white group's members are despondent about their futures, despise school, do not believe that schooling is a pathway to a better job or a better life, do not participate in after school activities, and, as a consequence, most have dropped out before finishing high school (7, 98). The Brothers, by contrast, all attend high school on a regular basis, eschew many of the habits and pastimes the white group models (smoking cigarettes, drinking alcohol, and using drugs), participate in extracurricular activities like sports and believe that education will provide them entrée into better jobs and a better way of life after they graduate (45, 99). While MacLeod's in-depth interviews reveal a wealth of fascinating details about the lives of those he began interviewing in 1983, our interest here is limited to those sections of his book which shed light on class mobility in the United States. The easiest way to sum up his findings is to succinctly profile the members of both groups when he first returned to interview them in 1991 and again in 2006–7.

MacLeod first re-visits the Hallway Hangers' occupational lives in a chapter entitled "Dealing with Despair." Stoney has moved from "pizzeria to pizzeria and from prison to prison" since MacLeod first met him. Dependent on Valium, Stoney has tried to take his life several times. In 1988 he robbed a convenience store and spent two years incarcerated. He later held up a pizza delivery man for $45 and received a five-year sentence in maximum security. In 1991 he was still in minimum security at the time of MacLeod's interview (158).

Steve had also been in prison – five times in the last seven years. "Apart from occasional babysitting, Steve offers little financial support to the mothers of his two children." He rotates in and out of constructions job and selling crack (158).

Shorty was incarcerated for thirteen months after stabbing a boy in the stomach (who recovered). He had a few construction jobs and then suffered a stabbing himself. He still lives with his mother, works only sporadically, and uses crack (159).

Chris and his girlfriend were homeless for the past several years prior to the 1991 interview. Once Chris held big plans to make it in the cocaine trade, but he became "his own best customer" (159), lost everything, and began cycling in and out of jail and prison. Most recently, he had been convicted of robbing three college students and received a seven-year sentence (159).

Boo-Boo had been working at a car wash in 1985 for $4.30 per hour. He quit, did a stint in jail for stealing a car, then went into the armed services for five weeks until he was medically discharged for bad feet. He married, but his wife had the marriage annulled; then, he re-married and lived with his second wife with her family in a different set of low-income projects. He and his second wife had two daughters, but Social Services took them away, essentially for neglect. Both he and his wife became involved in the crack life, and while they have extricated themselves, Chris told MacLeod his family life had totally disintegrated (160).

Slick joined the Marines but was discharged just several months later. He worked in construction and roofing but was arrested for involvement in a brawl and had his probation revoked when he missed AA meetings, spending six months in jail. When he came out, he began supplementing roofing with dealing cocaine. His work is irregular, and while he was earning more than any member of the group ($12/hour), he gets laid off every winter (160).

Jinx jumped from job to job before taking up drug trafficking. Like Slick, he eventually got out of the trade. He now works at a warehouse (161).

Frankie went out of state with his mother in 1984. He now lives within a mile of Clarendon Heights. He lives quietly with his girlfriend but is unemployed (161).

The title of MacLeod's companion chapter about the Brothers he interviewed in 1991 is "Dreams Deferred." Employed in the service sector of the economy, MacLeod recounts the Brothers have "bagged groceries, stocked shelves, flipped hamburgers, delivered pizzas, repaired cars, serviced airplanes, cleaned buildings, moved furniture, driven tow trucks, pumped gas, delivered auto parts … washed dishes … worked as mail carriers, cooks, clerks, computer operators, bank tellers, busboys, models, office photocopiers, laborers, soldiers, baggage handlers, security guards and customer service agents" (198). Only Mike, who holds a union job, had moved out of low-wage, high turnover work (198–9).

Like the Hallway Hangers, the Brothers come from families in which their parents hold jobs at the bottom of the urban occupational structure (or do not hold jobs at all) (126). While the Brothers fully accepted their high school's achievement ideology, the fact that they were in low educational tracks in high school and posted poor grades did not help them, even though most graduated (or finished later with a GED). Other than the fact that the Brothers had a decidedly less dramatic record of time spent imprisoned compared to the Hallway Hangers, they shared the same lower tier of the labor market (127–8).

MacLeod spends 175 pages summarizing and updating the lives of both groups after he returns to the field in 206–7 (275–450). We needn't spend that long. Frankie got hired in 1993 by the Housing Authority that runs low-income projects and stayed more than 12 years, moving over to the Highway Department just before MacLeod re-interviewed him (278–9). Jinx works on a landscape crew and was making $12.50 an hour in 2006–7 (292–3). Shorty regaled MacLeod with dramatic stories of work injuries, dismal treatment by former friends, health problems and surgeries, and lots of roofing and construction. In the end, he was still doing "bull work" – hard labor – and expected to do more of it as long as he lives (300–10).

Steve, who had been in and out of prison prior to 1991, now lived with his mother in a small house. From 1992 to 1995 he was back in prison for a stabbing. He was arrested again in 1995 and did two more years (through 1997) in prison. He obtained a license to work on boilers but couldn't get hired because he was a felon. He lied about his criminal history and worked sporadically. His licenses were eventually taken for non-payment of child support; he began using heroin and lost whatever he had (311–6). Stoney had been in state prison in 1991. He spent four years there, was out for a month, and robbed a 7–Eleven convenience store. He received a 7–10 year sentence for the robbery and spent five more years in prison. Since then, he worked at a friend's pizzeria, was a laborer in a welding shop, became certified to work at a Harley-Davidson franchise, and got into the music business as a drum-tech for rock bands (317–27). MacLeod found Chris in a rural jail 50 miles from Clarendon Heights. Chris told MacLeod he had been inside institutions almost all of the 15 years since MacLeod had last seen him (328–34). Only Slick had done well for himself: tried for murder but acquitted, Slick went with a roofing company down South after Hurricane Andrew. He worked for the company for three years, quit, and started his own company. When MacLeod found him, they went fishing on his 24-foot boat. He was having a new house built for he and his family and managing his successful company (335–49).

Some of the Brothers have made some strides, but many have not moved far beyond the service job tier in the labor market; MacLeod calls his chapter on them "Finally Finding a Foothold." Mokey is the night shift manager for a company that scans documents for law firms. He manages eight employees who stand for eight hours at copiers to do their work (350–9). MacLeod speculated that he would find Super "in prison or dead" (360). Instead, he found him with three daughters, one of them in jail, separated from both mothers of his children, and working as a furniture mover. Super told MacLeod, like many of the Hallway Hangers did, his stories of moving in and out of imprisonment and selling drugs (360–9).

When he was 16 years old, Mike went along with an older co-worker and took a test to work for the post office. At 18, he was called in and went to work carrying mail and driving the postal truck. He made good money at that time, and in the 1990s, he bought some rental properties. He started working in real estate so he could eventually get a realtor's license. When he did, he went out on his own. He's done well financially but tells MacLeod, "To be honest, luck had a lot to do with why I'm here ..." (370–5).

Juan began working as a mechanic right out of high school in 1983. He's mostly worked in the shop and as a tow truck driver for the same company since (376–85). James had not worked for a year when MacLeod last spoke to him in 1991. He began working part-time shortly thereafter for a temp agency; he did "computer stuff" for a bank. From learning on the job, he later moved to a full-time computer job. Later, he moved to another computer job at the fashion firm Calvin Klein. The work has been steady, but even as he has assumed more responsibility and received better pay, he has not moved beyond the lower echelon computer work of running reports and manning the help desk (386–95).

Derek moved to Utah in 1996 to work for a major airline. He did so to get away from Clarendon Heights. He rents the basement of a house in a working-class part of town. He began in reservations in a giant call center and remains in customer service. From there, he moved to another company as an hourly paid trainer for customer service (396–406).

As MacLeod summarizes, "[t]he majority of the men [from Clarendon Heights] may still be mired at the bottom of society, but some have achieved working class stability and even penetrated middle class" (407). Seeking more objectivity, MacLeod enlisted two of his mentors – Katherine McClelland and David Karen – to offer their own summary commentary on what he found. Their approach emphasized the constraints that structure and institutions imposed on the two groups' lives – even 25 years later. As they note, schools impose institutional limits on students as they pass through the educational system that reduce the number of possible pathways their lives may follow (409). The consequence, in their view, is that the "dynamics of social reproduction are clearly visible" (410). Overall, McClelland and Karen conclude that the young men's "habitus," in Bourdieu's terms, made a notable impact on their life chances. They conclude that "failures in school, and in particular their inability to complete college, …" were critical in their life trajectories (418). This was obviously enhanced by their lack of social capital as members of both groups lacked economically valuable social ties they could call upon growing up in Clarendon Heights (419). Indeed, one may call it "reverse social and cultural capital" that the young men acquired: habits, attitudes, a network, and patterns of speech that keep one mired in the lower class and blue-collar worlds. Ultimately, the men's habitus is also the source of the start of their respective "slides" down the social ladder into the demi-monde of drugs, alcohol, and crime for those who took the plunge. Clearly, there were many points at which access to greater resources would have helped halt an addiction, support a more permanent recovery, and shunt members back onto a better path had they been middle class or above (427–31).

Women without Class

Another well-known and highly regarded study of working class, high school youth – albeit one focused on girls and women – is Julie Bettie's *Women Without Class* (2014), her account of participant observation field work in "Waretown," a pseudonym, in central California's agricultural heartland. Bettie's study is very self-consciously about how inequalities are reproduced and how "the performance of class" constitutes one of the most significant barriers to class mobility in the United States (2014: xiv). The setting for her observations, and her conclusion that schools are often the locale for reinforcing inequality rather than solving it, is Waretown High, a public high school in a small city of 40,000 people.

Bettie's observations revealed six peer cliques within the Waretown High study body. Focusing principally on the seniors, Bettie identified them as the Smokers from the white working class; Cholas/Cholos, Mexican-American students from low income, "hard living" families; Las Chicas, Mexican-American girls from more settled, stable, working-class families who participated in "Chola" style when younger but had "matured out" by the time they were seniors; the Skaters, the largest group, who were white and whose principal characteristic was that they did not fit into any of the other groups; "Hicks," who were predominantly white students with interest in agriculture, the city and valley's predominant economy; and the Preps, primarily white students from the middle class with definite plans for attendance at four-year colleges (14–6).

Bettie's adept fieldwork produced an array of highly descriptive, discrete details about each of the six cliques. By her own admission, though, she was most interested in young women from families of modest means and generally low educational attainment. Moreover, Bettie was interested in how female students identified with, and then "performed," their culture of origin – such as lower-class Mexican-American – and whether their socialization into their early cultural influences was amenable to change.

Bettie's conclusion is that school is one of the principal venues for reinforcing and reproducing class inequality, not solving inequality. As MacLeod found with respect to the Hallway Hangers in particular, Bettie observed that the subcultural values of the working-class Mexican-American girls at Waretown were antithetical to the official middle class, academic/achievement culture that is the pathway to college (and therefore the pathway out of the working class) at Waretown High. Bettie came to believe that "with few exceptions," the working-class Mexican-American girls she observed would end up living "working class futures" (192). Bettie believed that the performative elements of the Las Chicas' working-class heritage were especially influential in slotting them toward a similar class future. The white prep girls, for example, looking ahead to acting out the anticipated future of their middle class lives, accepted the adult middle class norms of the high school's academic achievement-oriented college prep curriculum; Las Chicas did not. As Bettie was able to observe, Las Chicas used their class time, whenever possible, to talk about heterosexual romance and "girl culture" – which included conversations about fashion, shopping, and recent episodes of the television soap opera *Days of our Lives* (60). Prep girls stuck to the official curriculum in their classes. Anticipating no future in the transitioning middle class world of higher education, Las Chicas began adopting and performing adult expressions of sexuality, as well as talk of pregnancies and babies for some, thereby appropriating lifestyle forms of discourse that would not advance them toward further education or middle class status. Their adoption of elaborately stylized approaches to hairstyles, clothes, shoes, particular colors of lipstick, lip liner, and nail polish, along with the discourse manner and content reflective of their working-class Mexican-American identity, worked well as bonding agents but also embedded them in a restrictive cultural space (62). Almost identical to Ray's (2018) interview subjects, who we will hear about next, Bettie found that for these girls, graduating from high school – or even adding a year or two of community college – deceptively persuaded them they were achieving more than their parents when in reality most of Las Chicas would end up in clerical or retail service jobs (82).

The Making of a Teenage Service Class

A more recent study of poor high school youth from an East Coast city is Ranita Ray's, *The Making of a Teenage Service Class* (2018). Ray conducted her ethnographic observations in Port City, a small northeastern town with one of the highest poverty rates and lowest four-year high school graduation rates in the country (1). Ray followed and interviewed sixteen youth, mostly female, intensively for three years as she moved about and worked in a community organization in Port City. Her highly descriptive portraits of these young people's lives offer vivid testimony to the struggle the lower classes face in their fight for upward mobility in the contemporary United States.

Angie, born in Puerto Rico but brought by her mother to the United States when she was six months old, lives with her grandparents in Port City.[3] Her mother was raising Angie's five sisters in Philadelphia, where she lived after she and her husband, Angie's father, split up. Angie's father moved "in and out" of her grandparent's home, coming home drunk (or under the influence of drugs), eating food Angie had made for herself, and stealing money she had hidden at the bottom of a drawer (1).

Angie had an aspiration to attend college. She wanted to obtain a college degree, find a good job, start a family of her own, "and live the middle-class American dream" (2). This meant to her that "[B]ecoming pregnant was out of the question" (2). Her dream faced some potential road-blocks though. Angie's grades were only average, putting part of the plan in jeopardy because of her unpreparedness. Angie remained hopeful, and after graduation from high school in 2011, she moved to Florida with plans to attend Miami Dade College and live with her aunt and two cousins. Her aunt owned and operated a food truck and offered her a job there (2–3).

A few weeks after arriving in Florida, Angie called to say her aunt was unable to offer the promised job. While she had already applied for ten other jobs, none materialized. Unhappily, Angie returned to Port City not long after. Angie's dream did not end there; she soon enrolled in classes at the local community college, Port City Rivers, but she had already missed some weeks of classes. Moreover, she felt she needed a job – but all of the prospective jobs conflicted with her community college class times. Angie elected to withdraw from Port City Rivers and work three jobs, trying to earn the money she felt she needed (3–4).

Angie reenrolled at the community college the following semester, right on time. She learned to drive over the summer and bought a used car, but halfway through the semester, the car broke down. Trying to manage both school and work by using public transportation began to wear on Angie. Eventually, Angie faced what seemed to her an incontrovertible fact: she would need to choose, again, between continuing her classes and keeping her jobs. She dropped her classes and, under the influence of a bakery manager who she worked for, adjusted her dream to one of attending a well-known culinary school the following year. However, that did not happen; rather, she re-enrolled again at the local community college but often now took nutrition classes with a food industry future still in mind (4–5). In sum, Angie's dilemma was one typical of her peers and the subjects of Ray's study generally: Ray's youth all needed a job to continue school, even community college, but work schedules often conflicted with classes. While Angie – and Ray's respondents generally – had some family support, families also created obstacles – as did Angie's father in her case. The convergence of factors like these made dreams of upward mobility difficult to realize.

While I characterize Angie's situation as "typical" of those Ray reports, her circumstances are, by no means, among the most serious situations found among Ray's respondents. While Angie's situation was difficult enough to impede and derail her own plan for achieving the American dream, other lower class youth in Port City faced even more daunting challenges. Two young people Ray calls Cassy and Aaron are exemplary.

Cassy's parents had moved to the United States from Honduras and had limited fluency in English. Her father worked as a custodian while her mother maintained the home; consequently, their income was modest. The family lived in a two-bedroom apartment; Cassy's younger sisters slept on a bed in the living room. When the family budget was strained, her father would rent out the living room to a cousin and his wife, forcing Cassy's sisters to move into her bedroom (62).

Cassy was a self-described "nerd." She held firmly conceived aspirations to go to college and become a psychologist. She told Ray, "I want to help people and not be like my parents, just frustrated about money" (61). Like all of the youth Ray knew from her study, money figured prominently as a factor in Cassy's life. In spring 2012, Cassy was unable to pay her phone bill for one month. As Ray mentions in an aside, this was frequently the case for youth in her study, "when they lost a job or had to use their money other purposes such as rent or food" (62). She used her father's cell phone while he was asleep to call her boyfriend and, in doing so, saw that her father had exchanged "sexually suggestive messages" with a woman he apparently met on a dating site (62). At first, Cassy refrained from doing anything and decided to simply monitor her father's phone. After a month, though, he was still exchanging messages with the woman, and Cassy confronted him. Her father said he knew he had made a mistake and would stop, but Cassy told Ray that she knew he would not stop. Still, she did not tell her mother because the family could not really endure a disruption that might lead to a separation. As Cassy told Ray, in part:

> I'm not really gonna do anything anyway … Like we're broke as hell. I'm like [my sisters'] mother … I want to go to college for my sisters … I told my mom that she should learn to drive because it would make her independent, but she doesn't listen and she hasn't worked in the last five years, so she got nothing. (63)

As Ray describes, the emotional dynamic portrayed in Cassy's situation was not uncommon among her subjects, and older siblings often carried the emotional burden of keeping the family together to shield younger ones from parental quarrels and other family disruptions (63). Cassy worried that a wedge between her parents might leave her younger sisters to fend for themselves due to the tight economics under which the family functioned.

If Cassy's story ended there, it would sound in broad outline much like Angie's; that is, a story of constricted economics with the wrinkle of different details here and there. In Cassy's case, though, there is much more to tell. Although Cassy often stated she wanted to be a role model for her younger sisters and acted as an alternative mother figure to them, Cassy also acted to pass on knowledge about how to shoplift without getting caught. Indeed, she encouraged her younger sisters to shoplift small luxuries they could not afford, like shampoo, lip balm, or snacks. Cassy taught them how to remove security stickers, watch out for undercover shoppers, identify products that don't have security beepers, open CD covers in bathrooms, and look out for security cameras (64). Cassy tried to pass on what she considered to be the ethical parameters that should be applied when shoplifting:

> Like if I find an iphone, I'll even give it back, like if it's someone's. But who cares about Walmart anyway? Don't steal from no one that bought something with their blood money. (64)

Yet what started as an instrumental response to a constant shortage of funds turned into an expenditure of funds a few months later when Cassy's younger sisters were caught stealing some small items and a bottle of shampoo worth $8. The store manager called their father and charged the girls a $300 fine, which their father paid; Cassy gave $250 to her father because she felt responsible. Further, Cassy's effort to avoid family disruption and shield her sisters from turmoil also suffered since they were chastened both by the store manager and their father (64).

This, too, might have been the extent of Cassy's poverty struggles, but like many of her peers, her class circumstances often were the backdrop for an extended saga.

Cassy, like most of the young women in Ray's study group, had an interest in boys and viewed marriage as a pathway out of poverty (87). In a nutshell, what this boiled down to in the lower strata of Port City was looking for a good boy. In contrast to all the "bad boys," who were readily available, good boys were those who held jobs; earned at least average grades in school, aspired to attend college, and demonstrated a reasonable amount of effort to sustain the relationship, even amidst the usual financial strains of living in poverty (87). Often, though, as Ray documents, even relationships that begin with what is perceived to be a "good boy" can be derailed by disruptive minor events that then assume major proportions.

Cassy had been dating Aaron, a nineteen years old black man, for six years, a long time in the context of Port City's lower class youth. Although they occasionally fought, the relationship was vital and real. Aaron, for example, provided Cassy support when she fought with her mother or struggled with mental health issues (101). At the end of 2010, though, Aaron felt compelled to leave Port City because his mother's adiction had become worse. He moved to Ohio to live with his father and stepmother, leaving Cassy behind, who was devastated. Once Aaron moved, Cassy, worried that he would begin seeing someone else. He did not call for weeks, and Cassy barely ate, missed work often, and isolated herself playing video games until Aaron finally called, explaining that there was no money for a phone and his father did not have internet. Within a couple of weeks, Cassy was excited, telling Ray, "I finally get to see him! I am so excited!" (101).

As it turns out, Cassy, who had saved a $1,000 for her college expenses, ended up spending most of it on Aaron's trip to Port City to visit her (101). The disruption caused by Aaron's departure also seems to have had other deleterious effects on Cassy's plan to attend college and become a psychologist. Although she had finished her final year of high school, she had not taken the SAT nor begun the college admission process in time for many colleges. When Cassy finally got around to asking Ray to help with the FAFSA application, she said, "I decided to go to Port City Rivers (the local community college) for now …, it's too late" (102). When Ray arrives to help with the application forms, Cassy and her mother are fighting – because Aaron is now in jail and calling (likely collect) on their home phone. Aaron, who had been a relatively stable and positive influence for Cassy for over six years, had gotten into a physical fight with his stepmother because she had fraudulently used his Social Security number to take out a loan (102).

Perhaps a fitting epilogue for these lower and working class vignettes of mobility projects in the United States is Ray's account of Angie's circumstances after she came back from Florida. Angie asked for help in creating a resume. She was working at Bed, Bath, and Beyond (as a retail floor crew, stocking shelves, and cleaning) and working a second job taking care of seniors. She wanted to quit her care job and find something "better" (145). Her search was futile; a few months later, Bed, Bath, and Beyond started cutting her time.

Finally, after more time, Angie found a job at a coffee franchise. It was the end of another school year in Port City, and Angie ruefully reflected, "While everyone gets ready for prom and shit, I'm going to work" (146). She continued, "I don't know, nothin' working out the way I want, I hate my job, Ranita" (146). Ray, summing up Angie's dilemma for herself and her readers, observes,

> After Angie had returned from Florida, sometimes she planned to enter a culinary school in Minnesota to "make it" as a chef. At other times she planned to move to Miami again to attend Miami Dade College to become a dancer. Still other times, she adopted a dimmer view of what adulthood looks like: low wage coffee shop jobs. (146)

After Ray leaves Connecticut and Port City to take a faculty job, Angie, still in Port City in the minimum wage world, often asks Ray, "What's out there [in Las Vegas]? Is it cheap? Maybe I'll move up there if you find me a job" (241).

Middle and Upper Middle Class Families: Maintaining Class Boundaries

Studies of working and lower class youth and family life are focused on the financial, emotional, and relational struggles that these Americans face in order to stay afloat in our capitalist economy and the routine disruptions they experience in doing so. Their struggles come into hard relief when counterposed against the relative ease with which middle and upper middle class families act to secure their place in the class system by strengthening their claims for status through "concerted cultivation" of their children's acquisition of cultural and social capital (Lareau 2011, 2, 5). These families do so because they are able to afford to do so since they are in possession of more economic capital than the working and lower class, but also because they understand that increasingly the competition for upward economic mobility, status achievement, and status maintenance is waged on the battlefield of social and cultural capital and not, principally, on the sole basis of financial capital. Arguably, economic capital principally arises from the possession of cultural and social capital in the contemporary world and not the other way around.

Shalini Shankar, an anthropologist, became fascinated with the local, regional, and national worlds of spelling bees in the United States. Shankar began attending spelling bees and interviewing youthful competitors, their parents, Bee organizers, and experts. For six years, she attended the National Spelling Bee as she wove together the story she saw emerging in her book, *Beeline* (2019). While Shankar writes about her observations as though they may reveal something distinctive about Generation Z (roughly, those born between 1997 and 2012, following the generation referred to as Millennials), she concedes that generational analysis has its limitations. More to the point, Shankar realizes, although she does not spend a great deal of time addressing the point, that she is really only examining a very narrow slice of Generation Z – that is, those from the middle and upper middle class who engage in one form of competitive "brain sport." And, why should she? It is apparent from the opening paragraph of her book that the youth world of competitive spelling bees in the United States is the exclusive domain of those with enough discretionary income to afford the time for hours of weekly intense study and who live in a setting largely free of the distractions and disruptions that members of the working and lower classes in our society must endure.

Shankar's book is unabashedly about a specific form of competition for children that is organized by adults, most prominently including the children's parents. Spelling bees have proliferated in direct response to the amount of money, other resources, and effort invested in it by the middle class and upper middle class patrons it serves. As Shankar (2019 notes, 11 million U.S. children participate in spelling bees annually as of the date of her book (10). As Shankar recites, the National Spelling Bee has been called the "orthographic Super Bowl," tying it rhetorically to an exalted sports competition for adult males in our society in an "industry" that is a multibillion dollar economic juggernaut. In some ways, the comparison is apt: families spend serious money to support a child's participation in the spelling bee world as they ascend from local, to regional, to the national competition. Shankar often only hints at the costs a family might incur ("Professional spelling bee coaching was out of the question for Sai's family, …") (31). Yet statements from a former champion ("I don't feel it would be fair to serve as a coach who charges $200 an hour to study root words.") (269) and from several Gen Z elite spellers who have aged out at 15–16 years old about whether to charge from $35 to $100 per hour for various types of coaching (23), make the issue of costs more explicit. Travel, food, and lodging costs associated with spelling bee competition are likewise not fully explored but rather are submerged within the generalized talk of sponsors. Yet, as Shankar concedes, "… economic diversity is sadly lacking" (24) among the youthful competitors, especially as they become successful locally and then regionally and move upward in the competition. She adds, in a way that almost seems to suggest it is unnecessary to state the obvious, "Spelling bees, like many high-powered extracurricular activities today, require *significant* investments of time and money" (24; emphasis added).

Shankar realizes that as amazing as the young successful spellers who populate the National Spelling Bee competition are, they are – in a sense – byproducts of their heritage and, more specifically, the daughters and sons of their parents. These parents' style is the kind of personal attention, encouragement, and supervision that Lareau (2011) defined, through its various features, as concerted cultivation. Shayley Martin is a case in point. Shayley's grandmother taught her to read when she was a toddler, although her mother did not realize her daughter could read until "well after she turned three" (Shankar 2019, 129). By then, her daughter was reading works of poetry and "anything else she could find" (129). Ultimately, Shayley competed in four National Spelling Bees, although she did not win.

Mrs. Martin is a first-generation high school graduate and first-generation college graduate in her family. In this regard, Mrs. Martin is not very representative of the parents of "Bee" children. She is in another important way, though: as Shayley moved through the educational system, Mrs. Martin advocated for educational opportunities for her daughter that otherwise wouldn't have existed. She had Shayley take the SAT in the eighth grade, in which she received a perfect verbal score; urged the schools to let Shayley take German, followed by Mandarin, earlier than normally permitted. She followed by persuading the high school to make an exception so her daughter could take classes at the community college prior to the eleventh grade (148–9). As Shankar completes her study, Shayley is studying linguistics at Yale University.

Shankar's tentative conclusion, based on many observations like this one, is that a critical factor in supporting the desire and ability for children to compete in local, regional, and national bees is some variation on "stealth-fighter parenting," or what may be its close cousin, the manner in which many immigrant parents value educational achievement highly and set goals for their children to achieve, which Shankar refers to as "Bee Parenting" (131). In either case, what we are talking about is a style that requires a substantial investment of time and energy, and a less – but not inconsiderable – investment of money, into child support, encouragement, resource allocation, and monitoring. (Dhingra [2020, 199, 201], who also includes observations of spelling bees in his recent book, echoes these findings. "Parents were willing to go to great lengths to facilitate their children's success [in extracurricular academic competitions]. Some flew across the country, ... Time and energy were not the only kinds of investments. Registering for and attending ... can start to add up financially, ...".)

Chetan Reddy began competing in North South Foundation spelling bees in the first grade and entered the South Asian Spelling Bee in the third grade. In fourth grade, he became eligible to compete in the Dallas, Texas, regional bee but didn't advance from there to the national level until the following year, when he was in fifth grade. Over the next three years, he advanced further, finishing 22nd nationally when he was in seventh grade (Shankar 2018, 136–7). In his final year of competition, 2013, Chetan finished in 7th place (139).

Shankar found that Chetan's parents "worked closely with him for years on his spelling preparation" (137). Each of his parents holds a master of science degree in electrical engineering and computer science from the University of Texas at Dallas. Mr. Reddy also earned an MBA degree from the University of Dallas (137). His parents' support took many forms. "His father prepared word lists for him. His mother designed software using Excel and Visual Basic [that permitted Chetan] to test and review about 1000 words an hour" (138). In this way, Chetan could study over 100,000 words per month during his final bee season. As Chetan became more committed to spelling bee competition, he increased his study time – from two hours per day in fourth grade to four hours per day in eighth grade while studying up to eight hours per day on weekends and holidays. As his father observed, the aptitude and passion [and time] "to spend hours doing something tedious, day after day, month after month, year after year, ... is limited to an elite few" (138). As with other families of elite spellers, Shankar found that Chetan's family "prioritized his spelling career over their own leisure, ..." Their son's progress became "a focal point in their lives." In short, Chetan's parents were able to display the sort of engaged parenting that Lareau (2011) identified as "concerted cultivation," which supports children in their acquisition of skills, behaviors, and attitudes that lend themselves to making successful life adaptations, attaining educational achievement, and mastering cultural competency.

Although Shankar's study of local, regional, and national spelling bee participants and their parents provides a comprehensive picture of this social world and the parenting styles that seem to make their children's success possible, Shankar is not the only trained social scientist to examine the phenomenon. Pawan Dhingra, in his recent book *Hyper Education* (2020), also investigates the spelling bee world as part of a broader look at the growth of extracurricular education in the United States. The value of this sort of replication – often undervalued in social science – is the check on reliability that re-examination of social phenomena offers.

Dhingra's study, in addition to replicating Shankar's findings, also expands her earlier examination of the spelling bee world in the United States by locating it within the broader movement of extracurricular academic competitions for youth generally and within the burgeoning practice of private teaching and coaching on academic subjects for children, whether in science, technology, mathematics (STEM), spelling, or other subjects. In doing so, Dhingra confirms the core understanding at the heart of Shankar's observations: these phenomena – from spelling bees to private learning centers to math competitions to private tutoring or "coaching" – are exclusively the province of middle class and upper middle class families who are engaging in "concerted cultivation." As the founder of a math learning commercial franchise told Dhingra, these activities are pursued by families that value education "and are willing to pay for more" (2020, 6). These activities are not intended to "keep children up to grade level," provide remedial opportunities for those already falling below minimum academic requirements, nor are they designed to compensate for under-resourced and underperforming public schools (7). As Dhingra notes, none of the children he studied started their extra schooling activities because they needed academic help. Rather, all of the children attended highly ranked schools, whether public or private, in which they were "doing well," and all were the children of "highly educated professionals" (7). In short, these families and children live in social worlds that could hardly be further from Clarendon Heights, Waretown High, or Port City. All of the details Dhingra presents make that difference abundantly clear. (*See* Dhingra's (2020) Chapters 1 and 6 on Over-Programmed Families and "Everyone in the Family was Involved.")

Public Schools in the Context of the American Class Structure

The above accounts of working and lower-class youth in three communities often reference issues related to the local public high schools. This is significant for two reasons. First, over the last century and a half, schools have become the default institution for maintaining the illusory but very real meritocracy that governs and reproduces the American class system[4] (Sorokin 1959, 188). Second, working class and poor families have no other choice than public schools; wealthier families have not only a choice among public school districts but have private schools to choose from, too. Moreover, it is widely understood that these factors, plus residential sorting according to wealth and income, produce unequal educational opportunity, often further divided by race/ethnicity and class culture (Hauhart 2019, 48). Both of these points are critical because it has long been established that "parental social class and other aspects of economic status are passed on to children in part by means of unequal educational opportunity, ..." (Bowles and Gintis 2011 [1976], x). Indeed, Bowles and Gintis

(2011, 8) later go so far as to assert that the history of education in this country needs to be re-written because, in their view, "[E]ducation over the years has never been a potent force for economic equality." They assert that to understand the impact of the schools on economic standing, we must first examine the social structure (9), as I have contended here. Their principal observation with respect to the organization of American public schools, then and now, may be boiled down to this: public education in this country is organized hierarchically because its primary goal is to socialize students into becoming subordinate workers in a capitalist economy. Thus, the real message of the type and quality of public school one attends is simply an implicit signal as to who you are and who you may become. If the public school you attend is not well maintained, does not have resources for enough quality learning materials, does not pay teachers well, and does not convey a high regard for achievement and academic standards, then the message is simply that you are not well positioned in the American class system and you are not slated to achieve anything better than your present class position in the future.[5] In Bowles and Gintis' view, this suggests that "beneath the façade of the meritocracy lies the reality of the [American] educational system ..." (103). Rather than helping students learn and then evaluating merit, they suggest that the actual effect of our public schools is to legitimate inequality and assure the relatively frictionless process of inter-generational status transmission. The working out of this process can be seen in the evidence supplied by MacLeod, Bettie, and Ray in their descriptions of the schools in Clarendon Heights, Waretown, and Port City.

It is unnecessary to re-state all of the observations about the local schools that MacLeod, Bettie, and Ray documented for their descriptions are there for anyone to read. MacLeod's account of Lincoln High School in Clarendon Heights confirms what has been said above: "Many schools in poor neighborhoods lack the most basic resources ..." (266). Ashley, one of Ray's (2018) youth, is quite specific in her comments about Port City high in a discussion:

> Just so, like, when you look at Port City, the school is old, it hasn't been remodeled for God knows how long. ... There are cockroaches there, the stalls in the bathrooms don't have doors, the glasses [windows] are broken, there is not enough books for every student in the classroom, not enough chairs, not enough teachers for students in the classrooms, and you don't get enough attention if you don't understand, you know. (118)

Perhaps equally as important, MacLeod emphasizes the merciless sorting that the (LHS) school's tracking system imposes after the eighth grade, which does not seem to serve the students there well (2009, 84–9). In that system, students are required to choose among the several tracks available before they enter high school. Many of MacLeod's teens chose the Occupational Education track, the Fundamental School curriculum, or were placed, often involuntarily, in the Adjustment Class, which according to the teacher, was there for students "who've been in fights and are general pains in the ass" (87). All three programs are light on traditional academics; their principal purpose – particularly true with regard to the Adjustment Class – seems to have been to provide oversight for (male) students until many drop out of school at 16 years of age or otherwise provide a high school diploma to any student who can stick it out until graduation. Ultimately, the effect of a high school diploma is negligible, as Super confirms: "Now I see you can't get no decent job with just a high school diploma" (216). MacLeod, taking the point further, cites to studies that suggest there "is often very little at the end of the line" for community college certificate programs either[6] (217). In the end, it is the American class structure – of which school tracking is a somewhat invisible but crucial part – that MacLeod finds to be the most pernicious culprit in the reproduction of social class.

Bettie's (2014) study of Mexican-American working class high school girls is perhaps even more devastating in its implications for class stratification than MacLeod's observations, for her girls were not committed to the forms of disqualifying lower class male behavior that steered the Hallway Hangers and Brothers into engagement with crime. For the working class girls in Waretown, the effect of academic tracking and other exclusionary practices was to make them believe that success in school was not intended for them. For Bettie, the crucial impact of class could be found in the "preps" mastery of standard American speech and the working-class girls' non-standard grammar patterns (in English), parents who could not help with school work because of their own limited education and lack of time, and related deficiencies in cultural knowledge that were endemic in the working class *habitus*. As Bourdieu (1986, 241) struggles to impress upon us, the social world is not like the game of roulette. Society does not generally hold out "the opportunity of winning a lot of money in a short space of time, and therefore of changing one's social status quasi-instantaneously, …" Rather, the forms of capital take time to accumulate, whether one speaks of financial capital, cultural capital, or social capital. Lower and working class members of society, by definition, lack financial capital. Consequently, they must gain either cultural or social capital (or both) to move up in the class structure, where they may eventually acquire more economic capital. The message from MacLeod's, Bettie's, and Ray's studies is clear: short of cultural capital and social capital (as well as economic capital) due to their working-class *habitus*, youth growing up in the lower classes must successfully navigate environs that are culturally unfamiliar, somehow learning to perform a different "class" as they go, and only then will they be accepted by the next higher class on the social ladder. All of this is easier said than done, as each of the studies makes clear.

Ray's observations, too, attest to the persistence of the constricting, rather than enabling, character of education in contemporary United States society with respect to upward mobility. Echoing Super's view above, Ray (2018) notes, "… Port City youth understand that a high school diploma did not carry much weight in the job market" (109). Still, even to achieve a high school diploma, the youth Ray observed and interviewed had to navigate the world of low-wage work *and* school, at one and the same time, due to their family's (often unstable) economic circumstances. This often remained true for those students who later tried to attend community colleges, where they often found themselves overburdened by the combination of school and work, many times pursuing neither one successfully due to the conflict between the two (109). Moreover, while the number of community colleges has expanded, and four-year universities and their regional campuses have proliferated over the decades, educational inequality has not been affected because, at most, the elite schools have simply introduced more stringent screens for sorting individuals and otherwise raising standards (137).

For the youth Ray (2018) met, this was compounded by weaknesses in English language facility and general cultural knowledge, much like Bettie's (2014) Cholas and Las Chicas. As Ray quoted one of her respondents who, like many in Port City, grew up in Spanish-speaking households, "… I can't write well, my English is all fucked up, so I gotta work on it [before I can try for college]" (115). Finally, Ray's youthful subjects also shared immersion in some of the non-academic cultures that Bettie's (2014) working class women favored, while at the same time rhetorically honoring the achievement ideology of using education to gain upward mobility. As Sandra told Ray,

> I don't know what I wanna do. I wanna make money and do something, maybe fashion, 'cause like, I work in the mall now and I'm learning about the fashion

industry and I don't know what I wanna do with whatever classes I'm taking now, and like I gotta work two jobs. I don't even know when I'll finish college. (133)

Ray sums up some of her observations about working class youth who aspire for upward mobility by saying, "Their deep unfamiliarity with middle class cultural capital made tasks that middle-class students are familiar with excruciating for the Port City youth" (136).

The centrality of language and the importance of effective command of language, in school interactions is critical. As Bourdieu and Passeron (1977, 109–10) have noted, pedagogic communication via linguistic manipulation owes its particular influence to the institutional space it occupies and the legitimacy that space confers on the speaker and the style of speech the speaker transmits. Students who can "perform" the class attributes of their teachers – at any level of the educational system – because "they are prepared for [it] by a childhood that is spent in a family circle where words define the reality of things" (119), will academically prosper, as contrasted to those children whose habitus is working class, with its communicative limitations. Alize, one of Ray's Port City youth quoted above, recognized in her comment that her English speech and writing were not at the level of standard high school English. She knew her language skills were a barrier, saying further, "I'm gonna go to college, I made my mind. Like if my English is not good, I'm just gonna go to like Puerto Rico but I'm gonna go to school every day ..." (2018, 115).

Alize and a number of Ray's other respondents often characterized certain behaviors of themselves and their high school peers as "ghetto," including their own and others' style of speech. There are many verbatim examples of Ray's interviewees expressing themselves in her book, and in many of those, it is apparent that her subjects speak a style of English that most likely does not correspond to the schools' conception of how educated Americans should speak. As one example, Alize spoke about the fear of outsiders of Port City's youth and does so in her distinctively unique voice and style of speech:

> Niggas made me fucking change my tights 'cause they think all the motherfuckers in there ghetto – 'cause some of them real gangbangers. The principal told us how they fucking scared of us out there 'cause we like always fightin' and getting' into shit. (118)

Alize was speaking to Ray and some of her peers in an informal discussion and not in a school or work setting. However, it would ask a lot for one to believe that Alize, and her peers, could radically transform their use of the English language to fit more formal, non-profane institutional settings on a whim. Certainly, Ray does not suggest that is the case. Indeed, when Ray and another of the youth center workers were giving Franklin job seeking advice, they thought it important enough to say, "... look them in the eyes, use full sentences, and don't use cuss words" (150). Clearly, one doesn't need to give such targeted guidance about another person's speech unless one can anticipate such disqualifying speech in a job interview could happen. Like Bettie's Mexican-American high school girls, Ray's interview subjects cannot simply pick up, leave their lower, working class culture behind, and "perform" middle class. If they could, they would not be the subject of Ray's observations.

By way of contrast, the young spelling bee competitors Shankar interviewed often attend highly ranked high schools, even if public ones. Sai Chandrasekhar, who made it to the 2015 semifinal round of the National Spelling Bee, commutes daily from Flushing, Queens, to the upper east side of Manhattan, where she attends Hunter College High School (2019, 8). The school has often been ranked among the best public high schools in the United States. The school reports that students accepted to Hunter represent the top one-quarter of 1%

of students in New York City, based on test scores. The same was commonly true for the competitors Dhingra interviewed. Dhingra (2020) notes that he interviewed three different groups: educators, who were mainly from the Boston area, especially the suburbs; parents of competitors in math learning centers, spelling bees, and math competitions; and the competitors themselves (that is, school-age children). Dhingra provides two pieces of data that further delineate his sample. First, the educators were generally from "school districts … consistently rated as among the best in the state and in the country by *Boston Magazine* and *U.S. New and World Report*" (277). Second, he informs us that his predominantly South Asian Indian adult interviewees were immigrants "who arrived [in the U.S.] as married professionals in the middle and upper-middle class" and whose household incomes [at the time he interviewed them] ranged "from $100,000 to $400,000 [annually] …" (279). Dhingra's interviews confirm the class standing of those families who compete in academic competitions. For example, Deepak and his family [a wife and two children] flew to the east coast for the national South Asian Spelling Bee competition from Houston, Texas. (Both of his children were competing.) Kavita, the mother of child competitors, observed, "It costs $600 to $700 for regionals registration and travel. For the finals [the previous year], it was $3,000" (201). It can be worth it though; winners of regional to national spelling bees can receive from $10,000 to $40,000 USD, although sometimes lower winner's prizes, perhaps $3,000, or supplemented by separate scholarship award, round trip airfares, or other valuable benefits (Dhingra 2020, 1, 87) These sums, for a weekend or week of travel, lodging, and sustenance, are neither available – nor conceivable – to MacLeod's, Bettie's or Ray's interviewees, whose worlds are circumscribed by the Clarendon projects or the city limits of Port City.

So, just what is it that Shalini and Dhingra's subjects receive from these better schools, academic, extracurricular competitions, and the travel associated with them (other than the occasional financial windfall that comes from a win)? The answer is more of what they already possess. They refine and enhance their ability to "perform middle class." As MacLeod (2009, 101) recognizes, citing Karabel and Halsey (1977), dominant social groups determine what is valued in the educational system and subordinate social groups are evaluated as "not living up to" the standards of the higher class. While proponents of an academic meritocracy may contend this is exactly what the schools should do, critics abound (Hauhart 2019, 190–2, 206–8, 212–5) since the assessments are not limited to academic competence but more closely resemble what Bourdieu (1986, Bourdieu and Passeron 1977), and his associates, term cultural competence. Those who receive and profit from what schools have to offer are typically those who already possess the requisite cultural attributes, such as linguistic facility that reflects their class origin. This is apparent from the children Shankar (2019) and Dhingra (2020) interview: they are poised, they speak English well, they are comfortable speaking with adults, and speaking in public in competitive situations and to the media. They did not learn these things in schools; rather, they brought skills and attitudes to the schools that are received well by school authorities. Then, these middle class and upper middle class students take away from academic activities at school enhanced measures of the skills and attitudes they already possess. When these same students engage in extracurricular academic competitions, the same phenomenon repeats itself: they bring superior forms of "class performance" to these activities and leave with their attitudes and skills affirmed, applauded, and expanded.

For working class youth, it is precisely the opposite. The manners, deportment, dress, style of interaction, and linguistic facility – in short, all the elements and features of their working class performance – are at odds with the norms and attitudes prevalent in the schools. Moreover, the values, skills, and attitudes that they have acquired from their origin class often impair their ability to learn to "perform middle class."

Conclusion

I have argued that any number of responsible social sciences studies have shown over time that the United States is clearly a class-stratified society and that social change, including individual upward mobility, is highly restricted by the indicators, economic constraints, and social boundaries related to one's class position. From these studies, I have selected only a handful to make the point. While it is true that individuals can transcend class origins and move upward economically and socially in the United States (Vance 2016), evidence collected over time suggests that, more often than not, social classes in the United States reproduce themselves. That is, parents within each class raise children who themselves will shortly take their place in the same class as their parents and, then, when they become parents, repeat the process again. This is not to say that even within a class, it is not possible for children to do better than their parents, whether economically or socially, or both. Yet, to discount the power and influence of class in impacting life chances in the contemporary United States is akin to jumping out of an airplane without a parachute: it is nearly a comparable denial of reality.

There are many reasons that societies and cultures change incrementally, and that class boundaries persist over time. One important factor in the United States is the culture's long-standing commitment to competition, often at all costs. More than 50 years ago, in the first edition of *The Pursuit of Loneliness* (1970), Philip Slater lamented our individualistic, competitive ethos. Slater revised the book twice: in 1976 and 1990 (on the 20th anniversary of its release). While Slater deleted some materials and re-wrote some of what remained, he saw no need to change what he had to say about our competitive instincts. Slater (1990, 8–9) noted that competitive behaviors were firmly ingrained in our dominant institutions (politics, sports, business, education – even religion and the family), and the attention, money, and effort devoted to nurturing cooperative practices and institutions was minimal; such initiatives were treated as secondary and relegated to the periphery of our culture where they could be (and are) ignored for the most part. Slater was convinced that our society would persist in idolizing individuality and competition. Shankar (2019) and Dhingra's (2020) studies of middle class and upper middle class American culture, among others, seem to have proven him correct.

In the end, extracurricular academic competition is all for the purpose of ensuring social class reproduction; parents are passing social and cultural capital to their children that they hope will enable them to maintain their grasp on their class position, if not increase it. As Shankar (2019) states, it is a somewhat mysterious process that unfolds with the transfer of "assets, skills, social knowledge, and social networks" (258). Still, there is little dispute among social scientists that the process works: most members of those classes who have the capital to transfer will produce a new generation that takes their place in our class society.

Notes

1 By citing Merton (1938) and Hochschild (1995) here, I am not suggesting that either is principally – and certainly not solely – responsible for redefining Adams' approach to the American dream. Rather, I am just noting that each was among those who adopted reconfigured notions of the American Dream in their work.

2 The popularity of these exercises may be attributable, in part, to our proclivity for monitoring "who's up and who's down" in society, as we do in politics and other realms. This is entirely understandable; it is just not related to how Adams defined the American Dream.

3 Names of places and people within Ray's study are generally pseudonyms.

4 For a fascinating, brief history of the shifting institutional influence among the church, the army, education, and politics in sorting and selecting people for upward mobility, ending with our current reliance on an avowed meritocracy operated by schools, *see* Sorokin (1959, esp. 164–201).

5 It is instructive to note that while the decision in the case ultimately turned upon the language of the Fourteenth Amendment to the U.S. Constitution, the Supreme Court took notice of, and ordered remediation of, the fact that segregated Negro schools were inferior in physical plant, curricula, and transportation in the four consolidated cases in *Brown v. Board of Education*, et al., 347 U.S. 483 (1954). The point is: since schools are the *de facto* gatekeepers for upward mobility, their condition and the education that students receive in them matter.

6 In any event, as Ray (2018, 235) points out, less than 30% of students who attend community colleges graduate within three years.

References

Adams, James Truslow. 1931. *The Epic of America*. Boston, MA: Little, Brown & Co.

Adams, James Trulow. 1933. *The Epic of America*. Garden City: Garden City Books.

Bettie, Julie. 2014. *Women Without Class*. Oakland, CA: University of California Press.

Bourdieu, Pierre. 1986. "The Forms of Capital" in John G. Richardson, Ed., *Handbook of Theory and Research for the Sociology of Education*. New York: Greenwood Press.

Bourdieu, Pierre and Jean Claude Passeron. 1977. *Reproduction, in Education, Society and Culture*. London: Sage.

Bowles, Samuel and Herbert Gintis. 2011 [1976]. *Schooling in Capitalist America*. New York: Basic Books.

Dhingra, Pawan. 2020. *Hyper Education: Why Good Schools, Good Grades, and Good Behavior Are Not Enough*. New York: New York University Press.

Gerth, H.H. and C. Wright Mills. 1946. *From Max Weber: Essays in Sociology*. New York: Oxford University Press.

Hauhart, Robert C. 2016. *Seeking the American Dream: A Sociological Inquiry*. New York: Palgrave Macmillan.

Hauhart, Robert C. 2019. *The Lonely Quest: Constructing the Self in the Twenty-First Century United States*. New York: Routledge/Taylor and Francis.

Hochschild, Jennifer L. 1995. *Facing Up to the American Dream: Race, Class, and the Soul of the Nation*. Princeton, NJ: Princeton University Press.

Karabel, Jerome and A.H. Halsey, Eds. 1977. *Power and Ideology in Education*, New York: Oxford University Press.

Lareau, Annette. 2011. *Unequal Childhoods: Class, Race, and Family Life*. Berkeley, CA: University of California Press.

MacLeod, Jay. 2009. *Ain't No Makin' It: Aspirations and Attainment in a Low-Income Neighborhood*. Boulder, CO: Westview.

Merton, Robert K. 1938. "Social Structure and Anomie." *American Sociological Review*, 3(5), 672–82.

Ray, Ranita. 2018. *The Making of a Teenage Service Class: Poverty and Mobility in an American City*. Oakland, CA: University of California Press.

Sandel, Michael J. 2012. *What Money Can't Buy: The Moral Limits of Markets*. New York: Farrar, Straus and Giroux.

Shankar, Shalini. 2019. *Beeline: What Spelling Bees Reveal About Generation Z's New Path to Success*. New York: Basic Books.

Silva, Jennifer M. 2019. *We're Still Here: Pain and Politics in the Heart of America*. New York: Oxford University Press.

Slater, Philip. 1990. *The Pursuit of Loneliness*. Boston, MA: Beacon Press.

Sorokin, Pitirim A. 1959. *Social and Cultural Mobility*. New York: Free Press.

Vance. J.D. 2016. *Hillbilly Elegy*. New York: HarperCollins.

INDEX

Note: Page references in *italics* denote figure, in **bold** tables and with "n" endnotes.